PATTERN DIRECTED INFORMATION ANALYSIS

Dwijesh Kumar Dutta Majumder
Emeritus Professor
Indian Statistical Institute
Kolkata

Bhabatosh Chanda
Professor
Indian Statistical Institute
Kolkata

PUBLISHING FOR ONE WORLD

NEW AGE INTERNATIONAL (P) LIMITED, PUBLISHERS

New Delhi • Bangalore • Chennai • Cochin • Guwahati • Hyderabad
Jalandhar • Kolkata • Lucknow • Mumbai • Ranchi

Visit us at www.newagepublishers.com

Published by New Age International (P) Ltd., Publishers
First Edition: 2009

Branches:

- 36, Malikarjuna Temple Street, Opp. ICWA, Basavanagudi, **Bangalore**. ✆ (080) 26677815
- 26, Damodaran Street, T. Nagar, **Chennai**. ✆ (044) 24353401
- Hemsen Complex, Mohd. Shah Road, Paltan Bazar, Near Starline Hotel, **Guwahati**. ✆ (0361) 2543669
- No. 105, 1st Floor, Madhiray Kaveri Tower, 3-2-19, Azam Jahi Road, Nimboliadda, **Hyderabad**. ✆ (040) 24652456
- RDB Chambers (Formerly Lotus Cinema) 106A,1st Floor, S.N. Banerjee Road, **Kolkata**. ✆ (033) 22275247
- 18, Madan Mohan Malviya Marg, **Lucknow**. ✆ (0522) 2209578
- 142C, Victor House, Ground Floor, N.M. Joshi Marg, Lower Parel, **Mumbai**. ✆ (022) 24927869
- 22, Golden House, Daryaganj, **New Delhi**. ✆ (011) 23262370, 23262368

ISBN: 978-81-224-2358-7

Rs. 695.00

C-08-05-2574

Printed in Saras Graphics, Rai.
Typeset at Printek India, New Delhi.

PUBLISHING FOR ONE WORLD
NEW AGE INTERNATIONAL (P) LIMITED, PUBLISHERS
4835/24, Ansari Road, Daryaganj, New Delhi-110002
Visit us at **www.newagepublishers.com**

PREFACE

One of the goals of research in Pattern Recognition and related sub-areas such as Image/speech/Signal/Language processing, analysis and understanding for the last three decades or so has been to develop fundamental techniques for non-numerical data processing. In this endeavor Pattern Directed Information Analysis is used as a core function for flexible interactive, intelligent man-machine interface for diverse application in industry, and to reduce the alienation between the machines and the society.

The present volume contains some selected papers and overviews by internationally distinguished authorities and some state-of-the-art contribution by active researchers in these related fields. It is well known that the core of the Fifth and subsequently Future Generation of Computing Systems (FGCS) are (i) Problem Solving and Inference making Functions and (ii) Intelligent Man-Machine Interface Functions based on Knowledge Based Computing Systems or KBCS Technology. This book consists of following five Units.

Unit I: Trends of Research and Current Development in Pattern Directed Information Analysis

Unit II: Methods and Techniques in Pattern Recognition and Cluster analysis

Unit III: Speech and Signal Processing and Applications

Unit IV: Image Processing and Compression

Unit V: Image Analysis and Recognition

The central theme of the book is set in Unit-I by D. Dutta Majumder in the paper entitiled, " A unified Framework for Pattern Recognition (PR), Image Processing (IP), Computer vision (CV) and Artifical Intelligence (AI) in Future Generation Computer Systems: A Cybernetic Approach". The paper after providing a full-fledged overview about the technical objectives of the evolution to the Fifth Generation Computer Systems (FGCS) technology combining highly parallel processing and knowledge based systems for flexible interative intelligent man-machine interface is to be upgraded to future generations using a parallel logic language as the kernel of the new computer technology. Some new developments treated in this paper are constraint logic programming (CLP) as a new paradigm for image processing/computer vision and an architecture for soft computing based PR/IP/CV for a new class of bio-signals such as gesture, intention, emotion recognition for man-machine interface in service robots. H Fujisaki (Japan) in his paper entitled, "Problems and Prosepects of Speech Recognition Research" after an overview on the current status discusses in some depths several issues that are believed to be crucial for further progress in recognition and understanding of natural utterances with less and less resrictions on the speaker, manner of speech, dialect and topic. A. Rosenfield (USA) in his paper "Pyramid Algorithms for Finding Global Structures in Images" presents his approach making use of the pyramid cellular architecture to rapidly compute global information about an image in the methodology of CV system design which was established as a path breaking work. S. C. Kak (USA) presented a survey of the advanced techniques used in natural language processing and knowledge representation therein – and in this connection presented the case study of "The Paninian Approach to Natural Language Processing"

Unit II comprises of eight contributions on advanced methods and techniques in classification and pattern recognition out of which seven are on theoretical developments and the other on cluster analysis. The paper by C A Murthy and D Dutta Majumder (India) provides a "Consistent Estimation of compact Regions in R^2" that can be used to estimate clusters, the convergence of the methodology is also proved. Some interesting probability models for classifications based on Scale Invariant Discriminatn Functions are reported in the paper by T M Pukkila and C R Rao (USA). W A Mahmoud and L A M Bennett (UK) presents a new clustering method for speaker independent word recognition in their paper entitled "Creating reference Pattern via a Vector Quantization Algorithm. A Pal (Pathak) and S k Pal (India) in their paper entitled "Effect of Mislabelled Training Samples on the Convergence of a learning Process" have treated m-class N-feature parametric pattern recognition problem. The paper entitled "Cluster Analysis of Iconometric Measurements of Hoy Sala Sculptuers" by G Gobindaraju, M Bugbandar and G Siromoney (India) presents an extremely interesting study on the identification of temple sculptures – in this case of ancient Pallava, Pandeya, and Chola Dynastys. Z A Azmi, M Alaa and E Younis (Egypt) presents an interesting "Comparison Study of Classical Statistical and Fuzzy Tools in Medical Diagnostics" in order to establish the fuzzy logic as a possible candidate for medical diagnositcs applications. S K Pal and P K Pramanik (India) presents some results on their scheme "Seed Point Extraction using Fuzzy Measures: An applcation to clustering vowel sounds" in connection with speech recognition and speaker identification problem. The paper entitled "An Advaned Pattern Classification Scheme using Genetic Algorithms (with a case study on the point classifiction problem)" by P dutta D Dutta Majumder (India) presents results of investigation on the application of evolutionary class of algorithms on PR problems namely a critical appreciation of other soft computing approaches, along with a comparative study and how and why their version of GA outperforms the existing benchmark.

Unit III comprises of six contributions of some advanecd methods and techniques of speech and signal processing and their applications to real life problems of generation and recognition of pattens. K K Paliwal (USA) presents "A study of Nonlinear Transformations of Partial Correlation Coefficeints for vowel recognition" and established that vowel recognition performance is best with Log-area ration. The second paper by M Ganessan, S S Agrawal, A M Ansari and D Pavate (India) also describes some successful experiments on "Recognition of Hindi Vowels and Speakers using Sequential Pattern Matching Techniques". The paper by Z D Bai, P R Krishnaiah and L C Zhao (USA) entitled "Signal Processing using Model Selection Methods," presents technical review of some developments on multivariate statistical techniques for detection of the number of signals using eigen values. Next two papers are on atmospheric science related signal processing entitled "Diffractoin Pattersns as observed in T V signal Propagation" and "Echo Patterns is SODAR during Winter over Calcutta" that present the results of three collaborative multi-institutional projects funded by Dept. of Science and Technology, Government of India. The project were "Statistical Studies of the Troposphere for Design of Microwave Links," at Indian Statistical Institute, Calcutta University. In both the projects Bengal Engineering College at Shibpore and Radio Science Division of National Physical Laboratory were the collaborators. The results are of great national relevance to India. The last paper of the Unit is an invited paper on a frontier subject relating to signal processing and atmospheric science entitled "Fractal/Multifractal and Mutual Information in the study of Atmospheric Dynamcis with a case Study of Complexity of Wind Direction" presents the results of an in-dpeth study of the comparative usefulness of some of the most important mathematical formalisms, along with some measures of complexity in wind direciton.

The Unit IV consists of five papers covering mainly preprocessing tools and techniques and image data compression. The first paper of this Unit is by P C Mali and D Dutta Majumder (India) entitled "Some Analytical Properties and Fast Algorithms of a Discrete Linear Basis in Image Processing" which describes the properties of an image processing tool, namely discrete linear basis transform, and compares its performance with other standard 2D transforms. A more recently introduced image-processing tool is multi-scale morphology. The second paper by S Mukhopadhyay (Singapore) and B Chanda (India) entitled "Local Contrast Enhancement of Color Images using Multi-scale Morphology" presents an application of this tool in color image enhancement. Bezier curve approximation is used for curve drawing in computer graphics. However, a two-dimensional extension of the concept may be used to model image intensity. The paper entitled "Segmented Bezier Curve Approximation with a Control Parameter" by B B Chaudhuri and S Dutta (India) presents an efficient method for segmented curve approximation and studies its properties. Rests of the papers are on image compression. First one is the paper by S K Mitra (USA), M K Kundu, C A Murthy and B B Bhattacharya (India) which is based on relatively recently emerging concept called fractal dimension and iterated function system entitled "A New Probabilistic Approach for Fractal Based Image Compression". Finally, the paper entitled "LUT Based Color Quantization for Image compression" by P Pal and K Dutta (India) presents a simple but efficient color image compression method using a pre-computed color-palette.

The papers that are grouped in Unit V are on mid-level processing like segmentation to analysis. The first one "Image Segmentation Using Grayleel Co-occurrence Matrix" by B Chanda and D Dutta Majumder (India) is on a classical method of threshold selection using graylevel co-occurrence matrix and thereby segmenting the image. Another method of threshold selection is presented in the paper entitled "Adaptive Thresholding Based on Human Psychovisual Charactersistics" by M K Kundu and S K Pal (India). The proposed method utilizes the characteristics of human visual system to determine the threshold. D P Mukherjee (India), in his paper entitled "Image Segmentation using Level Set Analysis," has presented a newly developed concept for image segmentation using level set, where object boundary is estimated through energy minimization. The next paper also presents a currently widely explored technique, namely "Remote Sensing Image segmentation using

M-band Wavelet Packet Frames and Neuro-Fuzzy Tools" by M Acharya and M K Kundu (India). Remaining three papers in this Unit are basically on image analysis, firs of which is "Some Results of Shape and Digitization of Bi-level Pictures" by S K Parui and D Dutta Majumder (India). The authors present fundamental concepts, properties and analysis of shape of 2D binary (i..e, crisp) objects. A complete system is presented in the paper entitled "A Complete System for Document Image Segmentation" by A K Das, S P Chowdhury and B Chanda (India). Here a fully automatic system for decomposing a document page image into its constituents like text, half-tone, line-drawing, table, heading etc. is presented. Finally, the concluding paper entitled "Knowledge Based Apporach to Medical Image Processing: With Some Case Studies"by Mahu Bhattacharya and D Dutta Majumder (India) comprises of two parts. In the first part the authors developed a theoretical formalism for developing uni-model and multi-modal knowledge based image processing and analysis including a cybernetic approach for man-machine interface for medical diagnostics system. In the second part authors present some case studies of real-life applications, such as (i) tumor grading and cancer screening in CNS (ii) breast cancer screening and gradation using mammography images, (iii) quantitative measure of bone erosion process in osteoporosis, and (iv) multi-modal image registration and fasion of ventricular region for making quantitatie assessment of Alzheimers' disease.

After an analytical study of the contents of the Units the first important reliaztion would be the practical implementation of the theoretical advances in PR, IP, CV, AI and the basic mechanism of assocation, inference and learning. The methodologies described in the book are essential in order to realize man-machines interface in natural mode for diverse applications. The next significant realization would be software productivity enhancement and application of knowledge-based techniques with mangement and retrieval of information from data/knowledge-base with highly parallel hardware. Researchers will be very much benefited as several authors have indicaed the limitations of different concepts and technologies and need for future research to achieve break through in some fields. Finally, it may be realized that the present book may be treated as a documentation of evolution of KBCS technologies over a significant period of time as it presents both classical as well as state-of-the-art concepts under a single cover.

Though the full responsibilities for publication and obligation for the shortcomings are with us, the credit goes to our colleagues in the Electronics and Communications Sciences Unit, Indian Statistical Institute who helped us bringing out this volume. We also acknowledge with thanks the assistance we received from our colleagues of the National Center for Knowledge Based Computing, Machine Intelligence Unit and Computer Vision and Pattern Recognition Unit of ISI. We also gratefully acknowledge the help and encouragement we received from the colleagues at the Institute of Cybernetics Systems & Information Technology (ICSIT) in completing this task.

D. Dutta Majumder
B. Chanda
Editors

Contents

Preface

UNIT I: TRENDS OF RESEARCH AND CURRENT DEVELOPMENT IN PATTERN DIRECTED INFORMATION ANALYSIS

1. A Unified Framework for Pattern Recognition, Image Processing, Computer Vision and Artificial Intelligence in Fifth Generation Computer Systems: A Cybernetic Approach — 3
D Dutta Majumder

2. Problems and Prospects of Speech Recognition Research — 60
Fujisaki

3. Pyramid Algorithms for Finding Global Structures in Images — 75
A Rosenfeld

4. The Paninian Approach to Natural Language Processing — 87
S C Kak

UNIT II: METHODS AND TECHNIQUES IN PATTERN RECOGNITION AND CLUSTER ANALYSIS

5. Consistent Estimation of Component Regions in R^2 — 101
C A Murthy and D Dutta Majumder

6. Pattern Recognition based on Scale Invariant Discriminant Functions — 111
T M Pukkila and C R Rao

7. Creating Reference Patterns via a Vector Quantization Algorithm — 120
W A Mahmoud and L A M Bennett

8. Effect of Mislabeled Training Samples on the Convergence of Learning Processes — 131
A Pal (Pathak) and S K Pal

9. Cluster Analysis of Iconometric Measurements of Hoysala Sculptures — 140
S Govindaraju, M Bhagavandas and G Siromoney

10. Comparative Study on Classical Statistical and Fuzzy Tools in Medical Diagnosis 150
Zaki Ahmed Azmi and Mohamed Alaa El Din Younis

11. Seed Point Extraction using Fuzzy Measures: An Application to Clustering Vowel Sounds 160
S K Pal and P K Pramanik

12. A Comprehensive Study on Pattern Classification Problem (With a Case Study on Application of Genetic Algorithms on Point Classification Problem) 174
P Dutta and D Dutta Majumder

UNIT III: SPEECH AND SIGNAL PROCESSING WITH APPLICATIONS

13. A Study of Nonlinear Transformations of Partial Correlation Coefficients for Vowel Recognition 215
K K Paliwal

14. Recognition of (Hindi) Vowels and Speakers Using Sequential Pattern Matching Techniques 221
M Ganesan, S S Agrawal, A M Ansari and K D Pavate

15. Signal Processing Using Model Selection Methods 228
Z D Bai, P R Krishnaiah and L C Zhao

16. Diffraction Patterns as Observed in TV Signal Propagation 242
A K Sen, S K Chatterjee, J Das, A K De, S Chowdhury, N C Deb, D Dutta Majumder, S Basu Mullick and P K Sinha Roy

17. Echo Patterns in SODAR during Winter over Kolkata 246
D Dutta Majumder, J Das, N C Deb, S Chowdhury, S Basu Mullick, P K Sinha Roy, S K Chatterjee and A K Sen

18. Fractal/Multifractal and Mutual Information in the Study of Atmospheric Dynamics: A Case Study on Complexity of Wind Direction 251
A Chanda, J Das and D Dutta Majumder

UNIT IV: IMAGE PROCESSING AND COMPRESSION

19. Some Analytical Properties and Fast Algorithms of a Discrete Linear Basis in Image Processing 269
P C Mali and D Dutta Majumder

20. Local Contrast Enhancement of Color Images using Multi-scale Morphology 287
S Mukhopadhyay and B Chanda

21. Segmented Bezier Curve Approximation with a Control Parameter 313
B B Chaudhuri and S Dutta

22. A New Probabilistic Approach for Fractal Based Image Compression 325
S K Mitra, M K Kundu, C A Murthy and B B Bhattacharya

23. LUT Base Color Quantization for Image Compression 345
P Pal and K Dutta

UNIT V: IMAGE ANALYSIS AND RECOGNITION

24. Image Segmentation using Graylevel Co-occurrence Matrix 357
B Chanda and D Dutta Majumder

25. Adaptive Thresholding Based on Human Psychovisual Characteristics 369
M K Kundu and S K Pal

26. Image Segmentation using Level Set Analysis 381
D P Mukherjee

27. Remote Sensing Image Segmentation using M-band Wavelet Packet Frames and Neuro-fuzzy Tools 392
M Acharya and M K Kundu

28. Some Results on Shape and Digitization of Bi-level Pictures 425
S K Parui and D Dutta Majumder

29. A Complete System for Document Image Segmentation 430
S. Mandal, S P Chowdhury, A K Das and B Chanda

30. Knowledge Based Approach to Medical Image Processing: With Some case Studies 454
M Bhattacharya and D Dutta Majumder

UNIT I

TRENDS OF RESEARCH AND CURRENT DEVELOPMENT IN PATTERN DIRECTED INFORMATION ANALYSIS

1

A Unified Framework for Pattern Recognition, Image Processing, Computer Vision and Artificial Intelligence in Fifth Generation Computer Systems: A Cybernetic Approach

D DUTTA MAJUMDER
Professor Emeritus
Electronics and Communication Sciences Unit
Indian Statistical Institute,
Kolkata 700108, India

ABSTRACT

One of the aims of research for the last three decades in pattern recognition and its sub-areas such as, image processing, analysis and understanding, speech processing, analysis and understanding, natural language processing and understanding, computer vision techniques etc. has been to develop fundamental techniques for flexible interactive intelligent man-machine interfaces for computers. In this paper, the author attempts to argue that for evolution to the Fifth Generation Computer Systems (FGCS) as defined by Japanese and other scientists, [1,2] some of the things required are realisation and implementation of the advances in pattern recognition and its sub-areas, not only to achieve the man-machine interface with a natural mode of communication, but also the realisation of basic mechanism of inference, association and learning, which are inherent in pattern recognition and vice versa for the core functions of FGCS. The next generation computers will be knowledge-based systems which is a sub-domain of artificial intelligence (AI) techniques, and so AI provides the essential link between the above mentioned pattern recognition domains and different application systems. The present paper is an upgradation of the earlier papers by the present author [36, 37, 39, 83].

After introducing natural and intrinsic link between the evolving subjects of Artificial Intelligence and Computer Vision research, particularly in the context of next generation of computer system research, the paper presents an overview of the framework of current image understanding research from the points of view of knowledge level, information level and complexity. Since a general purpose computer vision system must be capable of recognizing 3-D objects, the paper attempts to define the 3-D object recognition problem, and discusses basic concepts associated with this problem. The major applications often mentioned are an industrial vision system and scene analysis in aerial photography.

No attempt is made to discuss about other essential conceptual building blocks, such as software engineering, computer architecture and VLSI technology unless these become very relevant in the discussions of concerned topics of the paper. The author has added a section on limitations of perception, learning and knowledge for computing machines.

The FGCS project aimed at development of a new computer technology combining highly parallel processing and knowledge processing using a parallel logic language as the kernal language of the new computer technology. Another important development treated in this paper is the constraint logic programming (CLP) a new paradigm for image processing.

In the end, we propose an architecture of soft computing based pattern recognition [6,36,46,82,85] for a class of bio-signals such as gesture, intention, emotion including voice for application to robotics application: Especially, the problem of inferring emotion and intention is considered to be an important research for future generation of computing systems (FGCS) research.

Keywords: Pattern Recognition; Artificial Intelligence, Image Processing, Computer Vision, Fifth-Generation-Computers, Knowledge Based Systems, Man-Machine-Interface, Speech Recognition, Language Processing, Emotion Intention Recognition, Parallel Inference Machine, Constraint Logic Processing.

1.1 INTRODUCTION

During the joint session of Eighth World Computer Congress and IFIP Congress 1980 in Tokyo, September 1980 a very important Japanese national project was presented. This project was known as Pattern Information Processing Systems (PIPS); a 14-year old project, it was just completed and was also the subject of a small concluding symposium in the Congress. Some of the work was demonstrated on one of the floors of a high rise building called Sunshine City in which the Congress took place. PIPS covered 12 main areas of research with more than 20 application programmes divided into 4 main parts -(1) devices and materials, (2) information processing systems, (3) integrated system prototype and (4) pattern recognition systems. It was announced that the work involved around ten thousand man-years of work. There were diverse reactions to this project among the commentators and scientists, particularly some adverse remarks by some Japanese commentators themselves, whereas the other including foreign visitors which included the present author realised that PIPS will eventually procure a prominent place in the history of information technology.

During the same IFIP congress some preliminary information about a nascent national computer project the fifth generation computer systems (FGCS programme) was distributed to some select visitors. As a member of the IFIP Technical Committee on digital systems design I received a copy of that information sheet. Actually, the first English version of the Japanese views in some detail came out in proceedings of the International Conference on Fifth Generation Computer Systems of 1981 edited by its Programme Committee Chairman Professor T Moto Oka [1].

In 1979, the Japanese constituted a task force drawn from various Universities and industrial and national research laboratories, which was charged with the task of formulating the image of computers of the '90s. This task force reviewed a 10 years' research project divided into three periods of 3-4-3 years that would lead to what was called the fifth generation computer systems (FGCS). The project started in 1982 and their programme is now being carried out by Institution of New Generation Computer Technology (ICOT). After that, there have been several national, cooperative and corporate efforts in this field outside Japan, in USA, UK, FRG, France, EEC and India, as a result of which a new framework of R & D in Information Technology is emerging which will differ from past R & D environments and different literatures on diverse aspects of FGCS research are being published. No attempt will be made here to present a complete review of the status of FGCS research.

From the information depicted in the first two paragraphs it should be clear to us that the project PIPS, the main motivation of which was to investigate the R & D requirements in terms of devices, circuits and systems (hardware, software logic and mathematical algorithms) for Pattern Information Processing was of crucial importance in deciding about FGCS R & D programme. Secondly, a certain amount of humanlike intelligence structure or capability of learning to gather knowledge from the continuous processing and handling of information patterns, needs to be incorporated in the next generation of computers.

An acceptable science of intelligence, or an information processing theory of intelligence in cognitive sciences, perhaps would guide us in the development of design technology of intelligent machines as well as explicate intelligent behaviour as it occurs in humans or other animals. Since such a general theory is still very much a goal, attention should be limited to those principles relevant to the engineering goal of building intelligent machines. In the author's view, in this process, one can contribute more to the development of general theory of natural intelligence, as speech pattern recognition and computer vision experiments in the last three and a half decades have contributed to the speech understanding and image understanding processes of living beings.

However, the next generation computing may be a general Information Technology System evolved from unification of several current state-of-the-art concepts, where no individual subsystem need be identified as the next generation computer. Intelligent interfaces will make communication easy, whereby identification of a typical device becomes irrelevant, and knowledge-based systems can extend the range of services, that computers can perform. At the intellectual level, some of the current disciplines will merge, and some new disciplines will emerge, such as Cybernetics, Information Science and Statistical Sciences are merging at theoretical level, and communication, computation and control systems are merging at the technological level [13, 14].

In this paper, an attempt is being made to highlight salient features of FGCS research in relation to some of the selected topics as mentioned in the title of this paper, and their relevance and future directions to objectives, architectures and applications.

1.2 SOCIAL AND TECHNICAL OBJECTIVES OF FGCS RESEARCH

It is well known that computers were designed by mathematicians and engineers mainly to solve numerical problems and even in fourth generation computers with VLSI architecture there has not been any significant change in that respect. Whereas in the world to-day, if we conduct a survey about the information generated as a result of the interaction between modem science and society that needs to be processed for decision making purposes in different sectors of the society, we are bound to conclude that more than 80 per cent of the information are non-numerical in nature, such as natural languages, speech sounds, printed characters, cursive scripts, photographic images, ECG, EEG, EMG, X-ray photographs and many other diverse non-numerical documentary information.

Present day computers have not been able to demonstrate their processing power in a satisfactory way in these applied fields. The future computer systems will have to have the capability to obviate these difficulties and will be used to process with numerical processing capability of the fourth generation computers. An incomplete possible list of applications including current ones [2] may be as follows:

Application Areas

FGCS application areas may be as follows:

1. *Man-Machine Communication:* *(a)* Automatic Speech Recogni-tion, *(b)* Speaker Identification And Recognition, *(c)* OCR Systems, *(d)* Cursive Script Recognition System, *(e)* Speech Understanding System, *(f)* Image Understanding and *(g)* Natural Language Processing.
2. *Bio-Medical Applications:* *(a)* ECG, EEG, EMG Analysis, *(b)* Cytological, Histological and other Stereological Application, *(c)* X-ray Analysis, *(d)* Diagnostics, *(e)* Mass Screening of Medical Images such as Chromosome Slides for Detection of Various

Diseases, Cancer Smears, X-ray and Ultrasound Images and Tomography and *(f)* Routine Screening of Plant Samples.

3. *Application in Physics: (a)* High Energy Physics and *(b)* Bubble Chamber and other forms of Track Analysis.
4. *Crime and Criminal Detection*: *(a)* Fingerprint, *(b)* Handwriting, *(c)* Speech Sound and *(d)* Photographs.
5. *Remote Sensing and Natural Resources Study and Estimation: (a)* Agriculture, *(b)* Hydrology, *(c)* Forestry, *(d)* Geology, *(e)* Environment, *(f)* Cloud Pattern, *(g)* Urban Quality, *(h)* Cartography, the Automatic Generation of Hill-shaded Maps, and the registration of Satellite Images with Terrain Maps, *(i)* Monitoring Traffic along Roads, Docks, and at Airfields, *(J)* Exploration of Remote or Hostile Regions for Fossil Fuels and Mineral Ore Deposits.
6. *Stereological Applications: (a)* Metal Processing, *(b)* Mineral Processing, *(c)* Biology and *(d)* Mineral Detection from Microphotographs of Ore Sections.
7. *Military Applications:* All the above six areas of applications plus *(a)* Detection of Nuclear Explosions, *(b)* Missile Guidance and Detection, *(c)* Radar and Sonar Signal Detection, *(d)* Target Identification, *(e)* Naval Submarine Detection, *(f)* Reconnaissance Application, *(g)* Automatic Navigation based on Passive Sensing, *(h)* Tracking of Moving Objects and *(i)* Target acquisition and Range Finding.
8. *Industrial Applications: (a)* Computer Aided Design and Manufacture, *(b)* Computer Graphic Simulation in Product Testing, *(c)* Automatic Inspection in Factories, *(d)* Non-Destructive Testing, *(e)* Object Acquisition by Robot Arms, for example by "Pin Picking", *(f)* Automatic Guidance of Seam Welders and Cutting Tools, *(g)* Very Large Scale Integration related processes, such as Lead Bonding, Chip Alignment, and Packaging, *(h)* Monitoring, Filtering and thereby containing the flood of Data from Oil Drill Sites or from Seismographs, *(i)* Providing Visual Feedback for Automatic Assembly and Repair, *(J)* Inspection of printed circuit boards for spurs, shorts and bad connections and *(k)* Checking the results of casting processes for impurities and fractures.
9. *Robotics, Computer Vision and Artificial Intelligence: (a)* Intelligent Sensor Technology, *(b)* Natural Language Processing, *(c)* All Computer Vision Applications, *(d)* Object Acquisition and Placement by Robots and *(e)* Designing Expert Systems for Specific Applications that require non-numerical Information Handling.

10. *Management Applications: (a)* Management information systems that have a communication channel considerably wider than current systems that are addressed by typing or printing and *(b)* Document reading and other office automation work.

From a cursory glance of the above list one can summarise that the role of FGCS is to enhance productivity in low productivity areas among non-standard operations in the tertiary industries, overcoming constraints on resources and energy consumption, realisation of mass level health-care, education and other support systems and step towards transition to a world society.

From this incomplete list of application areas we should also conclude that FGCS research should be aimed at two major objectives: one being social, namely, to reduce or eliminate the alienation between man and machines and to make available the machines as cheaply as possible, the second being the technological objective of overcoming the deficiencies in processing of huge amount of non-numerical information. The Japanese task force suggested a systems approach known as knowledge information processing systems (KIPS) that would support a high logic level and at the same time remain friendly and familiar to human beings. KIPS will have knowledge bases and will be able to infer from knowledge and solve problems and take decision in a way similar to the human approach. Such knowledge based systems will evolve out of the present-day machines, which are designed around a numerical computer system. But these new machines will have the ability to have access to the meaning of information and understand the problems described in human languages for solution, so that these machines will be aiding human beings in their different socio-economic tasks at a higher level of intelligence instead of replacing the human being.

1.3 EVOLUTION TO THE NEXT GENERATION COMPUTING SYSTEM

For evolution to the next generation some of the things required to be realised are practical implementation of the advances in pattern recognition, image analysis, computer vision and artificial intelligence, not only to realise man-machine interface with a natural mode of communication, but also the realisation of basic mechanism for inference, association and learning, which are inherent in the pattern recognition, image analysis, computer vision and artificial intelligence research, and methodology so as to form the core function of the fifth generation computer.

Next important point is the realisation of enhanced software productivity and application of AI techniques in order to utilise the above functions, along with retrieval and management of knowledge bases in hardware and software.

It is needless to state that in order to equip these FGCS of tomorrow with human-type senses and logical process, larger and faster chips than the VLSI must be fabricated, and chip designers are therefore looking towards the production of super chips by Ultra Large Scale Integration (ULSI).

It is estimated that it will be possible to place approximately 10 million transistors on a single IC chip. At present the size of the chips vary from 5 and 7 mm on a side for most complex functions. By 1990, the size was increased to 25 cm on a side, and the size of the individual features used for the circuits on the chip will be approximately one micrometer (one millionth of a meter), which means 100 million rectangular shapes on the chip surface. Previously these shapes have been specified manually for the designs. For a reasonably sized design team it is impossible to carry out the job in a way that can be expected to lead reliably to circuits that satisfy the desired function. Though, basic fabrication technology is capable of implementing these shape features, but to provide methods such that a designer can quickly, correctly and economically convert a high level functional specification into an accurate representation of shapes that will lead to properly functioning circuits is a challenge which can be met by designing an "intelligent ULSI-CAD" System associated inspection mechanism incorporating the latest results of shape analysis, pattern recognition, computer vision and robotics.

Apart from that as we have little guidance as to how such a high level description should be formally specified, a substantial experimentation with the variety of formal languages known as Hardware Design Languages (HDLs) is needed before any consensus can be obtained about the best means of expression.

It should be understood that interplay between performance strategy, functional specification, architecture and choice of technology (CMOS, NMOS or bipolar current mode logic-such as ECL) are of overriding importance. There are even more exotic technologies, such as the use of super-conducting Josephson junctions [3], or the use of gallium arsenide instead of silicon as a semiconductor. It can be safely expected that, in the FGCS research all these are being explored, but practical systems will be built using silicon as a semiconductor substrate, in either NMOS or CMOS or some hybrid technology that combines the virtues of both.

1.4 OVERVIEW OF FGCS AND INTELLIGENT INTERFACE SYSTEM

The main functions of fifth generation machines were (83) broadly classified under three headings:

1. Problem solving and inference making functions,
2. Knowledge-based management functions and
3. Intelligent man-machine interface functions, these we still to be realised.

These functions will have to be realised by making individual software and hardware subsystems to correspond with each other in the general FGCS framework. A conceptual framework of the system (1) is shown in Fig. 1.1. The descriptions of the blocks in the diagram are to some extent self-explanatory. In this diagram the upper half of the modeling (software) system circle corresponds to the problem-solving and inference functions, the lower half to the KBMS functions.

The portion that overlaps the human system circle corresponds to the intelligent interface function. From this diagram it should be understood that the intelligent interface function relies heavily on the two former groups of functions.

In my view, high speed computer communication (14) and local area networking will also constitute an important infrastructure in the final FGCS usage as shown in modified version of Fig.1.2.

A problem, as presented by the application system, through some end-user language that can use voices, figures and images etc., is analysed, recognized/ understood by using knowledge about the language and images/pictures. This is then translated into intermediate specifications, which are given to the programming system. Here an effort is made to understand the problem, using the knowledge about the problem domain, and as a result processing specifications are formulated. Those specifications are transformed into a program and optimized through referencing the knowledge about the machine system and the knowledge representation. The program, written in some algorithmic programming language, is then processed by the problem-solving and inference mechanisms and the knowledge-base machines. The numerical computation, symbolic manipulation and database machines in Fig.1.2 are coprocessors of the problem-solving and inference, as well as the database machine.

Though all these four above mentioned functions are integrally related to each other, the defined plan for developing an intelligent interface comprises: *(a)* patterns recognition and image processing and understanding, *(b)* natural language processing and *(c)* automatic speech

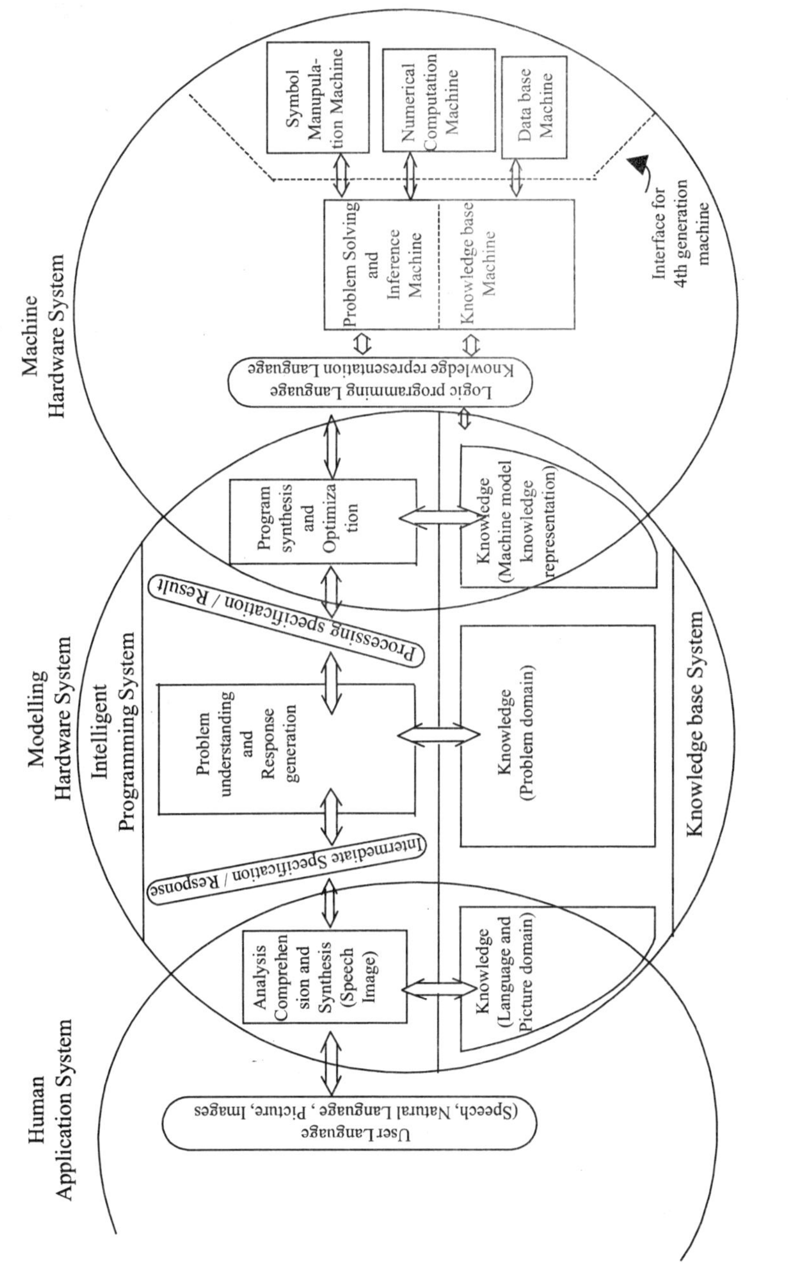

Fig. 1.1 Conceptual diagram of the fifth-generation computer system

recognition and understanding [4 -12]. Actually in the FGCS scheme the intelligent man-machine interface system constitutes front-end processor for input/output using spoken and written natural languages and pictures and images, as shown in Figs. 1.1 and 1.2 giving the basic configuration

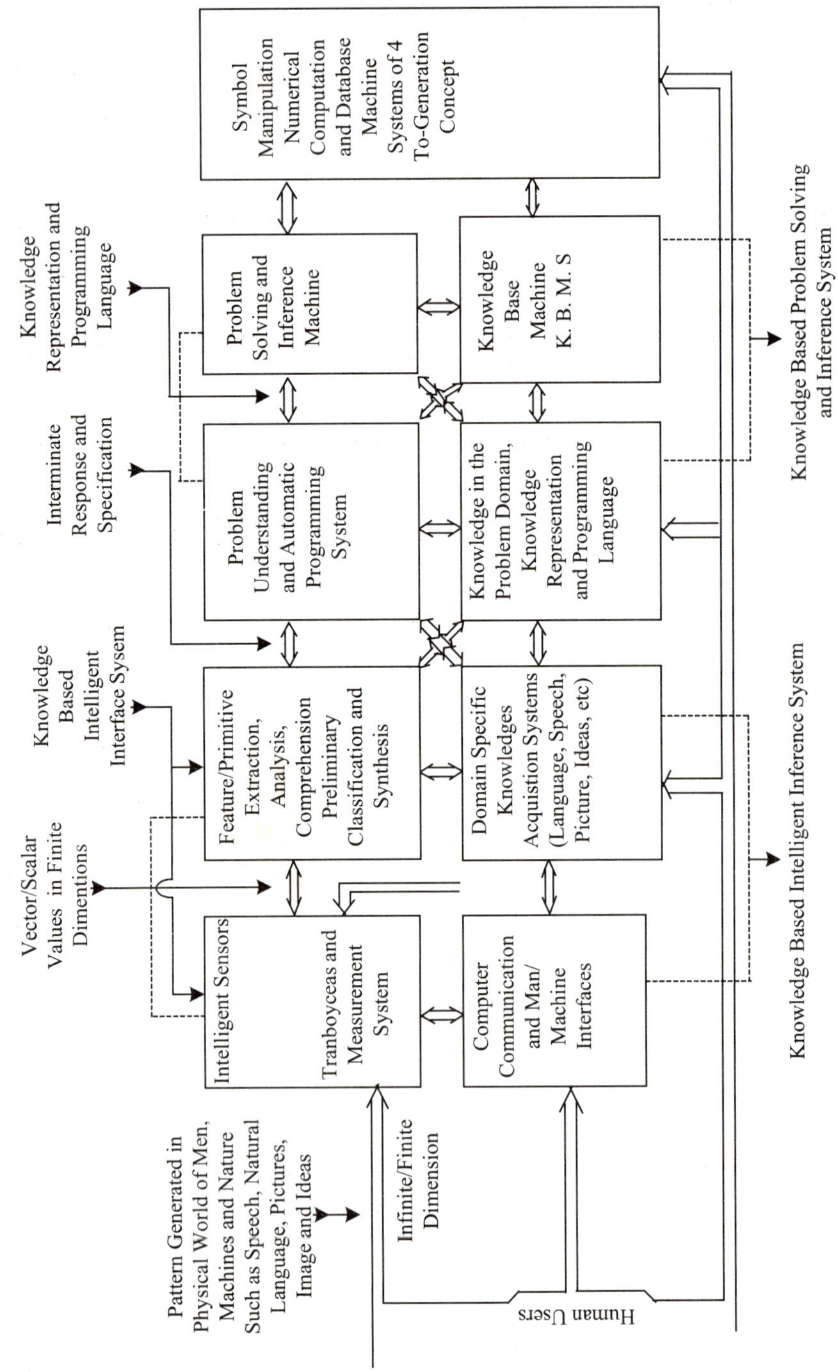
Symbol Manipulation Numerical Computation and Database Machine Systems of 4 To-Generation Concept
Knowledge Representation and Programming Language
Problem Solving and Inference Machine
Knowledge Base Machine K. B. M. S
Knowledge Based Problem Solving and Inference System
Interminate Response and Specification
Problem Understanding and Automatic Programming System
Knowledge in the Problem Domain, Knowledge Representation and Programming Language
Knowledge Based Intelligent Interface Sysem
Feature/Primitive Extraction, Analysis, Comprehension Preliminary Classification and Synthesis
Domain Specific Knowledges Acquistion Systems (Language, Speech, Picture, Ideas, etc)
Knowledge Based Intelligent Inference System
Vector/Scalar Values in Finite Dimentions
Intelligent Sensors
Tranboyceas and Measurement System
Computer Communication and Man/ Machine Interfaces
Pattern Generated in Physical World of Men, Machines and Nature Such as Speech, Natural Language, Pictures, Image and Ideas
Infinite/Finite Dimension
Human Users

Fig. 1.2

and the conceptual structure of FGCS. The theoretical approach should make FGCS imply a unified approach of Cybernetics and General Systems Theory as implied by Dutta Majumder's Noblest Wiener Award winning paper [13].

The FGCS aim of developing systems that are highly user-friendly suggest that current high level computer languages are inadequate for many purposes. A corollary to this interpretation is that natural languages (English, Japanese, Hindi, French, Bengali, etc.) will become the ultimate programming languages assuming that sufficiently intelligent man-machine interface can be designed. Existing natural language systems are less flexible than normal English and make more demands of the users. These systems work on a limited vocabulary where jobs are fed into the system via keyboard. One purpose of FGCS research will be to overcome the limitations of existing natural language system and the demand for oral communications in FGCS requires speech recognition, speaker identification and speech understanding systems.

In order to provide flexible interactive intelligent man-machine interfaces in the final FGCS, the plan for research will have to be motivated to develop fundamental techniques in all the three categories of pattern recognition research namely, natural language processing, speech processing and graph and image processing. However, in the research and development stage, state-of-the-art terminals will have to be used in all FGCS projects, because, an intelligent man-machine interface system will itself be a kind of KBMS composed of a front-end processor of various input/output forms, flexible KBMS and problem solving/inference systems. However, in the FGCS context we use the term "intelligent interface system" to denote the front-end processor for input/output in the form of natural languages, both spoken and written, pictures and images (computer vision).

1.5 PERCEPTION, LEARNING AND LIMITATIONS OF KNOWLEDGE FOR MACHINES

Again if we look back towards the history of modern computer science and information technology, two major approaches will come to light: that of the so-called 'hard' school and the soft 'school'. Members of the first group are concerned with building a strong theoretical component to their work based on pure mathematics. Members of the second group consider that the strong theoretical component is not only unnecessary but positively harmful. The first group on the other hand looks down upon the second school as being solely involved with mundane applications. But practical realisations usually come from theoretical and experimental co-ordination of findings of both the schools.

Innovations often came from reassessment of old ideas from both schools. The development of succeeding generations of computers is marked by new views of current activities and these new views encourage extensions to the techniques employed. Sometimes these new views come well before the technology can support them, or the mathematical tools and techniques are well obstructed for the purpose beforehand. Consequently, these views remain in the backwaters of mainstream science waiting to be re-discovered. *Some examples are the ideas of Charles Babbage and that of Alan Turing* (83).

The FGCS specifications about the inference machines and knowledge-based systems on the face of it seems to be influenced by the "hard" school. The important results of PR and AI in the last decade that interest designers have been to show that a higher level of problem specification can be achieved by engineering 'knowledge' and pattern-directed inferences and it is this principle that should underlie new design objectives.

In the last four decades since the advent of digital computers there has been a constant effort to expand the domain of computer applications. Pattern Recognition (PR) is an area of activity to process the huge amount of non-numerical information generated as a result of the interaction between science and society. Computer scientists were interested in designing machines that can speak, write and understand like humans do. That area of activity gave rise to what is now known as Artificial Intelligence (AI). Both of these motives are inherent in that area which we sometimes call Machine Learning (ML) or Machine Perception (MP).

At present the ability of machines to perceive their environment is very limited. A variety of transducers are available for converting the sound, light, temperature, pressure, etc. to electrical signals. *When the environment is carefully controlled, the perceptual problems become trivial. But as we move beyond having a computer read magnetic tapes to having it read hand-printed characters or analyze biomedical photographs, we move from problems of sensoring the data to problems of interpreting and understanding them.*

The apparent ease with which vertebrates and even insects perform perceptual tasks is both encouraging and frustrating. Psycho-physio-physical studies have given us many interesting facts, but not enough understanding to duplicate their performance with a computer. We are all experts at perception but none of us knows much about it. Since there is no general theory of perception, we had to start with modest problems. Many of these involve pattern classification-the assignment of a physical object or event or idea to one of several prespecified categories. Extensive study of classification problems led to some mathematical models [4]-[8] that provide theoretical basis for classifier designs. Of course, in any specific application one ultimately must come to grips with special characteristics of the problem at hand. A general mathematical theory of pattern recognition and machine learning is yet to be formulated.

1.5.1 Limitations of Knowledge for Machines

Without entering into the brains and the machines and mathematics [15] controversies, it can be safely argued that these controversies relate to our logical mind, whereas we have other inspirations and experiences that give us a clue to deeper levels of consciousness and intelligence. Most of the neurophysiological theories and mathematical models so far are based on grossly simplified view of the brain and central nervous system. There are a variety of properties--memory, computation, communication, control, learning, purposiveness, reliability despite component malfunction-which it seems difficult to attribute to mere mechanisms. The mind and intelligence we ordinarily use, is limited to reception of sensory data from the outer physical world, and usually not the inner mental world, which we use to assemble, to observe, to control, to regulate and to communicate for the purpose of learning, organising, planning and calculating analogues to the computer. Published literature on FGCS research from Japan and elsewhere more or less concerns this logical mind which is attempted to be made computer (IBM)-compatible.

In his famous incompleteness theorem, Kurt Godel has shown the limitations of the logical process [16]. According to Nagel and Newman [17], the axiomatic method, which lies at the foundations of our modern theory of logic programming and probability, has certain inherent limitations. They proved that it is impossible to establish the internal logical consistency of a very large class of deductive systems. Sir Arthur Eddington, in his *Philosophy of Science* [18] terms logical mind as "the group structure of a set of sensations in a consciousness ? The late Nobel Laureate Professor Dennis Gabor's [19] compromise formulation is *I have a consciousness, which receives sensory data from an outer, real, physical world, and images, concepts and urges from my unconscious mind.* In this partition of mental structure to conscious and unconscious mind does not seem to me to be a realistic concept. It is more likely that there are different levels of consciousness which are interactive in nature from unconscious, extra conscious, superconscious and other non-cognitive levels of awareness to ordinary consciousness which performs the day-to-day information processing, and motivates psychodynamic activities (D. Dutta Majumder 93, 94, 95).

Without attempting to put forward any coherent theory of intelligence, it can be safely argued that the nature of intelligent messages [20] in different types of flashes of inspirations and other usual experiences is entirely different from artificial intelligence of the FGCS Logic Programs talked about in literature. It should be understood that all this is at a far lower level than that exhibited by a human being, and that many differences between man and machine are not only qualitative but enormously quantitative. Even to partially bridge this gap some kind of a theoretical breakthrough will be required.

1.6 AUTOMATIC SPEECH PATTERN RECOGNITION AND FGCS RESEARCH

We have explained in previous sections that FGCS will be intelligent knowledge-based systems (IKBS) and they should be more congenital to the non-specialised computer user. Naturally, user languages will be in non-numerical forms such as speech, natural language, picture, image, etc. Obviously these machines will not be a carbon copy of human behaviour. Rather their objective will be to enhance the human information processing abilities and so they will be firstly, complementary in nature, secondly, able to tackle the problem of matching between two information processing systems, namely man and machine. From this point of view, IKBS will be usable in its real sense of the term only with an intelligent user interface and these two are mutually dependent on each other.

For the FGCS programme the forms of information transfers have been identified as:

1. Natural language;
2. Speech: and
3. Photographs and images.

Speech being the most natural mode of communication, speech interactive communication with machines presents the most interesting study.

It is well known that natural language in its spoken form is mostly ambiguous and largely depends on the listener[7]. Unambiguous communication with speech, say, military communication on radio channels will always require restricted vocabulary and well-structured communication protocols. So it can be summarised that man-machine communication with IKBS will also be in restricted manner. Factors that causes variability in spoken continuous sentences may be listed as:

1. Position of sound within a word;
2. Position of a word within a sentence;

3. Speed of talking;
4. Vocal characteristics;
5. Temporal effects, such as cold, fatigue, mood, etc.,
6. Dialect differences; and
7. Extraneous noise.

The status of speech understanding systems as envisaged in ARPA project in Hearsay-II system is well known[8]. But the Japanese FGCS plan aims to produce over what was achieved in ARPA project. As for example ARPA accepts connected speech from many co-operative speakers in a quiet room using a good microphone with slight tuning/ speaker accepting 1000 words using an artificial syntax in a constraining task yielding 10 per cent semantic error in a few times real time on 100 MIPS machine, whereas FGCS proposes continuous speech with multiple speakers in accurate and careful mode and with moderate adaptation 50000-word vocabulary with 95 per cent word recognition rate at three times the real time. Some of the major problems that ought to be looked into from the very beginning are:

1. Nature of the communication process itself and normal human expectation;
2. Minimizing the number of errors and misunderstandings;
3. Mistakes may be made either by the machine or by the man; and
4. From (3) we should conclude that there should be a logical method for correcting the human errors or may be correction is introduced through repetitions.

An important aspect is the emerging VLSI technology vis-a-vis speech synthesis and recognition as the technology has proved itself to be worthy of supporting these complex algorithms, which means FGCS will be approachable by novice computer users.

Looking at the state-of-the-art in published literature [2], [8], [9], it seems that speech recognition is more difficult than speech synthesis. Earlier in speech recognition research we tacitly assumed that all the information needed to recognise the utterance was in fact present in the speech waveform. But recent understanding reveals that there are many periods during an utterance when the words being spoken are not clearly recognisable in the waveform, if present at all, which means that to build an ASR system comparable with human being, a wide variety of knowledge must be brought to bear during the perceptual process in order to understand what has been spoken. Such a complete understanding system does not seem to be realisable in this decade and so one need not expect that the FGCS will lead to speech understanding system with multiple speakers utilising large vocabularies in a realistic syntax.

Whether one uses formant or LPC representation, some parametric analysis becomes inevitable to reduce amount of information to be analysed retaining the essential information for recognition process. Next problem, however, is normalisation of the input speech in time and frequency.

From these and several other considerations one can conclude that it is the basic understanding, which limits our progress, and recognising continuous speech remains an elusive goal for this decade at least.

1.6.1 Speech Understanding System

The five year ARPA Speech Understanding System (SUS) project (1971-76) made a clear distinction between CSR and SUS [8], [9]. In CSR, every element of a spoken message has to be identified whereas in SUS one aims at capturing 'meaning of a message' even though all its elements are not identified correctly.

Following Liberman's [10] model of human speech perception, various processes involved in ASR can be summarized as illustrated in Fig.1.3. Different processing levels correspond to knowledge sources (KSs), such as syntax, semantics and pragmatics which will be used in the system.

The role of syntactic knowledge is firstly to determine whether a particular sequence of words can belong to the processed language, and secondly to predict the words which can occur at a given place within a sentence. *Semantic knowledge will determine if a syntactically correct sentence is meaningful. Semantic information will also be used in order to predict sentence constituents (words or phrases) on a meaningful basis.*

Pragmatic knowledge will determine whether a meaningful sentence is plausible according to the context of the ongoing dialogue. Pragmatics can also be used for prediction, and man-machine dialogue control.

The scheme in Fig. 1.3 does not reflect the architecture of a particular system, but the usual functional levels of an ASR/SUS and forms the basis of experiments conducted at the ECSU of ISI at Calcutta. The levels indicated were merged in HARPY system, but we intend to experiment separately.

The understanding of a sentence implies the cooperation and communication of various knowledge sources, namely phonetics, phonology, prosody, lexicon, syntax, semantics, pragmatics, etc., which can be very different and have to be activated at the right moment when certain conditions are verified [11]. This principle of SUS functioning is indicated in Fig. 1.4.

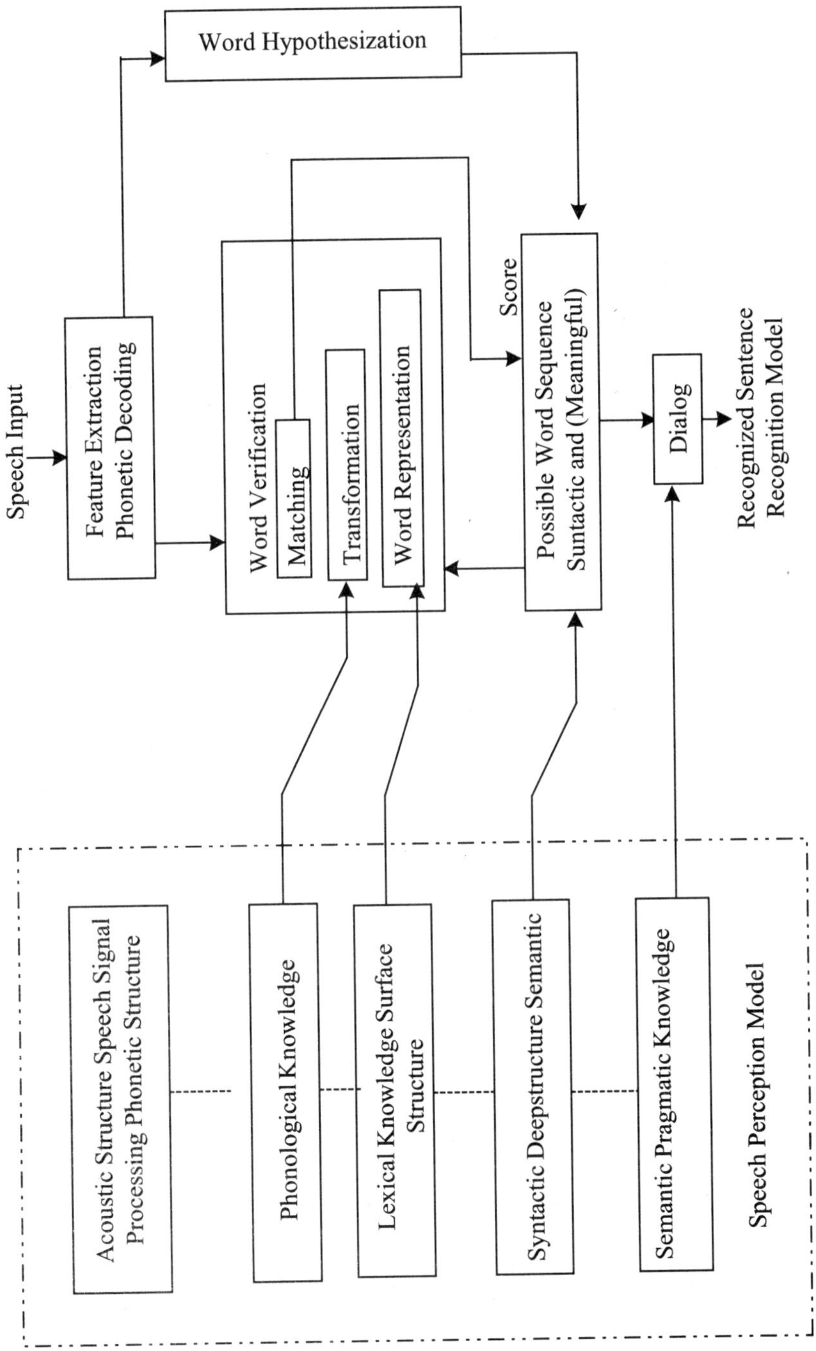

Fig. 1.3 Typical process in continuous speech recognition

The world hypothesization can be carried out either in a top-down or bottom-up way as illustrated in Fig. 1.4.

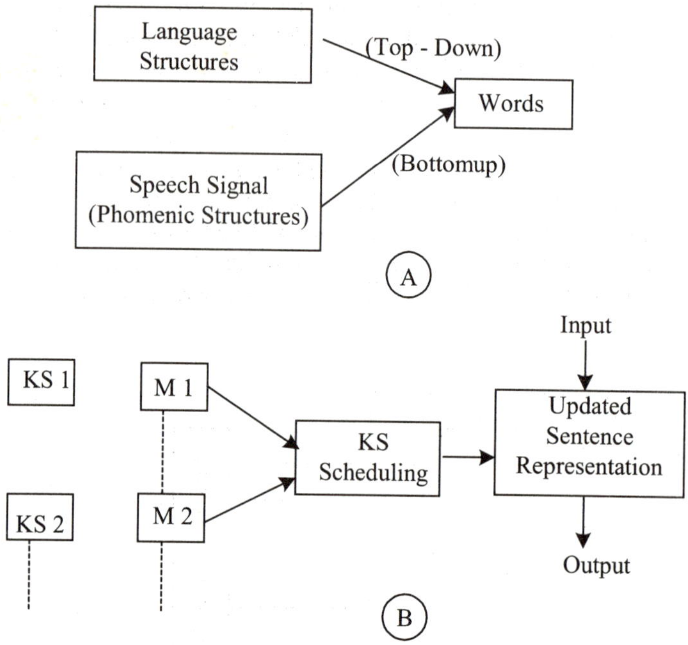

Fig. 1.4 (*a*) Lexical word level, (*b*) Principle of Speech understanding system

To each KS is associated a specific activation mechanism which varies from KS to KS, and the KS scheduler shown in the Fig. 1.4(*b*) will be incharge of assigning priorities between the KSs, and therefore controls the communication and interaction between the KSs.

There are two general models of KSs interaction, namely, the hierarchical model and the blackboard model. The blackboard model is data-driven and was used in HEARSAY-II of CMU. The hierarchical model is straightforward and can be developed with small minicomputers and are being experimented at ISI, largely for competence build-up and solving some inherent problems of speaker independence and large vocabulary.

Coming to the stated objective of Japanese FGCS effort of building a speech-activated typewriter with a vocabulary of 10,000 words by voice patterns of hundreds of speakers has many difficult problems. To realize such a device in the next five years will require some break-through and large amount of investment.

1.7 STATUS OF NATURAL LANGUAGE (NL) PROCESSING RESEARCH

The economically developed societies in the current age are shifting their emphasis from an economy based on the manufacture and dissemination of goods to one based on the generation and dissemination of information and knowledge, because it enables them to achieve better quality of life with given resources. This should have been equally, if not more, applicable for developing countries, as the resources are more limited here, but for the technological gap.

Much of this information is expressible in common man's language, and the task of gathering, manipulating, acting on and disseminating for social usage can be aided by computers, and this power can be made available to segments of population that are unable or unwilling to learn a formal computer language.

According to David Waltz of the University of Illinois [21] the following applications are either commercial product now or will be in the market in the next years or so:

1. NL database front-ends,
2. NL interfaces for operating systems, Library Search Systems, and other software packages,
3. Text filters and summarizers,
4. Machine-aided translation systems (that will need editing) and
5. Grammar checkers and critics.

There has not been much work in the area of systems control such as: *(a)* controlling industrial robots, missiles, or power generators, *(b)* diagnostic advices about medical problems, mechanical repairs, investment analysis etc. *(c)* creation of graphic displays, *(d)* teaching courses etc.

Such important applications as document understanding and document generation in the strict sense of the term are still far away[12].

However, because it is now possible to produce special purpose chips with relative ease, the desire to find and exploit potential parallelism in NL has lead to several parallel language processing models. To be useful, NL systems must be capable of handling a large vocabulary and large data base. A small system cannot be very natural.

FGCS goals in NL processing as envisioned by Japanese group is difficult to be realised in the next 10 years; but the scientific and technological fallout of this research will bring about fundamental changes in certain aspects of quality of life and work.

1.8 ARTIFICIAL INTELLIGENCE AND COMPUTER VISION – PERSPECTIVE AND MOTIVATION

Without entering into the philosophical issues involved in an attempt to define the meaning of artificial intelligence, the author intends to attempt a working definition delineating the approximate boundary of the evolving concept of Artificial Intelligence (AI) which will be automatically and intrinsically linked with the ideas inherent in the development of Computer Vision Systems (CVS). AI is the study of how to make machines to do some types of mental and associated activities, which at the moment man can do better than computers. Such tasks to mention a few are writing computer programmes, perceiving and understanding languages, pictures, photographs and visual environments, game playing and theorem proving, medical diagnosis, chemical analysis and engineering design, doing mathematics and problem solving, engaging in commonsense reasoning etc. The systems that can perform such tasks possess some degree of AI.

Perception of the world around had been crucial to the survival of living beings. Animals with much less intelligence than man are capable of very sophisticated visual perception. Early effort at simple static visual perception by machines led in two directions, namely pattern recognition and machine learning, and secondly image processing and understanding systems. The first group of activities, being based on strong mathematical foundation, are yet to fully collaborate with Al which from loosely structured and empirical orientation is improving very fast. Whereas, because of inherent flexibility latter group is typically regarded as falling within the purview of AI.

During the past two decades, the field of Computer Vision (CV) including its subfields of image processing and image understanding or scene analysis, has developed from the seminal work performed by a small number of researchers at the few centers of AI research into a major sub field of AI with widespread involvement. The intellectual climate for progress and theoretical basis for IUS & CVS has improved with the work conducted under the US DARPA IU program at CMU, University of Maryland, MIT, SRI, University of Rochester, Stanford University, The Virginia Polytechnic and State University and University of Southern California and Electronics and Communication Sciences Unit, Indian Statistical Institute, Calcutta, India. The goals and motivations of these researchers in the last decades were varied in nature, such as understanding and modelling of human vision system, development of comprehensive theories of perception and solution of some fundamental problems in AI. Most of the others were engaged in solving practical problems in applications of Computer Vision Systems. Research in designing computer systems to 'see' continues to be fascinating, challenging, exciting and to some extent bewildering. Bewildering, because the construction of effective general purpose CVS has proven to be exceedingly difficult, though vertebrates carry out this task with very high level of sophistication easily. Though Human Visual System (HVS) need not be considered as the best possible vision system, but it is definitely the best known one, so we shall often try to understand our perceptual mechanism, in course of our discussion.

The field of CVS now contacts such diverse disciplines and areas as cognitive psychology, pattern recognition, image processing, computer systems hardware and software, geometrical optics, computer graphics, electrical engineering, neurophysiology, psychophysics, and mathematics, and shares common problems from areas in automatic speech recognition, knowledge base management systems, robotics and artificial intelligence. The boundaries of this research are rather amorphous, particularly when we consider the important application domains in the context of designing next generation (commonly called fifth generation) of computer systems (FGCS).

As major motivation for developing computer vision was to develop application-oriented tool for solution of some contemporary problems, most of the successful scene analysis systems were based on *adhoc* working principles [22]-[24], with a limited domain of specialised applications. In the last decade there were several proposals to obviate these limitations [25]-[27], aimed at developing competent re-usable, extensible but general tools at the system level. Although concern for generality would appear natural in the context of biological vision or abstract vision theory, it is not necessarily a desirable characteristic of a methodology directed towards application-oriented vision system[26]. This realisation has resulted in gradual transition in AI from general purpose solvers to knowledge-specific systems. At general CVS comparable to HVS implies large range of objects and background with invariant system performance to large changes in viewing angle, illumination angle, contexts and obscured areas, along with ability to withstand rapid contextual changes such as indoor and outdoor environment.

It seems very difficult to achieve any of these characteristics, in the present state-of-the-art, and we should look at the necessary system characteristics in terms of a range of real problems from several application domains. We should also understand that the human vision and reasoning cannot be so neatly subdivided as: *(a)* sensing, *(b)* segmentation, *(c)* recognition, *(d)* description and *(e)* interpretation as in computer vision. An elementary machine vision principle is illustrated in Fig.1.5, which is self-explanatory. As for example recognition and interpretation are very much interrelated in HVS but is not understood to the point that they can be analytically modeled. We should look at these five subdivisions of functions for limited practical implementation of the state-of-the- art CVS.

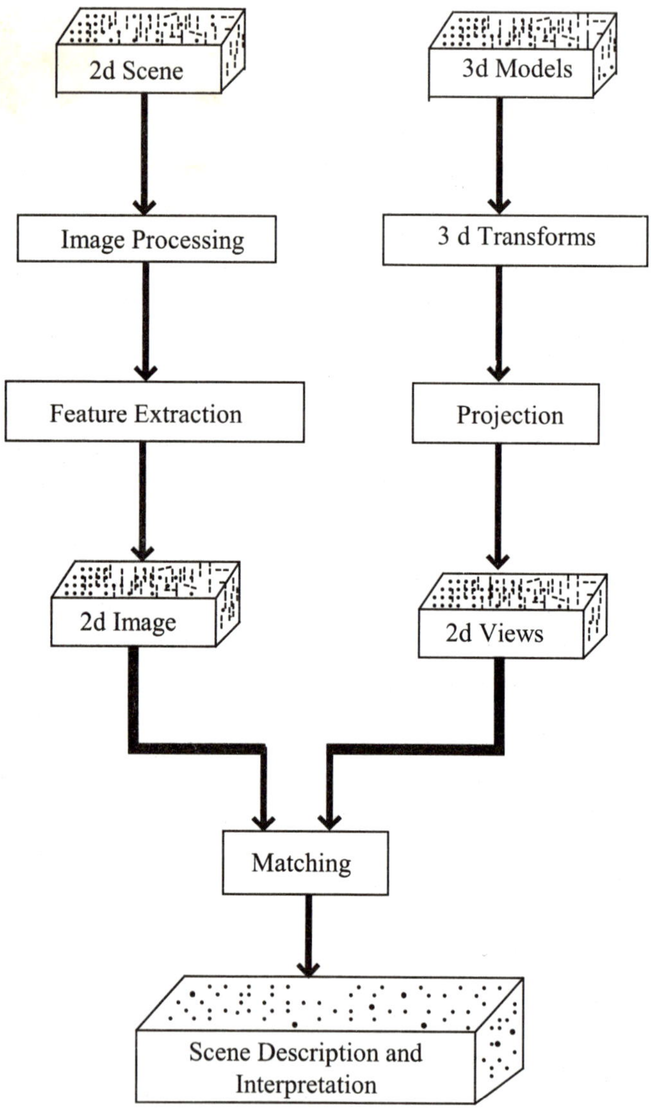

Fig. 1.5 Machine-vision principle

1.8.1 Levels of Vision

Taking into account the above developments we see that in some sense we may divide the general purpose CVS arbitrarily into several and at least three basic levels of vision. Levels proposed by Tennenbaum and Barrow [40: are-Level 0: Original image; Level 1: Intrinsic surface characteristics; Level 2: 3-D Surface descriptions; Level. 3: 3-D Object descriptions; Level 4: Symbolic description of scene. But most CVS are based on three-step process. The computational problems involved in deriving Level 1 from Level 0 are fairly well understood now. The next step from Level 1 to Level 2 is being extensively studied. But the choice of object representation at Level 3 will influence surface extraction and so the Level 2.

Computer vision efforts have advanced over the past 30 years along three fronts: low-level vision, the extraction of basic features such as edges from an image, inter- mediate level vision, the deduction of the three-dimensional shape of objects from the images: and high level vision, the recognition of objects and their relationships. Some representative research projects include the Hard-Eye robotic vision project initiated at the Massachusetts Institute of Technology in Cambridge and at Stanford University in Palo Alto, Calif: the pattern-information processing system (PIPS) project in Japan one of the earliest focused research programmes sponsored by the Ministry of international trade and industry, the US Defence Advanced Research Project Agency's image understanding system (IUS) project and the current Darpa next-generation project.

In Fig. 1.6 we present development in CVS research efforts over the past 25 years or so along the three fronts in some very significant projects in USA and Japan. At the lowest level (LLV) (sensor information – usually an intensity image) pictures are segmented into regions of similar primary features to extract 'primitive' information from a scene ranging from modelling the characteristics of incident and reflected light properties of a body to the detection of edge segments [41]-[44] and connecting them into lines or curves or regions with uniform properties[29] (Fig. 1.7). The next intermediate level of vision (ILV) refers to the procedures that use the results from ILV to produce structures in the picture or portions of the picture where complete knowledge regarding model features and topological structure are available. Techniques are edge linking, segmenting, shape analysis [45H 47], description and recognition of objects. Techniques such as local graph search and global optimization using dynamic programming as developed in AI can be employed to merge regions and to assign label sets to them [30]. The highest level vision (HLV) may be viewed as the process that attempts to emulate cognition, encompassing a broader spectrum of processing functions. HLV may use a relational database to store knowledge and a vision strategy akin to production system, which has to be based on knowledge-directed or goal-oriented analysis. Although this three-level process applies to many vision systems, several systems omit or add one or more steps depending on complexity of environments.

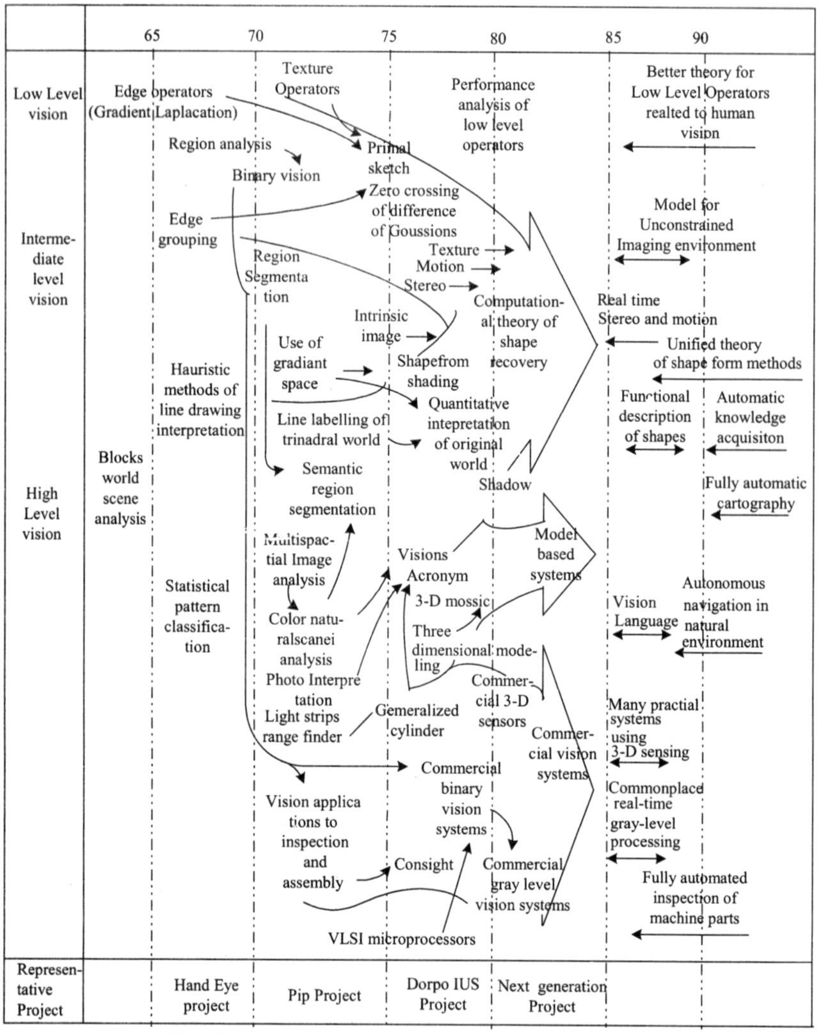

Fig. 1.6 Development of CVS research efforts

There are several competing paradigms to achieve the goal in this rapidly evolving field. It may not be possible for the author to discuss in depth the paradigms and research issues facing the field. Rather, he intends to provide a state-of-the-art overview of the breadth of problems which must be considered in the development of general computer vision systems.

The overview will include the framework of current image understanding research from the point of knowledge, information and complexity levels along with knowledge organisation and control structure in image understanding system (IUS). Different computational approaches to IUS will also be discussed briefly.

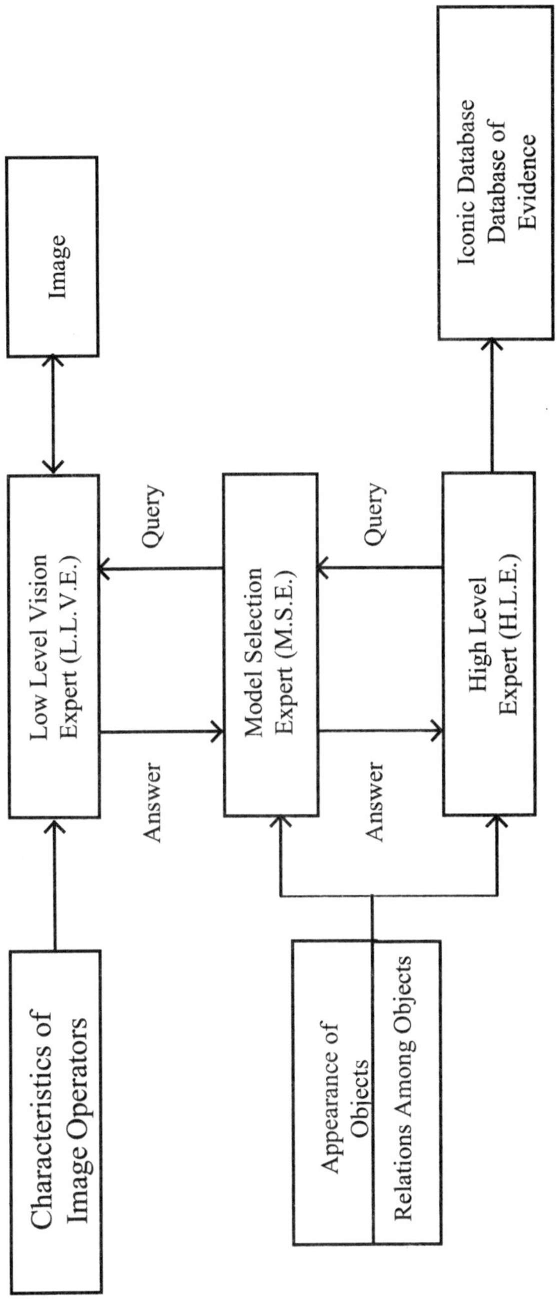

Fig. 1.7 A knowledge-based image understanding system with three levels of expertise for combining evidence

We shall try to present examples of problems in designing knowledge-based computer vision system [36], [37] for applications such as organization of aerial image analysis and industrial inspection system.

1.8.2 Framework of Image Understanding Research

Binford [31] gave a good survey of the different IUSs developed during the late seventies as feasibility studies. Some of them were proved to be good in some application areas as indicated in the earlier section of this paper, but several crucial problems became clear [32]. These are *(a)* viewpoint-dependent image model, *(b)* weak segmentation ability and *(c)* limited number of object classes in restricted environments. Though the scenes were essentially 3-D, the systems model scenes by 2-D image features, and weak segmentation produced erroneous results.

It was pointed out by Takeo Kanade [33] that the discrimination between 2D-image features and 3D scene features is essential in IUS, and the interpretation must be based on 3D features and relations. Michael Brady [34] indicated the extensive researches that are conducted to extract 3D features from 2D imagery. Banow and Tanenbaum [35] proposed to use the photo-geometry as the theoretical basis to recover intrinsic properties of 3D objects such as range (depth), orientation, reflectance and incident illumination of the surface element visible at each point in the image. The idea finds good support as these are useful for higher level scene analysis, humans can determine these characteristics irrespective of viewing conditions, and such a description is obtainable from noncognitive process. It has been shown that 3D shape of object surface can be recovered from 2D image features such as shading, textures, and contour shape.

David Man [26] advocated segmentation methods based on HVS with symbolic representation of pictorial information known as primal sketch. Haralick proposed a functional approximation of local gray level distribution to capture more informative pictorial characteristics. Chanda, Chowdhury and Dutta Majumder recently suggested some preprocessing techniques [41]-[43] useful for improved segmentation work, where the importance of segmentation based on 3D scene characteristics rather than 2D image features was also indicated [35]. Paul Besl and Ramesh Jain [48] proposed an effective utilization of all the information present in range images, as according to them range image understanding problem is a well-posed problem in contrast with the ill-posed intensity image understanding problem. Most segmentation work for single intensity images is based on thresholding, conelation, histograms, filtering, edge detection, region growing, texture discrimination or some combination of the above. The key issues in range image processing are planar region segmentation, quadratic surface region segmentation, roof-edge detection etc.

Methods and techniques of Artificial Intelligence can be used in this problem (of segmentation), above which is a central issue in realising intelligent computer vision systems. Intelligence often implies smart selection from a huge number of alternatives, in the sense that if the number of alternatives is small, not much intelligence is required for the system to work well. The problem now is how to increase the level of intelligence of IUS by using different Al ideas.

Levels of Knowledge for IUS

Problem *(a)*, *(b)* and *(c)* mentioned above in this section are closely related to the levels of knowledge required in IUS and CVS:

Physical Knowledge: The physical laws governing imaging process in the multidimensional physical world along with the geometry among camera, light source and object, and spectral properties of light source, sensor and material of the object provides powerful knowledge sources. Shape from X, (X : shading, texture, motion, object contour) and stereo vision can use this knowledge to recover 3D shape from projected 2D image features.

Visual Perception Knowledge: Gestalt laws of proximity, similarity, continuity, smoothness, symmetry etc. are used for the grouping of primitive pictorial entities into more global ones. This knowledge plays an important role in segmentation and also to group primitive 3D features into global characteristics.

Semantic Knowledge: For recognition of objects, knowledge about properties and relations between them is essential. The first two types of knowledge are general and domain-independent but semantic knowledge is domain-specific.

Levels of Information

Fig. 1.8 shows information levels in IUS and the processes developed so far to transform information across the levels. Here also we observe three levels of analytic processes. In the low level process, (LLP), physical and neuro-physiological knowledge are to be utilized to define and extract the most informative image features (primal sketch).

Fig. 1.8. Information levels in IUS [facts about brightness values are explicit in the image; brightness changes, group of similar changes, blobs, and texture are explicit in the primal sketch surfaces are explicit in the 2½D sketch; volumes are explicit in the world model].

In the middle level process (MLP), the local features of LLP are to

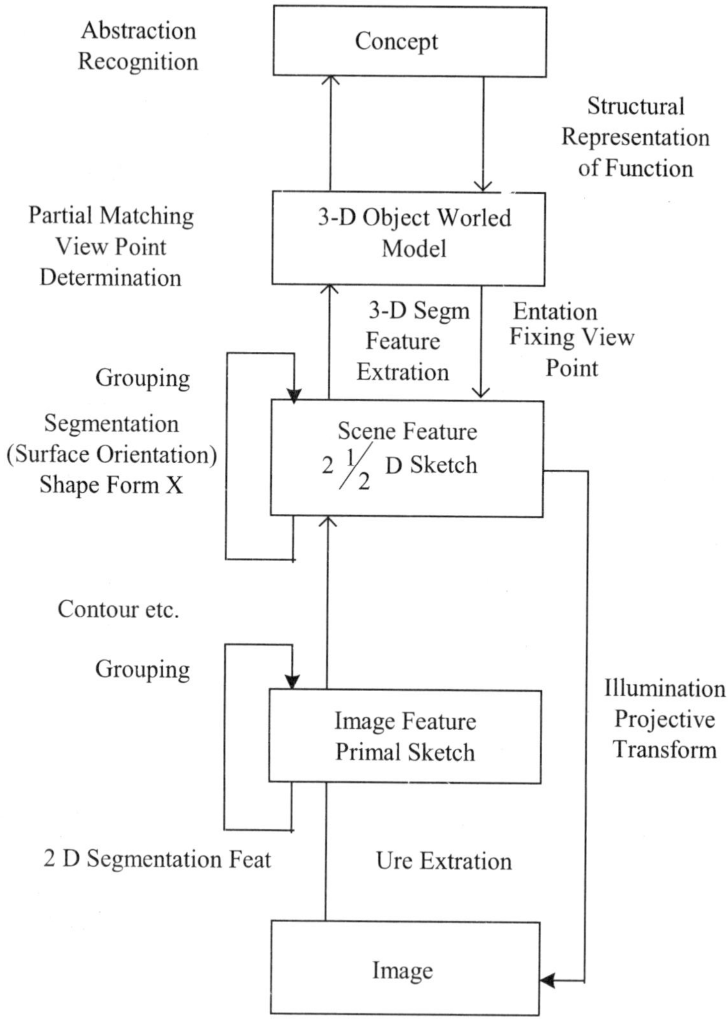

Fig. 1.8 Information levels in IUS

be grouped into global image features using the perceptual knowledge, again the image features are to be transformed to scene features (2-D features) using the physical knowledge so that matching can be performed with the 3D object model. There are many possibilities in the grouping and also 3D interpretations of a projected 2D image feature which calls for use of AI techniques. Probabilistic relaxation labeling [49] is a useful computational scheme to reduce such ambiguities.

The major task of the high level process (HLP) is to find the object model which matches with the information extracted from the input image. Problems in this are: *(a)* Depending on the viewing angle and the time of observation, 2-D appearance of 3-D and moving objects changes very much, *(b)* If an object is occluded by others it is *difficult* to predict its appearance, and *(c)* an abstract object can have widely varying appearances. These are the problems of under constraint to be solved by sophisticated model representation and utilisation of the semantic knowledge.

It should be understood that knowledge representation and control structures are key issues in the HLP in both IUS and AI and so also in CVS.

Levels of Complexity of a Scene

Depending on several environmental and other factors the levels of complexity of a scene can be assessed. These are, to mention a few: *(a)* Natural vs Artificial; *(b)* 3D vs 2D; *(c)* Flat vs Curved Surface; *(d)* Non-isolated vs Isolated Object, *(e)* Generic vs Specific Model; *(f)* Uncontrolled vs Controlled Imaging Environment.

Important factors in assessing complexity levels in motion understanding are: *(a)* Solid vs Deformable object; *(b)* Constrained vs Unconstrained Motion; and *(c)* Physical vs Semantic Description.

It is well known that because geometric relations and shapes of man-made artificial objects are often composed of analytically well-defined open and closed curves such as [45],[47] line segments and disks, it is easier to recognise and group them by such knowledge. Homogeneity and texture are also usual characteristics of artificial and natural scenes respectively. Hough transformation [46], [50] is an effective method to extract well-defined global image features such as straight lines and ellipses (2D appearance of a flat disk). Some scenes are essentially 2D such as maps, design charts, documents etc. It should be noted that partial matching is inevitable in 3D object recognition. In 3D scene analysis flat vs curved surface can be used as a measure of complexity. In the case of non-isolated occluded (overlapped) object, local property measurement is to be performed and partial matching is a must.

Most of the CVS developed so far are for specific models, such as for recognition of industrial parts with specific properties of shape, material, colour, texture etc. Generic models are abstract objects such as airplane, boat, table, house etc. If the imaging environment is under control as in industrial CVS the SN ratio and information level can be increased. Active sensing using a laser range finder and a structured pattern projector greatly facilitates the feature extraction process [77]-[80].

Regarding the factors of complexity in motion understanding it is obvious that if the motion of the camera can be constrained the analysis is facilitated. Description of the motion of deformable objects such as clouds is difficult because the shapes can change during the motion. It is also to be understood that the exact physical description of the motion is to be interpreted to obtain the semantic description.

1.8.3 From Images to Object Models

There is a wide gap between raw images and understanding of what is seen. It is too difficult to bridge this wide gap for CVS design. To identify, describe and localize objects, we need intermediate representations that make various kinds of knowledge explicit and that expose various kinds of constraint. Visual interpretation of completely unconstrained scene is far beyond the current state of the art of IUS and CVS. This view has led many researchers to the development of general, mainly 3D feature extraction methods. The other aspect of understanding is of course recognition, which again requires feature measurement. The difference between recognition and measurement is that, the former is in terms of generic objects and the latter is of a specific object instance.

The principle of recent IUS researches toward 3D object recognition is based on the proposition that 3D objects are generic models to understand a scene, and the features measured from an image are their specific appearances.

3-D Object Recognition

P J Besl and Ramesh Jain [48] reviewed the object recognition problem in the following subject areas:

1. 3-D object representation schemes
2. 3-D surface representation schemes
3. 3-D object and surface rendering algorithms
4. Intensity and range image formation
5. Intensity and Range image processing
6. 3-D surface characterisation
7. 3-D object reconstruction algorithms
8. 3-D object recognition systems using intensity images; and
9. 3-D object recognition systems using range images.

There are several overview papers on computer vision treating 3-D issues using intensity images as inputs[40], [34], [51], [31].

3-D Object Representation: In the area of Computer Aided-Design (CAD) geometric solid-object-modelling systems, several representations are commonly used. I shall mention them without any explanation for the sake of completeness. These are

1. Wire-frame representation

2. Constructive solid geometry representation (CSG)
3. Spatial-Occupancy representation consisting of *(a)* Voxel, *(b)* Octree, *(c)* Tetrahedral or *(d)* Hyperpath representations,
4. Surface boundary representation.

Most 3-D object representations in CVS literature can be categorized as one of the above mentioned schemes or as one of the schemes mentioned subsequently.

Generalised Cylinders or Sweep Representation: Generalised cones or generalised cylinders are often called sweep representations because object shape is represented by a 3-D space curve that acts as the spine or axis of the cone, a 2-D cross-sectional figure, and a sweeping rule that defines how the cross section is to be swept and possibly modified along the space curve. Fig. 1.9(*a*) and (*b*) illustrates the idea, which like many great ideas is quite simple. An ordinary cylinder can be described as a circle moved along a straight line through its centre. A wedge can be described as a triangle moved along a straight line through its centre. The shape is kept at a constant angle with respect to the line. The shape may be any shape. The shape may vary in size as it is moved. The line need not be straight. For some objects with varying cross-sections, the circle shrinks or expands linearly as it moves.

Fig. 1.9 (*a*) The generalized cylinder representation is good for a large class of objects. The simplest generalized cylinders are fixed, two-dimensional shapes projected along straight axes. In general, the size of the two-dimensional shape need not remain constant, and the axis need not be straight. Also, the two-dimensional shape may be arbitrarily complex, (*b*) Complicated shapes can be described as combinations of simple generalized cylinders. A telephone is a vaguely wedge-shaped cylinder with *u*-shaped protrusions.

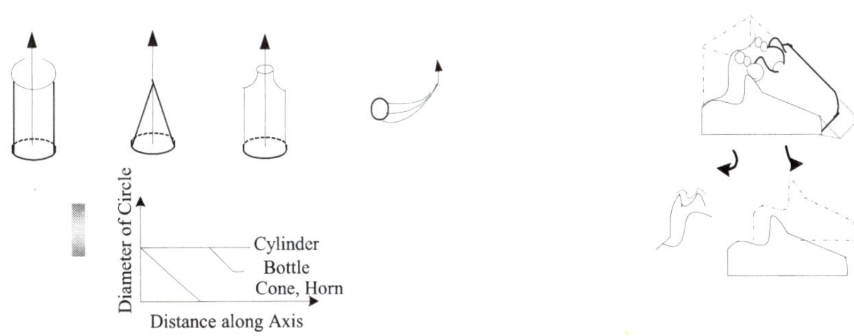

Fig. 1.9

Though this is most suitable for many real world problems, is not very general as it is almost impossible to describe an automobile or human face by this technique. But despite its limitations this is most suitable for vision purposes.

Multiple 2-D Projection Representation: In this method 3-D objects are represented by 2-D silhouette projections. Silhouettes have also been used to recognize aircraft in any orientation against the well-lit sky background. A more detailed approach of a similar nature is the characteristic-views technique described in Chakravorti and Freeman [52].

Skeleton Representation: A skeleton can be considered [53] an abstraction of the generalised cylinder description and consists of only the spines or axis curves, the idea of which is similar to the medial axis or symmetric axis transform of Blum [54].

Generalised Blob Representation: Generalised blobs have been used as a 3-D object shape description scheme in Mulgaonkar *et al.* [55] by sticks (lines), plates (areas), and blobs (volumes).

Spherical Harmonic Representation: For convex objects and a restricted class of non-convex objects, shapes can be represented by specifying the radius from a point as a function of latitude and longitude angles around that point.

Overlapping Sphere Representation: In this scheme[56] many spheres are required to represent a relatively smooth surface. Though it is a general-purpose technique, it is rather awkward for precisely representing most man-made objects.

The object recognition problem requires a representation that can model arbitrary solid objects to any desired level of detail and can provide abstract shape properties for matching purposes, which none of the existing schemes are capable. But whatever representations are used, it will be necessary to evaluate surfaces explicitly in at least one module of a vision system, because *(a)* range images consist of sampled object surfaces and *(b)* intensity images are strongly dependent on object surface geometry. Object recognition is largely dependent on surface perception.

Both intensity and range image formation and their processing has been studied by researchers in detail. The book by Ballard and Brown (1982) [57] provides a thorough treatment of these and also object reconstruction aspects of vision and graphics, and in order to save space and time we have to avoid these aspects in this paper.

Some Distance Measures for Shape Discrimination and Recognition: Several authors suggested distance measures [72]-[74] for 2-D shape matching and understanding in addition to the usual Fourier and other descriptors which are computationally complex. In the recent past Dutta Majumder and Parui suggested six new shape distance measures [45], [47], [75], [76] out of which five were information-preserving and satisfy all the metric properties (None of the previous shape distance measures satisfy all the metric properties). The formal approach of Dutta Majumder and Parui is mathematically rigorous. Two distance functions are for simple curves and four are for regions without holes.

Another originality of this approach is the use of the major axis in normalising the orientation of a region in order to construct the shape distance functions explicitly as a result of which they can deal with almost any shape which is based on Dutta Majumder's generalized Mathematic Theory of Shape [96].

The directional codes used to construct some of the shape distances are also a generalization of Freeman's Chain Codes. There have been several extensions to higher order ([37], [45] etc.) chain codes. But in our case the codes are much more general in the sense that they can take real value between 0 and 8 which has not been used before.

In order to extend some of the shape definitions and algorithms to 3-D, we intend to define 3-D continuous directional codes in 3 dimensions. Some of the shape distances can be extended to 3-D cases in a straight forward manner. The 2-D shape distance based on shape vector can be extended to 3-D by considering concentric spheres instead of concentric circles. Similarly, other shape distances are also extendable-in some cases one has to consider skeletal voxels instead of pixels. Similarly, theoretically speaking some of the definitions of measure of degree of symmetry and antisymmetry can also be extended. The approach of Dutta Majumder and Parui along with the approach of generalized cone/cylinder will lead to a more meaningful solution to the shape recognition problem.

1.8.4 Model-based 3-D Object Recognition Using AI Techniques

We have already mentioned about several 3-D object recognition schemes based on intensity images. Consistency among local features and ambiguity in data and knowledge are essential problems in CVS and IUS. The role of control strategy in recognition process is to resolve such ambiguity and to identify global objects by examining the consistency among local image features.

Control Structure

In order to control the recognition process knowledge is crucial to reduce the necessity for "search". On the other hand search can compensate for lack of knowledge. Nagao [58] gave a survey of control strategy in IUS. At this point it may be worthwhile if we look at how model-based 3-D interpretations are possible using an actual rule-based system such as ACRONYM [59], [60], which is often mentioned in CVS literature. This is probably because of the flexibility and modularity of its design, its use of view-independent volumetric object models, its domain independent qualities, and its complex, large scale nature. Fig. 1.10 shows a block diagram of the ACRONYM system and its hierarchical geometrical reasoning process. The system based on prediction-hypothesis-verification paradigm has three main data structures namely object graph, restriction graph and prediction graph, which are found on the basis of the world model and a set of production rules. Nodes of the object graphs are generalized cone object models, arcs are spatial relationships among the nodes and the subpart relations (e.g. is-part-to). Nodes of the restriction graph are constraints on the object models; and directed arcs are subclass inclusions. Nodes of the prediction graph are invariant and quasi-invariant observable image features of objects, and arc are image relationship among the invariant features-which are of the types: must be, should-be and exclusive.

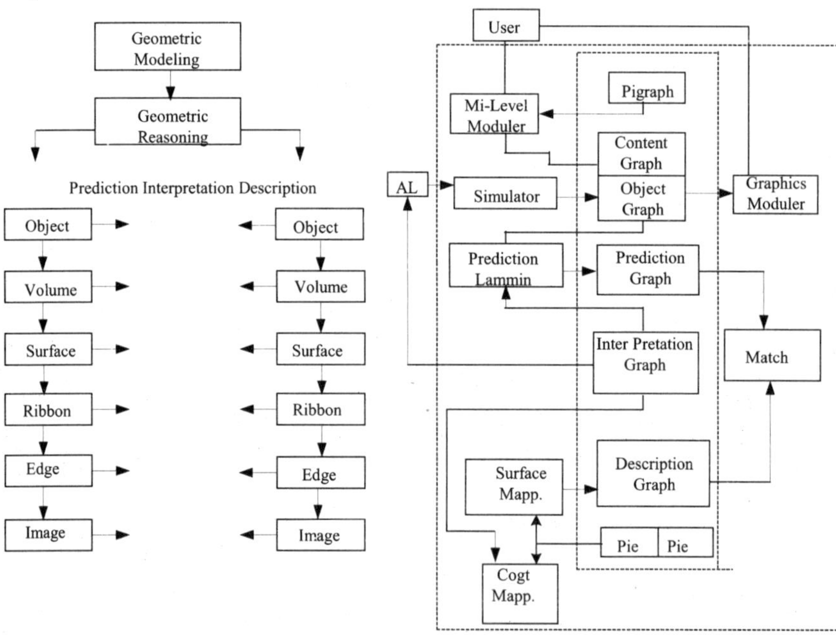

Fig. 1.10 The ACRONYNM system. (From Brooks et al.)

Every data 'unit' of the object has 'slots', such as a cylinder has a length slot and a radius slot which accept fillers or quantifier expressions. The image is processed in two steps. First, an edge operator is applied to the image. Second, an edge linker is applied to the output of the edge operator and is directed to look for ribbons and ellipses, which are 2-D image projections of the elongated bodies and the ends of the generalized cone models. The higher level 3-D geometric reasoning and searches in ACRONYM is based entirely on 2-D ribbons and ellipse symbolic scene descriptions. The heart of the system is a nonlinear Constraint Manipulation

System (CMS) that generalizes the linear SUP-INF methods of Presburger arithmetic [61]. Constraint implications are propagated top-down during prediction and bottom-up during interpretation. ACRONYM system is implemented in MACLISP. Its prediction subsystem consists of approximately 280 production rules and in a typical prediction phase approximately 6000 rule firings occur. But we have not yet come across any published results of 3-D interpretation using ACRONYM except that of some jets on runways.

In the recent past, as we have already mentioned some, there are several other 3-D object recognition schemes based on intensity images which have been developed such as Mulgaonkar *et al.* (1982) [55] using generalized blobs. Fisher (1983) [62] has implemented a data-driven object recognition program called IMAGINE, in which surfaces are used as geometric primitives. Though there are several criticisms of this system, the program did achieve its goal of recognizing and locating a robot and "understanding" its 3-D structure in a test image. Valuable ideas concerning occlusion are also presented in the paper. In all these and in several others including in automatic speech recognition system, unification of bottom-up and top-down process is very important.

Control Strategy For Unification of Bottom-up and Top-down Processes in Spatial Reasoning

It should be noted as above, that geometric relations are used for consistency verification in bottom-up analysis and hypothesis generation in top-down analysis. Hwang Matsuyama, Davis, and Rosenfeld (1983) proposed a control scheme [67] named "Evidence Accumulation for Spatial Reasoning in Aerial Image Under-standing" an important characteristic of which is that it integrates both bottom-up and top-down processes into a single flexible spatial reasoning process. There are three levels of representation and control in that system as discussed earlier.

A binary geometric relation between two classes of objects, 01 and 02 is denoted by REL (01,02) and is used as a constraint to recognize objects from these two classes, at first by extracting pictorial entities satisfying the intrinsic properties of 01 and 02, and then checking that the geometric relation is satisfied by these candidate objects (Fig.1.11). In this bottom-up recognition scheme, analysis based on geometric relations cannot be performed until pictorial entities corresponding to objects are extracted. In general, however, some of the correct pictorial entities often fail to be extracted by initial image segmentation. So one must additionally incorporate top-down control to find pictorial entities missed by the initial segmentation as described by Selfridge (1982) [64]. At this point it may be noted that ACRONYM does not have any top-down goal-oriented segmentation for detecting missing image features.

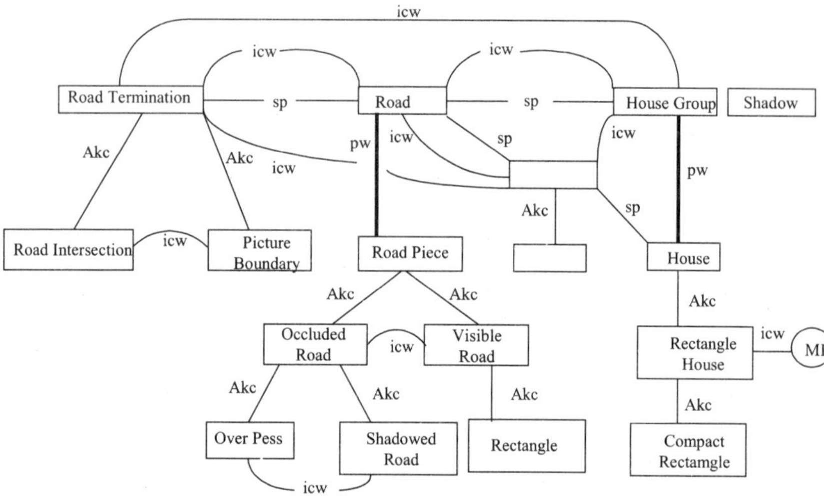

Fig. 1.11 Organization of knowledge about surburban scenes. Links: AKO: a kind of; PW: part whole relation; SP: spatial relation; IO: instance of; ICW: in conflict with.

The above relation can be functionally expressed as

$$01 = f(02) \text{ and } 02 = g(01).$$

Given an instance of 02, say *r*, function f maps it into a description of an instance of 01, f *(r),* which satisfies the geometric relation, REL, with *r*. The analogous interpretation holds for the other function, *g*.

In this system knowledge about a class of objects is represented using the frame theory as enunciated by Minsky (1975) [2], and a slot in that frame is used to store a function such as f or *g*. Whenever an instance of an object is created, and the conditions are satisfied, the function is applied to the instance to generate a hypothesis or expectation for another object which would, if found, satisfy the geometric relation with the original instance. A hypothesis is associated with a prediction area (locational constraint) where the related object instance may be located. In addition to this area specification, a set of constraints on the target instance is associated with the hypothesis. In the case of a road hypothesis the frame name is: Road, and Slot names are: Length, Direction, Left-adjacent-road-piece, Right-adjacent-road-piece, Left connecting-road-terminator, Right-connecting-road-terminator, Left-neighbouring-house-group, Right-neighbouring-house-group etc. All hypothesis and instances are stored in a common database, the iconic date-base (Fig.1.7) where accumulation of evidence i.e. recognition of overlapping sets of consistent hypotheses and instances is performed. Similar ideas have been proposed by Haar [65] and McDormitt [66] to solve spatial layout problems and to answer queries about map information.

Two types of geometric relations "spatial relation" (SP) and part-whole relation (PW) are used. SP represent geometric and topological relations and PW represent AND/OR hierarchies. "A-kind-of" (AKO) relations are used to construct object specialization hierarchies. There are restrictions to avoid redundant hypothesis generation. Fig.4 shows the organization of the entire system in which HLE undertakes the following iterative step:

1. Each Instance of an object generates hypotheses about related objects using functions stored in the object model (frame).
2. All pieces of evidence -both instances and hypotheses are stored in the common data-base-called iconic database. They are represented using an iconic data structure which associates highly structured symbolic descriptions of the instances and hypotheses with regions in a 2-dimensional array.
3. Pieces of evidence are combined to establish "situations", consisting of consistent evidences.
4. Most reliable situation is selected.
5. The selected situation is "resolved" which results either in the verification of predictions on the basis of previously detected/ constructed image structures or in the top-down image processing to detect missing objects.
6. Instantiation of objects at the very beginning of interpretation is performed by the MSE which searches for object models that have simple appearances, and directs the LLVE to detect pictorial entities which satisfy the appearances. The instances thus constructed are seeds for reasoning by the HLE.
7. The HLE maintains all possible interpretations and maximal consistent interpretation is selected.

In order to resolve a situation one of two actions are taken: confirm relations between instances or activate top-down analysis. In the paper [67] mentioned earlier, the MSE analysed the partial knowledge structure of a suburban scene detecting visible road, occluded road, overpass shadowed road etc. (Fig. 1.11).

Some of the problems that need to be solved are as follows: knowledge organization should have the knowledge of how to reason about failures depending on their causes. Secondly, some sort of meta-knowledge about the dependency among geometric relations should be established, so that which one should be examined first, which one is prohibited, which one cannot be done unless some others are established etc. can be coped with. Thirdly, ways to manage mutually conflicting interpretations should be found and it should be possible to perform reasoning on them.

To cope with the problems of ambiguity in data and knowledge because of partial information-all attempts should be made to increase the amount of information. Range sensing is a typical example. The Bayesian probabilistic model has been widely used to compute reliability values, but there are some basic problems in them. The concept of dependency graph as enunciated by Lowrence [68] seems to be a useful method in IUS.

Lee and Fu (69) proposed a design for a general purpose CVS that allows for the proper interaction of top-down (model-guided) analysis and bottom-up (data-driven) analysis. Chakravorti and Freeman [52] also developed an interesting technique using characteristic views as a basis for intensity image 3-D object recognition.

Before concluding this section, for the sake of completeness I have to mention about object recognition using range images, which for lack of space and time, I am not dealing with in this paper. Range image understanding is quickly becoming an important and recognised branch of CVS, as these contain a wealth of explicit information that is obscured in intensity images. In certain environments range-image CVS will be more suited -and this research will perhaps give us new insights into the whole problem of general purpose CVS. Some relevant references for this are Nevatia and Binford [70], Birbhanu [71] and Besl and Jain [48].

1.9 KNOWLEDGE INFORMATION PROCESSING BY HIGHLY PARALLEL PROCESSING: A MODIFIED ICOT MODEL

At this point it may be worthwhile to come back to the suitability of FGCS (highly parallel) architecture for knowledge information processing application like IUS and scene analysis for CVS applications.

The FGCS project aimed at development of a revolutionary new computer technology combining highly parallel processing and knowledge processing technology using a parallel logic language using KL1 as the kernel language of the new computer technology which is called the FGCS technology.

The parallel hardware consists of five models of parallel inference machines (PIMs) having about 1000 elementary processors in total. The PIMOS is fully written in KL1 and has an efficient parallel programming environment for the KL1 [81].

Parallel processing of this kind is classified as parallel symbol processing and much wider applicability to not only knowledge processing applications but also more general problems than conventional parallel processing technology.

1.10 CONSTRAINT LOGIC PROGRAMMING: A NEW PARADIGM FOR KNOWLEDGE INFORMATION PROCESSING IN IP / CV

Historically, the concept of constraint emerged in image processing and computer vision community within the context of the consistent interpretation of the scene analysis from local conditions. This problem can be booked upon as a search problem, in which a search is undertaken for combination of local conditions by which the entire scene can be expressed, in other words the relationship between the local conditions, are named constraints. As an example, if an end of an edge is convex, the opposite end also is a convex edge.

There are two models of the Constraint Logic Programming (CLP) - namely sequential one CAL (Constraint Avec Logic) Fig. 1.12 and parallel one known as GDCC (Guarded Definite Clauses with Constraints) Fig. 1.13.

The describing of problems by stating the relations is called constraint a language describing problems by stating the relations that hold within the problems is called logic programming language, combining the two we get CLP.

1.11 CAL SYSTEM

The CAL system as indicated in Fig. 1.12 consists of the translator, inference engine and constraint solvers.

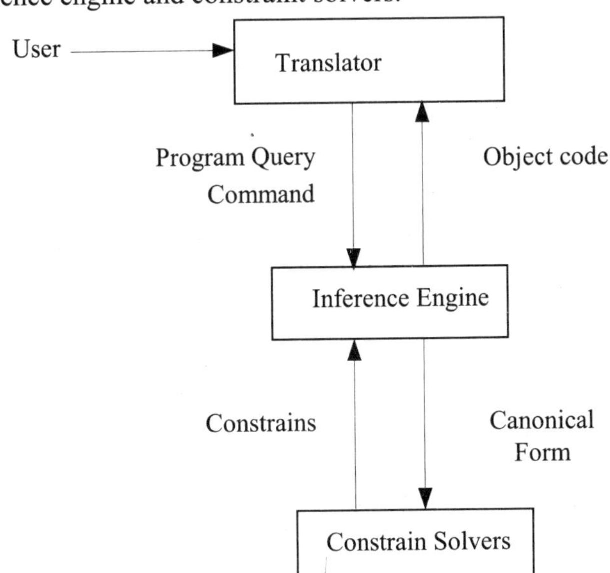

Fig. 1.12 Configuration of the CAL system.

The translator translates a CAL source program into the required object program. While executing a program, if the inference engine encounters a constraint, as constraint solver is invoked to handle it. There can be different types of constraint solver for different versions of CAL system, such as Algebric, Boolean, Linear etc.

1.11.1 The GDCC System

The configuration of the GDCC system is shown in Fig. 1.13. which speaks for itself.

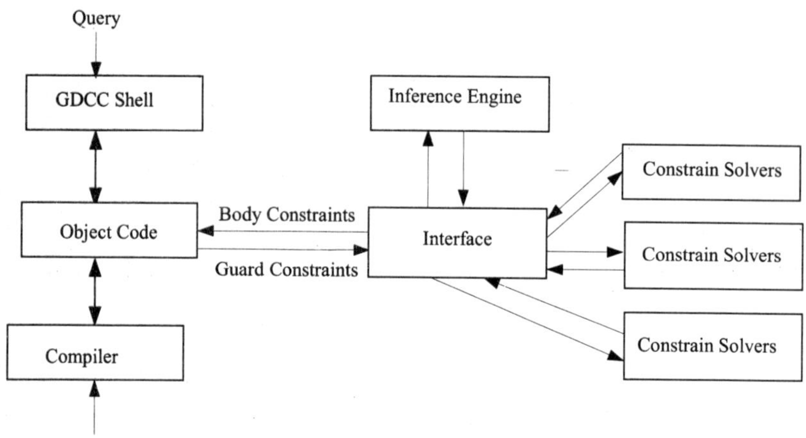

Fig. 1.13 The GDCC system Configuration

1.11.2 GDCC Source Program

The configuration of the GDCC system is shown in Fig. 1.13. Components of the system as depicted in the diagram are conceptually parallel process, and are synchronized, if necessary, in the guard constraints. Each subsystem of the GDCC system performs and communicates the function as indicated in the diagram. The constrain solvers receives constraints in the order that the inference engine generates them, evaluates them and converts them into canonical forms and uses them to evaluate the guards. In GDCC there is no difference between logical variables constraints variables, and all constraints in GDCC are treated as global ones.

Multiple environments can be realized by making each of the local constraint sets a context. Further, the synchronization of the inference engine and the constraint solvers can be accomplished by using the end of evaluations of local constraint sets as the synchronization point. A mechanism called 'Block' has been introduced, consisting of local variables and global variables.

1.12 MAJOR ACHIEVEMENTS OF THE FGCS PROJECT WORLD OVER

The Japanese FGCS project was started in April 1982 as a Japanese national project. This project was unique among other national projects because it aimed at contribution to the advance of global computer science and technology through the development of revolutionary computer technology which was far advance from market technologies of those days. ICOT was established as a central research Institute to carry out this project. Several other countries such as USA, UK, FRG, EEC and India followed suit.

In this projects the fifth generation computer was defined that it would have an inference mechanism using knowledge bases for its kernel function and would fully use highly parallel processing technology for its implementation as shown in Fig. 1.14.

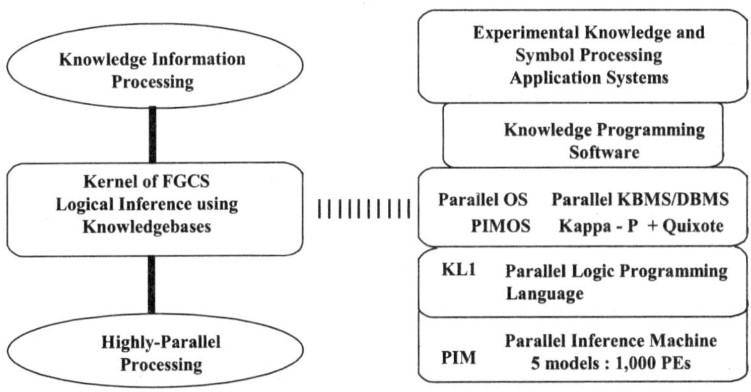

Fig. 1.14 FGCS Prototype system

After the eleven year research and development effort, the FGCS project achieved its initial goals and established the FGCS technology. To attain the goals, many new ideas, theories, small to large software and hardware technologies were created, evaluated, improved and extended. Finally, they were consistently integrated into an FGCS prototype system as shown in Fig. 1.14 and Fig. 1.15 .

It is probably the world's fastest and largest scale computer for knowledge information processing which is actually being used for practical application. To discuss many elementary technologies contained in the prototype system from macroscopic scientific view point, we roughly divide them into two categories: one is technologies related to parallel symbol processing and the other is parallel knowledge processing.

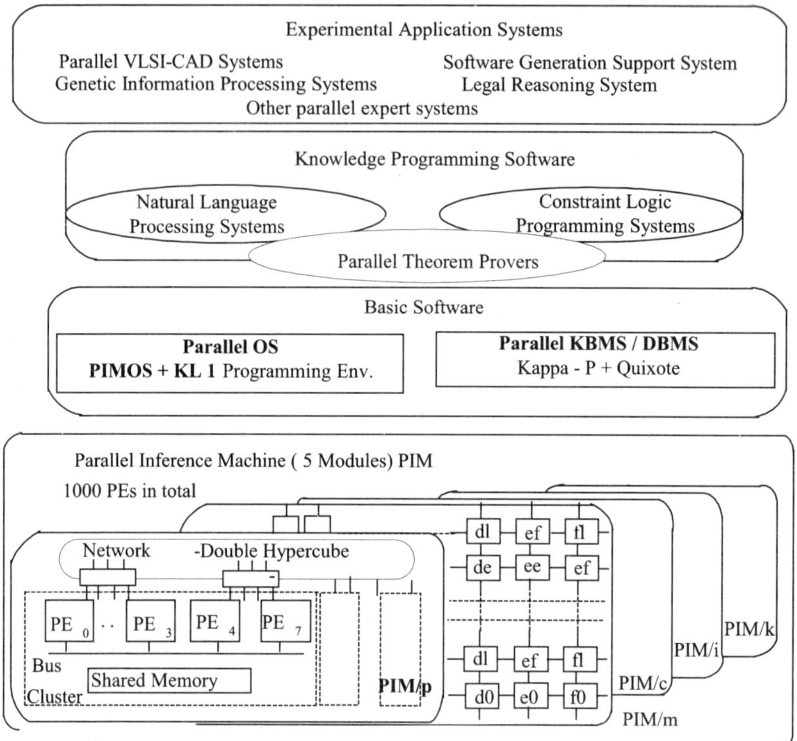

Fig. 1.15 Architecture form of parallel inference machine

1.13 KNOWLEDGE VERIFICATION SYSTEMS AND KNOWLEDGE REPRESENTATION LANGUAGES

Some of the most interesting work in KBCS project are:

1. Knowledge verification system with assumption based reasoning for expert systems for diagnostic reasoning, and
2. Knowledge representation languages suitable for natural language processing, object oriented data bases, legal reasoning etc.

1.14 PARALLEL INFERENCE MACHINE AND ITS OPERATING SYSTEM (PIMOS)

The Parallel Inference Machine (PIM) and its operating system (OS) (Fig 1.14) was developed as apart of FGCS / KBCS program. PIMOS which was written in logical programming language employs a hierarchical and distributed management policy to avoid the possible bottleneck in large scale parallel computing system. PIMOS features I/O resource management functions that virtualizes and multiplex physical

I/O devices, also virtualizes resource required for software development in coherent manner, under client - server model.

An OS for dynamic load - balancing shell with multi tasking feature into parallel processing capability was also developed.

1.15 SOFT COMPUTING BASED EMOTION/ INTENTION/ GESTURE RECOGNITION FOR MAN-MACHINE INTERFACE (A CYBERNETIC APPROACH TO ROBOTIC RESEARCH) A FUTURISTIC R & D PROGRAM

The service robots are mainly designed to serve humans directly or indirectly by helping or replacing humans in the works that usually require human flexibility under unstructured, possibly varying environments and sometimes intense-interactions. They immensely differ from the industrial robots that repeat only those works predefined in a structured workspace.

The service robots take various' forms and functions. For examples, they include housekeeping home robots, entertainment robots, rehabilitation robots for the disabled, intelligent robot house, etc. For these service robots, an important basic technology which needs a special attention is "human friendly interface" including voice recognition, gesture recognition, object recognition, user's intention reading, etc. This technique focuses on human-machine interaction because the service robots receive direct human command or cooperate with human.

To recognize bio-signs such as voice, gesture, facial expression and bio-signals, we need an intelligent recognition method that is tolerant of imprecision, uncertainty and partial truth of bio-sign. Here, bio-signals' include ECG (Electrocardiogram: heart signal), EMG (Electromyogram: muscle signal), EEG (Electroencephalogram: brain signal), etc. The soft computing method, which differs from the conventional hard computing paradigm, is known to have those characteristics and potential to solve; many real-world problems. The soft computing techniques contain fuzzy logic, neural network, probabilistic reasoning, evolutionary algorithms, chaos theory, belief networks, and Baysian learning theory [81, 82, 85].

The word 'emotion' is used very often in our daily lives. According to [85], it is very difficult to answer the question such as 'What is the emotion?' because of its wide usage and subjective characterization. However, we use the term 'emotion' to express our natural feeling of happiness, joy, sadness, surprise, anger, greeting, love, hate and so on. In this paper, the word 'emotion' is also used to represent such feelings as well as mood and affection.

Intention is an act or instance of determining mentally some action or result. It is a direct representation of the user's purpose, whereas emotion is an indirect one. For example, "bringing the cup to the user's mouth" is a good example of direct representation of the user's purpose, and we may relate it with an intention of the user. On the other hand, a negative reaction such as "shutting the user's mouth when the robot serves" may be interpreted as an emotional state to express that the user does not want to eat anything, which may be interpreted as a kind of indirect representation of the user's purpose, and we may relate it with emotion of the user.

From a psychological point of view, there have been many attempts to understand "how a human can recognize emotions/intentions of the other humans". Mehrabian proposes an emotion-space model called "PAD Emotional State Model" [46]. It consists of three nearly independent dimensions that are used to describe and measure emotional states: *Pleasure-displeasure, Arousal-nonarousal and Dominance-suhllziveness.* "Pleasure-displeasure" distinguishes the positive negative affective quality of emotional states, while "arousal-nonarousal" refers to a combination of physical activity and mental alertness. And "dominance-submissiveness" is defined in terms of control versus lack of control. Visual stimuli-based approach by Ekman et al. is also very popular. They proposed that many emotions or intentions in human's face may be recognized by combination of various facial muscular actions, so called "AU (Action Unit)" [87]. Dellaert et al. attempted to find elements that can affect emotions from speech signals [88].

On the basis of these psychological approaches, many researchers have been also trying to recognize human emotions for engineering purpose. An emotional agent proposed by Breazeal can recognize emotions *of* human beings based on PAD emotional state model [85]. This agent can recognize and represent many emotions based on PAD emotional model with mechanical structures. Vision-based approaches based on Ekman's theory show promising results. With soft computing techniques, machine can effectively recognize emotions *of* human beings based on images *of* facial expression. Nicholson made an attempt to recognize emotions from speech signals using artificial neural networks [85].

1.15.1 Soft Computing Tool Box

Soft computing techniques are convenient tools to solve many real world problems. It is known to exploit the tolerance for uncertainty and imprecision to achieve tractability, robustness, and low solution cost. Key methodologies include the Fuzzy Logic Theory (FL), Neural Networks (NN), Evolutionary Computation (EC), and the Rough Set

Theory (RS). Complementary combination of these methodologies may exhibit a higher computing power that parallels the remarkable ability of the human mind to reason and learn in an environment of uncertainty and imprecision.

Two concepts play a key role within FL [82]. One is the concept of *linguistic variable* and the other is the *fuzzy if-then rules,* FL mimics the remarkable ability of the human mind to summarize data and focus on decision-relevant information.

NN is a massively parallel computing system made up of simple processing units, called *neurons,* which has a natural propensity for storing experiential knowledge and making it available for use in decision making. Nonlinearity of neuron,' input-output mapping, adaptivity, and fault tolerance are useful properties of NN.

EC can be described as a two-step iterative process, consisting of *random variation* followed by *selection.* In the real world, EC offers considerable advantages such as adaptability to changing situations, generation of good enough solutions quickly, and so on [88,89].

By applying RS into a data set that is incomplete, imprecise, and vague, we can extract knowledge in a form of a minimal set of rules [90]. RS provides many advantages including efficient algorithms for finding hidden patterns in data, data reduction, methods for evaluating significance of data, etc.

To summarize, FL, NN, EC and RS can be appropriate tools for rule induction leaning, optimization and rule reduction, respectively.

1.16 SIGNAL FLOW IN MAN-MACHINE INTERACTION SYSTEM

Fig. 1.16 shows a model which was proposed to describe signal flow from human's *mind level* to machine's *action decision making module.* Emotion and intention in mind level induce various biosigns through many human's physical organs such as face, hand, muscle, brain and vocal cord in the *body level.* These biosigns include bio-signals, gesture, facial expression, voice, eye gaze, etc [85].

The machine senses biosigns using various sensors in *acquisition module* and recognizes emotion and (or) intention in the *emotion/ intention reading module* [Fig. 1.16]. Finally, the machine's actions are made between human and service robots.

To deal with the biosign, which has imprecision, uncertainty and partial truth, soft computing tool box is used in emotion/intention reading module and *action decision making module.* The detailed part from the acquisition module to emotion/intention module is dealt in subsequent

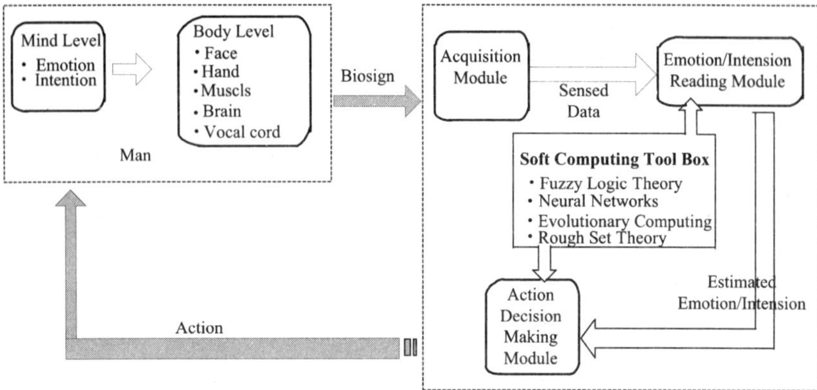

Fig. 1.16 Soft computing-based emotion/intention reading procedure from human mind level to action decision making level

section. As the man shows some biosign to the machine and the machine recognizes the biosign and produces some actions to the man, it makes the man-machine, interaction.

1.16.1 An Architecture of Soft Computing-Based Recognition System

As in cases of human, the partner's intention or emotion can be inferred not only from language but also from behavior. Typically, inferred, intentions or emotions are vague' and not necessarily expressible, but they play a key role for conservative decision making as in the case of design in consideration of safety or for smooth cooperation for comfort. A human being also tries to read the other party's intention or emotion subjectively. Thus, any classical probability or statistics may not be appropriate to express one's intention or emotion in a mathematical way [91]. Hence, we need appropriate methods, such as soft computing techniques, to deal with these types of vague and uncertain knowledge [82].

We propose a soft computing-based recognition system for the biosign as shown in Fig. 1.17. It is a modified figure of the fundamental step of digital image processing [92]. The input of the architecture is biosign and the output is the recognized intention, emotion, information and exogenous event.

The starting block of the system is "data acquisition", that is, acquiring bio-signs. The sensors for acquisition could be microphone, camera, glove device, motion capture device, EMG signal detector, etc. After the bio-sign is obtained, the next step deals with preprocessing. The preprocessing block typically deals with enhancing the signal and removing noise. The next stage deals with segmentation. It means partitioning a bio-sign into constituent signals. In general, it contains two

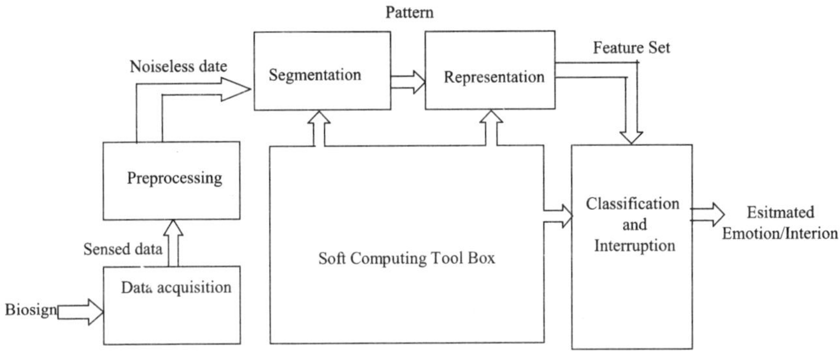

Fig. 1.17 An Architecture of soft computing-based recognition system

segmentation parts: spatial segmentation and temporal segmentation. The former means selecting the meaningful signal from a signal mixed with background signal, and the latter means selecting isolated signal from a continuous signal.

The output of the segmentation stage needs to be converted into a form suitable for computer processing. This involves representation of raw data. It contains the feature extraction process. The last stage of Fig. 1.17 involves classification and interpretation. Classification is the process that assigns a label to an object based on the information provided by its features. Interpretation involves assigning meaning to an ensemble of objects after classification.

To deal with biosign, we need prior knowledge in the processing modules in Fig. 1.17. We implement it with soft computing technique. As we mentioned, FL, RS, EC and NN may be appropriate method for rule induction, rule reduction, optimization and learning respectively. So, we propose to apply FL and NN to the segmentation stage, FL and RS to the representation stage, and FL, NN and EC to the classification and interpretation stage. As auxiliary methods, state space automata and Hidden Markov Model are proposed for segmentation and classification stage.

To overcome inconveniences of human-machine communication tools such as key-boards and mouse, the hand gesture method has been developed to accommodate a variety of commands naturally and directly. In spite of its usefulness, however, hand gesture is difficult to recognize by a machine.

Construction of a hand gesture recognition system involves structural categorization of gesture, real-time dynamic processing, pattern classification in a hyper dimensional space, coping with deterioration on recognition rate in case of expansion of gesture, dealing with ambiguity and nonlinearity constraints of the sensors, etc. Naturally several intelligent processing methods such as soft computing technique have been evolved to overcome these difficulties. In our works, we use state space automata to segment a continuous gesture into a set of individual gestures and we use *fuzzy* min-max neural network in the hand posture and hand orientation classification [85]. Also, we propose FL and Hidden Markov Model in the hand motion classification.

1.17 FACIAL EMOTIONAL EXPRESSION RECOGNITION SYSTEM

In general, the problem of recognizing emotion from a face is known to be very complex and difficult because; individuality may come in expressing and observing emotions. It is interesting to note, however, that human beings can successfully understand facial expressions in a seemingly easy way. Various soft computing techniques are used effectively for recognizing a positive expression of happiness [85]. This work has adopted NN, FS, and RS theory. To handle the recognition system by employing a traditional FL framework, a novel concept termed as "fuzzy observer" was proposed to indirectly estimate a linguistic variable from conventionally measured data.

1.17.1 Bio-Signal Recognition System

The EMG control is well known from the operation of some prosthesis with small DOF, Its application to the user's high level of movement paralysis is limited because the useful signals often interfere with the EMG signals from another muscle groups. The soft computing technique allows effective extraction of informative signal features in cases of high interference between the useful EMG signals and another muscle EMG signals.

To read the user's movement intentions effectively, it has been proposed the minimal feature set extraction algorithm [85] based on the fuzzy c-means algorithm (FCM), and RS. We can obtain the intervals of each feature by FCM to make condition rules, and then apply the rough set theory to extract a minimally sufficient set of rules for classification. After extracting numerous rules for classification and reduction done by RS, one can find the best feature set by measuring, the separability of each feature in each rules. By use of fuzzy min-max neural network (FMMNN) as a pattern recognizer with the extracted mini-max feature sets, one can classify the eight primitive arm motions with high classification rates [86].

1.17.2 Service Robot System with Emotion Monitoring Capability

To help human mentally and emotionally, a service robot system is designed to understand the user's emotion and react depending on the monitored information [85].

An intelligent robot agent is built for emotion-invoking action and emotion monitoring to combine the user's emotion and emotional model of the agent. For emotion monitoring the robot is to observe the user's behavior pattern that may be caused by some changes in the surroundings or by some initial robot action, to understand the user's emotional condition and then act by ingratiating itself with the user. For learning, the robot agent gets a feedback from the user's response so that it can behave properly, depending on any situation for the user's sake. Most important problem is to establish a mapping concept from the user's behavior pattern to the user's emotional state and from the emotional state to the robot's action ingratiating the user. Since each mapping rule depends on the personality of the user, it will be difficult to determine universal affective properties in the user's behavior pattern and robot's action. By the proposed NN structure, it is proposed that the robot would understand the user's emotional condition and how it shows its reaction, depending on the user's emotional state as a service robot.

1.18 CONCLUSION

The purpose of this paper has been to outline the role and impact of pattern information processing researches such as inference, estimation, and recognition procedures in statistical, syntactic and fuzzy set theoretic approaches and other soft computing approaches like, ANN, GA & RST and their combination in general pattern recognition problems of speech, natural languages, pictures images and other biosignals in Future Generations of Computer Systems Research. The author has attempted to show that developments in PR and AI in the last two and half decades are not only crucial for intelligent interfacing machines but also for the realisation of core functions of KBMS and inference Engine. It should also be understood that with the typical next generation system no single item of technology should be identified as the next generation computer. But the most important subdomains are AI-based KBMS, Language understanding and speech and picture recognition. Language understanding can be useful as interpreters for other programs or for translation. Speech and picture recognition can not only speed up the input to the computer, but will also revolutionise the uses of autonomous devices-robots that plan their actions in response to their environment, or in industrial manufacturing systems.

This paper also explains how the research in the fields of Artificial Intelligence (AI), Image Understanding systems (IUS) and some aspects of Pattern Recognition (PR) are unified in the CVS research largely motivated by the galaxy of applications.

The development of a general purpose CVS that can approach the abilities of the human eye and brain is remote at present, despite recent progress in understanding the nature of HVS.

There are many factors that are confounded in the image. A surface may look dark because of low reflectance, shallow angle of illumination, insufficient illumination or unfavourable viewing angle. The objects such as houses, cars, ships, roads, trees, ponds etc. to be interpreted require a large body of knowledge, not only about them-but also how they fit in together.

Though the architectural aspects have not dealt with in this paper, it should be noted that CVS involves large amount of memory and many computations. For an image of 1000 pixels some of the simplest procedures require 10^{10} operations. The human retina with 10^{10} cells operating at roughly 100 HZ performs at least 10 billion operations per second, and the visual cortex of the brain has undoubtedly higher capacities.

The status of research in different levels of vision and problems of determining 3-D shapes from 2-D images have been reviewed in depth which is on its way to systematic solution. The progress at the higher level problem of recognising the shapes deduced as objects and identifying them is limited. So it can be concluded that much research remains to be done. To develop generic systems, much more knowledge from the world has to be incorporated into the program. There must be a mechanism to store large-scale spatial information about an area, from which relevant data can be extracted and into which newly acquired information can be fed. Finally, there must be dramatic rise in the speed of CVS processors. Once such high speed processors are available, highly computationally intensive methods may be attempted that have not been tried so far, leading to more versatile systems. Next generation of computing systems with non-Von Neumann architecture will provide a greater opportunity. In the end the author presents briefly the principles of Constraint Logic Programming and parallel inference machine architecture as a new paradigm for knowledge information processing for in the context of PR/IP/AI.

At the end, the paper presents a soft computing based emotion/ intention/gesture recognition for man-machine interance in service robot applications. Soft computing techniques can deal with many real-world problems effectively. Among many possible applications of soft computing techniques [Fuzzy Logic (FL), Artificial Neural Network (ANN), Evolutionary Computing (EC), & Sough Set Theory (RST)], human-machine Interface or interaction procedure for the service robots are found to be very suitable because of its capability to deal with uncertainty and ambiguity. In this paper, we have also proposed a novel scheme for emotion/intention reading based on various soft computing techniques, And four successful applications are given as examples based on the proposed scheme.

Acknowledgement

The author wishes to acknowledge all his colleagues of ECSU, CVPR and MIU of Indian Statistical Institute and those who were involved FGCS/KBCS programme. In particular and also of Institute of Cybernetics Systems and Information Technology for their help in carrying out the work reported in this paper and to Mr. Dilip Kumar Gayen for his help and patience in completing this manuscript.

References

1. T Moto-Oka, H Tanaka, K Hirata, Maruyama (1981) "Challenge for Knowledge Information Processing Systems" (Preliminary Report on Fifth Generation Computer Systems). *Proc Int Conl Fifth Gen Comp Systems,* Oct. 19-22, pp 1-85.
2. D Dutta Majumder (1983) "On Some Contributions in Computer Technology and Information Sciences" *J Int. Elec. Tel. Eng.,* vol. 29, pp 429-449.
3. J Allen (1983) VLSI "Overall System Design", FGCS State-of-the-art report. *Pergamon Infotech Rep*, pp 33-39.
4. K S Fu (1968) Sequential Methods in Pattern Recognition and Machine Learning, New York: Academic Press.
5. K S Fu (1982) *Syntactic Pattern Recognition and Applications* Prentice Hall. Englewood Oiffs, N.J.
6. D Dutta Majumder and S K Pal (1985) *Fuzzy Mathematical Approach to Pattern Recognition* Wiley Eastern, New Delhi.
7. D Dutta Majumder and A K Dutta (1968) Some Studies on Automatic Speech Coding and Recognition Procedure. *Indian J. Phys.* Vol. 42, pp 425-443.
8. W A Lea (Ed) (1980) *Trends in Speech Recognition,* Prentice Hall. Englewood Cliffs, N.J.
9. J P Haton (1982) Speech Recognition and Understanding Proc. *6th ICPR, Munich,* Oct 19-22, IEEE Computer Society.
10. A M Liberman (1970) The Grammar of Speech and Language, *Cognitive Psychology,* 1, pp 301-323.
11. J P Haton (Ed) (1982) *Automatic Speech Analysis and Recognition,* D Reidal, Dordrecht.
12. M. J. Underwood (1983) Intelligent User Interfaces, *Pergamon Infotech Rep*, pp *33-39.*
13. D Dutta Majumder (1979) Cybernetics and General Systems Theory-A Unitary Science *KYBERNETS*, 8, pp 7-15.

14. D Dutta Majumder (1984) Trends in Computer Communication System and Distributed Database, *In Pattern Recognition and Digital Technique*, ISI, pp 499-529.
15. A Michael *Arbib* (1964) *Brains, Machines, And Mathematics* McGraw Hill Book Company, New York.
16. Kurt Godel (1931), *On Formally Decidable Propositions of Principia Mathematica and Related Systems* (Trans by B Meltzer) Basic Books Inc. Publishers, New York.
17. Nagel Ernst and R James Newman (1958) *Godel's Proof,* University Press, New York.
18. A Eddington (1939) *The Philosophy of Physical Sciences,* Cambridge University Press, pp 148.
19. D Gabor et al (1960) *Proc. IEEE* 108, 422-438.
20. Haneef Fatmi (1984) *A Theory of Processing Intelligent Messages,* London University Press, University of London, London SW6.
21. David Waltz (1983) Helping Computers Understand Natural Languages *IEEE Spectrum,* pp 81-84.
22. P Winston (1975) *The Psychology of Computer Vision* McGraw-Hill, New York.
23. M Minsky (1975) "A framework for representing knowledge". The Psychology of Computer Visions Ed. P Winerton McGraw Hill, New York.
24. D Marr (1977) Artificial intelligence -a personal view *Artificial intelligence.*
25. S Zucker A Rosenfeld and L Davis (1975) "General-Purpose Models: Expectations about the unexpected". RT-347, Computer Science Center, Univ. Maryland.
26. D Marr(1976) Analyzing natural images *A I Memo* 334 Al Lab, M.I.T.
27. P Wintson (1976) Proposal to ARPA *AI Memo* 366 Al Lab, M.I.T.
28. B L Bullock (1978) The necessity for a theory of specialised vision Ed A P Hauson and E M Riseman In: New York Vision Systems. Academic Press, New York.
29. Takeo Kanade and Raj Reddy (1983) Computer vision: the challenge of imperfect inputs, *IEEE Spectrum*, November.
30. Martin D Levin (1978) A knowledge-based computer vision system *In Vision Systems (Ed.* A.P. Hauson and E.M. Riseman,) Academic Press, New York.
31. T O Binford (1982) Survey of model-based image analysis systems Int. *Robotics Res* 1, No.1, pp 18-64.

32. Takashi Matsuyama (1984) Knowledge organisation and control structure in image *understanding, Proc* 8th *ICPR, IEEE,* pp 1118-1127.
33. Takeo Kanade (1980) Region segmentation signal vs semantics *CGIP/13* No.4. pp 279-297.
34. Michael Brady (1982) Computational approaches in image understanding ACM *Computing Surveys.* 14, No.1.
35. H G Barrow and J M Tanenbaum (1978) Recovering intrinsic srene characteristics from images In: *Computer Vision Systems* (Ed. A R Hauson and E M Riseman) (1986) Academic Press, New York, pp 3-26.
36. D Dutta Majumder (1986) Pattern recognition and artificial intelligence techniques in intelligent robotic system. *Proc nat Convention Production Eng* Division of Institute of Engineers (India) August 17-18.
37. D Dutta Majumder (1986) Pattern Recognition, Image Processing, Artificial Intelligence and Computer Vision in Fifth Generation Computer Systems *Sadhana, Proc Indian Aca Sci* Bangalore, 9, Part 2, pp 139-156.
38. T Moto-Oka *et al.* (1981) Challenge for knowledge information processing systems (prelim Re on *FGCS) Proc int. Conf FGCSOct.* 19-22, pp 1-85.
39. D Dutta Majumder (1986) Impact of Pattern Recognition and Computer Vision Research in FGCS *Framework Proc. Int. Conf.* APRDT, Kolkata, 6-10 Jan.
40. J M Tanenbaum and H G Barrow (1977) Experiments in Interpretation of guided *segmentation Artificial Intelligence* 8, pp 3.
41. B Chanda and D Dutta Majumder (1985) A hybrid edge detector and its properties *Int. J. System Sci Vol* 16, No. 1. pp 71-80.
42. B Chanda and D Dutta Majumder (1985) On image enhancement and threshold selection using grey level co-occurrence matrix *Patt Recog Lett* 3, No.4 pp. 243-251.
43. M Kundu, B B Chowdhury and D Dutta Majumder (1985) *A generalized digital contour coding scheme*, *CVGIP* 30 (3), pp. 269-278.
44. S N Biswas, B B Chowdhury and D Dutta Majumder (1986) An interactive curve design method through circular areas and straight line segments,. Fall Joint Conf on Computer, Univ. of Dallas, Texas
45. S K Parui and D Dutta Majumder (1982) *A New Definition of Shape Similarity* PRL, pp. 37-42.

46. D Dutta Majumder and B B Chowdhury (1980) Recognition and fuzzy description of sides and symmetries of figures by computers. *Int. J. Syst. Sci* 11. pp.1435-1445.

47. D Dutta Majumder and S K Parui (1982) How to quantify shape distance for 2-D regions *Proc 7th ICPR.*

48. P B Besl and R C Jain (1985) Three-dimensional object recognition *Computing Surveys,* 17, No.1.

49. A Rosenfeld, R A Hummel and S W Zucker (1980) Scene labelling by relaxation operations *IEEE Trans SMC* 10, No .2.

50. R C Duba and P E Hart (1972) Use of the Hough transformation to detect lines and curves in pictures *Commun ACM.* 15, January. pp 11-15.

51. A Rosenfeld (1984) Image analysis: problems, progress and prospects *Pattern Recognition*, 17,1. pp. 3-12.

52. I Chakravorti and H Freeman (1982) characteristic views as a basis for 3-D object recognition *IPL-TR-O34,* Rensselar Polytechnic Inst. Troy, N.Y.

53. K J Udupa and I S N Murthy (1977) New concepts for 3-D shape analysis *IEEE Trans Comp.,* C-26, 10 Oct. pp 1043-1048.

54. H A Blum (1967) Transformation for extracting new descriptors of shape. In: *Models for the Perception of Speech and Visual Form Ed. W Wathan Dunn* MIT Press, Cambridge 1967.

55. P G Mulgaonkar, L G Shapiro and R M Haralick (1982) Recognizing 3-D objects single perspective views using geometric and relational reasoning. *Proc PR & IP Con! IEEE,* Lasvegus.

56. J O Rpurke and N Badler (1979) Decomposition of 3-D objects into spheres *IEEE Trans. PAMI.* 3. (July).

57. D H Ballard and C M Brown (1982) *Computer Vision.* Prentice Hall Inc. 1982.

58. M Nagao (1984) O:Jntrol strategies in pattern analysis. *Patt Recog* 17. No.1 pp 45-56.

59. R A Brooks, R Greiner and T O Binford (1979) The ACRONYM model based vision system 6th Int. Jt. O:Jnf. AI, TOKYO, IJCAI.

60. R A Brooks (1983) Model-based 3-d interpretation of 2-d images *IEEE Trans PAMI5*, 2 pp.140-150.

61. W W Bledsoe (1974) The Sup-inf method in Presburger *arithmetic Dept. Math CS Memo A TP-18,* Univ. Texas, Austin.

62. R B Fisher (1983) Using surfaces and object models to reorganize partially obscured objects. 8th IJCAI.

63. T. Matsuyama, V Hwang and L S Davis (1984) Evidence Accumulation for Spatial Reasoning. *CAR-TR-54,* Univ. Maryland.
64. P G Selfridge (1982) Reasoning about success and failure in aerial image understanding. *Ph. D. Thesis,* Univ. Rochester.
65. R L Harr (1980) The representation and manipulation of position information using spatial relations. *TR-923,* CVL, Univ. Maryland.
66. D McDormitt (1980) A theory of metric spatial inference. Proc. fiat. *Artificial Intelligence conf.*
67. V Hwang, T Matsuyama, L S Davis and A Rosenfeld (1983) Evidence Accumulation for Spatial Reasoning in Aerial Image Understanding *CAR-TR-28,* Univ. Maryland.
68. J D Lowrence (1982) Dependency-graph models of evidential support. *Coins Tech. Rep,* Univ. Mass, USA.
69. H C Lee and K S Fu (1983) Generating object descriptions for model retrieval *IEEE Trans. PAMI-5*. pp. 462-471.
70. R Nevatia and T O Binford (1977) Description and recognition of curved objects. *Artificial Intelligence,* 8.1.
71. Bir Bhanu (1984) Representation and shape matching of 3-D objects. *IEEE Trans PAMI*-6 pp 340-351.
72. E Bribiesca and A Guzman (1980) How to describe pure form and how to measure differences in shapes using shape numbers. *Patt Recog.* 12, NO.2.
73. L S Davis (1977) Understanding shape: symmetry. IEEE Trans *SMC-7,* pp 204-212, 1977.
74. R L Kashyap and B J Oommen (1982) A geometrical approach to polygonal dissimilarity and shape matching *IEEE Trans PAMI*-4. pp 649-654.
75. S K Parui and D Dutta Majumder (1983) Symmetry analysis by computer of open curves *Patt Recog* vol 16, pp 63-67.
76. S K Parui and D Dutta Majumder (1983) Shape similarity measures for open curves. *Patt Recog* Lett 1 pp. 129-134.
77. B R Suresh, R A Fundakowski, T S Levittand J E Overland. Areal-time automated visual inspection system for hot steel slabs. *IEEE Trans PAMI-5,* No.6, pp. 563-572.
78. G J Agin (1980) Computer vision systems for industrial inspection and assembly. *IEEE Comp.*
79. W A Parkins (1983) INSPECTOR: A computer vision system that learns to Inspect posts. *IEEE Trans PAMI-5* No.6, pp- 584-592.
80. Michael Brady (1985) Artificial intelligence and robotics. *Artificial Intelligence,* 26, North Holland, pp 79-121.

81. Youji Kohda and Munenroi Maeda " Evolution of parallel systems: From Batch Processing to Multi - tasking " IPSJ Symposium, Japan, 1991.
82. D Dutta Majumder, "Fuzzy Mathematics and Uncertainty Management for Decision making in science and society" Journal of Computer Science and Information, vol.23, no.3, Sept. 1993, pp 1-31.
83. D Dutta Majumder "A Unified Approach to AI, PR, IP, CV in Fifth Generation Computer System", Int. J. Of Inf. Sc., Elsevier Science, New York, 1988.
84. Akira Aiba, ICOT, " Constraint Logic Programming, ICOT Journal, Tokyo, No. 35, 1992.
85. Z Zem Bien, Jung-Bae Kim, Jeon Su Han, "Soft Computing Based Emotion/Intention Reading for Service Robot" AFSS, 2002, pp 121-128, Springer - Verlog, Berlin Heidelberg, 2002.
86. A Mehrabian, "Basic Dimensions for a General Psychological Theory: Implications for Personality, Social, Environmental, and Developmental Studies" Oelgeschlager, Gannd Hain, Cambridge, MA, USA, 1980.
87. P Ekman, W V Friesen, "The Facial Action Coding System" Consulting Psychological Press, Inc. Sam Fransisco, CA, USA, 1978.
88. P Dutta and D Dutta Majumder, "Coverenge of an Evolutionery Algorithm" Proc. Fourth International on Soft Computing", 1996, pp 515-518.
89. P Dutta and D Dutta Majumder, "Performance Analysis of Evolutionery Algorithms", 13th ICPR, Vienna, 1996.
90. Z Pawlak, "Why Rough Sets", Proc. Fifth IEEE International Conference on Fuzzy Systems" Vol. 2, pp 738-743, 1996.
91. Y Inagaki, et. al. "Behaviour based intension inference for intelligent robots cooperating with human", Proc. Int. Conf. 4th Fuzz, IEEE, vol.3, pp 1695-1700,1995.
92. B Chanda and D Dutta Majumder, "Digital Image Processing and Analysis", Prentice Hall of India, 2002.
93. D Dutta Majumder, "Mind -Body Duality: Its Impact on Pattern Recognition and Computer Vision Research" Third APRDT, P. C. Mahalanobis Birth Centenary Volume, ISI, pp 3-17, Dec. 1993.
94. D Dutta Majumder, "Mind-Body Problem and Artificial Consciousness for Computing Machines: A Cybernetic Approach", Recent Advances in Cybernetics and Systems, Tata McGraw Hill, New Delhi, pp 337-345, 1993.

95. D Dutta Majumder and P K Roy, "Evolution of Group Consciousness - A Cybernetic Approach", KYBERNETS, vol.30, no.9/10, 2001, MCB University Press, Bradford, UK.
96. D Dutta Majumder "A study on a Mathematical Theory of Shapes in relation to PR & ev", Indian Journal of theoretical physics, vol 43, No. 4, pp 19-30 1995.

2

Problems and Prospects of Speech Recognition Research

HIROYA FUJISAKI[1]

ABSTRACT

The ultimate goal for speech recognition research is to be able to recognize and understand natural utterances without any restrictions on the speaker, manner of speech, dialect and topic. With increased awareness of the difficulties of the problem, however, recent efforts have been concentrated mainly on two separate directions: (1) word recognition, and (2) sentence understanding, usually allowing training of the system for each speaker.

This paper briefly reviews current techniques and results obtained along the two lines, and mentions national projects on new generation computer technology and their approaches to speech and language processing.

On the basis of the overview of the current approaches, the paper discusses in some depths several issues that are believed to be crucial for further progress in speech recognition and understanding.

Keywords: Word recognition; Sentence understanding; New Generation Computer Technology; Language processing.

2.1 INTRODUCTION

The human abilities of thought and communication owe very much to the use of language as a unique system of codes by which the information is expressed as messages. Communication by language, however, is achieved only when messages are converted into physical signals, i.e. either into speech as their acoustic manifestations or into characters as their optical manifestations. The primary importance of the spoken language as compared to the written language is apparent from its exclusive use by many of the primitive cultures as well as from the order of acquisition by infants.

The reason for its primary importance resides partly in its simplicity as a means of communication; it requires only the respiratory air flow for the source of energy, nothing but a part of our body as the instrument for production, nothing but the ambient atmosphere for transmission, and requires very little effort both from the speaker and from the listener. And yet, speech can provide by far the highest rate of information emission among all the output models available to man. The rate of 40 bits/sec is achieved by simultaneous control of several articulators,

---

[1] Faculty of Engineering, University of Tokyo, Bunkyo-ku, Tokyo, 113 Japan.

each of which can operate only at much slower rates. Every normal human being beyond infancy establishes, through continual training in his daily life, his ability as an expert both in emission and reception of speech.

On the other hand, communication through speech by itself suffers from both spatial and temporal restrictions, in that the signal can be received only at the immediate vicinity of its sender and at the instant of its generation. It is thus quite natural, that a large amount of scientific efforts has been expended for the alleviation of these restrictions. These efforts have been first materialized by the invention of telephone and gramophone about one century ago, and the techniques have since developed to such an extent that the use of trans-oceanic cables and communication satellites allows almost instantaneous telephone conversation without restrictions on the distance, and the use of magnetic recording permits storage and reproduction of spoken messages at any desired instant. Thus it may be said that the spatial and temporal restrictions inherent to speech communication have now been almost completely eliminated by these techniques.

With the widespread use of automatic information processing in the modern society, there is a strong need for more efficient means of man-machine communication than via keyboards and switches. Because of the basic advantage of speech over other means of human communication, it is obvious that man-machine communication would be optimal in most cases if it is mediated by speech. There exists a basic difference in difficulty of realizing speech synthesis and speech recognition by machine. The primary reason for this asymmetry is obviously the difference in the intelligence of the receiver. Furthermore, speech recognition in a most general sense will have to accept any speakers and thus will have to cope with individual differences of speakers, while speech synthesis usually will have to simulate only a few, if not only one, speakers.

In the following sections, a bird's eye view is presented on the basic problems of speech recognition, and then review of current efforts and their results. A brief comment on national projects and a discussion on crucial issues are presented.

2.2 PROBLEMS OF SPEECH RECOGNITION

The human speech is characterized both by its regularity and its variability. The regularity comes mainly from the structure of the language for which speech is the manifestation, and gives rise to redundancy which can be utilized in speech recognition. On the other hand, the variability of speech comes from various factors involved in the process of converting linguistic messages to sound, and presents difficulties for accurate recognition.

2.2.1 Hierarchical Structure of Language and Redundancy of Linguistic Messages

The essential function of a language as a coding system is quantization in the broadest sense, by which continuous or discrete phenomena, both physical and mental, are represented in terms of discrete units for the sake of reliable transmission and storage. Its function is achieved by three levels of units : symbols, codes and messages. The symbol of a spoken language is the phoneme, or the smallest discrete unit of acoustic representation which can be identified as such. To be discriminable from each other, and to avoid errors in the processes of generation, transmission and reception, the number of phonemes used in a language is usually limited below 30, and they are actualized by the combination of coarse (mostly binary) controls of several phonatory and articulatory dimensions. The distinctive features may be interpreted as dimensions of auditory sensation elicited by the acoustic consequences of the above control.

These phonemes are combined into a sequence of finite length to constitute a code, namely a word, which is the smallest discrete unit of conceptual representation. The arrangement of phonemes in a word is subject to both phonological and morphological constraints. Even with these constraints, however, the number of permissible phoneme sequences increases exponentially with their length, and exceeds 10^4 if word lengths of up to 10 phonemes are to be accepted, the number being almost sufficient for representing basic semantic units.

The information to be transmitted by language is concerned, however, not only with the individual events or concepts, but also with their relationships in specific situations. Though these relationships may be multi-dimensional, the sequential nature of linguistic expressions requires their representation in terms of a uni-dimensional sequence of words which constitute a message, namely a sentence. The arrangement of words within a sentence is also subject to both semantic and syntactic constraints, namely the grammar, which reduces the number of acceptable sentences to a large extent. Yet their number is apparently infinite if there are no restrictions on their lengths, and is practically infinite even if their lengths are limited to 10 words out of a vocabulary of 10^4. It is this capability of generating an unlimited number of sentences from a limited vocabulary that endows language its expressive and creative power.

The constraints imposed by the structure of a language upon possible messages give rise to redundancies which can be profitably utilized in speech recognition even if some of the constituent units are not correctly identified. Furthermore, in many situations of practical interest, the number of words and sentence types are only small subset of all the possibilities of a language. There also exist pragmatic constraints in the form of restrictions on the topic as well as on the situations where the language is being used. Strictly speaking, these pragmatic constraints are extra linguistic factors, but can also be utilized to increase the overall accuracy of speech recognition.

2.2.2 Causes of Variability in Speech Recognition

Although the aforementioned levels of linguistic expressions are all discrete, and linguistic messages invariably consist of sequences of discrete phonemes, they undergo complex smoothing and are superposed with various factors of statistical and systematic variations in the process of their actualization as speech, and are observed as a continuous acoustic signal. Namely, as indicated by Fig. 2.1, which illustrates major steps in generation, transmission and reception of speech in man-to-man communication, the phoneme strings organized as codes and messages at the centre of speech are converted into neuro-motor commands at the motor speech centre and are sent out in parallel to various phonatory and articulatory organs such as vocal chords, mandible, tongue body and tongue tip, lips as well as velum. These commands undergo several stages of smoothing during neural transmission and muscular contraction, and cause individual or concurrent inertial motions of the respective organs. The resultant deformations, both general and local, of the vocal tract in turn affect the acoustic characteristics of the speech signal in such a way that successive phonemes heavily overlap with each other and generally leave no trace of discreteness in the speech signal itself or in its acoustic characteristics.

The phenomenon is commonly called coarticulation or concatenation, and corresponds to the inter-symbol interference in digital transmission, but is conspicuous in that the interference occurs as the result of various smoothings at the articulatory level and is reflected on the speech wave through the overall characteristics of the mechanisms of speech production. Furthermore, there exist instances where the coarticulation can be regarded, not as a simple smoothing process at the phonatory and articulatory level, but rather as a logical process at the level of discrete neuro-motor commands. Consequently, the characteristics of phonemes in connected speech are almost always transient and are generally quite different from those of isolated phonemes even at points where the speech signal may seem to be most stationary, and there exists no simple operation to restore the discreteness of the original sequence of units.

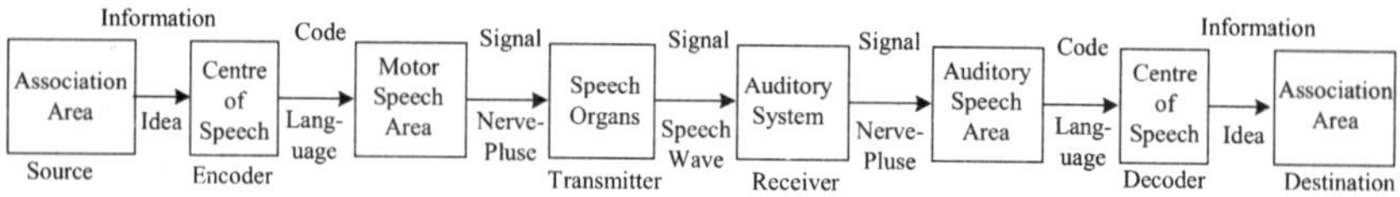

Fig. 2.1 Steps in generation, transmission and reception of information through speech

In addition to the contextual variability caused by coarticulation, there exist two other kinds of variabilities that are intrinsic to a speaker: the statistical variability due to physiological fluctuations in the mechanisms of speech production, and the systematic variability due to individual differences both in static and dynamic characteristics of phonatory and articulatory systems. The former is inevitably introduced into speech since activities for speech production, like any other physiological activity, are never exempt from statistical fluctuations. Thus two utterances of the same speaker in the same context can never be exactly identical, but differ both in spectral and temporal charcteristics. Since the speech signal is also used to transmit extra-linguistic information, namely speaker's emotion, which, unlike linguistic information, is actualized mainly through systematic but continuous control of prosodic features such as stress, accent and intonation, variability is observed in the intensity, pitch and duration of a particular unit such as a syllable, a word or even a sentence, relative to those of adjacent units. Thus the resultant changes in prosodic features may be regarded as irrelevant random fluctuations from the point of view of speech recognition.

The systematic variability due to idiosyncrasy of speakers, on the other hand, is mainly caused by individual differences in the static dimensions of the vocal tract as well as in the manner of dynamic control of various speech organs, and can be remarkably large if the age and sex of speakers are left completely unspecified. Dialects also cause systematic variability both in segmental and prosodic features of speech, which can be theoretically removed if we know the exact influences of a particular dialect on each of the features. In the absence of such knowledge, however, dialectal variations also tend to be regarded as irrelevant fluctuations in speech recognition.

The causes of variability thus far enumerated are all intrinsic to speakers, but there are also extrinsic factors, both stochastic and systematic, that introduce variability into speech. Statistical variability may be caused both by natural factors such as ambient noise and by artificial factors such as noise and distortion in communication systems used for transmission of speech, while systematic variability may be caused by changes in the constitution and the pressure of the ambient atmosphere in artificial environments such as in space- and underwater crafts.

Of all these factors that contribute to variability of acoustic characteristics of speech, which are summarized in Table 2.1, some are systematic so that their effects may be theoretically separable from linguistically relevant properties of speech by systematic transformations, while effects of stochastic factors can only be minimized by methods of statistical inference. Although it may be possible to devise and apply a method to cope with a particular cause of variability, it may not prove effective in more generalized situations where other causes of variability are left uncontrolled. Thus it may be easy to understand that formidable difficulties exist in the realization of speech recognition in its broadest sense, whose objective is to accept, without restrictions on vocabulary and speaker, connected utterances of a language and to identify each of the linguistic units and their interrelationships, and thus extract and process the semantic information therein contained.

Table 2.1 *Classification of variabilities encountered in speech recognition*

Intrinsic vs. Extrinsic		Systematic vs. Stochastic		Causes
		Systematic	**Stochastic**	
Intrinsic	Linguistic	Contextual		concatenation at phonological and articulatory levels
		Dialectal		difference of dialect of speakers
	Extra-Linguistic	Idiosyncratic		individual difference of dimensions and manners of control of speech organs
			Physiological	random fluctuations inherent to all physiological activities
			Emotional	control of prosodic features irrelevant to linguistic factors
	Natural		Environmental	ambient noise
Extrinsic	Artificial	Environmental		constitution of ambient atmosphere in space or underwater craft
			Technological	noise and distortion in communication systems

With the increased awareness of the difficulties involved, recent efforts in speech recognition seem to have been concentrated mostly on placing certain restrictions on the set of utterances to be recognized, thus automatically eliminating most of the causes of variability, and on testing the validity of specific methods of approach to problems of limited scopes. One of such directions is the recognition of words from a limited vocabulary and spoken in isolation, the other is the understanding of spoken sentences with heavy restrictions on vocabulary, syntax and topics.

2.3 TECHNIQUES AND TYPICAL RESULTS OF SPEECH RECOGNITION

Limited Vocabulary Spoken Word Recognition

By "spoken word recognition" is meant the case where each word in a vocabulary has an independent meaning, and thus can be uttered in isolation or as a connected sequence, such as digits and proper nouns, etc. In general, there is very little, if any, syntactic relationship between successive words even if the words are pronounced in a sequence. In this case the isolated utterances are not unnatural, and an ordinary speaker do not find it difficult to put almost equal stress on every item. On the other hand, the required accuracy of word recognition has to be very high since there is very little redundancy that can be exploited.

The success in this restricted task domain was brought about first by limiting the speaker and the vocabulary size. Thus a whole word, rather than its constituent phonemes, can be regarded as direct objects to be recognized. The problem of speech recognition is then reduced to that of pattern matching, where each word, uttered by a speaker in advance, can be used as standard templates against which each unknown input word is to be compared, thus circumventing the variability of acoustic characteristics of phonemes due to contextual and individual difference. There still remains, however, one factor of variability, i.e., involuntary fluctuations of the speech rate in multiple utterances of the same word by the same speaker. A change in the speech rate causes non-uniform durational changes; vowel durations are generally much more variable than consonant durations, hence the necessity of non-linear warping of the time axis in template matching. The technique of dynamic programming, first applied by Vintsyuk has been successively elaborated to suit the purpose of isolated word recognition, and then extended to apply to connected word recognition. It would not be an overstatement to say that speech recognition found its practical applications only after the introduction of this technique. In fact, most of the currently available speech recognition system are based on this technique. Rather than going into detailed descriptions of various systems, the author has shown a comparison of performances of commercially available speech recognizers, tested under the same condition, in Table 2.2.

While the technique is essentially suited for a small vocabulary, speaker trained recognition system, research efforts are of course being made to extend the success to two directions, i.e., larger vocabularies (typically of the order of 10^3 to 10^4 words) or speaker-independence.

An increase in the vocabulary size causes two problems. One is the increase in the amount of time for training the system for each speaker,

Table 2.2 *Performance comparison of commercially available spoken words recognizers*

Manufacturer	Type	Error Rate (%)
Verbex	1800	0.2
NEC	DP-100	1.2
Threshold Technology	T-500	1.4
Interstate Electronics	VRM	2.9
Heuristics	7000	5.9
Centigram	MIKE4725	7.1
Scott Instruments	VET/1	12.6

Test conditions:
16 speakers of American English (8 male and 8 female), 20 -word vocabulary 16 utterances each, system trained for each speaker.

and the other is the increase in the necessary computation time for template matching. Of these two, the second is not an essential one in view of the recent progress in LSI technology and hardware design, while the first one remains to be rather difficult to solve. If one can adopt sub-word units such as syllables, demisyllables, or phonemes (or more accurately, allophones), as stored templates to be prepared for each speaker, both the training time and the memory capacity for storing templates will be primarily independent of the vocabulary size. Because of the greater contextual variability in such smaller units, however, it usually becomes necessary to provide multiplicity of templates for each such sub-word unit. The choice of a proper sub-word unit is heavily dependent on the specific language. For example, if we adopt the syllable as the unit of template matching, the necessary number will be at least several thousands in the case of English, but is only a low hundreds in the case of Japanese. It is of course possible to define sub-word units independently from such phonetic entities as syllables and allophones. A recent work at IBM utilizes 200 pre-stored prototype feature vectors and identifies the unknown input word as a sequence of such sub-word unit of 10 msec duration each. The sequence is converted into strings of phonetic symbols by using a hidden Markov model, and then identified as a word. As an experimental discrete dictation recognizer for creation of office memoranda, it works on a 5000-word vocabulary, at an average error rate of 3.1% for read speech and 5.7% for spontaneous speech when the system is speaker-trained for each of five speakers (four male and one female). The training takes about 20 minutes.

Efforts toward speaker-independent word recognition have to cope with inter-speaker variability, which manifests itself not only as changes in the speech rate, but also as changes in spectral characteristics. One way to cope with the two-way variability is to use a single word template but introduce warping of both time and frequency axes. The other method is to adopt multiple templates for one word if inter-speaker variability is large and has multimodal distributions. Although a truly speaker-independent system has to cover utterances of male and female speakers over the entire range of age, most of the studies thus far have dealt only with utterances of adult speakers.

Understanding of Connected Speech

While the spoken word recognition as described in the previous section provides a practical solution for the machine, it is certainly not the most practical mode of speech communication for human speakers. In natural speech communication, one seldom utters the words in isolation but as a continuous string, and not all the words are uttered with equal degree of carefulness. Unimportant words are often uttered quite casually, and may even be left out. This is because in ordinary speech communication the main purpose of the speaker is to have the meaning of his utterance understood by the listener. In the same view, we need not be concerned so much with recognizing each sound and each word, but should aim at establishing a machine-understanding of the whole utterance if we are to deal with connected speech. This is the rationale for research in speech understanding started by R. Reddy in 1971 in a large scale ARPA Project. Even though the project was terminated in 1976, it has stimulated a number of research groups, both in Europe and in Japan, to continue research along similar lines. Since the results of the ARPA Speech Understanding project were described and commented in detail elsewhere, I will only mention briefly their merits and demerits.

The greatest merit of the ARPA Speech Understanding project was that it brought into foreground the necessity of formulating and utilizing knowledge sources at various levels (lexical, syntactic, semantic and pragmatic) other than the acoustic level. The use of such higher-level knowledge added a top-down processing to the conventional bottom-up analysis. The project also contributed much to the techniques of segmentation and labelling of phonetic units, as well as to procedures for word matching and verification. On the other hand, it left much to be desired in the acoustic-phonetic analysis. The results of typical ARPA projects as well as other speech understanding projects in U.S., Europe, and Japan are briefly summarized in Table 2.3.

2.4 SPEECH AND LANGUAGE PROCESSING IN LARGE-SCALE NATIONAL PROJECTS

Research efforts toward a new generation computer technology, first conceived in 1979 and started in 1982 in Japan as the FGCS project, have stimulated similar efforts in other countries, especially in the United

Table 2.3 *Performance comparison of various speech understanding projects*

Institution	Vocabulary Size	Task	Word Recognition Rate (%)	Sentence Understanding Rate (%)
CMU (Harpy)	1,011	Information Retrieval	91	95
BBN (HWIM)	1,097	Budget	–	44
IBM	1,000	Patent Documents	92	–
CNET	60	Directory Assistance	–	90
Kyoto Univ.	101	Computer Architecture	93	66
Kyoto Inst.	50	Computer Programming	–	86
Yamanashi Univ.	99	Computer Programming	–	78
NTT	112	Seat Reservation	–	85

States (DARPA Strategic Computing Project) and in the United Kingdom (Alvey Programme). These projects all claim natural language man-machine interface as an important feature of the new generation computer, though there is much difference in emphasis in the actual projects. I will present a brief overview of each project in relation to speech and language processing.

2.4.1 Japanese FGCS Project

The initial targets for the Japanese FGCS Project, as shown in Table 2.4, listed speech understanding as one of the goals for its 10-year-research. During the course of the initial 3-year period (1982-1984), however, the emphasis has been shifted toward establishing basic technology such as Inference Machines, Knowledge Base Machines, and a Logic Programming Language. Natural language processing is adopted as the main area of application, where parsing, discourse understanding, and compilation of large-scale machine-readable dictionaries are the three current projects. Although at present there is no project directly related to

Table 2.4 *The frame of targets for Japanese FGCS project*

Basic application	Expert System, Machine Translation System, CAD System
Man-machine interface	Speech Understanding, Image Understanding, Natural Language Understanding
Basic system	Intelligent Programming System
Basic mechanisms	Knowledge Base Inference, Problem-Solving
Kernel language	Logic Programming Language
Architecture	Inference Machine Knowledge Base Machine (High Level Language Machine) (Relational Database Machine) (Highly Parallel Machine)
Device	VLSI Technology

speech understanding, the above-mentioned projects will certainly provide powerful tools and favourable environment for speech understanding research (Fig. 2.2).

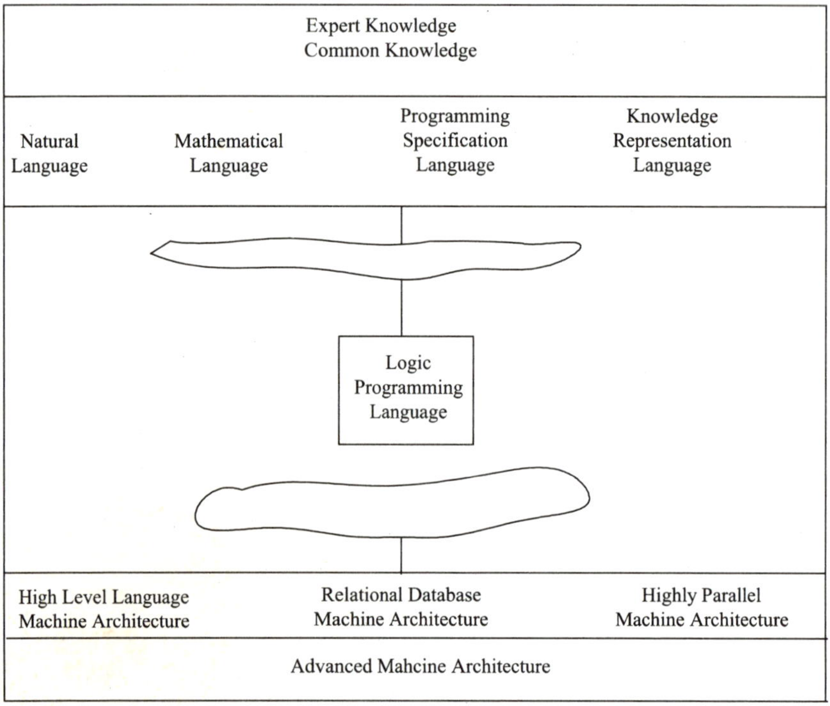

Fig. 2.2 Approaches adopted in the Japanese FGCS project

2.4.2 Darpa Strategic Computing Project (U.S.)

The Strategic Computing Project was announced in 1983 by the Defence Advanced Research Projects Agency (DARPA), as a 10-year plan to develop machine-intelligence technology. It is aimed at simultaneously advancing the computer technology at several levels: new materials and fabrication processes for creating faster chips, new parallel computer architectures for more rapid computation, and new software technology for endowing machines with flexible and intelligent behaviour. The program structure and goals for the project are shown in Fig. 2.3.

One of the conspicuous features of the Strategic Computing Project is that it has three mission programs: an autonomous land vehicle, a pilot's associate, and an aircraft-carrier battle-management system. Speech recognition is involved in the two latter programs. In the pilot's associate program, it aims at achieving limited vocabulary in a high-noise, high-stress environment, while in the battle-management program it aims at accomplishing continuous-speech recognition of very large vocabulary in a moderate noise environment. The following milestones are given for the speech subsystems:

1986 100-word vocabulary. Speaker-dependent recognition under conditions of severe noise and moderate stress.

1988 1000-word, continuous-speech recognition ability adaptable to the speaker. Intermediate sized grammar. Low noise and stress.

1990 Like 1986, except 200-word vocabulary and speaker-independent.

1992 Like 1988, except 10000 words, natural grammar, and speaker-independent.

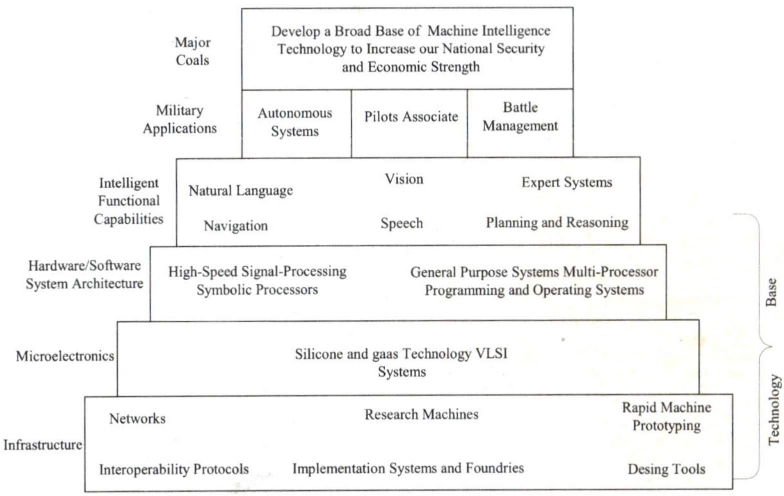

Fig. 2.3 Program structure and goals for the DARPA Strategic Computing Project

Research and development of these subsystems are carried out a several institutions including two universities (CMU and MIT). Unlik the first ARPA speech understanding program, there seem to be planned division of tasks and a better cooperation among the variou groups involved.

2.4.3 Alvey Programme (U.K.)

The Alvey Programme of U.K. was started in 1983 as a 5-year project tc make the most of the U.K.'s expertise in Information Technology research, based on a close collaboration between universities and industries. The following four areas are selected for intensive efforts foi development: software engineering, man-machine interface (MMI), intelligent knowledge base systems (IKBS), and VLSI.

Speech research occupies an important position in the MMI part of the Alvey Programme. A set of ten projects was announced in May 1985, bringing together the majority of speech researchers in U.K. in a coordinated effort at extending the possibilities for interacting with machine using speech. Four other projects are also reported to be under consideration. The relationship among these projects is shown in Fig 2.4.

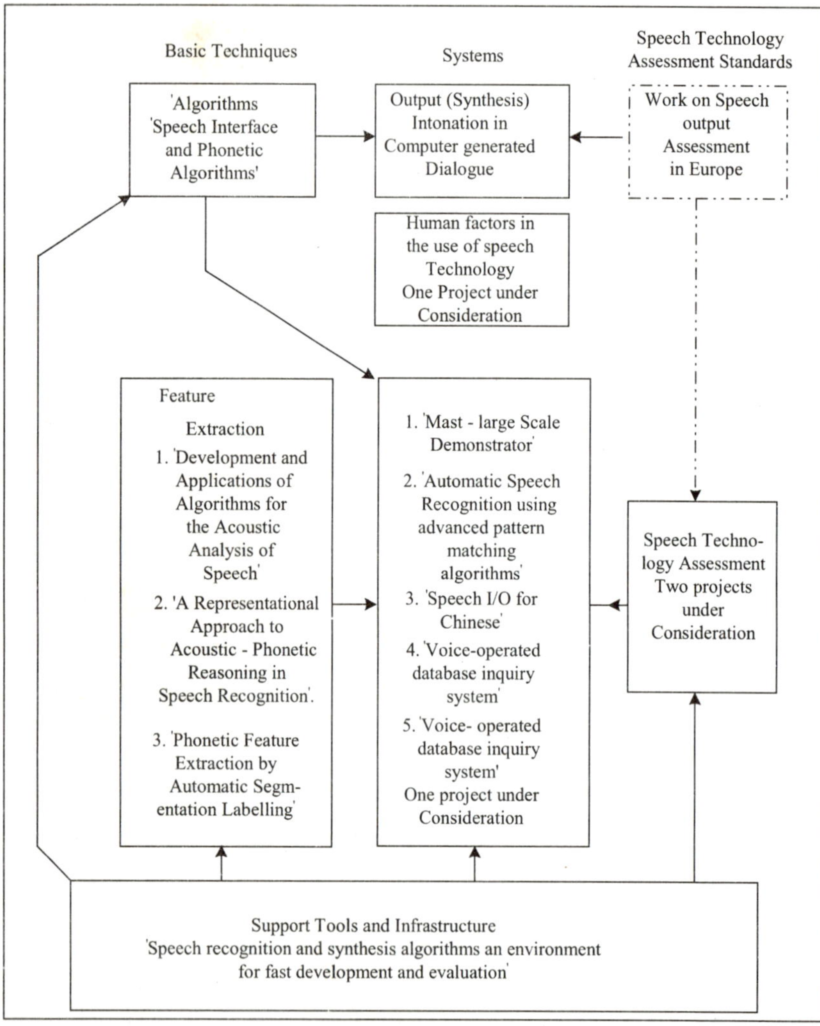

Fig. 2.4 Relationships among projects in the Alvey Speech Programme

Although the financial scale is smaller than the Japanese and the U.S. counterparts, the Alvey Speech Programme looks to be the best organized from the point of view of utilization of human resources in the academic institutions and industries.

2.4.4 Japanese Interpreting Telephony Project

Because of its peculiar structure which is quite different from all other languages of the world, the Japanese language is a barrier in international communications, and is making Japan culturally isolated from the rest of the international community. The realization of the interpreting telephony, though it may sound to be quite a remote and unrealistic target, is a task to be accomplished by the Japanese. The author was especially pleased that his proposal for a long-range research was adopted by the Ministry of Post and Telecommunication, and a study group was formed to draft a preliminary master plan for the next 15 to 20 years of research in speech recognition, language translation and speech synthesis. An International Symposium on Prospects and Problems on Interpreting Telephony is being organised to discuss various problems and possible approaches toward the goal.

2.5 AREAS OF FUTURE RESEARCH

Although the goals of speech recognition research in the above mentioned projects are certainly quite ambitious, their methods of approach are found to be rather conventional. For a real breakthrough in speech recognition, critical re-examination of some of the basic postulates may become necessary, as will be discussed in the following sections.

2.5.1 Units of Speech Recognition

While it is true that all the phonetic segments are clearly manifested in a careful utterance, it is also true that their manifestations are heavily distorted by their context, or even deleted in casual speech. While such distortions and deletions are treated as allophonic changes in conventional phonetics, it is more likely that a human listener do not require detailed phonetic analysis to recognize a familiar word or a sequence of words. This does not deny his capability of phonetic perception for clearly-pronounced words, especially when they are unfamiliar to him. These considerations lead us to believe that the basic unit of human speech perception is not unique but rather multiple. They also suggest that the unit of automatic speech recognition need not be unique. Although such a system has never been studied before, work is under way to construct a speech recognition system based on multiple units.

2.5.2 Recognition vs Understanding

What is the ultimate goal of speech recognition? Should we aim at deriving a linguistically well-formed output, or should we be satisfied with retrieving the semantic or pragmatic contents of the speaker's utterance? There are of course special cases where the answer is affirmative for the former question, but in the ultimate form of man-machine communication, the answer is affirmative for the latter. In fact, almost all the utterances in our daily life conversation are linguistically and phonetically ill-formed. The deviations from well-formed prototypes, which are called coarticulation, neutralization, omission ellipsis, etc., are found to be more common than the prototypes themselves, but these ill-formed utterances play the same communicative role as the most well-formed ones.

2.5.3 Speaker-adaptive *vs* Speaker-independent Systems

Although speaker-independence is often mentioned as if it was a realizable goal, few studies have ever faced the problem of individual differences of speech in a large number of speakers differing in age, gender, region, etc. Our own investigation of the acoustic characteristics of vowels of the common Japanese (not the dialects of Japanese), reveals that individual and regional differences are so large as to discourage the notion of speaker-independence in speech recognition. It may still be possible to speak of the speaker-independence for a fairly uniform group of speakers from the same region, but it seems to be more realistic to design a system that can be made to adapt to a speaker through an efficient learning procedure.

2.5.4 Deductive Inference *vs* Inductive Inference

Although at present much emphasis is being placed on realizing efficient hardware and software for deductive inference, especially in the Japanese FGCS Project, a real breakthrough in speech recognition is expected to come from the realization of efficient and systematic methods of inductive inference. For example, the automatic selection of acoustic features for phonetic recognition, the learning process (not the training process) in a speaker-adaptive system, understanding ill-formed utterances, as well as guessing the meaning of words, not found in previously acquired knowledge, are essential features of the human process of language acquisition and learning, and will only be possible for a machine by endowing it an ability of inductive inference.

2.6 CONCLUSIONS

Following an exposition of various problems of speech recognition, the state of the art has been briefly reviewed comparing the results of recent works. Several large-scale national projects have then been mentioned in their relation to speech recognition. Some of the basic postulates of conventional works have been critically reviewed, in order to provide a breakthrough in speech recognition. Finally, the author believes that it is inevitable to learn much more from the human processes of speech recognition and understanding, if we are going to construct a system with a similar performance to that of a human listener.

3

Pyramid Algorithms for Finding Global Structures in Images

AZRIEL ROSENFELD[1]

ABSTRACT

Multiresolution, or "pyramid", approaches to computer vision provide the capability of rapidly detecting and extracting global structures (features, regions, patterns, etc.) from an image. The human visual system too is able to spontaneously, or "preattentively", perceive various types of global structure in its input; this process is sometimes called *perceptual organization*. This paper describes a set of pyramid-based algorithms that can detect and extract these types of structures; these include algorithms for inferring three-dimensional information from images and for processing time sequences of images. If implemented in parallel on cellular pyramid hardware, these algorithms require processing times on the order of the logarithm of the image diameter.

Keywords: Pyramid; Algorithms; Global Structures; Images; Perceptual Organization; Image Diameter; Blobs & Ribbons; Bimodality.

3.1 INTRODUCTION

During the past few years the use of multiresolution ("pyramid") image representations in image analysis and computer vision has created interest. Several research groups have designed or built image processing machines based on this approach. A pyramid-structured array of multiprocessors can perform many types of operations on an image (input to the base of the pyramid, one pixel per processor), in time proportional to the log of the image diameter. A recent collection of papers on pyramid methods in image processing and analysis is Ref. [1].

One of the most important potential applications of pyramid machines is the fast detection and extraction of global structures (features, regions, patterns, etc.) in an image, by rapidly combining information collected from many parts of the image. A number of pyramid-based methods of extracting global image structures have been developed at our laboratory, and some have been proposed, as follows:

The rapid detection of global structure in images is an important, but not well understood, capability of the human visual system. Humans tend to spontaneously, or "preattentively", perceive various types of global structures in their visual input; this process is sometimes called *perceptual organization*. About 50 years ago, the Gestalt psychologists

[1] Center for Automation Research, University of Maryland, College Park, MD 20742, USA.

formulated a set of principles, or "laws":, that describe how image parts tend to "group" into global structures [2]. These include the "laws" of similarity, proximity, good continuation, and closure. In Sections 3.2 – 3.5, it is shown how each of these types of groupings can be detected using fast pyramid algorithms.

Fast detection of global structure in an image seems to be an essential component of 'real-time' perception. Humans are able to recognize objects in unexpected, complex images in one second or less, a period of time during which only on the order of 100 neural computational steps could have taken place. Obviously, the human visual system is highly parallel, but conventional parallel processing concepts are not powerful enough to account for this performance. For example, a human can "immediately" detect a long straight line in the visual field; since the line may be several hundred retinal receptor cells ("pixels") long, conventional methods would require several hundred computational steps, even on a two-dimensional parallel machine, to extract the line from the input image. Pyramid-style parallelism provides a much faster method of doing this; as we shall see below, a pyramid scheme can extract long straight lines from an image in tens, rather than hundreds, of steps. Schemes of this type seem to be essential in achieving fast recognition of global patterns. Such patterns cannot be reliably organized using conjunctions of local features; some means of explicitly extracting global structures is needed. The techniques described in the following sections provide such a means.

The grouping algorithms discussed here will be primarily two-dimensional, but similar pyramid-based techniques can be applied to the analysis of images of three-dimensional scenes, or to time-varying images. These extensions will be briefly discussed in Section 3.6.

3.2 "SIMILARITY": DETECTING BIMODALITY

According to the Gestalt "Law of Similarity", if an image consists of a mixture of two different types of local patterns, humans can "group" the patterns of one type together and perceive them as a "figure", where the remaining patterns become part of the background.

On the other hand, a mixture of three types of local patterns is hard to distinguish from a uniform distribution of pattern types, as illustrated by the pattern (taken from [3]). Apparently, the human visual system can detect bimodality (of a local property such as size or slope), and can "segment" an image containing a bimodal population of local patterns (in the sense that the two subpopulations can be perceived as distinct from one another); but the visual system cannot easily handle multimodal distributions, and tends to treat them as though they were uniform.

In a computer vision system, it is easy to compute the histogram of values of a local image property, and to detect multiple peaks in the histogram (provided they do not overlap). However, constructing a histogram is a somewhat slow process, since each of the distinct values must be separately counted. (A simple pyramid algorithm can be used to count the number of occurrences of any one value in time proportional to the log of the image diameter; but in order to compute a complete k-valued histogram, this algorithm must be repeated k times). We now describe a pyramid-based technique that directly detects bimodality, without computing a histogram; it is possible that a scheme of this type could serve as a model for humans' bimodality detection ability.

Our scheme is based on a simple pyramid structure in which each cell at level h receives inputs from a block of cells (its "children") at level $h - 1$. The image is initially input to the base of the pyramid (level 0), and the given local property is computed (wherever applicable), yielding a (sparse) array of local property values.

Each cell at level 1 now examines the set of values in its block of the (level-0) array, and finds the partition of these values into two subsets that minimizes the variance of each subset about its mean. (This partition is sometimes called the "bimean" [4].) Let the means of the subsets be μ and ν, let the sizes of the subsets be r and s, and let the standard deviations be σ and τ. The cell then computes the "Fisher distance" $d \equiv |\mu-\nu| / \sqrt{\sigma^2+\tau^2}$ between the two subsets. Note that a large Fisher distance means that the population of values in the cell's block is strongly bimodal (the means are many standard deviations apart). If the Fisher distance is not sufficiently large, the cell flags itself "as not bimodal".

Each cell on level 2 now examines the data computed by its "children" on level 1. Suppose that all (or nearly all) of the children have bimodal populations, say with means and standard deviations μ_1, ν_1, ...,μ_m, ν_m and σ_1, τ_1,....,σ_m, τ_m. The cell finds the partition of the μ's and ν's into two subsets that minimizes the variance of each subset about its mean. (The means of the subsets can be computed as weighted averages from the μ's and ν's and their corresponding r's and s's; the variances can be estimated from the μ's, ν's, r's, s's, σ's and τ's.)

Finally, the cell estimates the Fisher distance for this new partition, and decides whether its combined population of values is still bimodal. If several of the cell's children do not have bimodal populations, the cell does not carry out these computations, but simply flags itself as "not bimodal".

This process is repeated for the cells on levels 2, 4, ... We suggest that bimodality is "perceptually conspicuous" if a cell on a sufficiently high level (representing a large block of the image) has a bimodal population.

In principle, this scheme could be generalized to detect trimodality, ..., k-modality,..., but the amount of computation that the cells would need to perform would grow rapidly with k. In any case, since our method is based on repeatedly estimating the variances of subsets, it is not capable of fine discriminations between subsets whose means are close together; thus the method will detect bimodality only when the means are very far apart or the variances are very small, and there would be little value in attempting to detect k-modality for $k > 2$. [In general, it would be of little value for the brain to perform computations whose results would be so inaccurate as to provide no useful information. Note that if the brain contains pyramid-like structures, they would not be perfectly regular (i.e., the image blocks seen by the cells would not all be of equal sizes nor have equal degrees of overlap); thus it would be pointless to attempt to use them, e.g., for exact counting, but only for rough population size estimation.]

3.3 "PROXIMITY": DETECTING COMPACT REGIONS

The Gestalt "Law of Proximity" states that local patterns that lie close together tend to be grouped together as a "figure". We will deal in this section only with groupings that are "compact", or "blob-like". The detection of elongated, or "ribbon-like", figures (or parts of figures) probably involves other processes, in addition to proximity-based grouping; it will be discussed further in Section 3.5.

Several pyramid-based methods of detecting compact figures have been developed at our laboratory [5, 6]. A recently developed, simpler method [7] seems to yield even better results; it will be described below. We shall assume, as in Section 3.2, that the image is input to the base of pyramid and that the local property is first computed, so that the input becomes an array (not necessarily sparse) of local property values (e.g. gray levels).

Each cell on level 1 computes the mean and variance of the values in its block, and this process is repeated at levels 2, 3.... (In this case the variance of a cell at any level can be computed exactly from the means and variances of its children, because the children's population sizes are all equal [8].) Let P be a cell on level h, and let $Q_1, ..., Q_k$ be the cells on level $h + 1$ whose blocks of the image contain P's block. Let σ be the variance of P, and $\tau_1, ..., \tau_k$ the variances of Q's; let the area of P's block be s, and the areas of Q's blocks be t. We call P a "root node" if $\tau_1/t,...,\tau_k/t$ are all significantly higher than σ/s. Intuitively, this will happen if P's block lies (mostly) within a "homogeneous" region of the image (e.g., a region whose values are independent samples of the same normal distribution), but the Qs' blocks are too big to lie inside that region. [Note that for low levels h, if the image is noisy, this criterion will not be reliable, because the τ's may be too variable to be good estimates of the variability of the region's population of values; but for larger values of h, the estimates will be more reliable, and τ_i / t will be smaller than σ/s (since t is larger than s) if Q_i's block lies inside the region. Thus for large h's, the "root nodes" will represent maximal blocks of the image that approximately coincide with homogeneous regions.][2]

The homogeneous regions detected in this way can be extracted from the image by a top-down tree growing process such as the following: Take the root node P as the root of the tree. Let P' be a cell on some level $i < h$, and let $Q'_1, ..., Q'_k$ be the cells on level $i + 1$ whose image blocks overlap that of P'. Let Q' be that one of the Q's having smallest Fisher distance from P'. Then we make P' a tree node if and only if Q' is a tree node. This process is carried out for $i = h - 1, h - 2$ .... The leaves of the tree at level 0 are the pixels constituting the region. (There are several variations on this tree growing procedure; the details will be described in [7]).

The region extracted from the image in this way is necessarily compact, since it cannot contain pixels that are far away from the original root node's block of the image. (Indeed, at successive stages of the tree growing process we can only add to the tree cells whose blocks overlap that of P, then cells whose blocks are exponentially decreasing.) Of course, we can also lose parts of P's block, since some blocks that overlap P's block will not meet the criterion for inclusion in the tree. Note that at the levels immediately below h, it is likely that the cells whose blocks are contained in P's block will nearly all join the tree, since they represent relatively large samples of the same image region; thus the union of these blocks will define a "solid" region. At still lower levels, the blocks may no longer resemble that of P, due to noise, but if they are near the center of P's block they will have no choice but to join the tree, so that the region will remain solid. Blocks near the edges of the region, however, will not be forced to join the tree, so the tree growing process will be able to closely approximate the shape of the region.

Preliminary experiments [7] indicate that this approach is quite effective at extracting compact homogeneous regions from an image, even if they have irregular shape. We plan to conduct a more extensive

---

[2] Many variations of this simple root node selection criterion can be formulated, based on different assumptions about the distribution of local property values in the image.

series of experiments in which the approach is applied to the detection and extraction of various types of homogeneously textured regions (i.e., regions having stationary distributions of the values of local properties other than gray level). Note that in a textured image, our method will be able to detect both "texture primitives" (= pieces of the image having nearly constant gray levels) and textured regions (= clusters of these pieces); the former should give rise to root nodes at low levels, and the latter to root nodes at higher levels. Our approach can also be generalized to nonstationary distributions; for example, we can extract regions over which the distribution of property values varies linearly by least-squares fitting linear functions to the sets of property values in each image block, and calling P a root node if the fits to the Q's are all worse than P's fit. [Recall that when we compute the mean and standard deviation of a block, we are least-squares fitting a constant function to the values in the block.]

A related approach can be used to extract compact regions that are smoothly varying, but not necessarily homogeneous (i.e., their spatial distribution of property values does not globally fit a linear (etc.) function). To do this we call P a root node if its pairs of adjacent children (= cells on level $h - 1$, whose blocks are contained in P's block) all have small Fisher distances (i.e., P contains no "edges"), but none of the Q's (on level $h + 1$) whose blocks contain P's have this property. [Note that if the values in P's block vary smoothly, two adjacent children of P cannot have a large Fisher distance; their variances and the difference between their means will both be large if the variation is steep, and small if it is gradual.] We can then use tree-growing methods similar to those described above to extract the detected region.

3.4 "GOOD CONTINUATION": DETECTING SMOOTH CURVES

Approaches analogous to those in Section 3.3 can be used to detect and extract smooth curves, or curves that are good global fits to given functions (e.g. to straight lines). We first apply a local edge or curve detection operation to the image, and input the resulting set of feature points to the base of the pyramid.

To detect smooth curves, each cell at level 1 examines its block of the image; if (many of) the feature points in the block lie on a smooth curve, the cell records the positions and slopes of the end points of the curve, and also stores pointers to the feature points that constitute the curve. Each cell at level 2 now examines the data provided by its children at level 1. If (many of) the end point data are consistent (i.e., they can be arranged in a sequence such that successive end points coincide in position and slope), the level 2 cell records the positions and slopes of the first and last end points, and stores pointers to the level 1 cells that contributed the consistent data. This process is repeated at levels 3, 4, ... Thus if the image contains a long, smooth curve, some high level cell will contain its endpoint data, and will also be the root of a tree of pointers whose leaves are the feature points comprising the curve.

This approach requires only a bounded amount of computation by the cells at each level, and so can be carried out in O (log image diameter) time, even if the curve is long. It has difficulties, however, if the image contains several long, smooth curves, or a single curve that doubles back on itself. In such cases, some of the cells will detect more than one smooth curve, and will need the capacity to store several sets of endpoint data. In an early implementation of this approach, the cells were given the ability to store up to five sets of data [9]. Another possibility, currently under investigation, is to use a higher-dimensional "pyramid" in which the "base" is a three-dimensional space having coordinates (x, y, θ), where θ is slope. In this space, curves that cross at large angle will be far apart in θ; but tangent or closely parallel curves will still lie close together (and indeed, are perceptually harder to separate).

A similar approach can be used to detect curves that are good global fits to given functions—e.g., straight lines [9]. Here each cell at level 1 fits a straight line to the feature points in its block of the image (possibly discarding outliers); each cell at level 2 estimates a straight line fit to these fits (again, possibly discarding outliers); and so on. As in Section 3.3, the fit error measure should be divided by the number of points being fitted; this reflects the intuitive fact that the fit to a long piece of wiggly straight line is "better" than the fit to a short piece. A cell *P* is called a "root node" if its fit is significantly better than those of the cells overlying it on the level above it (the *Q*'s of Section 3.3). This should happen if (most of) the feature points in *P*'s block lie on or near a straight line segment, but the larger blocks of the *Q*'s contain parts of other curves. As in Section 3.3, it should be possible to use a top-down tree growing process, starting at *P*, to extract *P*'s straight line segment more precisely.

This recursive fitting process can also be used to detect corners, or angles, on a curve [10]. A cell detects an angle if two of its children contain good straight line fits that have different slopes and that (approximately) meet at a common endpoint. The closer the fits, the smaller the slope difference need be for an angle to be detected.

As in the smooth curve case, difficulties arise if the image contains several straight lines or curves. One way to deal with this is to build a "pyramid" starting from a three-dimensional (x, y, θ) "base", as described above. Another possibility is to allow each cell to store more than one fit, i.e., to find a "best" partition of its data in terms of the goodness of the fits to the parts. (Compare the "bimean" bimodality detection scheme in Section 3.2.) This latter possibility seems more plausible from a perceptual standpoint, since "good" straight lines do not perceptually interfere with each other even if they intersect at a shallow angle; in this situation the lines pass near each other in (x, y, θ) space, but they may still have a high "Fisher distance" if their individual fits are very good.

3.5 "CLOSURE": DETECTING BLOBS AND RIBBONS

Another pyramid-based approach to extracting regions from an image is based on detecting parts of the image that are "surrounded" by edges or curves. This approach can be used to extract "ribbon-like" as well as "blob-like" (= compact) regions.

We begin by detecting edges (or curves) in the input image, and inputting the resulting set of feature points to the base of the pyramid. We then pass this information up through the pyramid, condensing and "summarizing" it at each stage, e.g., by straight line fitting, as in Section 3.4. The cells at each level also examine their neighbouring cells (e.g., in a 5-by-5 neighbourhood) and check whether they are locally (nearly) "surrounded" by lines that run (approximately) broadside to them (and in the case of edge data, that have consistent contrasts, i.e., their dark sides all face inward or all face outward). If a cell discovers that these conditions are satisfied, it has detected a "blob".

An early implementation of this blob detection scheme is described in Ref. [6]. A non-pyramid implementation, which detected blobs by searching out from each pixel in a set of directions, up to a distance equal to the maximum expected blob radius, is described in Ref. [11]. The pyramid approach has the advantage that it requires only local searches; blobs of any size will become locally detectable at some level of the pyramid.

The edge-based approach to blob detection may be more perceptually plausible than the function fitting scheme described in Section 3.0. In the absence of edges, a region may look uniformly bright even when its brightness varies substantially from one side to another, due to shading; this suggests that the visual system cannot easily determine the slope of a (e.g.) linear fit to the brightness data. Conversely, suppose a region is surrounded by "pseudoedges" at which there is a local brightness change, but where the change smoothes out as we move away from the edges in either direction, so that the regions inside and outside the edges actually have the same uniform brightness (except near the edges). In this situation the region on the dark side of the edges looks uniformly darker than the region on the bright side, even though the brightness of the regions are actually the same; this phenomenon is known as the Craik-O'Brien-Cornsweet illusion [12]. This suggests that the visual system assigns a brightness to a region based on the local brightnesses along the edges surrounding the region, rather than by fitting a function globally to all the gray levels in the region.

In Ref. [6], a relatively complicated scheme is described for extracting and "colouring in" a blob detected using the edge-based approach. Another way of defining the precise boundaries of the blob is to project its surrounding edges downward through the pyramid, one level at a time, and at each level locally adjust them so as to maximize the gray level gradient magnitude along the edges. However, if this simple method of edge adjustment is used, noise at the lower levels of the pyramid will cause the edges to break-up, since we are not constraining them to be continuous [13]. Better results are obtained if we start with a connected region (the union of the pixels surrounded by the edges), project it downward through the pyramid, and at each step, adjust its border by adjoining or deleting pixels in such a way as to maximize the contrast around the border. This method constrains the border to remain continuous, and yields good region delineations even for noisy images [14].

An edge- (or curve-) based pyramid technique can also be used to extract ribbon-like regions from an image. Here too we begin by inputting the feature (edge or curve) points to the base of the pyramid, and performing repeated (e.g.) straight line fitting at successively higher levels. The cells at each level also examine their neighbourhoods (e.g. 5-by-5) and look for "antisymmetric" pairs of edges located on opposite sides of them i.e., pairs of edges such that the given cell is on the dark side of both of them, or on the light side of both. In effect, this process detects "smoothed local symmetries" [15] at each level of the pyramid. When a cell detects such a configuration, it stores the estimated position and orientation of the local axis of symmetry, as well as the distance and angle between the pair of edges; the latter information defines a linear fit to the "width function" defined by the pair of edges. Cells on higher levels can then link pieces of symmetry axis into smooth curves along which the width function varies smoothly, by a straightforward generalization of the methods described in Section 3.4. [Global functions (such as straight lines) can also be fit to the axes and to the width function, if desired]. Such a smooth curve defines a generalized ribbon [16]. By storing links between the axis segments and their associated edge segments, we can find the edges of the ribbon and then project them downward through the pyramid to extract the ribbon from the image, using the methods described in the previous paragraph.

3.6 EXTENSIONS TO THREE-DIMENSIONAL AND TIME-VARYING SCENES

In the preceding sections, for simplicity, the image data has been treated two-dimensionally, without reference to the fact that the underlying scene may be three-dimensional or that the image may be part of a time sequence. However, this approach can also be applied to infer three-dimensional scene information from an image, and to analyze optical flow in a sequence of images.

Global nonlinear variations in the gray level of a region may be an indication that the region is the image of a curved surface. Some work has been done using global function fitting to the image gray levels to detect specific types of surfaces in a scene [17]; this type of computation could be efficiently implemented using pyramid techniques such as those described in Section 3.3. Similarly, global variations (linear or nonlinear) in the sizes and spacings of texture elements over a region can serve as an indication that the region is the image of a slanted or curved surface. Thus the function fitting methods of Section 3.3 can serve as aids in the computation of surface shape from either shading, texture, or both.

Our function fitting methods can be applied to vector-valued as well as scalar-valued data; for example, they can be applied to colour data. If we are given a time sequence of images, and can estimate a set of displacement vectors relating points in one image to those in the next, we can also apply the function fitting approach to detect global patterns in the resulting (possibly sparse) "optical flow field". This approach has been successfully used to segment noisy synthetic optical flow fields into regions representing different types of motions, including translation, planar rotation, and scale change [18]. It should also be applicable to real data. [The global grouping of pixels having common velocity vectors was called the "Law of Common Fate" by the Gestaltists]. It may also be possible to detect surfaces in a stereopair of images by applying function fitting techniques to the (sparse) "disparity field" [19].

It should be pointed out, in conclusion, that the pyramid techniques described in this paper are quite different from the ways in which pyramids have been used by other investigators (see, e.g., [1]). Pyramids are often used to generate a set of bandpass-filtered, sampled versions of an image. This approach is appropriate when using pyramids to implement multiscale feature detection processes such as edge detection. Our use of pyramids is quite different; we employ them for model *fitting* rather than for *filtering*.

3.7 SUMMARY

The concepts outlined in this paper constitute a basic contribution to the methodology of vision systems design. The author's approach makes use of the pyramid cellular architecture to rapidly compute global information about an image in a recursive fashion, but its main contribution lies in the nature of the computations that are performed, which involve model fitting rather than filtering. The following are some of the key aspects of the approach.

- It provides a unified method of detecting various types of global patterns by bottom-up recursive fitting of low-order polynomial models to the data.
- It provides a method of delineating the detected patterns by top-down recursive refinement of the fitted data.
- It allows for the detection of more complex types of global patterns by applying local feature detection processes to the fitted models.
- The methods can be applied to gray level surfaces, to edges or curves, or to vector-valued data such as disparity or optical flow fields.

The transition from local to global—from pixel arrays to descriptive data structures has traditionally been a major point of discontinuity in vision systems. Our approach offers the promise of making this discontinuity much less abrupt.

References

1. A Rosenfeld (ed.) (1984) Multiresolution Image Processing and Analysis, Springer, Berlin.
2. M Wertheimer (1958) Principles of perceptual organization in: Readings in Perception (eds. D C Beardslee and M Wertheimer) van Nostrand, Priceton, NJ, 115–135.
3. D Marr (1982) Vision, Freeman, San Francisco, 95.
4. S M Dunn, L Janos and A Rosenfeld (1983) Bimean clustering, Patt Recog Lett 1, 155–160.
5. T H Hong and A Rosenfeld (1984) Compact region extraction using weighted pixel linking in a pyramid IEEE Trans PAMI-6, 222–229.
6. T H Hong and M Shneier (1984) Extracting compact objects using linked pyramids, IEEE Trans PAMI-6, 229–237.
7. A Gross M.S. Thesis (under preparation).
8. P Burt (1979) Hierarchically derived piecewise polynomial approximations to waveforms and images, TR-838, Computer Vision Laboratory, Univeristy of Maryland, November.

9. T H Hong, M O Shneier, R L Hartley and A Rosenfeld (1983) Using pyramids to detect good continuation, *IEEE Trans SMC*-13, 631–635.

10. R L Hartley and A Rosenfeld (1985) Hierarchical line linking for corner detection *In: Integrated Technology for Parallel Image Processing* (ed. S Levialdi), Academic, Press New York, 101–119.

11. L G Minor and J Sklansky (1981) The detection and segmentation of blobs in infrared images, *IEEE Trans SMC*-11, 194–201.

12. T N Cornsweet (1970), *Visual Perception*, Academic Press, New York, 27.

13. A Rosenfeld, M Thurston, and Y H Lee (1972) Edge and curve detection: further experiments *IEEE Trans* 21, 677–715.

14. E S Baugher and A Rosenfeld (1985) Boundary localization in an Image Pyramid TR-1488 Computer Vision Laboratory, University of Maryland, May.

15. J M Brady and H Asada (1984) Smoothed local symmetries and their implementation, AIM 757, Artificial Intelligence Laboratory, MIT, February.

16. A Rosenfeld Axial descriptions of shape, Computer Vision, Graphics, and Image Processing (In press).

17. R M Bolle and D B Cooper (1984) Bayesian recognition of local 3-D shape by approximating image intensity functions with quadric polynomials *IEEE Trans PAMI*-6, 418–429.

18. R L Hartley (1985) Segmentation of optical flow fields by pyramid linking *Patt Recog Lett* 3, 253–262.

19. R D Eastman and A M Waxman (1985) Using disparity functional for stereo correspondence and surface reconstruction TR-1547-Computer Vision Laboratory, University of Maryland, October.

4

The Paninian Approach to Natural Language Processing

Subhash C Kak[1]

ABSTRACT

Panini is not only the oldest grammarian whose work has come down to us—he is also the greatest.

H. Scharfe [1]

This paper is a survey of several techniques used currently in natural language processing and knowledge representation. It is shown that the most effective of these conform to the constructive approach presented more than twenty five hundred years ago by Panini. Panini's grammar is an algebraic structure that has rules on generation of words and sentences, as well as rules about rules. His grammar describes the Sanskrit language as it was spoken and used in his age. This structure can also be taken as a model for a universal grammar, so his ideas could be exploited in the development of computer based natural language processing systems. Furthermore, the fact that his grammar is nearly a complete description of Sanskrit suggests that the language dichotomy into the classes natural and artificial may not be a real one. Panini's grammar thus contains extremely important clues and insights for the researcher in artificial intelligence. Some implications of the Paninian approach to natural language processing are described.

Keywords: Panini; Grammar; Natural Language Processing; Artificial Intelligence; Machine Translation.

4.1 INTRODUCTION

Computer processing of a natural language, as against an 'artificial' language of the type used in writing computer programs, has gone through two distinct phases in the past thirty five years. It was first thought that machine translation (MT) of a language into another should be an easy matter once one had compiled dictionaries and obtained mathematical representation of the grammars of the languages in question. It was believed that actual translation would proceed by replacing the words in the text by their equivalents, followed by a rearrangement and modification of these new words according to the grammar of the target language.

It was soon found that this task was not easy since a word can have several equivalents, where the correct one can only be decided by the context. The mathematical representation of the grammar of a natural

[1] Department of Electrical and Computer Engineering, Louisiana State University, Baton Rouge, LA 70803, USA.

language so that the sentences are unambiguous was also given up as an intractable problem. Machine translations were often incomprehensible, or they totally distorted meaning. By the mid-1960's the MT program, as envisaged originally, was dead. The focus in the recent years has shifted away from MT to providing a preliminary translation, which can then be worked upon by an editor to produce the finished work. The other area to which attention has been given is the definition of a constrained language form and vocabulary, more flexible than in artificial languages, so that there is no ambiguity in meaning. These efforts have brought the problem of knowledge representation to the fore. Such a representation assumes a certain knowledge of the application environment, and a knowledge of the intended audience. Various techniques of knowledge representation have been incorporated in current systems: these include semantic networks, first order logic, frames, and production systems. Each of these techniques may offer special advantages for specific situations.

These techniques of knowledge representation also suffer from certain shortcomings. In the semantic network approach, where relationships between objects and classes are specified, it is not known how to distinguish between information related to an object as against that of a class and how to deal with exceptions. The first order logic approach, which has led to the development of Prolog, cannot deal with incomplete knowledge or with situations where non-deductive inference may be called for. In the frames approach the knowledge-base is decomposed into highly modular chunks, a procedure not always possible. In the production system approach rules connecting 'patterns' and 'action' (say in human reasoning) are defined. The memory required to define a pattern may be unobtainable, however. The development of the so-called fifth generation computers would be predicted on the success of the definition of 'constrained' variants of natural languages and efficient knowledge representation systems.

If there are limits to the nature of natural language processing by the computer, the question arises as to what the nature of these limits is. It appears that the best one can do to find these limits is to devise actual systems—in other words, use a constructive approach. The greatest success a constructive approach to the description of a natural language has ever had was when Panini devised his grammar for the Sanskrit language, an achievement termed by the famous linguist L. Bloomfield as '*one of the greatest monuments of human intelligence*' [2]. We would expect that the insights of Panini, '*the greatest linguist of antiquity, if not of all time*' [3] could be exploited to help answer the question regarding limits to computers, as well as define an approach that could yield powerful text and speech processing systems. The knowledge representation methodology in the grammar of Panini and his successors is, in many ways, equivalent to the more powerful currently researched AI schemes. Furthermore, it includes rules about rules, analogs of which are not known for other languages, or for a flexible enough subset of, say, English language that would qualify for most Al applications. This paper is a brief introduction to this Paninian approach, aspects of which have already been incorporated in the current computer understanding systems. This introduction also provides an overview of the 'standard' approach to natural language processing, so that one may appreciate the commonality between the two as well as main points of difference.

4.2 PANINI'S GRAMMAR

Dakshiputra Panini is believed to have lived during the 5th or 6th century B.C. He was born in the town of Shalatura, modern Lahur, in Northwest India. Panini's grammar Ashthadhyayi (The Eight Chapters) deals ostensibly with the Sanskrit language; it, however, is really a model for a universal grammar, applicable to any language. His book consists of a little under 4000 rules and aphorisms. Panini's grammar attempts to completely describe Sanskrit as the spoken language of its time. Two important commentaries on his grammar, which are often studied along with it are those by Katyayana, and Patanjali (2nd century B.C.). Its philosophical underpinnings were discussed in an important work in the 5th century A.D. by Bhartrhari. Modern translations and/or commentaries may be found in the books by Bohtlingk, Renou, Kiparsky, Staal [3,14], Scharfe [1,15] and Misra [16].

Panini's grammar begins with metarules, or rules about rules. To facilitate his description, he establishes a special technical language (or metalanguage [14]). This is followed by several sections on how to generate words and sentences starting from roots, as well as rules on transformations of structure. The last part of the grammar is a one-directional string of rules, where a given rule in the sequence ignores all rules that follow. This anticipates in form and spirit by more than 2500 years the idea of a computer program. The structure of this part of Panini's grammar should rightly be termed The Panini Machine.

Note that in Panini's system a finite set of rules is enough to generate an infinity of sentences. The algebraic character of Panini's rules was not appreciated in the West until very recently, when a similar generative structure was rediscovered by Chomsky and others. Before this, in the nineteenth century, Panini's analysis of root and suffixes and his recognition of ablaut had led to the founding of the subjects of comparative and historical linguistics.

Despite similarities between Paninian and the modern generative grammars, there exist striking differences as well. Some of these differences are related to the nature of the languages under study: Sanskrit in the case of Panini, and modern European languages in the other case. Furthermore, the contemporary evaluation of Panini is still going on, a process that is slowed down by the fact that the original is inaccessible to most linguists and computer scientists. In any event, for the purpose of this paper, we would define an approach to language processing as being Paninian if it uses:

1. Root and suffix analysis
2. Linear string of rules and analysis by rule sequence
3. Analysis by functional structure; and
4. An exhaustive description.

Since the current grammars for English do not satisfy condition (3), we would constrain the allowed structures so as to fit the capabilities of the grammars. It should be noted that as the significance of the Paninian structure for a universal grammar is further revealed and understood, our definition of this approach will change accordingly.

4.3 AMBIGUITY

Let us enumerate some of the ambiguities that make machine translation such a difficult task. These ambiguities need to be resolved, if at all possible, in various steps to obtain a translation.

Each kind of ambiguity is addressed separately in a sequence of steps, which constitutes the usual form of a computer based understanding system.

4.3.1 Lexical Ambiguity

This arises from a single word having two or more different meanings, all of which are potentially valid. Consider ‘stay away from the range’ which could be advice to a child to keep away from either the kitchen stove or the meadow. ‘The court was packed’ is a more complex example. The court here may refer to a judicial court or a rectangular space and packed might mean a deceitful composition or a crowding by people.

4.3.2 Structural Ambiguity

One source of this ambiguity is the many ways words in a sentence may be combined into phrases and then interpreted. Thus in ‘He saw the crane fly outside’ one might be referring to the crane fly, a long-legged two-winged fly. Other examples of this ambiguity are: ‘My friend came home late last night’ and ‘Flying kites can be tricky.’ Another kind of structural ambiguity is where the sentence has a unique grammatical structure but it still allows different meanings owing to different underlying ‘deep structure.' For example, 'The policeman's arrest was illegal' does not tell us who was arrested. Another example is 'That leopard was spotted.'

4.3.3 Semantic Ambiguity

An example of this is the sentence 'I like to eat brown grapes.' This could either mean that the speaker liked a particular bunch of grapes in front of him, or that he merely expressed a preference for brown grapes.

4.3.4 Pragmatic Ambiguity

This is related to the context of the sentence. Thus in 'She put the brick in the washer and spoilt it,' the meaning would be different depending on whether the brick was made of metal or wax. Likewise the meaning of 'John loves his wife and so does Bill' would be unambiguous only if it were known that Bill was a bachelor.

A further discussion of ambiguities of various kinds as well as approaches to theoretical and computational linguistics may be found in the list of references [7-13].

These difficulties are inherent in English but are not fundamental to all natural languages. Shastric (Scientific) Sanskrit is one natural language that appears to be particularly precise [18].

4.4 LINGUISTIC ANALYSIS

A language may be described at several hierarchically organized levels. At the lowest level a spoken language may be characterized in terms of elementary sounds, the study of which constitutes phonology. A group of similar speech sounds which function in the same way, and which may be substituted for each other without changing the meaning of an utterance, is called a phoneme. Natural languages are generally characterized by 30 to 80 phonemes. English is usually described in terms of about 40 phonemes. Sanskrit is described in terms of 48 phonemes, each of which is represented by a unique symbol in its alphabet [13 vowels and 35 consonants]. Each basic unit of the written language, that includes letters of the alphabet and the punctuation marks, and the blank separating words, is called a grapheme.

The study of the next level of linguistic analysis is termed morphology. Simple words, as well as inflectional sounds like the plural endings, prefixes and suffixes that convey meanings, are morphemes. Written words must be analyzed for their morphemic components in a natural language processing system. Thus a system might process 'unknowing' by finding its root form 'know', and then determining the change in meaning affected by each of the additional morphemes 'un-' and '-ing.'

Syntax deals with the manner in which the meaningful constituents are put together to form an utterance or sentence. The structure is usually represented in terms of a tree. The sentence ‘I like to eat the fruit from my garden’ may be represented by a parse tree as in Fig. 4.1.

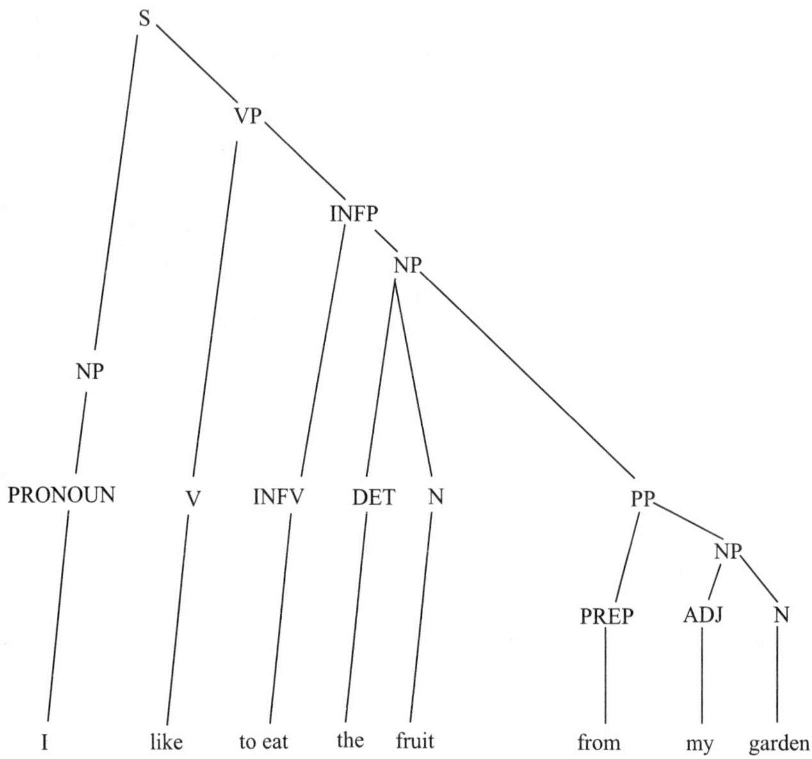

S	:	sentence	PP	:	prepositional phrase
NP	:	noun phrase	PREP	:	preposition
VP	:	verb phrase	ADJ	:	adjective
INFP	:	infinitive phrase	N	:	noun
INFV	:	infinitive verb	V	:	verb
DET	:	determiner			

Fig. 4.1 A parse tree

Some sentences can be parsed in many different ways, leading to different meanings. As example “Traffic jams were caused by slow trucks and buses carrying heavy loads” may be parsed in at least four different ways. In these different parse trees slow may qualify trucks only, or trucks and buses, and similarly heavy loads may qualify buses only, or both trucks and buses.

A parse tree is generated by rules of the kind

$$S \rightarrow NP \rightarrow VP$$
$$NP \rightarrow ADJ + N$$
$$NP \rightarrow DET + N + PP$$
$$PP \rightarrow PREP + NP$$

etc.

A collection of such rules is one way to generate a grammar. Most traditional English grammars have this form.

The grammatical tradition that grew out of Panini's work did not analyze sentences in the above noun-phrase/verb-phrase form. Rather, the description was a generative one, where the structure of the sentence was derived from a number of primitive syntactic categories such as verbal action, agents, objects, etc.

4.5 COMPUTER PROCESSING OF SPEECH

A computer based system of speech or text understanding must perform several operations in sequence. For speech the first operation is that of phonological analysis that transcribes sound waves into a series of phonemes. These may then be expressed as written words. The first analysis performed for written language is morphological, where each word is decomposed into its root and inflections. This is followed by lexical analysis where the words are assigned to different lexical categories such as noun, verb, adjective, etc. The next operation is that of syntactic analysis or parsing, where the rules of grammar are used to yield the structure of the sentence. The next step is that of semantic analysis, where the sentence is converted into a form so that inferences can be drawn easily. The last step is that of pragmatic analysis, which makes the context of the sentence explicit. At the end of the sequence the computer can announce its inferences and respond to questions. For such a sequence of operations to proceed effectively, it is necessary that the meaning underlying the sentences be represented in a convenient form. Different knowledge representation systems have been devised for this purpose. The sequence of operations in the understanding system is then a means of first generating information about the knowledge representation system which is followed by analysis.

Until now the most effective parsers have been the ones that are based on grammars designed with computers in mind. An early system (1971) that was quite impressive in reaching its limited aims was Winograd's SHRDLU where the parsing was done by interpreting grammars written as programs. SHRDLU simulates a robot which lives in a tabletop world of blocks containing a box and several coloured pyramids and cubes of assorted sizes. SHRDLU, keeps track of the locations of the blocks and can pick them up and rearrange them. The system accepts natural English input and responds by executing commands and answering queries about this world of blocks.

Syntactic classification in SHRDLU is done in terms of unanalyzable markings (features). The interdependence of these features can be represented by a graph. Each lexical entry for a word consists of a list of features and a semantic entry, the latter being a data structure which acts as the 'meaning' of the word. The parser, which is written in a language called PROGRAMMAR builds a syntactic tree where each node has a category label (such as noun, verb phrase, etc.), a list of features, and an associated semantic structure. SHRDLU was a successful system because its domain was very limited: a few actions with a set of blocks.

A representation of SHRDLU is given in Fig. 4.2. MONITOR initiates and terminates the processing of an input sentence. INPUT, together with DICTIONARY, carries out a morphemic analysis of the input sentences, and provides GRAMMAR with strings of words. Programmar does the parsing of sentences and ANSWER converts the system response into grammatical English and keeps track of context. PLANNER is used for analysis and deduces facts about the environment. BLOCKS is a subset of PLANNER theorems that embody the system's knowledge about its physical environment and DATA contains Planner statements that describe the object in the current scene.

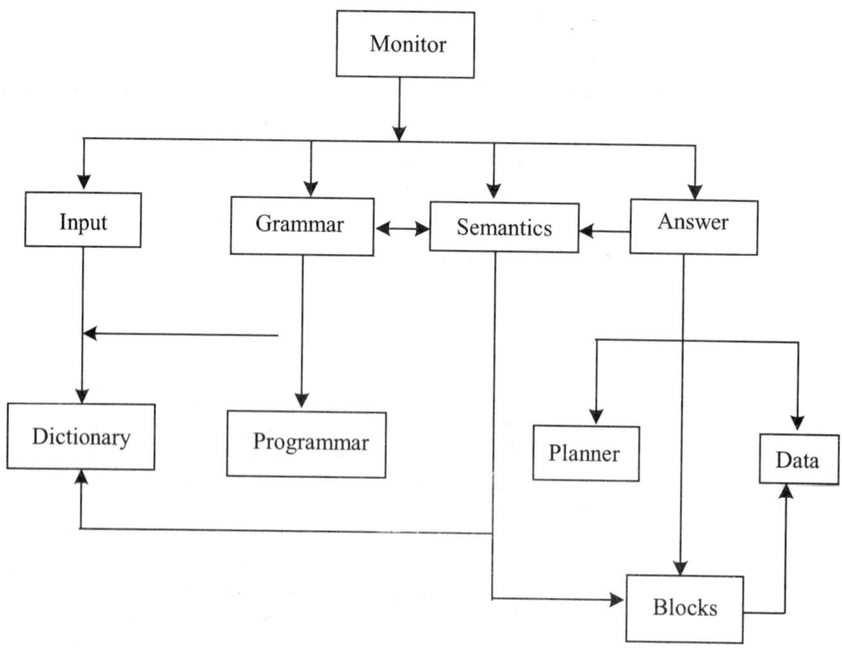

Fig. 4.2 Winograd's SHRDLU

Other systems that deal with domains much larger or different than that of SHRDLU have been designed in recent years. Many of these constitute parts of expert systems. They also use a variety of grammars.

4.6 KNOWLEDGE REPRESENTATION

A grammar may be coded in terms of a network where transitions between the constituents of a sentence are coded as transitions across the nodes. The arcs in the network contain additional information that instruct the parser as to what action it should take in order to generate a specific meaning structure. Such networks are called augmented transition networks (ATNs).

The ATN grammar is a standardized set of tests and operations that are performed on each sentence. Graphically, this can be represented by a directed graph, where arcs represent test-operation pairs and nodes indicate common points joining arcs. The tests are generally conditions on an input word and the network represents the several ways a sentence can be analyzed. All operations are carried out in order and a complete analysis is produced by a path through the network on which all the tests are satisfied by the input words. Another useful grammar is the 'lexical function grammar' (LFG). In LFG grammatical functions are expressed in a form so that categories such as head, number, person, tense subject, object, etc., are tied to the words and phrases that serve these functions. Such a categorization is a part of the Sanskrit grammar of Panini where modifiers identify subject and object, for example, and word order is free [14] and dictated mainly by style and convention. The LFG approach allows a sentence to be represented in a nested form, if a part of it plays a role in another part.

For semantic analysis one needs to represent the sentence in a form so that reasoning procedures can be applied on it. One may use the semantic network approach to classify objects through their relationships, which information can then be used with predicate calculus for further processing for the computer to draw its inferences. An example of simple semantic network is in the one in Fig. 4.3. Such a network is often at the basis of most knowledge representation systems.

The analysis in the grammars of Panini and his successors is done by analyzing the forms of the various words in the sentence. The transformations define agents, recipients as well as time and space relationships.

For example consider

Ratrau tvya mathmadhye na praveshtavyam, meaning

At night you must not enter the monastery.

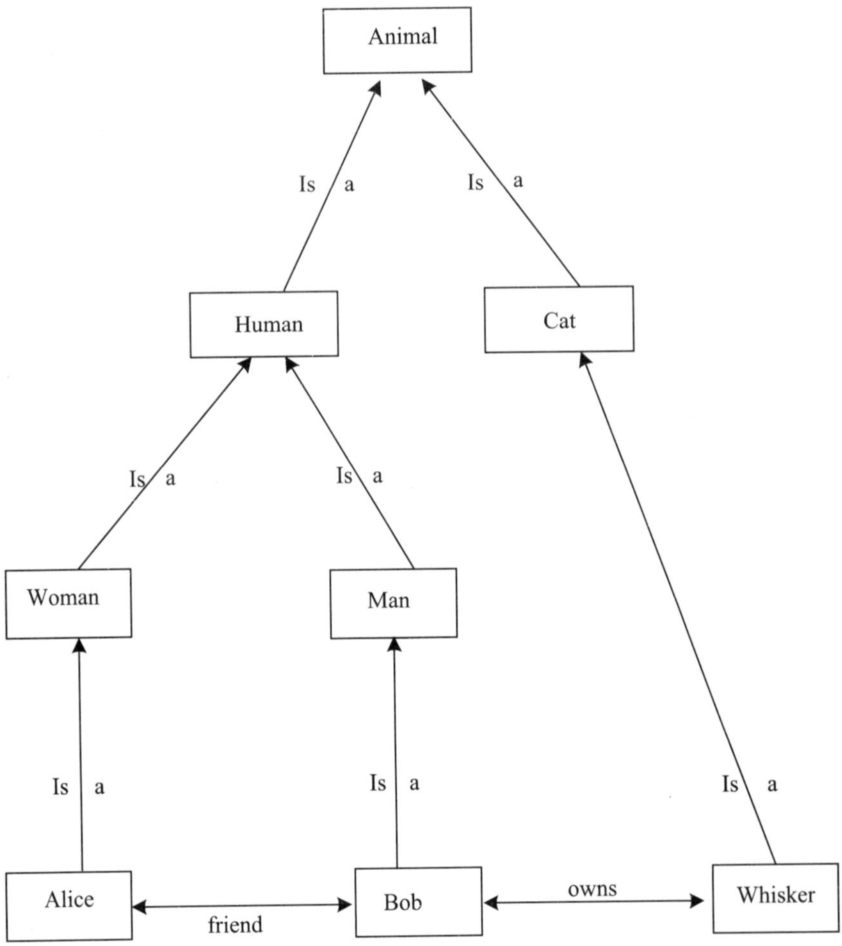

Fig.4.3 A simple semantic network

The future passive participle is formed with the suffix *tvya* that transforms *pravish* (enter). *Ratri* (night) is modified to express an event at night, and *mathmadhye* (within the monastery) represents the dative singular, *tvya* is you in the instrumental form, and *na* is not. This shows how the action, agent, time aspects are made clear.

Briggs has discussed, more fully, the question of equivalence between knowledge representation in AI models and in Sanskrit grammar.

4.7 CONCLUSIONS

The current natural language understanding systems have evolved into a form that fulfills certain attributes of the Paninian approach. Current systems appear to be promising only in severely restricted universes of objects and relationships. It appears that to make significant progress a two pronged attack on the problem is required:

1. Restricting the domain of allowed grammatical relationships in the language and
2. Expanding the understanding of the grammar by drawing upon the insights of Panini, as summed up in his grammar.

A comparison of the work of the later Indian grammarians [such as Nagesha (1730–1810)] and various recent knowledge representation schemes of AI has been given by Briggs in a recent paper [18]. According to Briggs: *"Among the accomplishments of the grammarians can be reckoned a method for paraphrasing Sanskrit in a manner that is identical not only in essence but in form with current work in Artificial Intelligence. [And] a natural language [can] serve as an artificial language also, and that much work in AI has been reinventing a wheel millenia old."*

To summarize, the current knowledge representation systems of AI agree with the requirements of the Paninian approach. This makes analysis systematic once the knowledge in a text has been represented. However, this does not answer the question of a successful extraction of knowledge since, as has been indicated earlier, natural language is full of ambiguity of one kind or the other. There are two different ways one can face this issue squarely. One may use Sanskrit as an intermediary natural language, because its grammar is exhaustive. This is unlikely to happen, however. The other way is to seek new, generative, Paninian style grammars for the English language.

It has been argued by Chomsky and others that the process of language acquisition by the child suggest that the generative principles of universal grammar must be innate to human mind. Also that "*the general features of language structure reflect not so much the course of one's experience, but rather the general character of one's capacity to acquire knowledge—in the traditional sense, one's innate ideas and innate principles*."[19]. This argument implies that it should be possible to find Paninian grammars for the English and other modern languages. As is well known, Panini was driven by the considerations of finding the smallest set of rules and metarules [17]. A development of a Paninian style of grammar would then involve a search for generative rules and metarules.

References

1. H Scharfe (1977) *Grammatical Structure* Otto Harrassowitz Wiesbaden.

2. L Bloomfield (1933) *Language* Holt, Rinehart and Winston New York.
3. J F Staal (1972) *A Reader on the Sanskrit Grammarians*. The MIT Press.
4. O Bohtlingk (1887) *Panini's Grammatik.* Leipzig. (*Reprinted* 1964).
5. L Renou (1966) *La Grammaire de Panini.* Paris.
6. P Kiparsky (1979) *Panini as a Variationist.* The MIT Press.
7. J Lyons (1968) *Introduction to Theoretical Linguistics.* Cambridge Univ. Press.
8. J Lyons (Ed.) (1970) *New Horizons in Linguistics.* Penguin Books.
9. R C Schank and K M Colby (Ed.) *Computer Models of Thought and Language*. Freeman.
10. T Winograd (1983) *Language as a Cognitive Process.* Addison Wesley.
11. H Tennant (1981) *Natural Language Processing,* Petrocelli Books.
12. J Bresnan (Ed.) *The Mental Representation of Grammatical Relations*. The MIT Press.
13. G D Ritchie (1980) *Computational Grammar.* Harvester Press/Barnes & Noble.
14. J F Staal (1967) *Word Order in Sanskrit and Universal Grammar*. D Reidel.
15. H Scharfe (1971) *Panini's Metalanguage.* American Philosophical Society, Philadelphia.
16. V N Misra (1966) *The Descriptive Technique of Panini.* The Hague: Mouton & Co.
17. B Shefts (1961) *Grammatical Method in Panini* American Oriental Society, New Haven.
18. R Briggs (1985) Knowledge representation in Sanskrit and artificial intelligence. *The AI Mag* **6**, Spring.
19. Noam Chomsky (1965) *Aspects of the Theory of Syntax.* Cambridge. MIT.

UNIT II

METHODS AND TECHNIQUES IN PATTERN RECOGNITION AND CLUSTER ANALYSIS

5

Consistent Estimation of Compact Regions in R^2

C A Murthy and D Dutta Majumder[1]

ABSTRACT

A consistent estimation procedure for compact regions is provided. This can be used to estimate clusters. The convergence property is established.

Keywords: Consistency; Compact; Region; Uniform Distribution; Lebesgue Measure; Minimal Spanning Free; Path Connected; Closure; Interior; Boundary; Symmetric Difference; Finite Measure.

5.1 INTRODUCTION

One of the problems faced by the researchers working in pattern recognition is to find the 'shape' of a set of points in plane [l, 2]. 'Shape' is not a clearly defined idea. Naturally, there are various methods of getting the rough shape of a set of points [3, 5]. One of the ways of solving this problem may be to estimate the set on the basis of the points and in the process getting the shape.

Clustering problem in R^2 also may be looked upon as a problem of estimation of sets. The problem formulation is as follows: $Q_1, Q_2, ..., Q_k$ are k disjoint sets in R^2 and $x_1, x_2, ..., x_n$ are points from them. The problem is to estimate $\bigcup_{i=l}^{k} Q_i$ on the basis of $x_1, x_2, ..., x_n$. Grenander [6] defined consistent estimator of a set and devised an estimation procedure in R^2 which is consistent when the distribution is uniform. But it cannot be applied when the sample size is finite. A paper on estimation of line classes has also appeared [7].

In this paper, the authors propose a method of consistent estimation of sets so that it can be used when the sample size is finite. The method is still not a panacea of all the problems. The parameter space is assumed to be the set of all compact regions in R^2 where a region is considered to be an open connected set with some, none or all the limit points included in it. Apostol [8] defines a region to be a *union* of open connected sets with some, none or all the limit points included in it. Union of connected sets is not considered here because connectivity is necessary for shapes and clusters. Closed region is assumed for mathematical convenience.

In the following section, the definition of consistency and Grenander's theorem [6] are stated.

---

[1] Electronics and Communication Sciences Unit, Indian Statistical Institute, Kolkata 700035.

Definition

An estimator α_n^* is said to be consistent estimator of α if $E_\alpha[\mu(\alpha_n^* \Delta \alpha)] \to 0$ as $n \to \infty$, where Δ is symmetric difference and μ is a σ-finite measure.

Theorem 1

Let $\alpha \subset R^2$ be borel such that $\mu(\delta\alpha) = 0$. [μ represents lebesgue measure in R^2. $\delta\alpha$ is the boundary of α]. Let $\varepsilon_n \to 0$ and $n\varepsilon_n^2 \to \infty$. Let X_1, X_2, ..., be independent and identically distributed random vectors from Ω to R^2 following uniform distribution over α. Let P_α be the probability measure on Ω which induced uniform distribution on α.

Let $$\alpha_n^*(w) = \bigcup_{i=l}^{n} \left\{ x \in R^2 : \| x_i(w) - x \| \le \varepsilon_n \right\} \forall\, w.$$

Then $$\int \mu(\alpha_n^*(w) \Delta \alpha)\, dP_\alpha(w) \to 0 \text{ as } n \to \infty.$$

Proof

Let $D(\varepsilon_n)$ be a closed disc of radius ε_n around origin.

Let $\alpha_n^{\text{in}} = \alpha \cap [\alpha^c \oplus D(\varepsilon_n)]^c$ where $\oplus$ represents Minkowski addition.

$\alpha_n^{\text{out}} = [\alpha \oplus D(\varepsilon_n)]^c$

$$\text{Let } I_n(x,w) \left.\begin{aligned} &= 1 \text{ if } x \in \alpha_n^*(w) \\ &= 0 \quad \text{otherwise} \end{aligned}\right\} \forall\, x \in R^2 \text{ and } \forall\, w$$

$$I_n(x,w) \left.\begin{aligned} &= 1 \text{ if } x \in \alpha \\ &= 0 \quad \text{otherwise} \end{aligned}\right\} \forall\, x \in R^2 \text{ and } \forall\, w$$

Then, $E_\alpha[\mu(\alpha_n^* \Delta \alpha)] = \int_\Omega \left(\int_{R^2} |I_n - I|\, d\mu \right) dP_\alpha$, where $d\mu$ represents integration with respect to lebesgue measure

$$= \int_{\alpha_n^{\text{in}}} \left(\int_\Omega |I_n - I|\, dP_\alpha \right) d\mu + \int_{\alpha_n^{\text{out}}} \left(\int_\Omega |I_n - I|\, dP_\alpha \right) d\mu$$

$$+ \int_{\left(\alpha_n^{\text{in}} \cup \alpha_n^{\text{out}}\right)^c} \left(\int_\Omega |I_n - I|\, dP_\alpha \right) d\mu.$$

$= J_1 + J_2 + J_3$ where, *Ji*'s are the respective integrals.

$\int I_n \, dP_\alpha = 1 - \left[1 - \frac{\pi \varepsilon_n^2}{\mu(\alpha)}\right]^n$ which goes to 1 as n goes to ∞ for $x \in \alpha_n^{\text{in}}$. So J_l goes to 0 as n goes to ∞.

$x \in \alpha_n^{\text{out}} \Rightarrow \int I_n \, dP_\alpha = 0$. $J_3 \le \mu\left(\alpha_n^{\text{in}} \cup \alpha_n^{\text{out}}\right)^c$ goes to μ $(\delta\alpha)$ which is equal to 0 as n goes to ∞.

So, $J_1 + J_2 + J_3$ goes to 0.

But this procedure cannot be applied for finite samples. In any sequence, first finite terms do not have any impact on the limit, if it exists. So ε_n can be any number for that sample size n.

We shall make ε_n a function of $X_1, \ldots, X_n$ and modify the proof accordingly. That is, ε_n will be determined automatically on the basis of $X_1, X_2, \ldots, X_n$. It will be determined by drawing minimal spanning tree (mst). In the next section a few definitions on mst are stated.

Definition

For any two points $x, y \in R^2$ let

$$[x, y] = \{z \in R^2 : z = \beta x + (1-\beta)y, \ 0 \le \beta \le 1\}. \text{ So, } [x, x] = \{x\}$$

Definitions

Let $B = \{x_1, x_2, \ldots, x_n\} c \ R^2$.

(a) A subset G of R^2 is called a graph of B if

$$G = \overset{k}{\underset{i=1}{U}} [x_{i1}, x_{i2}], B_1 = \overset{k}{\underset{i=1}{U}} \{x_{i1}, x_{i2}\} \subset B, \text{ where } k \text{ is a positive integer} \ge 1.$$

B_1 is called the node set of G and each $[x_{i1}, x_{i2}]$ is an edge. A curve also can be considered to be an edge. Here, only line segments are considered as edges.

(b) A graph G of B is said to be connected if for every two points $y_1, y_2 \in B, y_1 \neq y_2$, there exists $x_{j1}, x_{j2}, \ldots, x_{jm}$ such that

(i) $x_{j1}, x_{j2}, \ldots, x_{jm} \, \varepsilon \, B_1$ and

(ii) $\overset{m}{\underset{\beta=0}{U}} \left[x_{j\beta}, x_{j\,(\beta+1)}\right] \subset G$ where $x_{jo} = y_1$ and $x_{j(m+1)} = y_2$.

(c) A graph G of B is said to be a spanning tree if

$$G = \overset{n-1}{\underset{i=1}{U}} [x_{i1}, x_{i2}], B_1 = B \text{ and } G \text{ is connected.}$$

(d) Length of a spanning tree G is defined as

$$\wedge(G) = \sum_{i=1}^{n-1} \|x_{i1} - x_{i2}\|.$$

(e) A spanning tree G is said to be minimal if

$\wedge(G) \leq \wedge(G_1) \; \forall$ spanning trees G_1 of B.

In graph theory, mst is defined to be a spanning tree whose sum of edge weights is minimum. Here the edge weight is taken to be the distance between the two nodes. In effect, the definitions in graph theory are restricted to line segments and Euclidean distances.

(f) $L(G) = \underset{i}{Max}\left\{\left\| x_{i1} - x_{i2} \right\| : \left[x_{i1} - x_{i2}\right] \text{ is an edge of } G\right\}$ for an mst G of B.

The intuitive idea behind mst is as follows:

The maximum likelihood estimate (mle) of a convex set is the convex hull if the distribution is uniform. But maximum likelihood estimate does not exist if it is not known whether the set is convex or not. MLE does not exist even if the set is known to be path connected and no information about convexity is known. But if the original set is path connected then the minimal path connected set (minimal in the sense of length) that can be obtained from the given points is mst. Grenander filled the space with discs around the given points in estimation procedure. Discs may be drawn not only around the given points but also around every other point in mst so that connectivity can be preserved. But for the present paper, our consideration is to get an estimate of the set so that the human bias in the selection of constants is less and also one must be able to put it to use.

In the following a few results are proved.

Lemma 1

Let $A, B \subset R^2$.

Let $g_n(A)$ = sup $\{ \wedge(G_n), G_n$ is mst of n point subset of A where n points need not be distinct$\}$.

Similarly $g_n(B)$ is also defined.

Then $A \subset B \Rightarrow g_n(A) \leq g_n(B)$.

Proof

Let $D_n = \{T_n$: T_n is an n point subset of A where the n points need not be distinct$\}$.

$E_n = \{T_n$: T_n is an n point subset of B where the n points need not be distinct$\}$.

Then $D_n \subset E_n \; \forall_n$.

Let $|D_n| = \{\wedge(G_n) : G_n$ is mst of T_n, where $T_n \in D_n\}$.

$|E_n| = \{\wedge(G_n) : G_n$ is mst of T_n, where $T_n \in E_n\}$

$|D_n| \subset |E_n|$ since $D_n \subset E_n$.

So, sup $|D_n| \leq$ sup $|E_n|$ i.c. $g_n(A) \leq g_n(B)$.

Lemma 2

For a set $A \subset R^2$, $g_n(A) \leq g_{n+1}(A)\ \forall\ n$, where

$g_n(A) = \sup\ \{\wedge(G_n) : G_n$ is mst of an n point subset of A where the n points need not be distinct$\}$.

Proof

Let $D_n = \{T_n : T_n$ is an n point subset of A where the points need not be distinct$\}$.

Let $|D_n| = \{\wedge(G_n) : G_n$ is mst of T_n where $T_n \in D_n\}$.

Then $|D_n| \subset |D_{n+1}|$. (If the same node is repeated, the edge between the repeated node has length zero.)

So $\sup |D_n| \leq \sup |D_{n+1}|$ i.e., $g_n(A) \leq g_{n+1}(A)$.

Lemma 3

Let $A = [0, b] \times [0, b]$, where $b > 0$. Let $g_n(.)$ be as defined in lemma 2. Then $g_{(k+1)^2}(A) = (k + 2)b$ for every positive integer k.

The proof of lemma 3 is not given here due to lack of space.

Theorem 2

Let $\phi \neq \alpha \subset R^2$ be such that

(a) $Cl\ (\text{Int}(\alpha)) = \alpha$,
Cl represents closure and Int represents interior.

(b) α is compact and path connected and $\mu(\delta\alpha) = 0$ where μ is lebesgue measure and δ represents boundary.

Let $g_n(\alpha) = \sup\ \{\wedge(G_n) : G_n$ is mst of n point subset of α where the n points need not be distinct$\}$.

Let $\varepsilon_n = \sqrt{g_n(\alpha)/n}$. Then $n\ \varepsilon_n^2 = g_n(\alpha) \to \infty$, and $\varepsilon_n \to 0$

Proof

Int α cannot be empty because $\alpha \neq \phi$ i.e., there exists an open disc υ of radius 'a' which is completely contained in α. Draw discs of diameter $a/5$ as shown in Fig. 5.1 and name them as F_1, F_2, F_3, F_4, F_5, F_6, and F_7. Choose one point from each one of these discs. The length of the mst generated by these points is at least $6a/5$ as shown in Fig. 5.1.

Let $g_n(\upsilon) = \sup\ \{\wedge\ (G_n) : G_n$ is mst of n point subset of υ, where the points need not be distinct$\}$.

$g_n(\upsilon) \leq g_n(\alpha)$ from lemma 1. It suffices to show that $g_n(\upsilon) \to \infty$ as $n \to \infty$.

Now $g_7(\upsilon) \geq 6a/5$. Draw 7 discs of diameter $a/25$ in each of F_i $i = 1, \ldots, 7$, as was done in Fig. 5.2.

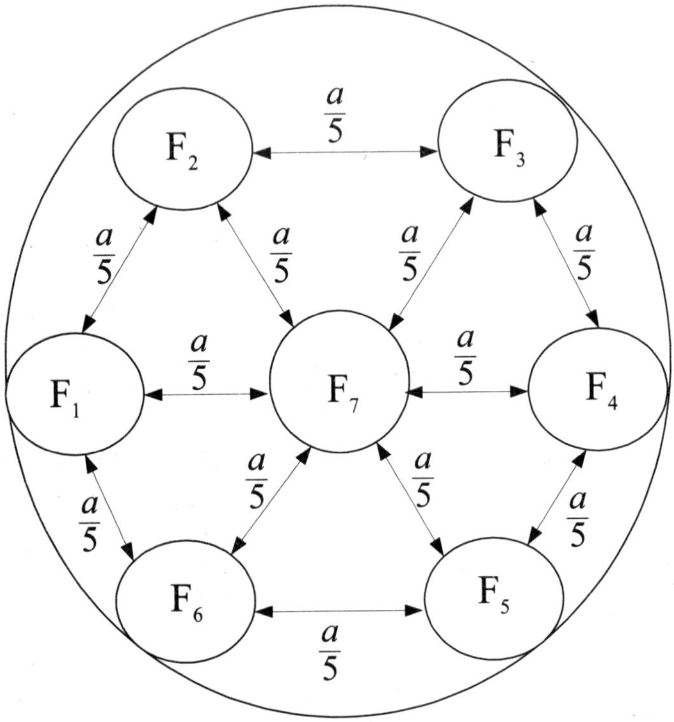

Fig. 5.1 Illustrates dires

Then $$g_{49}(\upsilon) \geq \frac{6a}{5} + 7 \cdot \frac{6a}{5}.$$

Similarly, $$g_{7^3}(\upsilon) \geq \frac{6a}{5}\left(1 + \frac{7}{5} + \left(\frac{7}{5}\right)^2\right)$$

i.e., $$g_{7^k}(\upsilon) \to \infty \text{ as } k \to \infty.$$

From lemma 2, $g_n(\upsilon)$ is a nondecreasing sequence.

So, $g_n(\upsilon) \to \infty$ i.e. $g_n(\alpha) \to \infty$

$$\varepsilon_n = \frac{\sqrt{g_n(\alpha)}}{n}$$

Since α is a bounded set, there exists a square H of side $b > 0$ such that $\alpha \subset H$.

Then $g_{(k+1)^2}(H) = (k+2)b$ for every positive integer k.

$$\frac{g_{(k+1)^2}(H)}{(k+1)^2} = \frac{(k+2)b}{(k+1)^2} \to 0 \text{ as } k \to \infty.$$

So $\varepsilon_n \to 0$ as $n \to \infty$. Since $g_n(\alpha) \leq g_n(H)$ from lemma 1.

Theorem 3

Let α, $g_n(\alpha)$ and ε_n be as defined in Theorem (2).

Let X_1, X_2,... be independent and identically distributed random variables defined on Ω, following uniform distribution on α.

Let P_α be the prob measure on Ω which induced uniform distribution on α.

Let $nh_n^2(w)$ = length of mst of $X_1(w), X_2(w), ..., X_n(w)$ $\forall$ $w \in \Omega$.

Then (*a*) $h_n(w) \to 0$ and (*b*) $nh_n^2(w) \to \infty$ in P_α.

Proof

(*a*) $h_n(w) \leq \varepsilon_n$ & $\varepsilon_n \to 0$. So $h_n(w) \to 0$ $\forall$ w.

(*b*) Int $\alpha \neq \phi$. So there exists an open disc ϑ of diameter 'a'.
such that ϑ *c* α. Consider open discs of diameter $F_1, F_2, ..., F_7$ of diameters $a/5$ as shown in Fig. 5.2.

Then $P(X_1 \notin F_1, X_2 \notin F_1, X_3 \notin F_1, ...) = \lim_{n \to 0} \left[\frac{\mu(F_1)}{\mu(\alpha)}\right]^n = 0.$

μ represents lebesgue measure.

So $P\{w : \exists$ a positive integer M_1 such that $X_{M_1}(w) \in F_1\} = 1$.

Similarly P $\{w$: $\exists$ a positive integer M_i such that $X_{M_i}(w) \in F_i\}$ $= 1$ $\forall$ $i = 2, ...,7$.

So P $\{w$: $\exists$ positive integer M_1, M_2, ..., M_7 such that $X_{M_i}(w) \in F_i$ $\forall = 2, ...,7.\} = 1$

i.e., P $\{w$: MST generated by $X_1(w), X_2(w)$,... has length $\geq \frac{6a}{5}\} = 1$.

Similarly, it can be proved (theorem 2) by considering discs of radius $a/25$ that

$$P\{w\text{:MST generated by } X_1(w), X_2(w), \text{..... has length} \geq \frac{6a}{5} + 7 \cdot \frac{6a}{5}\} = 1.$$

$$\text{i.e., } P\left\{w : nh_n^2(w) \geq \frac{6a}{5}\left(1 + \frac{7}{5}\right)\right\} \to 1 \text{ as } n \to \infty.$$

$$\text{Similarly, } P\left\{w : nh_n^2(w) \geq \frac{6a}{5}\left(1 + \frac{7}{5} + \frac{7^2}{5^2}\right)\right\} \to 1 \text{ as } n \to \infty.$$

So, for any positive M, find out k such that

$$t_k = \frac{6a}{5}\left(1+\frac{7}{5}+\frac{7^2}{5^2}+....+\frac{7^k}{5^k}\right) > M.$$

and $P\{w: nh_n^2(w) \geq t_k\} \to 1$ as $n \to \infty$.

Theorem 4

Let α, g_n, ε_n, h_n, be as defined in theorem 3.

Let $\alpha_{n1}^*(w) = \overset{n}{\underset{i=1}{U}} \{x \in R^2 \| X_i(w) - x\| \leq h_n(w)\}$

Then $E_\alpha\, \mu(\alpha_{n1}^*(w) \Delta \alpha) \to 0$ as $n \to \infty$.

Proof

$P\{nh_n^2 > M\} \to 1$ as $n \to \infty$. $\forall$ M (From theorem 3).

Let N_k be such that $P\{nh_n^2 \geq k\} \geq 1 - \varepsilon_k \;\; \forall_n \geq N_k$ where $k = 1, 2, 3, ….$

Let $S_i = 1 \;\; \forall \;\; i = 1, 2, ….., N_2$

$\quad = k \;\; \forall \;\; i = N_k + 1, N_k + 2, ….., N_{k+1}$

Let $\gamma_n = \dfrac{\sqrt{S_n}}{n}$.

Let $A_n = \{w : h_n(w) \geq \gamma_n\}$. So $\gamma_n \to 0$ and $n\gamma_n^2 \to \infty$.

$P(A_n) \to 1$ as $n \to \infty$.

i.e. $P(A_n^c) \to 0$ as $n \to \infty$.

Let $\alpha_n^*(w) = \overset{n}{\underset{i=l}{U}} \{x \in R^2 : \| X_i(w) - x \| \leq \varepsilon_n\}$

Let $\left.\begin{aligned} I_{1n}(x, w) &= 1 \text{ if } x \in \alpha_n^*(w) \\ &= 0 \text{ otherwise} \end{aligned}\right\} \;\; \forall \; x \in R^2 \text{ and } \forall \; w \in \Omega$

$\left.\begin{aligned} I_{2n}(x, w) &= 1 \text{ if } x \in \alpha_{n1}^*(w) \\ &= 0 \text{ otherwise} \end{aligned}\right\} \;\; \forall \; x \in R^2 \text{ and } \forall \; w \in \Omega$

$\left.\begin{aligned} I(x, w) &= 1 \text{ if } x \in \alpha \\ &= 0 \text{ otherwise} \end{aligned}\right\} \;\; \forall \; x \in R^2 \text{ and } \forall \; w \in \Omega$

i.e. I_{1n}, I_{2n} and I are defined on $R^2 \, x \, \Omega \to \{0, 1\}$.

Let $\alpha_n^{\text{in}} = \alpha \cap \{\alpha^c \oplus D(\varepsilon_n)\}^c$

$\alpha_n^{\text{out}} = [\alpha \oplus D(\varepsilon_n)]^c$

where $\oplus$ represents Minkowski addition and $D\ (\varepsilon_o)$ is the closed disc around origin of radius ε_n.

Let $J_n = E_\alpha\ [\mu(\alpha_{n1}^{*}\,\Delta\alpha)]$

$$= \int_{\alpha_n^{in}} \left(\int_{A_n} |I_{2n} - I|\, dP_\alpha \right) d\mu + \int_{\alpha_n^{in}} \left(\int_{A_n^c} |I_{2n} - I|\, dP_\alpha \right) d\mu$$

$$+ \int_{\alpha_n^{out}} \left(\int_{\Omega} |I_{2n} - I|\, dP_\alpha \right) d\mu + \int_{(\alpha_n^{in}\ U\ \alpha_n^{out})^c} \left(\int_{\Omega} |I_{2n} - I|\, dP_\alpha \right) d\mu$$

$$= J_{1n} + J_{2n} + J_{3n} + J_{4n}.$$

where, J_{in}'s are the corresponding integrals.

$$J_{4n} \le \mu\left(\alpha_n^{in}\ U\ \alpha_n^{out}\right)^c \to \mu(\delta\ \alpha) = 0.$$

$$J_{3n} \le \int_{\alpha_n^{out}} \left(\int_{\Omega} I\, dP_\alpha \right) d\mu = 0$$

$$J_{2n} = \int_{\alpha_n^{in}} \left(\int_{A_n^c} (I - I_{2n}) dP_\alpha \right) d\mu \le \mu(\alpha)\ P\left(A_n^c\right) \to 0, \text{ since } P\left(A_n^c\right) \to 0$$

$$J_{1n} = \int_{\alpha_n^{in}} \left(\int_{A_n} (I - I_{2n}) dP_\alpha \right) d\mu$$

$$= \int_{\alpha_n^{in}} \int_{\{w: h_n(w) \ge \gamma_n\}} \left(1 - I_{\bigcup_{i=1}^{n} \{(x,w)\, :\, \| X_i(w) - x \| \le h_n(w)\}} \right) dp_\alpha\ d\mu.$$

when I_A is indicator function of A.

$$= \int_{\alpha_n^{in}} \left(\int_{\{w: h_n(w) \ge \gamma_n\}} I_{\bigcap_{i=1}^{n} \{(x,w)\, :\, \|X_i(w) - x\| \ge h_n(w)\}}\ dp_\alpha\ d\mu \right)$$

$$\le \int_{\alpha_n^{in}} \left(\int_{\{w: h_n(w) \ge \gamma_n\}} I_{\bigcap_{i=1}^{n} \{(x,w)\, :\, \|X_i(w) - x\| \ge \gamma_n\}}\ dp_\alpha\ d\mu \right)$$

$$\le \int_{\alpha_n^{in}} \int_{\Omega} I_{\bigcap_{i=1}^{n} \{(x,w)\, :\, \|X_i(w) - x\| \ge \gamma_n\}}\ dp_\alpha\ d\mu$$

$$\le \mu(\alpha) \left[1 - \frac{\pi\, \gamma_n^2}{\mu(\alpha)} \right]^n \to 0 \text{ since } \left[1 - \frac{\pi\, \gamma_n^2}{\mu(\alpha)} \right]^n \to 0 \text{ and } \mu(\alpha) \text{ is bounded.}$$

So, $J_n \to 0$ as $n \to \infty$.

From the results proved in the previous section, the estimation procedure is as follows:

(a) Draw minimal spanning tree of the given n points.

(b) Find out the length L_n of it.

(c) Let $h_n = \frac{\sqrt{L_n}}{n}$.

(d) Draw discs of radius 'h' around each given point and take the union. That is the set from which the observations have come.

But note that the given distribution is assumed to be uniform and the set is assumed to be bounded. The usefulness of minimal spanning tree can be a matter of further investigation if the distribution is not uniform and the set is not bounded. Usually in pattern recognition problems, the classes or clusters are bounded sets. But the distribution of the observations need not be uniform.

The method suggested here has the positive aspect of not having to select any constant in the sense that h_n's are determined on the basis of the observations. The experimenter's bias on the constant will not be present.

But one drawback of this method is the following. The original set α is assumed to be connected and the value of h_n may be so small that the estimated set may get disconnected. If the discs are drawn around every point on the mst then the resultant set will be connected and it may be an acceptable solution.

In the other procedure[5] ad hoc selection of a constant is necessary. In this procedure, the human bias is not present.

References

1. S G Akl and G T Toussaint (1978) Efficient convex hull algorithms for pattern recognition applications *Proc 4th int Joint Conf Patt Recog Kyoto* 483–487.

2. R A Jarvis (1977) Computing the shape hull of points in the plane *Proc IEEE Comp Soc Conf Patt Recog Image Processing,* 231–241.

3. J Fairfield (1979) Contoured shape generation forms that people see in dot patterns *Proc IEEE Conf Cybernet Soc* 60–64.

4. G T Toussaint (1980) Pattern recognition and geometrical complexity *Proc* 5th *int Conf Patt Recog Miami Beach, Florida,* 1324–1347.

5. H Edelsprunner, D G Kirkpatric and R Seidel (1983) On the shape of a set of points in the plane *IEEE Tr Inform Theory IT-29,* No.4, 551–559.

6. U Grenander (1981) *Abstr Inference* John Wiley, New York.

7. C A Murthy and D Dutta Majumder (1986) On classification of bounded line classes *Proc* 8*th int Conf Patt Recog Paris.*

8. T M Apostol (1981) *Mathematical Analysis* Addison Wesley.

6

Pattern Recognition Based on Scale Invariant Discriminant Functions[1]

Tarmo M Pukkila[2] and C. Radhakrishna Rao[3]

ABSTRACT

Some probability models for classifying individuals as belonging to one of two or more populations using scale invariant discriminant functions are considered. The investigation is motivated by practical situations where the observed data on an individual are in the form of ratios of some basis measurements or measurements scaled by an unknown non-negative number. The probability models are obtained by considering a p-vector random variable X with a known distribution and deriving the distribution of random vector $Y = [G(X)]^{-1} X$, where $G(X)$ is a non-negative measure of size such that $G(\lambda X) = \lambda G(X)$ for $\lambda > 0$. Explicit expressions are obtained for the densities of what are called Angular Gaussian, Compositional Gaussian, Type 1 and Compositional Gaussian, Type 2 distributions.

Keywords: Angular Gaussian Distribution; Compositional Gaussian Distribution; Discriminant Function; Scale Free Methods.

6.1 INTRODUCTION

We consider the problem of classifying an individual as belonging to one of two or more populations using scale invariant discriminant functions. The investigation is motivated by practical situations where the observed data on an individual are in the form of ratios of some basic measurements or measurements scaled by an unknown non-negative number. In this paper we derive some probability models for applications to such data.

If $X' = (x_1, \ldots, x_p)$ is a vector of p basic measurements which may be known apart from a positive scaling factor, then we may consider transformed measurements.

$$(y_1, \ldots\ldots, y_p)' = Y = [G(X)]^{-1} X, \tag{1}$$

which are scale free if G is some non-negative measure of size such that $G(\lambda X) = \lambda G(X)$ for $\lambda > 0$. Some typical examples of $G(X)$ are

$$G(X) = \|X\| = \left(\sum x_i^2\right)^{1/2}, \tag{2}$$

---

[1] Research sponsored by the Air Force Office of Scientific Research (AFSC) under Contract F49620-85-C-0008. The United States Government is authorized to reproduce and distribute reprints for governmental purposes notwithstanding any copyright notation hereon.

[2] Department of Mathematical Sciences, University of Tampere, P.O. Box 607, SF-33101 Tampere, Finland.

[3] Center for Multivariate Analysis, University of Pittsburgh, Pittsburgh, PA 15260.

$$= \left| \Sigma \, x_i \right|. \tag{3}$$

The corresponding transformed variables $Y = X / \|X\|,\ X / \left| \Sigma \, x_i \right|$ are called directional and compositional data respectively. We note that the term compositional data is usually applied to a set of non-negative proportions [1], but our definition is more flexible. However, we refer to $Y = X / \left| \Sigma \, x_i \right|$ as compositional data of type 1 and $Y = X / \Sigma \, x_i$ as of type 2 even when x_i are not non-negative.

It is also interesting to note that when we have compositional data with non-negative proportions, $(y_1, ..., y_p)$ such that $\Sigma \, y_i = 1$, when we may transform them into directional data by considering $\left(\sqrt{y_i}, \ldots\ldots, \sqrt{y_p}\right)$ and use appropriate probability models for directional data (with non-negative components) for statistical analysis as suggested by Stephens [2].

One way of generating probability models for directional and compositional data is to consider a probability distribution for the basic measurements X and then derive the induced distribution for $Y = [G\,(X)]^{-1} X$. In this paper, we assume that $X \sim N_p\,(\mu, \Sigma)$, i.e., as p-variate normal with mean vector μ and variance-covariance matrix Σ, and derive the distribution of Y for different size functions G.

Once an appropriate probability model is chosen, the problem of discrimination can be handled in the usual way.

We also comment on non-parametric methods for estimation of density for directional and compositional data.

6.2 CLASSES OF DISTRIBUTIONS FOR DIRECTIONAL DATA

6.2.1 Angular Gaussian Distribution (AGD)

Let $X \sim N_p\,(\mu, \Sigma)$ and define $y = R^{-1} X$ where $R = \|X\| = (X'X)^{1/2}$, so that Y is the vector of direction cosines with the condition $Y'\,Y = 1$. The marginal distribution of Y on p-dimensional unit sphere Ω_p is called the AGD (Angular Gaussian Distribution). For the special case when $\Sigma = \sigma^2$, Bingham obtained the distribution of Y in the form of an infinite series [3, p. 226]. In this section, we obtain the distribution of Y in the general case in a closed form involving a finite number of terms.

Consider a polar transformation from X to (R, θ), where θ is a vector of $p-1$ angles in which case the Jacobian is of the form

$$\frac{D\,(X)}{D\,(R,\theta)} = R^{p-1} f(\theta)\,. \tag{4}$$

The transformed probability density functions (p.d.f.) is

$$|2\pi\Sigma|^{-1/2} R^{p-1}\ f(\theta)\ \exp\,[-2^{-1}(R^2 Q_3 - 2RQ_2 + Q_1)], \tag{5}$$

where

$$Q_3 = Y'\,\Sigma^{-1}\,Y,\ \ Q_2 = \mu'\,\Sigma^{-1}\,Y,\ \ Q_1 = \mu'\,\Sigma^{-1}\,\mu$$

and Y is a function of θ only. Changing from R to $r = R\sqrt{Q_3}$, the p.d.f. (5) transforms to

$$|2\pi\Sigma|^{-1/2}\,Q_3^{-p/2}\ f(\theta)\ \exp\,[-2^{-1}(Q_1 - Q_2^2\ Q_3^{-1})]$$
$$\times\ r^{p-1}\exp\,[-2^{-1}(r - Q_2\ Q_3^{-1/2})^2]. \tag{6}$$

Integrating out for r from 0 to ∞, the p.d.f. at Y w.r.t. the surface element $d\omega_p$ on Ω_p is

$$p\,(Y\mid\mu,\Sigma) = |2\pi\Sigma|^{-1/2}\,Q_3^{-p/2}\ I_p\ (Q_2\,Q_3^{-1/2})$$
$$\exp\,[-2^{-1}(Q_1 - Q_2^2\ Q_3^{-1})], \tag{7}$$

where

$$I_p\ (\alpha) = \int_0^\infty r^{p-1}\exp\,[-2^{-1}(r-\alpha)^2]\,dr. \tag{8}$$

The function I_P satisfies the recurrence relation

$$I_p(\alpha) = (p-2)\,I_{p-2}(\alpha) + \alpha\,I_{p-1}(\alpha)\ \text{ for }\ p > 2 \tag{9}$$

with the initial values

$$I_2\ (\alpha) = e^{-\alpha^2/2} + \alpha I_1\ (\alpha),\ I_1\ (\alpha) = \sqrt{2\pi}\ \phi\ (\alpha),$$

where $\phi\ (\alpha)$ is the distribution function of $N_1\ (0, 1)$.

It may be noted that the p.d.f. (7) remains unchanged if μ and Σ are replaced by $a\mu$ and $a^2\Sigma$ for any $a > 0$. However, we can make the parameters unique by imposing the condition $\|\mu\| = 1$.

6.2.2 Langevin Distribution

We can generate other distributions for Y from (5) and (6) as suggested by Fisher [4] by considering conditional instead of marginal distributions. Thus, from the expression (6) the conditional p.d.f. of Y on Ω_P given $r = 1$ is

$$\text{const.}\ Q_3^{-p/2}\ \exp\ (Q_2\ Q_3^{-1/2})$$
$$= \text{const.}\ (Y'\,\Sigma^{-1}\ Y)^{-p/2}\ \exp\ (\mu'\,\Sigma^{-1}\ Y/\sqrt{Y'\,\Sigma^{-1}\ Y}) \tag{10}$$

where we may impose the restriction $\|\mu\| = 1$. When $\Sigma = \sigma^2 I$ we have the Langevin–von Mises–Fisher distribution.

$$\text{const.}\ \exp\ \kappa\mu' Y, \tag{11}$$

on the surface of a p-dimensional sphere.

From the expression (5) we find that the conditional p.d.f. of Y on Ω_p given $R = 1$ with respect to $d\omega_p$ is

$$\text{const. exp } [-2^{-1} (Y-\mu)' \Sigma^{-1} (Y-\mu)], \tag{12}$$

where $\|\mu\| = 1$.

We add two other classes of distributions found to be useful in practical applications as possible models for directional data.

Scheideggar-Watson p.d.f. $\quad [b_p\ (\kappa)]^{-1} \exp\ (\kappa' Y)^2$. (13)

Bingham p.d.f $\quad [b\ (k)]^{-1} \exp\ Y'\ KY$, (14)

where K is $p \times p$ symmetric matrix.

6.2.3 Estimation of Parameters

The model (7) which is the angular normal distribution, can be used to construct scale invariant discriminant functions provided the parameters μ and Σ are known. If they are unknown, we may have to estimate them from past observations $Y_1, \ldots, Y_n$ on Y. Using the density function (7), the likelihood on past data is

$$\prod_{i=1}^{n} p\ (Y_i \mid \mu, \Sigma)$$

with the restriction $\|\mu\| = 1$. The method of maximum likelihood for estimation of parameters can be implemented without much difficulty since the derivatives of all the expressions involved in (7) with respect to μ and Σ can be easily evaluated. However, there are too many parameters to be estimated and a very large sample may be necessary to obtain reasonably good estimators.

We may consider an alternative method by considering the marginal bivariate distributions of Y, where $Y = (x_1 / \|x\|, \ldots\ldots, x_n / \|x\|)$ and $X - N N_p (\mu, \Sigma)$. If y_1 and y_2 are the first two components of Y, then it is easily seen that

$$P_\alpha = P(y_1 \leq \alpha y_2) = P\ (x_1 - \alpha x_2 \leq 0)$$

$$= \phi\ [(\alpha\mu_2 - \mu_1)/(\alpha^2\ \sigma_{22} - 2\alpha\sigma_{12} + \sigma_{11})^{1/2}] \tag{15}$$

where ϕ is the distribution function of N_1 (0, 1). If we have a sample of size n on Y with the first two components (y_{1i}, y_{2i}), $i = 1, \ldots, n$, we can estimate p_α for any given α by

$$\hat{p}_\alpha = \text{proportion of } i\text{'s such that } y_{1i} \leq \alpha y_{2i} \tag{16}$$

Then we have the observational equations

$$\phi\ [(\alpha\mu_2 - \mu_1)/(\alpha^2\ \sigma_{22} - 2\alpha\sigma_{12} + \sigma_{11})^{1/2}] = \hat{p}_\alpha\ \forall\ \alpha. \tag{17}$$

or $\quad (\alpha\mu_2 - \mu_1)^2 = [\phi - (\hat{p}_\alpha)]^2 \ (\alpha^2 \sigma_{22} - 2\alpha\sigma_{12} + \sigma_{11}) \ \forall \ \alpha \qquad (18)$

$p\ (p - 1)/2$ families of equations of the kind (17) or (18) are available involving all the elements of μ and Σ by considering every pair of components in Y. From the equations (17) or (18), it is clear that only ratios of the parameters can be estimated.

They can be made unique by using a restriction like $\|\mu\| = 1$. An appropriate method may be used to combine the equations (17) or (18) to produce the requisite number of consistent equations to estimate the parameters.

We describe one of the methods. First, we note that by smoothing $\hat{p}_\alpha$ in (17), we can estimate $\alpha_{-1}, \alpha_0, \alpha_1$, such that $P_{\alpha_1} = 1/4$, $P_{\alpha_0} = 1/2, P_{\alpha_1} = 3/4$.

Writing

$$\phi^{-1}\ (1/4) = q_{-1},\ \phi^{-1}\ (1/2) = 0,\ \phi^{-1}\ (3/4) = q_1, \qquad (19)$$

the equations (18) for $\alpha_{-1}, \alpha_0, \alpha_1$, can be written as

$$(\alpha_0\ \hat{\mu}_2 - \hat{\mu}_1) = 0 \qquad (20)$$

and $(\alpha_s\,\hat{\mu}_2 - \hat{\mu}_1)^2 = q_s^2(\alpha_s^2\,\sigma_{22} - 2\alpha_s\,\sigma_{12} + \sigma_{11}), s = -1, 1 \qquad (21)$

There are p equations of kind (20) obtained by considering all pairs of the components of Y. They yield estimates of the ratios of $\mu_1, ..., \mu_p$, which can be standardised to satisfy the restriction $\|\mu\| = 1$. Then we have $p\ (p - 1)$ equations of the type (21) involving the $p\ (p + 1)/2$ parameters in Σ. Observing that the equations are linear in σ_{ij}, we may combine them by least squares method to produce $p\ (p + 1)/2$ equations by solving which we obtain the estimates of σ_{ij}.

The estimates obtained by the above method may still require large samples. Other methods of combining the equations (17) or (18) have to be explored.

6.3 CLASSES OF DISTRIBUTIONS FOR COMPOSITIONAL DATA

6.3.1 Compositional Gaussian Distribution Type 1. [CGD(1)]

Let $X \sim N_p\ (\mu, \Sigma)$ and define $Y = \left|\Sigma x_i\right|^{-1} X$, so that $\left|\Sigma Y_i\right| = 1$. The distribution of Y on the set is

$$S = \{Y : \left|\Sigma y_i\right| = 1\}, \qquad (22)$$

which is the Compositional Gaussian Distribution, Type 1. We distinguish two sets

$$S_+ = \{Y : \Sigma Y_i = 1\},\ S_- = \{y : \Sigma Y_i = -1\} \qquad (23)$$

and note that $S_+ \cup S_- = S$ and

$$P(Y \in S_+) = P(\Sigma x_i > 0) \text{ and } P(Y \in S_-) = P(\Sigma x_i < 0) \quad (24)$$

In S_+ we consider the transformation

$$x_i = Ry_i, \; i = 1, ..., p-1$$

and

$$x_p = R(1 - y_1 - ... - y_{p-1}) = Ry_p \quad (25)$$

and in S_-

$$x_i = -Ry_i, \; i = 1, ..., p-1$$

and

$$x_p = R(1 + y_1 + ... + y_{p-1}) = -Ry_p \quad (26)$$

The Jacobian of the transformation in either case is

$$\frac{D(x_1, ..., x_p)}{D(R, y_1, ..., y_{p-1})} = R^{p-1} \quad (27)$$

The p.d.f. of X in S_+ transforms to

$$(2\pi)^{-p/2} |\Sigma|^{-1/2} R^{p-1} \exp[-2^{-1}(Q_3 R^2 - 2Q_2 R + Q_1)], \quad (28)$$

where

$$Q_3 = Y'\Sigma^{-1} Y, Q_2 = \mu' \Sigma^{-1} Y, \; Q_1 = \mu' \Sigma^{-1} \mu.$$

Making the transformation $r = RQ_3^{1/2}$, the expression (27) changes to

$$(2\pi)^{-p/2} |\Sigma|^{-1/2} Q_3^{-p/2} \exp[-2^{-1}(Q_1 - Q_2^2 Q_3^{-1})]$$
$$\times r^{p-1} \exp[-2^{-1}(r - Q_2 Q_3^{-1/2})^2] \quad (29)$$

Integrating out with respect to r from 0 to ∞, the p.d.f. of Y in S_+ with respect to the volume element $dy_1 ..... dy_{p-1}$ is

$$(2\pi)^{-p/2} |\Sigma|^{-1/2} Q_3^{-p/2} I_p(Q_2 Q_3^{-1/2}) \exp[-2^{-1}(Q_1 - Q_2^2 Q_3^{-1})] \quad (30)$$

where $I_p(\alpha)$ is as defined in (8)

In S_-, under the transformation (25), the expression corresponding to (29) is

$$(2\pi)^{-p/2} |\Sigma|^{-1/2} Q_3^{-p/2} \exp[-2^{-1}(Q_1 + Q_2^2 Q_3^{-1})]$$
$$\times |r|^{p-1} \exp[-2^{-1}(r + Q_2 Q_3^{-1/2})^2] \quad (31)$$

Integrating out with respect to r from $-\infty$ to 0, we obtain the same expression as in (30) for the p.d.f. of Y in S_-.

It may be noted that in the expression (30), we can impose a suitable restriction on μ_1 to make the parameters identifiable.

6.3.2 Compositional Gaussian Distribution, Type 2, [CGD (2)]

Let $X \sim N_p(\mu, \Sigma)$ and define $Y = (\Sigma x_i)^{-1} X$. For this we consider the transformation

$$x_i = Ry_i, \ \ i = 1, \ldots, p-1$$
$$x_p = R\,(1 - y_1 - \ldots - y_{p-1}) = Ry_p \tag{32}$$

so that $\Sigma y_i = 1$. We define the marginal distribution of Y on the simplex

$$S = \{Y : \Sigma Y_i = 1\}$$

as the Compositional Gaussian distribution, Type 2. Making the transformation (32), proceeding as in Section 3.1 and integrating the expression corresponding to (29) with respect to r from $-\infty$ to ∞ we obtain the p.d.f. of Y with respect to the volume element $dy_1 \ldots\ldots dy_{p-1}$ as

$$(2\pi)^{-1/2}\,|\Sigma|^{-1/2}\,Q_3^{-p/2}\,[I_p\,(Q_2\,Q_3^{-1/2}) + I_p\,(-Q_2\,Q_3^{-1/2})]\ \exp\,[-2^{-1}\,(Q_1 - Q_2^2\,Q_3^{-1})], \tag{33}$$

where Q_1, Q_2 and Q_3 are as in (28) and I_p is as defined in (8).

As in the other cases, the p.d.f. remains unchanged if μ and Σ are replaced by $a\mu$ and $a^2\Sigma$ respectively for any scalar $a > 0$.

As in (10), the conditional distribution of Y given $r = \kappa$ (a constant) is

$$\text{const.}\ \ Q_3^{-p/2}\ \exp\ (\kappa\,Q_2\,Q_3^{-1/2}) \tag{34}$$

which could be used as a probability model for compositional data.

If we define $Y = x_p^{-1}\,X$, then the distribution of $y_1, \ldots\ldots, y_{p-1}$ is the same as in (34). In the computation of Q_2 and Q_3, we substitute the value 1 for y_p. A natural way of normalising the parameters μ and Σ is to consider

$$|\mu_p|^{-1}\,\mu \ \text{ and } \ \mu_p^{-2}\,\Sigma \tag{35}$$

6.3.3 Logistic Gaussian and Related Distributions

Let Y be a vector of non-negative components $y_1, \ldots\ldots, y_p$ such that $\Sigma\, y_i = 1$. Then, one possible model which has been studied in detail, is the logistic Gaussian distribution which assumes that

$$X' = (x_1, \ldots, x_{p-1}) = (\log y_1\,y_p^{-1}, \ldots, \log y_{p-1}\,y_p^{-1}) \tag{36}$$

has a $(p-1)$-variate Gaussian distribution [7], [8]. In such a case the p.d.f. of Y can be written in the form

$$(2\pi|\Sigma|)^{-1/2}\,(y_1 \ldots\ldots y_p)^{-1}\ \exp\,[-2^{-1}\,(X-\mu)'\,\Sigma^{-1}\,(X-\mu)], \tag{37}$$

where X can be expressed in terms of Y as in (36)

In building a model for Y we could have used other transformations from the basic $(p-1)$-dimensional Gaussian variable X such as

$$x_i = \lambda^{-1}\,[(y_i / y_p)^{\lambda} - 1],\ i = 1, \ldots, p-1 \tag{38}$$

which is the Box and Cox transformation, [9] or more generally any appropriate transformation

$$x_i = h_i\ (Y),\ i = 1, \ldots\ldots, p-1 \tag{39}$$

suggested by data.

A well-known distribution for compositional data with non-negative proportions is the Dirichlet class D_P (β) with the typical density function

$$[\Delta\ (\beta)]^{-1}\ y_1^{\beta_1 - 1} \ldots\ y_p^{\beta_p - 1}, \tag{40}$$

where $\Delta\ (\beta) = \Gamma\ (\beta_1)\ \ldots\ \Gamma\ (\beta_p)/\Gamma\ (\beta_1 + \ldots + \beta_p)$.

Aitchison [1] considered a mixture of Dirichlet and a logistic Gaussian distributions, but imposing some relationship between the parameters μ and β to reduce the number of free parameters in the model. He also provided a computational procedure for obtaining the maximum likelihood estimators of the parameters in such a mixture of distributions.

6.4 ESTIMATION OF THE DENSITY FUNCTION

Let $Y_1, \ldots, Y_n$ be independent observations on a random variable Y defined on Ω_p, the p-dimensional unit sphere. If a suitable model for the distribution of Y is not available, we may use non-parametric methods and estimate its p.d.f. based on $Y_1, \ldots, Y_n$. For this purpose we define a window function defined on Ω_p, which is indexed by two parameters x and θ, $x \in \Omega_p$ and $0 \le \theta \le \pi/2$,

$$\phi_{x,\,\theta}\ (Y) = \begin{cases} 1 \text{ if } x'Y \ge \cos\theta, \\ 0 \text{ otherwise.} \end{cases} \tag{41}$$

The set of points Y satisfying the first equation in (4) defines a cup on Ω_p with x as a central point, whose area is

$$a\ (\theta) = \frac{2\pi^{(p-1)/2}}{\Gamma\left(\dfrac{p-1}{2}\right)} \int_0^\theta \sin\psi\ d\ \psi. \tag{42}$$

The number of points falling on this cup is

$$\sum_1^n \phi_{x,\,\theta}\ (Y_i) \tag{43}$$

By choosing a small value of $\theta = \theta_n$ an estimate of the p.d.f. of Y at x may be obtained as

$$P_n\ (x) = n^{-1} \sum_1^n\ [a\ (\theta_n)]^{-1}\ \phi_{x,\,\theta_n}\ (Y_i). \tag{44}$$

More generally we could use any suitable p.d.f. on Ω_p as a window function. In particular we suggest the use of the Langevin density (11)

$$c\,(\kappa_n)\,\exp\,(x'Y/\kappa_n) \tag{45}$$

and estimate the p.d.f. of Y as

$$P_n\,(x) = n^{-1}\sum_{1}^{n} c\,(\kappa_n)\,\exp\,(x'\,Y_i/\kappa_n). \tag{46}$$

We can choose κ_n by the method of Hebbema *et al.* [10] as the value κ at which the pseudo-likelihood

$$\prod_{i=1}^{n} (n-1)^{-1} \sum_{j \neq i} c\,(\kappa)\,\exp\,(Y_i'\,Y_j/\kappa) \tag{47}$$

is maximised. Further work on density estimation will be reported elsewhere.

References

1. J Aitchison (1985) A general class of distributions on the simplex. *J R Statist Soc* B **47** 136–146.
2. M A Stephens (1980) Use of the von Mises distribution to analyse continuous proportions. *Biometrika,* **69,** 197–203.
3. G S Watson (1983) *Statistics on Spheres.* Wiley Interscience, New York.
4. R A Fisher (1953) Dispersion on a sphere *Proc R Soc London* **A217**, 295–305.
5. P Langevin (1905) Magnetisme et theorie des electrons. *Ann Chim. Phys.* **5**, 70–127.
6. R Von Mises (1918) Uber die "Ganzzahligkeit" der Atomgewicht und Verwandte Fragen *Physik* **Z 19,** 490–500.
7. J Aitchison and S M Shen (1980) Logistic normal distributions: some properties and uses *Biometrika* **67,** 261–272.
8. J Aitchison (1982) The statistical analysis of compositional data (with discussion) *J R Statist Soc* B **44** 139–177.
9. G E P Box and D R Cox (1964). The analysis of transformations (with discussion) *J R Statist Soc* B **26** 211–252.
10. J D F Hebbema, J Hermans and K van den Brock (1974) A stepwise discriminant analysis program using density estimation. In: *Compstat.*
11. K V Mardia (1972) *Statistics of Directional Data.* Academic Press New York.
12. C Radhakrisna Rao (1973) *Linear Statistical Inference and its Applications.* Wiley, New York.

7

Creating Reference Patterns Via a Vector Quantization Algorithm

W A Mahmoud[1] and L A M Bennett[1]

ABSTRACT

A new clustering algorithm for selecting reference templates for speaker-independent isolated-word recognition is described. It is demonstrated that the vector quantization algorithm can be a powerful tool for selecting reference templates for isolated-word recognition.

The advantages of this new clustering algorithm over previous once include ease of use, robustness of the templates, and recognition accuracy comparable to previous systems with a smaller number of templates.

The proposed algorithm has been applied to a large speech database consisting of five repetitions of the 26 letters of the English alphabet and ten repetitions of the English digits for each of ten speakers, five male and five female. The results of the recognition performance show that the clusters are highly structured.

Keywords: Speaker-independent; Isolated-word Recognition; Vector Quantization Algorithm; Statistical Clustering.

7.1 INTRODUCTION

The three aspects of a statistical approach to a pattern recognition problem are: (1) the selection of features; (2) the choice of a measure of similarity; and (3) a method for creating the reference patterns (templates) used in the statistical test.

The rationale for choosing a feature set is related both to the features and to the efficiency with which the features can represent this information. For the work in this paper the features selected were the LPC parameters for each frame of the input speech. This set of features was chosen because of the fidelity with which the LPC parameters are capable of representing the speech waveform.

'Once the set of features is chosen, the next important step is the choice of a pattern similarity measure, which quantitatively tells how close a reference template is to the unknown spoken word. The choice of a similarity measure is intimately related to the chosen set of features. For the LPC coefficients, Itakura [1] has proposed a very powerful measure of similarity, which is used here, and is based on assumed statistics for the LPC parameter sets.

---

[1] Department of Electrical and Electronic Engineering, University College of Swansea, Swansea, U.K.

The third and final aspect of pattern recognition system for isolated words is the creation of the reference templates for use in the recognition phase. This paper deals with the problem of how to create reference patterns from a large number of isolated words, for both the speaker-adaptive and the speaker-independent speech recognition, *via* the vector quantization (VQ) algorithm.

Next we present a criterion on possible ways of handling the problem of covering the outliers in creating templates, and give numerical results on word recognition accuracy which illustrate the typical performance achieved with two representative systems.

7.2 EXISTING ALGORITHMS

The existing algorithms for creating reference templates for speaker-adaptive and speaker-independent isolated-word recognition can be broadly placed into three classes:

(a) *Adaptation methods* — Each speaker is asked to contribute several versions of each word in the vocabulary and a reference template is created from each spoken word. The problem associated with this class is that one cannot establish the reliability or robustness of the word templates without actually attempting to do recognition. This method is suitable for a small vocabulary size or for micro-processor-based speech recognition systems [1, 2].

(b) *Averaging methods* — The speaker (or several speakers in the case of speaker-independent systems) utters each word of the vocabulary V times, and the V versions of each word are averaged to give a single reference template. Averaging techniques for creating reference templates tend to minimize the risk of totally unreliable templates. However, these methods run the risk of averaging highly discrepant versions, and thereby creating a reference template that does not provide good representation of the given word. Commercial systems have performed extremely well using this type of training [3, 4].

(c) *Statistical clustering methods* — The speaker (or set of speakers) utters each word of the vocabulary V times, where V is large in the order of 50 - 100. The V versions are grouped into clusters based on pattern similarity, and one reference template is obtained containing C or more versions. This class of training methods has shown great promise for both speaker-independent and speaker-adapted isolated-word recognition [5, 6].

7.3 SUMMARY OF RELATED TECHNIQUES

Before describing the proposed clustering algorithm some general information of the framework will be given in order to simplify the understanding of some techniques involved in the procedure of proposed algorithm.

Advantages of Vector Quantization

Vector quantization (VQ) is a data compression technique in which the vector of acoustic parameters which represents a segment of speech is replaced by a single symbol or codeword [7, 8]. This symbol is an index number to an entry in a pre-determined ordered set of reference segments, referred to as the codebook, which represents a partitioning of the acoustic space in the domain of the speech being quantized.

Thus, the VQ algorithm is an automatic iteration scheme which will find any specified number of clusters for a given database. The iteration consists of three basic steps: classification, computation of cluster centres, and convergence testing [8]. Based on the above description it would seem that the VQ algorithm can be used to solve the reference templates problem.

Speech Recognition via Pattern Matching (DTW)

The most popular form of isolated word recognition is the classification pattern recognition approach. In the first stage of such an approach the system is responsible for collecting and storing the speech samples using segmentation, pitch analysis and data framing. Next the framed signal is converted to a more invariant spectral pattern by different ways of spectral estimation, such as linear predictive coding (LPC) spectra. These patterns need to be compared with pre-determined reference patterns of the stored templates using a distance measure [1].

One of the most serious types of variability among different utterances of the same word, even spoken by the same speaker, is the variation in time scale. Therefore, some form of time normalization needs to take account of these changes in the time scale. The most successful time normalization algorithm incorporates a non-linear time scale matching, whose mathematical basis is known as dynamic time warping (DTW) [1]. The final stage of the classical pattern recognition model is the decision rule that makes a recognition decision, or possibly a set of decisions or similarity scores provided by the pattern comparison block.

Speech Recognition via Vector Quantization (DTW/VQ)

To perform the classical pattern recognition approach via vector quantization, we need a predesigned codebook. Then, the reference segments are required to be labelled (quantized) to the nearest codewords of the codebook to them. Similarly, the test segments are required to be vector quantized. The remaining steps in the recognizer are essentially those of the classical pattern recognition model described in the previous section. The DTW alignment compares the test pattern to each reference pattern, coded as a series of codebook codewords, and generates a distance score [4, 7, 8].

7.4 PROPOSED ALGORITHM

Based on the discussion of section 7.3, it is seen that there are several key issues in the creation of an adequate set of reference templates for speaker-independent recognition of isolated words. These are:

(a) How to recognize clusters;

(b) How to average several versions within a cluster to create the reference template;

(c) Which parameter set should be averaged in creating the reference template;

(d) How many templates should be created for each word in the input set; and

(e) How to handle outliers.

Assume we are given a training set of words. For each of the W words in the vocabulary, there are V versions of the word by S speakers. For each word there is the LPC parameter set $A\ (i, j, k)$, where

i = frame number, $i = 1, 2, ..., F\ (j, k)$,

j = word number, $j = 1, 2, ..., W$ and

k = version number, $k = 1, 2, ..., V$

where $F\ (j, k)$ is the number of frames of the kth version of the jth word.

Therefore, the problem is how to create reference templates by a suitable way of combining the V versions of each word to give one or more templates whose properties reflect those of the distribution of the LPC parameters for that word. The way in which the proposed clustering procedure operates is as follows:

(a) For each word j in the vocabulary, calculate its average length (in frames) from its replications V. Thus find the average of $F\ (j, k)$ for each j for $k = 1, ..., V$ and repeat until $j = W$. Let these temporary averaged lengths equal $FA\ (j)$.

(b) Select that version of the word which has the nearest length to $FA\ (j) + 2$, and denote this selected word as $ws\ (j)$. It has been observed experimentally that this has the effect of linear transformation of the different versions of the word. Replace the values of the averaged lengths $FA\ (j)$ with the lengths of the selected words.

(c) Perform the dynamic time warping of each version of the word with the selected one to the standard duration FA (j).

(d) For each word in the vocabulary, group the coincident individual LPC segments from its replications V, hence for each word we have FA (j) groups of LPC vectors. Thus the elements of these groups G (i, j, k) are the warped A (i, j, k) LPC vectors of the different versions V of each word.

(e) Cluster each group of LPC segments G (FA (j), j, V) for each word via the vector quantization algorithm. Here for each group, codebooks of sizes of 2, 4, 8, and 16 codewords were produced. Note that the size of codebook depends mostly on the complexity of the words of the vocabulary.

(f) In order to identify and cover the outliers inside the clusters, we have implemented a covering criterion. The novelty of this criterion lies in its ability to merge existing codewords in order to give the actual number of codewords for each codebook, and hence to minimize similar templates at the latest stage. The principle of the covering criterion proposed here is that the VQ algorithm puts the number of codewords (level clusters) in the final iteration into a codebook of pre-determined size. Therefore, there is a probability of producing similar codewords and this necessitated the need for a criterion to merge these similar codewords. The codewords are merged under the following conditions:

   (a) If the size of the VQ codebook is larger or equal to 4.

   (b) If the number of vectors classified to each codeword is less than the threshold value Cmin.

   (c) If the distance between the *i*th codeword and the *j*th codeword is less than some threshold Tmin.

(g) Search for all possible combinations of the clustered frames (codewords) from the different levels (codebooks). Here equivalently we apply the Viterbi algorithm [9], where the optimum path is that one which gives the average minimum distance (or recognition error) from the V versions of the word (or may be from a set of test words). Denote these minimum distances by DM (j, c), where j = 1,..., W and c = 1, ..., C, the number of reference templates. Also, calculate the number of test words that are classified to each cluster formed, and denote these counts by M (j, c).

(h) The proposed covering criterion was imposed for merging the produced templates (word clusters), under the following conditions:

   (a) If the present number of templates exceeds the size of codebook used in generating the individual clusters.

   (b) If the number of test words classified to the template is less than 5% of the test words.

(c) If the warped average distance between the *i*th template and the *j*th template is less than a present threshold *Tw*.

Put the selected reference templates in descending order, according to their minimum distances *DM* (*j*, *c*), in order to facilitate the selection of the required number of templates per word.

Therefore, the procedure is a multi-level *k*-means iteration in an automatic procedure which will find the detailed structure of the data, given information from other procedures. The basic iteration scheme is designed to give increasingly accurate estimates of cluster centre location.

In fact, it enables the user to refine his estimate of the number of templates, while the multilevel *k*-means iteration is based on the estimated size of VQ codebook.

Additionally, it provides a more general solution than those reported elsewhere [3, 5, 6], and it avoids the poor reference templates. This appears to be true because the produced templates span an appropriate space representing variations in pronunciation and voice characteristics.

7.5 EXPERIMENTAL BACKGROUND

Ten speakers, five male and five female, generated the database of spoken English alphanumeric words. In one session, each speaker was asked to contribute fifty digits and 130 letters as isolated utterances. In a second section, each speaker was asked to read out as isolated words a list of fifty digits in random order. The first recorded session was used to generate the reference templates, using the three classes of generating reference templates. Both recordings were used in the recognition experiment as test patterns.

The data were pre-emphasised, a 12-bit ADC and a sampling rate of 10 k sample/sec was used. Hamming windows of five different lengths were used, which were 9.6, 12.8, 19.2, 25.6 and 38.4 m sec. A twelfth-order LPC analysis autocorrelation method was used based on previous experimental results [10]. The dynamic time warping (DTW) method of Itakura [1] was used to time-align utterances.

7.6 RECOGNITION PERFORMANCE

To evaluate the various methods of creating speaker-independent word templates, a series of experiments was carried out, using the DTW and DTW/VQ systems.

Recognition Results on the Digit-Vocabulary

As mentioned before, 50 versions of each word were used in the training set with equal number of male and female speakers. For the test set, four distinct sets of reference templates were created. For each set a total of five test results obtained corresponding to the five Hamming window lengths under consideration. The four sets using the DTW recognizer were the following:

Set 1— Ten templates per word for each of the 10 speakers in the training set using the adaptation method [2].

Set 2— Two individual templates per word using proposed clustering method. Note that a codebook of size 4 was used in clustering the individual segments of the training words.

Set 3— One template per word, based on averaging the autocorrelation coefficients and then transferring them back to LPC coefficients.

Set 4— Two individual templates per word, using the clustering method of reference [3].

In creating reference set 2 and 4, values for the cluster and codewords thresholds were obtained experimentally (these thresholds determined which word went into the cluster, or which codewords were to be covered).

A complete breakdown of the results for each of the above conditions is given in Table 7.1. By examining the data of this table some observations can be made.

1. The average templates of set 3 produced the highest error rate of all four sets, for all the 10 speakers.
2. Templates of the proposed method set 2 have lowest error rates in comparison with the other sets. The error rate scores for the proposed method were from 0.3% to 0.7% only and much lower than the error rate of the templates of other methods of clustering [5].
3. The error rates for the proposed method insignificantly differ from one speaker to another in comparison with all other methods. Furthermore, the results indicate that for almost all the speakers, the new training procedure gave the best performance and this performance as mentioned was significantly better than that obtained from equivalent templates of previous methods.
4. The adaptive templates have higher error rates in comparison with the clustering method but its error rate is lower than the average method.

Table 7.1 *Recognition error for the four sets using the DTW recognition system for five different window lengths*

Window Length	**9.6 msec**				**12.8 msec**				**19.2 msec**				**25.6 msec**				**38.4 msec**			
Set No.	1	2	3	4	1	2	3	4	1	2	3	4	1	2	3	4	1	2	3	4
***SPEAKER* BOB**	3.6	0	4	2	6.4	0	9	6	3.7	0	7	3	4.1	0	12	3	4.9	0	10	7
FARZ	4.1	0	8	1	4.4	0	7	1	4.0	1	9	0	4.6	0	8	1	4.2	0	11	1
IAN	1.2	1	8	0	0.9	1	15	1	0.8	1	6	0	1.3	1	14	2	0.8	2	11	2
JHON	1.1	0	9	0	1.2	1	9	0	0.5	0	7	0	1.0	1	19	0	0.2	0	15	0
RICH	5 5	0	4	2	5.9	2	11	1	3.3	0	5	1	5.1	3	17	9	4.1	1	11	3
CRIS	1.8	0	2	0	1.8	0	2	0	1.6	0	3	0	2.8	0	6	0	2.7	0	8	2
LYNDA	0.7	0	3	0	1.2	0	2	1	0.7	0	3	0	1.1	0	0	0	0.8	0	4	0
JULY	8.9	0	15	3	13.2	0	25	11	8.3	0	19	3	10.5	0	27	9	7.5	1	24	5
WIDGE	3.2	0	10	2	4.5	1	11	1	2.5	0	9	0	3.5	1	12	3	2.5	0	12	0
CATHY	3.4	2	20	0	5.4	1	17	2	3.5	2	21	2	6.9	1	23	4	5.9	2	20	1
AVERAGE	3.35	0.3	8.3	1.0	4.49	0.6	10.8	2.4	2.89	0.4	8.9	0.9	4.09	0.7	13.8	3.1	3.36	0.7	12.6	1.6

Table 7.2 shows the recognition results on the same vocabulary for two of the above sets, namely, set 1 and 2 using the DTW/VQ recognizer. The recognition test was performed for various size of codebook, from 16 up to 256 codewords, and for the 19.2 msec Hamming window length only. Again a good performance can be seen for the proposed method of generating templates.

Table 7.2 *Recognition error rate of the digits vocabulary using the DTW/VQ recognition system*

The Speaker Symbol	% Error using (Adaptation) for Different Codebook Size					% Error using (VQ/New) for Different Codebook Size				
	16	32	64	128	256	16	32	64	128	256
B	17.6	14.4	13.3	10.3	8.5	26	13	8	3	2
F	20.2	13.5	10.8	9.8	5.9	31	18	5	4	3
I	28.8	14.3	10.5	4.2	3.5	16	8	7	6	4
J	9.2	4.2	3.1	1.8	2.1	6	4	3	2	0
R	30.0	12.9	12.5	16.7	8.8	21	20	10	5	2
C	13.3	10.0	7.7	6.2	6.7	18	12	8	7	4
L	12.6	7.0	7.1	4.4	2.1	10	4	4	6	2
P	22.1	16.4	6.2	15.5	12.1	18	15	15	11	7
W	20.6	12.2	13.8	11.8	7.8	18	19	17	12	8
Y	21.2	20.4	17.3	12.9	7.2	25	17	10	7	5
The mean	19.56	12.59	10.23	8.76	6.47	18.9	13.0	8.7	6.2	3.7

Recognition Results of the Alphabet Vocabulary

In this section, some results are mentioned in respect of the application of the clustering techniques to the alphabet vocabulary under consideration. The two series of experimental tests were carried out corresponding to set 1 and set 2. In set 1 only five templates were used per word instead of ten, while two templates were used in set 2. Again the proposed method worked faithfully and a good recognition performance for such a complex vocabulary was obtained.

Table 7.3, shows that results of these two sets for the Hamming window length 19.2 msec., where the average recognition error was 7.788%.

Table 7.3 *Recognition results of alphabet vocabulary*

Speaker	B	D	I	J	M	C	H	K	L	N	The mean
Set 1	10.81	15.4	16.82	11.77	13.94	18.02	18.75	16.34	12.25	15.86	14.97
Set 2	0.96	11.53	7.69	1.92	10.57	7.69	9.61	10.57	3.84	13.46	7.78

7.7 DISCUSSION AND FURTHER REMARKS

In this paper, a new clustering procedure is proposed for creating reference templates for speaker-adaptive and speaker-independent isolated word speech recognition systems. Although the main purpose of this paper was to propose and study alternative methods of creating reference templates for isolated-word recognition system, the paper compares the recognition results obtained here with other studies. The systems were tested on 1000 digits and 1300 letters of English alphabet contributed by ten speakers, five male and five female. A recognition accuracy of up to 99.7% were achieved using the proposed method for the digit vocabulary, and up to 92.212% for the alphabet vocabulary.

The proposed method is more reliable and robust than the adaptation method, and has some of the advantages of averaging and clustering techniques. The new training procedure is applicable primarily to speaker-independent systems. With this method each reference word can be represented by a number of templates depending on the word complexity.

An interesting question here is: what is the source of the high variability for some speakers? Informal examination of the test data indicated that a large percentage was due to speaker generated artifacts (e.g., breath noise, mouth clicks, lip smackings, pops, etc.) which made end point detector somewhat unreliable. The advantages of this method is that versions with artifacts are generally extended by the VQ clustering procedure. Therefore, the resulting word reference templates are a good representation of the actual spoken words.

The existence of outliers is important in recognition tasks because an outlier is a potential cause of misclassification. If a version of one word is very dissimilar from all other versions of that word, it may well be similar to some versions of another word. The proposed algorithm treated such bad data points automatically, instead of eliminating them as in most existing cluster algorithms. Thus its novelty lies in its ability to merge the cluster to find the best configuration.

The proposed algorithm uses the VQ algorithm which gives at least a locally optimum solution in the individual cluster levels. However, it uses the power of the Viterbi algorithm in the combination stage whose optimality increases the probability of producing global solution.

Finally, due to the nature of the VQ, as more speakers are added to the training set, the better the produced templates. Unlike the proposed method, this has been seen to cause great difficulty in other clustering algorithms [5, 6].

7.8 ACKNOWLEDGEMENTS

The authors wish to acknowledge the kind assistance and helpful discussion of Dr S Levinson, AT&T Bell Laboratories in USA.

References

1. FItakura (1972) Minimum prediction residual applied to speech recognition *IEEE Trans* **ASSP-23,** 67–72.
2. W A Mahmoud and L A M Bennett (1985) Recognition of Arabic digits by a microcomputer *Proc Jordan IEEE Conf Amman,* 200–203.
3. T B Martin (1976) Practical application of voice input to machines *Proc IEEE* **64**, pp. 487, 501.
4. W A Mahmoud and L A M Bennet (1986) Speech recognition based upon segment classification and labelling technique and hidden Markov model presented at *Montreal Symposium on Speech Recognition* Canada, Montreal July 21–22, 1986.
5. L R Rabiner (1988) On creating reference templates for speaker independent recognition of isolated words *IEEE Trans* **ASSP-26,** 34–42.
6. S E Levinson, L R Rabiner, A E Rosenberg and J G Wilpon (1979) Interactive clustering techniques for selecting speaker-independent reference templates for isolated word recognition *IEEE Trans* **ASSP-27** 134–141.
7. W A Mahmoud and L A M Bennett (1985) Automatic recognition of spoken arabic digits *Via* vector quantization algorithm Presented at *Modelling and Simulation Conference,* Tunisia, 25 Nov. 1985.
8. W A Mahmoud and L A M Bennett (1985) The distortion measure of the segment classification and labelling technique of different window lengths *Proc IEEE ELECTRONICOM'85* 7–9 Oct. Canada 161 –164.
9. G D Forney Jr. (1973) The Viterbi algorithm *Proc IEEE* **61,** 268–278.
10. W A Mahmoud and L A M Bennett (1976) The effect of LPC order on the performance of vector quantization in isolated word recognition Presented at *Montreal Symposium on Speech Recognition* Canada, Montreal July 21–22, 1986.

8

Effect of Mislabeled Training Samples on the Convergence of Learning Processes

Amita Pal (Pathak)[1] and Sankar K Pal[1]

ABSTRACT

For the problem of parameter learning in pattern recognition, when there is a possibility of training samples being mislabeled, the authors have investigated the convergence of stochastic approximation-based learning algorithms. In the cases considered, it is found that estimates converge to non-true values in the presence of labeling errors. The general *m*-class *N*-feature pattern recognition problem is considered.

Keywords: Parameter Learning; Pattern Recognition; Convergence of Algorithms; Stochastic Approximation.

8.1 INTRODUCTION

The learning of unknown parameters of classifiers is an indispensable part of pattern recognition problems. If a sufficiently large set of correctly labeled training samples is available, then 'reasonably good' estimates of the parameters can generally be obtained. In many real-life situations, however, it is either difficult or expensive to obtain labels, so that mislabeling of training samples can become one of the spectres a pattern recognition scientist has to contend with. It is, therefore, useful to know how this problem can affect the learning procedure. A reasonable amount of work has been done for the two-class classification problem. The effects of random training errors on Fisher's discriminant function have been studied by several workers [1, 2, 3, 4, 5, 6]. They concluded that the effect is to underestimate distance, overestimate error rate, introduce bias into estimates of the discriminant function, make the maximum likelihood estimates of the discriminant function converge to non-true values, and affect the asymptotic relative efficiency (ARE) relative to a completely correctly classified sample of the same size.

In the context of recursive learning of parameters, the usefulness of stochastic approximation procedures cannot be overemphasized [7]. Briefly, a stochastic approximation procedure for recursively estimating by $\hat{\theta}_n$ a parameter θ by means of an unbiased statistic T, at the nth step, is:

$$\hat{\theta}_{n+1} = \hat{\theta}_n - a_n\,(\hat{\theta}_n - T_{n+1}),$$

---

[1] Indian Statistical Institute, Calcutta 700035, India.

where $\hat{\theta}_1$ is either a constant or $\hat{\theta}_1 = T_1$,

and $\{a_n\}$ is a suitable chosen sequence of positive numbers.

For instance, a recursive procedure for estimating the population mean μ of a variable X with the help of the sample mean $\bar{x}$ is:

$$\bar{x}_{n+1} = \bar{x}_n - \frac{1}{n}(\bar{x}_n - x_{n+1}),$$

x_{n+1} being the *(n* +1)-th observation on *X*.

In this paper, the particular case in which errors occur in the labeling of training samples is studied, for an *m*-class *N*-feature pattern recognition problem. The effect of mislabeling is to cause 'wrong' samples to be used in the recursive learning of the estimates, for any given class. A simple but realistic model [8] is adopted to describe this sort of situation. Under this model, the authors have investigated the convergence of recursive learning procedures of the type mentioned above. It is found that under certain conditions, these estimates do converge strongly, that is, with probability one, but to non-true values; to be more specific, to convex linear combinations of true parameters of all *m*-classes. This is obtained using some results on multidimensional stochastic approximation [9].

8.2 STATEMENT OF THE PROBLEM

Let us consider a general *m*-class pattern recognition problem, C_i, $i = 1\ (1)\ m$ being the *m*classes, for which an *N*-dimensional feature vector

$$\underset{N\times 1}{\mathbf{X}} = [X_1, X_2, ..., X_N]', \mathbf{X} \in \mathbb{R}^N$$

has been specified. Let us assume:

(Al) The distribution of $\mathbf{X}$ in each class is continuous.

(A2) The probability densities $p\ (\cdot \mid C_i)$, of $\mathbf{X}$ for the classes C_i, $i = 1\ (1)\ m$, are of the same family and differ only in respect of values of parameters.

Let $d\,(\cdot)$ be a decision function based on $\mathbf{X}$, i.e., let

$$\mathrm{d} : \mathbb{R}^N \to \mathbb{R}$$

and let it depend only on the $p\ (\cdot \mid C_i)$, $i = 1\ (1)\ m$. For each i, let

$$\underset{q\times 1}{\varphi_i} = [\varphi_{1_i}, \varphi_{2_i}, ..., \varphi_{q_i}]'$$

be the vector of unknown parameters of $p\ (\cdot \mid C_i)$ and hence $d_i\,(\cdot)$.

Let us further assume:

(A3) An unbiased statistic exists for the parameter-vector $\boldsymbol{\varphi}$ with respect to the probability density function p.

Let us suppose that for the purpose of learning we have been given a set of independent samples, $X_1^{(k)}, X_2^{(k)}, X_{n_k}^{(k)}, k = 1\ (1)\ m,$ where the superscripts k denotes the labels given to the respective samples. For the learning itself, let us utilize a stochastic approximation algorithm LA1 defined below:

Let $\hat{\varphi}_t^{(k)}$ denote the estimate obtained at the t-th step for the class C_k.

Then $\hat{\varphi}_1^{(k)} = f(X_1^{(k)})$ (1a)

and for $t \geq 1$ and $k = 1\ (1)\ m$,

$$\hat{\varphi}_{t+1}^{(k)} = \hat{\varphi}_t^{(k)} - a_t(\hat{\varphi}_t^{(k)} - f(X_{t+1}^{(k)})), \tag{1b}$$

where $\{a_t\}$ is a sequence of positive real numbers such that $a_t \leq 1 \forall\ t$, and $f: \mathbb{R}^N \to \mathbb{R}^q$ is an unbiased statistic for φ.

8.3 A MODEL FOR LABELING ERRORS

The model to be used for this purpose was developed by Chittineni [8]. It can be specified as follows:

Let w and $\hat{w}$ denote respectively the true and the given labels. Clearly

$$w, \hat{w}\ \varepsilon\ \{1, 2, \ldots, m\}.$$

Let $\pi_i = P[w = i]$ denote the a priori probability for the class C_i, $i = 1\ (1)\ m$. Further, let $p_i(X) = p(X \mid w = i)$ be the class-conditional density of the feature vector X for C_i. Also, let β_{ji} denote the probability that a sample from C_j has been given the label i, i.e.,

$$\beta_{ji} = P(\hat{w} = i \mid w = j),\ i, j = 1(1)\ m \tag{2}$$

Clearly, we must have

$$\sum_{i=1}^{m} \beta_{ji} = 1 \tag{3a}$$

i.e.,

$$B'\ \varepsilon = \varepsilon \tag{3b}$$

where $\underset{m \times 1}{\varepsilon} = [1\ 1\ 1 \ldots 1]'$

and $B = ((\beta_{ij}))$.

Now, $$p(X \mid \hat{w} = i) = \frac{p(X, \hat{w} = i)}{p(\hat{w} = i)}$$

$$= \frac{1}{p(\hat{w} = i)} \sum_{j=1}^{m} p(X, \hat{w} = i, w = j)$$

$$= \frac{1}{p(\hat{w}=i)} \sum_{j=1}^{m} p(\mathbf{X}|\hat{w}=i, w=j)\, P(\hat{w}=i \mid w=j) \times P(w=j)$$

$$= \frac{1}{p(\hat{w}=i)} \sum_{j=1}^{m} \pi_j\, \beta_{ji}\, p(\mathbf{X}|\hat{w}=i, w=j) \tag{4}$$

However, $$P[\hat{w}=i] = \sum_{j=1}^{m} p(\hat{w}=i, w=j)$$

$$= \sum_{j=1}^{m} p(\hat{w}=i, \mid w=j)\, P(w=j)$$

$$= \sum_{j=1}^{m} \pi_j\, \beta_{ji} \tag{5}$$

Hence, Eqn. 4 becomes

$$p(\mathbf{X}|\hat{w}=i) = \sum_{j=1}^{m} \alpha_{ji}\, p(\mathbf{X}|\hat{w}=i, w=j) \tag{6}$$

where $$\alpha_{ji} = \pi_j\, \beta_{ji} \Big/ \left(\sum_{l=1}^{m} \pi_l\, \beta_{li} \right). \tag{7}$$

If we are prepared to assume

$(A4)$ $p(\mathbf{X}|\, w=j) = p(\mathbf{X}|\hat{w}=i, w=j)\ \forall\ i, j$

then Eqn. 6 becomes

$$P(\mathbf{X}|\hat{w}=i) = \sum_{j=1}^{m} \alpha_{ji}\, p(\mathbf{X}|\, w=j)$$

$$= \sum_{j=1}^{m} \alpha_{ji}\, p_j(\mathbf{X}) \tag{8}$$

8.4 CONVERGENCE OF THE LEARNING ALGORITHM

The convergence of a recursive discrete algorithm $\hat{\theta}_n$ for estimating a parameter θ, can be defined in various ways. For instance we say that

(i) the sequence $\{\hat{\theta}_n\}$ converges to θ *with probability 1* or *almost surely* (in symbols, $\hat{\theta}_n \xrightarrow{a,s} \theta$) if

$$P[\lim_{n \to \infty} \|\hat{\theta}_n - \theta\| = 0] = 1.$$

(ii) $\hat{\theta}_n$ converges to θ in the *mean square* if

$$\lim_{n \to \infty} E\left[\| \hat{\theta}_n - \theta \|^2 \right] = 0,$$

E being the Expectation operator.

For studying the behaviour of the learning algorithm LA1 given in section 8.2, use will be made of the following results, due to Schmetterer [9]:

Lemma 1: Let $\{a_n\}$ be a sequence of positive real number such that

$$\text{(C1)} \qquad \sum_{n=1}^{\infty} a_n^2 < \infty.$$

Let x_n and y_n be k-dimensional random vectors which satisfy

$$\text{(C2)} \qquad \boldsymbol{x}_{n+1} = \boldsymbol{x}_n - a_n \, \boldsymbol{y}_n, \; n \geq 1.$$

Let M_n be a measurable mapping from $\mathbb{R}^k$ to IR^k such that

$$\text{(C3)} \qquad E\,(\boldsymbol{y}_n \,|\, \boldsymbol{x}_1, \boldsymbol{x}_2, \ldots, \boldsymbol{x}_n) = \boldsymbol{M}_n\,(\boldsymbol{x}_n) \; a.e.$$

Let a, b, c be non-negative real numbers and let

$$\text{(C4)} \qquad E\,(\|\boldsymbol{y}_n\|^2 \,|\, \boldsymbol{x}_1, \boldsymbol{x}_2, \ldots, \boldsymbol{x}_n) \leq a + b\,\|\boldsymbol{x}_n\| + c\,\|\boldsymbol{x}_n\|^2 \text{ a.e.}$$

Also, for every $x \in \mathrm{IR}^k$ and $n > 1$,

$$\text{(C5)} \qquad \boldsymbol{x}'\,\boldsymbol{M}_n\,(\boldsymbol{x}) \geq 0.$$

If $\boldsymbol{x}_1$ is chosen in such a way that

$$\text{(C6)} \qquad E\,(\|\boldsymbol{x}_1\|^2) \text{ exists,}$$

then the sequence $\{\boldsymbol{x}_n\}$ converges with probability 1 i.e., almost surely and the sequence $E\,\{\|\boldsymbol{x}_n\|^2\}$ converges also.

Lemma 2: Suppose that the conditions (C1) - (C6) hold. If, further, there exists for every $\eta > 0$ a $\delta > 0$ such that for $n > 1$

$$\text{(C7)} \qquad \inf_{\eta < \|x\| < \eta^{-1}} [\boldsymbol{x}'\,\boldsymbol{M}_n\,(\boldsymbol{x})] \geq \delta,$$

then $\{\boldsymbol{x}_n\}$ converges almost surely to the k-dimensional null vector 0.

We shall prove the following:

Proposition1 Consider the set-up given in sections 8.2 and 8.3. If, in addition to assumptions (A1) - (A4), we also have

$$\text{(A5)} \qquad \sum_{n=1}^{\infty} a_n^2 < \infty,$$

(A6) $\qquad \rho_i = E\left(\|f(X)\|^2 \,\middle|\, w=i\right)$ exists, with respect to each class-conditional density $p_i\,(X)$, then $$\hat{\varphi}_t^{(k)} \xrightarrow{a.s.} \sum_{j=1}^{m} \alpha_{jk} \varphi_j,$$

where α_{ji} $i, j = 1\ (1)\ m$, is as in equation 7.

Proof- The validity of the proposition can be inferred directly from the lemmas 1 and 2, provided one can show that the conditions (Cl) - (C7) hold for. $\psi_t^{(k)}$,

where $$\psi_t^{(k)} = \varphi_t^{(k)} - \sum_{j=1}^{m} \alpha_{jk} \varphi_j.$$

We note that from Eqs. 1*a* and 1*b* we have, for $k = 1\ (1)\ m$,

$$\psi_{t+1}^{(k)} = \begin{cases} g_k(X_1^{(k)}) & \text{for } t = 1 \quad (9a) \\ \psi_t^{(k)} - a_t(\psi_t^{(k)} - g_k(X_{t+1}^k)) & \quad (9b) \end{cases}$$

where $$g_k(X) = f(X) - \sum_{j=1}^{m} \alpha_{jk} \varphi_j.$$

The condition (Cl) is seen to be true because of (A5). The condition (C2) is equivalent to Eq. 9*b*.

The condition (C3) also holds, with $M_t(x) = x$, since

$$E\,[\psi_t^k - g_k(X_{t+1}^{(k)}) \mid \psi_1^{(k)}, \psi_2^{(k)}, \ldots\ldots, \psi_t^{(k)}]$$

$$= \psi_t^{(k)} - E\ g_k(X_{t+1}^{(k)}),$$

since $X_{t+1}^{(k)}$ is independent of $X_1^{(k)}, \ldots\ldots, X_t^{(k)}$ and hence of $\psi_1^{(k)}, \psi_2^{(k)}, \ldots\ldots, \psi_t^{(k)}$.

$$= \psi_t^{(k)} - E\,[g_k(X) \mid \hat{w} = k]$$

$$= \psi_t^{(k)} - E\,(f(X) \mid \hat{w} = k) - \sum_{j=1}^{m} \alpha_{jk} \varphi_j.$$

$= \psi_t^{(k)}$, as by Eqn. 8, $E\,(f(X) \mid \hat{w} = k) = \sum_{j=1}^{m} \alpha_{jk} \varphi_j = \overline{\varphi}_k$, say.

Similarly, wc have

$$E\,(\| \psi_t^{(k)} - g_k(X_{t+1}^{(k)}) \|^2 \mid \psi_1^{(k)}, \psi_2^{(k)}, \ldots\ldots, \psi_t^{(k)})$$

$$= E\,(\| \psi_t^{(k)} \|^2 - 2\psi_t^{(k)'} g_k(X_{t+1}^{(k)}) + \| g_k(X_{t+1}^{(k)}) \|^2 \mid \psi_1^{(k)}, \psi_2^{(k)}, \ldots\ldots, \psi_t^{(k)})$$

$$= \| \psi_t^{(k)} \|^2 + E\,(g_k(X) \mid \hat{w} = k) + E\,(\| g_k(X) \|^2 \mid \hat{w} = k)$$

for the same reason as before ;

$= \| \psi_t^{(k)} \|^2 + E\,(\| f(X) - \overline{\varphi} \|^2 \mid \hat{w} = k)$

since $E(g_k(X) \mid \hat{w} = k) = 0$;

$= \| \psi_t^{(k)} \|^2 - \| \overline{\varphi} \|^2 + E(\| f(X) \|^2 \mid \hat{w} = k)$

$\leq \| \psi_t^{(k)} \|^2 + \| \overline{\varphi}_k \|^2 + \sum_{j=1}^{m} \alpha_{jk}\, \rho_j$ because of our assumption (A6);

$\leq \| \psi_t^{(k)} \|^2 + \sum_{j=1}^{m} (\| \varphi_j \|^2 + \rho_j)$

so that (C4) is seen to hold with

$$a = \sum_{j=1}^{m} (\| \varphi_j \|^2 + \rho_j),\ b = 0,\ c = 1.$$

The condition (C5) is seen to be true as

$$x'\, M_t\,(x) = x'x \geq 0.$$

The validity of (C6) follows from the fact that

$$\begin{aligned} E\,\| \psi_1^{(k)} \|^2 &= E\,\| g\,(X_1^{(k)} \|^2 \\ &= E\,(\| g\,(X) \|^2 \mid \hat{w} = k) \\ &\leq \| \overline{\varphi}_k \|^2 + \sum_{j=1}^{m} \alpha_{jk}\, \rho_j < \infty. \end{aligned}$$

Finally, (C7) follows from the fact that

$$\begin{aligned} &\inf_{\eta < \|x\| < \eta - 1} [x'\, M_t(x)] \\ &= \inf_{\eta < \|x\| < \eta - 1} x'x = \eta^2 > 0. \end{aligned}$$

Hence the proposition.

Implications: *(i)* If the matrix B is the identity matrix, i.e., if there is no mislabeling, then under our assumptions,

$$\hat{\varphi}_t^{(k)} \xrightarrow{a.s.} \varphi_k$$

as expected.

(ii) If $B \neq I_m$, then clearly, the estimates $\hat{\varphi}_t^{(k)}$ for the different classes converge to non-true values

$$\overline{\varphi}_k = \sum_{j=1}^{m} \alpha_{jk}\, \varphi_j,$$

i.e., a convex linear combination of the parameter vectors of all the classes, as

$$\sum_{j=1}^{m} \alpha_{jk} = 1 \;\forall\; k = 1\ (1)\ m.$$

(iii) Yet another implication can be stated formally as follows:

Proposition 2: Consider the set-up specified in sections 8.2 and 8.3. If assumptions (A1) - (A6) hold, then

$$\sum_{j=1}^{m} \gamma_{jk}\ \hat{\varphi}_t^{(j)} \xrightarrow{a.s.} \varphi_k,\ k = 1\ (1)\ m;$$

where $\underset{m \times m}{\Gamma} = ((\gamma_{ij}))$ is a generalized inverse [10] of the matrix

$$\underset{m \times m}{A} = ((\alpha_{ij}))$$

satisfying $$A\Gamma = I_m. \tag{10}$$

Proof Firstly, we note that the matrix A is not full-rank as shown by Eq 3*b*. Consequently,

$$\text{rank}\ (A) = r \le m - 1.$$

From proposition 1, it is known that

$$(\hat{\varphi}_t^{(1)} \vdots\ \hat{\varphi}_t^{(2)} \vdots \cdots \vdots\ \hat{\varphi}_t^{(m)}) \xrightarrow{a.s.} A'\ (\varphi_1 \vdots\ \varphi_2 \vdots \cdots \vdots\ \varphi_m).$$

element-wise,

By well-known results on almost sure convergence it follows that

$$(\hat{\varphi}_t^{(1)} \vdots\ \hat{\varphi}_t^{(2)} \vdots \cdots \vdots\ \hat{\varphi}_t^{(m)}) \xrightarrow{a.s.} A'\ (\varphi_1 \vdots\ \varphi_2 \vdots \cdots \vdots\ \varphi_m).$$

element-wise, and hence

$$(\hat{\varphi}_t^{(1)} \vdots\ \hat{\varphi}_t^{(2)} \vdots \cdots \vdots\ \hat{\varphi}_t^{(m)}) \xrightarrow{a.s.} A'\ (\varphi_1 \vdots\ \varphi_2 \vdots \cdots \vdots\ \varphi_m).$$

column-wise, because of Eq. 10

Q.E.D.

It may be mentioned in passing that one such Γ satisfying Eq. 10 is the Moore-Penrose Inverse [10] of A viz., A^+ defined as

$$A^+ = \sum_{i=1}^{r} \frac{1}{\lambda_i} u_i\, u_i',$$

where λ_i is the ith non-zero eigen-value of A, and u_i the corresponding eigenvector, $i = 1\ (1)\ r$.

8.5 CONCLUSION

For the general m-class N-feature pattern recognition problem it is found that in the presence of labeling errors for training samples, the recursive estimated for class parameters φ_k, defined by means of Eq. 1, do converge strongly under certain conditions. However, the values they converge to are not the true class-parameter values but certain convex linear combinations of true values for all the m-classes.

References

1. P A Lachenbruch (1966) Discriminant functions when the initial samples are misclassified, *Technomet* **8,** 657–662.
2. P A Lachenbruch (1974) Discriminant functions when the initial samples are misclassified II: nonrandom misclassification models. *Technomet* **16,** 419–424.
3. G J McLachlan (1977) Estimating the linear discriminant function from initial samples containing a small number of unclassified observations *J Am Statist Assoc* **72**, 403–406.
4. J E Michalek and R C Tripathi (1980) The effect of errors in diagnosis and measurement on the estimation of probability of an event. *J Am Statist Assoc.* **75**, 713–721.
5. T J O'Neill (1978) Normal discrimination with unclassified observations. *J Am statist. Assoc.* **73**, 821–825.
6. T Krishnan (1985) Efficiency of normal discrimination with misclassified initial samples Tech. Rep No ASC/85/3 Indian Statistical Institute, Calcutta.
7. M B Nevel'son and R Z Has'minskii (1973) Stochastic Approximation and Recursive Estimation, American Mathematical Society, Providence, Rhode Island.
8. C B Chittineni (1980) Learning with imperfectly labelled samples *Patt Recog* **12**, 281–291.
9. L Schmetterer (1968) Multidimensional stochastic approximation, In: Multivariate Analysis - II: Proc. 2nd Int Symp Multiv. Anal Dayton, Ohio (ed. P R Krishnaiah) Academic Press, New York.
10. C R Rao and S K Mitra (1971), *Generalized Inverse of Matrices and Its Applications.* John Wiley and Sons, New York.

9

Cluster Analysis of Iconometric Measurements of Hoysala Sculptures

S Govindaraju, M Bagavandas and G Siromoney[1]

ABSTRACT

This paper deals with the analysis of sculptures belonging to the Hoysala dynasty of the twelfth and thirteenth centuries. The work presented here is the continuation of our earlier studies of the sculptures of Pallava, Pandya and Chola dynasties.

The Channakesava temple at Belur, the Hoysalesvara temple at Halebid and the Kesava temple at Somnathpur are selected for the present study. Point-to-point distances for about one hundred and twenty randomly selected carvings from the three monuments have been measured and multivariate analyses such as cluster analysis and discriminant analysis are preformed.

Cluster analysis and discriminant analysis are carried out to check the closeness of the carvings of the different monuments. The characteristics that make carvings distinct from one another are extracted. After establishing that the monuments are different in terms of facial proportions, they are studied individually.

Keywords: Cluster Analysis; Iconometric Measurements; Hoysala Sculptures; Computer Applications for Arts.

9.1 INTRODUCTION

Cluster analytic techniques, applied to education, agriculture, engineering and medicine [1] can be extended to an even wider range of problems and subjects. Applied to the study of South Indian sculptures of the twelfth and thirteenth centuries A.D. they may contribute to the study of major problems in art history, such as dating of sculptures and hypothesizing about the number of sculptors.

In the Mysore region of Southern India, the monuments at Belure, Halebid and Somnathpur belong to the 12th and 13th centuries A.D. The region was ruled by kings belonging to the Holysala dynasty. Halebid was the capital city of the Hoysala Kings [2].

The Channakesava temple at Belur [3], the Hoysalesvara temple at Halebid and the Kesava temple at Somnathpur are the best known in Hoysala sculpture. These monuments are known for the rich variety of sculptures. The carvings found on these monuments were made in chloritic schist, a very fine trained stone which is much more tractable to

---

[1] Department of Statistics, Chennai Christian College, Tambaram, Chennai 600059, India.

the chisel than granite. The Channakesava temple was built by the King Vishnuvardhana [4] around 1117 A.D. [3]. The outer walls of this temple are adorned with exquisite bands of carvings. Hoysalesvara, built during 1141-1182 [5] is one of the finest and largest temples of the Hoysalas. The Kesava temple at Somnathpur, built in 1268 [5] is a temple in miniature and in typical late Hoysala style [4].

In this study of iconometry, we have measured point-to-point distances for about 120 carvings of the three monuments and we have also performed multivariate analysis of the data using a large computer.

Such a study of iconometric measurments will prove generally useful in dating sculptures, in restoration work and in hypothesizing the number of sculptors who executed the work. Guralnick [6, 7] pioneered the study of sculptural proportions and applied clustering techniques to analyse the proportions of Greek sculptures. The application of statistical techniques to iconometric data was undertaken for the first time in India by the authors and some of their studies were mainly concerned with the sculptures belonging to the Pallava [8,9,10,11,12], the Chola and the Pandya [13,14,15] dynasties. The objective method of studying the similarity between Indian sculptures introduced in this study will reveal special features that have been missed by earlier scholars. The average values of the iconometric features of different periods and regions will be useful in dating sculptures and these values will also be of use to the restorers.

In this paper, we shall consider the applications of multivariate analysis such as cluster analysis and discriminant analysis to the study of iconometric measurements of carvings of the three monuments.

Ancient and medieval Sanskrit texts called *Silpa Sastras* or art manuals contain information on architecture, temple rituals, iconography and iconometry [16]. They include instructions for painting, sculpting and making painted carvings. The canons prescribe that the length of the face should be twelve *angulas* (an *angula* is a proportional unit equal to the width of a finger) and they also prescribe the length and breadth of all the parts of human body. The carvings found on these monuments are in different postures and it is difficult to get meaningful measurements common to all of them. Since the facial measurements are common to all, the measurements are standardized by reckoning the length of face to be twelve units, corresponding to the 12 *angulas* of the canons.

9.2 ICONOMETRIC MEASUREMENTS

Random samples of 50 carvings from the monument at Belur, fifty-five carvings from Halebid and 19 figures from Somnathpur are considered for the present study.

Point-to-point measurements were made by one of the authors using anthropometric instruments on each sculpture. The data consist of seventeen facial measurements [17] from each of more than 120 sculptures. The facial measurements considered are total face-length, morphological face-length, nose-length, nose-to-chin distance, nose-breadth, lip-length, lip-breadth, eye-length, eye-breadth, face-breadth (excluding ears), breadth measurements taken across forehead, subnasale and across lips, subnasale arc, chin arc and neck arc. All measurements are standardized with respect to face-length and the number of variables considered for analysis was reduced to sixteen.

9.3 CLUSTER ANALYSIS

Cluster analysis is used for discovering related groups or clusters with complex data [18] and calculations involve comparison of objects pair by pair. Any clustering procedure starts with some proximity measure between every pair of objects belonging to a given data set. Proximity measures are often numerical values assigned to describe the closeness, or alternatively, distance between two objects. Some of the measures commonly used are the Euclidean distance, product moment correlation coefficient and Minkowski's measures [19, 20]. Mahalanobis'D^2 is also a distance measure that can be used to group individuals. Roy and Adikari [21] have used this measure to cluster twelve ethnic groups of people from the United Provinces based on nine anthropometric measurements. We have used Euclidean distance to group individual carvings and the Mahalanobis'D^2 to group the Hoysala monuments.

Clustering procedure can be classified as hierarchical and non-hierarchical types [22, 23]. The commonly used hierarchical clustering techniques are the single linkage and the complete linkage. Agglomerative clustering using the concept of mutual nearest neighbour proposed by Gowda and Krishna [24] is also a hierarchical clustering.

Among the various non-hierarchical clustering methods, MacQueen's K-means [25] is suitable for our data [26].

9.4 CLUSTERING TECHNIQUES FOR THE PRESENT STUDY

The authors have made use of single and complete linkages and Krishna's method to cluster the Hoysala monuments. Assuming that the samples are taken from multivariate normal populations, an attempt is made to identify various groups based on Mahalanobis' distance between different groups [Table 9.1].

From the group constellation and from the dendrograms, it is clear that all the three monuments stand out separately. Three methods are used to ascertain the real or natural groups and all the three methods yield the same type of clusters. These results are further verified by way of obtaining discriminant analysis.

Table 9.1 *Mahalanobis' distance between the facial proportions of carvings of different Hoysala monuments*

	Belur	Halebid	Somnathpur
Belur	–	6.729	12.785
Halebid	6.729	–	16.219
Somnathpur	12.785	16.219	–

9.5 DISCRIMINANT ANALYSIS AND MISCLASSIFICATION RATES

The existence of various groups among the carvings of the Hoysala monuments has already been established with the aid of cluster analysis. Discriminant analysis is used to determine how distinct these groups are. The authors also made an attempt to assign all the carvings that are used to obtain the discriminant functions, to one of the groups under consideration. Fisher's discriminant functions [27] and the misclassification rates are obtained for the data and presented in Table 9.2.

Table 9.2 *Discriminant functions for the Hoysala monuments*

Variables	BLR-HLB	BLR-SMP	HLB-SMP
MFLN: Morphological face-length	- 1.82	1.32	3.15
NSLN: Nose-length	2.13	- 0.69	- 3.37
NCHN: Nose-to-chin distance	1.71	- 1.34	0.30
NSBR: Nose-breadth	4.99	3.54	- 7.08
EYLN: Eye-length	- 1.10	- 0.64	0.47
EYBR: Eye-breadth	8.47	1.15	10.12
LPLN: Lip-length	0.08	- 1.13	0.26
LPBR: Lip-breadth	5.77	11.20	1.78
FBNE: Face-breadth without ear	2.51	5.13	- 3.98
FBAF: Face-breadth (forehead)	2.28	2.55	10.80
FBAS: Face-breadth (subnasale)	- 1.34	- 5.54	- 5.79
FBAL: Face-breadth (lips)	- 1.83	- 4.80	- 1.12
FNAC: Frontal arc	0.57	0.22	- 0.79
SBAC: Subnasale arc	- 0.48	- 2.30	- 0.75
CNAC: Chin arc	- 0.87	- 0.50	- 3.33
NKAC: Neck arc	1.69	2.00	3.83
Misclassification rates (in %)	10.91	3.64	4.00

If the facial proportions of the three monuments do not differ from one another one would expect a high misclassification rate. The results do not exhibit such a trend. Low misclassification rates between monuments indicate that the facial proportions of the three monuments do differ significantly from one another.

These results are in conformity with the conclusion drawn already based on cluster analytic techniques. This led us to study the characteristics that make the carvings distinct making use of analysis of variance and *t*-test.

9.6 ANALYSIS OF VARIANCE AND *t*-TEST

To test the hypothesis that the mean proportions of the carvings of different monuments are equal, analysis of variance is carried out and *t*-statistic values are computed to test the equality of means of a characteristic for a pair of monuments. These tests ultimately end up with mean proportions of the face that make monuments differ from one another.

The mean values and the standard deviations of the various facial proportions are presented in Table 9.3. The *F*-statistic and *t*-test values are listed in Table 9.4.

Table 9.3 *Mean values and standard deviations of the facial proportions of sculptures of the Hoysala period*

Variables	Belur	Halebid	Somnathpur
Face-length	12.000	12.000	12.000
MFLN	8.369(0.476)	8.142(0.436)	8.539(0.358)
NSLN	4.422(0.401)	4.165(0.330)	4.402(0.318)
NCHN	3.963(0.276)	3.957(0.312)	4.113(0.467)
NSBR	2.943(0.311)	2.554(0.218)	2.842(0.434)
EYLN	3.743(0.491)	3.734(0.411)	4.041(0.435)
EYBR	1.131(0.195)	0.849(0.178)	1.161(0.159)
LPLN	4.106(0.371)	3.910(0.328)	4.222(0.505)
LPBR	1.707(0.172)	1.539(0.127)	1.538(0.230)
FBNE	11.462(0.802)	11.464(0.636)	12.556(0.772)
FBAF	10.865(0.801)	10.963(0.659)	11.501(0.836)
FBAS	10.938(0.810)	10.996(0.644)	12.309(0.683)
FBAL	10.458(0.810)	10.524(0.646)	11.838(0.710)
FNAC	21.439(1.864)	20.477(1.556)	23.450(1.712)
SBAC	19.823(1.777)	19.046(1.611)	22.591(1.784)
CNAC	22.045(1.659)	21.249(1.554)	23.934(1.724)
NKAC	22.504(1.629)	21.668(1.554)	24.270(1.733)

Table 9.4 *Analysis of variance and student's t-test values for the difference between the mean values of carvings of different Hoysala monuments*

Variables	*F*-value	BLR-HLB	BLR-SMP	HLB-SMP
MFLN	6.397*	2.574*	1.424*	3.272*
NSLN	7.058*	3.584*	0.198	2.403*
NCHN	1.737	0.086	1.712	1.752
NSBR	21.961*	6.532*	1.240	3.512*
EYLN	3.519*	0.105	2.445*	2.491*
EYBR	36.751*	7.807*	0.590	6.243
LPLN	5.814*	2.614*	1.133	3.015*
LPBR	15.182*	5.086*	3.768*	0.033
FBNE	17.375*	0.017	5.529*	5.447*
FBAF	5.020*	0.659	3.132*	2.614*
FBAS	26.827*	0.404	6.993*	6.612*
FBAL	26.699*	0.459	6.993*	6.572*
FNAC	21.303*	2.823*	4.527*	6.517*
SBAC	28.953*	2.292*	5.997*	7.583*
CNAC	18.262*	2.469*	4.305*	6.041*
NKAC	17.211*	2.553*	4.056*	5.856*

*Note: * indicates significance at 5% level.*

Compared to the carvings of the Halebid temple, the carvings of Belur temple have broader noses, thicker lips and wider eyes. The carvings of Belur and of Somnathpur temples differ significantly in breadth measurements of the face, eye-length and lip-breadth. Carvings at Belur have elongated faces compared to sculptures at Somnathpur. Almost all facial characteristics of the carvings of Somnathpur are different from those of the Halebid monument. Somnathpur have broader faces, longer noses and thicker lips.

This analysis clearly indicates the facial characteristics that distinguish the three monuments. After making a comparative study of the three monuments, we turn our attention to study the monuments individually. This study may reveal the existence of several types of faces in each monument.

9.7 CARVINGS OF BELUR, HALEBID AND SOMNATHPUR MONUMENTS

The *k*-means clustering technique is applied to the data on facial proportions of carvings of Belur, Halebid and Somnathpur. The number of clusters obtained in each monument and the cluster centroids are presented in Table 9.5. The optimum number of clusters is obtained based upon the minimum overall *F*-ratio.

It has been found that there are four natural clusters obtained for the data on Belur monument. There are four clusters for the Halebid monument and five clusters for the data on Somnathpur sculptures. From this analysis we conclude that there are four different types of faces represented in the carving of the Belur temple; five different types in the sculptures of the Somnathpur monument and four different facial types among the sculptures of the Halebid monument.

Table 9.5 *Clusters and their ceutroids*

Variables:		MFLN	NSLN	NCHN	NSBR	EYLN	EYBR	LPLN	LPBR
	1.	8.18	4.28	3.90	2.82	3.73	1.13	3.84	1.67
Belur	2.	8.32	4.39	3.95	2.88	3.17	1.11	4.09	1.70
(4)	3.	8.42	4.48	3.96	3.04	3.73	1.14	4.20	1.68
	4.	8.95	4.67	4.21	3.14	4.12	1.27	4.35	2.04
	1.	8.30	4.03	4.00	2.44	3.53	0.81	3.73	1.53
Halebid	2.	8.22	4.28	2.92	2.63	3.78	0.88	3.99	1.57
(4)	3.	8.06	4.15	3.89	2.53	3.86	0.82	3.93	1.52
	4.	8.68	4.40	4.15	2.86	4.01	1.04	4.33	1.55
	1.	8.00	4.20	3.60	2.80	4.20	1.40	3.40	1.20
Somnathpur	2.	8.40	4.21	4.02	2.48	3.83	1.09	3.89	1.63
(5)	3.	8.49	4.27	4.22	2.92	3.98	1.09	4.39	1.42
	4.	8.80	4.87	3.93	3.20	4.14	1.12	4.70	1.62
	5.	8.75	4.55	4.39	3.03	4.32	1.32	4.35	1.57
Variables		**FBNE**	**FBAF**	**FBAS**	**FBAL**	**FNAC**	**SBAC**	**CNAC**	**NKAC**
	1.	10.66	10.22	10.10	9.68	20.40	17.51	19.39	19.80
Belur	2.	11.33	10.55	10.87	10.41	20.28	19.06	21.60	22.17
(4)	3.	11.77	11.29	11.19	10.69	22.57	21.07	23.29	23.70
	4.	12.70	12.13	12.19	11.51	25.12	23.65	24.49	24.71
	1.	10.90	10.37	10.48	10.06	19.22	17.43	19.82	20.28
Halebid	2.	11.67	11.23	11.14	10.63	20.86	18.89	20.89	21.28
(4)	3.	11.62	11.11	11.15	10.65	21.07	20.24	22.32	22.77
	4.	12.56	12.03	12.12	11.67	22.25	22.02	24.55	25.02
	1.	11.40	10.80	11.20	10.80	19.00	18.60	21.60	22.00
Somnathpur	2.	11.91	10.76	11.85	11.41	23.32	21.76	22.39	22.61
(5)	3.	12.64	11.45	12.27	11.73	24.17	22.14	23.57	24.04
	4.	12.82	11.83	12.39	11.94	22.49	22.81	25.01	25.38
	5.	13.51	12.60	13.26	12.80	25.01	25.24	26.50	26.78

Carvings belonging to the first cluster of the Belur monument have elongated faces and the objects of the fourth cluster have broader faces. Similarly, if comparison is made between clusters using the mean values of the lip-lengths, one could find a lot of variation for the different. clusters. Sculptures of the Halebid monument have more or less round faces and the faces of the Somnathpur have wide variations. The differences found in the facial proportions of carvings of the three monuments could be attributed to possible number of sculptors who had worked on these monuments.

9.8 CONCLUSION

The authors have used computer methods to answer many interesting questions in Indian art history. With reference to Hoysala monuments of the twelfth and thirteenth centuries A.D., the average facial proportions of sculptures on three monuments, the Channakesava temple at Belur, the Hoysalesvara temple at Halebid and Kesava temple at Somnathpur has been determined. It has been found that these monuments differ in facal characteristics one from the other. A detailed study of the carvings found each monument, clearly indicates that there are various types of facial proportions of these carvings.

Application of computer methods in the analysis of sculptures remains an exciting field in India, new methods are being developed by the authors to answer old questions.

References

1. C A Murthy and D Dutta Majumder (1983) Clusters-some ideas on a theoretical framework, *Proc int Conf Syst Man. Cybernet,* 577 – 580.
2. L Narasimhachar (1976) *Guide to Halebid* Government of Karnataka, Mysore.
3. L, Narasimhachar (1975) *Belur* Government of Karnataka, Mysore.
4. C Sivaramamurthy (1977) *The art of India* Harry N Abrams Inc., New York.
5. R Benjamin (1967) *The Art and Architecture of India.* Penguin Books, London.
6. E Guralnick (1976) The proportions of some archaic Greek sculp-tured figures: a computer analysis, *Comp Humanit* **10** (3) 153 – 169.
7. E Guralnick (1978) The proportions of *Kouroi Am J Archaeol* **82**, 461 – 472.
8. S Govindaraju (1982) *Computer Analysis of Measurements of the Pallava Sculptures of South India,* Ph.D. Dissertation, Univ. Chennai.

9. G Siromoney, M Bagavandas and S Govindaraju (1980) An application of component analysis to the study of south Indian sculptures. *Comp Humanit* **14** (1) 29 – 37.

10. G Siromoney, M Bagavandas and S Govindaraju (1980) An iconometric study of Pallava sculptures. *Kalakshetra Qly* **3** (2) 7 – 15.

11. G Siromoney, S Govindaraju and M Bagavandas (1982) Iconometric study of Pallava somaskandas. *Kalakshetra Qly* **5** (1) 31 – 38.

12. G Siromoney, S Govindaraju and M Bagavandas (1985) Temple carvings of southern India *Perspect Comput* **5** (1) 34 – 43.

13. M Bagavandas (1982) *Statistical Analysis of Measurements of South Indian Sculptures,* Ph.D. Dissertation, Univ. Chennai.

14. G Siromoney, S Govindaraju and M Bagavandas (1981) Computer analysis of early Chola and Pandya sculptures: an iconometric study *Proc V int Tamil Conf* Madurai, 3 – 16.

15. G Siromoney, S Govindaraju and M Bagavandas and R Chandrasekaran (1984) Cluster analysis of facial proportions of south Indian sculptures. *Proc ISI Golden Jubilee int Conf Adv Infor Sci Technol I Patt Recog Digit Tech Ed.* D Dutta Majumder, Calcutta, 137 – 146.

16. T A Gopinatha Rao (1971) *Elements of Hindu Iconography,* I and II. Indological Book House, Delhi.

17. I P Singh and M K Bhasin (1968) *Anthropometry* Bharathi Bhavan, Delhi.

18. J A Hartigan (1975) *Clustering Algorithms* John Wiley and Sons, Inc., New York.

19. R M Cormack (1971) A review of classification *J R Statist Soc* **A-134** 321 – 367.

20. P R Sokal and P H A Sneath (1963) *Principles of Numerical Taxonomy* W. H. Freeman and Co., San Fransisco.

21. J Roy and A K Adikari (1977) Cluster analysis as a tool for Pattern Recognition, *Proc ISI Symp Digital Tech Patt Recog* Calcutta.

22. M R Anderberg (1973) *Cluster Analysis for Applications.* Academic Press, New York, 1973.

23. B S Everitt (1974) *Cluster Analysis* Halstead Press, London.

24. K Chidananda Gowda and G Krishna (1978) Agglomerative clustering using the concept of mutual nearest neighbourhood. *Patt Recog* **10** 105 – 112.

25. J B MacQueen(1967) Some methods for classification and analysis of multivariate observations, *Proc Berkeley Symp Math Statist*

Probab (Eds) L M Lee Cam and J Neyman Univ. California Press, Berkeley 282 – 297.

26. G Siromoney, M Bagavandas and S Govindaraju (1983) Iconometric analysis of the sculptures of the Dharmaraja Ratha, *SRINIDHIH: Perspectives in Indian Archaeology, Art and Culture,* Shri K R Srinivasan Fetschrift (Ed.) K V Raman, New Era Publications, Chennai, 137 – 150.
27. R A Fisher (1936) The use of multiple measurements in taxonomic problems *Ann Eugen* 7, 179 – 188.

10

Comparative Study on Classical Statistical and Fuzzy Tools in Medical Diagnosis

Zaki Ahmed Azmi and Mohamed Alaa El Din Younis[1]

ABSTRACT

Both mathematical classical theories and theory of fuzzy sets are fairly new fields in their applications in the field of medical diagnosis.

In the application of the classical methods like discriminant function, Bayesian cluster methods we have to ignore some variables which are not abnormality (0,1).

In fact both symptoms and diseases are treated as fuzzy sets type 1 and type 2.

The present approach is an attempt to explain the role of fuzzy set in medical diagnosis in practical cases comparing with classical tools like: "Blood count-low red blood cell count-low hemoglobin etc..."

Keywords: Medical Diagnosis; Discriminant Function; Bayesian Cluster Method; Fuzzy Sets; Pattern Recognition.

10.1 INTRODUCTION

A pattern recognition task is concerned with a collection of objects or possible objects such as speech sounds, hand written characters, or, as in this case, symptom complexes.

The collection of possible objects is called the universe. A pattern is a subset of the universe.

In our application in medical diagnosis the universe is the set of all possible symptom complexes, a pattern is a subset of the universe composed of all symptom complexes caused by a particular disease. An object is a particular element of the universe, medical diagnosis is then a process of identifying a patient's symptom complex as belonging to a particular disease pattern.

The representation of symptom of complexes and feature extraction are preliminary steps to the actual classification of the symptom complexes into disease classes, and are called preprocessing procedures. A clinician diagnoses with the aid of his medical knowledge, accumulated experience and judgement. A computer diagnoses with the aid of stored medical information (including the medical data of patients), and programmed mathematical algorithms. Some of the mathematical techniques used to this end are Bayesian, conditional

[1] Department of Statistics, Faculty of Economics, Cairo University, Egypt.

probability likelihood ratio, clustering methods, linear decision functions, Chebychev polynomial discriminant method, sequential methods, and others.

Many of these techniques presently employed in medical diagnosis can be immediately translated into fuzzy set language. Given a symptom spaces (possibly n symptoms, each of which is expressible on the real line R throughout its total possible range of values, and hence SCR^n, it is desirable to identify if possible, given disease classes with definite subsets of R^n. In practice, these disease classifications tend to overlap and have "fuzzy" boundaries. Hence, identifying diseases with fuzzy subsets of R^n seems natural.

10.2 TYPOLOGY OF STATISTICAL MODELS

The statistical models may be grouped into three general types:

1. Probabilistic
2. Geometric
3. Heuristic

The Bayesian model, the likelihood ratio model, the dynamic sequential model and the sequential Bayesian model all use probabilities in the diagnostic process.

The clustering models are among those models that utilize the geometric concepts of space and distance.

Finally, the heuristic models try to translate a physician's diagnostic methods into computer program[2]. By decomposing the model into sectors and subsectors (sub-systems) to facilitate the solution of the model.

(Probabilistic Model) Bayesian Probability Method

Perhaps the most widely known screening technique thus far employed in computer diagnostic centers about Baye's Theorem is:

$$P(D/S) = P(S/D) \cdot P(D)/(P/S),$$

where $P(A/B)$ is the usual statistical notation for the conditional probability of A given B. $P(A/B) = P(A \cap B)/P(B)$.

If we are presented with a patient exhibiting symptom S, Bayes Theorem says that the Probability that this patient has disease D is precisely = tb the Probability of a patient in the given population having disease D exhibiting symptom S times the Probability of disease D

---

[2] By decomposing the model into sectors and subsectors (sub-systems) to facilitate the solution of the model.

occurring in this population divided by the Probability of symptom S appearing in the population.

If the diseases of D_i, ... D_m are disjoint and $\sum_{i=l}^{m} P(D_i) = 1$ for a given population, $P(S)$ may be rewritten as $P(S) = \sum_{i=l}^{m} P(D_i).\ P(S/D_i)$. Bayes' Theorem then becomes $P(D_k / S) = P(S / D_k)\ P(D_k) / \sum_{i=l}^{m} P(D_i).\ P(S/D_i)$.

The only information needed, then, to compute all of the probabilities of the various diseases given a fixed symptom complex S, $P(D_k/S)$ for $k = 1, \ldots, m$, are the probabilities of having the diseases for a fixed population, $P(D_k)$, $k = 1, \ldots, m$, and the probabilities of a person having the diseases exhibiting the symptom complex S, $P(S/D_k)$ for $k = 1, \ldots, m$.

$P(D/S)$, the percentage of people having symptom S in a population also having disease D, is generally difficult to measure and may depend on such variables as season and geography.

The percentage of people with disease D who also having symptoms[3] P(S/D) can be estimated from hospital records.

Applications of the Bayesian Approach—Bayesian methods have been widely applied to various medical problems and have had mixed results.

A jaundiced patient whose disease fails to differentiate after a month of observation can have one of the six diseases which mimic each other closely.

A principal task of the physician is to determine whether or not jaundice is caused by an extrahepatic obstruction. If so, surgical intervention becomes necessary, if not, surgery introduces an undesirable mortality risk.

It was found that physicians at best, through non-computer aided techniques, are able to make the correct surgical versus non-surgical decision with somewhat less than 90% accuracy. A computer tested program making use of Bayes' Theorem in the form

$$P(D_i / S_i, \ldots, S_n) = \frac{P(D_i).P(S_i / D_i, \ldots)\ (S_n / D_i)}{\sum_{k=1}^{m} P(D_k).P(S_l / D_k)\ , \ldots\ldots,\ P(S_n / D_k)}$$

for disjoint, all inclusive disease categories D_i, ..., D_m and assumed conditionally independent symptoms S_i, ..., S_n was able to make not only

3 $P(S/D)$ can be estimated from hospital records.

the correct surgical versus non-surgical diagnosis with 98% accuracy but was also able to correctly identify the specific disease causing the patient's jaundice with 77% accuracy.

If the symptoms are highly conditionally dependent or if the distribution of a given symptom is not accurately estimated, use of these approximations will of course make the Bayesian analysis yield poor results. The accuracy of this method can be no better than the accuracy of the assumptions.

(Geometric Model) Clustering

A more intuitive approach to the classification of diseases is a geometric method where symptom complex is represented by a point or a vector in an *N*-dimensional space. It is a plausible assumption that symptom pattern points of a particular disease tend to cluster together. Conceptionally, it would then be possible to partition the *N*-dimensional space into subspaces, each containing a cluster of symptom pattern points of one disease. If such a partition can be defined, then by the geometric location of patient's symptom complex the disease may be identified. This geometric classification method is called clustering.

Methods to Determine Clusters - If the number of clusters (or disease to be identified) is known *a priori,* then an iterative method may be used to classify the pattern points.

Let D_j^k be the cluster center of the k-th cluster at the j-th iteration.

Let D^{-k} be the cluster of the k-th cluster defined at the j-th iteration.

A two-step interaction is defined by the following procedure:

(i) Assign one of the pattern points S_i to the one cluster, the cluster center of which is closest to it, i.e.,

$$S_i \varepsilon D_j^k \; iff \quad d(S_i, D_j)^k = \min d\,(S_i, D_j),$$

where $i = 1 \ldots, K, K$ being the known number of clusters.

(ii) Define the cluster centers for the $(j + 1)$-th iteration.

$$D_{j+1}^k \rightarrow \sum_{S_i \varepsilon \; D_{i_j}^k} d(S_i, D_{j+1}^{-k}) = \min \sum_{S_i \varepsilon \; D_j^k} (S_i, S_r) \;\; S_i \varepsilon D_j^k$$

Clustering-application Examples in Medical Diagnosis

Templeton [1] employed clustering as one of the techniques to distinguish normal and abnormal hearts. The diagnosis of each abnormal case was verified by autopsy, surgery or by cardiac catheterization and angiography. Some normal cases had abnormal cardiac catheterizations.

The remaining cases were completely free of any signs or symptoms of heart disease.

750 cases were used for training and 157 cases for testing; there were 13 different types of heart diseases or normal hearts.

A radiologist picked out 25 roentgenographic signs and 3 clinical variables (age, sex, cyanosis) for a total of 28 measurements. The differential diagnosis of 13 disease classes has an accuracy level of 74%. When the diagnosis was made between normal and abnormal cases, an accuracy level of 98% was reached.

For each disease class D_k, consider 2 co-centric hyperspheres (n-dimensional spheres) of unequal radii T_{1k} and T_{2k} centered at the mode of D_k. New pattern points may be classified on the basis of their locations with respect to the aforementioned hyperspheres as follows:

The threshold T_{1k} (disease class D_k) is selected to be the average Euclidean distance between each training pattern point S_{ik} in disease class D_k and its nearest neighbours in class D_k. Thus

$$T_{1k} = \frac{\sum_{J=1}^{N_k} \min d\,(S_{ik}, S_{jk})}{N_k} \qquad i \neq j,$$

where S_{ik} is the i-th pattern point of Class D_k.

(S_{ik}, S_{jk}) is the Euclidean distance between the i-th and j-th pattern points of Class D_k and N_k is the number of training pattern points in Class D_k.

The threshold T_{2k} is selected to be the average Euclidean distance between all pairwise combinations of training pattern points in Class D_k:

$$T_{2k} = \frac{\sum_{J=1}^{N_{k-1}} \sum_{J=i+1}^{N_k} d\,(S_{ik}, S_{jk})}{\binom{N_k}{2}}$$

Chebychev Polynomial Discriminant Method

In the Chebychev polynomial discriminant method non-linear surfaces as well as linear ones may be generated to separate subsets of R^n identified with particular symptom classes associated with a given disease. If we are to generate a surface separating disease D_i from disease D_2 by this method, we need to know the *a priori* probabilities of having the diseases $P(D_i)$ and $P(D_2)$ together with cost function C_{ij} associated with misclassifying a person having disease D_i into disease class D_j, and conditional probability density functions $f_i\,(S_i, ..., S_n) = P\,(S_i, ..., S_n\,/D_i)$. Define $F = R^n \rightarrow R$ by,

$$F\ (S_i,\ldots, S_n) = f_i\ \ (S_i,\ldots, S_n) - \left(\frac{P(D_2)\cdot C_{21}}{P(D_1)\cdot C_{12}}\right)\cdot f_2\ \ (S_i,\ldots, S_n).$$

$F(S) = 0$ then defines a hypersurface in R^n which is called the Chebychev polynomial discriminant surface separating disease class D_2 from disease Class D_1.

If $F\ (S_i,\ \ldots,\ S_n) < 0$ the diagnosis is D_1 while if $F\ (S_i,\ \ldots,\ S_n) > 0$ diagnosis is D_2. If we have m diseases we will have $\left(\frac{m}{2}\right)$ such discriminant functions. This Chebychev polynomial method in effect is Bayesian with an additional cost factor thrown in. Those values $S = (S_i,\ \ldots,\ S_n)$ for which $P(S/D_i).C_{ji} > P(S/D_j)P(D_j).C_{ij}$ will be diagnosed as D_i over disease D_j.

An ordering of the possible diseases according to this measure then provides an ordering of the diagnosis. If we assume costs of misdiagnosis are equal in all cases, $C_{ij} = C_{ji}$, then this method is equivalent to Bayesian analysis.

$$\left(\frac{P(S/D_i).P(D_i)}{P(S)}\right) > \left(\frac{P(S/D_j).P(D_j)}{P(S)}\right) \text{ if}$$

$$P(S/D_i).P(D_i) > P(S/D_j).P(D_j)$$

for $P(S) \neq 0$, which implies disease D_i will be diagnosed over disease D_j.

Hence, if independence assumptions are forgotten, Bayesian analysis can be regarded as a type of discriminant, or clusters analysis. One requires much more information about the diseases for this method, however, than either the linear discriminant analysis or "nearest neighbour" analysis.

As is the case for Bayesian analysis, values of $P(S_i,\ \ldots,\ S_n\ /\ D_i)$ and $P(D_i)$ are needed. For the same reasons as before, it may be desirable to assume conditional independence of symptoms.

10.3 TRANSLATION OF METHODS USED IN MEDICAL DIAGNOSIS TO FUZZY SET LANGUAGE

General Approach

Many of the techniques presently employed in medical diagnosis can be immediately translated into fuzzy set language. Given a symptom space S (possibly n symptoms, each of which is expressible on the real line R throughout its total possible range of values, and hence ($S^C R^n$), it is desirable to identify, if possible, given disease classes with definite subsets of R^n. In practice, these disease classifications tend to overlap and have "fuzzy" boundaries.

Hence, identifying diseases with fuzzy subsets of R^n seems natural.

Definition of the Disease Membership Functions: Bayesian Approach

The problem of defining the membership function M_D for disease D in Symptom Space S is similar to the problem of separating disease clusters from each other.

In the fuzzy way of looking at disease the boundaries defined between disease clusters are no longer required to be "sharp".

Disease clusters need not be disjoint, but may have edges which merge. Assuming good Bayesian values can be obtained for the probability indices $P(D_i/S_i, ..., S_n)$ at each point $(S_i, ..., S_n)$ S, assignment of $\mu_{D_i}(S_i, ..., S_n) = P(D_i / S_i\ S_n)$ is entirely reasonable.

In fact calling $P(D_i/S_{i,}..., S_n)$ the value of membership function μ_{Di} at $(S_i, ..., S_n)$ in R_n is much more reasonable than calling it a probability, since the manner of estimating $P(D_i / S_i, ..., S_n)$ is very inexact.

Physicians' estimating based on their own medical knowledge have, also been used in computing $P(D_i / S_i, ..., S_n)$ from $P(S_i, ..., S_n / D_i)$ and $P(D_i)$, so these estimates could be used with equal validity for, $\mu_{Di}(S_i, ..., S_n)$.

Incorporation of a cost factor into the membership function μ_{Di} of D_i can be approached in a manner similar to the Chebychev polynomial discriminant method if we require that $0 \le C_{ij} \le 1, V, \forall\ i, j$. Then we may define

$$\mu_{Di}(S_i, ..., S_n)\, P(D_i / S_i, ..., S_n) / C_i = \frac{P(S_i, ..., S_n / D_i).P(D_i)}{\sum_{i=1}^{m} P(D_i).(S_i, ..., S_n / D_j).C_i}$$

where C_i can be taken as the average cost of misdiagnosis of a patient as $D_i, C_i = \sum_{J=1}^{m} C_{ji} / m$ or if preferred, as the greatest possible $C_i = \max C_{ji}$.

If the cost of misdiagnosis is not incorporated into the membership function for D_i, it should be used later in comparing the desirability of various possible diagnosis suggested by the membership functions.

A Clustering Criterion for Fuzzy Sets

The following approach is proposed to the clustering problem for the medical diagnosis situation. This approach defines the membership functions at the sample points depending on both *(i)* how many sample points belonging to the same disease lie "close" to the sample point and *(ii)* how many points belonging to different diseases lie "close" to the sample points? Let it be a metrix on the sample space SCR^n and C a positive constant.

(a) The affinity of point P_{ij} for a disease category D_k, to be denoted α_{ijk}, is given by

$$\alpha_{ijk} = \sum \frac{1}{(d\ (P_{ij}, P_{ki}))^{C_{+1}}}$$

(b) The clustering measure of point P_{ij}, to be denoted α_{ij}, is just the affinity of point P_{ij} for its own disease category D_i given by

$$\alpha_{ij} = \alpha_{iji} = \sum_{1} \frac{1}{(d\ (P_{ij}, P_{i1}))^{C_{+1}}}$$

(c) The average affinity of point P_{ij} to diseases other than D_i to be denoted B_{ij} is given by

$$B_{ij} = \sum_{k = i} B_{ijk} / (m - 1).$$

Then α_{ij} is a measure of how many other points in disease category D_i lie "near" to P_{ij} according to the metric and B_{ij} in a like manner average the closeness of P_{ij} to points in other disease categories.

10.4 COMPARISON OF METHODS

How would the fuzzified clustering method developed under 'Chebychev Polynomial Discriminant Method' be expected to differ from the more classical Bayesian and clustering approaches to medical pattern recognition? As with the traditional statistical approaches, no "known" relationships between symptom complexes and diseases are incorporated into this fuzzified approach. Rather, the data are expected to reflect all the relationships.

In other words, all of these methods are ways of treating data, independent of "knowledge". A "marriage" of these two approaches would seem desirable, but is as yet unexplored.

There have not been any empirical studies examining how this fuzzified clustering approach compares in actual diagnostic situations to Bayesian and classical clustering methods. Even so several global statements can be made as to when this fuzzified approach might be the most useful in analyzing medical data.

As pointed out, this conditional independence assumption is frequently made in Bayesian analysis to reduce the volume of data analysis required, although it is rarely, theoretically justified. In this respect, clustering method might be expected to yield better results than

Bayesian analysis with assumed conditional independence of symptoms when this independence assumption is unrealistic.

Even if the assumption of symptom independence is not made, the Bayesian approach usually makes other assumptions which have varying degrees of validity depending on the particular study.

A large advantage of the fuzzy clustering method described in Sec. 10.3 for such cases is that no assumptions about the global shape of the data is assumed. At a local level, a choice of shape of the membership function through each sample point is made.

The fuzzy clustering method will result in a very "bumpy" membership function locally, the shape of each bump a matter of choice (as the distribution in Bayesian analysis is a matter of choice). But the global (shape of the membership function is a much more accurate reflection of the actual data in the fuzzy clustering method than in the Bayesian method.

Another disadvantage of Bayesian method is that rare diseases, i.e., diseases with low $P(D)$, are often malrepresented.

The fuzzy clustering method which does not employ $P(D)$, should better represent data pertaining to rare diseases. Theoretically, the fact that Bayesian analysis takes account of the prevalence of diseases $P(D)$ and of symptoms $P(S)$ in a population, should give it an advantage over other methods.

In reality these probabilities are difficult to estimate and may actually be a large source of statistical error for the Bayesian method.

The fuzzy clustering method may help in analyzing medical data. In assessing the membership of a patient in disease D_i, this method not only takes account of how many sample points belonging to disease D_i are "close" to a patient's symptoms, but also the distance of the patient's symptom to sample points belonging to other disease categories.

The fuzzy clustering method, then can offer a more accurate reflection of medical data than either Bayesian or traditional clustering methods. This fact can be advantageous when the data assume unusual "shape" or when boundaries between disease classes are not "sharp".

References

1. R E Bellman, R Kalaba and L A Zadeh (1966) Abstraction and pattern classification *J math Anal Appl* **13**, 1 – 7.

2. J C Bezdek (1974) Cluster validity with fuzzy sets J *cybern* **3**(3) 58 – 73.

3. J C Bezdek (1976) Feature selection for binary data: medical diagnosis with fuzzy sets. *Proc AFIPS nat Compat Conf Expo* (Ed. S Winkler) pp.1057 – 1068.

4. D Dubois and H Prade (1980) *Fuzzy Sets and Systems. Theory and Applications* Academic Press, New York.
5. A Kandel (1982) Fuzzy Techniques In Pattern Recognition John Wiley, New York.
6. A Kaufmann (1975) *Theory of Fuzzy Subsets* Academic Press, New York.
7. C V Negotia and D A Ralescu (1975) *Application of fuzzy sets to System Analysis* John Wiley, New York.
8. M Shimura (1975) Applications of fuzzy sets theory to pattern recognition *J Jaace* **19,** 243 – 248.
9. L A Zadeh, Sun-Fu King and M Shimura (1975) Fuzzy Sets and their Applications to Cognitive and Decision Processes Academic Press, New York.

11

Seed Point Extraction Using Fuzzy Measures: An Application to Clustering Vowel Sounds

S K Pal[1] and P K Pramanik[2]

ABSTRACT

The present paper demonstrates an application of the theory of fuzzy sets in determining the initial seed points in clustering. These were achieved through the application of index of fuzziness, entropy and π-ness. Two membership functions in R^n have been defined such that the fuzzy measures possess maximum value when the cross-over point/central point of the membership functions correspond to the points around which the data have tendency to cluster.

The effectiveness of the said algorithm is compared with that of extreme point approach. DYNOC algorithm is chosen to make this comparison with speech data as input. It has been observed that DYNOC converges with less number of iterations along with significant improvement of performance index than in case of extreme point approach.

Keywords: Seed Point Extraction; Fuzzy Sets; Clustering; Vowel Sounds; Dynamic Optical Cluster; DYNOC Algorithm.

11.1 INTRODUCTION

Partitioning a feature space into some homogeneous groupings is the aim of a clustering technique. The criteria of clustering may follow a heuristic scheme or may be based on the optimisation of certain performance index or the combination of both. It has been observed that overall performance of an iterative algorithm such as ISODATA, DYNOC, etc. depends greatly on the initial choice of cluster centres (seed points). Different methods of selecting such seed points include extreme point approach, graph-theoretic approach, thresholding, etc. [1].

When the clusters to be detected are not compact and well separated (i.e., boundaries are ill-defined) the fuzzy set theoretic representation has been found to provide a useful tool for cluster analysis. In such cases, it is more natural to assign each object to a cluster with a degree of cluster membership than it is done with classical set theory where each point may either belong to a cluster or not [2,3].

The present work demonstrates an application of the theory of fuzzy sets in determining the initial seed points in clustering. These were

[1] Electronics and Communication Sciences Unit, Indian Statistical Institute, Calcutta, India.

[2] Electronics Commission, National Informatic Centre, Jadavpur, Calcutta, India.

achieved through application of index of fuzziness, entropy, π-ness which measure the amount of fuzziness present in a set. In implementing these measures, two membership functions have been defined in R^n.

The effectiveness of the above said algorithm is demonstrated on a set of 871 speech data and is also compared with extreme point approach when DYNOC [9] is considered as a clustering tool.

11.2 FUZZY SETS

Definition

A fuzzy set A with its finite number of supporting elements $x_1, x_2, ..., x_{n_0}$ in the universe of discourse U is defined as

$$A = \{(\mu_A(x_i), x_i)\} \qquad i = 1, 2, ..., n_0,$$

where the membership function $\mu_A(x_i)$ having positive values in the interval [0,1] denotes the degree to which an event x_i may be a member of A. x_i is said to be a crossover point of A if $= \mu_A(x_i) = 0.5$.

Membership Functions Standard S-function is defined [4] as

$$S(x;\ a, b, c) = 0,\ x \le a \tag{1a}$$

$$= 2\left(\frac{x-a}{c-a}\right)^2,\ b \ge x \ge a \tag{1b}$$

$$= 1 - 2\left(\frac{x-a}{c-a}\right)^2,\ c \ge x \ge b \tag{1c}$$

$$= 1,\ x \ge c \tag{1d}$$

π-function as defined in terms of S-function is

$$\pi\ (x; b, c) = S(x;\ c-b,\ c-\left(\frac{b}{2}\right),\ c),\ x \le c \tag{2a}$$

$$= 1 - S(x;\ c,\ c + \left(\frac{b}{2}\right),\ c + b),\ x \ge c \tag{2b}$$

In $S(x;\ a, b, c)$, b is the crossover point i.e., $S(b;\ a, b, c) = 0.5$

In $\pi\ (x;\ b, c)$, b is the bandwidth i.e., the separation between the two crossover points of π-function. c is the central point at which $\pi = 1$.

S-and π functions represent the compatibility functions corresponding to fuzzy sets 'x is large' and 'x is c' respectively.

Let us now define two membership functions for $\chi \in R^n$. First one is

$$\hat{S}(x; b, \lambda) = \frac{1}{2}(1 - \|x - b\| / \lambda)^2 \tag{3a}$$

or

$$1 - \frac{1}{2}(1 - \|x - b\| / \lambda)^2, \ \|x - b\| \leq \lambda \tag{3b}$$

$$= 0 \text{ or } 1, \text{otherwise,}$$

where $\|\cdot\|$ denotes any norm in R^n, $\lambda > 0$ is said to be the radius of $\hat{S}(x; b, \lambda)$ and b is the crossover point. It is to be noted that equation (3) is a two valued (values being complementary) function.

The second one may be defined in terms of equation (3) as

$$\hat{\pi}(x; c, \lambda) = \text{Min } \hat{S}(x; y, \frac{\lambda}{2}), \ \frac{\lambda}{2} < \|x - c\| < \lambda \tag{4a}$$

$$= \text{Max } \hat{S}(x; y, \frac{\lambda}{2}), \ 0 < \|x - c\| \leq \frac{\lambda}{2}, \tag{4b}$$

where $\|y - c\| = \frac{\lambda}{2}$, Min $\hat{S}(x; y, \frac{\lambda}{2})$ implies the minimum of the two values of $\hat{S}$-function (equation 3) at the point x. Similarly, Max $\hat{S}(x; y, \frac{\lambda}{2})$ implies the maximum of the two values of $\hat{S}$-function at the point x. c is the central point i.e., $\hat{\pi}(c; c, \lambda) = 1$ and λ is the bandwidth. On simplification, (4) reduces to

$$\hat{\pi}(x; c, \lambda) = \frac{1}{2}(1 - 2\|x - y\|/\lambda)^2, \ \frac{\lambda}{2} \leq \|x - c\| \leq \lambda \tag{5a}$$

$$= 1 - \frac{1}{2}(1 - 2\|x - y\|/\lambda)^2, \ 0 < \|x - c\| < \frac{\lambda}{2} \tag{5b}$$

with $\|y - c\| = \frac{\lambda}{2}$.

Considering Euclidean norm,

$$\|x - y\| = \|x - c\| - \frac{\lambda}{2} \text{ if } \frac{\lambda}{2} \leq \|x - c\| \leq \lambda$$

$$= \frac{\lambda}{2} - \|x - c\| \text{ if } 0 \leq \|x - c\| \leq \frac{\lambda}{2} \tag{6}$$

Using equation (6), we can further reduce equation (5) to

$$\hat{\pi}(x; c, \lambda) = 2(1 - \|x - c\|/\lambda)^2, \frac{\lambda}{2} < \|x \ \ c\| < \lambda \tag{7a}$$

$$= 1 - 2\frac{\|x-c\|^2}{\lambda^2}, 0 < \|x-c\| < \frac{\lambda}{2} \tag{7b}$$

Fuzzy Measures

Index of fuzziness — Index of fuzziness of A having n_o supporting points is defined as [5]

$$\gamma(A) = \frac{2}{n_o^{1/k}} d(A, \mathbf{A}), \tag{8}$$

where d (A, $\mathbf{A}$) denotes the distance between A and its nearest ordinary set $\mathbf{A}$ such that $\mu_A(x_i) = 0$ if $\mu_A(x_i) \leq 0.5$ and 1 if $\mu_A(x_i) > 0.5$. $k = 1$ for linear distance and 2 for Euclidean distance.

When d *is* linear, we have

$$d(A, \mathbf{A}) = \sum_{i=l}^{n_o} |\mu_A(x_i) - \mu_{\mathbf{A}}(x_i)|$$

and accordingly linear index of fuzziness r_l (A) can be written as,

$$r_l(A) = \frac{2}{n_o} \sum_i |\mu_A(x_i) - \mu_{\mathbf{A}}(x_i)| \tag{9a}$$

$$= \frac{2}{n_o} \sum_i \mu_{A \cap \bar{A}}(x_i) \tag{9b}$$

$$d = \frac{2}{n_o} \sum_i \text{Min } (\mu_A(x_i), 1 - \mu_A(x_i)) \tag{9c}$$

Extension

Considering equation (3) for $x_i \in R^n$, we may write

$$r_l(A) = \frac{2}{n_o} \sum_i \text{Min } \mu_A(x_i), \tag{10}$$

where Min $\mu_A(x_i)$ implies the minimum of the two μ-values at the point x_i of $\hat{S}$ (equation 3).

Entropy — It is defined for the set A as [6]

$$H(A) = \left(\frac{1}{n_o \ln 2}\right) \sum_i S_n(\mu_A(x_i)), \; i = 1, 2, ..., n_0 \tag{11a}$$

where, $$S_n(x) = -\mu_A(x) \ln \mu_A(x) - (1 - \mu_A(x) \ln(1 - \mu_A(x)) \tag{11b}$$

Extension

For $x_i \in R^n$, we may write considering equation (3)

$$H(A) = \left(\frac{1}{n_o \ln 2}\right) \sum_i S_n\,(\mu_A(x_i)), \tag{12a}$$

where, $$S_n(\mu_A(x_i)) = -\,(\text{Min } \mu_A(x_i) \ln\,(\text{Min } \mu_A(x_i))$$

$$-\,(\text{Max } \mu_A(x_i) \ln\,(\text{Max } \mu_A(x_i)) \tag{12b}$$

Min $\mu_A(x_i)$ and Max $\mu_A(x_i)$ imply the minimum and maximum of the two μ- values at the point x_i of $\hat{S}$ function respectively.

Equations (9) and (11) measure the average amount of difficulty (ambiguity) that arises when one has to take decision, whether x_i would be considered a member of A or not.

These values lie in the interval [0,1] such that

$$\gamma(A) \text{ or } H(A) = 0 \text{ (minimum), when } \mu_A(x_i) = 0 \text{ or } 1 \text{ for all } i \tag{13a}$$

$$\gamma(A) \text{ or } H(A) = 1 \text{ (maximum), when } \mu_A(x_i) = 0.5 \text{ for all } i \tag{13b}$$

$$\gamma(A) = \gamma(\bar{A}) \text{ and } H(A) = H(\bar{A}) \tag{13c}$$

$$\gamma(A^*) \le \gamma(A) \text{ or } H(A^*) \le H(A) \tag{13d}$$

where A^* is a sharpened version of A such that $\mu^*_A(x_i) \ge \mu_A(x_i)$ for $\mu_A(x_i) \ge 0.5$ and $\mu^*_A(x_i) \le \mu_A(x_i)$ for $\mu_A(x_i) \le 0.5$. It follows that $\gamma(A)$ or $H(A)$ increases monotonically in the interval [0, 0.5] and decreases monotonically in [0.5, 1] with maximum value 1 at $\mu = 0.5$.

π -ness [7] — It is defined for the set A as

$$I(A) = \frac{1}{n_o} \sum_{i=1}^{n_o} \pi(x_i;\, b,\, c), \tag{14}$$

where $\pi(x_i;\, b,\, c)$ is defined by equation (2).

For $x \in R^n$, π-ness is defined as,

$$I(A) = \frac{1}{n_o} \sum_{i=l}^{n_o} \hat{\pi}(x_i;\, c,\, \lambda) \tag{15}$$

Concept of Fuzzy Sets in Extracting Seed Points

Let $X = \{X_1, X_2, ..., X_N\}$ be the set of N pattern points in n-dimensional ($n \ge 2$) feature space. We define fuzzy set associated with the set X as

$$X(b, \lambda) = \{\mu_{X(b,\lambda)}(X_i),\, X_i\},\ i = 1, 2, \ldots.., N, \tag{16}$$

where, $\mu_{X(b,\lambda)}(X_i) = \hat{S}(X_i; b, \lambda)$ or $\hat{\pi}(X_i; b, \lambda)$;

b corresponds to crossover point for $\hat{S}$ function and central point for $\hat{\pi}$ function. If we keep λ constant and change b we get different fuzzy sets i.e., changing b we can generate a class of fuzzy sets. From the expressions (3), (4), (10), (12), (15) and (13) we see that the contributions towards $\gamma\,(x\,(b, \lambda))$ or $H(X(b, \lambda))$ or $I(X(b, \lambda))$ are mostly from those points which are around b and it decreases as the points move away from b. In other words, if the number of points around b are more there will be greater number of points X_i having $\mu \cong 0.5, l \cong 1$ while using $\hat{S}$ function / $\hat{\pi}$ function (resulting in γ, H and $I \approx 1$) and less number of points having $\mu \cong 0$ or $l \cong 0$ while using $\hat{S}$ function / $\hat{\pi}$ function (resulting in γ, H and $l \cong 0$) thus increasing the value of $\gamma\,(X\,(b, \lambda))$ or $H(X(b, \lambda))$ or $I(X(b, \lambda))$. Therefore, the more the points from fuzzy set $X(b, \lambda)$ be compact around b, the greater would be its γ or H or I value and b can be considered as a seed point (centre of an initial cluster).

This suggests that modification of the cross-over point/central point b will result in variation of the measures $\gamma\,(X\,(b, \lambda))$, $H(X(b, \lambda))$ and $I(X(b, \lambda))$ and so a set of seed points $\{b\}$ may be estimated for which the corresponding fuzzy measures are locally maximum.

11.3 ALGORITHM FOR DETERMINING SEED POINTS USING FUZZY MEASURES

Let $X_1, X_2, \ldots, X_N$ be the N pattern points each of them having N number of properties i.e., samples are from n-dimensional feature space. Let l_i, u_i be the lower and upper bounds of the ith property of the sample. Let us break the space $(l_i, u_i) \times (l_2, u_2) \times, \ldots\ldots, (l_n, u_n)$ into L'' grid points where L is given by $\left(\dfrac{u_i - l_i}{d}\right)$ for a fixed i and d is some preassigned positive constant called grid width. Let b_i, $i = 1, 2, \ldots, L^n$ be the grid points.

Choosing λ suitably, calculate the fuzzy measures using any of the equations given below:

$$\gamma_l(X(b_i, \lambda)) = \frac{2}{N} \sum_{j=1}^{N} \text{Min}\ (\mu_{x(b_i, \lambda)}\ (X_j)); \tag{17a}$$

$$H\ (X(b_i, \lambda)) = \frac{1}{N\ \ln 2} \sum_{j=1}^{N} S_n\ (\mu_{x(b_i, \lambda)}\ (X_j)); \tag{17b}$$

and $$I(X(b_i, \lambda)) = \frac{1}{N} \sum_{j=1}^{N} \hat{\pi}(X_j, b_i, \lambda) \tag{17c}$$

$$i = 1, 2, \ldots\ldots, L^n$$

The grid points $\{b_i\}$ for which the corresponding fuzzy measures are locally maximum may be taken as initial seed points.

11.4 DYNOC ALGORITHM [9]

In this section, DYNOC algorithm is described in detail.

Step 1

Determine initial clusters by the following method.

Extreme-Point Approach — Let X_1, X_2, ..., X_N be the N pattern points each of them having n number of properties i.e., samples are from n-dimensional feature space. The sample mean is given by

$$Z_0 = \frac{1}{N} \sum_{i=l}^{N} X_i \tag{18}$$

The intraset distance of the entire sample set is

$$D_o \sum_{i=1}^{N} \|X_i - Z_o\| / N \tag{19}$$

Let X_i, X_k, X_l, ..., be the sample pattern vectors containing one or more components of extremely large magnitude. From these pattern vectors X_k is an extreme point, if

$$\|X_j - X_k\| > a D_o \qquad k \neq j, \tag{20}$$

where $0.5 < a < 1$. We denote the extreme point by l_k. The distance between two extreme patterns should satisfy this condition.

We also consider a pattern point near the mean Z_o as an interior extreme pattern point. We determine initial clusters by grouping pattern points in the vicinity of the extreme points.

Let S_k be the subset of patterns assigned to l_k, and N_c be the number of cluster centres. Then

$$X \in S_k, \text{ if } \|X - l_k\| < \|X - l_j\|, \tag{21}$$

$$\text{where } j = 1, 2, \ldots., N_c \text{ and } j \neq k$$

Step 2

Compute the centroid for each of the initial clusters.

Let N_j be the number of pattern points in the cluster C_j. Then the centroid for C_j is given by

$$Z_j = \frac{1}{N_j} \sum_{X_k \in C_j} X_k \qquad j = 1, 2, \ldots\ldots, N_C \tag{22}$$

Step 3

Compute the interset distances between clusters, and find the minimum of these distances.

Let the interset distances between clusters C_i and C_j be D_{ij}. Then

$$D_{ij} = \left\| Z_i - Z_j \right\|, \; i = 1, 2, \ldots\ldots., N_C - 1 \tag{23}$$

$$j = i + 1, \ldots.., N_C$$

We denote the minimum of all D_{ij}'s by Min D_{ij}.

Step 4

Perform statistical analysis of the sample patterns.

Find the standard deviation vector,

$$\sigma_j = [\sigma_{1j}, \sigma_{2j}, \ldots., \sigma_{nj}] \qquad j = 1, 2, \ldots.., N_C \tag{24}$$

for each of the clusters where σ_{ij} is the ith component and is given by

$$\sigma_{ij} = \sqrt{\frac{1}{N_j} \sum_{X_k \in C_j} (X_{ik} - Z_{ij})^2} \tag{25}$$

Compute the mean value of σ_j,

$$\bar{\sigma}_j = \frac{l}{n} \sum_{i=1}^{n} \sigma_{ij} \tag{26}$$

Find the maximum component of each σ_j and denote it by $\sigma_{j\,\max}$.

Step 5

Compute the intraset distance for each cluster, and find the maximum of these distances.

Let the intraset distance for cluster C_j be D_j. Then we have

$$D_j = \sqrt{2 \sum_{i=1}^{n} \sigma_{ij}^2} \tag{27}$$

we denote the maximum of all D_j's by Max D_j.

Step 6

Establish a performance index $\lambda(N_C)$ for determining optimal clusters.

Here $\lambda(N_C)$ is chosen as

$$\lambda(N_C) = \frac{\text{Min } D_{ij}}{\text{Max } D_j} \tag{28}$$

Optimal clusters occur when $\lambda(N_C)$ reaches a peak, and N_C is optimal if $\lambda(N_c)$ is a global maximum. N_c is increased by breaking a large cluster, and decreased by merging nearly small clusters.

Step 7

Split a large-size cluster.

A cluster C_j is broken into two new clusters with cluster centres Z_j^a and Z_j^b if one of the following conditions is satisfied

$$\sigma_{j\max} > \Theta_S$$

or

$$N_j > \Theta_n$$

or

$$D_j > D,$$

where Θ_S = standard deviation threshold $= \alpha\bar{\sigma}_j$

Θ_N = cluster size threshold $= \beta N / N_C$

D = intraset distance threshold $= \dfrac{1}{N} \sum_{j=1}^{N_C} N_j D_j$

The coefficients are chosen as

$$1 < \alpha < 2 \text{ and } 1 < \beta < 3$$

If cluster C_j is broken, cluster centre Z_j is deleted and N_C is incremented by 1.

New cluster centres are formed as follows

$$Z_j^a = Z_j + P_j \tag{29a}$$

and

$$Z_j^b = Z_j + P_j, \tag{29b}$$

where $p_j = [0, 0, ..., rD_j, ..., 0]$ whose non-zero component corresponds to maximum component of σ_j. The coefficient r is determined to ensure that the intraset distance is larger than a merging threshold. From this condition we have the coefficient r given by

$$r = \frac{\text{Min } D_{ik}}{2D_j} + \delta, \delta > 0 \tag{30}$$

Extremely small clusters are discarded.

Step 8

Merge small-size clusters.

Following cluster splitting, we compute new interset distances. The new interset distance D_{ij} is compared with merging threshold Θ_m, which is chosen as Min D_{ik}. If $D_{ij} < \Theta_m$ clusters C_i and C_j will be merged to form a new cluster with cluster centre given by

$$Z = (N_i Z_i + N_j Z_j) / (N_i + N_j) \tag{31}$$

Following the merge, cluster centres Z_i and Z_j are deleted and N_C is decremented by 1.

Step 9

Iterate the procedure.

Repeat steps 2-6 and find new $\lambda(N_C)$. If $\lambda(N_C)$ increases, go to step 7. If $\lambda(N_C)$ decreases, check whether $\lambda(N_C)$ is a global maximum. If not, go to step 7. Check the merging condition, if satisfied go to step 8.

If global maximum of $\lambda(N_C)$ is found, stop the procedure and record N_C.

Step 10

Analyse alternate groupings.

With optimal N_C found, patterns are reassigned to each cluster centre to obtain max $\lambda(N_C)$. If there are alternate groupings with equal number of clusters, choose the one with largest $\lambda(N_C)$.

11.5 IMPLEMENTATION AND RESULTS

The above mentioned algorithm was implemented on a set of 871 Indian Telugu vowel sounds in a Consonant-Vowel-Consonant Context uttered by three speakers in the age group of 30 to 35 years [8]. Fig. 11.1 shows the feature space of six vowels (δ, *a:*, *i*, *u*, *e*, *o*) corresponding to F_1 and F_2. F_1 and F_2 denote the first and second vowel format frequencies which were obtained through spectrum analysis of the speech data.

Table 11.1 shows the (F_1, F_2)-values for which the fuzzy measures γ, H and I were found to be locally maximum when d and λ were considered to be 50 and 100 respectively. A set of 5 to 7 maxima is observed for different measures. The seed points as given by these (F_1, F_2)-values are found to agree well with those of the classes in Fig.11.1.

In order to demonstrate the effect of the parameters d and λ on the selection of seed points, we have considered only the measure 'entropy' and Tables 11.2 and 11.3 illustrate such an effect when d and λ were chosen to be 25, 50 and 100 and 100, 150 and 200 respectively.

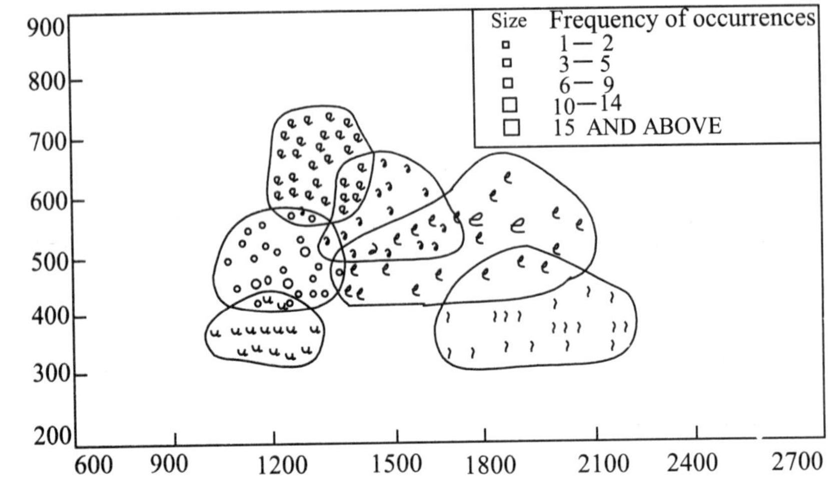

Fig. 11.1 Vowel classes in $(F_1 - F_2)$ plane

At low values viz, $d = 25$, $\lambda = 100$ (Table 11.2*a*), the number of seed points is found to be 9 and as we increase λ some of the weak local maxima get lost leaving behind only the strong ones. Similar effect is also found (from Tables 11.2(*a*), 11.1(*b*) and 11.3) to occur when one increases the grid width for a fixed value of λ.

With different values of the process parameters and with different processes of selecting initial clusters, DYNOC has been implemented. The groupings as DYNOC does for different processes of selecting initial clusters are shown through confusion matrices (Table 11.4). Tables 11.4*a* and 11.4*b* show the results corresponding to extreme point approach and the proposed approach for determining initial clusters.

Table 11.1 *Seed points and corresponding fuzzy measures when d = 50 and λ = 100, (a) rl (b) H (c) I*

Seed Point (F_1, F_2)	$\gamma \times 10^{-2}$	Seed Point (F_1, F_2)	$H \times 10^{-2}$	Seed Point (F1,F2)	$I \times 10^{-2}$
(350, 2265)	2.152	(350, 2265)	4.172	(350, 2265)	3.709
(400, 985)	3.316	(450, 985)	5.797	(500, 985)	5.464
(500, 985)	3.750	(500, 1981)	2.022	(500, 1981)	1.885
(500, 1981)	1.237	(550, 1554)	1.478	(550, 1554)	1.267
(600, 1411)	0.079	(750, 1269)	2.960	(600, 1838)	1.512
(600, 1838)	0.091	(*b*)		(750, 1269)	2.742
(750, 1269)	1.651				
(*a*)				(*c*)	

Table 11.2 *Seed points and the corresponding H-Values for d = 25 (a) λ = 100 (b) λ = 150 (c) λ = 200*

Seed Point (F_1, F_2)	H × 10^{-2}	Seed Point (F_1, F_2)	H × 10^{-2}	Seed Point (F_1, F_2)	H × 10^{-2}
(300, 1483)	0.106	(350, 2265)	7.301	(500, 1981)	2.022
(350, 2265)	4.172	(425, 985)	10.898	(525,1554)	1.498
(475, 985)	5.997	(525, 1838)	3.800	(600, 1838)	1.685
(500, 1838)	1.795	(550, 1554)	2.619	(650, 1198)	2.794
				(725, 1269)	3.158

(*a*)

Seed Point (F_1, F_2)	H × 10^{-2}
(700, 1269)	5.384

(*b*)

Seed Point (F_1, F_2)	H × 10^{-2}
(350, 2265)	10.200
(425, 985)	16.167
(500,1910)	6.258
(675, 1269)	8.016

(*c*)

Table 11.3 *Seed point and the corresponding H-values for d = 100 and λ = 100*

Seed Point (F_1, F_2)	H × 10^{-2}
(350, 2123)	2.430
(450, 985)	5.797
(550, 1838)	1.697
(750, 1269)	2.960

In Tables 11.4*a* and 11.4*b*, we considered $\alpha = 1.8$, $\beta = 2.6$, $a = 0.8$ and $\delta = 2.0$. Maximum value of performance index was found to be 0.86 and 0.62 for Tables 11.4*a* and 11.4*b* respectively. Number of iterations corresponding to those tables was found to be 5 and 2.

Table 11.4*a* *Clustering with the extreme point approach*

Cluster Found	Actual Classes									
	δ	*a:*	*i*	*i:*	*u*	*u:*	*e*	*e:*	*o*	*o:*
1	2	0	0	0	0	0	39	6	0	0
2	3	0	46	19	0	0	25	38	0	0
3	1	0	33	51	0	0	0	16	0	0
4	1	0	0	0	48	50	0	1	36	76
5	5	7	0	0	5	0	1	0	3	1
6	20	77	0	0	17	0	4	10	44	19
7	47	7	2	0	1	0	34	7	1	0
8	0	0	6	14	0	0	7	19	0	0

Table 11.4*b* *Clustering with the proposed approach*

Cluster Found	Actual Classes									
	δ	*a:*	*i*	*i:*	*u*	*u:*	*e*	*e:*	*o*	*o:*
1	0	0	35	47	0	0	8	15	0	0
2	1	1	0	0	63	80	0	1	54	24
3	18	1	2	0	1	0	24	12	5	0
4	7	0	16	0	0	0	43	35	0	1
5	31	83	0	0	7	0	3	4	25	0
6	1	0	0	0	0	0	29	7	0	0
7	0	0	34	38	0	0	0	23	0	0
8	14	4	0	0	0	0	3	0	0	0

11.6 CONCLUSION

A method has been outlined using the concept of fuzzy sets whereby a satisfactory choice of initial seed points for clustering a given data set may be determined. Effectiveness of the algorithm has been demonstrated on speech data and compared with extreme point approach when DYNOC is considered as a clustering tool.

Acknowledgement

The authors acknowledge Prof. D Dutta Majumder for his interest in this work and Mr J Gupta for typing the manuscript.

References

1. J T Tou and R C Gonzalez (1974) *Pattern Recognition Principles* Addison-Wesley Publishing Company, London.
2. J C Bezdek (1981) *Pattern Recognition with Fuzzy Objective Function Algorithms* Plenum Press, N.Y.
3. E Backer (1978) *Cluster Analysis by Optimal Decomposition of Induced Fuzzy Sets* Delftse Univ. Press.
4. L A Zadeh (1975) Calculus of Fuzzy restrictions In: *Fuzzy Sets and Their Applications to Cognitive and Decision Processes Eds. L A Zadeh et al.* Academic Press London, 1 – 39.
5. A Kaufmann (1975) *Introduction to the Theory of Fuzzy Subsets,* Vol.1, Academic Press, New York.
6. A De Luca and S Termini (1972) A definition of non-probabilistic entropy in the setting of fuzzy sets theory *Info Contr* **20**, 301 – 312.
7. S K Pal (1982) Fuzzy set theoretic approach - a tool for speech and image recognition In: *Pattern Recognition Theory and Applications eds. J Kittler et al.* D. Reidel Publishing Co. Holland, 103 – 117.

8. S K Pal and D Dutta Majumder (1977) Fuzzy sets and decision making approaches in vowel and speaker recognition. *IEEE Trans Syst Man and Cyberns* **SMC-7,** 625 – 629.

9. J T Tou (1978) DYNOC-A dynamic optimal cluster seeking technique *Int J Comp Info Sci* Vol. **8** No.6, 541 – 547.

12

A Comprehensive Study on Pattern Classification Problem (With a Case Study on Application of Genetic Algorithms on Point Classification Problem)

Paramartha Dutta[1] Dwijesh Dutta Majumder[2, 3]

ABSTRACT

In the present article, we have investigated the application of evolutionary class of algorithms on pattern recognition and as an instance, we have considered point classification problem, which is a specific variant of general classification problem. The problem has been tackled in a number of ways including various soft computing techniques. We try to present here a critical appreciation of all these soft computing methods before we present the paradigm of evolutionary computation (EC). However, for our present investigation, we have restricted within two dimensional case and taken up an existing genetic scheme as the benchmark. We have proposed our genetic schemes and have found how and why these schemes have outperformed the existing benchmark. As an extrapolation to the present initiative, we may explore higher dimensional possibilities of the present problem.

Keywords: Complexity; Clustering; Soft Computing Approach; Deterministic Algorithm; Objective Function of a Genetic Algorithm.

12.1 INTRODUCTION AND PERSPECTIVE

Two dimensional point classification is an interesting problem [8,9]. In this work, we restrict our attention to binary encoding of the search domain. Our basic focus is oriented towards exploring point classification problem. In order to make the present study comprehensive, we have also implemented a deterministic algorithm. We shall adopt a method, using an elitist model of genetic algorithm to partition two-dimensional feature space, into polygonal regions, by a given number of straight lines, such that, each region may be assigned to exactly one class.

The paper proposes some major improvements, over an existing algorithm presented in [4].

---

[1] Department of Computer Science and Engineering, Kalyani Government Engineering College, Kalyani 741 235, India. E-mail: paramartha.dutta@gmail.com

[2] Electronics and Communication Sciences Unit, Indian Statistical Institute, Calcutta, 203, B.T. Road, Kolkata - 700 108, India. E-mail: ddm@isical.ac.in.

[3] Institute of Cybernetics Systems and Information Technology (ICSIT), 155, Ashokegarh, Kolkata - 700 108, India.

- The space complexity of the existing algorithm is reduced from $O(2^H)$ to $O(H^2)$ (H being the number of straight lines). We shall provide a formal proof in due course, for the sake of completeness.
- A more effective and informative 'objective function' to estimate the fitness value, of a potential solution (a string in GA), is proposed, in a subsequent section. With this new objective function, the implementation of the modified algorithm, empirically shows expected rapid convergence to an optimal solution.
- A deterministic algorithm, carrying out exhaustive search, for the same problem has also been proposed. The deterministic algorithm has an exponential time complexity $O(n^{2H})$, where n is the number of feature points and H is the number of straight lines supplied. We shall see that, for all practical purposes, the optimal solution can be reached, much faster, using the GA based algorithm in comparison to deterministic algorithm.

12.1.1 A Brief Review of Pattern Recognition with Soft Computing Approaches

Pattern recognition (e.g. classification, clustering, feature evaluation) and machine learning form a major area of research and development activity, that encompass the processing of images and other non-numerical informations [1,2,3,4,5,6,7].

A motivation, for such activities, in this field is the need, for the people, to communicate with computing machines, in their natural mode of communication. Another important motivation is, that the scientists are concerned with the idea of designing and making machines 'intelligent', that can carry out certain tasks, as the human beings do.

The ability to classify and recognize a pattern is the first and foremost requirement for any intelligent entity. In terms of machine learning, it becomes the first prerogative to design a machine, which can classify and recognize different patterns. The area, encompassing pattern classification and recognition is an important component, for any *Intelligent Control System* (ICS), which involve processing and fusion of data from different sensors and transducers.

Various approaches have so far been proposed and experimented for designing pattern recognition systems. They can be broadly categorized into:

- decision theoretic approach (both deterministic and probabilistic),
- syntactic approach and
- neuro-fuzzy approach.

12.1.2 Different Available Approaches: A Critical Review

Clustering is useful in several exploratory pattern analysis, grouping and decision making situations including data mining [17, 20, 27, 30, 33], pattern classification [23, 29, 32], scene analysis [36], document retrieval [18, 19, 28, 29] and bio-informatics [25]. The common characteristic of most of these application domains is that, the size of the data involved, is very large. Typically, clustering algorithms work on pattern matrices, where each row of the matrix corresponds to a distinct pattern and each column corresponds to a feature [24]. As defined by Watanbe [39], a pattern is an entity, vaguely defined, that could be given a name. Typical pattern recognition using clustering or otherwise involves:

- **Feature extraction/selection:** The problem of feature selection means, selecting a subset (of size *m)* out of a set of *d* features, so that the classification error is minimum. Let, Y be the given set of features, with cardinality d and let m represent, the desired number of features in the selected subset X, $X \subseteq Y$. Let, the feature selection criterion function for the set X be $J(X)$. Higher functional value of J indicates, better feature subset. There are different methods of selection. Presented below in Table 12.1, is a comparative study of respective methods, adapted for selection. In addition to the search strategy, important are the choice of evaluation criterion function J and the value of m. Most feature selection methods use the classification error of a feature subset to evaluate its effectiveness. However, use of a different combination of classifier and error estimating method could lead to a selection, of different choice of feature subset altogether.
- **Domain specific similarity measure selection:** Depending on the context, different similarity measures have come up in the literature. For example, distance metrics like Manhattan metric, Euclidean metric, Mahalanobis distance, Minkawski's metric are used quite frequently. But the applicability of the above measures are very much dependent on the nature of application being handled. All the above measures are used to discriminate patterns, on the basis of the value of the measure, used in the problem. Apart from the above measures, there are other similarity measures, which do not satisfy the precise mathematical criteria of a metric, but may be used effectively for the purpose of discrimination. What is of importance, is to get hold of an effective, as well as, efficient similarity measure, with respect to a particular problem.
- **Classification in terms of the similarity measure:** This may consist of one of the following two tasks:
  - *Supervised classification* (e.g., discriminant analysis), in which the input pattern is identified as a member of a predefined class.

Table 12.1 *A qualitative comparison of different feature selection methods*

Method	Characteristics	Remarks
Exhaustive search	Evaluate all possible subsets.	Guaranteed to find the optimal subset, not feasible for even moderately large m
Branch and bound	Only fraction of all possible feature subsets be enumerated to find the optimal subset.	With any monotonic criterion function, optimal subset is guaranteed.
Best individual features	Evaluate all m features individually, select the best m features.	Computationally simple, not likely to lead to an optimal subset always.
Sequential forward selection (SFS)	Select best single feature and then add one feature at a time, which in combination with the selected features maximizes criterion function.	Once a feature is retained, it cannot be discarded, computationally attractive.
Sequential backward selection (SBS)	Start with all d features and successively delete one feature at a time.	Once a feature is deleted, it can not be brought back into optimal subset, more computation intensive than SFS.
"Plus l, take away r" selection	First enlarge the feature subset by l features, using forward selection and then delete r features, using backward selection.	Avoids the problem of feature subset "nesting", encountered in SFS and SBS methods, $l > r$.
Sequential forward floating search (SFFS) and sequential backward floating search	Generalization of "plus l take away r" method, l and r are determined automatically and updated dynamically.	Provides close to optimal solution at an affordable cost.

- *Unsupervised classification,* in which the pattern is assigned to a hitherto unknown class.

It is a generic label for a variety of procedures, designed to find natural groupings, based on measured/perceived similarities, among the patterns [24]. Unsupervised learning is a very difficult problem, because data can reveal clusters with different shapes and sizes. To compound the problem further, the number of clusters in the data, often depends on the resolution of viewing the data. Recent studies in cluster analysis suggest that, a user of a clustering algorithm should keep the following issues in mind:

(i) Every clustering algorithm will find clusters in a given dataset, whether they exist or not. The data should, therefore, be subjected to tests for clustering tendency, before a clustering algorithm is applied, followed by a validation of the clusters, generated by the algorithm.

(ii) There is no uniformly best clustering algorithm.

Therefore, a user is advised to:

(i) Try several clustering algorithms on a given dataset and

(ii) Apply a specific clustering algorithm on several datasets of different nature.

The most difficult and challenging problem in cluster analysis is the problem of effective representation. There is no hard and fast guideline in this regard and the problem itself is highly subjective. However, the intention is to isolate only the most descriptive and discriminatory features in the input set and process them exclusively in subsequent analysis. Once patterns are represented, using a collection of features, the goal of clustering is to partition them, into a number of clusters, on the basis of some meaningful measure of similarity. In the feature space, each pattern is nothing but a point in a typically multidimensional space. A large distance between two such points, is nothing but a resemblance of higher dissimilarity between the patterns. There may be a variety of similarity measures, depending upon the context, in which it is used. In order to frame such quantitative distance measures, the patterns have to be represented, using only quantitative features. Unfortunately, it is indeed difficult to capture qualitative aspects, using such a measure. In such a situation, a mixture of qualitative and quantitative features is typically required to represent patterns. This apart, the basic problem in computing similarity is not just the requirement of a numerical representation, but the notion of importance/weights, associated with each of the features. Distance functions, like the mutual neighbourhood distance [21], which are not metrics, have also been used successfully in pattern clustering. The most general similarity function between two objects is the conceptual cohesiveness, proposed and used in knowledge based clustering [26]. Typically, a grouping of patterns is meaningful, when the within group similarity is high and the between group similarity is low. Clustering algorithms are available, which yield crisp or fuzzy classification of points. Algorithms, used for the purpose of clustering can be broadly grouped into hierarchical and partitional categories. Partitional clustering techniques are used more frequently than hierarchical techniques. Most of the partitional clustering techniques implicitly assume continuous valued feature vectors, so that the pattern can be viewed, as being embedded in a metric space. If the features are on a nominal or ordinal scale, Euclidean distances and cluster centers are not very meaningful, and hierarchical clustering methods are normally applied. However, the most popular approach to partitional clustering is square-error clustering, whose general objective is to obtain the partition, which for a fixed number of clusters, minimizes the square-error. Suppose, that the given set of n patterns in d dimensions, has been partitioned into K clusters $\{C_1, C_2, \ldots., C_K\}$, such that, cluster C_i has n_i patterns and each pattern belongs to exactly one cluster in crisp sense, so that, $\sum_{i=1}^{K} n_i = n$. The centroid of the cluster C_i is defined as

$m^{(i)} = \frac{\sum_{l=1}^{n_i} x_l^{(i)}}{n_i}$, where $x_l^{(i)}$ is the lth pattern, belonging to cluster C_i. The within-cluster variation of cluster C_i is given by, $e_i^2 = \sum_{l=1}^{n_i} (x_l^{(i)} - m^{(i)})'$ $(x_l^{(i)} - m^{(i)})$ and the square-error for the entire clustering of K clusters, is given by, $E_K^2 = \sum_{i=1}^{K} e_i^2$. The objective of a square-error clustering method, is to find a partition, containing K clusters, that minimizes E_K^2, for a specific K. The resulting partition has also been referred to, as the minimum variance partition. If the Mahalanobis distance metric is used, instead of straight forward square-error, as described above, then the algorithm is even able to detect hyper-ellipsoidal shaped clusters. A big frustration, in using partitional clustering program is the lack of guidelines, available for choosing K, initial partition, updating the partition, adjusting the number of clusters, as well as the stopping criterion. A more general procedure of square-error clustering method is mixture decomposition method, which primarily constituted by well known method of expectation maximization.

Hierarchical algorithms are more versatile than the partitional algorithms. On the other hand, the time and space complexities of the partitional algorithms are typically lower than, those of the hierarchical algorithms. It is also possible to have hybrid algorithm, that exploits the good features of both categories. Hierarchical clustering algorithms are either divisive or agglomerative. Hierarchical divisive algorithms start with a single cluster, of all the given objects and keep splitting the clusters based on some criteria, to lead to a partition of singleton clusters. Typically they are computationally expensive. On the contrary, a hierarchical agglomerative algorithm begins with a clustering, in which each pattern is in a singleton cluster and continue to merge clusters, based on some within-cluster similarity value, until a one cluster solution is obtained. For this, they use a proximity matrix, that contains pre-computed similarities, between all pairs of patterns. The time complexity of construction of such a matrix is $O(n^2)$ and space complexity is $O(n^2)$, n being the number of patterns. For large n, the algorithm becomes computationally expensive either. Most of the agglomerative algorithms are variants of the singlelink (SL), complete link (CL) and variance algorithms. In the SL method, the nearest neighbours, across the patterns are considered, whereas, in the CL approach, the distance between two clusters is the maximum of all pairwise distances between patterns in the two clusters. In both the cases, two clusters are merged to form a bigger cluster, based on maximum similarity. The clusters, obtained by the CL algorithm, are more tightly bound or compact than those, obtained by the SL algorithm. On the contrary, SL algorithm is more versatile than the CL counterpart.

The *K*-means algorithm is the most successfully used square-error clustering algorithm. It starts with a random initial partition and keeps on reassigning the patterns into clusters, based on the similarity, between the patterns and the cluster centers, until a convergence criterion is met. The reason of popularity of *K*-means algorithm is that, it is easy to implement apart from its time complexity being $O(n)$. However, a major problem, with this method is that, it is very sensitive to the initial choice of partition and as a result, may suffer from premature convergence (convergence to a local optimum) [31]. Several variants of *K*-means algorithms have been reported in the literature, some of which address to the problem of effective choice of initial partition.

There are different approaches, that have come up, to solve the problem of clustering.

- **Artificial neural network (ANN):** This approach [22] is motivated by biological neural networks. Some of the features of the ANNs, that are important in respect of pattern clustering are as follows:
  - *(i)* For processing in ANNs, features have to be quantitatively represented,
  - *(ii)* ANNs are inherently parallel and distributed and
  - *(iii)* Weights are learned adaptively. More specifically, they can be adapted to normalize patterns and extract features thereof.

  Competitive ANNs are often used to cluster input data. In competitive learning, similar patterns are grouped by the network and represented by a single unit. This grouping is done automatically, based on data correlation. ANNs constitute Kohonen's learning vector quantization (LVQ), self organizing map (SOM) [44], and adaptive resonance theory (ART) models [46]. All of them are single layered nets. The weights between the input nodes and the output nodes are iteratively changed and as such learned, until a termination condition is satisfied. All the methods, mentioned above, are sensitive to the choice of learning parameters. All these methods are mainly used for data clustering and feature mapping. The learning process involves updating network architecture and connection weights, so that a network can efficiently perform a specific clustering task. The increasing popularity of neural network models, to solve pattern recognition problems has been primarily due to their seemingly low dependence on domain specific knowledge (relative to model based and rule based approaches) and due to the availability of efficient learning algorithms, for practitioners to use. Attempts have been made to improve the performance of *K*-means algorithm, by mapping it onto a neural network [43], for possibly efficient implementation. The most commonly used family of neural networks for pattern classification tasks is the feed-forward network, which includes multilayer perception (MLP) and radial basis function (RBF) networks. Neural networks offer several advantages such as, unified approaches for feature extraction and classification and flexible procedures for finding good, moderately non-linear solutions.

- **Evolutionary approach:** Various attempts have been carried out, to improve the performance of the basic *K*-means algorithm, by using simulated annealing, genetic algorithms to optimize the resulting partition [41]. A deterministic annealing algorithm has also been presented in [42]. Evolutionary approaches, motivated by natural evolution, make use of evolutionary operators and a population of solutions, to obtain the globally optimal partition of the data. The most well-known evolutionary algorithms are genetic algorithms (GA), evolution strategies (ES) and evolutionary programming (EP). Out of these three approaches, GAs have been most frequently used in clustering [4]. ES and EP differ from GAs in solution representation and the type of mutation operator used. EP does not use a recombination operator. EP uses only selection and mutation operators. All these three approaches have been used, to solve the clustering problem, by viewing it, as a minimization of the square-error criterion. In GAs, each point or chromosome represents a partition of n objects into K clusters and is represented by a K-ary string of length n. The major problem with GAs is that, they are sensitive to the selection of various parameters, like the encoding of the solution space, population size, selection strategy, crossover and mutation probabilities etc. It is possible to view the clustering problem, as an optimization problem, that finds out the optimal centroid of the clusters directly, rather than finding an optimal partition, using a GA. This view permits the use of ES and EP, because centroid can be coded easily, in these two approaches, as they support direct representation of a solution, as a real valued vector. It has been observed that, they perform better than their classical counterparts, *K*-means and fuzzy *K*-means algorithm. However, these approaches suffer like GAs and ANNs, from sensitivity to control parameter selection.
- **Fuzzy approach:** Numerous attempts have been made to improve the performance of the classical *K*-means algorithm by incorporating a fuzzy criterion function [16,40], resulting in a fuzzy *K*-means or (*c*-means) algorithm. The generated partitions, in a

traditional clustering approach contain patterns, where each pattern belongs to exactly one cluster. As a result, the clusters in a partition are disjoint. Fuzzy clustering extends this notion to associate, each pattern with every cluster, using a membership function. Even though, it is better than the hard *K*-means algorithm in avoiding local minima, fuzzy *K*-means algorithm can still converge to local minima of the square-error criterion [16]. The design of membership functions is the most important problem in fuzzy clustering. Different membership functions include those, based on similarity decomposition and centroid of clusters.

- **Support vector machine (SVM):** Over the recent years, a number of new concepts and techniques have been introduced. For example, the maximum margin objective was introduced in the context of SVM [13], based on structural risk minimization theory [15]. The maximum margin objective can be considered, as a special regularized cost function, where the regularizer is the inverse of the margin, between the two classes. SVM builds up a hyperplane as the decision surface, so that the margin of separation is maximized. During its operation, it estimates the function, classifying the data into two classes [37,38]. Many successful applications of SVM, have demonstrated the superiority of this objective function over others [14]. Other regularized cost functions, such as weight decay and weight elimination have also been used, in the context of neural networks. Supervised learning requires that, every training sample be labeled with its true category. Collecting a large amount of labeled data can sometimes be very expensive. In practice, we often have a small amount of labeled data and a large amount of unlabeled data. How to make use of unlabeled data, for training a classifier, is an important problem. SVM has been extended to perform semi-supervised learning [12]. Due to the introduction of SVMs, linear and quadratic programming optimization techniques are being extensively studied for pattern classification.
- **Incremental approach:** It is based on the assumptions, that it is possible to consider patterns, one at a time and assign them to existing clusters. Here, a new data item is assigned to a cluster, without affecting the existing clusters significantly. An important feature of this class of algorithms is that, they require a single database scan. Further they need store only the cluster representatives in the memory. So, they have the best time and space complexities. The LEADER clustering algorithm [45] is the simplest, in terms of $O(nk)$ time and $O(k)$ space complexities, where n and k are the number of patterns and number of classes resprectively. The ART network [46] may be viewed, as a parallel

and distributed implementation of the LEADER algorithm. There are other algorithms, like the shortest spanning path (SSP) algorithm, having $O(nk)$ space and $O(n^2)$ time, used to identify outliers and estimate missing values in databases [47]. Order independence is an important property of clustering algorithms. Unfortunately, all the incremental algorithms, enlisted above, have been found to generate different partitions, for different sequences of same data input.

- **Divide and conquer approach:** A major difficulty in clustering large data is that, it is not possible to store the entire data set, under consideration, in the main memory. So, a natural way of solving this problem, is to consider a part of the data set, at a time for clustering and store the corresponding cluster representatives in the main memory. Different algorithms guided by this philosophy, have been reported in the literature, like single pass *K*-means algorithm [48], CLARA [49], where clusters are represented in terms of medoids, instead of centroids, CURE [50], where extreme points in the cluster are used as representatives, rather than the centroids. It is possible to use different clustering algorithms at different levels. For example, in [51], LEADER algorithm is used in the first level, to loosely cluster the data and by taking one representative per cluster, the representatives are clustered, at the second level of a hierarchical algorithm. Such a hybrid approach permits us, to use an inexpensive scheme, at the first level to smart-size the data and then use an expensive and versatile algorithm, at the second level.

In order to make the present study comprehensive, provided below are different methodologies, presented in the literature. A qualitative comparison about the merits and demerits of them is presented.

12.1.3 A Qualitative Comparison among Different Algorithms Used for Clustering

After discussing the merits and demerits of different methodologies, used for clustering, whether handling huge volume of data or not, we can summarize them in Table 12.2.

Research articles on the integration of genetic algorithms and pattern recognition (classification) are quite common [10].

The methods developed for pattern recognition (classification) are usually problem dependent. Moreover, many tasks, involved in the process of classifying and recognizing patterns, need appropriate parameter selection and efficient search mechanism in complex spaces, in order to obtain optimal solution(s).

Table 12.2 *Comparative features of different methods of clustering*

Algorithm	Properties	Remarks
K-means	Identifies hyper-spherical clusters, by using some metric (Euclidean, Manhattan, Minkawski, Mahalanobis etc.) and computationally efficient.	Need to specify *K* and the initial cluster center. Additional parameters can be provided, like creating new clusters, merging existing clusters etc.
Fuzzy *K*-means	Every pattern has a degree of membership into the *K* clusters, which is a generalization of the classical *K*-means version.	Need to specify *K*, initial cluster centers and cluster membership function.
Minimal spanning tree (MST)	Clusters are formed, by deleting inconsistent edges in the MST of the data.	Need to provide the effective definition of an inconsistent edge.
Mutual neighbourhood	Computes the mutual neighbourhood value, for every pair of patterns.	Need to specify the neighbourhood depth.
Single link (SL)	A hierarchical clustering scheme, that accepts a proximity matrix and a dendrogram is generated. An SL cluster is a maximally connected subgraph on the patterns.	SL clusters easily chain together and cut the tree to form clusters using heuristic.
Complete link (CL)	A hierarchical clustering scheme, that accepts a proximity matrix and a dendrogram is generated. A CL cluster is a maximally complete subgraph (CLIQUE) on the patterns.	CL clusters tend to be small and compact, which combine into layer cluster, even when such a hierarchy is not desired. Heuristic is applied to form clusters.
Support vector machine (SVM)	Maximizes the margin between the classes, by selecting a minimum number of support vectors.	Scale dependent, iterative, slow training, non-linear, over-training insensitive, good generalization performance.
Nearest mean classifier	Assigns patterns to the nearest class mean.	Almost no training needed, fast testing, scale dependent.
k nearest neighbour (*k*-NN)	Assigns patterns to the majority class among *k* nearest neighbours, using a performance optimized value of *k*.	Asymptotically optimal, scale dependent, slow testing.
1-nearest neighbour	Assigns patterns to the class of the nearest training pattern.	No training needed, robust performance, slow testing, dependent on metric.
Perceptron	Iterative optimization of a linear classifier.	Sensitive to training parameters, may produce confidence values.
Multilayer perceptron (MLP)	Iterative MSE optimization of two or more layers of perceptrons, using sigmoid transfer function.	Sensitive to training parameters, non-linear classification function may produce confidence values, over-training sensitive, regulari-zation required.

(Contd...)

Radial basis Network	Iterative MSE optimization of a feed-forward neural network, with at least one layer of neurons, using Gaussian like transfer functions.	Sensitive to training parameters, non-linear classification function, may produce confidence values, over-training sensitive, regularization needed, may be robust to outliers.
Template matching	Assigns patterns to the most similar template.	Templates and metric have to be supplied by the user, procedure may include non-linear normalisations, dependent on metric.
Subspace method	Assigns patterns to the nearest class subspace.	Instead of normalising on invariants, the subspace of the invariants is used, dependent on metric.
Logistic classifier	Maximum likelihood rule for logistic (sigmoidal) posterior probabilities.	Linear classifier, iterative procedure, optimal for a family of different Gaussian distributions, suitable for mixed data types.
Bayes plug-in	Assigns patterns to the class, which has the maximum estimated posterior probability.	Yields simple classifiers for Gaussian distributions, sensitive to density estimation errors.
Fisher's linear discriminant	Linear classifier, using Mean Square Error optimization.	Simple and fast, similar to Bayes plug-in for Gaussian distributions, with identical covariance matrices.
Parzen classifier	Bayes plug-in rule for Parzen density estimates, with performance optimized kernel.	Asymptotically optimal, metric dependent, slow testing.
Binary decision tree	Finds a set of thresholds, for a pattern-dependent sequence of features.	Iterative training procedure, over-training sensitive, needs pruning, fast testing.
Simulated annealing (SA)	Finds decision boundaries, approximated by piecewise linear segments for classifying patterns.	Larger the size of training data set, SA classifier tends to provide Bayes boundary, inherently sequential, can not guarantee best classification.
Genetic algorithm (GA)	With suitable encoding, line segments are determined to minimize misclassification.	Inherently parallel, may suffer from premature convergence, performance enhanced for good choice of control parameters, no specific guideline for choosing control parameters as such.
Evolutionary programming (EP)	Fitness function is used, based on Davis-Bouldin index to cluster data, of crisp and spherical nature.	Inherently parallel, based on principle of stationary Markov chain, prone to premature convergence, independent of initial choice of cluster centers.
Our proposed evolutionary algorithms (EA)	Line segments are suitably encoded, so that fitness value computed, on the basis of misclassification, with respect to the position of the line segments, is minimized. It is done by efficiently discarding redundant region specification, out of the relative positions of the lines.	Inherently parallel, empowered with more informative fitness function and search domain is restricted within quadratic complexity, by intelligent manipulation of storage. As a result, performance becomes time efficient too. Premature convergence can not be ruled out. Performance is independent of the choice of initial population.

12.2 PROBLEM SPECIFICATION

In our present endeavour, we have a number of points (say, N), coming from K different classes. Our task is to distinguish them, as much as possible, into different regions, with the help of H many straight lines, so that the number of distinct classes, represented by so many points, within each region, becomes as small as possible. The mathematical sum of such numbers, over all possible regions, constructed by the classifier, gives the measure of *total misclassification.* Needless to say that, zero misclassification is the dream solution of such a problem. In other words, the problem boils down to generating decision boundaries, that can successfully distinguish various classes, in the feature space. However, with this formulation of the problem, each region ultimately will be a polygon. With the number of lines restricted to H, it may not always be possible to arrive at zero misclassification. If this restriction is relaxed, misclassification will tend to diminish. In fact, we require at most N number of lines to arrive at zero misclassification. In real life situation, the boundaries between different classes are usually non-linear, as depicted in Fig. 12.1.

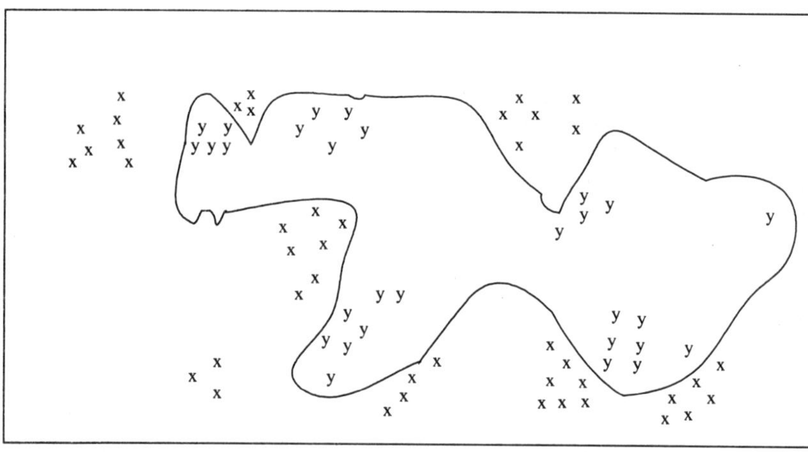

Fig. 12.1 Example of classification with non-linear boundaries

The present problem is, placing a given number of straight lines (say, H many) in the feature space, which can approximate the non-linear boundaries, in the best possible way, by polygonal bounded regions. The best such alternative corresponds to minimum misclassification [4].

The term, misclassification (represented by μ) of feature points in a bounded region, of the feature space is defined as number of different classes of feature points, present in that region minus one.

Thus, if a region in a feature space contains n feature points of q different classes, the misclassification of the feature points in that region is,

$$\mu = q - 1 \tag{1}$$

It may be noted that, μ is independent of the number (n) of feature points, actually present in the region.

The *total misclassification* of feature points, in the entire feature space, is defined as the sum of all such individual misclassifications, in the constituent regions.

So, if the feature space is divided into K distinct regions, such that, μ_i, $1 \le i \le K$, is the misclassification of feature points in region i, the total misclassification, of feature points in the entire feature space is,

$$\mu_{Total} = \sum_{i=1}^{K} \mu_i \tag{2}$$

As an illustration, the total misclassification $\mu_{Total,}$ of feature points as shown in Fig. 12.2 is 3, where $H = 3$ and $n = 10$.

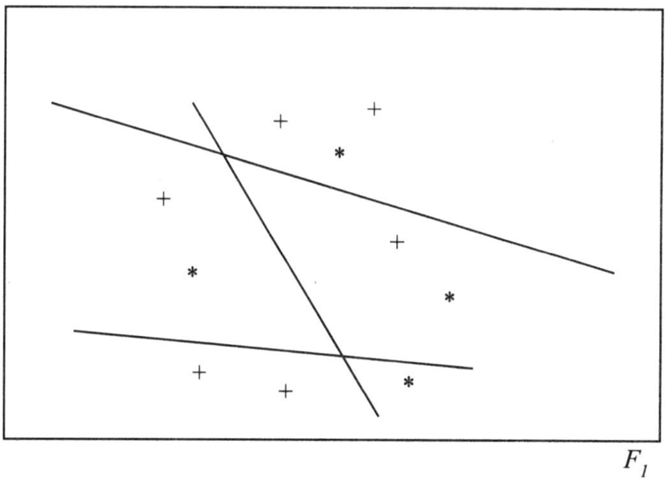

Example with $H = 3$, $n = 10$ and misclassification $= 3$

Fig. 12.2 An illustration of measuring misclassification

12.2.1 The Maximum Number of Regions Obtained by Placing *H* Straight Lines

In this section, our problem is, to find the maximum number $L(H)$, of regions defined by H number of lines, in a plane.

We start by looking at small cases, beginning with the smallest of all. The plane, with no line, has one region, whereas, with one line, it has two regions and with two lines, it has four regions, as illustrated in Fig. 12.3.

Although, with Fig. 12.3, one might feel inclined, to jump into a very tempting conjecture, that $L(H) = 2^H$, an expression exponential in H. But, this is not so. Pictorially, it will be immediately clear, if we consult Fig. 12.4. In fact, *L(H)* has an upper bound, which is quadratic in *H*. It is this observation, which we consider in designing our GA, and in due course, we shall come across, the improvement imparted by it. In this context, we need define a convex region, for the sake of completeness.

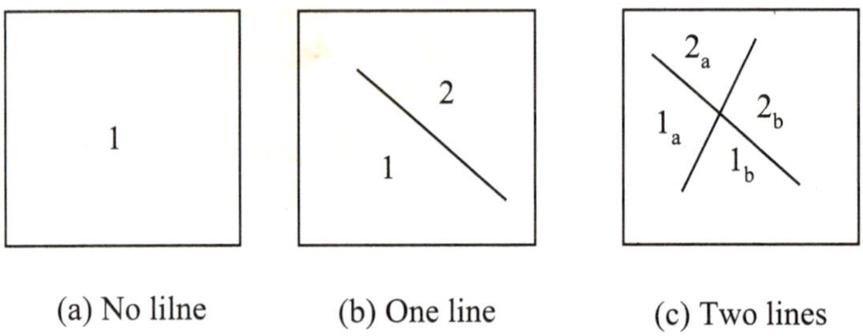

Fig. 12.3 Maximum number of regions with different number of lines

Definition

A region *R* is said to be *convex*, if for all $x, y \in R$, we have, $\lambda x + (1 - \lambda)y \in R \ \forall \lambda \in [0, 1]$.

Now, with the definition of a convex region, let us note that, a straight line can split a convex region, into at most two new convex regions. If, however, we follow Fig. 12.4, we see that, the introduction of the third line (the dotted one), only splits at most three of the old convex regions, instead of four, as the greedy conjecture suggests. Moreover, it does not depend on, how the first two lines were placed. This gives, $L(3) = 4 + 3 = 7$.

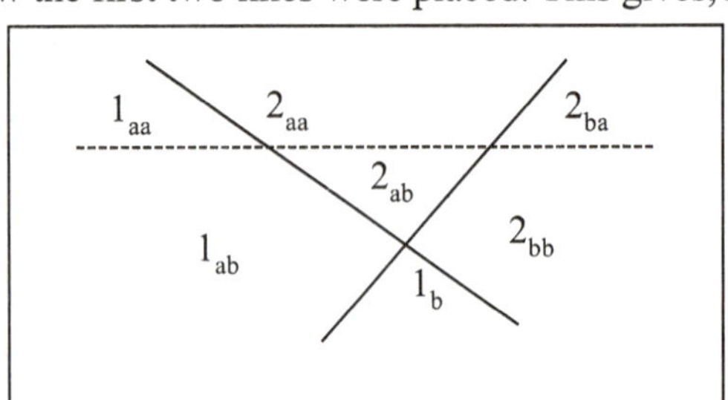

Maximum number of regions with *3* lines is *7*

Fig. 12.4 Number of regions with three lines

Be it noted that, the *H*th line ($H > 0$), increases the number of regions by *K*, if and only if, it splits *K* of the old regions.Moreover, it splits *K* old regions, if and only if, it hits the previous lines, in $K - 1$ different positions. Now, two lines can intersect, at most in one point. Therefore, the new line can intersect the $H - 1$ old lines in, at most $H - 1$ different points. This will ensure, $K \leq H$.

So, the upper bound comes out recursively as,

$$L(H) \leq L(H-1) + H, H > 0 \tag{3}$$

with $L(0) = 1$.

In this context, it may be of interest, as to, when exactly the upper bound is attained? The answer is:

- If the Hth line is placed, in such a way that, it is not parallel to any of the rest (in such a situation, it intersects all of them), and at the same time,
- If the Hth line does not go through, any of the existing intersection points (hence, it intersects all of them, at different places), then, the exact upper bound is achieved.

In that case, the recurrence relation becomes,

$$L(H) = \begin{cases} 1 & \text{if } H = 0 \\ L(H-1) + H & \text{if } H > 0 \end{cases} \tag{4}$$

It is to be noted that, the known values of $L(1)$, $L(2)$ and $L(3)$ agree, with this relation, with the boundary condition of $L(0)$, as already expressed. Unfolding the above recurrence relation, we have,

$$\begin{aligned} L(H) &= L(H-1) + H \\ &= L(H-2) + (H-1) + H \\ &= L(H-3) + (H-2) + (H-1) + H \\ &\vdots \\ &= L(0) + 1 + 2 + \cdots + (H-2) + (H-1) + H \\ &= 1 + \frac{H(H+1)}{2}, \; H \geq 0 \end{aligned} \tag{5}$$

Instead, of this approach, the above relation can be proved by induction also, noticing that, the result is true for $H = 0$. The key induction step assumes that, the relation holds good for index $H - 1$, $H \geq 1$. With this, we shall show that, it holds for index H, as well.

$$\begin{aligned} L(H) &= L(H-1) + H \\ &= \{(H-1)(H-1+1)/2 + 1\} + H \quad \text{(by induction hypothesis)} \\ &= \frac{H(H+1)}{2} + 1 \end{aligned} \tag{6}$$

So, in general,

$$L(H) \leq \frac{H(H+1)}{2} + 1 \tag{7}$$

The non-exact situation can be obtained in the same way, as we did in equation 5, with all the equality signs, being replaced by $\leq$. This completes the proof of the relation 7.

12.3 DESCRIPTION OF THE METHODOLOGY

The present investigation considers a fixed number of straight lines (say H), to denote a decision boundary, in a two-dimensional $F_1 - F_2$ feature space. The value of H varies from one problem to another, depending on the number of classes, as well as, the distribution of the feature points in the feature space. But, for a given instance, it is supplied as an input to the classifier system. It is to be noted that, this a priori estimation of H, may lead to the presence of redundant straight lines, in the decision boundary.

Now, each line provides two half-spaces, a positive half-space (not containing the origin), and a negative half-space (containing the origin), thereby yielding two regions, both of which are convex. So, apparently for H lines, the maximum number of such regions, is $\frac{H(H+1)}{2}+1$, as per our observation in section 12.2.1.

In course of our discussion, we shall see that, our suggested algorithm avoids searching, across all the 2^H apparent regions, by cleverly restricting the search operation, only within the valid regions, generated by itself. So, our improvement is two-fold, over our existing counterpart [4], both with respect to time, as well as space.

The improvements become obvious for large value of H. For example, when H is 20, 2^H is of the order of 1 million, whereas, the actual number of valid regions generated is at most 211. Moreover, it is worth mentioning that, in the proposed method, we are only selecting those regions, where, at least one feature point exists. As such, number of regions can at most be equal to the number of feature points or $\frac{H(H+1)}{2}+1$, whichever is smaller.

12.3.1 Search Space for Lines

The idea here, is to determine the appropriate finite search space (as a subspace of the two-dimensional feature space $F_1 - F_2$), for the possible straight lines, which may be considered as candidates, for the formation of an optimal decision boundary.

The maximum and the minimum values of each of the two features F_1 and F_2, associated with the feature points are calculated. Let, these be $maxF_1$, $minF_1$ and $maxF_2$, $minF_2$, for features F_1 and F_2 respectively.

Then, the rectangle, enclosing the feature points, is given by the vertices ($minF_1$, $minF_2$), ($maxF_1$, $minF_2$), ($maxF_1$, $maxF_2$) and ($minF_1$, $maxF_2$), as shown in the Fig. 12.5. This rectangle represents the required search space. Enclosing the feature space is vital from the computational as well as implementational points of view, since, it is not possible to algorithmically implement search space.of unbounded nature.

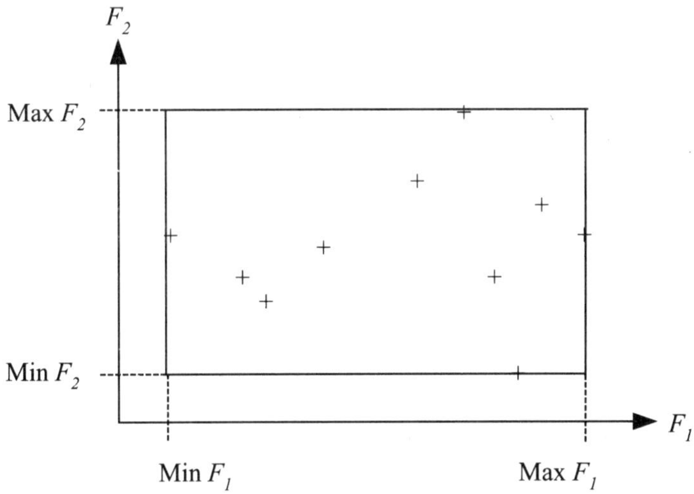

Fig. 12.5 Feature points and the enclosing rectangle

12.3.2 Straight Line Generation

This section describes how to generate a finite number of parallel lines, in a finite number of directions.

One way of representing a straight line in two-dimensional space is by the equation,

$$x \cos \theta + y \sin \theta - d = 0 \tag{8}$$

where, d is the perpendicular distance of the straight line, from the origin and θ is the angle, between the F_1-axis and the normal to the line. This particular equation of straight line is preferred, because here both the parameters, d and θ are finite in a finite search space. The way the two parameters θ and d are specified, is described below.

12.3.2.1 Angle/direction specification

The entire feature space will be spanned, if the angle θ is allowed to vary in the range, between 0 and π radians. The angle needs discretization, for machine implementation and is done so, into sufficiently small intervals, as 0, $\delta\pi$, $2\delta\pi$, ..., $N\delta\pi$. Then, the number of discrete angles considered, is equal to $N + 1$, and $\delta = 1/N$. The angle θ can then be specified, by a number *angle,* in the range [0, N], such that,

$$\theta = angle \times \delta\pi \tag{9}$$

12.3.2.2 Perpendicular distance specification

Once, the angle θ is fixed, the orientation of the line becomes fixed. For a given orientation, the perpendicular distances of the two lines, passing through the base points ($minF_1$, $minF_2$) and ($maxF_1$, $minF_2$) respectively, of the enclosing rectangle are computed, using equation 8. It will be seen that, the perpendicular distance d assumes negative value, if it lies in the negative half-space of the F_2-axis.

Of the two straight lines, the one, with the minimum value of d (say, d_{min}) is selected, as the base straight line. Clearly, the search space for straight lines, with this orientation is restricted at one end, by the base straight line. This can best be illustrated in Fig. 12.6. In other words, all straight lines, with $d < d_{min}$, are automatically discarded from the search space. It goes without saying that, this mechanism helps us downsizing our search space. Moreover, any straight line, at a distance *offset,* from the base straight line, can be specified by a number *offset* in the range [0, d_{length}], where d_{length} is the smallest integer, greater than or equal to the length of the diagonal (of the enclosing rectangle). The perpendicular distance d of that straight line, from the origin is therefore,

$$d = d_{min} + offset \tag{10}$$

A straight line can now be specified by two integer variables *angle* and *offset.*

It is worth mentioning that, for horizontal and vertical lines, equation 10 may lead to their justified rejection, on the ground that, they totally lie beyond the enclosing rectangle.

12.3.3 String Representation and Population Initialization

For the present purpose, we follow the string representation pursued in [4]. However, to make the present treatment self-contained, we formally provide a brief description of it. Each binary bit string is composed of H many representation of straight lines, with each straight line, being specified by two integer variables *angle* and *offset,* according to the above description. So, to encode a straight line, the numbers *angle* and *offset* are to be encoded. If the variable *angle* is represented by b_{ang} number of bits and the *offset* by b_{perp} number of bits, each straight line requires ($b_{ang} + b_{perp}$) many binary bits for its representation, where the first b_{ang} bits clearly encode the number *angle* and the next b_{perp} bits encode the number *offset,* associated with that straight line.

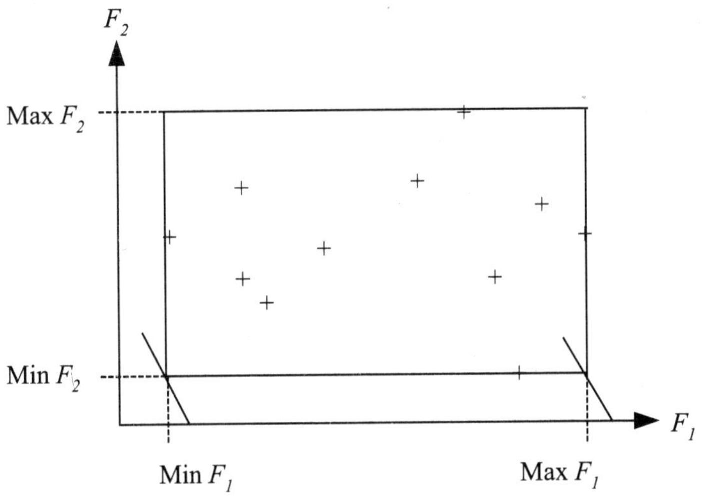

Fig. 12.6 Fixing the base line

Hence, the length of each string, *lchrom* (length of chromosome) equals

$$lchrom = (b_{ang} + b_{perp}) \times H \tag{11}$$

The number of bits, necessary to encode the diagonal of the enclosing rectangle is the value of b_{perp}. It is worth mentioning that, certain bit pattern in b_{perp} may represent an *offset,* which specifies a straight line, that lies totally beyond the enclosing rectangle. The values of b_{ang} and b_{perp} are decided, on the basis of the precision required, for the particular application.

12.3.4 Initialization

In our present realization of GA schemes, the size of the population *popsize* is fixed. Initially, each binary string of length *lchrom,* in the population is generated by selecting 0 or 1, with equal probability, for all *lchrom* bits of the string.

12.3.5 Region Identification

Each string i, $i = 1, 2, \ldots,$ *popsize,* represents H lines, denoted by L_{ij}, $j = 1, 2, \ldots, H$. L_{ij} represents the jth line of ith string of the population.

For each line L_{ij}, the values *angle* and *offset* are retrieved, and then the corresponding parameters θ_{ij} and d_{ij} are evaluated.

With (x_k, y_k) representing our kth point, $k = 1, 2, \ldots, n$, the sign with respect to L_{ij}, i.e., the sign of the expression,

$$E_{ijk} = x_k \cos(\theta_{ij}) + y_k \sin(\theta_{ij}) - d_{ij} \tag{12}$$

is determined. Taken note of that, n represents the total number of feature points present.

$$E_{ijk} = \begin{cases} 1 & \text{if } (x_k, y_k) \text{ lies on or in the positive side of line } L_{ij} \\ 0 & \text{otherwise} \end{cases} \tag{13}$$

The process is repeated with the point (x_k, y_k), for each $L_{ij}, j = 1, 2, ..., H$, of the ith string, at the end of which, we have a bit string denoted by SGN_{ik} of length H, for the point (x_k, y_k).

This bit pattern *SGN,* in fact, represents a particular enclosed (polygonal) region, in the search space. The index k in SGN_{ik} signifies that, the point (x_k, y_k) belongs to the region specified by *SGN*.

So, the string SGN_{ik} corresponds to the classification, yielded by the ith string of the population, for the kth feature point. This procedure is repeated, for all the n feature points.

It is to be noted here that, a binary bit string of length H can represent 2^H possible different bit patterns. We have, however, come across in section 12.2.1 that, H number of lines can divide a plane, into at most $\frac{H(H+1)}{2}+1$ distinct regions. So, out of this 2^H possible bit patterns, at most $\frac{H(H+1)}{2}+1$ different bit patterns correspond to some valid (feasible) regions and others do not.

12.3.6 Fitness Computation

According to the existing algorithm [4], the *total misclassification* is the measure of the fitness of a string. So, if a region contains 51 feature points of class 1, and another 49 points of class 2, then the *misclassification* of feature points in this region is 2 – 1 = 1. On the other hand, if another region contains 99 feature points of class 1, and only 1 point of class 2, the *misclassification* of the feature points in this region is also 2 – 1 = 1. So, the contribution to the *fitness* of this two regions is same, though the distribution of the points, coming from 2 different classes is completely different. We shall try, in our proposed algorithm, to overcome this apparently anomalous phenomenon, by introducing the following concept.

Let,

ϕ_i = number of points of class i, belonging to a particular region.

n = number of feature points, present in that region.

N = number of different classes, present in the feature space.

Then, average frequency β is given by,

$$\beta = \frac{\left(\sum_i \phi_i\right)}{N} = \frac{n}{N} \tag{14}$$

and variance σ^2 is as follows,

$$\sigma^2 = \sum_i (\phi_i - \beta)^2 / N \tag{15}$$

The normalized variance is,

$$\alpha = \frac{\sigma^2}{n} \tag{16}$$

The fitness of a string is the sum of this normalized variance, calculated for all the relevant regions, containing at least one feature point.

It is to be mentioned that, since N is fixed for a given data set, while calculating variance from equation 15, the division by N can be avoided, as is done in the implementation of this algorithm. It can be shown that, this method of estimating the fitness of a string, is highly sensitive to the relative distribution of feature points, belonging to different classes.

This definition of fitness is transparent, to the much cherished relative distributions. The two approaches are illustrated in Table 12.3, in which, f_1 and f_2 are the number of points of 1 and 2 respectively, belonging to a particular region.

Table 12.3 shows that, with the new definition of fitness introduced, the contributions due to fitness, of these two regions are drastically different, as expected. We shall incorporate it, in our algorithm and find noteworthy improvement.

12.4 ALGORITHMS

The next three sections 12.4.1, 12.4.2 and 12.4.3 describe the existing algorithm [4] and our two proposed methods, which are followed by the deterministic algorithm proposed in section 12.4.4.

12.4.1 Existing Method of Our Interest

A 'sign table', with 2^H slots (one for each of the 2^H possible bit patterns, that the 'sign string' can represent) is maintained. Each slot, corresponding to a particular bit pattern, of the *sign string* (the numerical value of the *sign string* is used to index through the *sign table)* contains a pointer variable. This pointer variable, which is initially NULL, will be pointing to a linked list. So, with each 'sign string', a linked list is maintained. The elements of each node, in such a list is an ordered pair, indicating the class and its cardinality. The cardinality of a class denotes the number of feature points of that class, which have been identified to fall into the region, represented by the 'sign string'.

Table 12.3 *Sensitivity of the two methods to relative distribution of feature points*

(f_1, f_2)	Misclassification μ	Variance σ^2	Normalised variance α
(100,0)	0	5000.00	50.00
(99,1)	1	4802.00	48.02
(98,2)	1	4608.00	46.08
(97,3)	1	4418.00	44.18
(96,4)	1	4232.00	42.32
(95,5)	1	4050.00	40.50
(94,6)	1	3872.00	38.72
(93,7)	1	3698.00	36.98
(92,8)	1	3528.00	35.28
(91,9)	1	3362.00	33.62
(90,10)	1	3200.00	32.00
(85,15)	1	2450.00	24.50
(80,20)	1	1800.00	18.00
(75,25)	1	1250.00	12.50
(70,30)	1	800.00	8.00
(65,35)	1	450.00	4.50
(60,40)	1	200.00	2.00
(55,45)	1	50.00	0.50
(50,50)	1	0.00	0.00

It is to be noted that, since there are at most $\frac{H(H+1)}{2}+1$ possible valid regions, only this many slots (among 2^H slots) can ultimately maintain a linked list. As such, rest of the slots will contain NULL pointer. To locate the non-empty slots (corresponding to the valid regions) during fitness calculation, a search, through the entire 'sign table' of length 2^H has to be made, thereby shooting up complexity. Also to be noted that, the non-NULL pointers in the slots indicate valid regions. Furthermore, since, most of the slots (for large *H*) remain unutilized, space usage seems to be inefficient in this method. But, this unnecessary search can be avoided, if we can somehow, identify the valid regions directly and provide appropriate data structure for that purpose.

12.4.2 Alternative Method 1

This method improves the time complexity of the search for slots, corresponding to the valid regions in the 'sign table', during fitness calculation. It still needs the 'sign table' of size 2^H, and hence, it does not achieve a better space complexity. At least,

$\left(2^H - \left(\frac{H(H+1)}{2} + 1\right)\right)$ slots of the table still remain totally unutilized. We need maintain a link between the valid slots, so that a search for the valid slots will be done directly, by following these links. For this, each slot of the 'sign table' need contain an integer variable, called the *last-index,* besides the pointer for the linked list (as mentioned before). Initially, this member variable, called *last-index* is initialized to '–1', and the pointer member to NULL, as before. A variable, called *next-index*, initialized to '–1' is also maintained.

Algorithm 1

begin

Step 1. repeat step 2 through step 15, for each feature point

Step 2. determine the *sign string*, of the feature point

Step 3. the numerical value of the *sign string* is decoded (this value is a non-negative integer and will be referred to, as the corresponding *index*)

Step 4. if the pointer member of the slot (of the *sign table*), indicated by the number *index* is NULL, then this slot is a virgin region (this feature point is the first point found to be in that particular region). In that case,

Step 4-1. perform step 10 through step 15

else

Step 4-2. go to step 5

Step 5. if the node, corresponding to the class of this feature is already in the linked list,

Step 5-1. update the node

else

Step 5-2. perform step 6 through step 9

Step 6. create a new node, corresponding to this class

Step 7. fill up the new node with the required information

Step 8. add it to the linked list

Step 9. go to step 1

Step 10. update the *last-index* member of the slot with *next-index*

Step 11. update the *next-index* with *index*

Step 12. create the first node of the linked list, corresponding to this slot

Step 13. fill it up with the required information

Step 14. update the pointer member of the slot to point to this node

Step 15. go to step 1

end

At the end of this algorithm, the variable *next-index* will be pointing to the slot, which is the last one to have lost its virginity. To locate all the slots, representing the non-empty valid regions, all that one need do is, to start from the slot, indicated by the final value of *next-index* and follow the links, indicated by the member variable *last-index,* to reach the next slot, until '–1' is reached.

12.4.3 Alternative Method 2

This method gets rid of the concept of 'sign table' completely and hence, achieves a significant improvement (particularly for large *H*), in terms of space usage. Instead of 'sign table', it maintains a dynamic linked list structure of 'sign strings'. For each new *sign string*, generated for the feature points, a *header* node is created. This *header* node contains three member variables as described below:

- The first member represents the pattern (actually its numerical value).
- The second member is a pointer variable, which will be pointing to the linked list mentioned before.
- The third member is also a pointer variable, but will be pointing to another *header* node.

This method maintains a linked list with these *header* nodes. So, by knowing the address of the initial node and following the header link, all valid non-empty regions can be traced and retrieved, whenever necessary. It goes without saying that, this structure is competent to recognize and maintain valid regions. So, by this, we avoid nurturing with invalid regions. The only disadvantage of this method is that, during the construction phase of this *header* linked list, a linear search through this list has to be carried out, for each of the feature points, unlike the previous two methods, where a particular slot of the 'sign table', was accessed directly, by using the numerical value of the decoded 'sign string', as the index of the 'sign table'. We think that, we are now in a position to describe our second algorithm.

Algorithm 2

Initialization: A pointer variable *start header* of the type, described above is initialized to NULL.

begin

Step 1. repeat step 2 through step 6, for each of the feature points

Step 2. determine the *sign string* for the feature point

Step 3. decode the *sign string* into a non-negative integer

Step 4. if *start header* points to NULL,

begin

Step 4-1. create a new *header* node

Step 4-2. update *start header* to point to it

Step 4-3. initiate the linked list, as described before in the other two methods for this header

Step 4-4. the second member of the header points to this linked list

Step 4-5. the third member points to NULL

end

else

Step 5. if *start header* is not NULL,

begin

Step 5-1. search the linked list, through the *third field*, of each node header (until NULL is found) trying to match their *first field*, with the decoded value of the *sign string*

Step 5-2. if such a header is found,

begin

Step 5-2-1. update the corresponding linked list of the *header* as before

end

else

Step 5-3. if *header* is not found,

begin

Step 5-3-1. create new *header*

Step 5-3-2. fill it up with necessary information

Step 5-3-3. append it to the *header* linked list at the end

end

end

Step 6. go to step 1

end

The implementation of this method is found to work efficiently, even for very large value of *H,* unlike the implementation of the methods, described in sections 12.4.1 and 12.4.2. This is because, the number of non-empty regions (containing at least one feature point) and thereby the number of *header* nodes required, are both bounded above either by $\frac{H(H+1)}{2}+1$ or the number of training points, whichever is smaller. So, empirically saying, even if the number of feature points (n) is of the order of 100 and H is very high (say, 100 and the number of valid regions is 5051), the number of relevant regions (non-empty regions) can at most be 100.

12.4.4 Deterministic Algorithm

It is to be noted that, each line provides two half-spaces - a positive half-space (not containing the origin) and a negative half-space (containing the origin), as depicted in Fig. 12.7. We may pose the same problem in a different way. In this new perspective, we intend to place a line, with respect to fixed position(s) of a line(s). Let us encompass different cases, by building up one after another.

When the feature plane contains only one feature point, there are only two ways to place a straight line, as per Fig. 12.7.

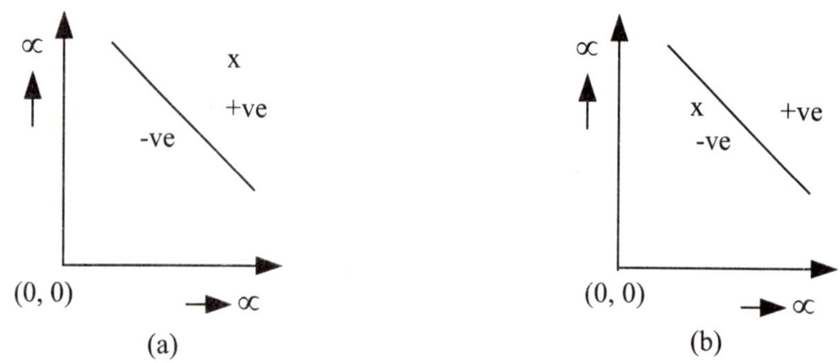

Fig. 12.7 (*a*) Point contained in positive half space, (*b*) Point contained in negative half space

With two feature points, there are four different ways, in which, one may place a straight line, as in Fig. 12.8.

Expressed in words,

- Both the points are contained in the negative half-space.
- Both the points are in the positive half-space.
- The first point is contained in the positive half-space and the second point is in the negative half-space.
- The first point falls in the negative half-space, whereas, the second one does so in the positive half-space.

Now, for N number of feature points in the feature plane, there are ${}^{N}C_2$ different choices of pair of points. For each pair of points, there are four possible ways to place a straight line, as illustrated in Fig. 12.8. So, the total number of straight lines, that is to be considered for N distinct feature points is $4 \times {}^{N}C_2$. Thus, the number of ways, one can select H lines from $4 \times {}^{N}C_2$ lines is ${}^{4 \times {}^{N}C_2}C_H$, which equals ${}^{2N(N-1)}C_H$. In terms of computational complexity, it is equivalent to $O(N^{2H})$. Now, we go to construct this deterministic algorithm, in the next section, but not before explaining some outstanding points.

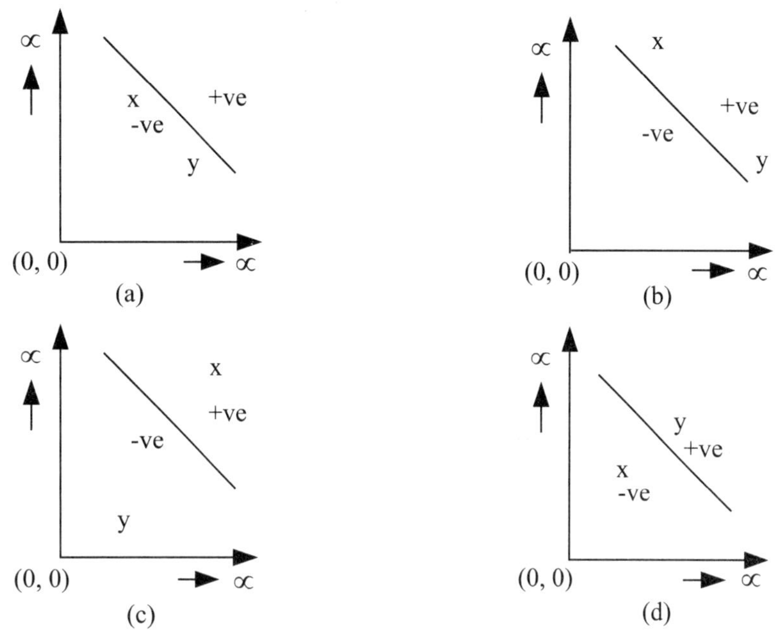

Fig. 12.8 Four different ways of placing a straight line in IR^2 with two points

Our set-up consists of N feature points, which are labelled by the indices i, $i = 1, 2, ..., N$ and there are H straight lines. A pair of points is uniquely represented by the ordered pair (i, j), $i = 1, 2,..., N - 1$ and $i < j. \leq N$

For each ordered pair (i, j) of points, there are four different types of straight lines, as already illustrated. Let us represent the type of a straight line by the index t. So, the ordered sequence (i, j, t) for $i = 1, 2, ..., N - 1$ and $j > i, j = 2, 3,..., N$ and $t = 1, 2, 3, 4$ uniquely specifies the position of a straight line, which is referred to as a *state,* in our future discussion. Hence, in our set-up, there are ${}^{2N(N-1)}C_H$ possible states, with each state representing a straight line. Our nomenclature of (1, 2, 1) and ($N - 1$, N, 4) are respectively the 'firststate' and the 'laststate'. So far as the implementation of the present deterministic algorithm is concerned, we maintain a 'statevector' of size H, to represent H straight lines, in the two-dimensional feature space.

The algorithm

begin

Step 1. initial processing

begin

Step 1-1. state ← firststate

Step 1-2. $k \leftarrow 1$

Step 1-3. statevector $[k]$ ← state

Step 1-4. done ← False

Step 1-5. $k \leftarrow k + 1$

end

Step 2. repeat the following steps until done = True

Step 3. if $k < H$

go to step 4

else

perform step 13 through step 17

Step 4. state ← nextstate(state) if state is a valid state

perform step 5 through step 7

else

perform step 8 through step 10

Step 5. statevector$[k]$ ← state

Step 6. $k \leftarrow k + 1$

Step 7. go to step 3

Step 8. $k \leftarrow k - 1$

Step 9. if $k = 0$

begin

Step 9-1. done ← True

Step 9-2. terminate with *failure* message

end

else

Step 10. if $k \neq 0$

begin

Step 10-1. perform step 11 through step 12

end

Step 11. state ← statevector$[k]$

Step 12. go to step 3

Step 13. $k \leftarrow H$

Step 14. state ← statevector$[k]$

Step 15. map statevector into line

Step 16. construct sign string table

Step 17. calculate misclassification

Step 18. if misclassification = 0

begin

Step 18-1. terminate with *success* massage

end

else

Step 19. if misclassification ≠ 0

begin

Step 19-1. go to step 2

end

end

In the above procedure, we have used the function 'nextstate (state)', which is as follows:

nextstate (state)

begin

Step 1. if state = 1

begin

Step 1-1. state ← 2

Step 1-2. return state

end

Step 2. if state = 2

begin

Step 2-1. state ← 3

Step 2-2. return state

end

Step 3. if state = 3

begin

Step 3-1. state ← 4

Step 3-2. return state

end

Step 4. if state = 4

begin

Step 4-1. state ← 1

Step 4-2. go to step 5

end

Step 5. if $j < N$

begin

Step 5-1. $j \leftarrow j + 1$

Step 5-2. update the state

Step 5-3. return state

end

else

go to step 6

Step 6. if $i < N - 1$

begin

Step 6-1. $i \leftarrow i + 1$

Step 6-2. $j \leftarrow j + 1$

Step 6-3. update state

Step 6-4. return state

end

else

go to step 7

Step 7. return Errorstate

end

12.5 IMPLEMENTATION AND RESULTS

In this work, we have taken a fixed population size, with crossover probability p_c, lying between [0.9 - 0.99] and a mutation probability p_m, lying between [0.01 - 0.02], both the probabilities remaining fixed throughout the generations. The program has been executed for a maximum of 800 iterations.

A comparison of the performance of the new method, with the existing method [4], is shown in Table 12.4 and Table 12.5 on two data sets, each comprising 50 points. In this context, Figs. 12.9, 12.10, 12.11 and 12.12 present the original data points of these two data sets and their classification, with respect to algorithms suggested in [4] and the one, suggested by us. Points coming from different classes are represented by different symbols like '*x*', '*y*' etc.

Table 12.4 *Comparative illustration of two algorithms on the first data set*

Gen_{max}	Classes	H	Population	p_c	p_m	Gen_{old}	μ (old algo)	Gen_{new}	μ (new algo)
800	4	4	24	0.90	0.010	800	3	76	0
800	4	4	24	0.99	0.015	800	3	82	0
800	4	8	24	0.99	0.015	800	3	24	0

Table 12.5 *Comparative illustration of two algorithms on the second data set*

Gen_{max}	Classes	H	Population	p_c	p_m	Gen_{old}	μ (old algo)	Gen_{new}	μ(new algo)
400	2	3	24	0.90	0.010	400	1	83	0
400	2	4	24	0.90	0.010	400	1	29	0
400	2	6	24	0.90	0.010	339	0	30	0
400	2	10	24	0.90	0.010	236	0	10	0
400	2	12	24	0.90	0.010	136	0	3	0

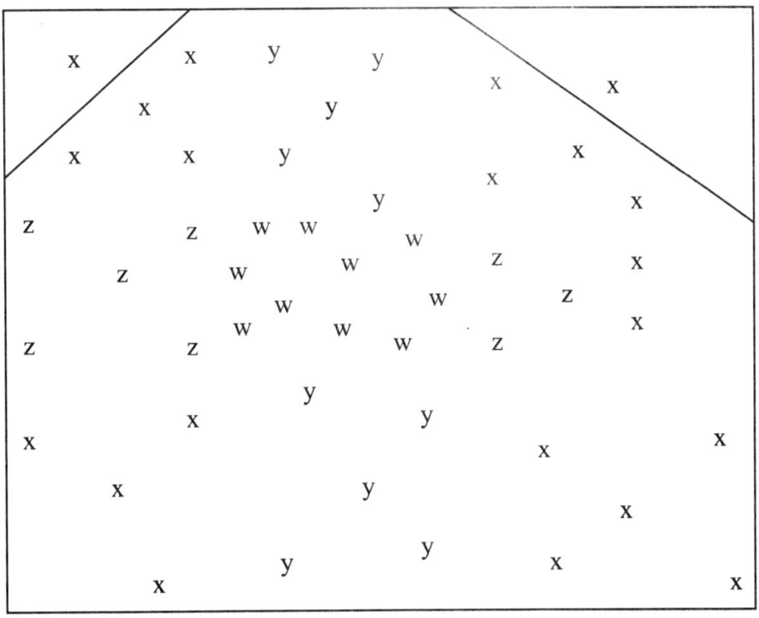

Fig. 12.9 Existing algorithm with $p_c = 0.9$, $p_m = 0.012$, $H = 4$, number of generations = 800 and misclassification = 3 on the first data set

It is empirically apparent from Tables 12.4 and 12.5 that, the new method is performing better than the existing method [4]. We conducted our experiment on 50 different data sets, with 50 different parameter conditions, and on each and every occasion, we found, our suggested algorithm, outperforming the present one. We have presented a few typical representation figures. The deterministic algorithm is also run on a small artificial data set, but because of its exponential time complexity, our GA gives a solution relatively much faster.as expected. With data size 50, that we considered in the supplied data sets, the deterministic exhaustive search took practically infeasible amount of time, which we prefer not presenting here for obvious reasons.

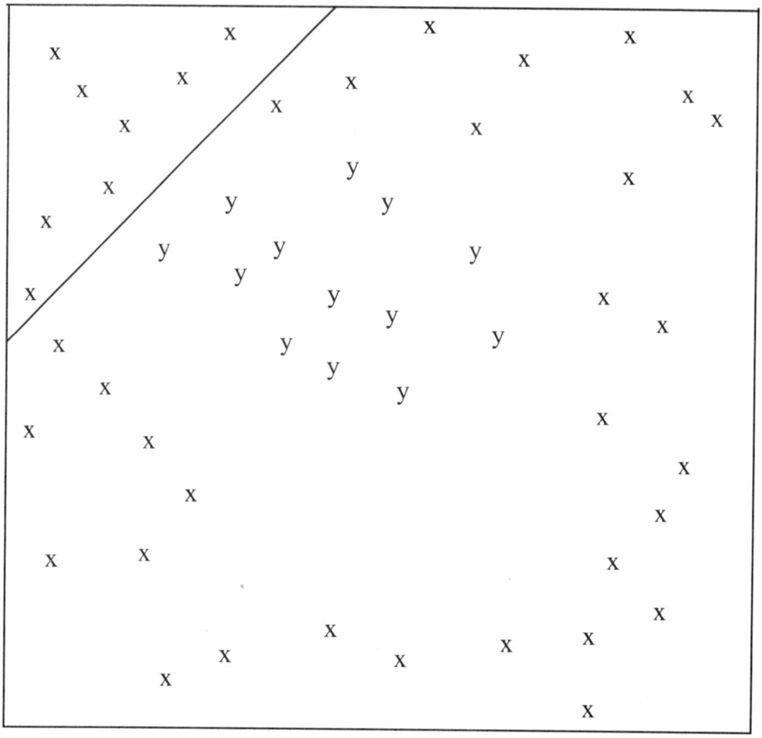

Fig. 12.10 Existing algorithm with $p_c = 0.9$, $p_m = 0.012$, $H = 3$, number of generations = 400 and misclassification = 1 on the second data set

12.6 DISCUSSION

The functioning of GAs may be visualized, as a balanced combination of exploration of new regions in the search space and the exploitation of already sampled regions. The balance between exploitation and exploration, which critically controls the performance of GAs, is determined, by an appropriate choice of control parameters. Some of the trade-offs, that arise with the choice of the optimal control parameters, are determined by the following issues:

- Increase in the crossover probability, increases recombination of build-blocks, while it also increases the disruption of good strings.
- Increase in the mutation probability, tends to transform the genetic search into a random search, while it also aids in reintroducing lost genetic material into the string.
- Increase in the population size, enhances the density in the population and the probability, that the GA does not prematurely converge to a local optimum, while it also increases the time required for the population, to converge to the optimal regions in the search space.

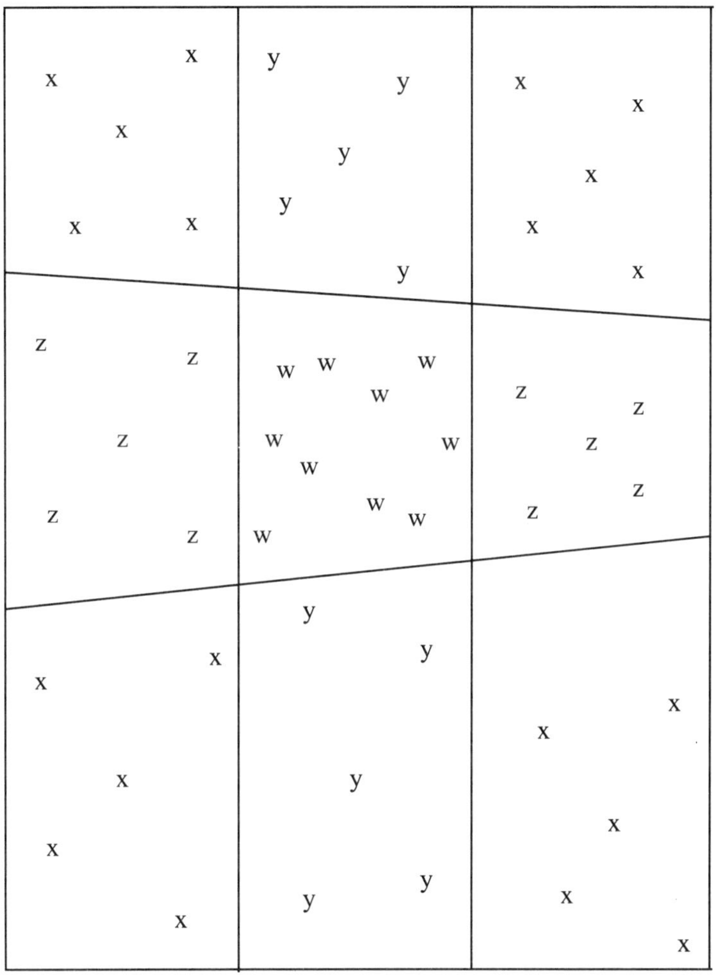

Fig. 12.11 Our algorithm with $p_c = 0.9$, $p_m = 0.012$, $H = 4$, number of generations = 76 and misclassification = 0 on the first data set

More importantly, the control parameters have to be chosen, after considering the interaction between the genetic operators. They cannot be determined independently, and the choice of the control parameters itself, has been viewed as a complex, non-linear optimization problem [10]. Further, it is becoming evident, that the optimal control parameters critically depend on the nature of the objective function [10].

However, it is not easy to choose optimal control parameters for a given problem. Even till this date, there is very little reliable theoretical guidelines, for choosing control parameters, with respect to a given problem [35].

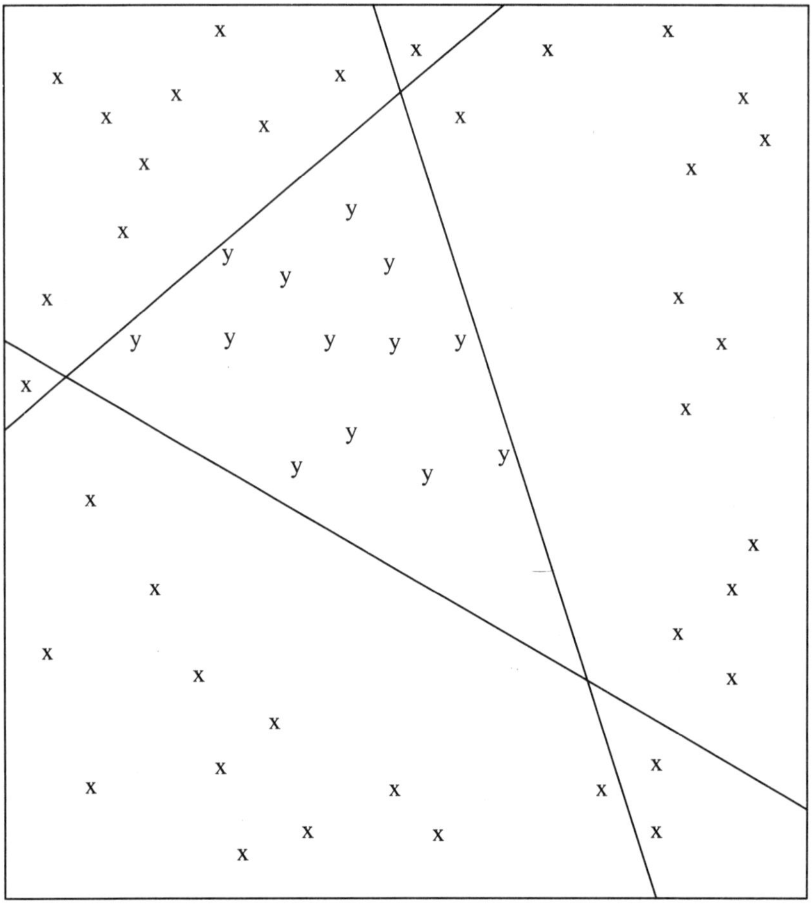

Fig. 12.12 Our algorithm with $p_c = 0.9$, $p_m = 0.012$, $H = 3$, number of generations = 83 and misclassification = 0 on the second data set

An observed feature of the methodology is that, an increase in the number of straight lines, results in a quicker convergence to an optimal solution.

It is known in the literature [11], that as the number of iterations moves towards infinity, the elitist model of GA will certainly result in an optimal string. Rudolph [34] has underlined convergence issues in EA set-up. However, for the problem under consideration, for infinitely many iterations, any value of *H*, will certainly provide the minimal misclassification for that *H,* provided a solution exists. However, a proper choice of *H,* that provides the least misclassification, is of crucial practical importance.

References

1. K S Ray and J Ghoshal, "Neuro genetic approach to pattern recognition", in *Proceedings of the Fourth International Conference on Soft Computing, IIZUKA* - 96, Japan, Vol. 1, 1996.
2. M Fukumi and N Akamatsu, "A genetic approach to feature selection for pattern recognition systems", in *Proceedings of the Fourth International Conference on Soft Computing, IIZUKA* - 96, Japan, Vol. 2, 1996.
3. S Forrest, B Jovornik, R N Smith and A S Perelson, "Using genetic algorithms to explore pattern recognition in the immune system", *Evolutionary Computation*, Vol. 1, No. 3, 1993.
4. S Bandyopadhyay, C A Murthy and S K Pal, "Pattern classification with genetic algorithms", *Pattern Recognition Letters*, Vol. 16, No. 8, pp 801 – 808, 1995.
5. S McClintock, T Lunney and A Hashim, "An application of genetic algorithms to star pattern recognition", in *Proceedings of the Fourth International Conference on Soft Computing, IIZUKA* - 96, Japan, Vol. 2, 1996.
6. C A Ankenbrandt, B P Buckles and F E Petry, "Scene recognition using genetic algorithms with semantic nets", *Pattern Recognition Letters*, Vol. 11, 1990.
7. W Siedlecki and J Sklansky, "A note on genetic algorithms for large-scale feature selection", *Pattern Recognition Letters*, Vol. 10, No. 11, 1989.
8. P Dutta and D Dutta Majumder, "An improved genetic scheme for 2D point classification problem", in *Proceedings of the Fourth Joint Conference in Information Sciences*, 1998.
9. P Dutta and D Dutta Majumder, "An improved genetic scheme for two dimensional point classification problem", *Information Sciences*, Communicated 1998.
10. S K Pal and P P Wang, *Genetic Algorithms for Pattern Recognition.* CRS Press, Inc., 1996. Edited.
11. D Bhandari, C A Murthy and S K Pal, "Genetic algorithm with elitist model and its convergence", *International Journal on Pattern Recognition and Artificial Intelligence.* Communicated.
12. K P Bennett, "Semi-Supervised Support Vector Machines", in *Proceedings of Neural Information Processing Systems*, Denver, 1998.
13. C J C Burges, "A Tutorial on Support Vector Machines for Pattern Recognition", *Data Mining and Knowledge Discovery*, Vol. 2, No. 2, pp. 121 - 167, 1998.
14. M A Hearst, "Support Vector Machines", *IEEE Intelligent Systems*, pp. 18 - 28, July/August. 1998.

15. V N Vapnik, "Statistical Learning Theory", John Wiley & Sons, New York, 1998.
16. J C Bezdek, "Pattern Recognition with Fuzzy Objective Function Algorithms", Plenum Press, New York, 1981.
17. R Agrawal, J Gehrke, D Gunopulos and P Raghavan, "Automatic subspace clustering of high dimensional data for data mining applications", in *Proceedings of the ACM-SIGMOD International Conference on Management of Data,* Seattle, Washington, 1998.
18. F Can, "Incremental clustering for dynamic information processing", *ACM Transactions on Information Systems*, Vol. 11, No. 143, 1993.
19. P Drineas, A Frieze, A Kannan, S Vempala and V Vinay, "Clustering in large graphs and matrices", in *Proceedings of SODA, SIAM,* 1999.
20. M Ester, H P Kriegei, J Sander and X Xu, "A density based algorithm for discovering clusters in large spatial databases with noise", in *Proceedings of the second International Conference on Knowledge Discovery in Databases and Data Mining*, Montreal, Canada, 1995.
21. K C Gowda and G Krishna, "Agglomerative clustering using the concept of mutual nearest neighbourhood", *Pattern Recognition*, Vol. 10, No. 105, 1977.
22. S Haykin, "Neural Networks - a Comprehensive Foundation", second edition, Prentice Hall, Englewood Cliffs, 1999.
23. O Heinonen and H Mannila, "Attribute-oriented induction and conceptual clustering", *Report No. C-1996-2, Dept. of CS,* University of Helsinki, Finand, 1996.
24. A K Jain and R C Dubes, "Algorithms for Clustering Data", Prentice-Hall, New Jersey, 1988.
25. A Krause, "Large Scale Clustering of Protein Sequences", *Ph.D Thesis,* University of Bielefeld, Berlin, Germany, 2002.
26. R S Michalski and R E Stepp, "Automated construction of classifications: conceptual clustering versus numerical taxonomy", *IEEE Transactions on Pattern Analysis and Machine Intelligence*, Vol. 5, No. 396, 1983.
27. S Mitra, S K Pal and P Mitra, "Data Mining in soft computing framework: A survey", *IEEE Transactions on Neural Networks*, Vol. 13, No. 3, 2002.
28. M N Murthy and A K Jain, "Knowledge-based clustering scheme for collection, Management and retrieval of library books", *Pattern Recognition*, Vol. 28, No. 949, 1995.
29. R Natarajan, "Exploratory data analysis in large, sparse datasets", *IBM Research Report, RC 20749*, 1997.
30. A K Pujari, "Data Mining Techniques", University Press, New Delhi, India, 2001.

31. S Z Selim and M A Ismail, "K-means type algorithms: A generalized convergence and characterization of local optimality", *IEEE Transactions on Pattern Analysis and Machine Intelligence*, Vol. 6, No. 81, 1984.
32. D V Susheela and M N Murty, "Hand-written digit recognition using soft computing", in *Soft Computing for Image Processing* edited by S K Pal, A Ghosh and M K Kundu, Physica-Verlag, Hiedelberg, 2000.
33. T Zhang, "Data Clustering for Very Large Datasets Plus Applications", *Ph.D Thesis,* University of Wisconsin - Madison, 1997.
34. G Rudolph, "Convergence Properties of Evolutionary Algorithms", Kovac, Hamburg, Germany, 1997.
35. J D Schaffer et.al., "A study of control parameters affecting online performance of genetic algorithms for function optimization", in *Proceedings of the Third International Conference on Genetic algorithms*, pp. 51 - 60, Morgan Kaufmann, San Mateo, California, 1989.
36. R O Duda and P E Hart, "Pattern Classification and Scene Analysis", John Wiley & Sons, New York, 1973.
37. V N Vapnik, "The Nature of Statistical Learning Theory", Springer, New York, 1995.
38. B Moghaddam and M H Yang, "Gender classification with support vector machines", in *Proceedings of the 4th IEEE International Conference on Automatic Face and Gesture Recognition*, pp. 306 - 311, 2000.
39. S Watanbe, "Pattern Recognition: Human and Mechanical", Wiley, New York, 1985.
40. L A Zadeh, "Fuzzy logic = Computing with words", *IEEE Transactions on Fuzzy Systems*, Vol. 4, No. 103, 1996.
41. S K Mishra and V V Raghavan, "An Empirical Study of the Performance of Heuristic Methods for Clustering", *Pattern Recognition in Practice*, E S Gelsema and L N Kanal eds., North Holland, pp. 425 - 436, 1994.
42. K Rose, "Deterministic Annealing for Clustering, Compression, Classification, Regression and Related Optimization Problems", *Proceedings IEEE*, Vol. 86, pp. 2210 - 2239, 1998.
43. J Mao, K Mohiuddin and A K Jain, "Parsimonious Network Design and Feature Selection through Node Pruning", in *Proceedings of the 12th International Conference on Pattern Recognition*, pp. 622 - 624, 1994.
44. T Kohonen, "Self Organizing Maps", *Springer Series in Information Sciences*, Vol. 30, Berlin, 1995.

45. H Spath, "Cluster Analysis Algorithms for Data Reduction and Classification of Objects", Ellis Horwood Limited, West Sussex, U.K., 1986.
46. G Carpenter and S Grossberg, "ART3: Hierarchical search using chemical transmitters in self-organizing pattern recognition architectures", *Neural Networks*, Vol. 3, No. 129, 1990.
47. R C T Lee, J R Slagle and C T Mong, "Towards automatic auditing of records", *IEEE Transactions on Software Engineering*, Vol. 4, No. 441, 1978.
48. F Farnstorm, J Lewis and C Elcan, "Scalability for clustering algorithms revisited", *http://citeseer. nj. nec. com,* 2000.
49. R T Ng and J Han, "Efficient and effective clustering methods for spatial data mining", in *Proceedings of the VLDB Conference*, Santiago, Chile, 1994.
50. S Guha, R Rastogi and K Shim, "CURE: an efficient algorithm for clustering large databases", in *Proceedings of ACM-SIGMOD International Conference on Management of Data*, Seattle, 1998.
51. H Stahl, "Cluster Analysis of Large Data Sets", *Classification as tool of research*, W. Gaul and M. Schader eds., Elsevier, Amstardam, 1986.

UNIT III

SPEECH AND SIGNAL PROCESSING AND APPLICATIONS

13

A Study of Nonlinear Transformations of Partial Correlation Coefficients for Vowel Recognition

KK Paliwal[1]

ABSTRACT

The partial correlation (PARCOR) coefficients derived through linear prediction (LP) analysis of speech have a number of desirable properties which make them attractive for quantization in speech coding applications. However, these coefficients have the drawback of their spectral sensitivities being non-uniform. Recently, three nonlinear transformations of the PARCOR coefficients have been reported which make their spectral sensitivities uniform. In the present paper, the PARCOR coefficients and their nonlinear transformations (log-area ratios, log-error ratios and inverse sine PARCORs) are compared as to their performance in a vowel recognition task. Vowel recognition performance is found to be the best with the log-area ratios.

Keywords: Nonlinear Transformation; Partial Correlation (PARCOR) Coefficient; Linear Prediction (LP) Analysis; Vowel Recognition; Log-area and Error Ratio.

13.1 INTRODUCTION

The Linear prediction (LP) analysis technique is one of the most popular techniques of speech processing [1,2] and has been extensively used for speech recognition, speech coding, speech synthesis and speaker recognition. The LP analysis technique provides a number of parametric representations [3,4] which provide equivalent information about the speech spectrum envelope. Out of these parametric representations, the PARCOR coefficient representation has certain desirable properties which make it suitable for quantization purposes in speech coding. These properties are as follows: *(i)* The PARCOR coefficients may be obtained as a result of orthogonalization of the basis vectors for the LP coefficients [5]. *(ii)* The values of PARCOR coefficients k_i, $i < M$ (where M is the order of linear predictor used in LP analysis), do not change as M increases [2]. *(iii)* The stability of the estimated all-pole filter can be ascertained by verifying the magnitudes of the PARCOR coefficients to be less than unity [1,2].

The facts that the PARCOR coefficients are representations is an orthogonal system of coordinates and that these coefficients can be

[1] Computer Systems and Communications Group, Tata Institute of Fundamental research, Homi Bhabha Road, Bombay 400005, India and Bell Telephone Laboratory, New Jersey, U.S.A.

computed efficiently using the lattice structure make them desirable for speech recognition where template matching is used for pattern classification. Recently, the PARCOR coefficient representation has been compared with the other LP parametric representations in a isolated-word recognition task by Ichikawa *et al.* [6] and in a vowel recognition task by Paliwal and Rao [7]. It has been found that the recognition performance of the PARCOR coefficient representation is inferior to that of the other LP parametric representations.

The poor recognition performance of the PARCOR coefficients has been attributed by Makhoul [5] to non-uniform spectral sensitivities of these coefficients. Viswanathan and Makhoul [4] have shown that the variation of spectral sensitivity with respect to a PARCOR coefficient is a U-shaped curve; i.e., a small change in the value of a PARCOR coefficient near ± 1 causes a relatively large deviation in the all-pole spectrum. This causes a problem when Euclidean-type distance measures are used for pattern classification. In order to overcome this problem, three non-linear transformations have been proposed in the literature [4,8]. The transformed PARCOR coefficients result in uniform spectral sensitivity functions. These transformed coefficients are given below in terms of PARCOR coefficients k_i, $i = 1, 2, ---, M$

Log-area Ratios [4]:

$$f_i = \log \frac{1 - k_i}{1 + k_i}, \qquad i = 1, 2, ----, M.$$

Log-error Ratios [4]:

$$g_i = \sin (k_i) \log \frac{1}{1 - k_i^2}, \qquad i = 1, 2, ----, M.$$

Inverse sine PARCORs [8]:

$$h_i = \sin^{-1} (k_i), \qquad i = 1, 2, ----, M.$$

The aim of the present paper is to study the effect of these nonlinear transformations on the speech recognition performance. Since most of the phonemes (about 38.2 per cent [9]) occurring in conversational English are vowels, we will compare here the four representations (PARCOR coefficient, log-area ratio, log-error ratio and inverse sine PARCOR) in terms of their vowel recognition performance.

13.2 DATA ACQUISITION AND PREPROCESSING

The speech data used in the present study consist of 900 utterances, having 30 repetitions of 10 different */b/*-vowel-*/b/* syllables, spoken by 3 speakers (2 male and 1 female). The vowels used here are 10 Hindi vowels:/i/, /I/, /e/, /æ/, /∧/, /a/, /)/, /o/, /U/ and /u/. Recording of these utterances is done in an ordinary office room. The speech signal is digitized at a sampling rate of 10kHz by means of a 12 bit analog-to-digital converter. A low-pass filter with a cutoff frequency of 4kHz is used as an anti-aliasing filter.

The steady-state part of the vowel segment is manually located for each of the 900 utterances and a 20msec segment is excised from its centre. A 10th order LP analysis is performed and the PARCOR coefficients are derived from each of these 20msec segments. The autocorrelation method of linear prediction (with 20 msec Hamming window and without preemphasis) is used here for analysis.

13.3 RECOGNITION PROCEDURE

The aim here is to classify the *M*-dimensional vectors (each vector has *M* (=10) transformed PARCOR coefficients as its components) representing the vowel segments into ten vowel classes. This is a standard problem in statistical pattern recognition and has been treated exhaustively in the literature [10]. In the present paper, the classification scheme used is the forced decision pattern matching method and is studied using the Euclidean distance measure which, for the *i*th class, is given by

$$\boldsymbol{d}_i = \left[(\boldsymbol{x} - \boldsymbol{m}_i)\,(\boldsymbol{x} - \boldsymbol{m}_i)\right]^{1/2},$$

where $\boldsymbol{x}$ is the test vector and $\boldsymbol{m}_i$ the mean vector of the *i*th class. The superscript *t* denotes here the transpose of the vector. The test vector $\boldsymbol{x}$ is classified here into the *i*th class if $d_i < d_j$ for all $j \neq i$.

The mean vector for all the ten vowel classes are computed from the data in the training set by using the following relation:

$$\boldsymbol{m}_i = \frac{1}{N_i} \sum_{j=1}^{N_i} \boldsymbol{y}_{ij}, \qquad i = 1, 2, ---, 10.$$

where N_i is the number of preclassified vectors in the *i*th class and $\boldsymbol{y}_{ij}$ the *j*th vector of the *i*th class.

13.4 RESULTS AND DISCUSSION

Vowel recognition performance of the PARCOR coefficient representation, the log-area ratio representation, the log-error ratio representation and the inverse sine PARCOR representation is studied here separately for each of the three speakers. In the present study, a speaker-specific training is used; i.e., both the training and test data sets are derived from the same speaker.

In order to estimate the vowel recognition performance, we have here a fixed sample of 300 preclassified vectors for each speaker (obtained from 30 repetitions for each of the 10 vowel classes). This fixed sample can be used in many ways to compute the vowel recognition performance [11]. However, in the present study, we use the following two procedures for computing it. In the first procedure, the training and test data sets are kept the same. This procedure has the drawback that it results in biased (optimistic) estimate of the vowel recognition performance [11]. In the second procedure, the training and the test data sets are kept different. Here, for each vowel class, twenty-nine repetitions are used for training the classifier and the remaining thirtieth repetition for testing. It is repeated 30 times and a total of 300 decisions are made by the classifier for each speaker.

Vowel recognition performance of the four PARCOR parametric representations is studied for each of the three speakers. Results are shown in Tables 13.1 and 13.2. Table 13.1 lists the vowel recognition accuracies when the training and test data sets are same and Table 13.2 when the training and test data sets are different. Average recognition performance over the three speakers is also listed in these tables for each of the four representations. It can be seen from these tables that two of the three nonlinear transformations (i.e., log-area ratios and inverse sine PARCORs) show an improvement in performance over the PARCOR coefficient representation, while the third nonlinear transformation (i.e., log-error ratios) shows a deterioration. Similar results have been reported in the speech coding literature where the log-area ratios and the inverse sine PARCORs are the preferred choices for quantization [4,12].

Table 13.1 *Vowel recognition performance of different PARCOR coefficient representations when training and test data sets are same.*

PARCOR Coefficient Representation	**Vowel Recognition Score (in per cent)**			
	Speaker 1	*Speaker 2*	*Speaker 3*	*Average*
PARCOR coefficients	87.3	86.7	80.7	84.9
Log-area ratios	91.7	88.0	83.0	87.6
Log-error ratios	80.0	75.7	79.7	78.4
Inverse sine PARCORs	87.3	87.7	83.3	86.1

Table 13.2 *Vowel recognition performance of different PARCOR coefficient representations when training and test data sets are different.*

PARCOR Coefficient Representation	**Vowel Recognition Score (in per cent)**			
	Speaker 1	*Speaker* 2	*Speaker* 3	*Average*
PARCOR coefficients	84.7	84.7	78.3	82.6
Log-area ratios	89.7	86.0	79.7	85.1
Log-error ratios	78.7	74.0	77.3	76.7
Inverse sine PARCORs	86.7	84.3	78.7	83.2

The better performance of the log-area ratio and the inverse sine PARCOR representations can be attributed to the spectral sensitivity measures which are defined in these cases in terms of difference between the two log spectra under consideration. (Specifically, the spectral sensitivity measure is the average of the absolute value of the difference between the two log spectra for the log-area ratios [4] and the root-mean square value of the difference for the inverse sine PARCORs [8]. The spectral sensitivity measure for the log-error ratios is defined as the average of the ratios of the two spectra under consideration [4]. Thus, these results indicate that for speech recognition the difference between two log spectra provides a better measure for spectral deviation than the ratio of two spectra.

Thus, we have seen that out of the four PARCOR parametric representations the log-area ratio representation results in the best vowel recognition performance. It might be interesting to compare these results with other LP parametric representations [7]. Since the cepstral coefficient representation results in the best performance among the eight LP parametric representations studied in [7], we compare here the vowel-recognition performance of the log-area ratio representation with that of the cepstral coefficient representation. Using the Euclidean distance measure for pattern classification, the cepstral coefficient representation results in an average vowel recognition performance of 92.9 per cent when the training and the test data sets are same and 91.4 per cent when they are different. The corresponding results for the log-area ratios are 87.6 per cent and 85.1 per cent, respectively. Thus, though the log-area representation gives the best performance among the different PARCOR parametric representations, it is still inferior to the cepstral coefficient representation.

13.5 CONCLUSION

In the present paper, the PARCOR coefficient representation and three other representations (obtained by nonlinear transformations of PARCOR coefficients) are studied as to their performance in a vowel recognition task. The Euclidean distance measure is used for vowel classification. It is shown that two of these nonlinear transformations (log-area ratios and inverse sine PARCORs) show an improvement in the vowel recognition performance over the PARCOR coefficient representation, while the third transformation (log-error ratios) show a deterioration. The log-area ratio representation results in the best performance among the four PARCOR representations. But, its performance is inferior to that of the cepstral coefficient representation which was shown in an earlier study [7] to be the best LP parametric representation for vowel recognition.

References

1. J D Markel and A H Gray, Jr (1976) *Linear Prediction of Speech,* Springer-Verlarg, Berlin.
2. J Makhoul (1975) Linear prediction: a tutorial review. *Proc. IEEE,* 63(4), 561–580.
3. B S Atal (1974) Effectiveness of linear prediction characteristics of the speech wave for automatic speaker identification and verification *J Acoust Soc Am* 55(6) 1304–1312.
4. R Viswanathan and J Makhoul (1975) Quantization properties of transmission parameters in linear predictive systems. *IEEE Trans Acoust Speech and Signal Process* ASSP-23 (3) 309–321.
5. J Makhoul (1974) Linear prediction in automatic speech recognition In: *Speech Recognition* (Ed. D R Reddy), Academic, New York, 183–220.
6. A Ichikawa, Y Nakano and K Nakata (1973) Evaluation of various parameter sets in spoken digits recognition, *IEEE Trans Audio Electroacoust* AU-21 (3); 202–209.
7. K K Paliwal and P V S Rao (1982) Evaluation of various linear prediction parametric representations in vowel recognition. *Signal Process* 4(4), 323–327.
8. A H Gray Jr and JD Markel (1976) Quantization and bit allocation in speech processing *IEEE Trans Acoust Speech and Signal Process* ASSP-24 (6), 459–473.
9. M A Mines, F Hanson and J E Shoup (1978) Frequency of occurrence of phonemes in conversational English. *Language and Speech,* 21(3); 221–235.
10. R O Duda and P E Hart (1973) *Pattern Classification and Scene Analysis* (1974) Wiley, New York.
11. G T Toussaint (1974) Bibliography on estimation of misclassification, *IEEE Trans Info Theor***IT-20** (4), 472–479.
12. N S Jayant and P Noll (1984) *Digital Coding of Waveforms: Principles and Applications to Speech and Video* Prentice Hall, New Jersey.

14

Recognition of (Hindi) Vowels and Speakers using Sequential Pattern Matching Techniques

M Ganesan, SS Agrawal, AM Ansari and KD Pavate[1]

ABSTRACT

Some experiments are described relating the recognition of vowels and speakers using a ten-dimensional discriminant function. The dimensions correspond to the ten acoustic parameters of Hindi vowels obtained by spectrographic analysis for 11 different speakers in four different contexts.

The data were used for creating the test and the reference samples for conducting a number of pattern matching experiments using a laboratory minicomputer. The effect of such factors as the number of training samples and use of weighting coefficients on recognition performance have been studied.

Keywords: Vowel (Hindi) Recognition, Speaker Recognition; Sequential Pattern Matching; Spectrographic Analysis, Fuzzy Set.

14.1 INTRODUCTION

The study of speech is a multidisciplinary subject. The techniques of pattern recognition and statistical methods play an important role in the study of the nature of speech communication and the development of man-machine communication systems using human voice. In general, these techniques are used for solving two types of problems, namely the feature selection and the classification based on some measurements pertaining to a given set of features. In most of the studies related to a speech, two different approaches are generally used i.e., the Fuzzy set theoretic approach and the statistical decision theoretic approach [l]. In the past few decades, a number of studies have been conducted to study the effect of these techniques on the feature selection as well as classification of different types of speech sounds extracted from isolated syllables, words as well as continuous speech signal [2-12].

In India, several studies have been conducted particularly, by using Indian languages, by ISI, Kolkata. In the study on recognition of Telugu vowels, the technique of sequential pattern recognition was used for recognizing the vowels using a three-dimensional feature vector based on the first three formant frequencies [13].

The present study was motivated to find the efficiency of sequential pattern matching technique for the classification of Hindi vowels and the

---

1 Central Electronics Engineering Research Institute, Delhi Centre, CSIR Complex, Hillside Road, New Delhi, India.

speakers using a ten-dimensional feature vector. The dimensions correspond to ten different acoustic parameters of the vowels spoken by male speakers in different phonetic contexts. The effect of different numbers of training samples and the use of weighting coefficient have been studied on:

(i) The recognition of Hindi vowels and their phonetic features,

(ii) The identifications of male speakers, and

(iii) The verification of male speakers.

In some cases, the performance of recognition has been studied and compared in the text-dependent and text-independent situations.

14.2 PROCEDURE

The speech material consists of ten pure Hindi vowels of frequent occurrence i.e., */i/, /I/, /e/, /ε /, /ʌ /, /a/, /ɔ/, /O/, /U/, & /u/* embedded in four different phonetic contexts of isolation, */h-d/, /w-w/* and */j-j/*. These were spoken by 11 different male speakers. For speaker recognition studies some vowels were spoken 10 times in the */h-d/* context. Thus different combinations of utterances were used for vowel recognition and speaker recognition experiments. The utterances were recorded on a cassette tape recorder in a studio. These were analyzed using a Kay Elemetrics Sound Spectrograph Model No.7030 AC in the linear frequency range of 80 to 8000Hz. Three different types of displays i.e., wideband, narrow band and section were obtained for each utterance. Ten acoustic parameters namely, the fundamental frequency (F_0), centre frequencies of the first four formants (F_1, F_2, F_3, F_4), amplitudes of these formants (A_1, A_2, A_3, A_4) and the duration of vowel segment was determined. Therefore, a data bank consisting of large number of acoustic parameters of vowels for different speakers was created and used to create the reference and test samples.

14.3 METHOD OF CLASSIFICATION

A. Vowels Recognition and Identification of Speakers

The discriminant function of sequential pattern matching techniques were used to classify the unknown input among the known classes. The weighted Euclidean distance was used to obtain the discriminant function. The Euclidean distance between the unknown input and the reference vector is given by

$$E.D_j = \left\{ \sum_{i=1}^{N} \left[W_{ij} (X_i - R_{ij}) \right]^2 \right\}^{1/2} \quad i = 1, 2, ... n....N \text{ and } = j = 1, 2, \ldots m \ldots M \qquad (1)$$

where X_i is the unknown sample corresponding to I-th feature in N-dimensional feature vector and R_{ij} is the mean reference vector corresponding to i-th feature and j-th class.

The discriminant function corresponding to jth class is given by

$$D_j = 1/E.D_j \quad (2)$$

The unknown input X is classified here as j–th class if $D_j > D_k$ for all $j \neq k$.

B. Verification of Speakers

A threshold value for the discriminant function was calculated to verify the speaker of the claimed input. The threshold value corresponding to jth speaker is given by

$$D_jT = \underset{Q}{\overset{\text{MAX}}{|}} D_{jq} \qquad q = 1, 2, 3, ... Q.$$

D_{jq} is calculated by computing the Euclidean distance between the Lth element with all the L–1 element in the L element reference sets using equation (1) and Q, the number of distances calculated within the reference set is given by $Q = \dfrac{L(L-1)}{2}$.

Accept the input as jth speaker if $D_j \le D_jT$, else reject.

14.4 RECOGNITION OF VOWELS AND THEIR PHONETIC FEATURES

For vowel recognition experiment 44 samples of each vowel obtained from 4 different contexts of 11 speakers were used. The number of test samples and reference samples were varied for 4 different test conditions. The nos. of reference samples were kept as 11, 22, 33 and 44 and the nos. of test samples 33, 22 and 1 respectively corresponding to 4 different conditions of test.

The effect of varying the number of training samples was studied on each vowel for the above conditions of test. The correct responses of the vowels as well as their confusions were noted down and confusion matrics made for each test condition.

The recognition was also studied for a set of distinctive features of vowels. Five different phonetic features namely, openness, place of articulation, lip rounding, tenseness and duration were used to classify ten Hindi vowels as shown in Table 14.1. Correct recognition scores for each feature were determined from the analysis of confusion matrices for each test condition.

The recognition scores for vowels and all the features (except in the case of tenseness) increases as the no. of training samples increases. This

Table 14.1 *Distinctive features used for classification of (Hindi) vowels*

Features/vowels	/i/	/I/	/e/	/ε/	/ʌ/	/a/	/ɔ/	/O/	/U/	/u/
Openness [A]	1	1	2	2	2	3	2	2	1	1
Place [B]	1	1	1	1	2	3	3	3	3	3
Lip Rounding [C]	1	1	1	1	2	2	3	3	3	3
Tenseness [D]	1	0	1	0	0	1	0	1	0	1
Duration [E]	1	0	1	1	0	1	1	1	0	1

A) Openness (1) Narrow; (2) Medium; (3) Wide

B) Place (1) Front; (2) Central; (3) Back

C) Lip Rounding (1) Stretched Lips; (2) Neutral Lips; (3) Rounded Lips.

D) Tenseness (0) Lax; (1) Tense

E) Duration (0) Short; (1) Long

observation is in conformity with the earlier observations [13, 14]. The performance of features shows that the features of lip rounding and place of articulation are recognised better as compared to the features of openness and duration. The scores for the feature tenseness are very low. This observation indicates that the vowels are confused with the sounds having same place of articulation rather than having the same manner of articulation-such as openness. These observations compare very well with the results obtained for the human recognition experiments for Hindi vowels [14].

These results indicate that the phonetic features play an important role in the recognition of speech sounds. It is remarkable to note that their relative importance remains the same in the cases of machine recognition and human recognition of speech.

14.5 SPEAKER IDENTIFICATION

Speaker identification experiments have been conducted using reference samples from the same context as well as from different contexts.

In the first test the data from four different contexts for all the vowels were used and the three utterances were used as the reference samples whereas the fourth utterance was used as test sample. A total of 440 combinations were used for decision making. In the other test, the data were collected from ten different utterances of the speakers for one context only. Out of 10 samples, the reference sample number was varied from 3 to 9 and the remaining samples were used as test samples. In all the cases, the test and the reference samples were interchanged in all possible ways to form maximum number of combinations. The recognition scores were obtained both by using and not using the weighting coefficient. These tests were also conducted by dividing the parameters into two groups. In the first group, frequency parameters namely F_0, F_1, F_2, F_3, F_4 were used whereas in the second group the amplitude parameters (A_1, A_2, A_3, A_4) and duration were used. The effect of these parameters on speaker identification was determined with and without weighting coefficient.

The correct recognition scores of speakers for the above test conditions indicate that the recognition performance improves significantly with the increase in number of reference samples, use of weighting coefficient and when the reference samples are used from the same context. Similar observations were made by earlier workers also in the case of speaker recognition experiments [15]. It also indicates that the first group of parameters (frequency parameters) gives better performance as compared to the second group of parameters (amplitude and duration). This indicates that the frequency parameters are more important for the recognition of speakers.

14.6 SPEAKER VERIFICATION

Speaker verification experiments have been conducted using reference samples from the same context. The data were collected from the different utterances of 11 speakers for one context only. Out of these, 9 utterances were used as reference samples and the 10th utterance was used as the test sample. These were interchanged to form all possible combinations. The verification scores were obtained using weighting coefficient as well as without using weighting coefficient.

The correct verification scores are shown in Table 14.2. It appears that the use of weighting coefficient does not have a significant effect on the verification scores. However, in both the cases, the tendency of correct elimination is better than that of correct verification [16].

Table 14.2

	Without W.C	With W.C.
Correct Verification	86	86
False Elimination	24	24
Correct Elimination	994	963
False Verification	106	137

14.7 CONCLUSIONS

The above mentioned studies on vowel recognition, speaker identification and speaker verification have been conducted using similar data on 10 acoustic parameters of Hindi vowels. It appears that the parameters selected for the study are important for both vowel recognition as well as speaker recognition. However, frequency-dependent parameters show greater importance than the amplitude-dependent parameters. Increase in the number of training samples and the use of weighting coefficient improves the performance of recognition significantly.

The recognition matrices for vowels have been analyzed using a set of distinctive features. The analyses shows two important findings. One is that the place feature is recognized much better than the other features. This means that most errors correspond to the adjacent place of articulation. Feature analysis can help in developing strategies for better speech recognition system. The other is that features follow the same rank of importance as it was obtained in the case of human recognition of vowels in a separate experiment.

The study of speaker identification suggests a possibility of identifying speakers in the text-independent condition. However, the recognition scores improve when the samples are collected from the same context. In both the cases of speaker identification and verification, the increase in number of training samples can improve the performance significantly.

Acknowledgement

The authors are thankful to the Director, CEERI, Dr GN Acharya for his kind encouragement and providing necessary facilities to conduct these experiments.

References

1. A K Dutta (1980) Statistical approach in ASR research, *Proc. Int. Symp. Speech process* TIFR, Mumbai, July 23–26, 11–1 to 11–22.
2. D Dutta Majumder and A K Datta (1968) Some studies on automatic speech coding and recognition procedure *Indian J Phys* **12**.
3. SEG Ohman (1966) Coarticulation in VCV utterances: Spectrographic measurements, *J Acoustic soc Am* **39,** 151–168.
4. F Itakuna and S Saito (1970) A statistical method for estimation of speech spectral density and formant frequencies. *Electron Commun* Japan 53 – A, 36 – 43.
5. D Dutta Majumder, A K Dutta and N R Ganguli (1973) Some studies on the acoustic features of human speech in relation to Hindi speech sounds. *Indian J Phys* **47** (1973) 598–613.
6. D Dutta Majumder and A K Dutta (1974) *On some application of statistical method in man-machine communication research* Presented at the International Symposium on Recent Trends in Statistics.
7. F Jalinek, L R Bahl and R L Mercer (1975) Design of linguistic statistical decoder for the recognition of continuous speech, *IEEE Trans Inf Theory* **IT-21**; 250–256.

8. JW Forgie and CD Forgie (1959) Results obtained from a vowel recognition computer programme. *J Acoust Soc Am* **30**.
9. BS Atal (1976) Automatic recognition of speakers from their voice *Proc IEEE* **64**, 475–485.
10. KK Paliwal and PVS Rao (1984) Synthesis based recognition of continuous speech *J Acoustic Soc Am* **71**, 1016–1024.
11. M Ganesan, SS Agrawal, AM Ansari and KD Pavate (1984) *Computer Recognition of (Hindi) vowels based on Spectrographic data* **3**, 04.01 to 04.14. CSI.
12. AE Rosenleng and MR Sambur (1975) New techniques for automatic speaker verification. *IEEE Trans ASSP*, **23**,169–176.
13. D Dutta Majumder, AK Datta and SK Pal (1976) Computer recognition of Telugu vowel sounds. *J Comp Soc India*, **7**, 14–20.
14. S S Agrawal and K D Pavate (1980) On the perception of Hindi speech sounds and distinctive features in different phonetic context. *Proc. int. symp. speech process* TIFR, Mumbai, July 23–26 pp 11–1 to 11–22.
15. H M Dante and V V S Sarma (1979) Automatic speaker identification for large population, *IEEE Trans ASSP* **27**, 255–263.
16. J L Flanagan (1976) Computers that talk and listen: man-machine communication by voice. *Proc. IEEE.*

15

Signal Processing Using Model Selection Methods[1]

Z D Bai, P R Krishnaiah and L C Zhao[2]

ABSTRACT

In this paper, the authors gave a review of some recent developments on multivariate statistical techniques for detection of the number of signals using eigenvalues. The main emphasis of the review is 'Efficient Detection Criterion (EDC)' procedures proposed by the authors recently. These procedures are strongly consistent.

Keywords: Signal Processing; Eigenvalues, Additive Model; Strong Consistency; Information Theoretic Criteria.

15.1 INTRODUCTION

In the area of signal processing, eigenstructure methods are becoming popular in determination of the number of signals and estimation of the parameters of the signals when noise is present. Problems of signal detection in presence of noise are quite complex and they arise in many situations. For example, in the area of active sonar detection, signals are transmitted and the echoes from the targets are recorded. The observations are corrupted by disturbances in the sea and we are interested in identification of the targets. In radar detection, pulses are sent and the reflections from the targets are recorded. Here, the observations may be subject to atmospheric disturbance and disturbances due to jammer and clutter. Eigenstructure methods were used in the past by several workers [1-10]. Recently, Wax and Kailath [11,12], Zaho, Krishnaiah and Bai [13,14] Bai, Krishnaiah and Zaho [15] and Paulraj and Kailath [6] considered the problem of determination of the number of signals using model selection approach. The object of this paper is to give a review of the work on model selection approach to determine the number of signals in presence of noise.

---

1 This work is supported Contract N00014-85-K-0292 of the Office of Naval Research and Contract F49620-85-C-0008 of the Air Force Office of Scientific Research. The United States Government is authorized to reproduce and distribute reprints for governmental purposes not withstanding any copyright notation hereon.
Invited paper presented at the Second International Symposium on Advances in Pattern Recognition and Digital Techniques held at the Indian Statistical Institute, January 6-9, 1986.

2 Centre for Multivariate Analysis, Fifth Floor, Thakeray Hall, University of Pittsburgh, Pittsburgh, PA 15260, U.S.A.

In the model considered in this paper, the observations from the sensors are expressed as the sum of noise and linear combinations of the wavefronts of the signals from the sources. When the noise is spatially white, the number of signals is related to the multiplicity of the smallest eigenvalue of the covariance matrix Σ_2 of the observation vectors. Various test procedures are available in the literature [17-19] for testing the hypothesis that the multiplicity of the smallest eigenvalue of the covariance matrix is equal to a specified value when underlying distribution is multivariate normal. The above tests can be used to test the hypothesis that the number of signals is equal to a specified value. When the noise is spatially coloured the number of signals is related to the multiplicity of the smallest eigenvalue of $\Sigma_2 \Sigma_1^{-1}$ where Σ_1 is the covariance matrix of the noise vector. Rao [19] considered the following problem.

Let S_1 and S_2 be distributed independently as central Wishart matrices with n_1 and n_2 degrees of freedom and $E(S_i) = n_i \Sigma_i$ for $i = 1, 2$. Also, let $\Sigma_2 = \Gamma + \lambda \Sigma_1$, where λ is a known or unknown scalar and Γ is nonnegative definite matrix. Rao [19] derived the likelihood ratio test statistic for testing the hypothesis on the rank of Γ when λ is unknown; when λ is known, he derived modified likelihood ratio test statistic. The results of Rao can be used to test the hypothesis that the number of signals is equal to a specified value in the case of spatially coloured noise.

There are many situations where the experimenter is confronted with the problem of making one of the various possible decisions instead of testing one specified hypothesis. In these situations, one can formulate the problem within the framework of model selection. In the context, one of the several possible models is chosen where each model corresponds to the statement that the number of signals is equal to a particular value. In the model selection approaches discussed in this paper, no threshold value (critical value) is needed. In tests of hypotheses, we need a critical value for implementation of the tests and it is quite complicated to compute the critical values in some situations. The model selection approaches discussed here involve using certain information theoretic criteria. Of course, model selection methods should have optimum properties to have an appeal. One such desirable property in our case is the consistency of the estimate of the number of signals. Consistency property of the model selection methods is also discussed in this paper. A description of the organization of the paper is given below.

Section 15.2 gives some preliminaries. Section 15.3 gives a review of the literature on detection of the number of signals in presence of white noise. Analogous problems are reviewed in Section 15.4 when the noise is spatially coloured. In Section 15.5 is reviewed the literature on detection of the number of signals when the subarrays are located at wide distances apart. The main emphasis of this review is on the *Efficient*

Detection Criteria (EDC) procedures developed by Zhao, Krishnaiah and Bai [13, 14] very recently. These procedures are strongly consistent. In the case of white noise, Bai, Krishnaiah and Zhao [13] gave exponential type bounds on the probability of wrong detection of the number of signals if the EDC procedures are used. These bounds tend to zero rapidly as the sample size increases. Similar bounds can be drived in the case of spatially coloured noise.

15.2 PRELIMINARIES

We now define complex multivariate and Wishart distributions since these definitions are needed in the sequel.

Let $\boldsymbol{x} = \boldsymbol{y}_1 + i\boldsymbol{y}_2$ where $(\boldsymbol{y}'_1, \boldsymbol{y}'_2)$ is distributed as $2p$-variate normal with mean vector $\mathbf{0}$ and covariance matrix.

$$\begin{pmatrix} \Sigma_1 & \Sigma_2 \\ -\Sigma_2 & \Sigma_1 \end{pmatrix} \tag{1}$$

$i = \sqrt{-1}$ and Σ_1 and Σ_2 are of order $p \times p$. Then $x : p \times 1$ is known to be distributed as complex multivariate normal with mean vector $\mathbf{0}$ and covariance matrix $\Sigma = 2(\Sigma_1 + i\Sigma_2)$. The density of x is of the form

$$f(x) = \{1/\pi^p |\Sigma|\} \exp(-\bar{x}\, \Sigma^{-1} x), \tag{2}$$

where $\bar{\boldsymbol{a}}$ and $\bar{\boldsymbol{A}}$ respectively denote the complex conjugate of a and transpose of $\bar{A}$. Next, let $\boldsymbol{x}_1 \ldots \boldsymbol{x}_n$ be distributed independently and identically as complex multivariate normal with mean vector $\mathbf{0}$ and covariance matrix Σ. Then $S = \sum_{j=1}^{n} \boldsymbol{x}_j \bar{\boldsymbol{x}}_j$ is known to be distributed as the central complex Wishart distribution with n degrees of freedom and $E(S) = \boldsymbol{n}\Sigma$. The complex multivariate normal distribution was considered by Wooding [20], whereas the complex Wishart distribution was investigated by Goodman [21]. Complex multivariate normal distribution belongs to the family of complex elliptically symmetric distributions studied by Krishnaiah and Lin [18]. For a review of the literature on complex multivariate distributions, the reader is referred to Krishnaiah [22].

15.3 DETECTION OF NUMBER OF SIGNALS IN PRESENCE OF WHITE NOISE

In this section, we discuss certain methods of detection of number of signals in presence of white noise. The model that is considered is given by

$$\boldsymbol{x}(t) = A\boldsymbol{s}(t) + \boldsymbol{n}(t), \tag{3}$$

where $\boldsymbol{A} = [\boldsymbol{A}(\phi_1), ..., \boldsymbol{A}(\phi_q)]$, $\boldsymbol{x}(t) = (\boldsymbol{x}_1(t), ..., \boldsymbol{x}_p(t))$, $\boldsymbol{s}'(t) = (\boldsymbol{s}_1(t), ..., \boldsymbol{s}_q(t))$, and $\boldsymbol{n}'(t) = (\boldsymbol{n}_1(t), ..., \boldsymbol{n}_p(t))$. Here the elements of jth column of A depend upon the parameters of jth signal. Also $\boldsymbol{n}(t)$ and $\boldsymbol{s}(t)$ are distributed independently as complex multivariate normal with $\boldsymbol{E}n(t) = \mathbf{0}$, $\boldsymbol{E}s(t) = \mathbf{0}$, $\boldsymbol{E}\{\boldsymbol{n}(t)\ \overline{\boldsymbol{n}(t)'}\} = \sigma^2 I_p$ $\boldsymbol{E}\{\boldsymbol{s}(t)\ \overline{\boldsymbol{s}(t)'}\} = \psi$. The covariance matrix Σ_2 of $\boldsymbol{x}(t)$ is given by

$$\Sigma_2 = \boldsymbol{A}\psi\overline{\boldsymbol{A}'} + \sigma^2 I_p. \tag{4}$$

In the model (3), $x_j(t)$ denotes the observation on jth sensor $n_j(t)$ denotes the noise component associated with jth sensor. and $s_j(t)$ is the signal due to the jth wavefront. Also, we assume that a uniform linear array of P identical sensors is used and q is unknown. In addition, we assume that $\boldsymbol{x}(t_1)$,..., $\boldsymbol{x}(t_n)$ are n independent observations. One special case (e.g., see Shan, Wax and Kailath [10]) of the A matrix is

$$\boldsymbol{A}(\phi_j) = (1, \exp(-i\,\omega_o\,\tau_j), ..., \exp(-i\,\omega_o\,(p-1)\,\tau_j)), \tag{4a}$$

where $\tau_j = (d \sin \theta_j)/c$, d is the distance between the sensors, c is the propagation speed of wavefront, and θ_j denotes the angle of arrival of jth signal.

One important problem in signal processing is to estimate q, the number of unknown signals. We will now discuss this problem from the point of view of model selection.

Let $\lambda_1 \geq ... \geq \lambda_p$ denote the eigenvalues of Σ and let $l_1 \geq ... \geq l_p$ denote the eigenvalues of $\hat{\Sigma}$ where $n\hat{\Sigma} = \sum_{j=1}^{n} \boldsymbol{x}(t_j)\overline{\boldsymbol{x}(t_j)'}$. Here we assume that $\boldsymbol{x}(t_1)$,..., $\boldsymbol{x}(t_n)$ are distributed independent of each other. Now, let $H_k : \lambda_k > \lambda_{k+1} = ... = \lambda_p = \sigma^2$, where σ^2 is unknown. Then H_k denotes the hypothesis that the number of signals is equal to k. It is known that the likelihood ratio test statistic for testing H_k is given by

$$L_k = \left\{ \prod_{i=k+1}^{p} l_i^n \ (1/(p-k)) \ \sum_{i=k+1}^{p} l_i^{n(p-k)} \right\}. \tag{5}$$

Since $-2\log L_k$ is distributed asymptotically as Chi-square with $(p-k)(p-k+1)-1$ degrees of freedom, we can use the above statistic for testing H_k for large samples. In most of the situations, we do not know as for what values of k we should test H_k. Also, if H_k is rejected, we should test for H_{k+1} conditional upon the rejection of H_k. The distribution problem in this case is complicated. We now discuss a model selection approach proposed by Zhao, Krishnaiah and Bai [13] for determination of the number of signals.

Let

$$EDC(k, C_n) = -\log L_k + C_n\, \gamma(k, p), \tag{6}$$

where $\gamma(k, p) = k(2p - k + 1) + 1$ is the number of the parameters that have to be estimated under H_k and C_n is chosen such that

$$\lim_{n \to \infty} \{C_n / n\} = 0 \tag{7}$$

and

$$\lim_{n \to \infty} \{C_n / \log \log n\} = \infty \tag{8}$$

Also, let $EDC(\hat{q}, C_n) = \min\{EDC(0, C_n), \ldots, EDC(p-1, C_n)\}$, (9)

Zhao, Krishnaiah and Bai [13] showed that $\hat{q}$ is a strongly consistent estimate of q. This criterion is known to be Efficient Detection Criterion (EDC). When $C_n = 1$ in (6) $EDC(\hat{q}, C_n)$ reduces to Akaike's AIC Criterion but C_n does not satisfy condition (8) in this case. When $C_n = 1/2 \log n$, $EDC(\hat{q}, C_n)$ reduces to Schwartz-Rissanen's minimum description length (MDL) criterion and it satisfies conditions (7) and (8). Wax and Kailath [11] used AIC and MDL criteria for determination of the number of signals. They have pointed out that AIC criterion is not consistent; whereas the MDL criterion is consistent, their proofs are incomplete [23]. Bai, Krishnaiah and Zhao [15] gave an exponential bound, under certain conditions, on the probability of wrong detection and this bound tends to zero rapidly as $n \to \infty$.

Let $H_k^* : \lambda_k > \lambda_{k+1} = \ldots = \lambda_p = 1$. Zhao, Krishnaiah and Bai [13] derived the following expression for the likelihood ratio test statistic L_k^* for H_k^*:

$$\log L_k^* = n \sum_{i = 1 + \min(\tau, k)}^{p} (\log l_i + 1 - l_i), \tag{10}$$

where τ denotes the number of eigenvalues of l_i which are greater than one. They also showed that $\hat{q}$ is a strongly consistent estimate of q where $\hat{q}$ is chosen such that

$$EDC(\hat{q}, C_n) = -\log L_k^* + C_n\, \gamma(k, p), \tag{11}$$

where C_n satisfies the conditions (7) and (8) and $\gamma(k, p) = k(2p - k + 1)$.

In the EDC procedure described above, it was assumed that $\boldsymbol{x}(t_1), \ldots, \boldsymbol{x}(t_n)$ are distributed independently as complex multivariate Gaussian. But these assumptions need not be valid in a number of situations. But, the proofs of the strong consistency of $\hat{q}$ given by Zhao, Krishnaiah and Bai for the case of unknown σ^2 and $\sigma^2 = 1$ are valid under the following weak conditions.

(i) $\{x(t_i, i = 1,2,....\}$ is a stationary and ϕ-mixing sample sequence with ϕ decreasing and $\sum_{j=1}^{\infty} \phi^{1/2}(j) < \infty$. (12)

(ii) $E(x(t_1)) = O$, $E(\{\bar{x}(t_1)x(t_1)\}^{2+\varepsilon}) < \infty$ for some $\varepsilon > 0$ and $i = 1, 2, \ldots$ (13)

If $x(t_1)$,..., $x(t_n)$ are not distributed as independent complex multivariate normal, L_k and L_k^* are not likelihood ratio test statistics for H_k and H_k^* but the procedures described in this section can be still applied if the conditions (12) and (13) are satisfied.

15.4 DETECTION OF NUMBER SIGNALS IN PRESENCE OF SPATIALLY COLOURED NOISE

Consider the model

$$x(t) = As(t) + \lambda^{1/2} n(t) \tag{14}$$

where λ is known or unknown. Also, $x(t) : p \times 1$, A, $s(t)$ $q \times 1$ and $n(t)$ are as defined in Section 12.3 with the following difference. The covariance matrix of $n(t)$ is Σ_1 that is, noise is spatially correlated. Here, the covariance matrix Σ_2 of $x(t)$ is related to Σ_1 as

$$\Sigma_2 = A\psi\bar{A}' + \lambda\Sigma_1 \tag{15}$$

Then, we are interested in finding out the number of signals q which is unknown. This problem is equivalent to the problem of finding the number of eigenvalues of $\Sigma_2\Sigma_1^{-1}$ which are different from its smallest eigenvalue.

Rao [24] considered the following problem which is very closely related to the above problem. Let S_1 and S_2 be distributed as central Wishart matrices with n_1.and n_2 degrees of freedom, respectively and $E(S_i) = n_i\Sigma_i$ for $i = 1, 2$. Also, let $\Sigma_2 = \Gamma + \lambda\Sigma_1$, where λ is known or unknown and Γ is of rank $q(< p)$ and is nonnegative definite. Rao [24] derived the likelihood ratio test and modified likelihood ratio test for the rank of Γ when λ is unknown and known, respectively. The above procedures, with minor modifications, can be applied to the case when S_1 and S_2 are distributed complex Wishart matrices. So, the results of Rao can be applied for testing the hypothesis that the number of signals is equal to a specified value. We will now describe certain model selection procedures proposed by Zhao, Krishnaiah and Bai [14] for determination of the number of signals.

When the data are collected at widely spaced time points $t_1, ..., t_{n_2}$, it is realistic to assume that $\boldsymbol{x}(t_1)$,..., $\boldsymbol{x}(t_{n_2})$, the observations on the sensors are distributed independently. In this case, we can estimate Σ_2 with S_2/n_2, where $\boldsymbol{S}_2 = \sum_{j=1}^{n_2} \boldsymbol{x}(t_j)\overline{\boldsymbol{x}(t_j)'}$. Now, let S_1/n_1, denote an unbiased biased estimate of Σ_1 obtained from an independent set of n_1 observations which consist of noise only and no signals. In this case S_1 and S_2 are distributed independently as complex Wishart matrices with n_1 and n_2 degrees of freedom and $\boldsymbol{E}(\boldsymbol{S}_i) = \boldsymbol{n}_i \Sigma_i$ for $i = 1, 2$ where the relationship between Σ_1 and Σ_2 is given by (4) with Σ_1 instead $\sigma^2 I$. Now, let $\lambda_1 \geq .... \geq \lambda_p$ denote the eigenvalues of $\Sigma_2 \Sigma_1^{-1}$ and let $\delta_1 \geq ... \geq \delta_p$ denote the eigenvalues of $\boldsymbol{S}_2 \boldsymbol{S}_1^{-1} \boldsymbol{n}_1 / \boldsymbol{n}_2$. Also let

$$H_q^* : \lambda_q > \lambda_{q+1} = ... = \lambda_p = 1. \tag{16}$$

Zhao, Krishnaiah and Bai [14] showed that the LRT statistic for H_q^* is given by

$$L_q^* = \prod_{i = 1 + \min(q,\tau)}^{p} (\alpha_n + \beta_n \delta_i)^{-n/2} \delta_i^{-n\beta_n/2} \tag{17}$$

where $n = n_1 + n_2$ $\alpha_n = n_1/n$, $\beta_n = n_2/n$ and τ denotes the number of δ_i's greater than one. Now, let

$$\boldsymbol{EDC}^*(k, C_n) = -\log L_k^* + \gamma^*(k,p) C_n, \tag{18}$$

where $\gamma^*(k,p) = k(2p-k)$ and C_n satisfies the following conditions:

$$(i) \quad \lim_{n\to\infty} (C_n / n) = 0 \tag{19}$$

and

$$(ii) \quad \lim_{n\to\infty} \{C_n / \log \log n\} = \infty. \tag{20}$$

An estimate of $\hat{q}$ of q is given by

$$\boldsymbol{EDC}^*(\hat{q}, C_n) = \min \{\boldsymbol{EDC}^*(0, C_n),...., \boldsymbol{EDC}^*(p-1, C_n)\}. \tag{21}$$

Zhao, Krishnaiah and Bai [14] proposed the above estimate and proved its strong consistency.

Next, let $H_q : \lambda_q > \lambda_{q+1} = ... = \lambda_p = \lambda$, where λ is unknown. In this case, the likelihood ratio test statistic is known [24] to be

$$L_q = \prod_{i=q+1}^{p} [((n_2 \delta_i + n_1 \hat{\lambda}_{k0})/n)^n / \delta_i^{n_2} \hat{\lambda}_{k0}^{n_1}], \tag{22}$$

where $\hat{\lambda}_{k,0}$ satisfies the equation

$$(p-k) = \sum_{j=k+1}^{p} \{\hat{\lambda}_{k,0} /(\alpha_n \hat{\lambda}_{k,0} + \beta_n \delta_j)\}, \tag{23}$$

Now, let

$$EDC(k, C_n) = -\log L_k + C_n \gamma(k, p), \tag{24}$$

where $\gamma(k, p) = k\,(2p - k) + 1$. Then, an estimate of $\hat{q}$ of q is given by

$$EDC(q, C_n) = \{\min EDC(0, C_n), ..., EDC(p-1, C_n)\}. \tag{25}$$

Zhao, Krishnaiah and Bai [14] proposed the above estimate and established its strong consistency. The property of strong consistency holds good even if the assumptions of independence and normality are violated provided the conditions (19) and (20) are satisfied and (12) and (13) are true for the two sets of observations used to estimate Σ_1 and Σ_2.

We will discuss the method proposed by Paulraj and Kailath [16] for the determination of the number of signals when the noise is spatially coloured. They considered the situations when two estimates of the array covariance are available by displacing the array. The two-measurement model considered by them is given by

$$\boldsymbol{x}_i(t) = \boldsymbol{A}_i \boldsymbol{s}_i(t) + \boldsymbol{n}(t) \quad i = 1, 2, \tag{26}$$

where $\boldsymbol{x}_i(t)$ and $\boldsymbol{s}_i(t)$ are respectively, the observation vector and vector of wavefront of ith measurement. The covariance matrices of the observation vectors for the measurements is given by

$$\Sigma_{2i} = \boldsymbol{A}_i \psi_i \overline{\boldsymbol{A}}_i' + \Sigma_1. \tag{27}$$

Also, Σ_{2i} is estimated with S_{2i}/n where

$$nS_{2i} = \sum_{j=1}^{n} \boldsymbol{x}_i(t_j) \overline{\boldsymbol{x}_i(t_j)}'.$$

In addition, let $\boldsymbol{P} = \Sigma_{21} - \Sigma_{22}$ and $\boldsymbol{R} = (1/n)\,(S_{21} - S_{22})$. Now, let $\lambda_1 \geq .... \geq \lambda_p$ denote the eigenvalues of P and let $l_1 \geq .... \geq l_p$ denote the eigenvalues of $\boldsymbol{R}$. If the volumes of $[A_1\ A_2]$ are distinct and $p \geq 2q$, then

$$\lambda_{q+1} = ... = \lambda_{p-q} = 0. \tag{28}$$

If Ψ_1 and Ψ_2 are positive definite and $\Psi_1 - \Psi_2$ is nonsingular and $A_1 = A_2$, then

$$\lambda_{q+1} = ... = \lambda_p = 0. \tag{29}$$

Taking advantage of (28) and (29), Paulraj and Kailath [16] proposed using methods similar to those used in Wax and Kailath [12]. But, unfortunately, the distribution of $\boldsymbol{S}_{22} - \boldsymbol{S}_{21}$ is very complicated since it is the difference between two complex Wishart matrices. So, we feel that the derivation of the likelihood ratio test statistics for testing the hypothesis that some of the eigenvalues are zero and the establishment of the consistency of the information theoretic procedures are difficult and may not be feasible. When $A_1 = A_2$, one may use some suitable function of $l_{k+1} .... l_p$ to test the hypothesis that $\lambda_{k+1} = ... = \lambda_p = 0$. One possible test statistic is l_{k+1}. But, unfortunately, the distributions of test statistics based upon $l_{k+1} .... l_p$ involve $\lambda_1, ..., \lambda_k$ as nuisance parameters. Remarks similar to the above may be made for testing the hypothesis that $\lambda_{k+1} = ... = \lambda_{p-q} = 0$ when Ψ_1 and Ψ_2 are positive definite and the columns of $[A_1\ A_2]$ are distinct.

15.5 DETECTION OF NUMBER OF SIGNALS IN DECENTRALIZED PROCESSING

In some situations, the arrays of sensors are located in locations which are wide apart. In these cases, the model can be written as

$$\boldsymbol{x}_h(t) = \boldsymbol{A}_h \boldsymbol{s}(t) + \boldsymbol{n}_h(t), \tag{30}$$

for $h = 1, 2, ...M$, where $\boldsymbol{x}_h(t) : \boldsymbol{p}_h \times 1$ denotes the vector of observation at t th time point using hth group of arrays. $\boldsymbol{s}(\boldsymbol{t}) : \boldsymbol{q} \times 1$ is the signal vector, $n_h(t)$ is the noise vector on hth subarray and $\boldsymbol{A}_h : \boldsymbol{p}_h \times \boldsymbol{q}$ is a matrix whose elements depend upon the parameters of the signals. We also assume that $\boldsymbol{s}(\boldsymbol{t})$ and $\boldsymbol{n}_h(\boldsymbol{t})$ are distributed independently as complex multivariate normal with $\boldsymbol{E}(\boldsymbol{s}(\boldsymbol{t})) = 0$, $\boldsymbol{E}(\boldsymbol{n}_h(\boldsymbol{t})) = 0$, $\boldsymbol{E}(\boldsymbol{s}(\boldsymbol{t})\overline{\boldsymbol{s}(\boldsymbol{t})'}) = \Psi$ and $\boldsymbol{E}(\boldsymbol{n}_h(\boldsymbol{t})\overline{\boldsymbol{n}_h(\boldsymbol{t})'}) = \sigma^2 I$. We also assume that $\boldsymbol{x}_1(\boldsymbol{t}), ..., \boldsymbol{x}_M(\boldsymbol{t})$ are distributed independent of each other. The covariance matrix Σ_{2h} of $\boldsymbol{x}_h$ *is* given by

$$\Sigma_{2h} = \boldsymbol{A}_h \Psi \overline{\boldsymbol{A}}_h' + \sigma^2 I_{p_h} \tag{31}$$

Now Let $\boldsymbol{S}_{2h} = \sum_{j=1}^{n} \boldsymbol{x}_h(\boldsymbol{t}) \overline{\boldsymbol{x}}_h(\boldsymbol{t}_j)$. Also, let $l_{1h} \geq ... \geq l_{p_h h}$ denote the eigenvalues of $\boldsymbol{S}_{2h}/\boldsymbol{n}$. Under the model (30) Wax and Kailath [12] proposed to estimate q, the number of sources, using AIC and MDL criteria. The same method can be used even if the noise variance differs from subarray to subarray. We now propose a method of estimation of the number of signals using the *EDC* criterion when the covariance matrix of $\boldsymbol{n}_h(t)$ is σ_h^2.

$$EDC(C_{nh};\ p_h) = -\log L_{kh} + C_{nh}\, \gamma(k, p_h), \tag{32}$$

where C_{nh} satisfies the conditions

$$(i) \qquad \lim_{n\to\infty} (C_{nh}/n) = 0$$

$$(ii) \qquad \lim_{n\to\infty} \{C_{nh} / \log \log n\} = \infty. \tag{33}$$

Also, $\gamma(k, p_h) = k(2p_h - k + 1) + 1$, and

$$L_{kh} = \left\{ \prod_{i=k+1}^{p_h} l_{ih}^{n} \Big/ \left(\sum_{i=k+1}^{p_h} l_{ih} / (p_h - k) \right)^{n(p_k - k)} \right\} \tag{34}$$

In addition, let

$$EDC(k) = \sum_{h=1}^{M} EDC(k, C_{Nh}; p_h) \tag{35}$$

Then, an estimate $\hat{q}$ of q is given by

$$EDC(\hat{q}) = \min \{EDC(0), \ldots., EDC(p-1)\}, \tag{36}$$

where $p = \min(p_1 \ldots, p_M)$. We may choose C_{nh}'s to be equal to C_n. The above procedure may be applied even if $\sigma_1^2 = \ldots. = \sigma_M^2$. Alternatively, we can use the procedure described below. Let L_k denote the likelihood ratio test statistics for testing the hypothesis that

$$\lambda_{k+1,}\ h = \ldots. = \lambda_{p_h} = \sigma^2 \quad h = 1, 2, \ldots\ldots, M$$

In this case

$$L_k = \left\{ \prod_{h=1}^{M} \prod_{i=k+1}^{p_h} l_{ih}^{n} \Big/ \left(\sum_{h=1}^{M} \sum_{i=p+1}^{p_h} l_{ih} / (p_0 - kM \right)^{n(p_0 - kM)} \right\} \tag{37}$$

where $p_0 = p_1 + \ldots + p_M$. Now, let

$$EDC(k, C_n) = -\log L_k + C_n \gamma(k, p_0), \tag{38}$$

where $\gamma(k, p_0) = k\,(2p_0 - kM + M) + M$ and C_n satisfies the condition

$$(i) \qquad \lim_{n\to\infty} (C_n / n) = 0$$

and

$$(ii) \qquad \lim_{n\to\infty} \{C_n / \log \log n\} = \infty$$

Then, the number of signals q can be estimated with $\hat{q}$ where $\hat{q}$ is given by

$$EDC(\hat{q}, C_n) = \min \{EDC(0, C_n), \ldots., EDC(p-1, C_n)\}, \tag{39}$$

where $p = \min\,(p_1 \ldots, p_M)$ as before. Here, we note that $\boldsymbol{x}_1(t), \ldots, \boldsymbol{x}_M(t)$ are not distributed independent of each other. If we assume that $\boldsymbol{n}_1(t)$,..., $\boldsymbol{n}_M(t)$ are distributed independent of each other, then $\boldsymbol{E}\,\{\boldsymbol{x}_i(t)\,\overline{\boldsymbol{x}_j(t)'}\} = \boldsymbol{A}_i\,\Psi\,\boldsymbol{A}_j^{-1}$. So L_k is not the likelihood ratio test statistics unless $\boldsymbol{A}_i\,\Psi\,\overline{\boldsymbol{A}}_j' = 0$ for $i \neq j$.

Next, let the covariance matrix of $\boldsymbol{n_h}(t)$ be Σ_h and other assumptions on the model (30) remain the same. Also, let $\hat{\Sigma}_{1h}$ denote an unbiased estimate of Σ_{1h} obtained from an independent sample of observations which consist of noise without signal. We assume that the size of this sample is n, and the observations in this sample are independent. We now propose an *EDC* procedure for the determination of the number of signals in this case.

Let $\lambda_{1h} \geq ... \geq \lambda_{p_h,h}$ denote the eigenvalues of $\Sigma_{2h}\,\Sigma_{1h}^{-1}$ and let $\delta_{1h} \geq ... \geq \delta_{p_h,h}$ denote the eigenvalues of $\hat{\Sigma}_{2h}\,\hat{\Sigma}_{1h}^{-1}$. If the number of signals is q, then

$$\lambda_{q+1,h} = ... = \lambda_{p_h,h} = 1 \tag{40}$$

for $h = 1, 2, ..., M$. Now let

$$EDC(k,\, C_{nh};\, p_h) = -\log L_{kh} + \gamma_h(k, p_h)C_{nh}, \tag{41}$$

where $\gamma_h(k, p_h) =$

$$L_{kh} = \prod_{i=1+\min(k,t_h)}^{p_h} (\alpha_n + \beta_n\,\delta_{ih})^{-n/2}\,\delta^{-nb_n/2} \tag{42}$$

and τ_h denotes the number of eigenvalues $\hat{\Sigma}_{2h}\,\hat{\Sigma}_{1h}^{-1}$ which are greater than one. Also, C_{nh} satisfies the following conditions:

$$(i) \quad \lim_{n\to\infty} (C_{nh}/n) = 0$$

and

$$(ii) \quad \lim_{n\to\infty} (C_{nh}/\log\log n) = \infty. \tag{43}$$

Here, we note that L_{kh} denotes the likelihood ratio test statistic for testing the hypothesis that $\lambda_{q+1,h} = ... = \lambda_{p_h,h} = 1$. Now,

$$EDC(k) = \sum_{h=1}^{M} EDC(k, C_{nh};\, p_h) \tag{44}$$

Then, an estimate $\hat{q}$ of q *is* given by

$$EDC(\hat{q}) = \min\{EDC(0), ..., EDC(p-1)\}, \tag{46}$$

where $p = \min(p_1, ..., p_M)$ as before. By following the same lines as in Zhao, Bai and Krishnaiah [14], the consistency of the above procedure can be established.

Now, let $\Sigma_{11} = ... = \Sigma_{1M}$ and let L_k denote the likelihood ratio test statistic for testing the hypothesis

$$\lambda_{k+1,h} = ... \geq \lambda_{p,h} = 1 \text{ for } h = 1, 2, ... M.$$

In addition, let

$$EDC(k, C_n) = -\log L_k + C_n \gamma(k)$$

where $\gamma(k)$, denotes the number of free parameters that have to be estimated and C_n satisfies the following conditions:

$$(i) \quad \lim_{n\to\infty} (C_n / n) = 0$$

and $$(ii) \quad \lim_{n\to\infty} (C_n / \log \log n) = \infty$$

Then, we can estimate q with $\hat{q}$ where $\hat{q}$ is given by

$$EDC(\hat{q}, C_n) = \min \{EDC(0, C_n), \ldots., EDC(p-1, C_n)\}$$

Acknowledgement

The Authors wish to thank Dr Neil Gerr of the Office of Naval Research for bringing their attention to some useful references.

References

1. S Haykins (1985) Radar array processing for angle of arrival estimation. In *Array Signal Processing* S Haykins Ed. 194–292. Prentice Hall.
2. R Kumaresan and D W Tufts (1980) Data adaptive principal component signal processing. *Proc 19th IEEE Conf Decision and Control Alburquerqe N M* 949–954.
3. W S Liggert (1973) Passive sonar fitting models to multiple time series. In *Signal Processing* (J W Griffith *et al.* Ed) 327–345. Academic Press Inc., New York.
4. N L Owsley (1977) Spectral signal set extraction. In *Aspects of Signal Processing* Part II (G Tacconi, Ed.) 469–475. Reidel.
5. N L Owsley (1985) Sonar array processing. In *Array Signal Processing* (S Haykins, Ed.) 115–193. Prentice Hall.
6. V F Pisarenko (1973) The retrieval of harmonics from a covariance function. *Geophys R astro Soc* **33**, 247–266.
7. S S Reddi (1979) Multiple source location—a digital approach. *IEEE Tran Aerospace Electron Syst* **AES- 15,** 95–105.
8. R O Schmidt (1979) Multiple emitter location and signal parameter estimation. In *Proc. RADC Spectrum Estimation Workshop,* Rome N.Y.
9. D W Tufts and R Kumaresan (1982) Estimation of frequencies of multiple sinusoids making linear prediction perform like maximum likelihood. *Proc. IEEE* **70**, 975–989.

10. M Wax, T J Shan and T Kailath (1984) Spatio-temporal spectral analysis by eigenstructure methods. *IEEE Trans Acoustics Speech, Signal Process* **ASSP-32** 817–827.

11. M Wax and T Kailath (1984) Determination of the number of signals by information theoretic criteria. *IEEE Trans Acoust Speech Signal Process* **ASSP-33**, 387–392.

12. M Wax and T Kailath (1985) Decentralized processing in sensor arrays. *IEEE Trans Acoustics Speech Process* **ASSP-33**, 1123–1129.

13. L C Zhao, P R Krishnaiah and Z D Bai (1985) On detection of number of signals in presence of white noise. *Tech Rep* No. 85–37. Center for Multivariate Analysis, University of Pittsburgh.

14. L C Zhao, P R Krishnaiah and Z D Bai (1985) On detection of number of signals in presence of coloured noise using information theoretic criteria. *Tech Rep* No.85–39. Center for Multivariate Analysis, University of Pittsburgh.

15. Z D Bai, P R Krishnaiah and L C Zhao (1985) On rates of convergence of efficient detection criteria in signal processing. *Tech Rep* No 85–45. Center for Multivariate Analysis, University of Pittsburgh.

16. A Paulraj and T Kailath (1986) Eigenstructure methods for direction of arrival estimation in the presence of unknown noise fields. *IEEE Trans Acoust Speech Signal Process* **ASSP 34,** 13–20.

17. M S Bartlett (1954) A note on multiplying factors for various X^2 approximations. *JRS Soc Ser B,* **16**, 296–298.

18. P R Krishnaiah and J Lin (1984) Complex elliptical distributions. *Tech Rep* No.84–19 Center for Multivariate Analysis, University of Pittsburgh.

19. C R Rao (1973) *Linear Statistical Inference and its Applications.* John Wiley, New York.

20. R Wooding (1956) The multivariate distribution of complex normal variables. *Biometrika,* **43**, 212–215.

21. N R Goodman (1963) Statistical analysis based on a certain multivariate complex Gaussian distribution (an introduction) *Ann Math Statist* **34**, 152–176.

22. P R Krishnaiah (1976) Some recent developments on complex multivariate distributions. *J multivar Anal* **6**, 1–30.

23. L C Zhao, P R Krishnaiah and Z D Bai (1985) Remarks on certain criteria for detection of number of signals. *Tech Rep* No. 85–43. Center for Multivariate Analysis, University of Pittsburgh.

24. C R Rao (1983) Likelihood ratio tests for relationship between two covariance matrices. In *Studies in Econometrics. Time Series and Multivariate Statistics* (T Amemiya, S Karlin and L Goodman, Eds). Academic Press Inc., New York.

16

Diffraction Patterns as Observed in T V Signal Propagation

A K Sen and S K Chatterjee[1], J Das, A K De, S Chowdhury, N C Deb, D Dutta Majumder[2], S Basu Mallick and P K Sinha Roy[3]

ABSTRACT

The present contribution is intended to provide brief and interesting results of diffraction patterns observed, for the first time, in a horizontally propagated VHF TV signal transmitted from Bangladesh. Classical knife-edge diffraction due to a sharply bounded elevated layer in the troposphere, acting as a phase changing screen is involved in interpreting the results. A study of such diffraction patterns observed during the monsoon season in 1985 over Kolkata with multistation TV receiving systems, is reported in this paper.

Keywords: Diffraction; TV; Signal propagation; VHF; Troposphere; Fresnel Half-period Zones; Gaussian Irregularity; Yagi Antenna

16.1 INTRODUCTION

Periodic variations of the intensity of a TV signal is often noticeable during the passage of an aircraft across the propagation path [1]. The variations originate presumably from the obstruction or reflection of successive Fresnel half period zones involved, resulting in a diffraction pattern observable in the signal strength records at such times. While carrying on investigations on the tropospheric propagation of TV signals in the fringe region, we have observed a similar diffraction pattern even when there was no aircraft in the propagation path and are presumed to originate from moving elevated inversion layer structure in the diffraction path. A study of such diffraction patterns was made with a multistation observation from the Indian Statistical Institute, Kolkata, Institute of Radiophysics and Electronics, University of Kolkata and B.E. College, Sibpore, Howrah. Some of the interesting results obtained are presented in this paper.

16.2 EXPERIMENTAL SET UP

It has been fairly established that microwave and ultra high frequency radio signals are propagated beyond the earth's horizon by scattering or partial reflection from refractive index variations or fluctuations in the

---

1 Institute of Radiophysics and Electronics, University of Kolkata.

2 Indian Statistical Institute, Kolkata.

3 B.E. College, Sibpore, Howrah.

troposphere, and that characteristics of these transhorizon signals are related to space and time variations in the refractive index structure of the troposphere itself. Some of the atmospheric parameters and related transhorizon propagation effects are:

(i) Drift (wind) and the internal motions as they affect the Doppler spectrum or fading of the radio signals.

(ii) Statistical characteristics or properties of the random fluctuations or variations in the atmosphere as they are related to frequency and angular dependence of the mean scattered power.

(iii) Nonuniformities in the statistical characteristics of the atmosphere such as inhomogeneity or anisotropy (including stratification tendencies) that exist to a scale resolvable by the measuring devices (sometimes antennas) or the technique.

Much of the early work in transhorizon radio propagation was concerned with communications system applications, and the parameters measured in the experiments were usually averaged over long periods of time and over large regions of space. In the present system of observation we have employed a TV receiver fed from an 11-element Yagi antenna installed at each of the stations. The gated AGC output of the receiver is recorded on a chart recorder. To record the minute variations of the signal level, a differential voltmeter technique is employed with a buck out voltage of about 1.8 volts. This was necessary to buck out the rather high mean signal level due to tropospheric bending of the ray over the region of 75 km involved.

16.3 RESULTS AND DISCUSSION

The mean signal level was found to vary over a range less than 0.1 volt about a mean level of the order of 1.8 volts.

The variations during the diffraction pattern lies in the range 10-50 mV. The diffraction patterns at three stations are usually uncorrelated. On certain occasions, they are observed at two or three stations with a characteristic time delay between stations. The patterns usually occur in pairs but there are also cases when those occur singly. Two typical records of the diffraction are shown in Fig. 16.1(*a*) and (*b*), obtained at ISI, Kolkata and B.E. College, Sibpore, Howrah respectively.

In the past, attempts have been made by several workers to simulate some of the observed quasiperiodic fluctuations of satellite signals by postulating a drifting diffraction pattern generated by a simple Gaussian irregularity. These attempts suggest that isolated ionospheric irregularities can be visualized as Gaussian fluctuations in the ambient density of the ionosphere. The patterns observed at three stations in Kolkata, resemble the Fresnel diffraction patterns of opaque (strips) or edges (half planes). The position of pattern minima can be calculated from a model in which

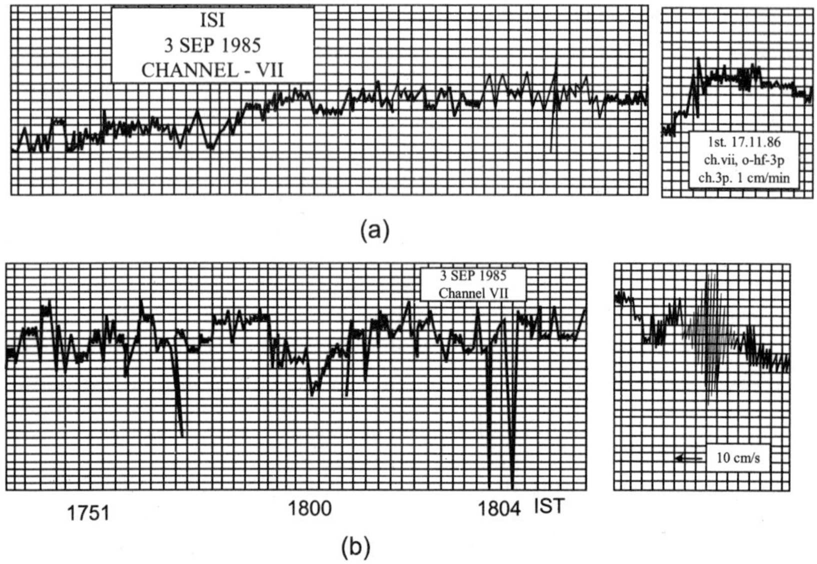

Fig. 16.1 (*a*) and (*b*)

the original wave from the source interferes with a wave reflected from the edge (with a phase change of π). This method of analysis was infact used eleswhere.

The problem of diffraction by random phase changing screen [2,3] is relevant to physical situations where waves of any kind pass through a region containing irregularities of refractive index. Examples are, twinkling of starlight in the turbulent atmosphere, the scintillation of satellite or cosmic radio sources caused by electron density irregularities in the ionosphere, and the inter-planetary scintillation of quasar radio sources caused by electron density irregularities in the solar wind. In each case, statistical analysis of the amplitude or intensity fluctuations enables inferences to be made concerning the properties of the relevant irregularities.

Analytic approaches to this problem have been confined to various limiting cases. When ϕ, the r.m.s. phase deviation imposed on the wave by the screen, is small, the statistical properties of the resulting diffraction pattern can be evaluated fairly readily. When ϕ is large, the problem is considerably more complex, when ϕ is of the order of 1 radian, however, no analytical solution or approximation is available.

The diffraction patterns were subjected to spectral analysis, the spectra exhibited a narrow band line structure which enables one to distinguish the diffraction spectra from the spectra of the usual random fading due to turbulence. A search for similar patterns in the signal strength records of microwave line of sight (LOS) links around 7.3 GHz over a 44 km path length indicated a complete absence of any such pattern. This suggests that the layers responsible for the diffraction patterns in the TV signal must indeed be located much higher up compared to the heights of the microwave antennas in the LOS links, which are typically about 100m. In case of the TV signal, the 11-element Yagi antenna is not directive enough to restrict the antenna beam to a horizontal path, and can easily see the tropospheric elevated layer structures at higher angles to the horizon. A radio interferometric technique is being planned to locate the height of the elevated layers and the results will be reported in due course.

Acknowledgement

The work is part of: (1) A collaborative project at ISI, Kolkata entitled 'Statistical Studies of Tropospheric Propagation from Signal Strength Records in the VHF, UHF and Microwave Links' sponsored by the Department of Science and Technology, Govt. of India. The Institute of Radiophysics and Electronics, University of Kolkata and B.E.College, Sibpore, Howrah are the collaborating organisations and (2) A project at the Institute of Radiophysics and Electronics, University of Kolkata, entitled, 'Modelling of the Atmosphere from Radio Propagation and Radio Refractive Index Data' sponsored by IMAP-UGC.

References

1. A K Sen, S Basu Mallick, A K Dev Gupta, M Rahaman, S Dev Barman, M K Pal and J Das (1985) Detection of aircraft from oscillations in TV signal strength', presented at the symposium on Navigational Electronics, organised by IETE, Kolkata Centre, Co-sponsored by the Department of Electronics, Govt. of India, held on June 6–7, 1985 at the Saha Institute of Nuclear Physics, Kolkata.
2. J A Ratcliffe (1956) Some aspects of diffraction theory and their application to the ionosphere, *Phys Soc Repo Progr Phys* **9**, p.188.
3. D T Gjessing (1969) Atmospheric structure deduced from forward scattered wave propagation experiments. *Radio Sci* **4**, 1195 – 1210.

17

Echo Patterns in SODAR During Winter Over Kolkata

D Dutta Majumder, J Das, A K De, N C Deb and S Chowdhury[1], S Basu Mallick and P K Sinha Roy[2], S K Chatterjee and A K Sen[3]

ABSTRACT

The use of radar in detecting echoes from atmospheric inhomogenities is well known and has been reported by various investigators in this field. In the present paper, the authors have made a study of the echo patterns reflected from the atmospheric strata by using sound radar at Indian Statistical Institute, Calcutta. The echo patterns obtained from the atmospheric layer revealed some typical characteristics of the atmospheric layers which are discussed.

Keywords: Echo; SODAR; Radar; Remote Sensing.

17.1 INTRODUCTION

Remote sensing of the atmosphere by an acoustic sounder called a SODAR (Sound Detection and Ranging) has been a subject of great interest during the last two decades [1-4]. In India, the SODAR studies spread over the country during the last decade [5-8]. In the eastern region of India, similar facilities have been created at the Indian Statistical Institute, Kolkata under a collaborative programme with the Institute of Radiophysics and Electronics, University of Kolkata and B. E. College, Sibpore, Howrah as collaborating organisations. Some of the interesting echo patterns observed in the SODAR during the winter months over Calcutta are presented in this paper. The results are compared with those obtained at such times over other parts of India and the peculiarities of the tropospheric layer structures occurring over this region are highlighted.

17.2 EXPERIMENTAL SET-UP

The experimental set-up of sound radar unit is shown in Fig. 17.1. The system utilizes acoustic signal in the frequency range of 2.35 kHz (variable) and is transmitted vertically through a parabolic reflector in the atmosphere. After transmission the signal is detected by the same

[1] Indian Statistical Institute, Kolkata.

[2] B.E. College, Sibpore, Howrah.

[3] Institute of Radiophysics and Electronics, University of Kolkata.

transducer unit, which is then amplified and processed for further investigations.

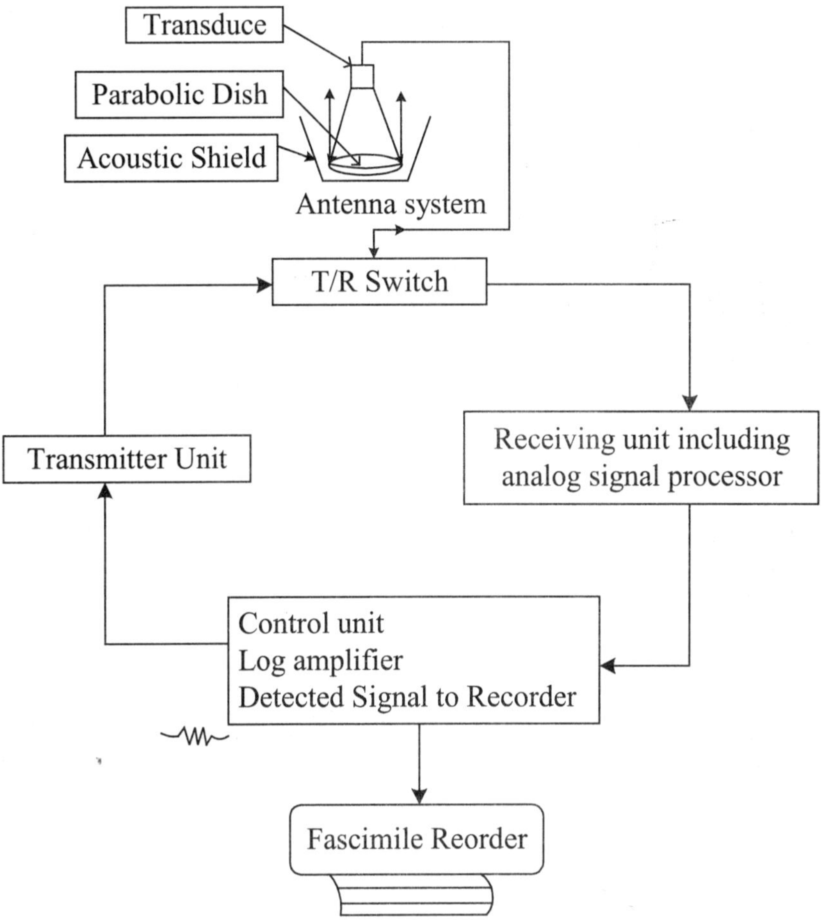

Fig. 17.1 Block diagram of Sodar system.

The SODAR equipment employed for the purpose was developed with the active co-operation of the scientists of the Radio Science Division, National Physical Laboratory, New Delhi. The specification of the equipment is given below:

Frequency of acoustic signal	:	1–2 kHz
Output power, acoustic	:	10 W, peak
Antenna	:	Parabolic reflector of diameter 6′ with $f/d = 0.35$, made of fibre glass
Pulse duration	:	20–100 msec
Pulse interval	:	20 sec
Operational range	:	1 km

17.3 OBSERVATIONS

The echo patterns, in general, appear to be extended in the time domain starting with delays varying between 200msec to several seconds after

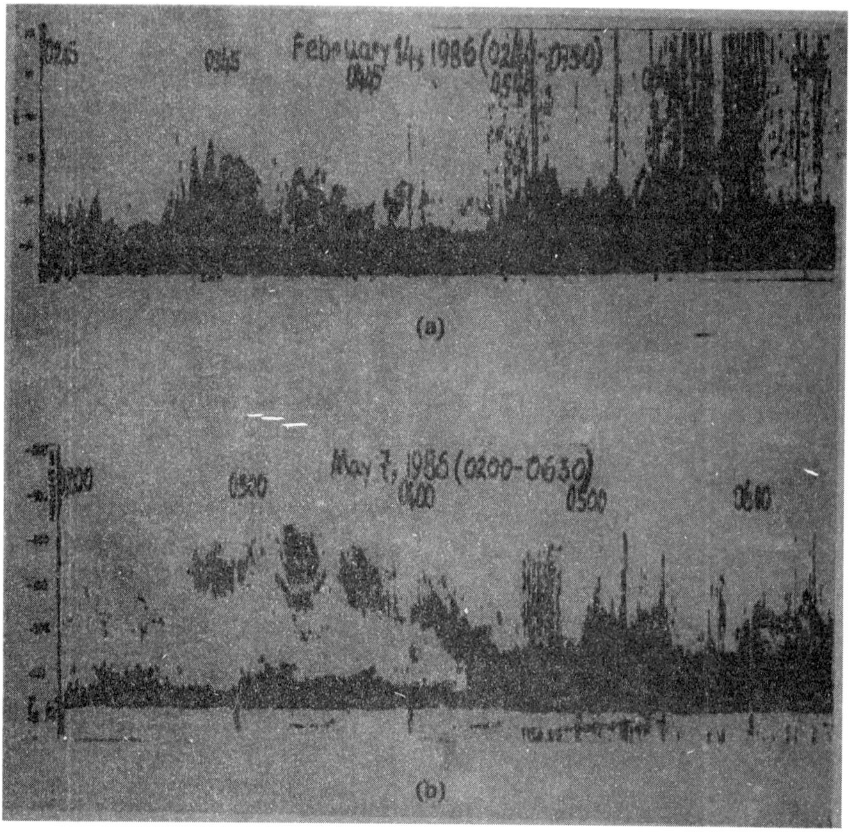

Fig. 17.2 (*a*) Stable nocturnal structure with small turbulence due to winds, (*b*) A remarkable multilayered structure during morning hours

the transmitted acoustic pulse. It has been found that long range echoes are predominant only in the morning and evening hours, when prominent elevated inversion layers occur in the troposphere.

The extent of lengthening of an echo increases with the range of the echo, as observed on the oscilloscopic display of an individual echo. A simultaneous three-dimensional record of range, time and amplitude on a facsimile recorder indicated the height of an echo at a particular moment. Some of these records called Sodar echogram are shown in Fig. 17.2(*a*) and (*b*).

17.4 DISCUSSION

The lengthening of an echo in the time domain appears to originate from the atmosphere behaving as a lowpass filter for the transmitted pulse waveform. For the attenuation to atmospheric oxygen increases sharply with increase of the spectral component of the pulse beyond about 1000 Hz. The successive layer of the atmosphere, in fact, acts as ground to the upward and downward journey of the acoustic pulse. It may be mentioned here that this sort of lengthening would be more remarkable at a frequency around 1000 Hz when the atmospheric attenuation exhibits a sharp minimum. In that case the atmosphere will behave as a high-Q bandpass filter tuned to 1 kHz. However, the background noise level at the site did not allow operation at the frequency of 1000 Hz with a reasonable signal-to-noise ratio and other low noise site are being explored to study this effect more systematically.

Acknowledgement

The work is a part of a collaborative project entitled, 'Statistical Studies of the Troposphere from Field Strength Measurements in the VHF, UHF and Microwave Links' at the Indian Statistical Institute, Kolkata, sponsored by the Department of Science and Technology, Govt. of India. The Institute of Radiophysics and Electronics, University of Kolkata and B. E. College, Sibpore, Howrah, are the collaborating organisations in the project. The work is also supported by the Indian Middle Atmosphere Programme (IMAP) entitled, 'Modelling of the atmosphere from radio propagation and radio refractive index data', sponsored by the UGC, and operative at the Institute of Radiophysics and Electronics, University of Kolkata. The authors are grateful to the scientists of the Radio Science Division, National Physical Laboratory, New Delhi for their active help and suggestion during the development of the SODAR.

References

1. G W Gilman, H B Coxhead and F H Willis (1945) *J Acoust Soc Am* **18**, 274.
2. L G McAllister (1968) *J Acoust Terr Phys* **30**, 1439.
3. C Little Gordon *Proc IEEE* **57** (1969) 571.
4. H Edmund, E H Brown and F F Hall (Jr) (1978) Advances in atmospheric accoustics *Rev Geophys Space Phys,* 16, No.1. 47.

5. S P Singal, H N Dutta, B S Gera, S K Aggarwal and M Saxena (1978) *CENTROP rep.* No.28 Centre of Research on Troposphere, National Physical Laboratory, New Delhi.
6. M Purnachandra Rao, A Raghu Kumar, J S R Murthy and C Poornachandra Rao (1980) *Indian J Radio and Space Phys* **10**, 176.
7. H S Gurm, H S Somal, Darshan Singh, G S Dhillon, H N Dutta, S K Sarkar and B M Reddy (1982) *Indian J Radio and Space Phys* **11**, 106.
8. K Sengupta and P K Kunhikrishnan (1980) 'Preliminary results on vertical wind velocities and temperature structure parameter in the boundary layer by Acoustic Radar,' presented at National Space Science Symp. held at IISc., Bangalore during Feb. 3–6,1982, In *Tropospheric and Middle Atmospheric Phenomena.* p.047.
9. S P Singal (1978) *Indian J Radio and Space Phys* **8**.

18

Fractal/Multifractal and Mutual Information in the Study of Atmospheric Dynamics: *A Case Study on Complexity of Wind Direction*

Amitabha Chanda[1], J Das[2] & D Dutta Majumder [1, 2]

ABSTRACT

After a brief introduction to the problems involved in the investigation of complexities and uncertainties in dynamical systems in general and atmospheric dynamics in particular the paper examines the comparative usefulness of fractal/multifractal dimensions and mutual information in the study of atmospheric dynamics. In the end we present some results of case studies that indicate some measures of complexity in wind directions.

Key words: Atmospheric Dynamics; Fractals; Multifractals; Mutual Information; Wind Direction; Measures of Complexities; Self-similarity.

18.1 INTRODUCTION AND PERSPECTIVE

Atmosphere is a dynamical system in space and time. It is a great and a unique laboratory as well. Number of natural processes are uninterruptedly taking place over millions and millions of years. In this laboratory it is possible to conduct many types of studies covering inter-alia studies on fluid dynamics in diverse boundary conditions. All these studies support decisive steps in agriculture, aviation, environmental pollution and many other areas of great social and economic importance. For example study of temporal change in atmospheric pressure gives valuable clue to the possibility of rain or otherwise in a particular location, which agriculturalists are interested to know in advance to plan for necessary irrigation. Study of wind direction and speed is necessary for airport authority to take decision regarding flights. If there is indication in advance of severe storm, realized from the study of wind direction, speed, pressure etc. the airport authority may not permit any aircraft to be airborne for some time.

Dynamical systems are broadly divided into two classes, deterministic and nondeterministic. By a dynamical system we mean a system which changes with respect to time. And for a dynamical system with imprecise or unknown information we should understand either one or both of the following:

---

[1] Institute of Cybernetics Systems & Information Technology, Kolkata-700108. India.

[2] Indian Statistical Institute, Kolkata-700108. India.

(a) a dynamical system, whose mathematical formulation in terms of a set of equations is not precisely known and

(b) even if the formulation is known, the quantities involved are not precisely measurable, that is, parameters and features are uncertain.

In the deterministic case it is possible to calculate accurately the development of the system, because it can be functionally related to time. But in the nondeterministic case, however, the behavior of the dynamical system is far from predictable. Accordingly, unlike the deterministic case whose analytical solution is theoretically possible, a nondeterministic case may be approached only statistically. It is a complex problem altogether.

From the standpoint of information a deterministic case is a system of known complexity. Theoretically, there is not much in a deterministic case that remains to be known. Hence not much information is there which has to be derived. But many things are unknown in a nondeterministic case. So there is lot of information here. Practically, information is related to complexity which is related to the uncertainty of the system. More complex the system, it is more uncertain and so more information is there.

With the application of the Theory of Information by Shannon & Weaver [1] study of complexity of a dynamical system gains lot of momentum. Entropy gets linked with information. Different types of entropy like conditional entropy, suggested by Kullback [2] have been studied and more and more information about the system is explored.

It is now known that there are several other different types of uncertainty. Their related complexity and mathematical formalisms has been properly investigated in some frameworks, such as, fuzzy set theory [3][4][5], probability and statistics [6] and fractals [7] and multifractals [8][9][10] and has been applied to diverse fields of image generation, turbulence [11], atmospheric science and bio-medical science. In this chapter we intend to examine the comparative usefulness of fractal/ multifractal dimensions and mutual information in the study of atmospheric dynamics.

In addition to entropy a geometrical approach also gained momentum during the last three decades. It is the study of geometrical self-similarity studied through fractal dimension, introduced by Mandelbrot [12]. The approach is based upon the broad assumption that natural objects follow similarity principle. It was later found that geometrical self-similarity is very seldom to come by. The possibility of self-similarity on statistical basis was then suggested. That introduced the concept of multifractal dimensions. Study of multifractal dimension of a system gives an idea of existence of patterns embedded in the system on statistical basis. This ultimately characterizes the level of complexity in the system.

18.2 COMPLEXITIES IN ATMOSPHERIC DYNAMICS

Atmospheric systems are generally nondeterministic systems, hence complex. Nobody can say with certainty when an atmospheric process like rain, thunderstorm will occur. Something, if at all, can be said, it can be said on probabilistic basis. However, that also requires the knowledge of the level of information it has. In this chapter we shall discuss how that knowledge can be derived from the study of entropy and fractal/multifractal dimensions.

But how is atmosphere studied? The study of a phenomenon may be subjective or objective. Practically these two types of studies are complimentary to each other. A subjective study is a pointer to in what direction the objective study has to be carried out. A subjective study may be expressed in terms of a sentence whereas an objective study is generally numerical. Say for example one may study the formation and color of cloud in the North-West and predict a storm. But in fact this leads to the necessity of studying the development of pressure and temperature fields in great details which is generally done by measuring these properties of the atmosphere over time.

Measurement of an atmospheric parameter/feature is done with the help of suitable instrument. Signals emitted by an atmospheric process are received by a sensor and subsequently measured by an instrument. On statistical sense there may be three types of measurement, over space, over time and on ensemble. For the sake of studying the development of a particular phenomenon measurement over time is more important than the other two. While measuring the value of a particular property of an atmospheric phenomenon over time data are generally done by collecting data at uniform interval. These data collected at equal interval make a time-series.

Signals, as realized by a sensor are hardly a deterministic time-series. Various types of irregularities are embedded in it. Study of these irregularities through statistical method is a standard process. The time-series values are decomposed into four different components either in an additive or a multiplicative way. These parts are Trend, Seasonal Variation, Cyclic Variation and Random Fluctuation.

In additive model a time-series value is given as

$$X = T + S + C + R \tag{1}$$

In multiplicative model this is given as

$$X = T \times S \times C \times R \tag{2}$$

where

X - Instantaneous value as in time-series

T - Trend component

S - Seasonal component

C - Cyclic component

R - Random fluctuation component

There are statistical methods to understand and evaluate different components in time-series. The most popular method is the method of moving average.

We have already observed that time-series data are the values of certain properties of an atmospheric phenomenon, collected at equal intervals. For example in order to study an impending storm we need to study the development of change of atmospheric pressure at a particular location. For the purpose pressure is sensed by a pressure sensor and is measured at equal intervals. Hence we may say that development of change of pressure at the location where the sensor is located is a signature of the atmosphere in the present case. Therefore it is expected that thorough study of the time-series of atmospheric pressure will reveal the present atmospheric dynamics that may lead to a storm.

But how this thorough study can be done? It has already been stated that statistical study of time-series will give some sort of insight into time-series. Besides statistical study there are other studies which may also throw light on the structure of the time-series vis-a-vis the dynamics it represents. These studies are directed towards exploring the inherent complexities of the dynamical system through time-series. In the subsequent paragraphs some of these methods to study the complexities of dynamical system through time-series data are discussed.

18.3 A FEW MEASURES OF COMPLEXITIES

Among various processes for studying complexities embedded in time-series there are two well-known processes. One is based on Information theory and the other on Dimension theory. The process based on Information theory measures mutual information of the time-series. On the other hand the process based on Dimension theory measures fractal and multifractal dimensions of the time-series. Both the processes have been used to study atmospheric dynamics like wind speed and direction [8][9].

In this chapter we shall examine these two processes individually and on comparative basis as well in order to understand their efficacies and their individual field of use. Initially we shall study how one process differs from the other from the theoretical viewpoint. Then it will be examined if the two studies concur in their results or give different sets of information.

18.3.1 Mutual Information

Mutual Information has its base in the Information Theory of Shannon & Weaver [1]. It may be noted in this context that as complexity in system increases information also increases. So measure of complexity or uncertainty as enunciated by Shannon is very much linked with information. Shannon's measure of complexity in terms of probability is given as

$$H\left(p(x)|x \in X\right) = -\sum_{x \in X} p(x)\log_2 p(x) \tag{3}$$

where $\left(p(x)|x \in X\right)$ is a probability distribution on a finite set X.

Let us first intuitively try to explain the significance of Shannon's entropy. Let us take an element x from our universal set. If the probability of occurrence of x is 0.99 i.e. $p(x)$ =0.99 then the actual occurrence is almost bound to take place. We are not surprised to see that x has actually occurred. So information regarding the occurrence of x is scanty. On the other hand when the probability of occurrence of x is very small, say 0.01, it is extremely difficult to foresee when x would occur. The uncertainty of occurrence of x is very high and so also information is very high.

Besides this intuitive explanation of Shannon's measures of information or Shannon's entropy we may also site another mathematical example. Let us take a finite binary string.

0010101001001010010010000010101111100111101111

We may observe that in the binary string obviously there are two elements 1 and 0. 1 is occurring for 23 times and 0 is occurring also for 23 times. Hence the probability of occurrence of 1 and 0 may be written respectively as

$$p(1) = 0.5 \text{ and } p(0) = 0.5$$

Accordingly, Shannon's entropy may be written as

$$\begin{aligned} H &= -\sum_{i=1,0} p_i \log_2 p_i \\ &= -\left(0.5\log_2 0.5 + 0.5\log_2 0.5\right) \\ &= \log_2 2 \\ &= 1 \end{aligned} \tag{4}$$

Let us now examine the lower and upper bounds of Shannon's entropy for this particular case of binary string. In the case of binary string in general Shannon's entropy is given as

$$H = -\left[p\log_2 p + (1-p)\log_2(1-p)\right] \tag{5}$$

It may be shown using L'Hospitals rule that as $p \to 0$ or $p \to 1$, $H \to 0$. Hence no information or complexity is there.

In order to find the extremum of H let us differentiate H w.r.t. p. We get

$$\frac{dH}{dp} = -\left[\log_2 p - \log_2(1-p)\right] \tag{6}$$

$$\frac{dH}{dp} = 0 \tag{7}$$

when $2p = 1$.

Again taking the second derivative we get

$$\frac{d^2H}{dp^2} < 0 \tag{8}$$

So the maximum value of entropy is achieved when $p = 0.5$ and the maximum value is 1.

It may be shown that maximum uncertainty is obtained when all probabilities are equal. If instead of a binary string we take an n-ary string maximum uncertainty is obtained when all the probabilities are equal to $(1/n)$. The bounds are

$$0 \le H(p_1, p_2, \ldots\ldots\ldots, p_n) \le \log_2 n \tag{9}$$

Based on this theory of information another information parameter, named Mutual Information is of great importance. It is based upon conditional entropy, suggested by Kullback [2].

Let us again take two sets of variables X and Y. Mutual Information between these two sets is given as

$$\begin{aligned} I(X,Y) &= \sum_{x,y} p(x,y)\log\frac{p(x,y)}{p(x)\,p(y)} \\ &= -\sum_{x} p(x)\log p(x) - \left(-\sum_{x,y} p(x,y)\log p(x|y)\right) \\ &= H(X) - H(X|Y) \end{aligned} \tag{10}$$

Since $I(X,Y)$ is symmetric it can be written also as

$$I(X,Y) = H(Y) - H(Y|X) \tag{11}$$

It may be noted that mutual information is a measure of complexity regarding a particular element when information about the other element is available. It is practically the intersection of $H(X)$ and $H(Y)$, as shown in Fig. 18.1.

Details of Mutual Information may be seen in Arndt [13] and Cover et al [14]. Lot of application of mutual information has already been done

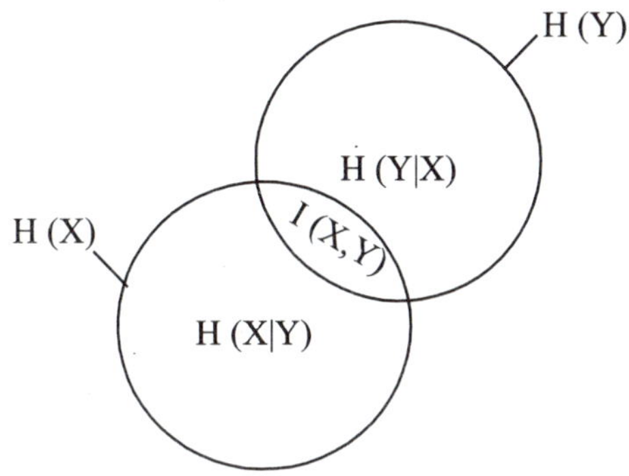

Fig. 18.1 Diagrammatic representation of mutual information

in many fields. Detailed work has been done by Gell-Mann [15], Palmer et al [16]. Chanda et al [8][9] have utilized mutual information to explain complexity in wind direction.

18.3.2 Fractal/Multifractal

Topological dimension of a line is unity and that of a surface is two. This is the convention of natural dimension. But what is the dimension of a curve. Conventionally it should be unity. Similarly the dimension of an undulated surface should be two. Then how to differentiate between a straight line and a curve or a plane and a curved surface. This necessity of distinguishing a straight line from a curve or a plane from a curved surface has been fulfilled with the introduction of fractional dimension.

The feasibility of fractional dimension popularly known as fractal dimension was discussed by many mathematicians from the stand-point of measure theory. Hausdorff suggested a type of fractal dimension. Hausdorff dimension is amply covered by Falconer [17]. The idea of Hausdorff dimension runs as follows.

Let E be a subset of the n-dimensional Eucledian space R^n and let s be a nonnegative number. For $\delta > 0$ define

$$H_\partial^s(E) = \inf \sum_{i=1}^{\infty} |U_i|^s$$

where infimum is over all countable δ-covers $\{U_i\}$ of E. For any E it has been shown that $H^s(E)$ is non-increasing as s increases from 0 to ∞. Moreover if $s < t$ then

$$H_\partial^s(E) \geq \partial^{s-t} H_\partial^t(E)$$

It implies that if $H^t(E)$ is positive then $H^s(E)$ is infinite. Thus there is a unique value dim E for which the following inequality holds.

$$H^s(E) = \infty \ \text{if} \ 0 \le s < \dim E, \ H^s(E) = 0 \ \text{if} \ \dim E < s < \infty,$$

dim E is called Hausdorff dimension.

Hausdorff dimension is derived from the concept of Measure Theory. It is difficult to calculate and hence it was long been confined to the books of measure theory. Mandelbrott [3] introduced the concept of generator to calculate fractional dimension and showed how fractal dimension can be used for some practical purposes like measurement of length of an irregular line, surface of an irregular surface etc. It led to intense application from various branches of science including physics [18], chemistry [19], biological sciences [20], atmospheric sciences 8][9] and turbulence [10].

Mandelbrott made an intuitive conjecture that natural objects are more or less self-similar. It means that the object looks similar in all magnification. This assumption appears to be very crude. Even then we may get some example in support of the assumption. Let us take the case of a casuarina tree. A small twig of the tree and the tree itself are of similar geometrical shape. Another example may be drawn from the structure of cloud. In some cloud formation it appears that the parts of the cloud are geometrically similar to the whole formation. Another important aspect of this assumption is that an object may be made out of repetitive application of a small building block. Artificially also iterative application of a particular elementary pattern in some cases may lead to a design that broadly looks similar to the pattern itself.

Calculation of Fractal Dimension: Box Counting Method

Box Counting method is a widely used method for calculating Fractal Dimension of lines and surfaces. Broadly the method is like this.

In the case of a line it is first embedded in a square. Then a small length of straight segment is chosen and the given line is measured by that straight line segment. It is used almost like a yardstick. Length of the line is calculated by counting how many times yardstick is rolled over the line. The length of the straight segment is further shortened and similar operation is done and length of the line is calculated. The process is repeated till the measured length becomes almost constant. Fractal dimension of the line is then calculated by the following formula.

$$D_0 = -\frac{\log(N)}{\log(l)} \tag{12}$$

where D_0 is the fractal dimension, N is the number of times the line segment is rolled over the line and l is the length of the line segment in fraction of the line.

For the time being let us digress a little and go back to the Cantor's view about dimension. Cantor suggested an algorithm which is well known as 'Cantor's Remove Middle-third' algorithm. It is as follows.

Let us take an unit interval and divide it in three equal parts. Let us now remove the middle part. So we are left with two parts of equal length. Let us again divide each of the two remaining parts into three equal parts and again remove the middle thirds. If we iterate this process for infinite times we shall be left with a set of infinite number of points. The measure of this set is zero. This set is sometimes called Cantor's dust. But what is the fractal dimension of Cantor's dust. Since it is a set of points with measure zero natural dimension is zero. But we shall show that it has a non-zero fractal dimension. It is as below.

After first iteration we have two line segments left each of length (1/3). After n iterations we shall have 2^n segments each of length $(1/3)^n$. Hence as n approaches to infinity according to the above discussed box counting method the fractal dimension of Cantor's dust is given as

$$D_0 = -\lim_{n\to\infty} \frac{\log(2^n)}{\log\left(\frac{1}{3}\right)^n} \tag{13}$$

$$= \frac{\log 2}{\log 3}$$

Hence we observe that there is an object whose fractal dimension is less than unity but non-zero.

Similarly we may have a different set of objects whose knowledge is essential for computer scientists. These are Koch curves. Let us give a short account of a Koch curve. We again take a unit interval and divide it in three equal parts as in the case of Cantor's algorithm. We then take out the middle segment and create a replica of it and make a tent like formation at the middle wherefrom the middle segment has been removed. This is explained in the three successive steps given in Fig. 18.2.

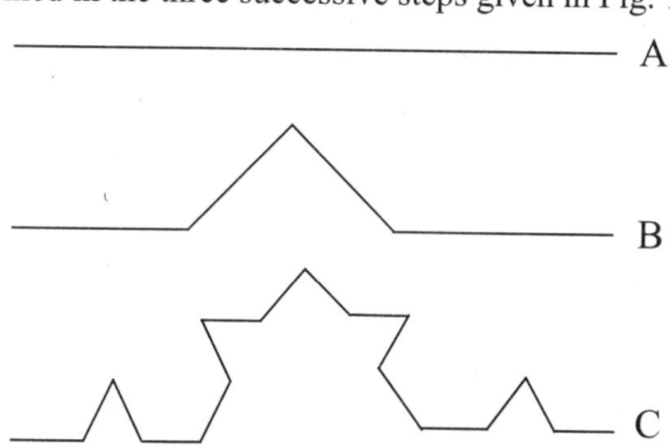

Fig. 18.2 Steps of generation of a Koch curve

First we start with a unit interval *A*. *B* shows the picture after first iteration and *C* after the second iteration. It may be noted that after the first iteration we have four segments each of length (1/3). So after *n* iteration we shall have 4^n segments, each of length $(1/3)^n$ length. So the fractal dimension of this Koch curve can be calculated as

$$D_0 = -\lim_{n\to\infty} \frac{\log\left(4^n\right)}{\log\left(\frac{1}{3}\right)^n} \tag{14}$$

$$= \frac{\log 4}{\log 3}$$

After the de-tour we again come back to our main point. We have discussed the method of calculating fractal dimension. But what is the relation of fractal dimension with complexity of a system. In fact if the object possesses perfect geometrical self-similarity then as opined by Cover et al [14] Kolmogorov complexity is zero. On the other hand we may say that a geometrically self-similar object has no information. Everything is known about it.

Halsey's Partition Function & Multifractal Dimensions

We have so far discussed objects possessing geometrical self-similarity. A Koch curve which is a geometrically self-similar object is practically made of one type of scale. In each step we have taken one third of length as our scale. But in practice geometrically self-similar object is hard to come by. Generally, a natural object is made by iteration of more than one scale. We may observe this again in the Cantor's algorithm.

If instead of dividing unit interval into three equal segments we divide it into four equal segments and then remove the third segment we shall obviously get two types of segments, one (1/2) and the other (1/4). If the iteration is continued we would have a result different from that of Cantor's "Remove Middle-third" algorithm. Same will be the situation in case of a Koch curve. In these cases we have a multiscale object which is not practically a geometrically self-similar object. And hence these objects cannot be characterized with the help of fractal dimension only. These objects unlike geometrically self-similar objects are complex.

In fact almost any object for which randomness is the basic issue that determines the structure of the object turns out to be fractal over some range of length scale.

Bunde et al [21] have observed that there are roughly of the order of 10^3 recognised fractal systems in nature, though at the time when

Mandelbrot's classic book Fractal Geometry of Nature was published many of these systems were not known to be fractal.

In order to calculate fractal and other dimensions, called multifractal dimensions we here mention the partition function suggested by Halsey et al. [22]

$$\chi = \sum (p_i)^q \tag{15}$$

where p_i is the probability that the curve has visited the i-th step and q is a nonnegative integer.

Based on this partition function multifractal dimensions are given as below.

$$D_q = \frac{1}{q-1} \lim_{l \to 0} \frac{\log(\chi)}{\log(l)} \tag{16}$$

It may be observed that D_0 takes the form of the expression of fractal dimension. Others D_1, D_2, ... are multifractal dimensions.

18.4 COMPARISON BETWEEN INFORMATION AND FRACTAL/MULTIFRACTAL DIMENSIONS

A few measures of complexities have been discussed in the foregoing paragraphs. It will now be shown that there is some relation between multifractal dimension and information entropy. For this purpose let us take the case of D_1.

It may be seen from the expression of multifractal dimensions that D_1 cannot be calculated easily. For calculating D_1 one has to calculate $D_{1+\delta}$ first, then to allow δ to approach zero. The limit can be found using Hospital's rule. In this way D_1 is given as

$$D_1 = \lim_{l \to 0} \frac{\sum p_i \log p_i}{\log(l)} \tag{17}$$

It may be observed that the numerator of the expression for D_1 is same as the term for information entropy. In view of this D_1 is named as Information dimension. It means that like entropy, mutual information etc. multifractal dimensions can also be used as measures for complexity.

Another interesting point regarding multifractal dimensions is that in case of self-similar fractal objects probability distribution is uniform distribution and hence a simple calculation will show that all multifractal dimensions are same and are equal to fractal dimension. Any deviation from this uniformity indicates multiscaling and increase in information. But if those are all same then there is absence of complexity vis-a-vis lack of information.

18.5 A CASE STUDY

Chanda et al [9] has conducted extensive study on sets of wind direction data to show the comparative relations of fractal/multifractal dimensions with mutual information to measure complexity in an atmospheric dynamics.

Wind directions have been studied both from the standpoint of fractal/multifractal dimensions and average mutual information (AMI). Three things have been compared. These are AMI, information dimension (ID) and difference between correlation dimension (CD) and fractal dimension (FD).

For calculation of AMI the method followed is given in brief. The time-series has been detrended first then binariased. Patterns of a particular length have been formed following all possible combinations. For each pair of pattern mutual information is calculated. The average of all mutual informations of all possible pairs is AMI.

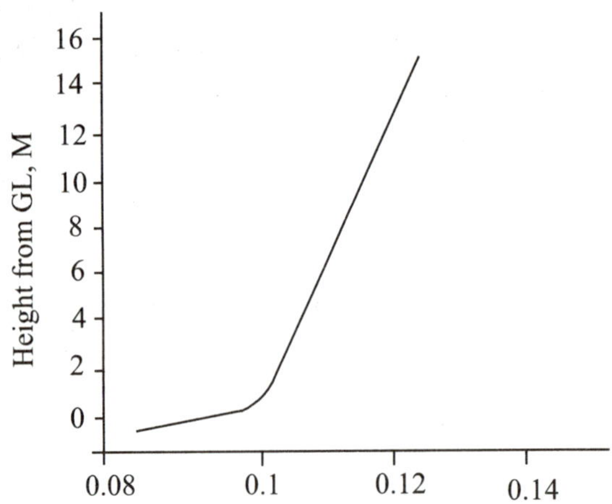

Fig. 18.3 AMI vs height from GL

The idea behind conducting these studies may be understood from what has been discussed in the foregoing. We have already observed that information entropy of a system is well connected with one multifractal dimension D_1, Information dimension. Moreover it has been observed that deviation of multifractal dimension from fractal dimension indicates existence of complexity. One such deviation viz. difference between correlation dimension and fractal dimension has been studied. However, selection of correlation dimension has been done arbitrarily.

It has been shown with increasing height AMI, ID and (CD-ID) all increase. It shows that AMI and ID are correlated and information increases as we go higher and higher. Increase of (CD-FD) indicates

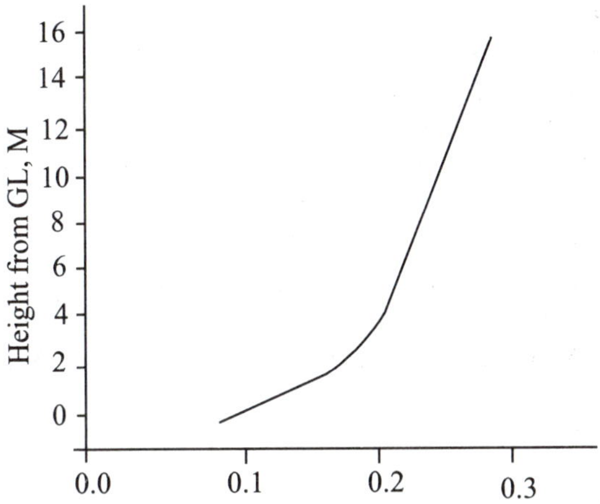

Fig. 18.4 Information dimension vs height from GL

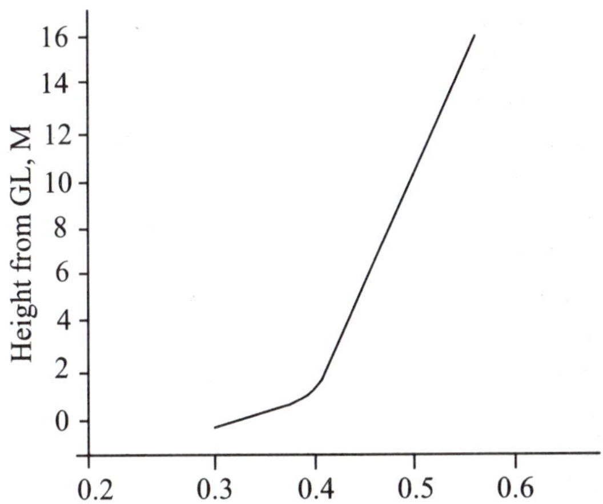

Fig. 18.5 (FD-CD) vs height from GL

replacing geometrical self-similarity by statistical self-similarity with increase in number of scales. It has been conjectured that the results indicate that near the ground wind is weak and as we go higher, wind not only becomes stronger but also is subjected to intermittent blows of wind from different directions. Figs. 18.3, 18.4 and 18.5 show the results obtained.

References

1. C E Shannon, & W. Weaver. *Mathematical Theory of communication.* University of Illinois Press. Urbana 1949.
2. S Kullback, *Information Theory and Statistics.* John Wiley, New York. (Reprinted by Dover, New York, 1968).

3. D Dutta Majumder, *Fuzzy Mathematics and Uncertainty Management for Decision Making in Science and Society*. J. Computer Science & Information, Vol 23, no. 3, Sept 1993, pp 1-31.
4. D Dutta Mazumder, K K Mazumder, *Complexity, Analysis, Uncertainty Management and Fuzzy Dynamical Systems. A Cybernetic Approach with Some Case Studies*. Int. J. Systems and Cybernetics (Kybernetics), Vol.33, no.7, 2004.
5. K K Majumder, & D Dutta Majumder, *Fuzzy Differential Inclusion in Atmospheric and Medical Cybernetics*. IEEE Trans. System, Man & Cybernetics, April 2004, Vol 34, no. 2, ISSN 1683-4419, pp 877-887.
6. A Chanda, A K Dey & J Das. *On the fractal characterisation of atmospheric velocity field.* Ind. J. of Radiophysics, Vol 26, pp 307-311, 1997.
7. A Chanda, A K Dey & J Das. *Fractal characterisation of temperature, field in the convective boundary layer.* FRACTALS, Vol 5, no. 2 (1997).
8. A Chanda, & J Das. *Self-similarity in Wind Direction in Turbulent Atmosphere.* J Tech. Phys. **39,** 2. 23-29. 1998.
9. A Chanda, & J Das. *Measures of Complexity in Wind Direction.* J Tech. Phys. **44,** 2. 207-214. 2003,
10. A Chanda, P Das & J Das. *On multifractal dimensions and their relations.* Proc. Int. Symp. Math. and Math. Sc., organised by Calcutta Mathematical Society, January 2000 (ISMMS 2000).
11. A Chanda, P De, P Das & J Das. *Selfsimilarity in the decay of homogenous and isotropic turbulence.* J. Technical Physics, Vol. 41(1), pp 13-I7, 1999.
12. B B Mandelbrot, *The Fractal Geometry of Nature.* W. H. Freeman. New York. 1982.
13. C Arndt, *Information Measures.* Springer. Berlin. 2000.
14. M Cover, and Joy A. Thomas. *Elements of Information Theory.* Wiley Series in Telecommunications. John Wiley & Sons Inc. New York. 1991.
15. M Gell-Mann, and S Lloyd. *Information Measures, effective complexity and total information.* Complexity, **2**, 44-52. 1996.
16. A J Palmer, and C W Fairall, W.A. Brewer. *Complexity in the Atmosphere.* IEEE Trans. on Geoscience and Remote Sensing. **38,** 4, 2056-2063. 2000.
17. K J Falconer, *The Geometry of Fractal Sets.* Cambridge University Press. Cambridge. 1985.
18. H Takayasu, *Fractals in the Physical Sciences.* Manchester University Press. Manchester. 1990.

19. D Avnir, ed, *The Fractal Approach to Heterogenous Chemistry.* Wiley. Chicester. 1989.
20. T Lahiri, and D Dutta Majumder. *Fuzzy MultiFractal Approach in the Study of Texture Complexity in Image database.* Fuzzy Set Theory and its mathematical Aspects and Application. A. K. Shrivastava (Ed.). Allied Publishers, New Delhi. pp 131-135. 2002.
21. Bunde, Armin, Shlomo Havlin (eds.). *Fractals and Disordered Systems.* Springer-Verlag, Berlin. 1996.
22. T C Halsey, M.H. Jenson, L P Kadanoff, I. Procaccia and B.I. Shraiman Physical Review A, **33**, 2. 1141-1151, 1986.

UNIT IV

IMAGE PROCESSING AND COMPRESSION

19

Some Analytical Properties and Fast Algorithms of a Discrete Linear Basis in Image Processing

P C Mali[1] and D Dutta Majumder[2]

ABSTRACT

For the suitability to carry out a comparative study of discrete linear basis transforms, a parametric class of these transforms have been considered. It has been shown that under certain conditions on the parameters, every member of this class is superior to Walsh-Hadamarad transform for first order stationary Markov process. For high correlation of this process, the class has been proved to be inferior to slant transform. A lower bound of the performance of this class has been found. The fast algorithms for finding the diagonal elements of two-dimensional discrete linear basis transform of a given matrix, have been presented. The speed of the algorithms has also been discussed.

Keywords: Image Processing; Discrete Linear Basis Transform; Walsh-Hadamard Transform; Performance Bound; Slant Transform; Fast Algorithm.

19.1 INTRODUCTION

Fast unitary transforms have been extensively used in feature selection, data compression and filtering in pattern recognition and image processing problems. Although frequently used, sinusoidal family of unitary transforms has been studied in detail by Jain[1], Ahmed *et al.*[2] and Hamidi and Pearl[3] both empirically and analytically, the study of non-sinusoidal family of unitary transforms consuming less computation time appears to be lacking. The experimental investigations of some members of this family e.g., Walsh-Hadamard transform (WHT), Haar transform (HT) and slant transform (ST) have been carried out by Pratt *et al.*[4]. Recently, some interesting analytical properties of these transforms have been discussed in [5] and [6]. The current paper is an extension of this work to another non-sinusoidal family member, discrete linear basis transform (DLBT) which was introduced and successfully used by Haralick and Shanmugam [7] in image data compression.

In this paper, at first, a relative performance measure of a unitary transform with optimum Karhunen-Loeve transform (KLT) has been defined. On the basis of this measure a comparative study of a parametric DLBT class WHT and ST for first order stationary Markov process, has

---

[1] Department of Mathematics, Jadavpur University, Kolkata - 700 032, India. To whom correspondence should be made.

[2] Electronics and Communication Science Unit, Indian Statistical Institute, Calcutta - 700 035, India.

been carried out. A lower bound of this class for positive correlation has been found. A transform giving supreme performance of this class is obtained, which may be generated by repeated application of Kronecker product operation on a discrete cosine transform (DCT). Finally, some fast algorithms for computing two-dimensional (2-D) DLBT of a given matrix, have been developed, which may be used to realize the relative performance measure, diagonal filter matrix [8] or transform domain variances of a data set for the DLBT.

19.2 COMPARATIVE STUDY OF DLBT AND WHT

In order to compare DLBT and WHT, we define relative performance measure R_{T_P} of a transform T_P of order 2^P (= N), operated on a given data set of dimensionality N as [3].

$$R_{T_P} = \frac{\sum_{i=1}^{N}\left(d_i^2 - r_i^2\right)}{\sum_{i=1}^{N}\left(\lambda_i^2 - r_i^2\right)} \tag{1}$$

where r_i is the ith diagonal element of the data domain covariance matrix and d_i and r_i are respectively the ith diagonal elements of the transform domain covariance matrices corresponding to T_P and KLT. We also assume that the image data follows the most frequently used, first order stationary Markovian property. In this case the covariance matrix of the image data may be represented in the form Tbeplitz matrix $X = \left[\rho^{|i-j|}\right]$, where ρ is the correlation coefficient between two adjacent pixels in the image data.

It is known that DLBT generated by k matrices of order $N_1, N_2, \ldots, N_k$ requires $N_1, N_2, \ldots N_k\, (N_1 + N_2 + \ldots + N_k)$ add and multiply operations to determine the projected components of a data set with dimensionality $N = \prod_{i=1}^{k} N_i$. It simply indicates that the computational load for implementation of DLBT will be increased if the order of the generator matrices are increased keeping N fixed. Considering this behaviour of DLBT and also the suitability for the comparison with WHT, we have used the generator matrices of order 4 only. Each of these matrices is of the form

$$\begin{bmatrix} 1 & 1 & 1 & 1 \\ r & -s & s & -r \\ s & r & -r & -s \\ 1 & -1 & -1 & 1 \end{bmatrix}$$

where r and s are positive integers. It is noted here that this DLBT class of order N requires $N \log_2 N$ additions/subtractions and $\frac{1}{2} N \log_2 N$ integer multiplications considering the fact that the generator matrices contain odd or even basis vectors and also ± 1. On the other hand WHT of the same order requires only $N \log_2 N$ additions/subtractions.

Without any loss of generality we assume that the generator matrices of this class (Say $\mathfrak{I}$) are of the form

$$M_{\alpha_q} = \begin{bmatrix} \frac{1}{2} & (1 \quad 1 \quad 1 \quad 1) \\ \frac{1}{\sqrt{2(1+\alpha_q^2)}} & (1 \quad -\alpha_q \quad \alpha_q \quad -1) \\ \frac{1}{\sqrt{2(1+\alpha_q^2)}} & (\alpha_q \quad 1 \quad -1 \quad -\alpha_q) \\ \frac{1}{2} & (1 \quad -1 \quad -1 \quad 1) \end{bmatrix}$$

Where α_q (a positive rational number) is the only parameter of the matrix M_{α_q} so that it become an unitary matrix.

We shall now establish an important theorem when the data series is a first order stationary Markov process with positive correlation.

Theorem: For the class $\mathfrak{I}$ of DLBT, $R_{DLBT} > R_{WHT}$ if all the parameters of $\mathfrak{I}$ lie in the interval (1, 3).

Proof: Let D_{q+1} and D_q be two transforms in the class $\mathfrak{I}$ such that $D_{q+1} = M_{\alpha_q} \otimes D_q$,

Where $q = \log_4 N$ and $\otimes$ is the Kronecker product operation. Now, the Tbeplitz matrix X_{q+1} of order $4N$ may be recursively defined as

$$X_{q+1} = \begin{bmatrix} X_q & Z_q^T & \rho^N Z_q^T & \rho^{2N} Z_q^T \\ Z_q & X_q & Z_q^T & \rho^N Z_q^T \\ \rho^N Z_q & Z_q & X_q & Z_q^T \\ \rho^{2N} Z_q & \rho^N Z_q & Z_q & X_q \end{bmatrix}$$

$$Z_{q+1} = \begin{bmatrix} \rho^{3N} & \rho^{2N} & \rho^{N} & 1 \\ \rho^{4N} & \rho^{3N} & \rho^{2N} & \rho^{N} \\ \rho^{5N} & \rho^{4N} & \rho^{3N} & \rho^{1N} \\ \rho^{6N} & \rho^{5N} & \rho^{4N} & \rho^{2N} \end{bmatrix} \otimes Z_q \qquad (3)$$

with $X_o = [1]$ and $Z_o = [\rho]$.

Then, the four diagonal blocks $D_{q+1}\ X_{q+1}\ D^T{}_{q+1}\ \left(= \widetilde{X}_{q+1}, \text{ say}\right)$ are respectively.

$$\widetilde{X}_q + a_q \frac{\widetilde{Z}_q + \widetilde{Z}_q^T}{2}$$

$$\widetilde{X}_q + b_q \frac{\widetilde{Z}_q + \widetilde{Z}_q^T}{2} \tag{4}$$

$$\widetilde{X}_q + c_q \frac{\widetilde{Z}_q + \widetilde{Z}_q^T}{2}$$

and $$\widetilde{X}_q + d_q \frac{\widetilde{Z}_q + \widetilde{Z}_q^T}{2},$$

and those of $D_{q+1} \dfrac{Z_{q+1} + Z_q^T + 1}{2} D_{q+1}^T \left(= \dfrac{1}{2}(\widetilde{Z}_{q+1} + \widetilde{Z}_{q+1}^T) \right)$ are respectively

$$e_q \frac{\widetilde{Z}_q + \widetilde{Z}_q^T}{2},\ f_q \frac{\widetilde{Z}_q + \widetilde{Z}_q^T}{2},\ g_q \frac{\widetilde{Z}_q + \widetilde{Z}_q^T}{2},\ h_q \frac{\widetilde{Z}_q + \widetilde{Z}_q^T}{2}, \tag{5}$$

where $$a_q = \frac{1}{2}(3 + 2\rho^N + \rho^{2N}),$$

$$b_q = \frac{1}{1+\alpha_q^2}(-\alpha_q^2 - \rho^{2N} - 2\alpha_q + 2\alpha_q \rho^N),$$

$$c_q = \frac{1}{1+\alpha_q^2}(-\alpha_q^2 \rho^{2N} - 1 + 2\alpha_q - 2\alpha_q \rho^N),$$

$$d_q = \frac{1}{2}(-1 - 2\rho^N + \rho^{2N}),$$

$$e_q = \frac{1}{4}(1 + \rho^N + \rho^{2N} + \rho^{3N})^2$$

$$f_q = -\frac{1}{2(1+\alpha_q^2)}(1 - \rho^{3N} - \alpha_q \rho^N + \alpha_q \rho^{2N})^2$$

$$g_q = -\frac{1}{2(1+\alpha_q^2)}(\rho^N - \rho^{2N} + \alpha_q - \alpha_q \rho^{3N})^2$$

and $$h_q = \frac{1}{4}(1 - \rho^N)^4\ (1 + \rho^N)^2.$$

Let x_{q+1} and y_{q+1} be the sum of the squares of all the diagonal elements of $\widetilde{X}_{q+1}$ and $\dfrac{\widetilde{Z}_{q+1}+\widetilde{Z}_{q+1}}{2}$ respectively.

Then using the fact that $a_q + b_q + c_q + d_q = 0$ the recursive relations of x_{q+1} and y_{q+1} in terms of x_q and y_q may be established from (4) and (5) as

$$x_{q+1} = 4x_q + (a_q^2 + b_q^2 + c_q^2 + d_q^2)y_q$$

and $$y_{q+1} = (e_q^2 + f_q^2 + g_q^2 + h_q^2)y_q \tag{7}$$

with $$x_o = 1,\; y_o = \rho^2.$$

It is observed that if all the parameters of the class $\mathcal{F}$ are equal to 1, the corresponding DLBT reduces to WHT. In that case a_q, d_q, e_q and h_q remain unchanged and b_q, c_q, f_q and g_q will reduce to the corresponding values

$$b'_q = \frac{1}{2}(-1 - \rho^{2N} - 2 + 2\rho^N)$$

$$c'_q = \frac{1}{2}(-\rho^{2N} - 1 + 2 - 2\rho^N)$$

$$f'_q = -\frac{1}{4}(1 - \rho^{3N} - \rho^N + \rho^{2N})^2 \tag{8}$$

$$g'_q = -\frac{1}{4}(1 - \rho^{3N} + \rho^N - \rho^{2N})^2$$

Hence, recursive relations corresponding to (7) are given by

$$x'_{q+1} = 4x'_q + (a_q^2 + b_q'^2 + c_q'^2 + d_q^2)\,y'_q$$

and $$y'_{q+1} = (e_q^2 + f_q'^2 + g_q'^2 + h_q^2)y'_q \tag{9}$$

with $$x'_o = 1, y'_o = \rho^2$$

From (6) and (8), it is noted that

$$b_q + c_q = b'_q + c'_q$$

and $$f_q + g_q = f'_q + g'_q. \tag{10}$$

After some algebric manipulation, it may also be easily shown that

$$b_q < b'_q < c_q \quad \text{if} \quad 1 < \alpha_q \le 3$$

and $$f_q > f'_q > g_q \quad \text{if} \quad \alpha_q > 1. \tag{11}$$

Combining these results and using (10), it can be proved that

$$b_q^2 + c_q^2 > b_q'^2 + c_q'^2$$

and $$f_q^2 + g_q^2 > f_q'^2 + g_q'^2 \text{ if } 1 < \alpha_q \le 3. \tag{12}$$

Then comparing (7) and (9), one may conclude that $x_q > x'_q \ \forall\ q$ if all the parameters involved in the DLBT lie in the interval (1,3) which follows the theorem.

19.3 LOWER BOUND OF DLBT

It has been experimentally verified that the performance measure R_{D_q} for first order stationary Markov process is monotonically increasing with the correlation coefficient ρ in (0, 1). Using this property of DLBT, the lower bound of R_{DLBT} for positive correlation may be found making $\rho \to 0$ i.e., ρ^3 term and all higher powers of ρ are neglected in the recursive relations (7). Hence, we obtain

$$x_{q+1} = 4x_q + \left\{\frac{7}{2} + \frac{2\alpha_q(2\alpha_q^2 + 3\alpha_q - 2)}{(1+\alpha_q^2)^2}\right\} y_q,$$

and $$y_{q+1} = \left\{\frac{3}{8} - \frac{\alpha_q^2}{2(1+\alpha_q^2)^2}\right\} y_q \tag{13}$$

with $x_o = 1, y_o = \rho^2$.

With the help of (13) and assuming that all the parameters of D_q are known the lower bound of R_{D_q} can be found from the relation

$$R_{D_q} = \frac{x_q - N}{2(N-1)\rho^2}. \tag{14}$$

Here the denominator of right side of (14) represents the value corresponding to that in (1) when only ρ^2 term is retained.

For the sake of simplification, if we assume that all parameters in the DLBT are equal to α then (13) reduces to

$$x_{q+1} = 4x_q + \beta y_q,$$

and $$y_{q+1} = \gamma\, y_q \tag{15}$$

with $x_o = 1,\ y_o = \rho^2,$

where $$\beta = \frac{7}{2} + \frac{2\alpha(2\alpha^2 + 3\alpha - 2)}{(1+\alpha^2)^2},$$

$$\gamma = \frac{3}{8} - \frac{\alpha^2}{2(1+\alpha^2)^2}.$$

Solving (14) one readily obtains

$$x_q = N + \beta \frac{N - \gamma^q}{4 - \gamma}.$$

Thus we get $R_{D_q} = \dfrac{\beta(N-\gamma^q)}{2(N-1)(4-\gamma)}$ (17)

which follows that $R_{D_q} \to \dfrac{\beta}{2(4-\gamma)}$ as $N \to \alpha$ (18)

As a particular case, substituting $\alpha = 1$ in (16) one may find the performance bound of WHT as [3]

$$R_{\text{WHT}} = \frac{2}{3}$$

It is also observed that if $\alpha = 3$, i.e. the DLBT is generated by the ST matrices of order 4 (the general ST matrix is defined in section 5.0), the performance bound of DLBT is given by

$$R_{\text{DLBT}} = \frac{250}{367}$$

It is interesting to note that this value is greater than the performance bound of WHT but less than that of ST [6]. However, for $\alpha = 2$, the corresponding value of R_{DLBT} may be shown to be greater than R_{ST}.

19.4 PERFORMANCE MEASURE OF DLBT FOR HIGH CORRELATION

In most of the images, it has been observed that the correlation coefficient between two adjacent pixels varies from 0.85 to 0.95. In some cases, this correlation exceeds 0.95 also. Keeping this in view, it seems that the study of behaviour of DLBT near $\rho = 1$ i.e., at $\rho = 1 - \varepsilon$ (ε is a very small quantity) is important. As we see from (1) that x_q plays a principal role in the behaviour of DLBT, we calculate x_q at $\rho = 1 - \varepsilon$ retaining up to ε^2 term.

Now, from (6) we obtain

$$\boldsymbol{a}_q = 3 - 2N\varepsilon + \frac{1}{2}N(3N-2)\,\varepsilon^2$$

$$\check{z}\boldsymbol{b}_q = -1 + \frac{2N(1-\alpha_q)}{1+\alpha_q^2}\varepsilon + \left.\frac{N\{(N-1)\alpha_q - (2N-1)}{1+\alpha_q^2}\right\}\varepsilon^2,$$

$$\check{z}\boldsymbol{c}_q = -1 + \frac{2N(\alpha_q^2+\alpha_q)}{1+\alpha_q^2}\varepsilon - \left.\frac{N\{(N-1)\alpha_q + (2N-1)\alpha_q^2}{1+\alpha_q^2}\right\}\varepsilon^2,$$

$$d_q = -1 + \frac{N^2}{2}\,\varepsilon^2,$$
$$e_q = 4 - 12N\varepsilon + N(23N-6)\varepsilon^2,$$
$$f_q = -N^2(3-\alpha_q)^2\,\varepsilon^2,$$
$$g_q = -N^2(1+3\alpha_q)^2\,\varepsilon^2 \tag{19}$$

and $h_q = 0$

Then using (7) we may establish the recursive relations as

$$x_{q+1} = 4x_q + \left[12 - 16N\varepsilon + \left\{N(20N-8) + \frac{8N^2\alpha_q(\alpha_q^2-1)}{(1+\alpha_q^2)^2}\right\}\varepsilon^2\right]y_q$$

and $$y_{q+1} = 16\left\{1 - 6N\varepsilon + \frac{1}{2}(41N-6)N\varepsilon^2\right\}y_q \tag{20}$$

with $x_o = 1$, $y_o = (1 - 2\varepsilon + \varepsilon^2)$.

This relation may be simplified to

$$x_{q+1} = 4x_q + N^2\left[12 - 40N\varepsilon + (78N^2 - 20N - 2)\varepsilon^2 + \frac{8N^2\alpha_q(\alpha_q^2-1)}{(1+\alpha_q^2)^2}\,\varepsilon^2\right] \tag{21}$$

with $x_o = 1$.

With the help of (21) we may determine x_q when all α_q's are known. The corresponding relation for WHT may also be obtained by letting $\alpha_q = 1 \;\forall\; q$

Thus $$x'_{q+1} = 4x'_q + N^2[12 - 40N\varepsilon + (78N^2 - 20N - 2)\varepsilon^2] \tag{22}$$

with $x'_o = 1$.

It is interesting to see that x_q obtained from (21) will be greater than x_q obtained from (22) if $\alpha_q > 1 \;\forall\; q$. In other words, we may conclude that performance of DLBT in $\Re$ superior to that of WHT near $\rho = 1$ if all the parameters of DLBT arc greater than 1.

It is also clear from (21) that one may obtain the best performance for DLBT in $\Re$ near $\rho = 1$ if α_q's are chosen in such a way that

$$S = \frac{\alpha_q(\alpha_q^2-1)}{(1+\alpha_q^2)^2} \text{ is maximum.}$$

Now, S is maximum at $\alpha_q = \sqrt{2} + 1$ implying that transform generated by DCT of order 4 will give the supremum performance and performance of DLBT in $\mathcal{F}$ may be improved by choosing the rational number α_q as close as the irrational number $\sqrt{2} + 1$. This result seems to dictate an important generalization which we conjecture as the performance of the general class of DLBT can not exceed that of DCT near $\rho = 1$.

For further simplification we let $\alpha_q = \alpha \ \forall\ q$. Then (21) may be solved giving

$$x_q = N^2 - \frac{2}{3}N(N^2-1)\varepsilon + \frac{N}{42}(N-1)(13N^2-N-8)\varepsilon^2 + \frac{2N(N^3-1)\alpha(\alpha^2-1)}{63(1+\alpha^2)^2}\varepsilon^2 \tag{23}$$

By substituting $\alpha = \sqrt{2} + 1$, we obtain

$$\sup_{\text{DLBT} \in \mathcal{F}} x_q = N^2 - \frac{2}{3}N(N^2-1)\varepsilon + \frac{N}{42}(N-1)(13N^2-N-8)\varepsilon^2 + \frac{1}{126}N(N^3-1)\varepsilon^2 \tag{24}$$

19.5 COMPARISON OF DLBT WITH ST FOR HIGH CORRELATION

In the last section, we have found a performance measure of DLBT near $\rho = 1$. To compare this transform with ST near $\rho = 1$, we need to determine the performance measure of ST in the same neighbourhood of ρ. In order to carry out this computation we first, define Hadamard ordered ST. The ST matrix of order $2^p (= N)$ denoted as S_p and represented recursively as [9]

$$\boldsymbol{S}_{p+1} = \frac{1}{\sqrt{2}}\boldsymbol{M}_{2N}\begin{bmatrix} S_p & S_p \\ S_p & -S_p \end{bmatrix}$$

where

$$\boldsymbol{M}_{2N} = \begin{bmatrix} I_{N/2} & r_{2N} & -S_{2N} & \\ & S_{2N} & r_{2N} & \\ & & & I_{N/2} \end{bmatrix}, \ r_{2N} = \left(\frac{3N^2}{4N^2-1}\right)^{1/2}, \ S_{2N} = \left(\frac{N^2-1}{4N^2-1}\right)^{1/2} \tag{25}$$

and $I_{N/2}$ is an identity matrix of order $N/2$ with the initial condition

$$S_o = [1],\ \boldsymbol{M}_2 = I_2.$$

The Tbeplitz matrix $\boldsymbol{X}^*_{p+1} = [\rho^{|i-j|}]$ of order 2^{p+1} can also be expressed in the following recursive manner.

$$\boldsymbol{X}^*_{p+1} = \begin{bmatrix} \boldsymbol{X}^*_p & \boldsymbol{Z}^{*T}_p \\ \boldsymbol{Z}^*_p & \boldsymbol{X}^*_p \end{bmatrix},\ \boldsymbol{X}^*_o = [1]$$

and
$$\boldsymbol{Z}^*_{p+1} = \begin{bmatrix} \rho^N \boldsymbol{Z}^*_p & \boldsymbol{Z}^*_p \\ \rho^{2N} \boldsymbol{Z}^*_p & \rho^N \boldsymbol{Z}^*_p \end{bmatrix},\ \boldsymbol{Z}^*_o = [\rho] \tag{26}$$

where the superscript T denotes the matrix transpose. Now, we denote x^*_p and y^*_p as the sum of the squares of the diagonal elements of

$\boldsymbol{S}_p\,\boldsymbol{X}^*_p\,\boldsymbol{S}^T_p$ and $\boldsymbol{S}_p \dfrac{\boldsymbol{Z}^*_p + \boldsymbol{Z}^{*T}_p}{2} \boldsymbol{S}^T_p$ respectively. Then the recursive relations of x^*_p and y^*_p can be developed with the aid of (25) and (26). These relations are given by

$$x^*_{p+1} = 2(x^*_p + y^*_p) + 2(\mu - \nu)(\mu - \eta)$$

and
$$y^*_{p+1} = \frac{1}{2}(1 + 6\rho^{2N} + \rho^{4N})y^*_p + 2(\mu_1 - \nu_1)(\mu_1 - \eta_1) \tag{27}$$

with $x^*_o = 1,\ y^*_o = \rho^2$,

where

$$\mu = \frac{1+\rho}{1-\rho} - \frac{3\rho\left(2N - 1 + \dfrac{2}{1-\rho}\right)}{N(4N^2-1)(1-\rho)^2}\left\{(2N-1)(1+\rho^{2N}) - \frac{2\rho(1-\rho^{2N-1})}{1-\rho}\right\}$$

$$\nu = \frac{1+\rho}{1-\rho} - \frac{3\rho}{N(N^2-1)(1-\rho)^2}\left\{(N-1)(1+\rho^N) - 2\rho\frac{(1-\rho^{N-1})}{1-\rho}\right\}$$

$$\left\{(N-1)(3+\rho^N) + \frac{4-2\rho+2\rho^N}{1-\rho}\right\}$$

$$\eta = \frac{1+\rho}{1-\rho} - \frac{\rho(1-\rho^N)(3-\rho^N)}{N(1-\rho)^2}$$

$$\mu_1 = -\frac{3\rho}{2N(4N^2-1)}\left\{\frac{2N-1}{1-\rho}(1+\rho^{2N}) - \frac{2\rho(1-\rho^{2N-1})}{(1-\rho)^2}\right\}^2 \tag{28}$$

$$\nu_1 = -\frac{3\rho(1+\rho^N)^2}{2N(N^2-1)}\left\{\frac{N-1}{1-\rho}(1+\rho^N) - \frac{2\rho(1-\rho^{N-1})}{(1-\rho)^2}\right\}^2$$

$$\eta_1 = -\frac{\rho(1-\rho^N)^4}{2N(1-\rho)^2}$$

Details of this derivation may be found in [6]. Now substituting $\rho = 1 - \varepsilon$ in (28) and retaining up to ε one can obtain

$$\mu-\nu = \frac{3}{5}N^2\varepsilon,\ \mu-\eta = \frac{2(N^2-1)}{15}\varepsilon,$$

$$\mu_1-\nu_1 = 0,\ \mu_1-\eta_1 = 0.$$

Consequently, discarding ε^3 and higher powers of ε, (27) gives

$$x^*_{p+1} = 2(x^*_p + y^*_p) + \frac{4N^2(N^2-1)}{25}\varepsilon^2 \tag{29}$$

and $$y^*_{p+1} = 4\left[1-2N\varepsilon + N(\frac{5}{2}N-1)\varepsilon^2\right]y^*_p$$

with $$x^*_o = 1,\ y^*_o = 1-2\varepsilon+\varepsilon^2.$$

Solving (29), we get

$$x^*_p = N^2 - \frac{2}{3}N(N^2-1)\varepsilon + \frac{N}{42}(N-1)(13N^2-N-8)\varepsilon^2$$

$$+\frac{2N}{175}(N-1)(N-2)(N+3)\varepsilon^2 \tag{30}$$

Noting that both x_q in (24) and x^*_p in (30) are the performance measure of DLBT and ST respectively for first order Markov process of finite length N and comparing them we conclude that $x^*_p > \sup x_q$ if $N \geq 16$

$$\text{DLBT} \in \mathcal{F}$$

Thus performance of ST is superior to that of DLBT in $\mathcal{F}$ near $\rho = 1$ but DLBT has the heavier computational load than that of ST. In this sense DLBT has a drawback for using it in images. However, there may be some DLBT, with higher order generator matrices, whose performance measure is better than that of ST. It is also experimentally verified that ST is more efficient than DLBT for high values of ρ

whereas, for its low values the result is reversed. However, WHT is inferior to both transforms DLBT and ST and superior to HT.

19.6 FAST ALGORITHMS FOR COMPUTING DIAGONAL ELEMENTS OF 2-D DLBT OF A MATRIX

Let $\boldsymbol{A_k}$ be a given matrix of order N and D_k be the DLBT of order N, which is generated by k matrices, M_1, M_2, ... M_k of orders respectively N_1, N_2 ,.... N_k with $N=\prod_{i=1}^{k} N_i$. Then diagonal elements computation of 2-D DLBT of A_k is characterised by three cases.

Case 1: When A_k is not symmetric

Before proceeding to establish an iterative procedure for finding the diagonal elements of the two-dimensional transform with $\boldsymbol{D_k}$ of the matrix $\boldsymbol{A_k}$ we consider, for example, the transform

$$\tilde{\boldsymbol{D}}=\begin{bmatrix} xD & yD \\ zD & wD \end{bmatrix}$$

and the matrix

$$\tilde{\boldsymbol{A}}=\begin{bmatrix} A & B \\ C & E \end{bmatrix}$$

where x, y, z and w are definite constants and $\boldsymbol{A}$, $\boldsymbol{B}$, $\boldsymbol{C}$, $\boldsymbol{D}$ and $\boldsymbol{E}$ are matrices of order N. Then, the two-dimensional transform of $\tilde{\boldsymbol{A}}$ is

$$\tilde{\boldsymbol{D}}\tilde{\boldsymbol{A}}\tilde{\boldsymbol{D}}^T=\begin{bmatrix} \boldsymbol{D}(\boldsymbol{x}^2\boldsymbol{A}+\boldsymbol{xyB}+\boldsymbol{xyC}+\boldsymbol{y}^2\boldsymbol{E})\boldsymbol{D}^T & * \\ * & \boldsymbol{D}(\boldsymbol{z}^2\boldsymbol{A}+\boldsymbol{zwB}+\boldsymbol{zwC}+\boldsymbol{w}^2\boldsymbol{E})\boldsymbol{D}^T \end{bmatrix}$$

Here * indicates some matrix which is unnecessary for our purpose. From (31), it is clear that the computation of the diagonal elements of $\tilde{\boldsymbol{D}}\tilde{\boldsymbol{A}}\tilde{\boldsymbol{D}}^T$ with order $2N$ may be carried out through the computation of two-dimensional transform of $F = x^2\boldsymbol{A} + xy\,\boldsymbol{B} + xy\,\boldsymbol{C} + y^2\boldsymbol{E}$ and $\boldsymbol{G} = z^2\boldsymbol{A} + zw\,\boldsymbol{B} + zw\,\boldsymbol{C} + w^2\boldsymbol{E}$ of order N. It should be noted the matrices $\boldsymbol{F}$ and $\boldsymbol{G}$ can be computed from the diagonal elements of the matrices like

$$\begin{bmatrix} x & y \\ z & w \end{bmatrix} \boldsymbol{H} \begin{bmatrix} x & z \\ y & w \end{bmatrix},$$

where $\boldsymbol{H}$ is a 2×2 matrix containing 4 elements and constructed by collecting the corresponding elements of the matrices $\boldsymbol{A}$, $\boldsymbol{B}$, $\boldsymbol{C}$ and $\boldsymbol{E}$ and placing them in the positions same as the matrices $\boldsymbol{A}$, $\boldsymbol{B}$, $\boldsymbol{C}$ are in A. This concept may be generalized to obtain the diagonal elements of 2-D DLBT of the matrix $\boldsymbol{A_k}$.

At first, the matrix $\boldsymbol{A_k}$ which is to be transformed, is divided into N_1^2 blocks, each of size $\frac{N}{N_1} \times \frac{N}{N_1}$. A matrix $\boldsymbol{H}_{ij}$ of size $N_1 \times N_1$ is constructed by collecting (i, j) th element of each block of $\boldsymbol{A_k}$ $(i, j = 1, 2, \ldots, \frac{N}{N_1})$. Then N_1 diagonal elements of $\boldsymbol{M}_1\ \boldsymbol{H}_{ij}\ \boldsymbol{M}_1^T$ are computed and stored in (i, j)th position of the diagonal blocks of $\boldsymbol{A_k}$. By this process, the matrix $\boldsymbol{A_k}$ is reduced to N_1 matrices $A_{K-1}^{(i)}$ $(i = 1, 2, \ldots\ldots N_1)$ and stored in the N_1 diagonal blocks of $\boldsymbol{A_k}$. This completes one iteration. It is noticed here that the generator matrix $\boldsymbol{M}_1$ is made unitary by multiplying suitable constants to each basis vector of $\boldsymbol{M}_1$. This multiplication may be avoided by adjusting suitable multipliers at the final stage of computation.

In the next iteration, the same procedure is applied to all the matrices $\boldsymbol{A}_{k-1}^{(i)}$ replacing the integer N_1 and the matrix $\boldsymbol{M}_1$ by N_2 and $\boldsymbol{M}_2$ respectively. In this way, the iterations are repeated q times and finally we obtain the diagonal elements of 2-D DLBT of the given matrix $\boldsymbol{A_k}$. The algorithm of this computation is described in the following.

A. Diagonal Computing Algorithm 1 (DCA1)

Step 1. Initialize the integers k, N, the matrix $\boldsymbol{A}$, the matrix $\boldsymbol{M}_i$ and integer N_i $(i = 1, 2, 3, \ldots\ldots, k)$.

Step 2. $i \leftarrow 1, e \leftarrow 1$.

Step 3. $j \leftarrow 1$.

Step 4. $t \leftarrow \frac{N}{eN_i},\ f \leftarrow \frac{N}{e}(j-1)$.

Step 5. Construct the matrix $\boldsymbol{H}_{mn}$ whose (r, s)th element is given by

$$h_{rs} = a_{f+m+(r-1)t,\ f+n+(s-1)t};$$

$$m, n = 1, 2, \ldots..t;\ r, s = 1, 2, \ldots., N_i.$$

Step 6. Compute 1th diagonal element u_{11} of $U = \boldsymbol{M}_i\, \boldsymbol{H}_{mn}\ \boldsymbol{M}_i^T$ for all $l = 1, 2, \ldots, N_i$; $m, n = 1, 2, \ldots, t$.

Step 7. $a_{f+m+(l-1)t,\ f+n+(l-1)t} \leftarrow u_{11}$,

$$l = 1, 2, \ldots.., N_i;\ m, n = 1, 2, \ldots., t.$$

Step 8. If $j = e$, go to step 4 otherwise next step.

Step 9. $e \leftarrow eN_i,\ i \leftarrow i+1$.

Step 10. If $i > q$ go to the next step, otherwise step 3.

Step 11. Print diag (A).

Case 2: When A_k is a symmetric matrix

For symmetric $\boldsymbol{A_k}$, we can take advantage of reducing the computation for the redundancy of the elements of $\boldsymbol{A_k}$. In this case, it is observed that the matrix $\boldsymbol{H_{mn}}$ constructed in step 5 of DCA1 is the transpose of $\boldsymbol{H_{nm}}$ implying that the diagonal elements of $\boldsymbol{M_i H_{mn} M_i^T}$ and $\boldsymbol{M_i H_{mn} M_i^T}$ are identical. Thus the computational load in step 6 will be reduced by varying m and n in the manner $m = n, n + 1, \ldots.., t; n = 1, 2, \ldots., t$.

Case 3: When A_k is a covariance matrix of first order stationary Markov process

If $\boldsymbol{A_k}$ is a matrix of the form $[\rho^{|i-j|}]$, further reduction of computation is possible. Let D_{i+1} be a DLBT matrix of order n_{i+1} constructed from $\boldsymbol{D_i}$ recursively by the relation

$$\boldsymbol{D}_{i+1} = \boldsymbol{M}_{k-i} \otimes \boldsymbol{D}_i \tag{32}$$

and $\boldsymbol{X_{i+1}}$ be a Tbeplitz matrix of order n_{i+1} which is generated by the recursive relations

$$\boldsymbol{X}_{i+1} = \begin{bmatrix} \boldsymbol{X}_i & \boldsymbol{Z}_i^T & \rho^{n_i}\, \boldsymbol{Z}_i^T \ldots.\, \rho^{n_i}\, (N_{k-i}-2)\boldsymbol{Z}_i^T \\ \boldsymbol{Z}_i & \boldsymbol{X}_i & \boldsymbol{Z}_i^T \ldots..\rho^{n_i}\, (N_{k-i}-3)\boldsymbol{Z}_i^T \\ \cdots & \cdots & \cdots\cdots\cdots\cdots \\ \rho^{n_i}\, (N_{k-i}-2)\boldsymbol{Z}_i & & \boldsymbol{X}_i \end{bmatrix}$$

and $$\boldsymbol{Z}_{i+1} = \boldsymbol{Z}_1' \otimes \boldsymbol{Z}_i$$

with $$\boldsymbol{X}_o = [1],\ \boldsymbol{Z}_o = [\rho]$$

where

$$Z_i' = \begin{bmatrix} \rho^{n_i}\, (N_{k-i}-1) & \rho^{n_i}\, (N_{k-i}-2) & \cdots\cdots & 1 \\ \rho^{n_i}\, (N_{k-i}) & \rho^{n_i}\, (N_{k-i}-1) & \cdots\cdots & \rho^{n_i} \\ \cdots\cdots\cdots & \cdots\cdots\cdots & & \cdots\cdots\cdots \\ \rho^{n_i}\, (2N_{k-i}-2) & \rho^{n_i}\, (2N_{k-i}-3) & \cdots\cdots & \rho^{n_i}\, (N_{k-i}-1) \end{bmatrix}$$

Now, if we divide the matrix $\boldsymbol{D_{i+1} X_{i+1} D_{i+1}^T}$ into the blocks, each of size $n_i \times n_i$, we may easily obtain from (32) and (33), jth diagonal block of $\boldsymbol{D_{i+1} X_{i+1} D_{i+1}^T}$

$$= \sum_{r>l} m_{jr}\, \rho^{n_i(r-l-1)}\, m_{jl}\; \boldsymbol{D}_i(\boldsymbol{Z}_i + \boldsymbol{Z}_i^T)\boldsymbol{D}_i^T + \boldsymbol{D}_i\, \boldsymbol{X}_i\, \boldsymbol{D}_i^T$$

$$= (j\text{th diagonal element of } \boldsymbol{M}_{k-i}\, \boldsymbol{X}_i'\, \boldsymbol{M}_{k-i}^T)\boldsymbol{X}$$

$$\boldsymbol{D}_i \frac{\boldsymbol{Z}_i + \boldsymbol{Z}_i^T}{2} \boldsymbol{D}_i^T + \boldsymbol{D}_i\, \boldsymbol{X}_i\, \boldsymbol{D}_i^T, \tag{34}$$

where m_{jl} is the (j, l)th element of $\boldsymbol{M}_{i+1}$ and

$$X_i' = \begin{bmatrix} 0 & 1 & \rho^{n_i} \cdots & \rho^{n_i}(N_{k-i}-2) \\ 1 & 0 & 1 \cdots & \rho^{n_i}(N_{k-i}-3) \\ \cdots & \cdots & \cdots & \cdots \\ \rho^{n_i}(N_{k-i}-2) & \cdots & \cdots & 0 \end{bmatrix}$$

Also, $$\boldsymbol{D}_{i+1}\, \boldsymbol{Z}_{i+1}\, \boldsymbol{D}_{i+1}^T = (\boldsymbol{M}_{k-i}\, \boldsymbol{Z}_i'\, \boldsymbol{M}_{k-i}^T \otimes \boldsymbol{D}_i\, \boldsymbol{Z}_i\, \boldsymbol{D}_i^T) \tag{35}$$

Noting that diag $(\boldsymbol{D}_i \boldsymbol{Z}_i \boldsymbol{D}_i^T)$ = diag $(\boldsymbol{D}_i\, \boldsymbol{Z}_i^T\, \boldsymbol{D}_i^T)$, we get from (35),

$$\text{diag}\left(\boldsymbol{D}_{i+1} \frac{\boldsymbol{Z}_{i+1} + \boldsymbol{Z}_{i+1}^T}{2} \boldsymbol{D}_{i+1}^T\right) = \text{diag}\,(\boldsymbol{M}_{k-i}\, \boldsymbol{Z}_i'\, \boldsymbol{M}_{k-i}^T) \otimes$$

$$\text{diag}\left(\boldsymbol{D}_i \frac{\boldsymbol{Z}_i + \boldsymbol{Z}_i^T}{2} \boldsymbol{D}_i^T\right) \tag{36}$$

Using the recursive relations (34) and (36) an algorithm may be developed which computes the diagonal elements of $\boldsymbol{D}_k\, \boldsymbol{X}_k\, \boldsymbol{D}_k^T$. The algorithm is described below.

B. Diagonal Computing Algorithm 2(DCA2)

Step 1. Initialize the integers k, N, the correlation coefficient ρ, the integers n_j and matrices $\boldsymbol{M}_j$, $j = 1, 2, 3, \ldots .\, k$.

Step 2. $i \leftarrow 0,\ n_1 \leftarrow 1,\ d_1^{(0)} \leftarrow 1,\ f_1^{(0)} \leftarrow \rho$.

Step 3. Compute the diagonal elements $\tilde{x}_{il}$ $(l = 1, 2, \ldots, N_{k-1})$ of $\boldsymbol{M}_{k-i}\, \boldsymbol{X}_i'\, \boldsymbol{M}_{k-i}^T$

Then, $d_{n_i(l-1)}^{(i+1)} + r \leftarrow d_r^{(i)} + \tilde{x}_{il}\, f_r^{(i)},\ r = 1, 2, \ldots, n_i$.

Step 4. if $i = k - 1$ go to Step 7, otherwise next step;

Step 5. Compute the diagonal elements $\tilde{z}_{il}$ $(\boldsymbol{l} = 1, 2, \ldots, \boldsymbol{N}_{k-i})$ of $\boldsymbol{M}_{k-i}\, \boldsymbol{Z}_i'\, \boldsymbol{M}_{k-i}^T$.

Then $f_{n_1(l-1)}^{(i+1)} + r \leftarrow \tilde{z}_{il}\, f_r^{(i)},\ r = 1, 2, \ldots, n_i$.

Step 6. $n_{i+1} \leftarrow n_i N_{k-i},\ i \leftarrow i+1$, then go to step 3.

Step 7. Print d_l^k, l=1, 2, ..., N.

19.7 SPEED OF THE ALGORITHMS

The straightforward method of computation of the diagonal elements of 2-D DLBT of a given matrix is performed through the repeated application of one-dimensional (1-D) DLBT and requires $2N^2 \sum_{i=1}^{k} N_i$ add and multiply operations for DLBT generated from the matrices of orders N_1, N_2, ..., N_k. A considerable reduction of computation is possible if one applies DCA1 or DCA2. In the DCA1, step 6 requires $\left(\frac{N}{N_1}\right)^2 \left(N_1^3 + N_1^2\right)$ add and multiply operations in the first iteration. In the 2nd iteration Step 6 is repeated N_1 times and in each time $\left(\frac{N}{N_1 N_2}\right)^2 \left(N_2^3 + N_2^2\right)$ add and multiply operations are needed leading to the total computation of $N_1\left(\frac{N}{N_1 N_2}\right)^2 \left(N_2^3 + N_2^2\right)$ operations. It is also observed that the algorithm will be completed after k iterations. Thus it requires $N^2\left(N_1 + 1 + \frac{N_2+1}{N_1} + \frac{N_3+1}{N_1 N_2} + \cdots + \frac{N_k+1}{N_1 N_2 \cdots N_{k-1}}\right)$ add and multiply operations to compute the diagonal elements of 2-D DLBT of A_k.

If A_k is a symmetric matrix then from case *2* of the last section we conclude that the first iteration of Step 6 in DCA 1 requires $\frac{1}{2}\left\{\left(\frac{N}{N_1}\right)^2 + \frac{N}{N_1}\right\}\left(N_1^3 + N_1^2\right)$ add and multiply operations and thus resulting in $\frac{1}{2}N^2\left(N_1 + 1 + \frac{N_2+1}{N_1} + \cdots + \frac{N_k+1}{N_1 N_2 \cdots N_{k-1}}\right) + \frac{1}{2}N\left(N_1^2 + N_1 + N_2^2 + N_2 + \cdots + N_k^2 + N_k\right)$ add and multiply operations needed for implementing the algorithm.

If A_k is Tbeplitz matrix of the form $[\rho^{|i-j|}]$ DCA2 shows that Step 3 is repeated k times and requires $\left(N_k^3 + N_k^2 + N_k\right) + \left(N_{k-1}^3 + N_{k-1}^2 +\right.$

$N_{k-1}\ N_k\big)+\ \cdots\ +N_1^3+N_1^2+N)$ operations whereas Step 5 iterated $k-1$ times and requires $\left(N_k^3+N_k^2+N_k\right)+\left(N_{k-1}^3+N_{k-1}^2+N_{k-1}\ N_k\right)+\ \cdots\ +(N_2^3+$ $N_2^2+N_2\ ....\ N_k)$ multiplications and $\left(N_k^3+N_k^2\right)+(N_{k-1}^3+N_{k-1}^2)+\cdots$ $+(N_2^3+N_2^2)$ additions. Thus the total number of operations required to execute the algorithm is $2(N_k^3+N_k^2+N_k)+2(N_{k-1}^3+N_{k-1}^2+N_{k-1}\ N_k)+$ $...+2(N_2^3+N_2^2+N_2\ ....\ N_k)+(N_1^3+N_1^2+N)$ multiplications and $2(N_k^3+N_k^2+N_{k-1}^3+N_{k-1}^2+...+N_2^3+N_2^2)+(N_k+N_{k-1}\ N_k+...+N)+N_1^3+N_1^2$ additions.

For example, we consider a particular case when $N_i = 4\ \forall\ i$. Then DCA1 requires $\frac{20}{3}N(N-1)$ add and multiply operations and for symmetric A_k, it requires $\frac{10}{3}N(N-1)+10Nk$ add and multiply operations. When A_k is a covariance matrix of first order stationary Markov process, the corresponding computation is only $\frac{1}{3}(5N-8)+80(2k-1)$ multiplications and $\frac{4}{3}(N-1)+80(2k-1)$ additions.

It should be noticed in the above computations that the redundancies of the even or odd basis vector elements of the generator matrices of the DLBT have not been used. Using these properties, the number of multiplications however, may be reduced to their respective halves at the places where multiplications of the generator matrices are involved in the algorithms, although the number of additions remains unchanged.

19.8 CONCLUDING REMARKS

A thorough in-depth study of a DLBT class has been carried out and compared with WHT and ST. The comparative study with WHT imposes a restriction on the DLBT class to obtain a superior performance and supports the experimentally demonstrated result shown in [7]. The lower bound of DLBT in (18) is useful and important and reveals that there are some members of the DLBT class whose performance may be superior to that of ST for small correlation coefficient. As the high correlation is the inherent property of image data, the comparison with ST seems to be very important and concludes that ST is more useful and efficient than DLBT for image data compression.

Furthermore, the fast algorithms developed in section VI is not restricted to applying in the diagonal filtering or variance calculation of a data set under 1-D DLBT. These may be used to study the same in the 2-D case of any unitary transform, because of the fact that the two-dimensional transform of a matrix is equivalent to the Kronecker product of two separate transforms operated on a vector whose elements are obtained by the concatenation of the rows of the matrix.

Acknowledgement

The authors wish to thank Dr B B Chaudhuri of ECSU, Indian Statistical Institute for his valuable help and inspiration to study this subject.

References

1. A K Jain (1979) A sinusoidal family of unitary transforms. *IEEE Trans Patt Anal Mach Intelligence* **PAMI-I** 356 – 365.
2. N Ahmed, T Natarajan and K R Rao (1974) Discrete cosine transform. *IEEE Trans Comp* **C-23** 90 – 93.
3. M Hamidi and J Pearl (1976) Comparison of the cosine and Fourier transforms of Markov-1 signals. *IEEE Trans Acoust Speech, Signal Process* **ASSP-24**, 428 – 429.
4. William K Pratt, Wen-Hsiung Chen and Lloyd R Welch (1974) Slant transform image coding. *IEEE Trans Commun* **COM-22**, 1075 – 1093.
5. P C Mali, B B Chaudhuri and D Dutta Majumder (1983) Performance bound of Walsh-Hadamard transform for feature selection and compression and some related algorithms. *Patt Recog Lett* **2**, 5 – 12.
6. P C Mali, B B Chaudhuri and D Dutta Majumder (1983) Some properties and fast algorithms of slant transform in image processing *Signal Processing* **9**, 233 – 244.
7. Robert M Haralick and K Shanmugham (1974) Comparative study of a discrete linear basis for image data compression. *IEEE Trans Sys Man Cybernet* **SMC-4**, 16 – 27.
8. N Ahmed and K R Rao (1975) *Orthogonal Transform for Digital Signal Processing.* Springer-Verlag, New York.
9. Zhong-De Wang (1982) New algorithm for the slant transform *IEEE Trans Patt Anal Mach Intelligence* **PAMI-4,** 551 – 555.

20

Local Contrast Enhancement of Color Images using Multi-scale Morphology

Susanta Mukhopadhyay and Bhabatosh Chanda[1]

Electronics and Communication Sciences Unit
Indian Statistical Institute
Calcutta, INDIA 700035
chanda@isical.ac.in

ABSTRACT

A multi-scale algorithm for contrast enhancement of color images using mathematical morphology is presented in this paper. Each pixel of a color image is a 3-tuple consisting of red, green and blue components which cannot be enhanced independently. The three color components are used to construct the magnitude image. The direction cosines of the color vectors at each pixel location are preserved. The magnitude image is subjected to multi-scale bright and dark top-hat transformation using flat-top circular SEs of increasing scales and the resulting filtered images are stacked in two morphological towers. The towers, so formed, keep the bright and dark features according to scale. The images in the tower are then combined with the input magnitude image in a suitable way so that the resulting image has improved contrast. The enhanced red, green and blue components are obtained by combining the enhanced magnitude image with the original direction cosines. The algorithm is tested on several color images and the results are compared with those of two other standard techniques. A performance measure based on the degree of contrast enhancement is also presented. The proposed method preserves shape of the color-features, and their color attributes like hue and saturation.

Keywords: Mathematical Morphology; Multi-Scale Morphology; Morphological Towers; Top-hat Transformation; Local Contrast Enhancement; Color Enhancement; Performance of Color Contrast Enhancement.

20.1 INTRODUCTION

Enhancement and restoration are very common operations in digital image processing. The formation of a digital image of an object or a scene involves several intermediate steps in each of which the visual quality and the information content of the image are prone toward degradation. Low contrast, noise contamination are examples of such degradations. Such a degraded image cannot render itself successfully for subsequent processing toward image understanding and interpretation. The technique usually adopted for improving the quality of the degraded image is broadly termed as *image enhancement* which is basically an

[1] corresponding author

ad-hoc technique [30, 10, 14] involving transformation of the image gray-levels based on some pre-defined criteria about them. An enhancement technique is developed on the basis of the purpose of the operation and often it is meant to be suitable for a restricted class of images. The contrast of the degraded image may be increased by *histogram stretching* [12, 30]. Another common image enhancement technique is *histogram equalization* [30, 10] in which the basic underlying concept is that the entropy of an image attains the maximum value when the gray-levels of the image are distributed uniformly. The histogram may be stretched using monotonic functions which may be linear, logarithmic, exponential [5]. The choice of the function depends on the purpose of the applications. There are few variations of histogram equalization technique e.g. histogram modification [8, 9].

The conventional histogram equalization technique treats the image globally and it employs the statistical knowledge about the entire image as a whole. In such enhancement techniques, there is hardly any scope of emphasizing on the local statistics of the image. Since the image characteristics may differ considerably from one region to another in the same image, it is reasonable to adopt a context-sensitive technique based on local contrast variation especially when the local histogram does not follow the global histogram. Dorst [6] adapted histogram stretching method over a neighborhood around the candidate pixel for local contrast stretching. While, various modifications [29, 28, 22] of histogram equalization (or modification) are suggested based on adapting the same over a sub-region of the image. Contrast stretching methods using local statistics are also reported [17, 18, 27]. Attas et. al [1] have devised a variational approach to local contrast enhancement through a suitable optimization of some desirable characteristics of gray-level histogram of output image. Similar approach for constrained local histogram equalization has been adopted by Zhu et, al [40].

With the rapid increase in the usage and applications of color video media, it has become a necessity to develop tools and algorithms for color image processing. Some concepts and tools used in gray-level image operations may be extended in case of color images. However, the treatments generally performed on gray-level images may not be readily extended to case of color images due to various practical issues. The visual appearance of a color image is controlled by various factors or attributes and uncontrolled modification of any of them may have undesired effect on the appearance and the purpose may be defeated. Unlike gray-scale images, color images keep the color information at each pixel location in the form of a triplet. The eye perceives an overall effect of these triplets. There is no definite guideline as such to alter the values in the 3-tuple at each pixel location so that the color in the resulting image may be viewed with high contrast. Different color models are used in representing and dealing with color information. The commonly used hardware-oriented color models are *(i) RGB (ii) CMY* and *(iii) YIQ*. These models, though are widely used in image processing algorithms, do not reflect intuitive color notions or perception of human vision. For such reasons other models namely *HLS, HSV* or *HVC,* for representing color are proposed. For a better description about the widely used color models [Foley et. al. [7]] may be consulted.

Several multi-scale or multi-resolution signal decomposition schemes where objects or features are treated according to their scale or size, provide effective ways to process information. The concepts of multi-scale processing were realized by researchers like Rosenfeld [31], Marr [20], Witkin [39], Koenderink [15]. The concepts and operations of mathematical morphology are also extended with the objective of multi-scale processing [37]. The advantages of morphological operations of being sensitive to the shape of the feature under study are combined with the concepts of multi-scale processing to realize a very powerful class of filters. Multi-scale morphological filters are used to solve a number of standard image processing problems. In multi-scale techniques information of scale-specific features are extracted from the image and are embedded as a stack of description in a space termed as *scale-space.* The *scale-space* used by the authors in this work is represented as *morphological towers* [25, 23, 24]. There exist various multi-scale and multi-resolution techniques for contrast enhancement. Boccignone and Picariello [3] have suggested a multi-scale approach to contrast enhancement using a non-linear scale-space representation of image generated by anisotropic diffusion. Another multi-scale contrast enhancement technique is developed by Toet [37] through non-linear pyramid recombination. A scheme for local contrast enhancement of gray-scale images using multi-scale morphology is also proposed by [23]. A scheme for color image enhancement employing genetic algorithm is proposed by Shyu et.al. [34]. Tang et. al. [36] have proposed a method of enhancing color images via Chromaticity diffusion. A hue preserving enhancement scheme for a class of color images is proposed by Gupta et.al. [11]. A multi-scale approach for color image enhance-ment has been proposed by Toet [38]. Strickland et. al. [35] have proposed a scheme for color enhancement based on saturation. A description of color equalization methods and its application to color images is given in [4].

In this paper we present a local contrast enhancement technique for color images using multi-scale morphology. We use usual notations of digital image processing and mathematical morphology [13] in the following description. Section 20.2 presents a brief description about mathematical morphology along-with multi-scale morphology and top-hat transformation. The proposed method is presented in section 20.3. The underlying theory of the proposed color image enhancement is discussed in section 20.3.1. Section 20.3.2 presents the theoretical formulation of the proposed enhancement using multi-scale morphology. The effect of the proposed enhancement scheme on the color properties like hue, saturation and lightness is also presented here. Section 20.3.3 presents elaborately various steps of the implementational aspects of the proposed algorithm. Section 20.4 presents the experimental results of the proposed scheme. The experimental results also include the outputs of other standard color enhancement schemes. A quantitative performance analysis is also provided to rate the efficacy of the proposed method. Finally, concluding remarks are cited in section 20.5.

20.2 MULTI-SCALE MATHEMATICAL MORPHOLOGY

In morphology, the objects in an image are considered as set of points and operations are defined between two sets: the object and the structuring element (SE) [33, 13]. The shape and the size of SE is defined according to the purpose of the associated application. Basic morphological operations are erosion and dilation and the operation like opening (closing) is sequential combination of erosion (dilation) and dilation (erosion). We adopt, here, *function and set-processing* (FSP) system [19]. FSP dilation and erosion of a gray-level image $g(r, c)$ by a two dimensional point set B is defined respectively, as

$$(g \oplus B)(r,c) = max\{g(r-k,c-l) \mid (k,l) \in B\} \tag{1}$$

$$(g \ominus B)(r,c) = min\{g(r+k,c+l) \mid (k,l) \in B\} \tag{2}$$

The shape of the structuring element B plays a crucial role in extracting features or objects of given shape from the image. However, for a categorical extraction of features or objects from the image based on shape and size we must incorporate an additional attribute to the structuring element which is its *scale.* A morphological operation with a scalable structuring element can extract features based on both shape and size. Also features of identical shape but of different size are now treated separately. Such a scheme of morphological operations where a structuring element of varying scale is utilized is termed as *multi-scale morphology* [33, 19]. Multi-scale opening and closing [37] are defined, respectively, as

$$(g \circ nB)(r, c) = ((g \oplus nB) \oplus nB)(r, c) \tag{3}$$

$$(g \bullet nB)(r, c) = ((g \oplus nB) \oplus nB)(r, c) \tag{4}$$

where n *is* an integer representing the scale factor of the structuring element. If B is convex nB is obtained by dilating B recursively $n-1$ times with B itself as [19]

$$nB = \underbrace{B \oplus B \oplus B \oplus \cdots \oplus B}_{n-1 \text{ times}} \tag{5}$$

By convention $nB = \{(0, 0)\}$ when $n = 0$.

The *top-hat transformation* originally proposed in [21] provides an excellent tool for extracting bright (respectively, dark) features smaller than a given size from an uneven background. Using gray-scale opening, one can remove from an image the brighter areas, i.e. features, that cannot hold the structuring element. Subtracting the opened image from the original one yields an image where the features that have been removed by opening clearly stand out. This holds good for closing operation also. Thus, dark features from a brighter background may be extracted by subtracting the original image from the closed one. Let us call it a *dark top-hat* transformation as opposed to *bright top-hat* transformation in case of opening. Therefore, the bright top-hat transformation decomposes an image into two parts as given by

$$g(r, c) = \underbrace{(g \circ B)(r, c)}_{\text{part 1}} + \underbrace{[g(r, c) - (g \circ B)(r, c)]}_{\text{part 2}} \tag{6}$$

where B is a disk in discrete domain. Fig. 20.1 shows an example of bright top-hat transformation for an one-dimensional signal. Let us call part 1 of equation (6) the *base image* with respect to $B(r, c)$ and part 2 of equation (6) the *feature image* at size of B as it contains all the bright features of $g(r, c)$ that are smaller than the size of B.

The multi-scale bright and dark top-hat transformation on being applied on an image, thus, extract scale-specific bright and dark features respectively from the image. In multi-scale techniques, the first and foremost objective is to collect or extract features at different scale. In the final stage of multi-scale techniques the scale-specific features need to satisfy the following criteria namely *(i)* causality *(ii)* edge localization and *(iii)* invariance under rotation. By the term *causality* it is meant that no new edge should be generated at higher scale. 'Edge localization' demands that no edge should drift from its original position. The system is also expected to be *scale-calibrated,* i.e. at a particular scale, all features of only that scale are present in the output image. The conventional opening and closing and hence the top-hat transformation do not satisfy the properties like causality and edge localization. The use of isotropic SE (circular disk for example) keeps the system rotation–invariant. A number of variants of rank order filters, morphological filters are proposed by different researchers to cope up with the problem of causality and edge localization [2, 16, 32]. Morphological filters by reconstruction employing geodesic dilation and erosion satisfy causality and edge localization criteria. The greater details are available in [24].

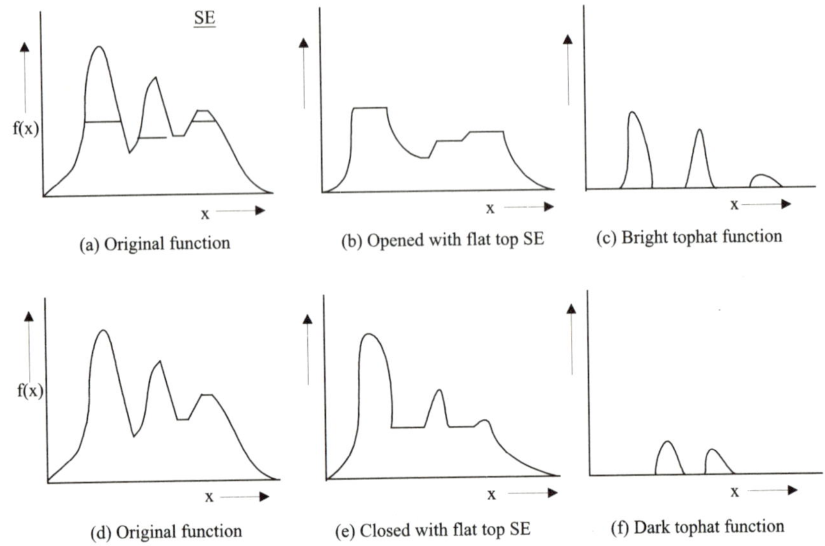

Fig. 20.1 Illustrating bright and dark top-hat transformation through gray-level opening and closing with flat–top SE.

However, morphological multi-scale filtering by reconstruction incurs large computational cost. Second, the issues like causality, edge localization are important when filtering takes place for large number of scales factors, e.g. multi-scale segmentation of gray-scale images [26]. However, in case of local contrast enhancement, the image is made to undergo filtering for small number of low-valued scale factors. Hence, the issues above are not so stringent and hence the conventional opening and closing may be used instead of opening and closing by reconstruction respectively.

An ordered sequence of morphological top-hat filtering through opening (closing) of the image with a disk structuring element at different scales extracts scale-specific bright (dark) features from the image. These scale-specific features can be amplified selectively to achieve local contrast stretching. Based on this notion we propose a local contrast enhancement method as described elaborately in the following section.

20.3 PROPOSED METHOD

The structure of a color image is first analysed from the point of view of optics. In the next subsection the authors have tried to model a transformation which serves the purpose of color enhancement preserving the hue.

20.3.1 The Color Model

The intensity of reflected light following Phong's model [7] is given by

$$C^x(\lambda_n)=\{E_a(\lambda_n)T_a S_x(\lambda_n)+f_{attn} E_p(\lambda_n)[T_d S^x(\lambda_n)\cos(\theta)+T_s \cos^m(\alpha)]\} \tag{7}$$

where

λ_n	n-th sample of wavelength range
x	a location on the surface
$C^x(\lambda_n)$	intensity of emitting light in the direction of the viewer
$S^x(\lambda_n)$	surface reflectance at location x
$E_a(\lambda_n)$	intensity of ambient light
$E_p(\lambda_n)$	intensity of a point light source
T_p	ambient reflection coefficient
T_d	diffuse reflection coefficient
T_s	specular reflection coefficient
θ	angle of incidence. Assumed to be constant for all x as the point is practically at infinity
α	angle of viewer with respect to angle of specular reflection
m	constant ≥ 1

In case of multi-sensor or multi-channel image acquisition system, if $R_k(\lambda_n)$ be the spectral sensitivity of the k-th receptor and ρ_k^x be the intensity recorded by the k-th receptor from the location x then

$$\begin{aligned}\rho_k^x &= \sum_{n=1}^{N} \{E_a(\lambda_n)T_a S_x(\lambda_n)R_k(\lambda_n)+f_{attn}E_p(\lambda_n) \\ &\qquad \left[T_d S^x(\lambda_n)\cos(\theta)+T_s\cos^m(\alpha)\right]R_k(\lambda_n)\} \\ &= \sum_{n=1}^{N}\{E_a(\lambda_n)T_a S_x(\lambda_n)R_k(\lambda_n)+\sum_{n=1}^{N} f_{attn}E_p(\lambda_n)\left[T_d S^x(\lambda_n)\cos(\theta)\right. \\ &\qquad R_k(\lambda_n) + \sum_{n=1}^{N} f_{attn}\, T_s \cos^m(\alpha)\left.\right]R_k(\lambda_n)\} \\ &= \rho_{a_k}^x+\rho_{d_k}^x+\rho_{s_k}^x \end{aligned} \tag{8}$$

The terms involving the wavelength λ_n may be expressed as combinations of orthogonal basis functions like *Fourier* or *Lagrange* basis of suitable dimensionality so that we may write

$$E_a(\lambda_n)=\sum_{i=1}^{D(E_a)} \varepsilon_{a_i}\xi_i(\lambda_n) \tag{9}$$

$$E_p(\lambda_n)=\sum_{i=1}^{D(E_p)} \varepsilon_{p_i}\xi_i(\lambda_n) \tag{10}$$

$$S^x(\lambda_n)=\sum_{i=1}^{D(S)} \sigma_i^x S_i(\lambda_n) \tag{11}$$

For notational simplicity we may assume $D(E_a) = D(E_p) = D(S) = N$ where N is also equal to the number of wavelength sample points. The equations given above may be written in terms of product of matrices corresponding to N sample points of λ as follows

$$\hat{E}_a = \begin{pmatrix} E_a(\lambda_1) \\ E_a(\lambda_2) \\ E_a(\lambda_3) \\ \cdots \\ E_a(\lambda_i) \\ \cdots \\ E_a(\lambda_N) \end{pmatrix} = \begin{pmatrix} \xi_1(\lambda_1) & \xi_2(\lambda_1) & \cdots & \xi_N(\lambda_1) \\ \xi_1(\lambda_2) & \xi_2(\lambda_2) & \cdots & \xi_N(\lambda_2) \\ \xi_1(\lambda_3) & \xi_2(\lambda_3) & \cdots & \xi_N(\lambda_3) \\ \cdots & \cdots & \cdots & \\ \xi_1(\lambda_i) & \xi_2(\lambda_i) & \cdots & \xi_N(\lambda_i) \\ \cdots & \cdots & \cdots & \\ \xi_1(\lambda_N) & \xi_2(\lambda_N) & \cdots & \xi_N(\lambda_N) \end{pmatrix} \begin{pmatrix} \varepsilon_{a1} \\ \varepsilon_{a2} \\ \varepsilon_{a3} \\ \cdots \\ \varepsilon_{ai} \\ \cdots \\ \varepsilon_{aN} \end{pmatrix} \quad (12)$$

$$\hat{E}_p = \begin{pmatrix} E_p(\lambda_1) \\ E_p(\lambda_2) \\ E_p(\lambda_3) \\ \cdots \\ E_p(\lambda_i) \\ \cdots \\ E_p(\lambda_N) \end{pmatrix} = \begin{pmatrix} \xi_1(\lambda_1) & \xi_2(\lambda_1) & \cdots & \xi_N(\lambda_1) \\ \xi_1(\lambda_2) & \xi_2(\lambda_2) & \cdots & \xi_N(\lambda_2) \\ \xi_1(\lambda_3) & \xi_2(\lambda_3) & \cdots & \xi_N(\lambda_3) \\ \cdots & \cdots & \cdots & \\ \xi_1(\lambda_i) & \xi_2(\lambda_i) & \cdots & \xi_N(\lambda_i) \\ \cdots & \cdots & \cdots & \\ \xi_1(\lambda_N) & \xi_2(\lambda_N) & \cdots & \xi_N(\lambda_N) \end{pmatrix} \begin{pmatrix} \varepsilon_{p1} \\ \varepsilon_{p2} \\ \varepsilon_{p3} \\ \cdots \\ \varepsilon_{pi} \\ \cdots \\ \varepsilon_{pN} \end{pmatrix} \quad (13)$$

$$\hat{S}_x = \begin{pmatrix} S^x(\lambda_1) \\ S^x(\lambda_2) \\ S^x(\lambda_3) \\ \cdots \\ S^x(\lambda_i) \\ \cdots \\ S^x(\lambda_N) \end{pmatrix} = \begin{pmatrix} s_1(\lambda_1) & s_2(\lambda_1) & \cdots & s_N(\lambda_1) \\ s_1(\lambda_2) & s_2(\lambda_2) & \cdots & s_N(\lambda_2) \\ s_1(\lambda_3) & s_2(\lambda_3) & \cdots & s_N(\lambda_3) \\ \cdots & \cdots & \cdots & \\ s_1(\lambda_i) & s_2(\lambda_i) & \cdots & s_N(\lambda_i) \\ \cdots & \cdots & \cdots & \\ s_1(\lambda_N) & s_2(\lambda_N) & \cdots & s_N(\lambda_N) \end{pmatrix} \begin{pmatrix} \sigma_{a1} \\ \sigma_{a2} \\ \sigma_{a3} \\ \cdots \\ \sigma_{ai} \\ \cdots \\ \sigma_{aN} \end{pmatrix} \quad (14)$$

The spectral sensitivity of the k-th receptor at the point x is then given by

$$\begin{aligned} \rho^x_{a_k} &= \sum_{n=1}^{N} E_a(\lambda_n) T_a S^x(\lambda_n) R_k(\lambda_n) \\ &= T_a[E_a(\lambda_1) S^x(\lambda_1) R_k(\lambda_1) + E_a(\lambda_2) S^x(\lambda_2) R_k(\lambda_2) + \cdots + \\ &\qquad E_a(\lambda_n) S^x(\lambda_n) R_k(\lambda_n) \\ &= \hat{E}_a^T [R_k] \hat{S}^x \end{aligned} \quad (15)$$

where

$$[R_k] = \begin{pmatrix} R_k(\lambda_1) & 0 & \cdots & 0 & 0 \\ 0 & R_k(\lambda_2) & \cdots & 0 & 0 \\ 0 & 0 & R_k(\lambda_3) & \cdots & 0 \\ \cdots & \cdots & \cdots & \cdots & \cdots \\ 0 & 0 & \cdots & R_k(\lambda_i) & 0 \\ \cdots & \cdots & \cdots & \cdots & \cdots \\ 0 & 0 & \cdots & \cdots & R_k(\lambda_N) \end{pmatrix} \tag{16}$$

Thus, for a 3–receptor system the above equation may be written as

$$\begin{pmatrix} \rho_{a1}^x \\ \rho_{a2}^x \\ \rho_{a3}^x \end{pmatrix} = T_a \begin{pmatrix} E_{a1}(\lambda_1)R_1(\lambda_1) & E_{a1}(\lambda_2)R_1(\lambda_2) & \cdots & E_{a1}(\lambda_N)R_1(\lambda_N) \\ E_{a2}(\lambda_1)R_2(\lambda_1) & E_{a2}(\lambda_2)R_2(\lambda_2) & \cdots & E_{a2}(\lambda_N)R_2(\lambda_N) \\ E_{a3}(\lambda_1)R_3(\lambda_1) & E_{a3}(\lambda_2)R_3(\lambda_2) & \cdots & E_{a3}(\lambda_N)R_3(\lambda_N) \end{pmatrix} \begin{pmatrix} S^x(\lambda_1) \\ S^x(\lambda_2) \\ S^x(\lambda_3) \end{pmatrix} \tag{17}$$

Combining equations (14) and (17) we have,

$$\hat{\rho}_a^x = T_a \Lambda_{E_a} \hat{\sigma}^x \tag{18}$$

where Λ_{E_a} is matrix obtained by multiplying the $3 \times N$ matrix of eqn. (17) with the $N \times N$ matrix of eqn. (14). Likewise for other components we have

$$\hat{\rho}_d^x = T_d \Lambda_{E_p} \hat{\sigma}^x \tag{19}$$

$$\hat{\rho}_s^x = T_s \Lambda_{E_p} \hat{u} \tag{20}$$

where $\hat{u}$ is a vector whose all elements are 1.

Let us assume that ambient light is generated mainly by repeated reflection of electromagnetic energy from the point light source. Then $\Lambda_{E_a} = \delta \Lambda_{E_p}$, where δ is a constant. As a result the total response becomes

$$\begin{aligned} \hat{\rho}^x &= \hat{\rho}_a^x + \hat{\rho}_d^x + \hat{\rho}_s^x \\ &= T\delta\Lambda_{E_p}\hat{\sigma}^x + v_2\Lambda_{E_p}\hat{\sigma}^x + v_3\Lambda_{E_p}\hat{u} \\ &= v_1\Lambda_{E_p}\hat{\sigma}^x + v_2\Lambda_{E_p}\hat{\sigma}^x + v_3\Lambda_{E_p}\hat{u} \\ &= (v_1 + v_2)\Lambda_{E_p}\hat{\sigma}^x + v_3\Lambda_{E_p}\hat{u} \end{aligned} \tag{21}$$

Now, for a color image, we may look at the vector $\hat{\rho}$ as representing the intensity values corresponding to the *red, green* and *blue* colors at each pixel location as given below.

$$\hat{\rho}^x = \begin{pmatrix} R^x \\ G^x \\ B^x \end{pmatrix} \tag{22}$$

From the above equation one may write

$$\begin{pmatrix} R^x \\ G^x \\ B^x \end{pmatrix} = \Lambda_E \left(\underbrace{v \begin{pmatrix} \sigma_1^x \\ \sigma_2^x \\ \sigma_3^x \end{pmatrix}}_{part\ 1} + \underbrace{v_3 \begin{pmatrix} 1 \\ 1 \\ 1 \end{pmatrix}}_{part\ 2} \right) \tag{23}$$

Thus each response vector consists of two parts. First part depends on the property of object surface, hence is the main contributor to the hue information. Second part is a constant term and contributes to the saturation component of color. However, they together along-with the matrix multiplier determine the total intensity. The color image may be enhanced keeping its hue and saturation unaltered by multiplying the right hand side of eqn. (23) as shown below.

$$\begin{pmatrix} \tilde{R}^x \\ \tilde{G}^x \\ \tilde{B}^x \end{pmatrix} = K^x \Lambda_E \left(\underbrace{v \begin{pmatrix} \sigma_1^x \\ \sigma_2^x \\ \sigma_3^x \end{pmatrix}}_{\text{part 1}} + \underbrace{v_3 \begin{pmatrix} 1 \\ 1 \\ 1 \end{pmatrix}}_{\text{part 2}} \right) \tag{24}$$

where $\tilde{R}^x$, $\tilde{G}^x$ and $\tilde{B}^x$ are the enhanced red, green and blue color component at location x and K^x is an amplification factor.

If x represents the actual location and $N(x)$ represents a predefined neighborhood of the location then the aim of the local contrast enhancement is to stretch the difference in the intensity values corresponding to x and $N(x)$. Let $\hat{\rho}^x, \tilde{\hat{\rho}}^x$ and $\hat{\rho}^{N(x)}$ represent the intensity vector at location x before and after contrast stretching, and the intensity vector in the neighborhood of location x respectively. The contrast may be improved by multiplying a function of intensity at a location with itself, where the function depends on the intensity at the location and that of its immediate neighborhood. Hence, the modified intensity would be

$$\tilde{\hat{\rho}}^x = f(\hat{\rho}^x, \hat{\rho}^{N(x)})\hat{\rho}^x \tag{25}$$

where $f(.)$ is a monotonic function such that

- $\| \hat{\rho}^x \| < \| \hat{\rho}^{N(x)} \|$ implies $\| \tilde{\hat{\rho}}^x \| \leq \| \hat{\rho}^{\tilde{N}(x)} \|$
- $\| \hat{\rho}^x \| > \| \hat{\rho}^{N(x)} \|$ implies $\| \tilde{\hat{\rho}}^x \| \geq \| \hat{\rho}^{\tilde{N}(x)} \|$
- $\| \tilde{\hat{\rho}}^x - \hat{\rho}^{\tilde{N}(x)} \| \geq \| \hat{\rho}^x - \hat{\rho}^{N(x)} \|$

In the next section we have developed a multi-scale morphological scheme for selecting a suitable function $f(.)$.

The red, green and the blue components at a pixel location x combine to yield the overall color sensation. In the *rgb* space this color is represented by a vector. The magnitude of this vector is given by

$$g^x = \| \rho^x \| = \sqrt{(R^x)^2 + (G^x)^2 + (B^x)^2} \tag{26}$$

The gray-level image constructed from its components is termed as *magnitude* or *intensity* image. In the next section the theory of the morphological multi-scale enhancement is developed starting with this magnitude image.

20.3.2 Multi-scale Contrast Enhancement

In case of a gray-scale image a contrast stretching method using local statistics [17, 18] amplifies the difference between gray-level $g(r, c)$ and mean gray-level $\bar{g}(r, c)$ over a predefined neighborhood surrounding the pixel at location (r, c) (same as location x) as given by

$$\tilde{g}(r, c) = \bar{g}(r, c) + k[g(r, c) - \bar{g}(r, c)] \tag{27}$$

where k is a global amplification factor and is greater than one. The amplification factor may be a function of local statistical parameters [27].

However, this kind of transformation using only local gray-level statistics cannot distinguish between consistent variation in intensity over a region and the variation in intensity due to presence of a feature (bright or dark) within a region. So it may stretch contrast evenly in both the cases. As a result, undesired contrast intensification (in supposedly smooth region) takes place at some regions of the image, which may require further processing such as *de-enhancement* [22]. On the other hand, if local contrast is stretched based on the presence of spatial features, then this problem can be avoided completely. As mathematical morphology is an appropriate tool for dealing with spatial features or shapes, we intend to modify equation (27) in terms of mathematical morphological operators.

The feature image [i.e., part 2 of equation (6)] gives a measure of local contrast in the original image due to presence of bright features. Hence, combining equations (27) and (6) we suggest the following transformation for local contrast stretching

$$\tilde{g}(r, c) = (g \circ B)(r, c) + k[g(r, c) - (g \circ B)(r, c)] \tag{28}$$

where k is again a global amplification factor and is greater than one. So this transformation makes bright features brighter and, thus, improves the local contrast. Now suppose $k = 2$. The equation (28) becomes

$$\tilde{g}(r, c) = g(r, c) + [g(r, c) - (g \circ B)(r, c)] \tag{29}$$

Let us denote $[g(r, c) - (g \circ B)(r, c)]$ by $F_B^o(r, c)$ i.e.; features of size less than that of B obtained by opening (more specifically, by bright top-hat transformation). Accordingly, we can rewrite equation (29) as

$$\tilde{g}(r, c) = g(r, c) + F_B^o(r, c) \tag{30}$$

Similarly we denote the bright-feature image at scale n by $F_{nB}^o(r, c)$ as it contains all the features of $g(r, c)$ that are smaller than nB. Hence, the value $F_{nB}^o(r, c)$ of bright-feature image at (r, c) gives a measure of local contrast in the original image due to presence of bright features at scale n. Note that $F_{0B}^o(r, c)$ is an all-zero image. Now, let us define

$$\delta_n^o(r, c) = F_{nB}^o(r, c) - F_{(n-1)B}^o(r, c) \tag{31}$$

It is evident that $\delta_n^o(r, c)$ contains bright features of $g(r, c)$ that are larger than scale $(n - 1)$, but smaller than scale n. Therefore, we obtain, using multi-scale approach, local contrast stretching of bright features as

$$\tilde{g}(r, c) = g(r, c) + k_1\, \delta_1^o(r, c) + k_2\, \delta_2^o(r, c) + k_3\, \delta_3^o(r, c) + \cdots \tag{32}$$

where $k_1 > k_2 > k_3 > \ldots$, since we know that smaller the size of a bright feature, more should be its intensity for detectibilty. Suppose the features up to the scale m are needed to be enhanced then

$$\tilde{g}(r, c) = g(r, c) + \sum_{i=1}^{m} k_i\, \delta_i^o(r, c) \tag{33}$$

Theoretically, m may correspond to SE as large as the entire image; however, for all practical purpose m is small. This is because large features, in general, contribute heavily to global histogram and thus can influence global contrast stretching in their favour. Secondly, the probability that $\delta_i^o(r, c)$ being all-zero image is more as i increases. So we ignore $\delta_i^o(r, c)$ for $i > m$. Now taking $k_{i-1} = k_i + 1$ for all i and choosing $k_m = 1$ we finally have local contrast stretching of bright feature as

$$\tilde{g}(r, c) = g(r, c) + \sum_{i=1}^{m} F_{iB}^o(r, c) \tag{34}$$

Selecting $k_m = 1$ we can avoid multiplication operation to compute enhanced image and, thus, the computational cost is reduced to some extent.

Proceeding in a similar way based on multi-scale dark top-hat transformations we achieve local contrast stretching of dark features as

$$\tilde{g}(r, c) = g(r, c) - \sum_{i=1}^{m} F_{iB}^{c}(r, c) \tag{35}$$

Hence, to obtain the modified image, in which contrast of both (bright and dark) types of features are stretched locally, we add equations (34) and (35) and divide the result by 2 to get

$$\tilde{g}(r, c) = g(r, c) + 0.5\sum_{i=1}^{m} F_{iB}^{o}(r, c) - 0.5\sum_{i=1}^{m} F_{iB}^{c}(r, c) \tag{36}$$

The constant multiplier 0.5 is used for assigning equal or impartial weightages to both dark and bright features. For the sake of generalization, we slightly modify equation (36) as

$$\tilde{g}(r, c) = \underbrace{g(r, c)}_{part1} + \underbrace{0.5\sum_{i=n}^{m} F_{iB}^{o}(r, c) - 0.5\sum_{i=n}^{m} F_{iB}^{c}(r, c)}_{part2} \tag{37}$$

where all the features, either dark of bright, smaller than scale n are assumed to be noise in the image.

Let us compare the equations (37) and (25). The part 1 of eqn. (37) corresponds to the magnitude of the original color image at the location (r, c) (*i.e.* x) and is analogous to $\|\hat{\rho}^x\|$ of eqn. (25). The second part corresponds to the component $\|\hat{\rho}^{N(x)}\|$ of eqn. (25), where the neighborhood $N(x)$ is chosen in a multi–scale sense. Therefore, the contrast stretching function $f(.)$ of eqn. (25) may be expressed as

$$f(\hat{\rho}^x, \hat{\rho}^{N(x)}) = \frac{\|\hat{\rho}^x + \hat{\rho}^{N(x)}\|}{\|\hat{\rho}^x\|} \tag{38}$$

The numerator $\|\hat{\rho}^x + \hat{\rho}^{N(x)}\|$ is now identical with $\tilde{g}(r, c)$ of eqn. (37). Therefore, the final stretched color image is given by

$$\begin{pmatrix} \tilde{R}^x \\ \tilde{G}^x \\ \tilde{B}^x \end{pmatrix} = \frac{\tilde{g}^x}{g^x} \begin{pmatrix} R^x \\ G^x \\ B^x \end{pmatrix} \tag{39}$$

It can be shown that the proposed multi–scale enhancement scheme, presented above preserves the color properties like hue and saturation of the image. The color parameters hue, saturation and the lightness are defined as follows.

The hue H is defined as

$$H^x = \begin{cases} h^x & \text{if } h^x \geq 0 \\ h^x + 360 & \text{if } h^x < 0 \end{cases}$$

where

$$h^x = \begin{cases} 60 * \left\{ \dfrac{G^x - B^x}{R^x - Min^x} \right\} & \text{if } R^x = Max^x \\ 60 * \left\{ 2 + \dfrac{B^x - R^x}{G^x - Min^x} \right\} & \text{if } G^x = Max^x \\ 60 * \left\{ 4 + \dfrac{R^x - G^x}{B^x - Min^x} \right\} & \text{if } B^x = Max^x \end{cases}$$

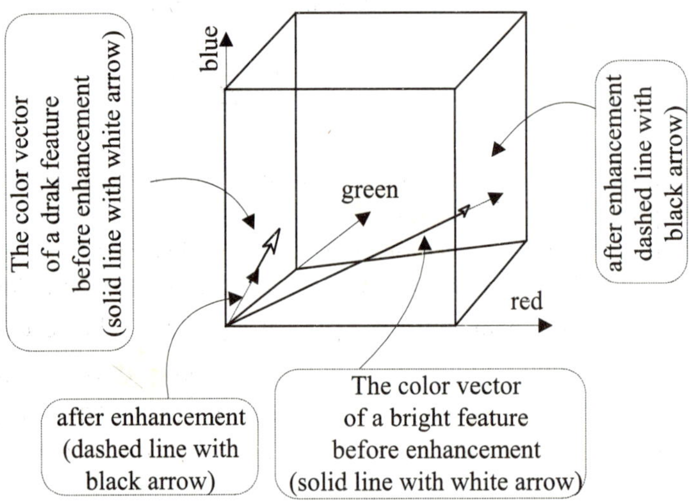

Fig. 20.2 Color contrast enhancement in rgb space

where

$$Min^x = minimum(R^x, G^x, B^x) \text{ and} \tag{40}$$

$$Max^x = maximum(R^x, G^x, B^x) \tag{41}$$

The saturation and lightness are defined (respectively) as

$$Sat^x = \frac{Max^x - Min^x}{Max^x + Min^x} \tag{42}$$

$$Lit^x = Max^x \tag{43}$$

If $\widetilde{R}^x$, $\widetilde{G}^x$ and $\widetilde{B}^x$ be the enhanced red, green and blue components at pixel location x as given by eqn. (39), the hue, saturation and the lightness of the enhanced image are given by

$$\widetilde{h}^x = h^x$$

$$\widetilde{S}at^x = Sat^x \quad \text{and}$$

$$\widetilde{L}it^x = \alpha Lit^x$$

where $\alpha = \dfrac{\widetilde{g}^x}{g^x}$.

20.3.3 Implementation

The implementation of equation (37) describing feature based local contrast enhancement involves construction of a number of morphological towers as elaborated below.

20.3.3.1 Construction of the magnitude image

The color image to be enhanced is used to construct the magnitude image for use in the subsequent steps. The magnitude image is constructed by taking the square root of the sum of the squares of the red, green and blue intensity values at each pixel location. The angles or the direction cosines of the three color components at each pixel location are saved for future use.

20.3.3.2 Construction of morphological towers

The image to be enhanced is subjected to a sequence of gray–scale morphological opening operations with a disk structuring element and its higher order homothetics. The resulting sequence of images are kept in a stack called the *opening tower* as shown in the Fig. 20.3. An identical tower, called closing tower, is constructed with the sequence of the images resulting from multi-scale closing of the input image. Thus the *i*–th entry in the opening (closing) tower contains the image opened (closed) with the structuring element *iB*.

20.3.3.3 Construction of difference towers

The gray-level at each pixel location of the opened image is less than or equal to that of the original image. Subtracting the opened image from the original one produces the feature image made up of bright features specific to the scale of the SE. Each entry of the opening tower is

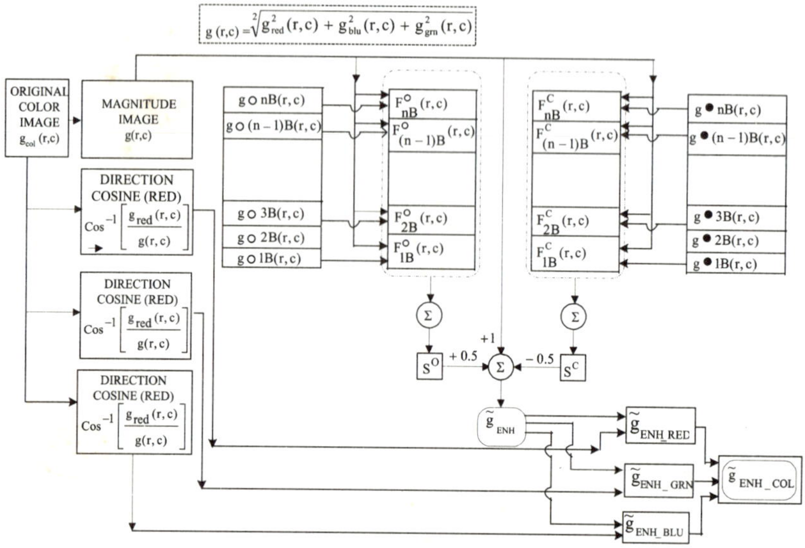

Fig. 20.3 Multi-scale color enhancement using morphological towers

subtracted individually from the original image and the resulting bright feature images are then kept in corresponding entries in another tower called the *difference tower.* An identical difference tower is constructed for the dark feature images obtained by subtracting the original image from each entry of the closing tower. Therefore the *i*-th entry in the difference tower for opening (closing) contains an image consisting of bright (dark) features which are smaller than or equal to *iB*.

20.3.3.4 Construction of the enhanced magnitude image

For reconstructing the final image we do the following:

- We sum up all the entries in the difference tower corresponding to the opening operation. This results in an image consisting of bright features of all possible scales of interest that are present in the original image.

$$S^{o}(r, c) = \sum_{i=1}^{n} F_{iB}^{o}(r, c) \tag{44}$$

  The summation, here, denotes pixel-wise sum of n images.

- We perform the same operation on the difference tower corresponding to the closing operation. This results in an image consisting of dark features of all scales of interest that are present in the original image.

$$S^{c}(r, c) = \sum_{i=1}^{n} F_{iB}^{c}(r, c) \tag{45}$$

Finally, the locally enhanced magnitude image is obtained by combining three images as given by

$$\tilde{g}(r, c) = g(r, c) + 0.5S^{op}(r, c) - 0.5S^{cl}(r, c) \tag{46}$$

The '+' and '–' operations are applied between corresponding pixels of three different images. However, it should be noted that at some pixels the value of $\tilde{g}(r, c)$ computed using equation (46) may exceed the allowed gray-level range. In that case the weights 0.5 may be replaced by α such that not more than 1% of total pixels are clipped. The value of α can be selected between 0 and 0.5 using binary search technique.

20.3.3.5 Construction of the enhanced color image

The enhanced magnitude image obtained in the previous step and the direction cosine information about the red, green and blue preserved in the first step are used to construct the enhanced red, green and blue components by taking the projections on respective axes. The final enhanced color image is obtained by combining these enhanced red, green and blue components. This follows from eqn. (39) as given below.

$$\begin{pmatrix} \tilde{R}^x \\ \tilde{G}^x \\ \tilde{B}^x \end{pmatrix} = \tilde{g}^x \begin{pmatrix} \dfrac{R^x}{g^x} \\ \dfrac{G^x}{g^x} \\ \dfrac{B^x}{g^x} \end{pmatrix} \tag{47}$$

Now the ratio $\dfrac{R^x}{g^x}$ is basically the *direction cosine* of the color vector at location x with respect to the *red* axis and may be written as $\cos(\theta_r^x)$. Thus eqn. (47) may be written as

$$\begin{pmatrix} \tilde{R}^x \\ \tilde{G}^x \\ \tilde{B}^x \end{pmatrix} = \tilde{g}^x \begin{pmatrix} \cos(\theta_r^x) \\ \cos(\theta_g^x) \\ \cos(\theta_b^x) \end{pmatrix} \tag{48}$$

The schematic diagram for multi-scale color image enhancement is shown in Fig. 20.4.

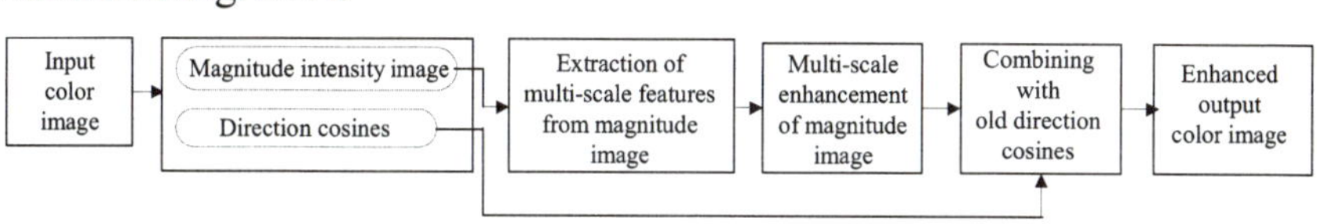

Fig. 20.4 Passes of the local contrast enhancement algorithm

20.4 EXPERIMENTAL RESULTS AND DISCUSSION

The proposed algorithm has been tested on a set of color images and the results have been compared with that of other methods [See Fig. 20.6]. Here we present the results with four real images shown in Figs. [20.6 (*a–d*)](*i*). Fig 20.5*(a)* shows a color image which is enhanced using conventional histogram equalization. The result [See Fig. 20.5*(b)*] reflects the in-applicability of the enhancement technique due to distortion of color components. Results of the proposed algorithm are shown in Figs. [20.6(*a–d*)](*iv*). In the experiment we have used $n = 1$ (as the images are assumed to be noise-free), $m = 5$ and B is a circular disk of radius 1 so as to get visually optimum results. That means largest SE used is disk of radius 5. The value of m can be made larger depending on demand or precision. However, it should be noted that very large value of m will not give noticeable improvement in the output since the feature images of progressively larger scales have gradually smaller weightages in enhancing the image. Moreover, very large value of m, in spite of incorporating generality in the scheme, increases the computational time unnecessarily.

(a) (b)

Fig. 20.5 *(a)* Original color image *(b)* histogram stretching of the original color image

The resulting images are seen to have more contrast than the respective original versions without any effect on the color content. The results of the proposed scheme are compared with those of two other methods namely *(i)* the multi–scale pyramidal approach of Toet [See Figs. (20.6(*a–d*)*(ii)*] and *(ii)* the method employing genetic algorithm [See Figs. (20.6(*a–d*)*(iii)*] due to [34]. Brief descriptions of these two methods are given below.

Multi-scale color image enhancement due to Toet [38]

In this work, the color image is first converted to its *hls* representation. The luminance and the saturation images are employed for the contrast

(a)(i)
(a)(ii)
(a)(iii)
(a)(iv)
(b)(i)
(b)(ii)

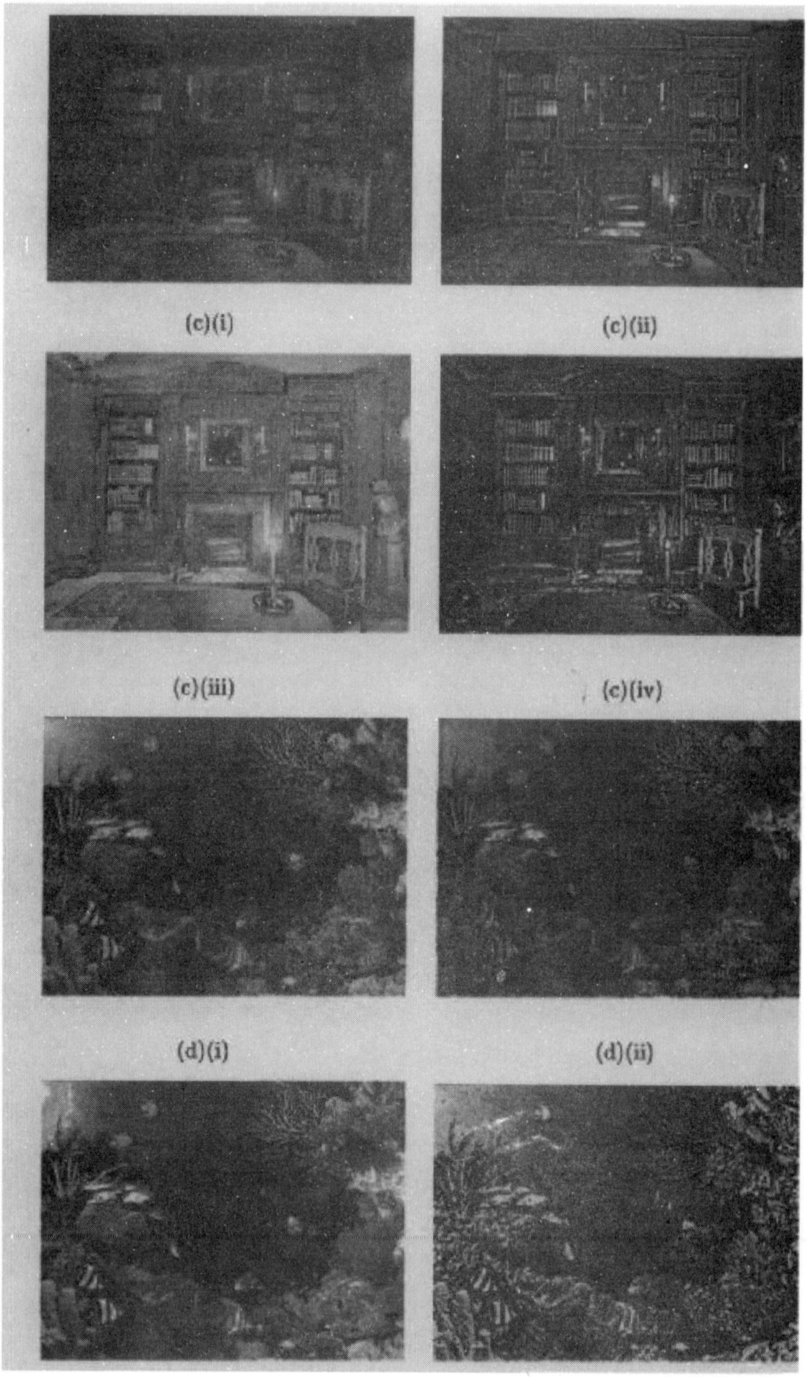

Fig. 20.6 Results: *(i)* Original image, *(ii)* Local contrast stretching using multi-scale pyramid (Toet), *(iii)* Local contrast stretching based on genetic algorithm due to Shyu et. al. and *(iv)* Local contrast stretching using multi-scale morphology.

enhancement of the color image. The luminance and saturation contrast primitives at each scale are examined by constructing pyramids at each scale. A new set of multi-scale luminance contrast primitives is constructed by modulating the original luminance contrast primitives at each scale using the saturation contrast primitives at that scale. The method involves construction of pyramids of luminance and saturation images for both down and up-sampling, and, for the implementation, the rectangular input *rgb* images were padded by "0" pixel values to make the image height and width same and equal to the nearest integral power of 2. The parameter used in the experiment are chosen according to the specifications given in the paper. For a greater detail [38] may be referred. Finally enhanced version of the luminance component along-with its original version are used to construct the enhanced *rgb* version of the image.

Color image enhancement employing genetic algorithm due to Shyu et. al. [34]

In this work too, the color image is first converted to *hls* representation. The luminance component is intended to undergo four types of contrast enhancement and the contribution of each component is realized in terms of normalized multiplier constants ω_1, ω_2, ω_3 and ω_4. The four types of contrast stretching methods for the luminance image are also characterized by five parameters p_1, p_2, ... p_5 as expressed by the following equations. The saturation component is made to undergo a transformation involving incomplete beta-gamma function characterized by two more parameters α and β.

$$T_1(l_{x,y}) = \frac{1}{p_1} ln[1+\exp^{(p_1-1)} l_{xy}] \tag{49}$$

$$T_2(l_{x,y}) = \frac{1}{p_2}[1+p_2)^{l_{xy}} - 1] \tag{50}$$

$$T_3(l_{x,y}) = \frac{1}{1+\left[\dfrac{(l_{max}-l_{xy})}{p_3}\right]p_4} \tag{51}$$

$$T_4(l_{x,y}) = \frac{p_3}{l_{max}} \frac{1}{\left(\dfrac{l_{max}}{l_{xy}} + p_5 - 1\right)p_4} \tag{52}$$

The luminance and the saturation images are modified using the following equations

$$l'_{x,y} = \omega_1 T_1(l_{x,y}) + \omega_2 T_2(l_{x,y}) + \omega_3 T_3(l_{x,y}) + \omega_4 T_4(l_{x,y}) \tag{53}$$

$$s'_{x,y} = \int_0^{s_{xy}} \frac{t^{\alpha-1}(1-t)^{\beta-1}}{B(\alpha,\beta)} dt \tag{54}$$

The eleven parameters are estimated using genetic algorithms. In this experiment, the total length of each chromosome has been taken as 88 while the number of iterations are limited to 50. The details of the original work is available in [34]. Finally the luminance and the saturation component corresponding to the best-fit parameters are used to construct the *rgb* version of the enhanced image. The standard algorithms for inter-conversion of *rgb* and *hls* formats are available in [7]

20.4.1 Comparative Performance

For a quantitative assessment of the degree of enhancement performed by the methods we have defined the *overall contrast* as follows. First, we compute the average value of the difference of the maximum and minimum pixel value (i.e. local contrast over a 3 × 3 mask) for the individual color components.

$$d\_red(i,j) = \sum_{p=i-1}^{i+1} \sum_{q=j-1}^{j+1} [max\_red - min\_red]$$

$$avg\_red = \frac{1}{MN} \sum_{i=0}^{M-1} \sum_{q=j-1}^{j+1} d\_red(i,j)$$

$$d\_grn(i,j) = \sum_{p=i-1}^{i+1} \sum_{q=j-1}^{j+1} [max\_grn - min\_grn]$$

$$avg\_grn = \frac{1}{MN} \sum_{i=0}^{M-1} \sum_{q=j-1}^{j+1} d\_grn(i,j)$$

$$d\_blu(i,j) = \sum_{p=i-1}^{i+1} \sum_{q=j-1}^{j+1} [max\_blu - min\_blu]$$

$$avg\_blu = \frac{1}{MN} \sum_{i=0}^{M-1} \sum_{q=j-1}^{j+1} d\_blu(i,j)$$

Table 20.1 *Relative performance of the contrast enhancement schemes for color images*

Image	Enhancement Scheme			
	Original image	*Toet's pyramidal scheme [38]*	*Shyu's Genetic algorithm [34]*	*MMS (Proposed)*
Garden	17.772835	36.173661	18.657312	72.822688
Flowers	30.241696	40.886359	30.110354	84.185133
Library	21.473958	69.872317	46.413833	74.809492
Pond	43.782650	62.703967	48.497008	113.058342

MMS: Multi-scale morphological scheme

The overall contrast is defined as the minimum of the average contrasts of the three color components as given below.

$$Cont = min(avg\_red, avg\_grn, avg\_blu) \quad (55)$$

The overall contrast is computed for the original color image and the enhanced images resulting from all the enhancement schemes. From the table it is evident that the overall contrast is the best for the proposed method.

20.5 CONCLUSION

In this paper the authors have proposed a scheme for local contrast enhancement of color images. The red, green and blue color components of the image under study are used to construct the magnitude (i.e. the intensity) image. For each pixel, the direction cosines corresponding to the primary colors in the *rgb* space are preserved for future use. The method employs multi-scale morphological filtering in extracting the scale specific dark and bright features from the input magnitude image through the implementation of a number of *towers*. The recombination of all such features at the time of reconstruction emphasizes on the basic requirement of local contrast enhancement which demands that features of progressively smaller scales should get more weights. The enhanced red, green and blue components are obtained by combining the enhanced magnitude image with the original direction cosine information preserved previously. A simple example in one dimension is provided to clarify the functionality of the algorithm. The scheme has been implemented and executed on a set of color images. The results have been compared with those of two standard methods. The results due to the proposed method have been found to be reasonably satisfactory. The proposed method while performing enhancement preserves the color attributes namely hue and saturation. The proposed multi–scale method takes care of color, shape and scale simultaneously and it is inherently parallel.

References

1. I Attas, J Louis, and J Belward. A variational approach to the radiometric enhancement of digital imagery. *IEEE Transactions on Image Processing*, 4(6): 845–849, 1995.
2. J A Bangham, P D Ling, R Harvey, and R V Aldridge. Morphological scale-space preserving transforms in many dimensions. *Journal of Electronic Imaging*, 5(3): 283–299, 1996.
3. G Boccignone and A Picariello. Multiscale contrast enhancement of medical images. *Proc. ICASSP'97, Munich, Germany, April* 21–24, 4:2789–1997.

4. I M Bockstein. Color equalization method and its application to color image processing. *Journal of Opt. Soc. Am.,* A 3(5): 735–737, 1986.
5. B Chanda and D Dutta Majumder. *Digital Image Processing and Analysis.* Prentice-Hall of India Pvt. Ltd., New Delhi, 2000.
6. L Dorst. A local contrast enhancement filter. In *Proc. of the 6th Intl. Conference on Pattern Recognition,* pages 604–606, Munich, Germany, 1982.
7. J D Foley, A Van Dam, S K Feiner, and J F Hughes. *Computer Graphics Principles and Practice.* Addison-Wesley Publishing Company, second edition, Reading, MA, 1997.
8. R C Gonzalez and B A Fittes. Gray–level transformations for interactive image enhancement. In *Proc. 2nd Conf. on Remotely Manned Systems,* pages 17–19, 1975.
9. R C Gonzalez and B A Fittes. Gray-level transformations for interactive image enhancement. *Mechanism and Machine Theory,* 12:111–122, 1977.
10. R C Gonzalez and P Wintz. *Digital Image Processing, 2nd ed.* Addison-Wesley, Reading, MA, 1987.
11. A Gupta and B Chanda. A hue preserving enhancement scheme for a class of color images. *Pattern Recognition Letters,* 17:109–114, 1996.
12. E L Hall. *Computer Image Processing and Recognition.* Academic Press, New York, 1979.
13. R M Haralick and L G Shapiro. *Computer and Robot Vision, Vol.* 1. Addison-Wesley, Reading, MA, 1992.
14. A K Jain. *Fundamentals of Digital Image Processing.* Prentice-Hall, Englewood Cliffs, N.J., 1989.
15. J Koenderink. The structure of images. *Biological Cybernatics,* 50:363–370, 1984.
16. C Lantuejoul and F Maisonneuve. Geodesics methods in image analysis. *Pattern Recognition,* 17:117–187, 1984.
17. J S Lee. Digital image enhancement and noise filtering by use of local statistics. *IEEE Trans. on Pattern Analysis and Machine Intelligence,* PAMI-2:165–, 1980.
18. J S Lee. Refined filtering of image noise using local statistics. *Computer Graphics and Image Processing*-4, 15:380–389, 1981.
19. P Maragos. Pattern spectrum and multiscale shape representation. *IEEE Trans. on PAMI,* 11:701–716, 1989.
20. D Marr. *Vision.* Freeman, San Francisco, CA, 1982.
21. F Meyer. Contrast feature extraction. In J L Chermant, editor, *Quantitative Analysis of Microstructures in Material Sciences, Biology and Medicine.* Riederer Verlag, Stuttgart, Germany, 1978.

22. D Mukherjee and B N Chatterji. Adaptive neighborhood extended contrast enhancement and its modification. *Graphical Models and Image Processing,* 57:254–265, 1995.
23. S Mukhopadhyay and B Chanda. Multi-scale morphological approach to local contrast enhancement. *Signal Processing,* 80(4):685–696, 2000.
24. S Mukhopadhyay and B Chanda. An edge preserving noise smoothing technique using multiscale morphology. *Signal Processing,* Vol 82, 527-544, 2002.
25. S Mukhopadhyay and B Chanda. Fusion of 2d gray-scale images using multiscale morphology. *Pattern Recognition,* 34(10): 1939–1949–2001.
26. S Mukhopadhyay and B Chanda. Multiscale morphological segmentation of gray-scale images. *Communicated to IEEE Transaction on Image Processing,*.Vol 12, 533–549, 2003.
27. P M Narendra and R C Fitch. Real-time adaptive contrast enhancement. *IEEE Trans. on Pattern Analysis and Machine Intelligence,* PAMI-3:655–661, 1981.
28. R B Paranjape, W M Morrow, and R M Rangayyan. Adaptive-neighborhood histogram equalization for image enhancement. *Graphical Models and Image Processing*, 54:259–267, 1992.
29. S M Pizer, E P Amburn, J D Austin, R Cromartie, A Geselowitz, T Geer, B H Romeny, J B Zimmerman, and K Zuiderveld. Adaptive histogram modification and its variation. *Computer Vision, Graphics and Image Processing,* 39:355–368, 1987.
30. A Rosenfeld and A C Kak. *Digital Picture Processing, 2nd ed., Vol.* 1 & 2. Academic Press, NY, 1982.
31. A Rosenfeld and M Thurston. Edge and curve detection for visual scene analysis. *IEEE Transactions on Computers,* C-20: 562–569, 1971.
32. P Salembier. Morphological multi-scale segmentation for image coding. *Signal Processing,* 38:359–386, 1994.
33. J Serra. *Image analysis using mathematical morphology.* Academic Press, London, 1982.
34. M Shyu and J Leou. A geneticle algorithm approach to color image enhancement. *Pattern Recognition,* 31(7):871–880, 1998.
35. R N Strickland, C S Kim, and W F McDonnell. Digital color image enhancement based on the saturation component. *Optical Engineering,* 26:609–616, 1987.
36. B Tang and G Sapiro. Color image enhancement via chromaticity diffusion. *IEEE Transactions on Image Processing,* 10(5): 701–707, 2001.

37. A Toet. A hierarchical morphological image decomposition. *Pattern Recognition Letters,* 11(4): 267–274, 1990.
38. A Toet. Multi-scale color image enhancement. *Pattern Recognition Letters,* 13(3): 167–174, 1992.
39. A Witkin. Scale-space filtering. In *International Joint Conference on Artificial Intelligence,* pages 1019–1021, Karlsruhe, West Germany, 1983.
40. H Zhu, F H Y Chan, and F K Lam. Image contrast enhancement by constrained local histogram equalization. *Computer Vision and Image Understanding,* 73(2):281–290, 1999.

21

Segmented Bezier Curve Approximation with a Control Parameter

B B Chaudhuri[1] and Sushanta Dutta[2]

ABSTRACT

This paper deals with Bezier approximation technique for curve drawing and curve fitting in Computer Graphics. A new method of Segmented Bezier approximation with a simple control parameter and its modified version are proposed for fast and efficient curve approximation. Some interesting properties of the proposed technique is proved and experimental results are presented. The results are compared with those using B-spline approximation technique.

Keywords: Segmentation; Bezier Approximation; Computer Graphics; B-Spline Approximation.

21.1 INTRODUCTION

Curve drawing and fitting problems occur most frequently in Computer Graphics applications. Interpolation and approximation are two basic approaches of curve fitting. Interpolation is the problem of finding a curve that passes through a set of given points. On the other hand, approximation is the problem of finding a curve that is guided by a set of given points called guiding points (GPs) but not necessarily pass through them.

The most popular techniques of interpolation use piecewise polynomial functions of various types. Spline functions are one of them. Spline functions, particularly the B-splines, are well suited for computer graphics use. B-splines are also very useful for approximation problems. Another popular technique of approximation is the Bernstein-Bezier Approximation. Both interpolation and approximation techniques have their respective advantages and disadvantages and their applicability depends on the problem in hand.

The present work is concerned with the Bernstein-Bezier approximation technique. For $n + 1$ GPs, the Bezier curves are nth degree polynomials derived using Bernstein basis functions [1,2]. Several modifications of the Bezier approximation techniques are reported in recent literature [3–9]. They deal mainly with segmented approximation,

---

[1] Electronics and Communication Sciences Unit, Indian Statistical Institute, 203, B.T. Road, Calcutta 700035, INDIA.

[2] Tata Consultancy Services, NICCO House, 2 Hare Street, Calcutta 700001.

order of continuity between successive segments and weight adjustment of different GPs.

One of the drawbacks of conventional Bezier method is that the resultant curve resembles the shape of the polygon well only near the two end points. It is possible to follow the GPs more closely by giving multiple weight at each GP location [9], but this approach is not computationally attractive because the degree of the Bezier polynomial increases with the number as well as multiplicity of the GPs. Again the curve is completely determined by the GPs and there is no controlling parameter by which the shape of the curve can be changed interactively. The only way to change the shape is through the multiplicity of GPs.

A new segmented Bezier approximation technique is presented here which provides a simple control parameter, so that the shape of the curve can be changed predictably by varying the parameter. The parameter may work in two ways. In the first, a new point is introduced in the line segment between each pair of successive GPs and a second order Bezier polynomial is fitted for each GP. It is seen that the resultant curve is 'titled', which may be objectionable in some applications. The effect of tilt is rectified in the second method where two points are introduced in the line segment between each pair of successive GP's. The positions of the introduced points depend on the control parameter. There are several interesting properties of the present method and its modification which are proved and the results are discussed.

21.2 BEZIER CURVE APPROXIMATION

Consider parametric representation of curves in $\mathbb{R}$ given by

$$x = P_x(S), \quad y = P_y(S), \quad 0 \le S \le 1 \tag{1}$$

For $m + 1$ ordered points in space denoted as $P_o(x_o, y_o), P_1(x_1, y_1), \ldots.$ $P_m(x_m, y_m)$, the parametric Bezier curve is the vector-valued Bernstein polynomial of order m given by

$$P(S) = \sum_{i=0}^{m} \Phi_i(S)\, P_i, \tag{2}$$

where $\Phi_i(S)$ are the binomial probability density functions

$$\Phi_i(S) = \binom{m}{i} S^i\,(1-S)^{m-i},\ i = 0, 1, 2, \ldots, m, \tag{3}$$

while $P(S)$ and P_i are the column vectors

$$P(S) = \begin{pmatrix} P_x(S) \\ P_y(S) \end{pmatrix} \text{ and } P_i = \begin{pmatrix} x_i \\ y_i \end{pmatrix}, \text{ respectively.}$$

The points P_0, P_1, ... P_m are the GPs of the curve defined by Eq.(2). Some of the interesting properties of the Bezier curve are that it lies inside the convex hull of the GPs and passes through P_0 and P_m. Also, the curve is tangential to line segments $P_0 P_1$ and $P_{m-1} P_m$ at P_0 and P_m, respectively.

Extension of (2) to $\mathbb{R}^n$, $n > 2$ is possible, but we are concerned with 2-D only. It is pointed out in Section 21.1 that a GP may be assigned multiple weightage so that the Bezier curve follows the GP closely. A GP of multiplicity k is treated as k GPs placed at the same position. The order of the polynomial defining the Bezier curve is increased by k because of the multiplicity of GP. In general, if P_i is a GP with multiplicity k_i then (2) is modified as

$$P(S) = \sum_{i=0}^{m} P_i \sum_{j=l_i}^{l_{i+1}-1} \Phi_j(S), \tag{2a}$$

where $$l_i = \sum_{j=0}^{i-1} k_j,\ i = 1, 2, \ldots.., m+1, \text{ and } P_0 = 0$$

21.3 SEGMENTED BEZIER APPROXIMATION WITH CONTROL PARAMETER

(A) Method

It is clear from (2) that the order of Bezier approximating polynomial and hence the computation increases with increase in the number of GPs. The situation is worse when multiple GPs are necessary. To reduce the computation, a *segmented Bezier technique* may be employed. In the specific case described below each of the *curve segments* is of degree two and the curve over all the GPs is obtained by concatenating all of the successive curve segments. Each *curve segment* is drawn using three points as follows.

A curve to be drawn may be closed or open. At first, the treatment for closed curve is discussed. For $m + 1$ distinct GPs P_0, P_1, ..., P_m, the closed Bezier curve is the one that approximates the polygon P_0, P_1, ..., P_m. Let c be a real number between 0 and 1. Let the points Q_0, Q_1, ..., Q_m be selected on the line segments P_0P_1, P_1P_2, ..., P_mP_0 as follows:

$$Q_i = (1-c)P_i + cP_{i+1},\quad i = 0, 1, 2, \ldots., m+1$$

and $$Q_m = (1-c)P_m + cP_0 \tag{4}$$

For convenience in closed curve approximation let $P_{m+1} = P_0$ and $Q_{m+1} = Q_0$. For i = 1, 2, ..., m + 1, the ith curve segment $F_i(t), 0 < t < 1$ is defined to be the second order Bezier curve with Q_{i-1}, P_i and Q_i as GPs. A second order curve is given by

$$F_i(t) = (1-t)^2\ Q_{i-1} + 2t(1-t)P_i + t^2Q_i \tag{5}$$

$$i = 1, 2, \ldots, m + 1$$

$Q_0, Q_1, \ldots, Q_m$ are the points where the successive segments meet when the segments are concatenated to form the complete curve. These points may be called the *joints* and the complete curve may be termed as *segmented Bezier curve.*

The treatment for open curve is the same except at the two end segments. An open curve is formed if the polygon P_0, P_1, ..., P_m is stripped off the line segment $P_m\ P_0$ and is approximated using Bezier technique. The curve segments for i = 1,2, ..., m – 1 are defined by (5) using (4). F_m and F_{m+1} are defined to be the line segments joining Q_{m-1} with P_m and P_0 with Q_0, respectively.

The parameter c may be used to control the shape of the resulting curve interactively. Hence, c is called the *controlling parameter.*

For example, consider Fig. 21.1 where P_0, P_1, ..., P_4 are the GPs and the shape of polygon P_0,P_1,P_2,P_3,P_4 is followed by the segmented Bezier

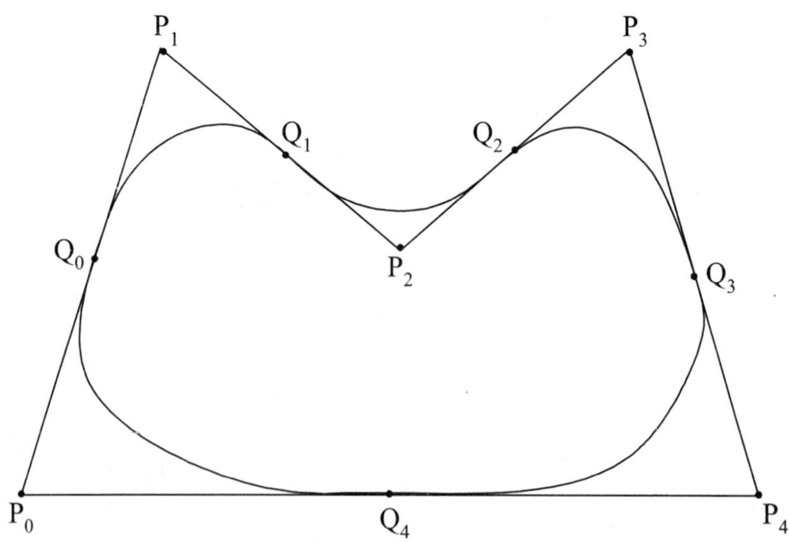

Fig. 21.1 Segmented Bezier approximation of a closed curve (for c = 0.5).

approximating technique using c = 0.5. The joints Q_0, Q_1, ..., Q_4 are found using this value of c in (4). Since c = 0.5, Q_i lies midway between P_i and P_{i+1}. Each curve segment is drawn using (5) and the concatenated form shows the complete approximated *closed curve.*

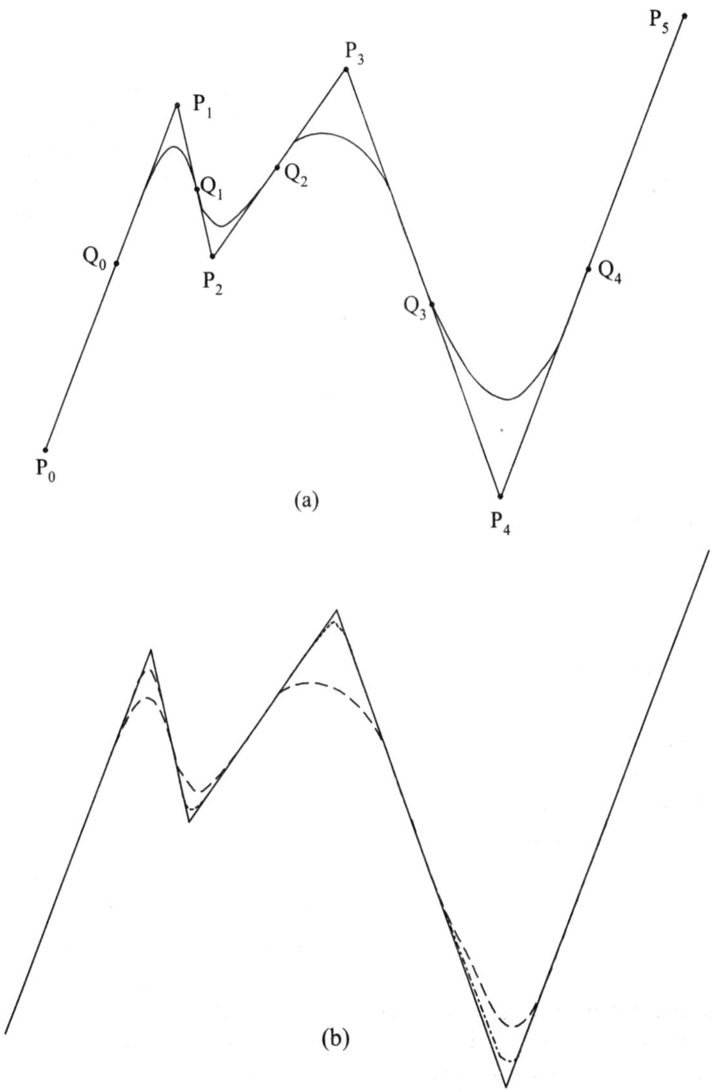

Fig. 21.2 *(a)* Segmented Bezier approximation of an open curve for $c = 0.5$
(b) Variation of the open curve with c for $c = 0.05$, … for $c = 0.2$.

In Fig. 21.2(*a*), an *open curve* is drawn using segmented Bezier technique on GPs P_0, P_1, ..., P_5 for c = 0.5. It is seen that the curve between Q_4 and P_5 as well as P_0 and Q_0 are the line segments Q_4P_4 and P_0Q_0, respectively. The variation of the shape of the curve with controlling parameter c is shown in Fig. 21.2(b). It is seen that the curve approaches the line segments as c approaches 0. It is shown below that the property is true as c approaches 1 as well. Also, it is shown there that at least first order continuity is maintained between curve segments. As can be seen from Figs (21.1–.2) that the segmented Bezier curve is visually quite smooth.

(B) Properties

There are several interesting properties of the present technique. The properties and their proofs are given below.

Property 1

The segmented Bezier curve lies in the convex hull of all the GPs.

Proof

The first curve segment in the case of open polygon is the line segment joining P_0 and Q_0, where Q_0 is a point in the line segment P_0P_1. Thus this curve segment lies in the convex hull of the two points P_0 and P_1. Similarly, the last curve segment for open polygon lies in the convex hull of P_{m-1} and P_m. The other curve segments for both types of polygons are of the form

$$F_i(t) = (1-t)^2\ Q_{i-1} + 2t(1-t)P_i + t^2 Q_i$$

Using the expressions for Q_1's this can be written as

$$F_i(t) = (1-t)^2[(1-c)P_{i-1} + c \cdot P_i] + 2t(1-t)P_i + t^2[(1-c)P_i + c \cdot P_{i+1}]$$

since the coefficients are non-negative and their sum is equal to 1, $F_i(t)$ is a convex combination of P_{i-1}, P_i and P_{i+1}. Thus each curve segment lies in the convex hull of two or three GPs, and hence lies in a convex hull of all the GPs.

Property 2

The segmented Bezier curve is continuous and at least once continuously differentiable at the joints.

Proof

Each Q_i is a common end point of the two neighbouring curve segments and at this point the lines Q_iP_i and $Q_i\ P_{i+1}$ are tangents to these two curve segments. From this it follows that the curve segments are continuous and have continuous slopes at their common joints.

Property 3

The segmented Bezier curve converges to the polygon as $c \to 0$ or $c \to 1$.

Proof

From equation (4), it can be seen that in the limit c tending to zero or one Q_i tends to P_i or P_{i+1}. Hence the Bezier curve segment for the three GPs Q_{i-1}, P_i, Q_i approaches the line segment P_{i-1} P_i or P_i, P_{i+1} according as c tends to 0 or 1.

Property 4

The segmented Bezier curve can be made to pass through a multiple GP.

Proof

Suppose two successive GPs are same, i.e., $P_i = P_{i+1}$ for some i. Then, $Q_i = (1 - c)\ P_i + c \cdot P_{i+1} = P_i$ which implies that P_i is a point on the approximating curve. Thus the segmented Bezier curve can be forced to pass through a GP, by repeating that point in the GP sequence.

There is another way of using multiple GPs. In this, the multiplicities are not considered at the time of selecting the joints Q_i's. Suppose P_{i-1}, P_i and P_{i+1} are three successive distinct GPs. If P_i is of multiplicity k, then the corresponding Bezier curve segment is taken to be the $k + 1$th degree Bezier polynomial for the $k + 2$ GPs Q_{i-1}, P_i with multiplicity k and Q_i, where

$$Q_{i-1} = (1-c)P_{i-1} + c \cdot P_i$$

and

$$Q_i = (1-c)P_i + c \cdot P_{i+1}$$

Hence, from (2*a*) the curve segment has the form

$$F(t) = (1-t)^{k+1} \cdot Q_{i-1} + \sum_{j=1}^{k} \binom{k+1}{j} t^j (1-t)^{k+1-j} P_i + t^{k+1} Q_i$$

Thus multiple GPs can also be used to force the curve to follow the GPs closely but not pass through them.

21.4 RESULTS AND MODIFICATION

The present technique has been applied to several sets of data in plane and some of the results are compared with the *B*-Spline approximating curves. In Fig. 21.3, the same set of GPs are taken to draw *B*-Spline curve, Bezier curve using (2) and segmented Bezier curve using (5). It is seen that Bezier curve using (2) follows the shape poorly. Both *B*-Spline and segmented Bezier curves are good approximations and their difference is little. The use of multiple GPs in segmented Bezier curve to follow a GP closely but not passing through it, as given in Property 4 is also shown at P_4 with multiplicity 2.

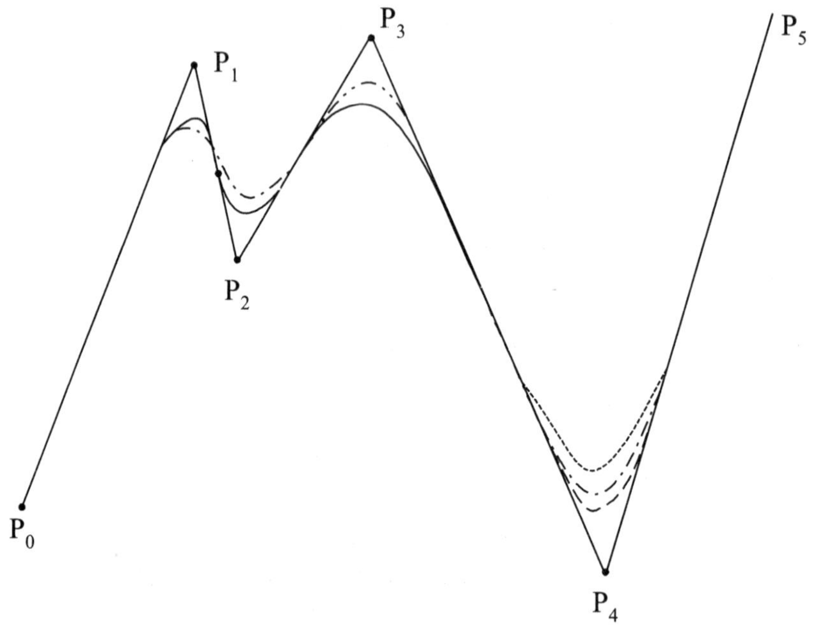

Fig. 21.3 Comparison of different curve approximation techniques. —— - —— - B-spline curve, —— Bezier curve using (2), …. Segmented Bezier curve using (5), —— Effect of using multiplicity at P4.

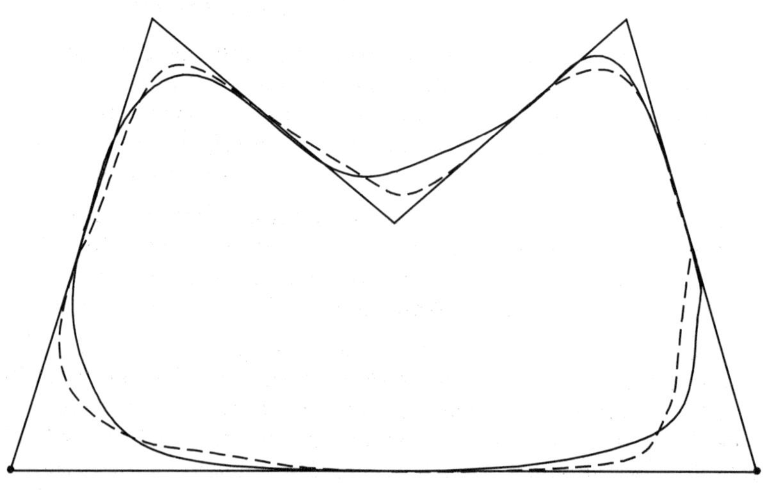

Fig. 21.4 Tilt of the curve with change in c. for c = 0 .25, for c = 0.75.

It is shown in Fig. 21.2 that c can be used to control the shape of the resultant curve. The effects of c away from 0.5 in both directions towards 0 and towards 1 are similar except for the tilt of the curve. The tilt is understood from Fig. 21.4 and Fig. 21.1 where in Fig. 21.4, the values of c are taken as 0.5 as well as 0.75, an offset of 0.25 in either direction from c = 0.5 of Fig. 21.1, respectively. In general, the curve segment between two successive edges of the polygon is tilted towards the later (former) side if the control parameter c is closer to zero (one) than to one (zero). Although c is constant over all segments here, it may be different for different segments.

However, in some applications, the tilt of the curve may be objectionable. To make the resultant curve more symmetric, a modified technique is proposed here. Instead of introducing a single point Q_i between two GPs P_i and P_{i+1}, we introduce two points $Q_{i,1}$ and $Q_{i,2}$ around P_i as follows

$$Q_{i,1} = \frac{c'}{2} P_{i-1} + \left(1 - \frac{c'}{2}\right) P_i$$

and

$$Q_{i,2} = \left(1 - \frac{c'}{2}\right) P_i + \frac{c'}{2} P_{i+1},$$

where c' is the modified control parameter and $0 \le c' \le 1$. Draw a segmented Bezier curve between $Q_{i,1}$, P_i and $Q_{i,2}$. Also, join $Q_{i,2}$ and $Q_{i+1,1}$ by a straight line. The process, when repeated for each value of i, generates the segmented Bezier curve with the modified control parameter.

It is seen that for $c' = 0$, $Q_{i,1}$ and $Q_{i,2}$ coincide at P_i, so that the curve segments on both sides of P_i are straight lines. For $c' = 1$ everywhere the resultant curve is the same as that of the previous method with $c = 0.5$. In general, the value of c' should be nearer to 0 for a segment to be more straight while it should be nearer to 1 for the segment to be smoothly curved.

Introduction of the current modification does not increase computation very much since the additional computation is needed only to draw straight lines between $Q_{i,2}$ and $Q_{i+1,1}$ and there exist very efficient line-drawing algorithms. It may be verified that the properties of the segmented Bezier curve described above is true for the modified control parameter also.

Applicability of the present technique for drawing a meaningful curve is investigated. For example, drawing the letter '*B*' in English alphabet is considered. Fig. 21.6 shows the results obtained for $c = 0.5$ on GPs shown in Fig. 21.5. Also, Fig. 21.6 demonstrates the use of double GPs to force the curve to pass through these GPs. The result obtained using B-Spline technique on the same set of GPs is also shown in Fig. 21.7 for comparison. A careful observation reveals that the B-Spline curve appears slightly more smooth than the curve obtained with the present technique for $c = 0.5$. One of the possible reasons is that the B-Spline technique maintains at least second order continuity while the present technique maintains the first order continuity at the joints. However, curve due to the present technique is visually quite acceptable.

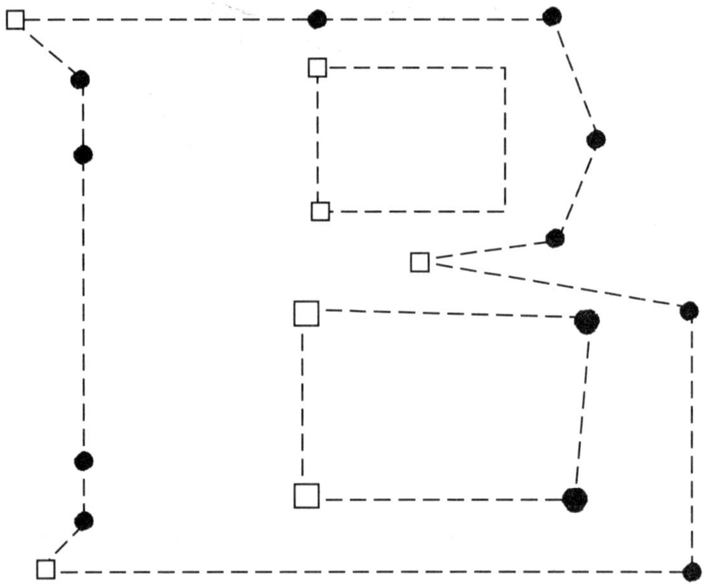

Fig. 21.5 GPs for drawing '*B*' in English alphabet ⊙ Simple GP, ▯ GP with multiplicity 2.

Fig. 21.6 Segmented Bezier approximation curve drawn with GPs of Fig. 21.5 (for $c' = 0.5$)

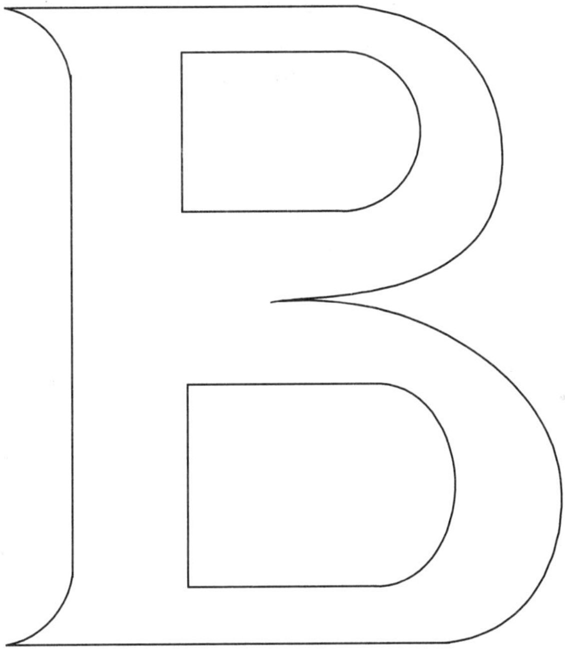

Fig. 21.7 B-spline approximation curve drawn with GPs of Fig. 21.5.

In all of the above examples we have found that the computational effort necessary by the present method is smaller than that for B-Spline and conventional Bezier technique. The current method may be extended to surface drawing and approximation for 3-dimensional computer graphics.

References

1. P Bezier (1968) How Renault uses numerical control for car body design and tooling. *Paper SAE 680010, Soc Automot Engrs Congr Detroit, Michigan,* USA.
2. P Bezier (1972) *Numerical Control* Transl. A.R. Forest. Wiley New York.
3. W J Gordon and R F Riesenfeld (1974) Bernstein-Bezier methods for computer aided design of free form curves and surfaces. *ACM* **21**, 293 – 310.
4. K Harada and E Nakamae (1982) Applications of the Bezier curve to data interpolation. *CAD* **14,** 55 – 59.
5. K Harada, K Kaneda and E Nakamae (1984) A further investi-gation of segmented Bezier interpolants. *CAD* **16,** 186–190.
6. L Hering (1983) Closed c^2 - and c^3 - continuous Bezier and B-spline curves with given tangent polygons. *CAD* **15,** 3–6.

7. H G Timmer (1980) Alternative representation for parametric cubic curves and surfaces. *CAD* **12,** 25–28.
8. A R Forest (1982) interactive, interpolation and approximation by Bezier polynomials. *Comp J* **15**, 71–79.
9. T Pavlidis (1972) *Algorithms for Graphics and Image Processing.* Springer Berlin.
10. P J Davis (1963) *Interpolation and Approximation.* Ginn-Blaisdell New York.

22

A New Probabilistic Approach for Fractal Based Image Compression

Suman K. Mitra[1]
Malay K. Kundu[2], C. A. Murthy[3], Bhargab B. Bhattacharya[4]

ABSTRACT

Approximation of an image by the attractor evolved through iterations of a set of contractive maps is usually known as fractal image compression. The set of maps is called iterated function system (IFS). Several algorithms, with different motivations, have been suggested towards the solution of this problem. But, so far, the theory of IFS with probabilities, in the context of image compression, has not been explored much. In the present article we have proposed a new technique of fractal image compression using the theory of IFS and probabilities. In our proposed algorithm, we have used a multiscaling division of the given image up to a predetermined level or up to that level at which no further division is required. At each level, the maps and the corresponding probabilities are computed using the gray value information contained in that image level and in the image level higher to that level. A fine tuning of the algorithm is still to be done. But, the most interesting part of the proposed technique is its extreme fastness in image encoding. It can be looked upon as one of the solutions to the problem of huge computational cost for obtaining fractal code of images.

Key words : Iterated function System (IFS); Collage theorem; measure; Markov operator; image compression.

22.1 INTRODUCTION

A set of contractive maps on a space is called iterated function system (IFS) on the same space. The most interesting property of IFS is that it produces a fixed point when the maps are used recursively starting with any arbitrary set. The fixed point is called the attractor of the IFS. The theory of image coding using IFS was first proposed by Barnsley [1]. He modeled real life images by the attractor evolved through iterations of an IFS. With the help of iterated function system, along with the Collage theorem, Barnsley laid the foundation stone of fractal image compression. However, in most of his published research papers, implementation part of the theory of IFS to real life images has not been very clear as the demonstrations are mostly restricted to binary images. Seemingly, a photocopying machine has been designed by means of which coefficients of maps are computed [2]. The concept of photocopying machine has

1 Institute for Neural computation, University of California
2,3,4 Indian Statistical Institute, Kolkata

also been extended to the case of gray scale images [2]. In this case, the machine is computing not only the coefficients of maps but also the probability values associated with each map. The reason behind using the IFS with probabilities is that a Markov operator associated with the probability measure whose support is the support of the given image can be defined. It has also been shown that the Markov operator is a contractive map on the space of all probability measures. Barnsley also presented the Collage theorem for measure [2] for which the Markov operator possesses an invariant measure in probability space. From this Collage theorem it has been found that an IFS with probabilities can produce an invariant measure such that the support of the invariant measure is the unique fixed point of the IFS concerned.

The first ever published algorithm of fractal image compression was suggested by Jacquin [3]. This scheme is based on partitioned or local IFS [4]. A variety of algorithms have been explored [5], [6], [7], [8], [9] thereafter. Most of these schemes are closely related to the technique described by Jacquin. Unfortunately, the theory of IFS with probabilities, in the context of image compression, has not been explored much. Though the theoretical results are existing in the literature for a long time [2], [10], [11], there are very few attempts to implement the theory on computer for images. It may be due to the fact that some of the mathematical terms need to be properly explained and interpreted in the context of computer programme on a digital images apart from considering all other implementation details.

An algorithm, which is not in the line of PIFS based fractal image compression has been suggested here. We have used a multiscaling division of the given image. At each level the coefficients of maps and the corresponding probabilities are computed using the gray value information. This is an attempt to implement the theory of IFS with probabilities for digital images. There are very few references [12], [13] in the literature on fractal image compression, besides the work done by Barnsley [2], on this particular aspect. The present algorithm is appeared to be extremely fast for encoding a given image. A comparison of the proposed method with a GA based fractal method [9] is provided. It is found that the present scheme is at least 300 times faster than that of the GA based methodology. Note that, previously it has been found that GA based fractal scheme is faster than the conventional fractal scheme which uses exhaustive search.

The algorithm described here utilizes the probabilistic relation exists in between pixel values of a given image. Contribution of a particular pixel, in terms of intensity (gray level value), towards the total intensity of the image is computed under a multiscaling partition. If 'p' is the proportion of the total intensity carried by a pixel then one can express the intensity of that pixel (say 'g') as $g = p \times G$, where 'G' is the sum of all pixel values. In this algorithm, 'p' is computed as a product of a set of probability values which were obtained from the image information (pixel values) after braking the image in multiscaling order. In the reconstruction process each pixel value is again regenerated using 'G' and the stored set of probability values. Note that 'G' is also stored within the code. The scheme performs very fast as no search is performed for finding appropriate domain blocks and maps for a set of range blocks. This sort of searching is very common in case of PIFS based image compression. In the present case, the range blocks are the image partitions at a particular subdivision and the domain blocks for these range blocks are the image partitions at immediate higher level subdivision. The same kind of partitioning is also utilized by Dudbridge [14]. As far as we understand, the present algorithm is only similar with the algorithm suggested by Dudbridge [14] in case of selection of domain blocks and range blocks under multiscaling partitioning. The procedure for computation of codes is not exactly the same as that of the method suggested by Dudbridge. Note that no computation such as 'least square' is adopted in our method.

There is a lot of scope for improving the present algorithm towards the efficiency in the sense of compression ratio as well as quality of the decoded image. It is obvious that a fine tuning of the scheme is needed. Work, in this regard, is in progress. Our main objective, in this article, is to investigate the art of finding a probabilistic approach for approximating the given image. The high speed of execution of the method appeared to be the main advantage.

The mathematical foundation of IFS with probabilities is outlined in Section 22.2. The methodology of the proposed probabilistic algorithm is described in Section 22.3. Section 22.4 presents implementation and the results. Discussion and conclusions are provided in Section 22.5.

22.2. MATHEMATICAL FOUNDATION

The detailed mathematical description is given in [1], [2]. Some relevant definitions and theorems are stated here. Proofs of the theorems have not been stated as all these are already given in [1]. Starting with the definition of complete metric space, IFS has been defined in the space of probability measures. Invariant measure of IFS in terms of Collage theorem has also been described in the same space.

The most important result which is being used here, is the theorem of invariant measure of IFS with probabilities defined on a probability space. Other definitions and theorems are stated for better understanding of the theorem of interest. To define the IFS with probabilities in the probability space, we need to define, the probability space and the IFS in that space. Again we need to define the probability measure and the contractive mapping theorem on this space. Let us start with complete metric space.

Definition 1

Let (X, d) be a complete metric space. Then $\mathcal{H}(X)$ denotes the space of all nonempty compact subsets of X. ♠

Definition 2

Let The map $w : X \to X$ is called a contractive map with contractivity factor s with $0 \le s < 1$ if

$$d(w(x), w(y)) \le s\, d(x, y) \;\; \forall x, y \in X. \spadesuit$$

Lemma 1

Let w be a contractive map on the complete metric space (X, d). Then w maps $\mathcal{H}(X)$ into itself where

$$w(B) = \{w(x) : x \in B\}, \forall\; B \in \mathcal{H}(X).$$

w is a contractive map on $(\mathcal{H}(X), h)$ with contractivity factor s. Here 'h' is called Hausdorff metric. ♠

Lemma 2

Let (X, d) be a complete metric space. Let $\{w_i : i = 1, 2, ..., n\}$ be contractive maps on $(\mathcal{H}(X), h)$. Let the contractivity factor for w_i be denoted by s_i for each i. Define $W : \mathcal{H}(X) \to \mathcal{H}(X)$ by

$$W(B) = \bigcup_{i=1}^{n} w_i(B), \;\; \forall B \in \mathcal{H}(X).$$

Then W is a contractive map with contractivity factor $s = max\{s_i : i = 1, 2, ... n\}$. ♠

Definition 3

An iterated function system (IFS) consists of a complete metric space (X, d) together with a finite set of contractive maps $w_i : X \to X$, with respective contractivity factors s_i, for $i = 1, 2, ..., n$. The notation for this IFS is $\{X ; w_1, w_2, ..., w_n\}$ and its contractivity factor is s where $s = max\{s_1, s_2, ..., s_n\}$. ♠

The preceding results are useful in proving the following theorem of the existence of a fixed point of IFS.

Theorem 1 (IFS Theorem)

Let $\{X ; w_1, w_2, \ldots, w_n\}$ be an IFS with contractivity factor s. Then the transformation $W : \mathcal{H}(X) \to \mathcal{H}(X)$ defined by

$$W(B) = \bigcup_{i=1}^{n} w_i(B), \ \forall B \in \mathcal{H}(X),$$

is a contractive map on the complete metric space $(\mathcal{H}(X), h)$ with contractivity factor s; i. e.

$$h(W(B), W(C)) \leq s.h(B, C), \ \forall B, C \in \mathcal{H}(X).$$

Also $W^N(B)$ is defined as

$$W^N(B) = W(W^{N-1}(B)); \ \forall B \in \mathcal{H}(X) \text{ and } \forall N \geq 2,$$

where

$$W^1(B) = W(B); \ \forall B \in \mathcal{H}(X),$$

It has a unique fixed point, called **attractor**, $A \in \mathcal{H}(X)$, which obeys

$$A = W(A) = \bigcup_{i=1}^{n} w_i(A),$$

and is given by

$$A = \lim_{N \to \infty} W^N(B); \ \forall B \in \mathcal{H}(X). \ \spadesuit$$

Besides the contractive maps, there may exist a condensation map. The theorem of IFS is also valid when the condensation map is included in the IFS along with the contractive maps.

Definition 4

Let (X, d) be a complete metric space and let $C \in \mathcal{H}(X)$. Define a transformation $w_0 : \mathcal{H}(X) \to \mathcal{H}(X)$ by $w_0(B) = C; \ \forall B \in \mathcal{H}(X)$. Then w_0 is called a condensation transformation and C is called the associated condensation set. ♠

The condensation map is also a contractive map with unique fixed point. Next we are going to state the Collage theorem of IFS.

Theorem 2 (Collage theorem)

Let (X, d) be a complete metric space. Let $T \in \mathcal{H}(X)$ and let $\in \geq 0$ be given. Choose an IFS $\{X ; w_1, w_2, \ldots, w_n\}$ with contractivity factor s such that

$$h(T, \bigcup_{i=1}^{n} w_i(T)) \leq \varepsilon,$$

where h is the Hausdorff metric. Then

$$h(T, A) \leq \frac{\varepsilon}{1-s},$$

where A is the attractor of IFS. ♠

Now we shall define IFS defined on the space of all probability measures. In particular, the Markov operator, which is a contractive map on the space of all probability measures, is defined below. For this purpose, one needs to first define a metric on the space of all probability measures.

Definition 5

An iterated function system with probabilities consists of an IFS $\{X; w_1, w_2, \ldots, w_N\}$ together with an ordered set of numbers $\{p_1, p_2, \ldots, p_N\}$ such that

$$p_1 + p_2 + \ldots\ldots + p_N = 1 \text{ and } p_i > 0 \ \forall i.$$

The probability p_i is associated with the transformation w_i. ♠.

Definition 6

Let $\square = \{(x, y) \in \mathbb{R}^2 : a \leq x \leq b, c \leq y \leq d\}$,

where $a < b$ and $c < d$ are real constants. Also let P denote the set of all probability measures on $\square$. The Hutchinson metric d_H on P is defined by $d_H(\mu, \nu) = \sup\{\int_\square f\, d\mu - \int_\square f\, d\nu : f : \square \to \mathrm{IR}^2$ is a continuous function.

and obeys $|f(x) - f(y)| \leq d(x, y) \ \forall\ x, y \in \square\}, \ \forall \mu, \nu \in P$ ♠

Theorem 3

Let P denote the set of all probability measures on $\square$ and let d_H denote the Hutchinson metric. Then (P, d_H) is a complete metric space. ♠

Definition 7

Let $\{\square; w_1, w_2, \ldots, w_2; p_1, p_2, \ldots, p_n\}$ be an IFS with probabilities. The Markov operator associated with the IFS is the function $M : P \to P$ defined by

$$M(\nu) = p_1\, \nu \circ w_1^{-1} + p_2\, \nu \circ w_2^{-1} + \ldots\ldots + p_n\, \nu \circ w_n^{-1}; \ \forall \nu \in P.$$

i.e. $$M(\nu) = \sum_{i=1}^{n} p_i\, \nu \circ w_i^{-1}. ♠$$

The preceding definitions and results are needed to prove the following theorem.

Theorem 4 (Hutchinson's Theorem)

Let $M : P \to P$ be the Markov operator associated with an IFS with probabilities, where each transformation has contractivity factor $0 \leq s < 1$. Then M is a contractive map, with contractivity factor s, with respect to the Hutchinson metric P; i. e.,

$$d_H\,(M(\nu),\, M(\mu)) \leq s\; d_H\,(\nu,\, \mu);\;\; \forall\, \nu, \mu \in P.$$

In particular, there is a unique measure $\mu \in P$ such that $M\mu = \mu$. Also, if $M^N(\nu) = M(M^{N-1}(\nu))$ for $\nu \in P$, $N \geq 2$, then

$$\lim_{N \to \infty} M^N(\nu) = \mu,\; \forall \nu \in P.$$

where the convergence is with respect to the Hutchinson metric on P. ♠

The Collage theorem for measures is stated below. The theorem states that any given probability measure is approximated by the fixed point (unique invariant measure) of an IFS with probabilities.

Theorem 5

Let $\{\square;\, w_1, w_2, \ldots, w_n;\, p_1, p_2, \ldots, p_n\}$ be an IFS with probabilities. Let μ be the associated invariant measure. Then the support of μ is the attractor of the IFS $\{\square;\, w_1, w_2, \ldots, w_n\}$. ♠

Theorem 6 (Collage Theorem for Measure)

Let $\{\square;\, w_1, w_2, \ldots, w_n;\, p_1, p_2, \ldots, p_n\}$ be an IFS with probabilities. Let μ be the associated invariant measure. Let $s \in (0, 1)$ be the contractivity factor for the IFS. Let $M : P \to P$ be the associated Markov operator. Let $\nu \in P$. Then

$$d_H(\nu,\, \mu) \leq \frac{d_H(\nu, M(\nu))}{(1-s)}. \;\; ♠$$

Note that the theory of IFS with probabilities can be extended to include a *condensation measure.* Once IFS with probabilities or the Markov operator associated with ν is at hand, one can approximate the measure ν by the invariant measure μ starting from any measure on the same space. In the context of image compression, the process of computing the Markov operator is called the encoding process. Likewise the process of finding the invariant measure μ, hence the attractor of the concerned IFS, starting from any initial measure, is called the process of decoding.

To implement the aforesaid theory on real life images the problem is to find a way of defining probability measure corresponding to an image. It is extremely difficult to define the probability measure of the image. However an algorithm called gray scale photocopying algorithm, seemingly, was suggested by Barnsley [2] as a part of his patented work.

We don't know the details of the patented work. A description of the algorithm is given in [2]. But the implementation part is not clear from this description. The methodology of the present algorithm is motivated by this description. We are presenting here only the salient features of the algorithm suggested by Barnsley [2].

The gray scale photocopying algorithm is a procedure for computing the invariant measure μ, the unique solution of $Q(\mu) = \mu$, $\mu \in P$. Consider a gray scale photograph supported on □. If light is passed through the photograph, it reflects a certain amount of light. Dark regions reflect relatively less light, while bright regions reflect relatively large. A function ν is introduced which describes the amount of light reflected from different regions of the photograph. The photograph is now represented by $\nu \in P$, where P is the set of all normalized Borel measures on □. The photocopying machine consists of some lenses and filters. The emitted light, from different parts of the given image, is controlled by system of lenses which apply the affine transformations w_i; $i = 1, 2, \ldots, n$. Each lens system has its own filter p_i, $i = 1, 2, \ldots, n$. A filter attenuates the light that passes through it by a factor proportional to the number p_i. The output of the machine is taken on a photographic plate. The resulting image is $Q(\nu)$.

The basic idea of the machine is adjusting the affine maps w_i and the probabilities p_i one by one starting from all set at zero. For example, first of all, the transformation w_1 and the probability p_1 are adjusted to make the output image as good an approximation as possible to a part of the target measure ν. The adjustment of w_1 and p_1 are such that $p_1 \nu \circ w_1^{-1}(B) < \nu(B)$ for every Borel subset B of □. Thus $(\nu - p_1 \nu \circ w_1^{-1})$ is a Borel measure. Next the affine transformation w_2 and probability p_2 are adjusted in such a way that $p_1 \nu \circ w_1^{-1} + p_2 \nu \circ w_2^{-1}$ is as good an approximation as possible of a larger part of ν. Again the adjustment is such that $\nu - (p_1 \nu \circ w_1^{-1} + p_2 \nu \circ w_2^{-1})$ is a Borel measure. New transformations and probabilities are added successively to the IFS with probabilities to improve the approximation of ν by $Q(\nu)$. At all stages the contractivity of the Markov operator is maintained to be s by insisting that each affine map has a contractivity factor less than s, where $0 \leq s < 1$. Once the output image looks sufficiently like the input image, the transformations and the corresponding probabilities are recorded.

In the next section we have described our proposed algorithm.

22.3 PROPOSED PROBABILISTIC APPROACH FOR IMAGE ENCODING

In the present work we have used a multiscaling division of the given image as described in Fig. 22.1. At each level of partitioning, the image or subimage is divided into four quadrants. Each quadrant is called the child of its parent image or subimage. The Markov operator is computed and the approximation of the image by means of the invariant measure of the Markov operator, as described in Theorem 6 [Section 22.2], is carried out at each level of partitioning. The process of partitioning the image, or the subimage as the case is, and computing the Markov operator are performed up to a predetermined level or up to a level at which no further division is required. No further division is required at any level indicates that the successful approximation of the given image through the obtained Markov operator. To compute the Markov operator, it is essential to find the maps and their corresponding probabilities. At each level, probabilities are computed by the ratio of sum of gray values of a child subimage to the sum of gray values of its parent subimage. This conforms the sum of four probabilities, at each level, to be unity. The ratio of the gray level value of a pixel to the sum of all gray level values of the entire image indicates the proportion of information carried by that pixel. Actually, contractive maps along with the probabilities try to approximate the ratio of each gray level value to the sum of all gray level values. So, in the proposed algorithm, it is essential to store the information regarding the sum of gray level values. Also the corresponding contractive maps are nothing but the maps from a parent subimage to its child subimages [Fig. 22.1]. The size of a parent subimage is double that of its child subimages. Hence, the map from parent subimage to its child is a contractive map.

We have already mentioned that the division of a parent subimage into its children depends on the performance of the approximation of the subimage by the Markov operators. Now if the complexity of the pixel values of the parent subimage is higher, then further division of the subimage is quite likely. On the other hand the image region where the complexity of the pixel values is low, no further division is required. In this case, if there is division, then we are losing in the sense of compression ratio. In order to avoid this problem we have introduced a simple classification scheme. The scheme classifies the child subimages into two groups according to the variability of the pixel values. If the variability is low *i.e.,* if the variance of the pixel values in the subimage is below a fixed value, called threshold, we call the subimage as smooth type. Otherwise we call it a rough type. Each pixel value in a smooth type subimage is replaced by the mean of all pixel values. The procedure can be looked upon as a condensation map. Note that under a condensation map, an image region is nothing but the copy of itself. Rough type subimages are approximated by the computed Markov operators. Hence, for each subimage we are to store either a probability value or the mean of the pixel values along with the information regarding the block type.

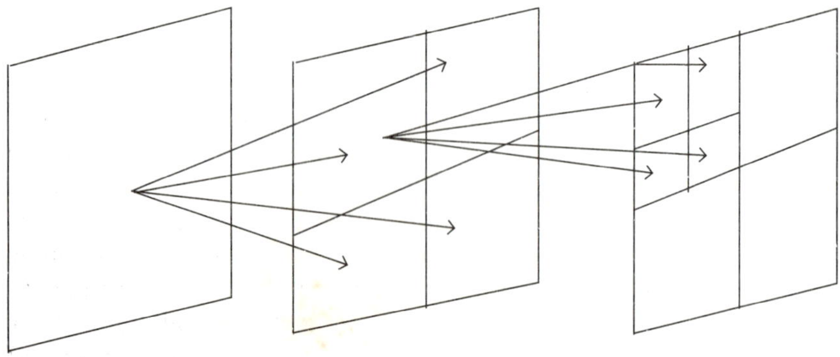

Fig. 22.1 Multiscaling type division of an image

It may be noted that there will exist a level at which no further division of the image blocks is required. When the size of a child image block becomes 1×1 [*i.e.,* the child image block is a pixel], it can't be further subdivided. It may also be observed that, in such a case, there will be a contractive map from the parent image block to the child image block such that the error in estimating the pixel value of the child image block is zero.

The description of the encoding algorithm, the computation of bit rates and the decoding process are described in the following subsections.

A. Description of the Encoding Algorithm

Step 1. Compute the sum of gray level values of the given image.

Step 2. Partition the image (I) into its four quadrants. Each quadrant is called child subimage (I_k, $k = 1, 2, 3, 4$) of I.

Step 3. Compute

(i) $$p_k = \frac{\text{sum of pixel values in } I_k}{\text{sum of pixel values in } I}; \qquad \sum_{k=1}^{4} p_k = 1.$$

(ii) Mean (I_k) = m_k (say), $k = 1, 2, 3, 4$.

(iii) Variance (I_k) = υ_k (say), $k = 1, 2, 3, 4$.

Step 4. If Variance (I_k) < Th, [Th is a prefixed value]

then approximate I_k by replacing each pixel value of I_k by m_k,

else compute $I_k^1 = p_k\, w(I)$, $k = 1, 2, 3, 4$. (A)

Here $w(I)$ is obtained by considering non overlapping windows of size 2×2 covering the entire image (I) and taking sum of four pixels within a window. Thus, the size of w (I) becomes equal to that of I_k, $k = 1, 2, 3, 4$.

Step 5. Compute I^1 by appending I_k^1, $k = 1, 2, 3, 4$. (B)

Repeat the process (A) and (B) until $I^N = I^{N+1}$, where $I_k^N = p_k.w(I^{N-1})$ is the approximation of I_k.

Note that I^N is an approximation of I by Theorem 6 [See Section 22.2]

Step 6: Check the difference between I_k and I_k^N.

If the difference is small (approximation is satisfactory) then STOP,

else replace I by I_k^1, $k = 1, 2, 3, 4$ and repeat steps 1, 2, 3, 4 and 5 until the size of I_k is equal to a prefixed value.

A schematic diagram of the encoding process is presented in Fig. 22.2.

B. Computation of Bit Rate

The complete description of an image in terms of its code, with respect to its storage or transmission requirements, is to be evaluated to get the compression ratio or bit rate. The important overhead costs which are to be considered for the proposed encoding method of an image are: *(i)* the description of the image partition, *(ii)* the nature of the blocks, *i.e.,* class information of blocks and *(iii)* the quantized values of the numerical parameters.

First of all, the sum of the gray level values or the average gray level value of the given image is to be stored. If the given image is a 8 bit/pixel image then 8 bits are required to store this average gray level value. Next a complete description of the image partition needs to be stored. Note that we have used here a multiscaling type division. At any stage, a block is either partitioned into its child blocks or remains unaltered. The partitioning of a block into its child blocks depends on the performance of the estimator of the parent block. In particular, for a parent block, there may exist either one or two or three or all four children blocks. Therefore, there are, sixteen possible coding configurations for a block at any stage and 4 bits are required for storing this information. Fig. 22.3 shows the sixteen possible configurations of a block at any stage. Each block is again, either smooth type or rough type. Thus for storing block information, we need to store one more bit for each block. Now, we are left with two most important numerical parameters, the mean gray level value of a smooth type block and probability corresponding to a block. The mean values and the probabilities are quantized and stored in the codes.

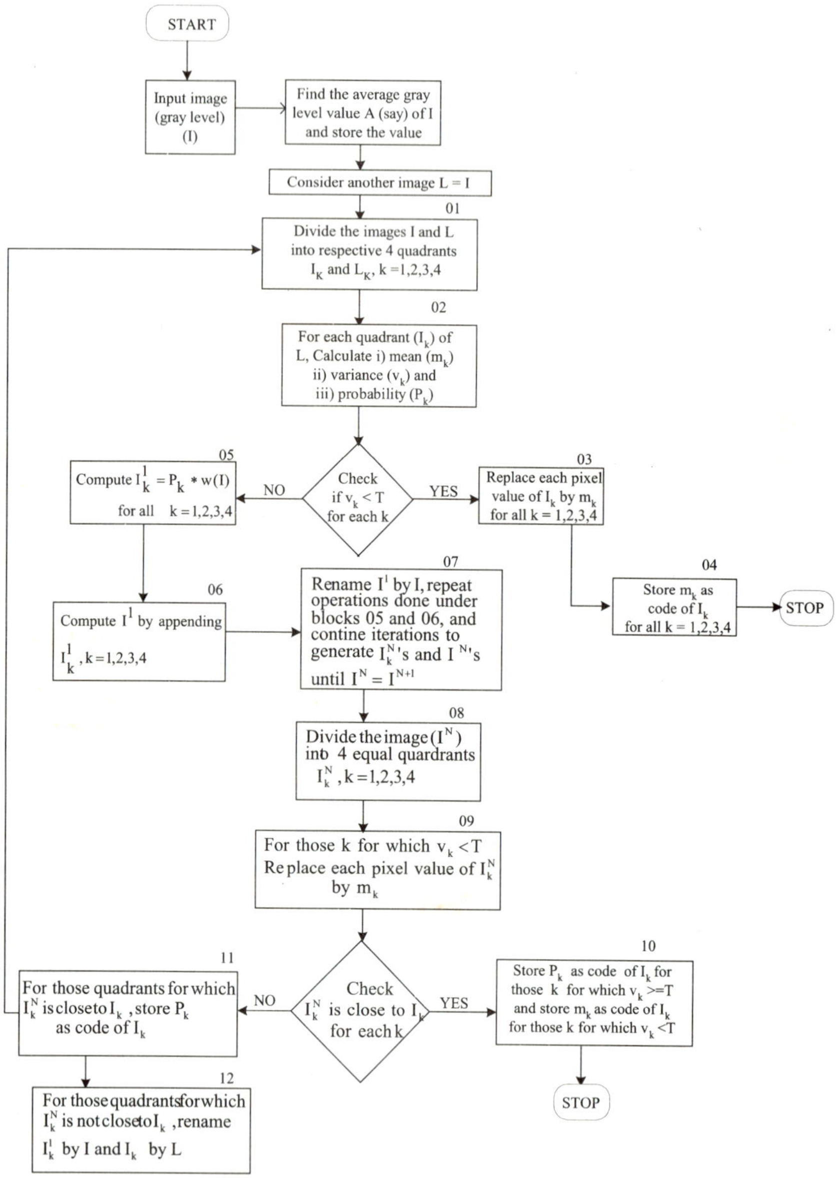

Fig. 22.2 Schematic diagram of the proposed encoding algorithm

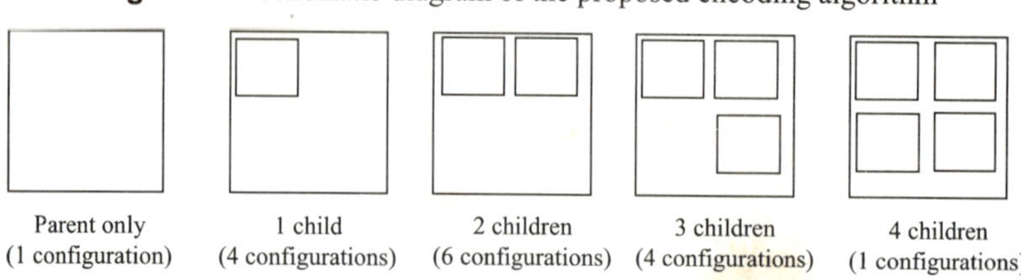

Fig. 22.3 Possible configurations of a subimage

C. Image Reconstruction from the Code

Image reconstruction is a process of decoding the obtained code. Here the decoding process is almost similar to the encoding process. The process starts with an arbitrary image with at least one pixel having nonzero pixel value. This starting image plays the role of a dummy image. In the decoding process no probabilities or contractive maps are computed. The starting image is partitioned following the partition rule stored in the codes. Using the block information, the mean gray level values or the stored probabilities and the maps are applied to the blocks of the starting image to get the stabilized value for each pixel of the starting image. These stabilized values are not the fixed points of the target image. The desired image [*i.e.,* the close approximation of the target image] is obtained by multiplying each stabilized value of the starting image by the ratio of sum of the gray level values of the original image, stored in the codes, to that of the starting image.

In the decoding, the number of iterations to get to the stabilized value of a pixel of the starting image is fixed, depending on the image size. Also, unlike the decoding of a PIFS code [3], [9], no intermediate reconstruction of the image is possible in this decoding scheme. Note that, the starting image should be such that, there exist at least one pixel with nonzero pixel value. Otherwise, whatever may be the subdivision of the image, we will always obtain the image with every pixel value being zero.

A schematic diagram of the decoding process is presented in Fig. 22.4.

22.4 IMPLEMENTATION AND RESULTS

The probabilistic approach for fractal image compression, discussed in Section 22.3 is tested with a wide range of gray scale images. We are presenting here the results obtained for some 256 × 256, 8 bits/pixel images. First of all, let us discuss the results obtained by implementing the algorithm on the benchmark image "Lena" (256 × 256, 8bits/pixel). The original image of "Lena" is shown in Fig. 22.5. The image is subdivided into four 128 × 128 subimages, each of which is encoded separately. Partitioning of each subimage has been carried out up to the level of subimages of size 2 × 2. The performance of the encoding methodology is also examined by considering the image partitioning up to the level of subimages of size 4 × 4.

For encoding the "Lena" image, the results of partitioning up to 2 × 2 subimages and 4 × 4 subimages are reported here. Also, the encoding

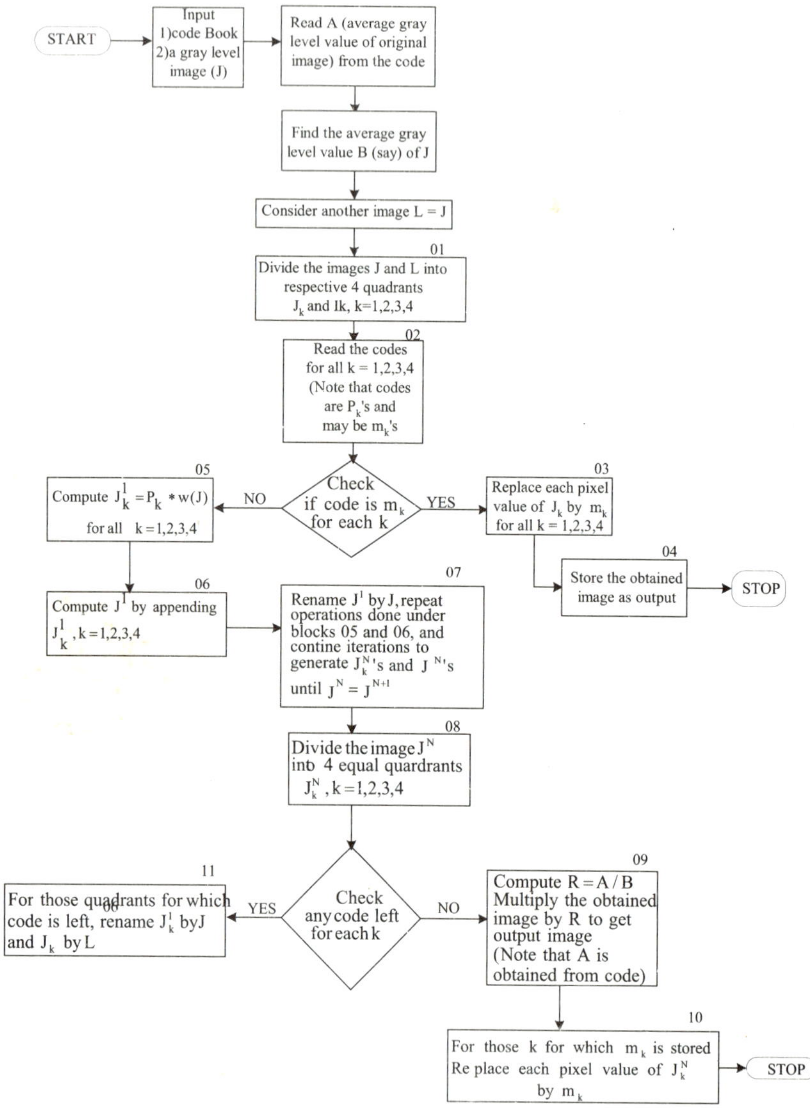

Fig. 22.4 Schematic diagram of the proposed decoding algorithm

using partitioning up to 2 × 2 subimages has been performed for different threshold values. Note that, successful approximation of an image block at any stage will be judged by the selected threshold value. Actually, the threshold is set to evaluate the error criterion (here, the error criterion is RMSE). All the test results and some statistics of both the cases are given in Table 22.1. The test result is showing how compression ratio increases with decrease in the PSNR value for encoding up to 2 × 2 subimages. The time taken for encoding is also computed to show the relative fastness of the proposed fractal image compression scheme using IFS with probabilities. The programming language used here is "c" and all the programs have been executed on a 133 MHz Silicon graphics (Indy) Workstation.

Table 22.1 *Test Results for 256 × 256, 8 Bit/Pixel "Lena" image using different threshold values*

Lowest level subimage size	Compression Ratio	PSNR, (in db)	bits/pixel (bpp)	Time elapsed (in Sec.)
4 × 4	20.1	22.43	0.40	8.34
2 × 2	3.20	30.49	2.50	23.39
2 × 2	5.08	28.23	1.58	16.40
2 × 2	8.81	27.11	0.90	10.93

The corresponding figures for the "Lena" image are shown in Fig. 22.9 to 22.12. Fig. 22.9 shows the decoded image of "Lena" where the encoding is carried out up to the subimage of size 4 × 4. Fig. 22.10, 22.11 and 22.12 are showing the decoded "Lena" for different threshold values when the encoding is processed up to the subimages of size 2 × 2. The decoding process is carried out with a starting image which is "White" image having all the gray level values fixed at 255.

Fig. 22.5 Original "Lena" image (8 bpp)

Fig. 22.6 Original "Girl" image (8 bpp)

Fig. 22.7 Original "LFA" image (8 bpp)

Fig. 22.8 Original "Seagull" image (8 bpp)

The algorithm is also tested for the "Girl" image, a "low flying aircraft (LFA)" image and a "Seagull image. All these images are 8 bit/ pixel images of size 256 × 256. The original images are shown in Figs. 22.6, 22.7 and 22.8. Experimental results of these images are shown in Table 22.2. Figs. 22.13, 22.14 and 22.15 are the decoded images of "LFA", "Girl" and "Seagull" respectively. For all the cases the starting image is considered as the "White" image having all the gray level values 255. Note that, images can also be reconstructed starting from any other image.

Table 22.2 *Test Results for several 256 × 256, 8 Bit/Pixel images*

Image	Compression Ratio	PSNR (in db)	bits/pixel (bpp)	Time elapsed (in Sec.)
Girl	10.41	27.75	0.76	9.68
LFA	4.46	24.23	1.79	15.46
Seagull	7.20	26.12	1.11	12.56

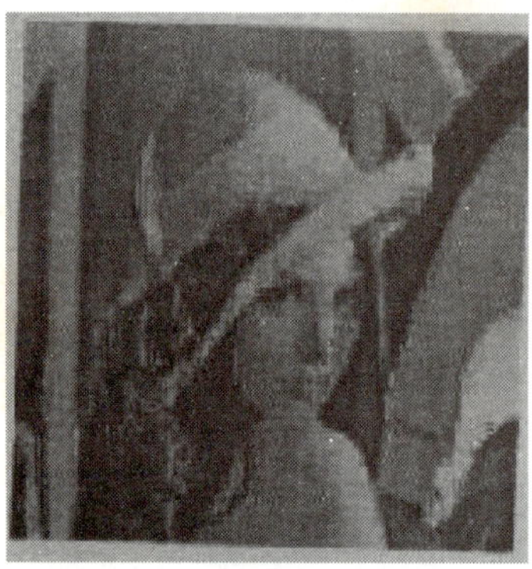

Fig. 22.9 Decoded Lena, 0.40 bpp, where subimage size is 4 × 4

Fig. 22.10 Decoded Lena where, 0.90 bpp, subimage size is 2 × 2

Fig. 22.11 Decoded Lena, 1.58 bpp, where subimage size is 2 × 2

Fig. 22.12 Decoded Lena, 2.50 bpp, where subimage size is 2 × 2

Fig. 22.13 Decoded LFA, 1.79 bpp, where subimage size is 2 × 2

Fig. 22.14 Decoded Girl, 0.76 bpp, where subimage size is 2 × 2

Fig. 22.15 Decoded Seagull, 1.11 bpp, where subimage size is 2 × 2

The proposed probabilistic approach for fractal image compression method is also compared, in terms of the computational time, with the GA based fractal image compression technique proposed by Mitra et al. [9]. The basic feature of GA based fractal image compression scheme is same as that of the scheme proposed by Jacquin [3] and is usually known as partitioned iterated function system (PIFS) based compression. A GA based compression technique tries to reduce the computational time for the implementation of the PIFS based compression technique. It has been found that almost 20 times reduction in the search space is achieved for the GA based compression technique in comparison to the usual PIFS based image compression technique. In the usual PIFS based image compression technique, an image is tiled with "range blocks", and for each range block a mapping on a larger "domain block" is found such that the transformed domain approximate the range block. The search for an appropriate domain block and transformation for each range block is carried out by exhaustive search mechanism. In GA based technique, the search is performed using GAs. Note that, the present probabilistic approach is introduced with no search mechanism. The test results of both probabilistic approach encoding and the GA based encoding techniques are presented in Table 22.3.

Table 22.3 *Results obtained by using probabilistic approach and the GA based technique for fractal image compression*

	Probabilistic approach			GA based technique		
Image	*Compression Ratio*	*PSNR (in db)*	*Time elapsed (in Sec.)*	*Compression Ratio*	*PSNR (in db)*	*Time elapsed (in Sec.)*
Lena	8.81	27.11	10.93	10.50	30.22	3141.47
Girl	10.41	27.75	9.68	11.37	30.74	2608.18
LFA	4.46	24.23	15.46	5.51	26.86	5838.17
Seagull	7.20	26.12	12.56	7.40	27.27	4240.02

It is very clear from the Table 22.3 that the proposed probabilistic approach for fractal image compression is very fast compared to the GA based fractal image compression technique. On the other hand, the compression ratio and the quality of the decoded image in terms of PSNR of the proposed method is not so impressive as compared to that of GA based technique. A few blocking effects, due to quantization, are visible in the decoded image of the present algorithm. But in respect of computational time, the proposed method is probably one of the fastest, if not the fastest.

22.5 CONCLUSIONS AND DISCUSSION

The proposed probabilistic approach for image compression is a direct outcome of the theory of IFS with probabilities. The algorithm is very fast in the sense of computational time. But at the same time, the technique is very much dependent on the partitioning scheme used. As we are using multiscaling type division to find the contractive maps and corresponding probabilities, it is assumed that, under a suitable transformation, there exists at least some similarity between image regions along this direction. But real life images need not necessarily possess similarity like this. To overcome this problem one has to divide the image up to subimages which are considerably small. Note that the algorithm will be a lossless one if one goes up to the pixel level division for every pixel. But, in that case, it would not be useful for compression as there will be hardly any compression.

The proposed method is also applicable in case of condensation maps included in the set of maps. A particular type of condensation map is used in the present case. Note that, due to this type of condensation map, each pixel value of an image region is replaced by the average of all pixel values of that region.

The present scheme is an attempt to find an image compression technique using IFS and probabilities. Some blocking effects are observed, though those are not very serious, in the final decoded image. It is true that some modifications have to be incorporated to make the algorithm more efficient to achieve a high compression ratio as well as quality decoded image. The information regarding multiscaling partition is taking a huge storage space causing reduction in the compression ratio. One way to increase compression could be to bypass this information. Towards the solution of this problem one can possibly make the multiscaling image subdivision mandatary up to a prespecified level. In particular, for the first few subdivision, one may consider all four subimages instead of going for option of selecting a few out of four depending on the image estimation obtained at that subdivision. This may reduce the burden of storing 4 bits for each subimage at each level. Another way of increasing compression could be done by adopting a lossless compression, *e.g*,. arithmetic or run length, scheme and applying it to the code obtained by the probabilistic approach.

The huge reduction in the computational time makes the present algorithm more attractive. The probabilistic approach technique for fractal image compression is at least 300 times faster than the GA based fractal image compression technique. The relative fastness of the proposed algorithm appeared to be its main feature. The method is found to be practically an online process. The fastness of the algorithm can be utilized to real time coding, for which reasonable compression may be delivered very rapidly.

References

1. M F Barnsley, *Fractals Everywhere.* New York: Academic Press, 1988.
2. M F Barnsley and L P Hurd, *Fractal Image Compression.* Massachusetts: AK Peters Ltd., 1993.
3. A E Jacquin, "Image coding based on a fractal theory of iterated contractive image transformations," *IEEE Transactions on Image Processing,* Vol. 1, no. 1, pp. 18–30, 1992.
4. A E Jacquin, "Fractal image coding : A review," *Proceedings of the IEEE,* Vol. 81, no. 10, pp. 1451–1465, 1993.
5. Y. Fisher, E. W. Jacbos, and R. D. Boss, "Fractal image compression using iterated transforms," in *Image and Text Compression* (J. A.Storer, ed.), pp. 35–61, Kluwer Academic Publishers, 1992.
6. Y Fisher, *Fractal Image Compression: Theory and Application.* New York: Springer Verlag, 1995.
7. L Thomas and F Deravi, "Region-based fractal image compression using heuristic search," *IEEE Transactions on Image Processing,* Vol. 4, no. 6, pp. 832–838, 1995.
8. Y Fisher, *Fractal Image Encoding and Analysis. NATO ASI Series F,* Vol. 159. Berlin: Springer Verlag, 1998.

9. S K Mitra, C A Murthy, and M K Kundu, "Technique for fractal image compression using genetic algorithm," *IEEE Transactions on Image Processing*, Vol. 7, no. 4, pp. 586–593, 1998.
10. J Hutchinson, "Fractal and self similarity," *Indiana Univ. J. Math.*, Vol. 30, pp. 713–747, 1981.
11. J H Elton, "An ergodic theorem for iterated maps," *Ergodic theory and Dynamical Systems,* Vol. 7, pp. 481–488, 1987.
12. B Forte and E R Vrscay, "Solving the inverse problem for measures using iterated function systems: a new approach," *Adv. appl. Prob.,* Vol. 27, pp. 800–820, 1995.
13. S Graf, "Barnsley's scheme for the fractal encoding of images," *Journal of Complexity,* Vol. 8, pp. 72–78, 1992.
14. F Dudbridge, "Linear time fractal coding schemes," in *Fractal Image Encoding and Analysis, NATO ASI Series F,* Vol. 159 (Y. Fisher, ed.), pp. 133–137, Springer Verlag, Berlin, 1998.

23

LUT base Color Quantization for Image Compression

Pinakpani Pal[1], **Kaushik Dutta**[2]

ABSTRACT

Resolution and depth of colors in PDA displays are smaller, making it difficult to display "**true**" color image (24 bit) from internet through wireless networks. Also access of such images will take longer time over slow wireless networks as the size (bytes) of true color images are larger than the corresponding low bit images. We present a methodology to determine the colors of a 4-bit palette (for LUT) which best represents 24-bit color combinations present in the image (there by reducing its size) yet retaining its visual appeal to an appreciable extent.

Key words: Color Image; Color Quantization Algorithm; Octree.

23.1 INTRODUCTION

Internet has become a standard way of getting various information and in many cases such information is represented as images such as satellite images in weather sites and images in news sites. Due to proliferation of high resolution digital camera, most of these images are in true form i.e. are represented by 24 bit color palettes.[3] These true color images can easily be displayed in modern desktop computers, but the internet is being accessed now days not only by desktops but also from PDAs (palm devices such as Cell phones, Palm Pilots. Palm computers). The resolution and depth of color in PDA displays are smaller than desktop monitors.[4] So high resolution true colors images can not be displayed as it is in such PDAs. Because of this separate images are prepared for mobile content of the Internet or in some cases ICAP technology is used to convert the content targeted towards desktop computers to content suitable for displaying in palm devices in web sites or proxies.

Moreover size of true images are much larger than the corresponding 8 bit or 16 bit images. So even if in next few years the display

---

1 ECSU, Indian Statistical Institute, Kolkata

2 Decision Science and Information Systems, College of Business, Florida International University.

3 8 bit each for red, green and blue bands providing 16.8 million ($2^8 \times 2^8 \times 2^8$) color combinations.

4 Very high end PDA such as Hewlett Packard iPAQ H2215 Pocket has 16 bit color pallets with screen resolution of 240×320.

technology of PDAs gets matured to display true color images, the access of such images will take longer time over slow wireless networks. Internet access from PDAs typically happen through wireless networks. The wireless network bandwidth of PDAs are much smaller than the broadband network bandwidth available for desktop computers. The modern 3G wireless network provides internet bandwidth of just 10 Kbps compared to 1.54 Mbps available through T1 or broadband cable/DSL connections from desktop computers. So even if in near future PDAs be able to display true images, it will take longer time to fetch such true color images through slow wireless network available from PDAs. The speed of wireless data transfer is so far behind the data transfer rate available in wired world, it is not likely to match in near future. In such environment it become essential to transfer true color images to much lower bit images of much lower size that will be transferred through wireless network in much less time. Such smaller size images are required to protect the view of the image as perceived by the end user to be kept intact as far as possible.

This paper introduces a variation of one such popular techniques of transferring true color images to just 16 color images that give better accuracy of the image with much lower size that can easily be transferred through slow wireless network. Such techniques can be added into ICAP proxy to do the image transfer suitable for a particular PDA requesting the image.

Different approaches can be taken for solving this problem. One may choose any standard classification algorithm like mean distance classifiers and may be even *fuzzy c-means* classification technique [5]. Algorithms like Min-cut [6], Color Quantization techniques such as *popularity algorithm* [7] are known to give satisfactory results. However almost all of them suffer from the serious drawback that they are extremely CPU and memory intensive and thereby impossible to execute online when such true images are being requested by an user.

The other alternative is to use *dithering patterns*, which are ordered combination of colored dots to represent a specific shade of color. However, even the sophisticated Floyed Steinberg dithering equation [3] has the problems of increasing the image size excessively with the decrease in image resolution and loss of image details. Thus dithering technique does not serve our basic objective of reducing the image sizes by having less number of colors (PDA displays have small screen resolution).[5]

Coming back to our problem of mapping 16.8 million combination to 16 colors, we concentrate on *color quantization* [4] approach in detail. The novelty of octree data structure and its dynamic updation give the unique advantage of implementation in Internet where online processing of such images are required. However, the straightforward extension of this algorithm to detect 16 color palette from "true" color image does not perform upto the mark. Our variation of "octree" approach in this respect has improved the image quality to a great extent without sacrificing in terms of CPU and memory. Our specific contributions are as follows:

- Finding optimum 16 color (red, green and blue) combinations out of maximum possible 16.8 million colors.
- The methodology retains the visual appeal of the original image to a great extent. It could be implemented with very limited memory and CPU making it perfect for online processing of images in the internet.

In the next section we detail color image fundamentals. In section 23.4, we present our approach followed by results and discussion.

23.2 COLOR IMAGE FUNDAMENTALS

The "true" color images keep 24-bit information (8-bit each for the three primary colors - red, blue and green) for each pixel. In case of 8-bit or 4-bit palette images the original palette is kept to some fixed location in the image file itself [2] (e.g. PCX, TIFF, JPEG, GIF file formats) and each pixel value represents an index to that palette. Displaying such image precedes dynamically setting up the display device's color palette and subsequently displaying images using that color palette.

23.3 COLOR QUANTIZATION

Color quantization groups "similar" pixel colors and replaces them with a single quantized color having visual effect comparable to the original color. This mapping method gives, in effect, a suitable set of quantized colors for a given set of colors (present in the image concerned). This can be done by first classifying the given set of colors into a predetermined number (k) of groups, mostly restricted by the hardware and the associated compiler. Each group is then replaced by a single color that is visually closest. In our case the value of k is 16.

---

[5] Images in the Internet are popularly represented in some compressed format such as JPEG or GIF. Size of such image format to a large extent depends on how many color requires to display the image.

The quality of the quantization therefore varies depending on various factors.

- The number of distinct colors in the original image.
- How intelligently the algorithm identifies the different colors and groups them.
- How the algorithm chooses a color which is visually closest to that group.

Till date many quantization [1] algorithms have been proposed, each having its own merits and demerits. One of the oldest algorithms is "**uniform quantization**" [4]. This approach divides the three dimensional color space into *k* colors. But the disadvantage of this process is that it is totally image independent; the quantization process may take into account those set of colors which may not even present in the image itself. Naturally, one does not get the most suitable representation of colors that are present in the original image.

"**Popularity**" algorithm has been proposed by Heckbert [7] that takes care of only those colors present in the image. It chooses the most frequently occurring colors to represent all the colors in the original image. Other suitable modifications of this algorithm have been developed subsequently in order to have a better visual effect. But the major disadvantage of these algorithms is that they require sufficient memory and processing time to store counters for each original color. Hence to implement them in online image processing at ICAP or original web site will be difficult due to its inherent requirement of high memory and CPU. In the next section we present our approach followed by result and discussion.

23.4 PROPOSED METHOD

Our aim is to determine the colors of a 4-bit palette (16 different colors) from a 24-bit color combinations present in an image which retains its visual appeal to an appreciable extent. The methodology must be implemented with limited memory available in application servers of proxies. The memory of application servers and proxy in a 32 bit machine is limited by 4GB. If such image conversion is required for multiple images at the same time for thousands of users connected to the site at the same time, the availability of memory and CPU will be a big concern particularly with the fact that modern application servers and proxies are already overburden to do multiple other complex tasks of running a full grown enterprise application. This limitation can be solved by applying octree color quantization [4] technique, however, the straightforward extension of this algorithm for our problem does not perform upto the mark to give a very accurate impression of the true color image.

23.4.1 Octree Color Quantization

With the help of an octree one can dynamically choose the most suitable set of quantized colors. The data structure used for this scheme is an octree with each node having a maximum of eight child nodes as shown in Fig. 23.1. A node with no child node is called a leaf-node. Nodes between the root-node and leaf-node are called intermediate nodes. For octree color quantization algorithm each leaf of the octree represents a color palette. The number of leaves in an octree represents the number of colors present in the image provided the octree is allowed to grow without any restriction. The intermediate nodes represent the path leading to a class of leaf-nodes. A complete octree has 16.8 million colors. But the octree color quantization algorithm stores only those leaf-nodes that represents the quantized colors and the intermediate nodes that lead to them from the tree's root.

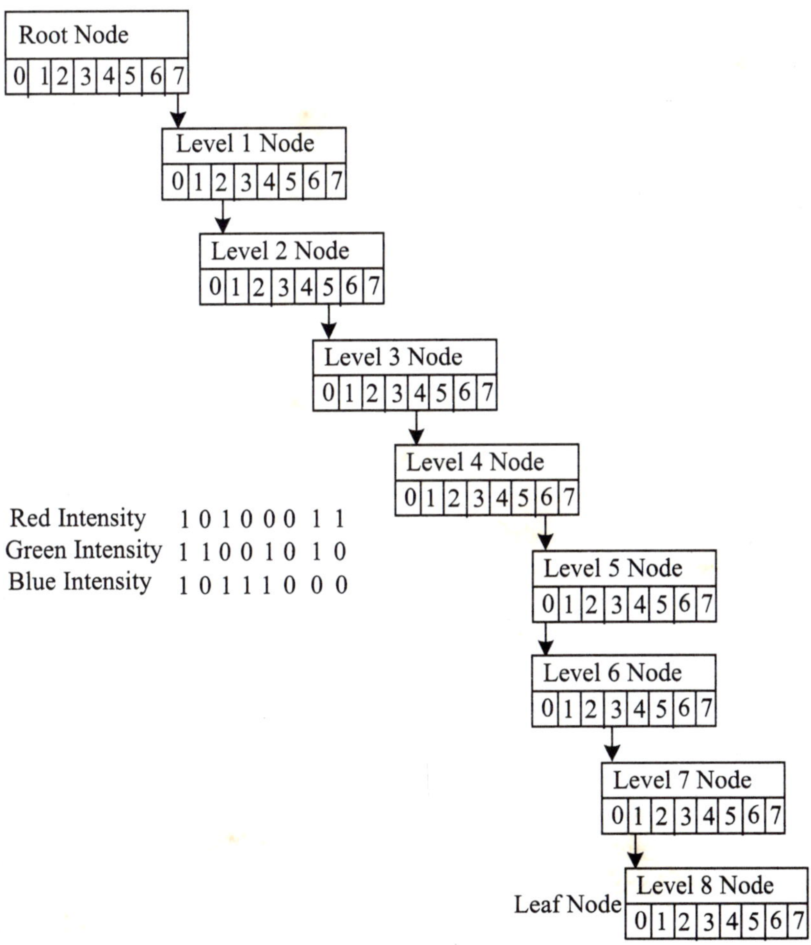

Fig. 23.1 Octree data structure

23.4.2 The Octree Quantization Algorithm

Octree color quantization [4] is a two-pass process. We have implemented the first pass in our method. In the first pass, it sequentially examines each pixel of a 24-bit color image and if necessary, inserts its color into the octree data structure. For inserting a 24-bit color in the octree, first the most significant bits of each 8-bit red, green and blue components are considered and the node represented by this 3-bit number is an intermediate node to which the color belongs. In Fig. 23.1 these bits are 0, 1 and 0 respectively and the third child-node (numbered 2) of the root is the intermediate node. Repeating this process for the next significant bit of each above mentioned byte (1, 1 and 1 in Fig. 23.1), places the color in the next level of the octree hierarchy. The algorithm maintains a pixel count for each node. When the number of inserted color (i.e. current number of leaf-nodes) exceeds a predetermined limit *k*, octree seeks to group similar colors in such a way so that the current number of leaf-nodes reduces to *k* or less. Any intermediate node with two or more children is a candidate of such group. Such nodes with the largest depth represent path of the color which is closest to one another, so they should be grouped first. If there are more than one such group there are two options to choose either the node with the smallest pixel count or the node with the largest pixel count. In the implementation of octree, in our methodology, we have chosen the node with the largest pixel count. The pseudo code is given below:

if number of leaf-node ≥ *k*

> *select the node at the deepest level in the tree which has maximum value of* **pixel_count**
>
> *delete all its descendants*
>
> *color of the node* ← *weighted average of the color value of descendants leaf-nodes*
>
> *mark the node as* **leaf_node**

endif

This in effect replace the detail color shading information by a single similar color. Actually by doing so we are reducing intra class distances and increasing the inter class distances. For example more weightage is given to distinguish shades of yellow from shades of red rather than to distinguish different shades of yellow among themselves. The color that represents the group is the sum of each primary color divided by the node's pixel count. After the first pass is over the octree contains maximum of *k* leaf-nodes.

In the second pass, it reads the image pixel sequentially. Each pixel color is now guaranteed to have an existing path in the octree to a leaf-node. The average color associated with this node represents the quantized color for the pixel.

This algorithm works well for $k = 256$, but for our problem ($k = 16$) does not perform upto the mark. Therefore we have modified the second pass and introduced hierarchical mapping to improve the visual quality.

23.4.3 Hierarchical mapping

Let the given color image (24-bit) is represented by matrix of vector $\{f(i, j)\} = \{(f_r(i, j)\ f_g(i, j)\ f_b(i, j))^T\}$ and $C = \{c_0, c_1, c_2, ..., c_{L-1}\}$ where c_l represents the lth color in the palette as $\{r_l, g_l, b_l\}$ which is generated from the input image $\{f(i, j)\}$ through the first pass of octree quantization algorithm (for $k = 256$, $L \leq k$). The proposed mapping may be described as

$$f'(i, j) = c_l \text{ if } d(f(i, j), c_l) < d(f(i, j), c_m),\ \forall m \text{ and } l \neq m$$

where d is the euclidean distance defined as

$$d(f(i, j), c_l) = \left[(f_r(i, j) - r_l)^2 + (f_g(i, j) - g_l)^2 + (f_b(i, j) - b_l)^2\right]^{1/2}$$

This gives $(f'(i, j)\}$ an intermediate color image with maximum 256 different color palettes.

However we have used

$$d(f(i, j), c_l) = \left[\,|\,f_r(i, j) - r_l\,| + |\,f_g(i, j) - g_l\,| + |\,f_b(i, j) - b_l\,|\right]$$

which produces exactly similar mapping but incurs less computational cost.

The octree quantization method is then applied on $\{f'(i, j)\}$ for $k =$ 16. The output image $\{f''(i, j)\}$ is an image with maximum 16 different color palettes (stored in LUT).

Since the mapping is done in two steps, we call it "Hierarchical mapping".

23.5 RESULT

Fig. 23.2 *(a)*, *(b)* and *(c)* are "true" color images. These images are mapped to 16 colors (4-bit palette) through the proposed method. The results are shown in Fig. 23.4 *(a)*, *(b)* and *(c)* respectively. The results of the straightforward extension of the octree algorithm to 16 color are shown in Fig. 23.3 *(a)*, *(b)* and *(c)* respectively. As mentioned in the introduction, it fails to retain the appeal of the original image, if compared with Fig. 23.3.

Table 23.1 supports our subjective claim. We have defined signal to noise ratio (S.N.R.) as

$$S.N.R. = 10\log\left[\frac{\sum_{i=0,\ j=0}^{row,\ col}(f(i,\ j))^2}{\sum_{i=0,\ j=0}^{row,\ col}(f(i,\ j) - f_{result}(i,\ j))^2}\right]$$

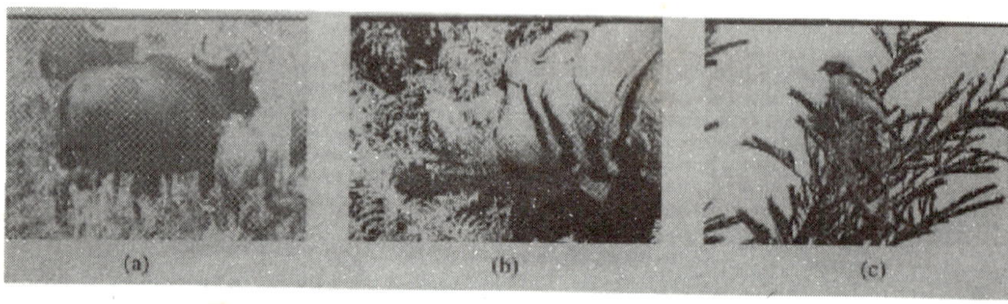

Fig. 23.2 Original image (a) Mosh (b) Gandar (c) Pakhi

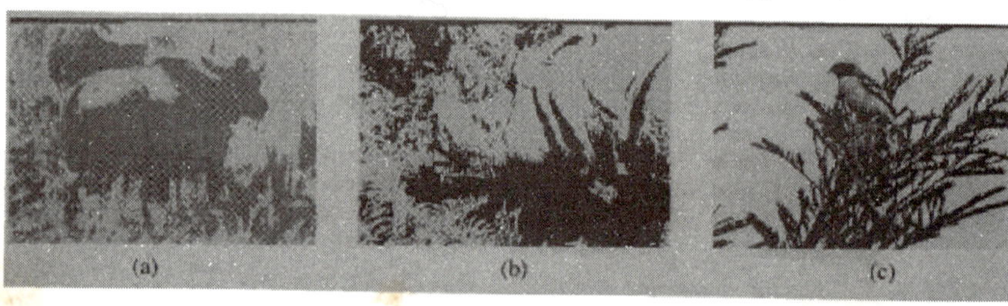

Fig. 23.3 Output of octree quantization (a) Mosh (b) Gandar (c) Pakhi

Fig. 23.4 Output of proposed method (a) Mosh (b) Gandar (c) Pakhi

The limitation of the algorithm is that larger the number of distinct colors present in the image poorer the visual effect.

Table 23.1 *S.N.R. (in dB) for octree quantization and proposed method*

	Mosh	**Gandar**	**Pakhi**
Octree Quantization	21.765	14.185	18.496
Proposed method	24.868	17.217	22.316

23.6 DISCUSSION

Transferring high resolution true color images through slow wireless network and displaying such images in limited resource PDA display is a major challenge to the graphic researchers. We have shown that our approach attracts attention considering image quality. This is more so that a huge lossy compression from 16.8 million to 16 could not distort the display quality to a large extent.

Table 23.2 *Color Palette examples*

Palette	*r*	*g*	*b*
Level	01234567	01234567	01234567
c_x	01100000	10100000	00100000
c_y	01011100	10011100	00011100
c_z	01011111	10011111	00011111

The important aspect that needs to be investigated in more details is whether the quality of visual appeal that is retained to a great extent could be substantiated with theoretical objective backup rather than subjective claim. Formation of octree is based on taking sequentially 1 bit from each 8-bit red, green and blue components of pixel. This may group two nearly equal palettes in two different branches. For example consider the color palettes in Table 23.2, palettes c_x and c_y are separated from 2nd level while forming the octree. The palette c_z although very close to c_x follow the same path of c_y upto 5th level. After node reduction c_y and c_z may be grouped together with some more palettes and represented by a single palette and similarly c_x by some other palette. These palettes depend upon all the palettes and their weightage present in those group. Therefore c_x and c_z are better represented by any one of these two resultant palettes. Our mapping scheme reduces such miss-classification.

References

1. B Chanda and D Dutta Mazumder, *Digital Image Processing and Analysis,* Printice Hall of India, 2000.
2. Ben Ezzell, *PC Magazine Windows* 3.1 *Graphics Programming,* BPB Publications, 1994.
3. Craig A Lindley, *Practical image processing in C : acquisition, manipulation and storage : hardware, software images and text,* Canada : John Wiley & Sons, Inc., 1991.
4. Ian Ashdown, Octree Color Quantization, *C/C++ users journal,* Vol. 3, pp. 31–44, 1995.
5. J C Bezdek,*Pattern recognition with fuzzy objective function algorithms,* NY, USA: Plenum Press, 1981.
6. J D Foley and A van Dam and S K Feiner and J F Huges, *Computer graphics principles and practice,* NY, USA: Addison Wesley, 1992.
7. P S Heckbert, Color image quantization for frame buffer display, *ACM SIGGRAPH'82*, Vol.16:3, pp. 297–307, 1982.

UNIT V

IMAGE ANALYSIS AND RECOGNITION

24

Image Segmentation using Graylevel Co-occurrence Matrix

B Chanda and D Dutta Majumder[1]

ABSTRACT

One of the most popular and economic techniques for image segmentation is graylevel thresholding. In this paper, some methods of threshold selection using graylevel co-occurrence matrix are discussed. Some of them are already reported and are well known. The rest are suggested in this report and are conceptually different from the former ones. Experimental results reveal that newly proposed techniques are more effective for segmenting the real-world noisy images.

Keywords : Image Segmentation; Graylevel; Thresholding; Real World Noisy Image; Scene Analysis.

24.1 INTRODUCTION

Scene analysis and image interpretation require images to be segmented into meaningful parts. Segmentation is basically a process of pixel classification which extracts the regions by assigning the individual pixels to classes. One of the most useful and economic techniques for image segmentation is graylevel thresholding which extracts the homogeneous regions by classifying pixels based on their graylevels. The main problem of this technique is the selection of threshold. In general, threshold is selected using graylevel histogram. Weszka [1] has surveyed a number of threshold selection techniques using histograms. Informations provided by histograms is often found to be inadequate to select a proper threshold. In such cases, graylevel co-occurrence matrix can be an aid to threshold selection.

Graylevel co-occurrence matrix gives an overall idea about the spatial variation of graylevel in image data. Different workers [2,3,4,5] have measured different properties from this matrix for all possible threshold values. Finally, proper threshold is selected corresponding to the optimum value of the measurement. Graylevel co-occurrence matrix has also been used in texture analysis and remote sensing applications [6,7].

---

1 This work is funded by the Department of Electronics, Govt. of India [No. 2(176)/84 – TDID].
Electronics and Communication Sciences Unit, Indian Statistical Institute, Calcutta, India.

This paper makes an attempt to study different measures using co-occurrence matrix and their use in threshold selection for image segmentation. Section 24.2 is devoted for this purpose. Section 24.3 describes experimental results using the approaches described in section 24.2. Finally, concluding remarks are sited in section 24.4.

24.2 DIFFERENT MEASURES OF IMAGE PROPERTIES

Let the discrete variable m represents the graylevel of pixel (j, k) and the discrete variable n represents the graylevel of pixel $(j - d \sin \theta, k + d \cos \theta)$ of a L-level graytone image $[g]$ i.e., $[g] = \{g(j, k) \mid j = 0, 1, 2,..., M - 1; k = 0, 1, 2, ..., N - 1\}$ and $m, n \in \{0, 1, 2, ..., L - 1\}$. We are interested in considering the co-occurrence of graylevels in pairs of pixels where one is lying at a distance of 'd' in the direction θ with respect to the other. Here we take value of d equal to 1 and θ as an integral multiple of $\frac{\pi}{2}$.

Now elements of graylevel co-occurrence matrix $[C_\theta]$ for the direction θ can be defined as

$$C_{\theta,m,n} = \sum_{j=0}^{M-1} \sum_{k=0}^{n-1} \#[g(j, k) = m \wedge g(j - \sin\theta, k + \cos\theta) = n] \tag{1}$$

where # $[.\wedge.]$ is equal to 1 if the argument is true and is equal to 0 if the argument is false. The element $C_{\theta,m,n}$ gives the frequency that a pixel having graylevels n occurs adjacent to a pixel having graylevel m in the direction θ. Considering all the directions, the co-occurrence matrix is obtained as

$$[C] = \{C_{m,n}\} = \frac{1}{4}([C_0] + [C_{\pi/2}] + [C_\pi] + [C_{3\pi/2}]) \tag{2}$$

Since $[C_\pi] = [C_0]^T$ and $[C_{3\pi/2}] = [C_{\pi/2}]^T$, Eq. (2) can be simplified to

$$[C] = \frac{1}{4}([C_0] + [C_0]^T + [C_{\pi/2}] + [C_{\pi/2}]^T)$$

So [C] is a symmetric matrix of size $L \times L$ and its elements are nonnegative, i.e.,

$$C_{m,n} = C_{n,m} \text{ and } C_{m,n} \geq 0.$$

For simplicity let us assume $g(j, N) = g(j, 0)$, $g(j, -1) = g(j, N - 1)$, $g(M, k) = g(0, k)$ and $g(-1, k) = g(M - 1, k)$

Then

$$\sum_{m=0}^{L-1} C_{m,i} = \sum_{n=0}^{L-1} C_{i,n} = h_g(i) \tag{3}$$

$h_g(i)$ is the ith entry of the graylevel histogram of the image, since both m and n represent the same physical quantity, i.e. the graylevel present in the image.

Let t be the graylevel threshold that maps the original image into two distinct sets of regions R_1 and R_2. This mapping consequently divides the graylevel co-occurrence matrix into four nonoverlapping blocks as shown in Fig. 24.1.

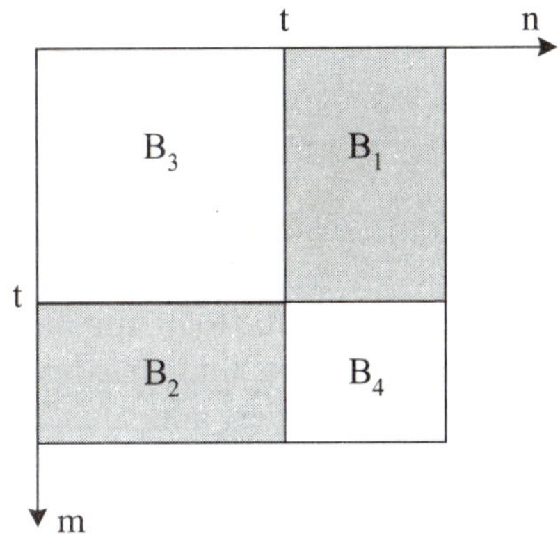

Fig. 24.1 Four non-overlapping blocks of graylevel co-occurrence matrix where t is value of threshold.

Respective blocks of [C] are representing:

(i) the co-occurrence of graylevel in region R_1 say, i.e., those $C_{m,n}$ for which $m \le t$ and $n \le t$ (shaded area B_3);

(ii) the co-occurrence of graylevel in region R_2, i.e., those $C_{m,n}$ for which $m > t$ and $n > t$ (shaded area B_4); and

(iii) the co-occurrence of graylevels in the border region of R_1 and R_2, *i.e.*, those $C_{m,n}$ for which either $m \le t$ and $n > t$ (shaded area B_1) or $m > t$ and $n \le t$ (shaded area B_2).

The methods of threshold selection using co-occurrence matrix can be divided into two classes. One looks, directly or indirectly, for the threshold for which number of pairs of border pixels i.e., sum of $C_{m,n}$ over the blocks B_1 and B_2 of Fig. 24.1 be minimum. In other words, it searches for a threshold which segments the image into the largest homogeneous regions possible. Measures like 'Busyness' [3], 'conditional probability' [4] and 'entropy' belong to this class.

Busyness Measure

Busyness measure [3] for threshold t can be defined as

$$\text{Busy}(t) = \sum_{m=0}^{t} \sum_{n=t+1}^{L-1} C_{m,n} + \sum_{m=t+1}^{L-1} \sum_{n=0}^{t} C_{m,n} \tag{4}$$

for t = 0, 1, 2, ..., L – 2. The method for selecting the threshold is as follows:

Search for minima in Busy(t). Select the value of t as threshold which corresponds to minimum among these minimas, if image contains only two types of regions. If image contains more than two types of regions, then every value of t corresponding to every minima is taken as distinct threshold.

Eq. (4) can also be written as

$$\text{Busy}(t) = MN - \left(\sum_{m=0}^{t} \sum_{n=0}^{t} C_{m,n} + \sum_{m=t+1}^{L-1} + \sum_{n=t+1}^{L-1} C_{m,n} \right), \quad (5)$$

for t = 0, 1, 2, …., L – 2. For acceptable threshold, for which Busyness measure is minimum among minimas, the portion within parentheses on right hand side of Eq.(5) which gives the total number of pixels in region R_1 and R_2 respectively is maximum among maximas. That means the threshold segments the image into largest homogeneous region possible. So the method is useful for segmenting images which consist of large smooth regions.

Again, computational cost of Busyness measure can be reduced by using the following recurrence relationship:

$$\text{Busy}(0) = 2\sum_{n=1}^{L-1} C_{0,n}$$

$$\text{Busy}(t) = \text{Busy}(t-1) + 2\left[\sum_{n=t+1}^{L-1} C_{t,n} - \sum_{m=0}^{t-1} C_{m,t} \right]$$

for t = 1, 2, 3, ….., $L-2$.

Conditional Probability

Deravi and Pal [4] measured the probability of pixel (j – sin θ, k + cos θ) lying in R_2 when (j, k) is known to lie in R_1 and of pixel (j – sin θ, k + cos θ) lying in R_1 when (j, k) is known to lie in R_2. So this conditional probability for a threshold t may be expressed as

$$\begin{aligned} \text{Cond. prob.}(t) &= \text{Prob.}\,(g(j - \sin\theta,\, k + \cos\theta) > t \mid g(j,k) \le t) \\ &\quad + \text{Prob.}\,(g(j - \sin\theta,\, k + \cos\theta) \le t \mid g(j,k) > t) \\ &= \frac{\text{Prob.}\,(g(j - \sin\theta,\, k + \cos\theta) > t,\ g(j,k) \le t)}{\text{Prob.}\,(g(j,k) \le t)} \\ &\quad + \frac{\text{Prob.}\,(g(j - \sin\theta,\, k + \cos\theta) \le t,\ g(j,k) > t)}{\text{Prob.}\,(g(j,k) > t)} \end{aligned}$$

Hence, from co-occurrence matrix we can write

$$\text{Cond. prob.}(t) = \frac{\sum_{m=0}^{t}\sum_{n=t+1}^{L-1} P_{m,n}}{\sum_{m=0}^{t}\sum_{n=0}^{L-1} P_{m,n}} + \frac{\sum_{m=t+1}^{L-1}\sum_{n=0}^{t} P_{m,n}}{\sum_{m=t+1}^{L-1}\sum_{n-0}^{L-1} P_{m,n}}, \tag{6}$$

for $t = 0, 1, 2, \ldots, L-2$, where $P_{m,n} = C_{m,n}/MN$.

Simplifying Eq., (6), we obtain

$$\text{Cond. prob.}(t) = \frac{MN\,Busy(t)}{2\sum_{i=0}^{t} h_g(i)\,[MN - \sum_{i=0}^{t} h_g(i)]}. \tag{7}$$

For this measure also a recurrence relationship similar to that for Busyness measure can be established.

However, for the image consisting of large homogeneous regions, the probability of pairs of pixels of which one is lying in R_1 and other in R_2, i.e., the probability of border pairs is less. So in this case also, threshold is selected in a similar way as in case of Busyness measures and satisfactory result for some images can be achieved.

Entropy Measure

Both the measures described above, directly or indirectly, counts the pairs of border pixels. Here is another measure, namely entropy or information content of border pixels, of similar category and is defined as

$$\text{Entropy}(t) = -\sum_{m=0}^{t}\sum_{n=t+1}^{L-1} P_{m,n}\log P_{m,n} - \sum_{m=t+1}^{L-1}\sum_{n=0}^{t} P_{m,n}\log P_{m,n} \tag{8}$$

for $t = 0, 1, 2, \ldots, L-2$. Since $\log P_{m,n}$ is a monotonic increasing function of $P_{m,n}$, then approach to select graylevel threshold is similar to that using Busyness measure. But the present measure has an advantage that it takes care of distribution $P_{m,n}$ (or $C_{m,n}/MN$) over areas B_1 and B_2 of Fig. 24.1 unlike Busyness measure which considers only aggregate of $C_{m,n}$ over these areas. To reduce computational cost following recurrence relationship can be used.

$$\text{Entropy}(0) = -2\sum_{n=1}^{L-1} P_{0,n}\log P_{0,n}$$

$$\text{Entropy}(t) = \text{Entropy}(t-1) + 2\left[\sum_{m=0}^{t-1} P_{m,t}\log P_{m,t} - \sum_{n=t+1}^{L-1} P_{t,n}\log P_{t,n}\right]$$

for $t = 1, 2, 3, \ldots, L-2$.

Other class of methods for threshold selection defines a suitable function of $C_{m,n}$ and then looks for the threshold for which the function attains an optimum value. Measures like 'average contrast' [5] and 'average entropy' belong to this class.

Average Contrast Measure

It is known that, in an image, contrast is maximum at the regions where different types of regions meet. So those $C_{m,n}$, where pixel having graylevel m and pixel having graylevel n lie in different types of regions, are responsible for the maximum contrast and the magnitude of contrast is an even function of difference in graylevels, i.e., $(m - n)$. Average contrast per pixel in the border region for the threshold t can be defined as [5].

$$\text{Av.cont.}(t) = \frac{\sum_{m=0}^{t}\sum_{n=t+1}^{L-1}(m-n)^2 C_{m,n}}{\sum_{m=0}^{t}\sum_{n=t+1}^{L-1} C_{m,n}} + \frac{\sum_{m=t+1}^{L-1}\sum_{n=0}^{t}(m-n)^2 C_{m,n}}{\sum_{m=t+1}^{L-1}\sum_{n=0}^{t} C_{m,n}} \tag{9}$$

For $t = 0, 1, 2, \ldots, L - 2$.

Average contrast can also be defined incorporating human visual response, specifically logarithmic response to brightness (Weber's law), as

$$\text{Av.cont.}(t) = \frac{\sum_{m=0}^{t}\sum_{n=t+1}^{L-1}\frac{|m-n|}{\min\{n,n\}} C_{m,n}}{\sum_{m=0}^{t}\sum_{n=t+1}^{L-1} C_{m,n}} + \frac{\sum_{m=t+1}^{L-1}\sum_{n=0}^{t}\frac{|m-n|}{\min\{m,n\}} C_{m,n}}{\sum_{m=t+1}^{L-1}\sum_{n=0}^{t} C_{m,n}} \tag{10}$$

for $t = 0, 1, 2, \ldots, L - 2$. However, Eq. (10) is not treated further in this report. Eq. (9) can be simplified to

$$\text{Av.cont.}(t) = \frac{\sum_{m=0}^{t}\sum_{n=t+1}^{L-1}(m-n)^2 C_{m,n}}{\text{Busy}\ (t)} \tag{11}$$

The method for selecting the threshold based on this measure is as follows:

Search for maxima in Av.cont. (t). Select the value of t as threshold which corresponds to maximum among these maximas, if image contains only two types of regions. If image contains more than two types of regions, then every value of t corresponding to every maxima is taken as distinct threshold.

Eq. (11) reveals that maximum among maximas found in Av.cont. (t) may not correspond to minimum among minimas found in Busy (t). So this method of threshold selection is conceptually different from those described earlier.

Average Entropy Measure

It is observed that edge points play the most important role in detecting and interpreting an object in an image by human observer. So one may argue that average entropy per pixel in the border region should be maximum. Average entropy per pixel for a threshold t may be defined as

$$\text{Av.ent.}(t) = \frac{\sum_{m=0}^{t}\sum_{n=t+1}^{L-1} P_{m,n}\log P_{m,n}}{\sum_{m=0}^{t}\sum_{n=t+1}^{L-1} C_{m,n}} - \frac{\sum_{m=t+1}^{L-1}\sum_{n=0}^{t} P_{m,n}\log P_{m,n}}{\sum_{m=t+1}^{L-1}\sum_{n=0}^{t} C_{m,n}} \tag{12}$$

for $t = 0, 1, 2, \ldots, L-2$.

Since, [C] is a symmetric matrix, Eq. (12) can be simplified to

$$\text{Av.ent.}(t) = \frac{\text{Entropy}(t)}{\text{Busy}(t)} \tag{13}$$

Eq.(13) reveals that a recurrence relationship for Average entropy measure can be found out to reduce computational cost. The approach to select the graylevel threshold is similar to that using Average contrast.

Spatial Variation Measure

Another new method of threshold selection may be described using Busyness measure and spatial homogeneity. Let us first compute average spatial variation V in graylevel over entire image, which is in other words average contrast, using the relation

$$V = \left[\frac{1}{MN}\sum_{m=0}^{L-1}\sum_{n=0}^{L-1}(m-n)^2\, C_{m,n}\right]^{1/2}. \tag{14}$$

Now the number of pixels K' for which spatial variation in graylevel is not more than average spatial variation over entire image is obtained by

$$K' = \sum_{m=0}^{L-1}\sum_{i=-V'}^{V'} C_{m,\,m+i} \tag{15}$$

where $V' = [V]$, i.e. V' is the greatest integer not exceeding V. So we can assume that K' number of pixels lying in the homogeneous region of the image. Then $(MN - K')$ should be the number of pixels lying in nonhomogeneous region. Busyness measure also tries to find same physical quantity for different values of threshold. But since $[C_\theta]$ cannot exhibit any indication for horizontal edge when $\theta = 0$ or π and for vertical edge when $\theta = \pi/2$ or $3\pi/2$, Busy (t) measured from [C] gives only half of the number of pixels lying in nonhomogeneous regions for the threshold t. So for comparing with Busy(t), we take $K = \frac{1}{2}(MN - K')$ as the number of pixels lying in those regions where spatial variation is high. Now the value of t is selected as threshold for which |Busy (t) – K| is minimum. The present method has an advantage that in some cases due to absence of proper minima in Busy(t) [for $t = 0, 1, 2, ..., L - 2$] graylevel threshold cannot be selected; whereas, |Busy (t) – K| will always show a minimum value for some value of t as graylevel threshold in every case. However, it has a disadvantage that it is applicable for segmenting the image which consists of only two types of regions.

24.3 EXPERIMENTAL RESULTS

The threshold selection techniques described above using graylevel co-occurrence matrix are implemented on several images. The thresholds selected automatically using different measures are used to segment biomedical images. In the present experiment, the authors have used both types of images: (i) images consisting of two types of regions, and (ii) images consisting of more than two types of regions. Here we will show the results of implementation of segmentation algorithm on one image from each class. Images are sampled into 200 × 200 pixels resolution and intensity values are quantized into 256 levels.

First, we consider Fig. 24.2(a), which is a microphotograph of a 'cell'. The image contains only two types of regions, namely (object) and cytoplasm (background). Fig. 24.2(b) shows the graylevel histogram of this image and reveals that being nearly unimodal it is not trivial to detect a threshold using this histogram. Figs 24.2(c-g) exhibit plots of different measures namely Busyness, conditional probability, entropy, average contrast and average entropy, respectively vs. threshold values (i.e., all possible graylevels). Segmented image obtained using the thresholds selected from average contrast measure is shown in Fig. 24.2(h). Note that the optimum threshold selected corresponds to the maxima in Fig. 24.2(f) producing visually good result as shown in Fig. 24.2(h).

The second image we have chosen to display the performance of different measures is shown in Fig. 24.3(a). Fig. 24.3(b) shows its graylevel histogram. This image of 'skin layer' consists of three types of

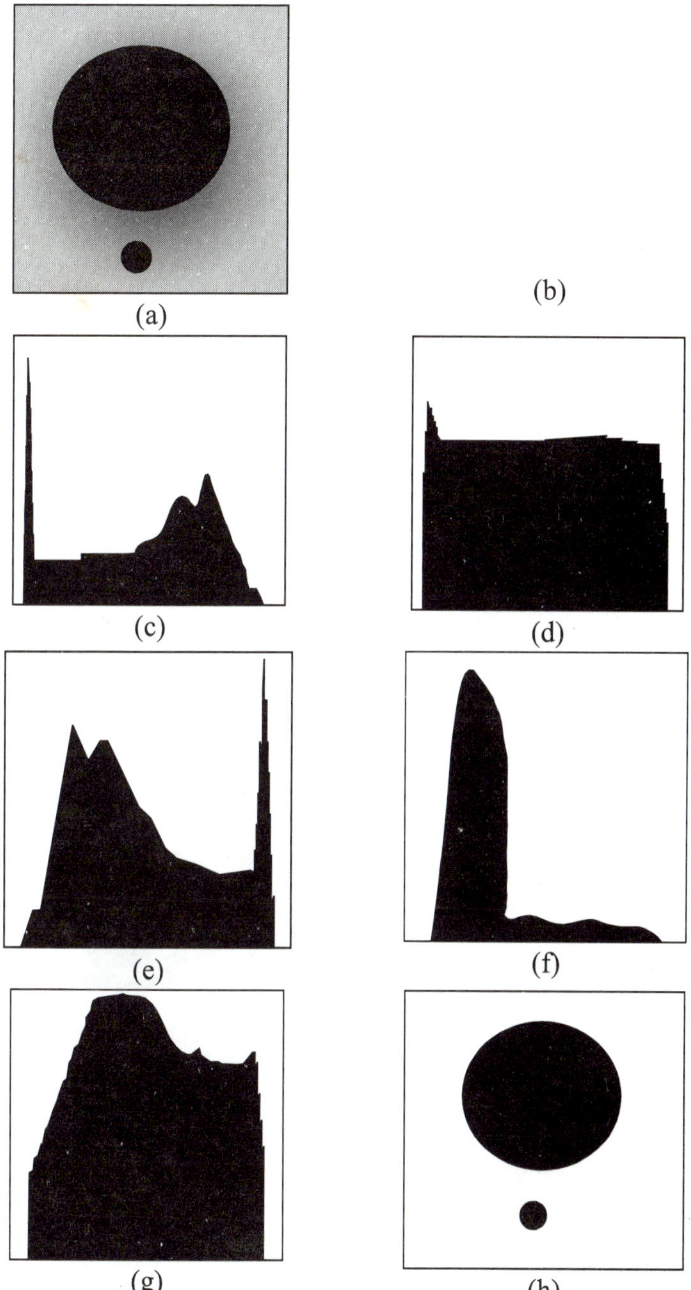

Fig. 24.2 (*a*) Original image of 'Cell' where graylevel varies from 0 to 255. (b) Graylevel histogram of (*a*). (c) Plot of Busyness measure vs threshold. (d) Plot of conditional probability measure vs. threshold (e) Plot of entropy measure vs. threshold. (*e*) Plot of entropy measure vs. threshold. (*f*) Plot of Average contrast vs threshold. (*g*) Plot of Average entropy vs threshold. (*h*) Segmented image using threshold detected corresponding to the maxima in (*f*).

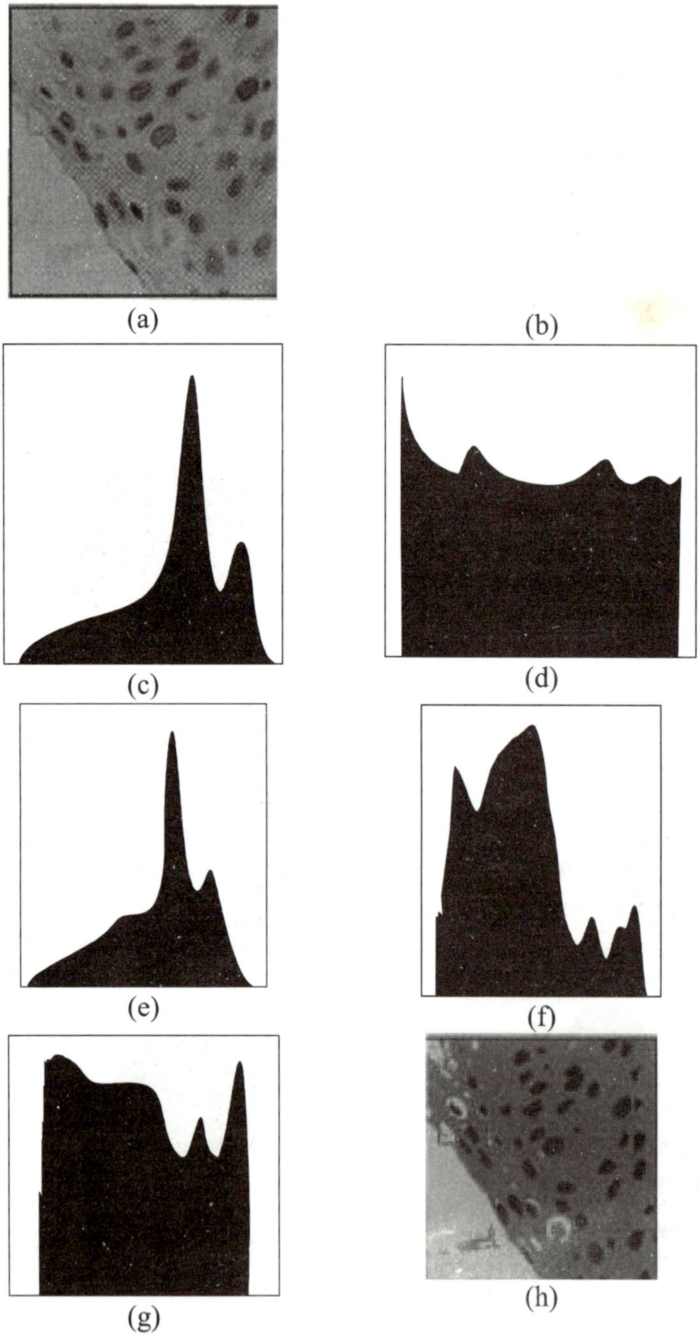

Fig. 24.3 (*a*) Original image of a 'Skin layer' where graylevel varies from 0 to 255. (*b*) Graylevel histogram of (*a*). (*c*) Plot of Busyness measure vs threshold. (*d*) Plot of conditional probability measure vs. threshold (*e*) Plot of entropy measure vs. threshold. (*f*) Plot of Average contrast vs. threshold. (*g*) Plot of Average entropy vs threshold. (*h*) Segmented image using threshold detected corresponding to two largest maxima in (*f*).

regions, namely nucleus, cytoplasm and background. Figs 24.3 (*c-g*) exhibit plots of different measures namely Busyness, conditional probability, entropy, average contrast and average entropy, respectively vs. threshold values (i.e., all possible graylevels). Segmented image obtained using the thresholds selected from average contrast measure is shown in Fig. 24.3(*h*). Note that the optimum threshold selected corresponds to the two largest maxima in Fig. 24.3(*f*) producing visually good result as shown in Fig. 24.3(*h*).

24.4 CONCLUSION

In this report, we have proposed four different measures using graylevel co-occurrence matrix for threshold selection. These are entropy, average contrast, average entropy and spatial variation. Their performances are compared with those of two well known measures, namely Busyness and conditional probability. For noise free good quality image, performances of all the measures are found comparable. But for real world images which are degraded and noisy, the results obtained by using Average contrast measure are the most reliable. The result of Average entropy measure in the nearest to them. However, results of Spatial variation measure are found best in most of the cases where image consists of only two types of regions. Unfortunately, this method is not applicable to those images which contain more than two types of regions. Results obtained by using conditional probability measure and entropy measure are seen to be comparable and are worse than those previous measures. Another point to note is that the plots of entropy and busyness measures are almost similar, the performance of the later is the worst among all.

However, we must conclude with the statement that the comparisons given here are based on our experiments and it is not wise to draw any general inference about their performances.

Acknowledgement

Authors like to express their thanks to Mr J Gupta for typing the manuscript.

References

1. J S Weszka (1978) A survey of threshold selection technique. *CGIP,* **7**, 259–265.
2. R M Haralick(1973)Textural features for images classification, *IEEE Trans SMC*, **SMC-3**, 610–621.
3. J S Weszka and A Rosenfeld (1978) Threshold evaluation techniques *IEEE Trans SMC,* **SMC-8**, 622–629.
4. F Deravi and S K Pal (1987) Graylevel thresholding using second order statistics *PRL* **1**, 417–422.

5. B Chanda B B Chaudhuri and D Dutta Majumder (1985) On image enhancement and threshold selection techniques using the graylevel co-occurrence matrix*PRL*, **3**, 243–251.
6. R W Conners, M M Trivedi and C A Harlow (1984) Segmentation of a high-resolution urban scene using texture operators *CGIP* **25**, 273–310.
7. R M Haralick and K S Shanmugan (1974) Combined spectral and spatial processing of ERTS imagery data, *Remote Sens Environ.* **3**, 3–13.

25

Adaptive Thresholding Based on Human Psychovisual Characteristics

Malay K Kundu[1] and Sankar K Pal[1]

ABSTRACT

An algorithm based on the characteristics of human visual system is presented here in order to select automatically (without human intervention) the thresholds for detecting the significant edges as perceived by human beings. The threshold value adapts with background intensity according to the criterion governed by characteristic of one of the De Vries-Rose, Weber's and saturated regions. The effects of different span length for those regions and also the different mid-range (constant) values are studied. The algorithm is found to provide satisfactory improvement in performance over the conventional edge detection process for wide ranges of input image.

Keywords: Adaptive Thresholding; Human Psychovisual Characteristics; Edge Detection; Graylevel; Gradient Image.

25.1 INTRODUCTION

Visual information is concentrated at points of large spatial variation of light intensity in the picture. The difference operators such as gradient, Robert gradient, Sobel and Prewitt gradients and Laplacian [l] give rise to high values at the places where the change in greylevel occurs. The greater the spatial variation of intensity, the easier is the detection of change and the stronger is the edge intensity. Thresholding of spatial difference of greylevels (gradient image) is one of the popular techniques for sharpening the edges (i.e., selecting valid or significant edge points according to human perception). The problem of edge detection therefore boils down to finding out an appropriate threshold which may be global, local or dynamic, such that if the spatial difference at a point that exceeds threshold, *then and only then* it will be considered as a valid edge point. [6]

The present work is an attempt to make this task automatic by providing an adaptive algorithm based on human psychovisual phenomena. The visual increment threshold curve [2] is piecewise linearly approximated here such that the spatial difference in greylevel at a point is thresholded depending on its background intensity by one of the criteria in De Vries-Rose, Weber and saturated regions.

---

[1] MACHINE INTELLIGENCE UNIT, Indian Statistical Institute, Calcutta 700108, India.

Effectiveness of the algorithm is demonstrated for the existing gradient operators when a set of different images is considered as input.

25.2 EDGE OPERATORS AND THRESHOLDING

Let x_{mn} be the greylevel of the (m, n) th pixel of an $M \times N$ dimensional, L level image $X = [x_{mn}]$, $m = 1, 2, ..., M$, $n = 1, 2, ..., N$. The gradient x'_{mn} denoting edge intensity at the point (m,n) may be defined as [3]

$$x'_{mn} = (|G_1| + |G_2|)/2, \tag{1}$$

where G_1 and G_2 are given by equations (2), (3) and (4) corresponding to ordinary gradient, Robert's gradient, and Prewitt's and Sobel's gradients–

$$G_1 = x_{mn} - x_{m,\, n+1} \tag{2a}$$

$$G_2 = x_{mn} - x_{m+1,\, n} \tag{2b}$$

$$G_1 = x_{mn} - x_{m+1,\, n+1} \tag{3a}$$

$$G_2 = x_{m,\, n+1} - x_{m+1,n} \tag{3b}$$

$$G_1 = \frac{1}{2+W}[(x_{m+1,\, n+1} + Wx_{m+1,\, n} + x_{m+1,\, n-1}) - (x_{m-1,\, n+1} + Wx_{m-1,\, n} + x_{m-1,\, n-1})] \tag{4a}$$

and

$$G_2 = \frac{1}{2+W}[(x_{m-1,\, n+1} + Wx_{m,\, n+1} + x_{m+1,\, n+1}) - (x_{m+1,\, n-1} + Wx_{m,\, n-1} + x_{m-1,\, n-1})] \tag{4b}$$

with $W = 1$ and 2 for Prewitt's and Sobel's gradients respectively. These are called the first difference operators. The second difference operator such as Laplacian can be expressed as

$$G_1 = \frac{1}{2}(x_{m-1,\, n} + x_{m+1,\, n} - 2x_{mn}) \tag{5a}$$

and

$$G_2 = \frac{1}{2}(x_{m,\, n-1} + x_{m,\, n+1} + 2x_{mn}) \tag{5b}$$

The simple gradient and Robert's gradient [equations (2) and (3)] not only respond strongly to the edges but also to the isolated points. The Laplacian does respond to the edges, but it responds more strongly to the corners, lines, line ends and isolated points. It has zero response to a linear ramp but it responds strongly where there is a change in rate of change of graylevel. Due to some smoothing effect, Prewitt and Sobel operators, on the other hand, possess better noise immunity and good edge response, added to this weighted average in Sobel operator [equation (4) with $W = 2$] reduces to a great extent the blurring effect of smoothing.

After applying these operators on an image X, an edge is deemed to be present at the point (m, n) if x'_{mn} exceeds a predefined threshold value T. The general form of T is

$$T = f(x_{mn,}\ N_{mn,}\ (m,n)), \tag{6}$$

where N_{mn} denotes some local property at the point (m, n) having pixel intensity x_{mn}.

The threshold is called 'global' if T depends on x_{mn}. When T depends on both x_{mn} and N_{mn}, it is called 'local'. If T depends on the co-ordinate (m,n) in addition to x_{mn} and N_{mn}, the threshold so computed is defined as 'dynamic'. A good review on different thresholding techniques is given by Wezka[4]. Selection of an appropriate threshold therefore poses an important problem in detecting the valid edge points in X.

In the following sections, we are going to present an automatic threshold selection procedure based on human psychovisual facts. The selection is made on the basis of both local and global information available from X such that for a particular x'_{mn} its threshold value adapts with its average background intensity B_{mn} following either $K_2\sqrt{B}_{mn}$ in De Vries-Rose region or $K_1\ B_{mn}$ in Weber region or $K_3\ B^2_{mn}$ in saturation region (K_1, K_2 and K_3 being positive constants).

25.3 HUMAN PSYCHOVISUAL PHENOMENA

Brightness is a psychological sensation associated with the amount of light stimulus. Due to great adaptive ability of eye, absolute brightness could not be measured by human eye. The relative brightness is an observer's feeling of difference in greyness between the objects. The term contrast is used to emphasize the difference in illuminance of objects. The perceived greyness of a surface depends on its local background and the perceived contrast remains constant if the ratios of contrasts between object and local background remain constant [3].

In psychology, perceived contrast C refers to the ratio of difference in luminance of an object B_0 and its immediate surrounding B_s i.e.,

$$C = |\,B_0 - B_s\,| / B_s = \frac{\Delta B}{B_s}. \tag{7}$$

The visual increment threshold (or just noticeable difference) is defined as the amount of light ΔB_T necessary to add to the visual field of intensity B such that it can be discriminated from a reference field of same intensity B. It therefore gives a limit for a perceivable change in luminance or intensity.

The major problems at low intensity level which any image processing system has to face are [5]:

(i) detection of changes occurring in a low steady but visible illumination (i.e., minimum detectable change); and

(ii) detection of mere presence or absence of light under dark adapted condition (i.e., absolute visual threshold).

At low intensity near absolute visual threshold, the visual increment threshold ΔB_T is constant. With increase in intensity *B*, ΔB_T converges asymptotically to Weber behaviour i.e., $\Delta B_T \propto B$. This type of behaviour is exhibited in brightness incremental threshold for white broad band spectra and monochromatic narrow band spectra [2]. (Buchsbaum).

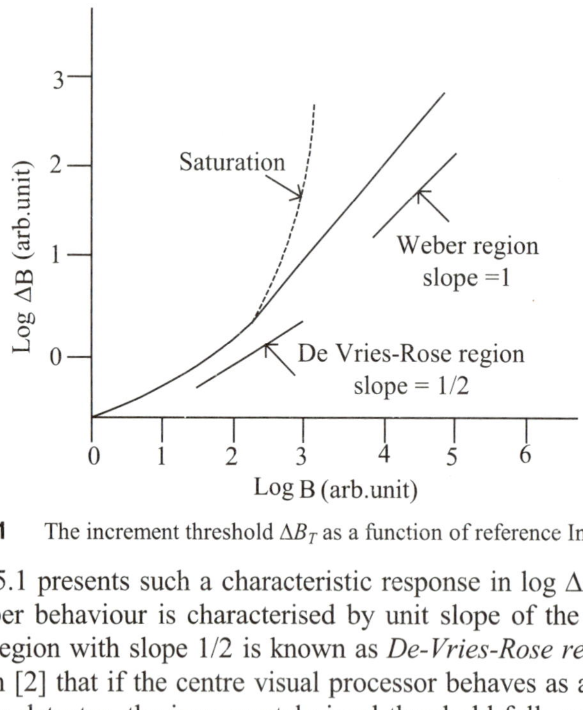

Fig. 25.1 The increment threshold ΔB_T as a function of reference Intensity *B*

Fig. 25.1 presents such a characteristic response in log ΔB_T – log *B* plane. Weber behaviour is characterised by unit slope of the curve. The preceding region with slope 1/2 is known as *De-Vries-Rose region.* It has been shown [2] that if the centre visual processor behaves as an optimum probabilistic detector, the incremental visual threshold follows the square root law i.e., $\Delta B_T \propto \sqrt{B}$. However, in actual case this rule is followed in a small restricted region (Fig. 25.1). The dashed curve shows the deviation from Weber's law. This deviation (which represents a *saturation region)* is not usually exhibited by retinal cone mechanism even under very high intensities but could happen in very restricted cases.

From Fig. 25.1, it is seen that variation of log ΔB against log *B* in De Vries-Rose region is slower than that in the Weber region. In other words, the discrimination ability in De Vries-Rose region is greater than in Weber region. The possible reason for this deterioration in discrimination ability can be attributed to inherent visual non-linearity.

Assuming the response curve (Fig. 25.1) to be piecewise linear, the Weber and the DeVries-Rose regions can be represented as

$$\log \Delta B_T = \log (K_1 B) = \log B + \log K_1 \tag{8}$$

and
$$\log \Delta B_T = \log (K_2 \sqrt{B}) = \frac{1}{2} \log B + \log K_2 \tag{9}$$

respectively. K_1 and K_2 are the constants of proportionality.

Furthermore, the saturation which might occur even rarely, only at very high intensities can be approximated as

$$\log \Delta B_T = 2 \log B + K_3, \tag{10}$$

K_3 being a constant.

Therefore, when brightness value of an object is higher (or lower) than its surrounding or background or a reference intensity B by an amount $\geq \Delta B_T$, it corresponds to a point on or above the curve (Fig. 25.1) and the object will appear either brighter (or darker). In case of variable object and background intensity, the visual system adopts to an average intensity.

Furthermore, Fig. 25.2 shows the variation of $\Delta B_T / B$ with B. It is seen that in the Weber region, the ratio $\Delta B_T / B$ remains fairly constant at about β % of its maximum value over very wide range of its B-value [1]. In the literature the value of β is said to be around 0.02.

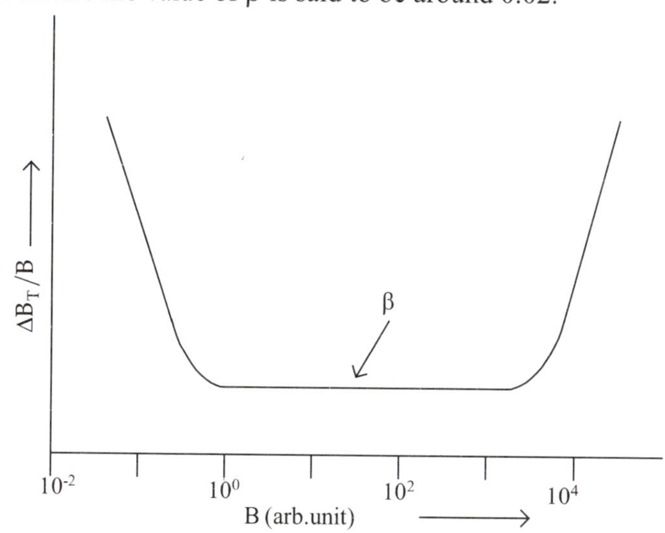

Fig. 25.2 The variation of contrast sensitivity $\Delta B_T / B$ with background intensity B for uniform background

25.4 ADAPTIVE THRESHOLDING

The piecewise linear approximation of the visual increment threshold curve (Fig. 25.1) is shown in Fig. 25.3. Here, the threshold values in the De Vries-Rose region, the Weber region and the saturation region are defined by the linear equations (8), (9) and (10) respectively. Although the demarcation between these regions represented by various equations is not very sharp and definite, we assume here for the sake of simplicity and ease of analysis that De Vries-Rose region extends between x_1 and x_2 (Fig. 25.3) (x_1 corresponds to absolute visual threshold), Weber region between x_2 and x_3 and saturation region beyond x_3. The value of B corresponding to log $B = x_i$ is assumed here to B_{x_i}, $i = 1, 2, 3$. In other words,

$$x_i = \log B_{x_i} \tag{11}$$

$$i = 1, 2, 3$$

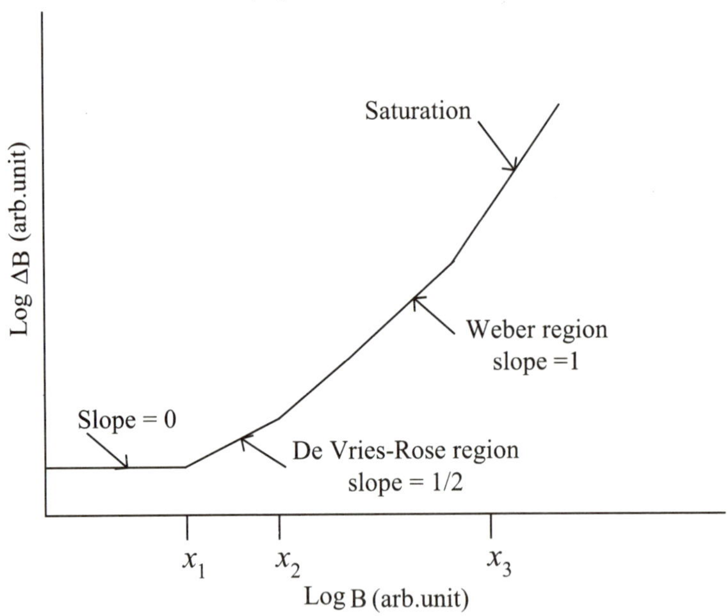

Fig. 25.3 The increment threshold ΔB_T vs. reference intensity B curve (Fig. 25.1) with linear approximation for different regions

Let x_0 and B_t be the maximum values of log B and B respectively. Let us assume further that

$$x_i = \alpha_i x_0, \qquad i = 1, 2, 3 \tag{12}$$

and

$$B_{x_i} = \alpha_i' B_t, \qquad i = 1, 2, 3 \tag{13}$$

where $$0 < \alpha_1 < \alpha_2 < \alpha_3 < 1$$
$$0 < \alpha_1' < \alpha_2' < \alpha_3' < 1.$$

As mentioned in Sec. l, the value of $\Delta B_T / B$ remains fairly constant over the entire Weber region with a value approximately equal to β% of $(\Delta B/B)_{max}$, maximum value of $\Delta B/B$ over the entire dynamic range. Therefore, from equation (8) one can write

$$K_1 = \frac{\Delta B_T}{B} = \frac{1}{100}\beta\left(\frac{\Delta B}{B}\right)_{max} \tag{14}$$

Now, equations (8) and (9) are both satisfied at the point (x_2, y_2) of Fig. 25.3. Therefore, we can write

$$y_2 = x_2 + \log K_1 = \frac{1}{2}x_2 + \log K_2$$

or $$\frac{1}{2}x_2 = \log(K_2 / K_1) \tag{15}$$

Using equation (11) for $i = 2$

$$\frac{1}{2}\log B_{x_2} = \log(K_2 / K_1)$$

or $$K_2 = K_1 \sqrt{B}_{x_2} \tag{16}$$

Similarly, considering equations (8) and (10) at the point (x_3, y_3), we have

$$K_3 = K_1 / B_{x_3} \tag{17}$$

The minimum values of increment threshold are therefore

$$\Delta B_T = K_2\sqrt{B} = \frac{\sqrt{B}}{100}\beta\left(\frac{\Delta B}{B}\right)_{max}\sqrt{B}_{x_2};\; B_{x_2} \geq B \geq B_{x_1} \tag{18a}$$

$$= K_1 B = \frac{B}{100}\beta\left(\frac{\Delta B}{B}\right)_{max};\; B_{x_3} \geq B \geq B_{x_2} \tag{18b}$$

$$= K_3 B^2 = \frac{B^2}{100}\beta\left(\frac{\Delta B}{B}\right)_{max}\frac{1}{B_{x_3}},\quad B \geq B_{x_3} \tag{18c}$$

corresponding to De Vries-Rose, Weber and saturation regions.

Equation (12) defines the minimum amount of brightness level, in three different regions, by which the intensity of an object must be greater or less than its background intensity B in order to make the object appear brighter or darker (i.e., detectable). In other words, for a particular point in a picture having intensity B_P, if we have either $$\frac{\Delta B}{\sqrt{B}} \geq K_2 \text{ when } \alpha'_2 B_t \geq B \geq \alpha'_1 B_t \quad (19a)$$

or $$\frac{\Delta B}{B} \geq K_1 \text{ when } \alpha'_3 B_t \geq B \geq \alpha'_2 B_t \quad (19b)$$

or $$\frac{\Delta B}{B} \geq K_3 \text{ when } B \geq \alpha'_3 B_t \quad (19c)$$

with $$\Delta B = |B_p - B|, \quad (20)$$

then and only then it can be considered as a detectable edge point having edge intensity ΔB.

25.5 ALGORITHM

Fig. 25.4 shows the flow chart and extracting valid edges of an $M \times N$ dimensional, L level image $X = [x_{mn}]$, $m = 1, 2, ..., M$, $n = 1, 2, ..., N$ using the above mentioned adaptive thresholding scheme.

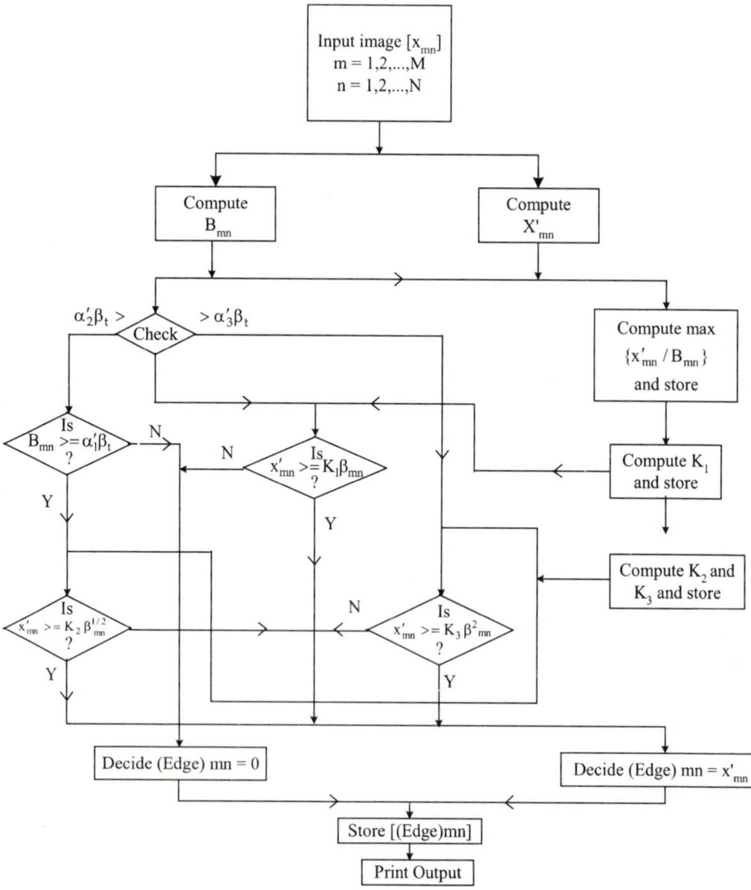

Fig. 25.4 Flow chart for the proposed thresholding algorithm

B_{mn} denoting the background intensity B at the point (m, n) was considered here to be the weighted average over its 8 neighbours i.e.,

$$B_{mn} = \left\{ \frac{1}{2} \left[\frac{1}{4} \sum_{Q} x_{ij} + \frac{1}{4\sqrt{2}} \sum_{Q'} x_{k1} \right] + x_{mn} \right\} \Big/ 2 \tag{21}$$

$$(i, j) \; \varepsilon \; Q, (k, l) \; \varepsilon \; Q'$$

where Q and Q' denote the set the neighbouring pixels x_{ij} and x_{kl} which are at a distance of 1 and $\sqrt{2}$ unit respectively from x_{mn}. Similarly, x'_{mn} denoting the ΔB-value at the (m, n)th point (difference in intensity of x_{mn} with respect to its neighbouring pixels) can be obtained by equations (1) to (5) corresponding to different spatial edge detection (gradient) operators.

Finally, for computing constants K_i, $i = 1, 2, 3$, we consider

$$B_t = \max \{x_{mn}\} - \min \{x_{mn}\} \tag{22}$$

and
$$\left(\frac{\Delta B}{B} \right)_{\max} = \max \{x'_{mn} / B_{mn}\}, \tag{23}$$

$m = 1, 2, ..., M, n = 1, 2, ..., N.$

Here B_t has been taken to be equal to the dynamic range of the input image.

As shown in Fig. 25.4, the task of thresholding is two-fold. At the first stage, each pixel intensity x_{mn} is decided, on the basis of its local information (namely, background intensity B_{mn}), to encounter the requirement in one of the three regions. The second stage consists of checking whether x'_{mn} satisfies its respective criterion (equation (19)). If that condition is satisfied, x_{mn} is then treated as a valid edge point having edge intensity x'_{mn}. Otherwise, edge intensity at the (m, n)th point is taken to be zero. It is to be mentioned here that the thresholding criterion (equation (18) or (19)) for a particular x'_{mn} is seen to be adaptive (i.e., changing with its B_{mn} value according to $K_2 \sqrt{B}_{mn}$ *or* $K_1 B_{mn}$ or $K_3 B^2_{mn}$ in the respective cases).

25.6 IMPLEMENTATION AND RESULT

The algorithm discussed in the previous section was simulated on EC 1033 computer. The output images were generated by overprinting technique as there is no facility for graphic display. An image of a Biplane (25.5(a)) was taken as test data of size 64 × 64 and with 32 graylevels. Although it was mentioned in the earlier section that Weber's region covers the major portion of the total dynamic range and both De Vries-Rose and saturated regions cover very small portion of it [2], there is no quantitative figure available for the length of span of each region discussed. To estimate the approximate length of span for different regions, four different combinations of a'_2 and a'_3 were taken. They are ($\alpha'_2 = 0.33$, $\alpha'_3 = 0.66$), ($\alpha'_2 = 0.1$, $\alpha'_3 = 0.7$), ($\alpha'_2 = 0.25$, $\alpha'_3 = 0.75$), and ($\alpha'_2 = 0.1$, $\alpha'_3 = 0.9$). These set of values were used in the present algorithm (Fig. 25.4) and four different results of thresholded edges for Biplane image Fig. 25.5(*a*) are shown in Figs 25.5(*c*)-(*f*) using Prewitt operator to calculate x'_{mn}.

It is evident that if the value of α'_2 increases or decreases, the pixel population for De Vries-Rose region (having lowest ΔB_T value) will increase or decrease. As a result, more or less number of edge points will be able to cross the threshold for detection. Similarly, as α'_3 increases or decreases the pixel population for saturation region will decrease or increase. Therefore more or less number of pixels will appear as significant edge points (due to comparatively high value of ΔB_T in saturated region). These facts are clearly demonstrated in the Fig. 25.5(*c*)-(*f*). It is seen from Fig. 25.5(*f*) that a thin and continuous edge appeared inside the biplane together with normal outline edges of the biplane. This is true only for the particular set of α' values ($\alpha'_2 = 0.1$, $\alpha'_3 = 0.9$). But for other set of values for α'_3s either the inner edge is not continuous or contours are thicker.

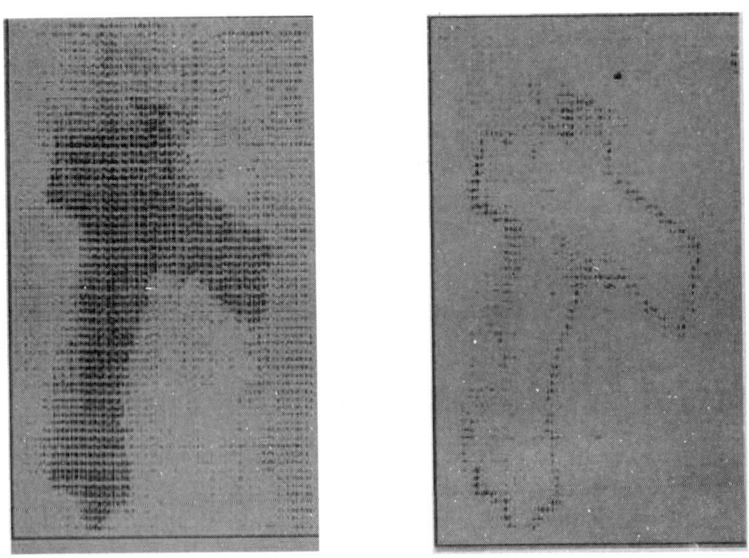

(a) (b)

Fig. 25.5 (*a*) Input Image Biplane. (*b*) Edge detected image using Prewitt operator.

It was also mentioned in the literature [1] that the value of $\beta \approx 0.02$. If the value of β is increased or decreased, then the values of $\Delta\ B_T$ Eq. 18(a)–(c) for all the regions will simultaneously increase or decrease, which results in overall thinning or thickening of edges. In the present

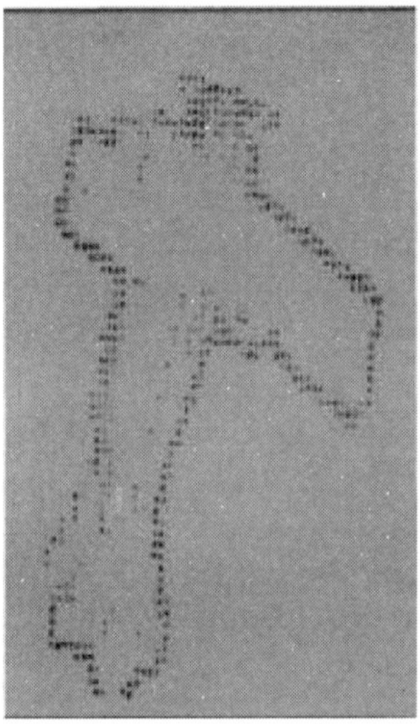

(c)

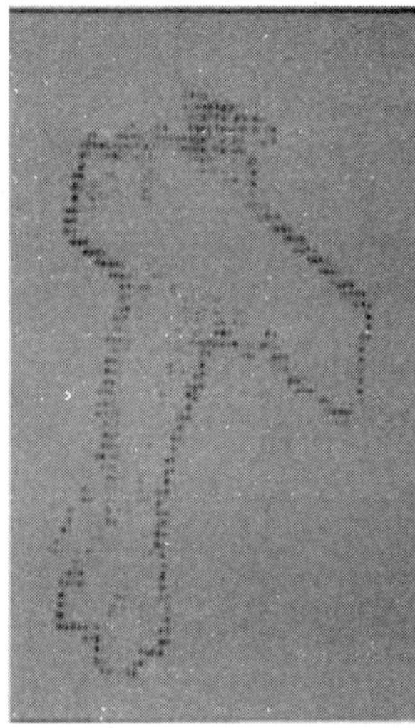

(d)

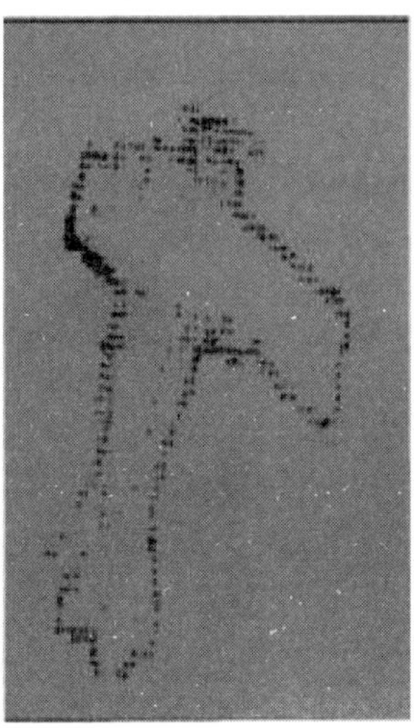

(e)

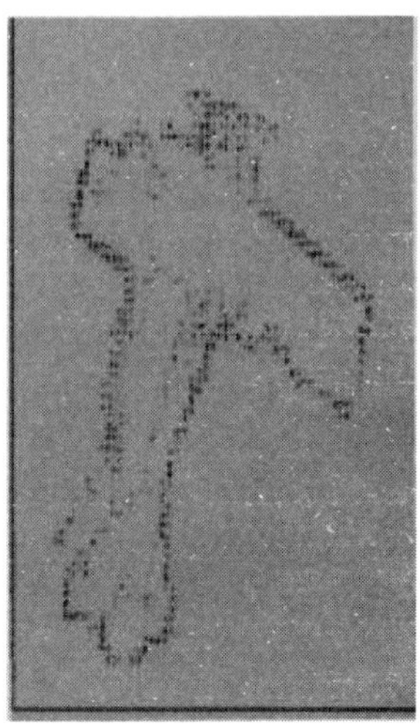

(f)

(*c*) Edge detected and thresholded image ($\alpha'_2 = 0.33$, $\alpha'_3 = 0.66$ $\beta = 0.045$)
(*d*) Edge detected and thresholded image ($\alpha'_2 = 0.1$, $\alpha'_3 = 0.7$ $\beta = 0.045$)
(*e*) Edge detected and thresholded image ($\alpha'_2 = 0.25$ $\alpha'_3 = 0.75$ $\beta = 0.045$)
(*f*) Edge detected and thresholded image ($\alpha'_2 = 0.1$, $\alpha'_3 = 0.9$ $\beta = 0.045$)

experiment different values of β such as 0.02, 0.03, 0.045, 0.055 and 0.07 were considered. As a typical illustration $\beta = 0.045$ were taken for all the results presented here for different images. It is obvious that as β increases threshold value for all the regions will be increased, and the number of detected edge points in each of the range will decrease. As a result the edge lines become thinner and finally become disconnected.

25.7 CONCLUSION

The thresholding technique proposed in this paper does not require any human intervention for the choice of threshold values. Although certain portion of the edges are found to be more than one pixel width, those could be thinned by using any standard edge linking technique.

Acknowledgement

Authors wish to thank Dr D Dutta Majumder, Former Head of Electronics and Communication Sciences Unit of the Indian Statistical Institute for his constant encouragement for this work.

References

1. R C Gonzalez and P Wintz (1977) Digital Image Processing Addison-wesley, Mass USA.
2. G Buchsbaum (1980) An analytical derivation of visual nonlinearity IEEE Trans biomedi Engg, 27, 237 – 242.
3. E L Hall (1979) Computer Image Processing and Recognition Academic Press N.Y.
4. J S Wezka (1978) A survey of threshold selection Comp graph *Image Process* **7**, 259–265.
5. P Zuidema *et al.* (1983) A mechanistic approach to threshold behaviour of visual system *IEEE Trans System, Man and Cybern* **13**, 923–934.
6. M K KUNDU and S K Pal (1986) Thresholding for edge detection using human psychovisual phenomena, Pattern Recognition Letters 4, 433–441.

26

Image Segmentation using Level Set Analysis

Dipti Prasad Mukherjee[1]

ABSTRACT

Image segmentation problem involves estimation of object boundaries present in an image. The object boundary detection problem can be visualized as drawing one or more initial curve(s) inside an image and then gradually deform the curve(s) under imaging constraints to take the shape of object(s) present in the image. In this paper the curve deformation process is implemented using level set analysis. Level set analysis has the advantage of adapting changes in topology of the curve while evolving the curve in entirety avoiding any individual pixel level motion calculation. The theory of level set based curve evolution is presented in this paper along with its applications in image segmentation on real images. The problems of extending the proposed approach as generalized segmentation tool is also discussed.

26.1 INTRODUCTION

Level set analysis is an emerging tool for geometric curve evolution. Given a curve it is possible to deform and evolve the curve under a set of constraints so that the deformed curve represents a shape. Consider the example shown in Fig. 26.1. The thin elliptic curve outside the dark circular object can be deformed and squeezed to ultimately take the shape of the circular object. The level set analysis can be used to achieve this curve deformation and evolution process. In this paper we first derive the theory of level set analysis and then show how the level set function constraints curve evolution process. As an application of the curve evolution process, we take the example of image segmentation.

The level set analysis is widely used in various disciplines of mechanical and applied sciences where the boundary detection, contour tracking and propagation of any physical variable are important. For example, level set propagation is used extensively in the study of fluid flow [11]. The effect of any external force on a mechanical or civil structure can be visualized as propagation of stress and/or strain inside structure components. This stress and/or strain propagation is modeled using level set analysis [9]. Similarly the applications ranging from metal deposition in semiconductor chips to pattern morphing are successfully implemented using level set analysis [2,3,8]. In a related development constrained active contours based on level set analysis are used for object boundary detection [5,6]. Detailed application driven theoretical developments of level set analysis can be found in [1,7,8].

[1] ECSU, Indian Statistical Institute, Kolkata.

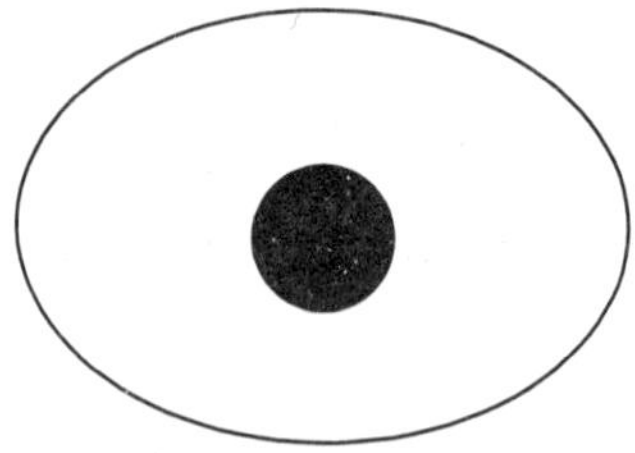

Fig. 26.1 A thin elliptic curve that can be evolved and deformed to take the circular dark object.

Let us understand how level set analysis can represent the curve evolution process. Look at the sort of "bowl" shaped surface in Fig. 26.2. This surface is the *level set function* of the elliptic curve of Fig. 26.1. Before we discuss how we can get the level set function, assume that the thin elliptic curve in Fig. 26.1 is embedded in the "bowl" shaped surface in any arbitrary position parallel to the horizontal X-Y plane. Let us also assume that the elliptic curve can move up or down along Z axis of the "bowl" surface of Fig. 26.2 but always staying embedded inside the surface. Therefore, moving up the "bowl" surface along increasing Z direction the size of the embedded elliptic curve increases while its size decreases moving in the opposite direction along negative Z. If the circular 2D dark object is somewhere on the "bowl" surface of Fig. 26.2, the elliptic curve as it is moving down the "bowl" shaped surface touches the object boundary. In case the "bowl" shaped surface gradually deforms to take the shape of the circular object, the embedded curve while moving down exactly fits in the object boundary. That is object boundary detection through curve evolution where the curve is evolving inside the level set function! Why the curve has to move down along negative Z direction of "bowl" shape? This is because the size of the elliptic curve is bigger than the circular object. In case we want to capture a bigger object than the curve, the curve has to move up the surface along positive Z direction. In any case the surface should gradually deform to take on the shape of the target object. So, there are four major issues:

(a) To fabricate surface similar to the "bowl" shaped surface, the visualization of *level set function.*

(b) To move the embedded curve either in positive or negative Z direction of the level set surface.

(c) To define mechanism for continuous deformation of level set function such that situation like an elliptic curve exactly fits the contour of a circular object can be implemented, and finally,

(d) the evolution of curve must stop as soon as it finds the object.

We explore these issues in subsequent sections. In the next section we derive the mechanism to build the level set function. This is followed by the derivation of the theoretical basis to move and deform the curve embedded in the level set function. In Section 26.4, we present the specific application of image segmentation where the termination criterion for level set evolution is also explained. Results on different real images including bottlenecks for implementing generalized image segmentation routine are explained in Section 26.5.

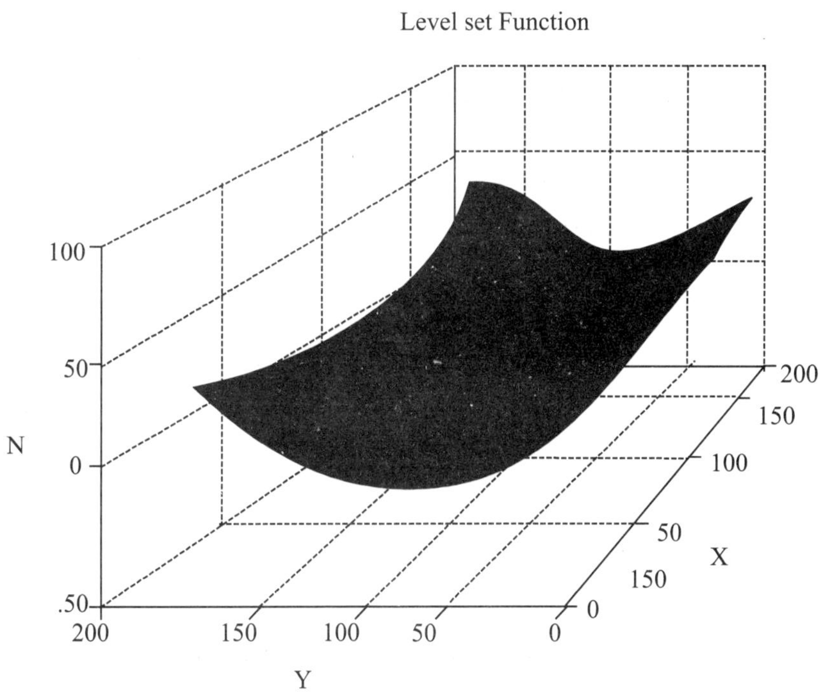

Fig. 26.2 The level set function for the elliptic curve of Fig. 26.1.

26.2 LEVEL SET FUNCTION

An easy way to visualize the level set function is as a distance function of the initial curve, for example the thin elliptic curve of Fig. 26.1. Assume that the curve is embedded in a 2D matrix. We can find distance of every matrix point from each of the curve points. For n number of curve points, there are n distance values for each matrix point. Let us put minimum of those n distance values for each matrix point. Let us also give a small twist to this definition. Let us set all the distance values those are outside the curve as positive distance values and those inside as negative distance values. For the matrix points, which are on the curve the distance values are obviously zero. If we plot these distance values along Z-axis with X-Y plane representing the horizontal image plane, then the proposed distance function for the thin ellipse of Fig. 26.1 should exactly look like the "bowl" shaped surface of Fig. 26.2. So we have designed the level set function, which is essentially a signed distance function. The position where the curve is embedded in the level set function has distance value zero. So, the curve can be found as the intersection of a plane $Z = 0$ with the level set surface. The position of the curve inside the level set surface is therefore referred as *zero level set.*

If φ denotes the level set function and at any instance t, $c(s, t)$ represents the curve that is embedded in a 2D image matrix $I \subset Z^2$, then the level set function is given by:

$$\varphi(x, y, t) = \min\{d((x, y), c(s, t))\}, \tag{1}$$

where $d(.,.)$ represents distance function between (x, y), an element of the image matrix I of dimension row × column, $0 \le x <$ row and $0 \le y <$ column, and the curve $c(s)$ at time t. Also, by definition, $\varphi(x, y) > 0$ if (x, y) is outside $c(s)$, $\varphi(x, y) < 0$ if (x, y) is inside $c(s)$ and $\varphi(x, y) = 0$ if (x, y) is on the curve $c(s)$. As the time evolves the curve which is the zero level set moves up or down within the level set. By definition the zero level set containing the curve has a constant level set function value 0. Formally, the zero levels set representing the curve is given by

$$\varphi(x, y, t) = 0 \tag{2}$$

But what would be the mechanics of the movement of the curve? We explore this in the next section.

26.3. CURVE EVOLUTION USING LEVEL SET FUNCTION

Consider a simple geometric curve evolution process. Look at the Fig. 26.3. We would like to evolve the curve towards any specific direction ($\vec{P}$). This direction can be decomposed into its normal component ($\vec{N}$) and tangential component ($\vec{T}$). So the rate of evolution of the curve $\vec{c}(s)$ in time can be written as

$$\frac{\partial \vec{c}(s)}{\partial t} = \alpha(s)\vec{T}(t) + \beta(s)\vec{N}(t), \tag{3}$$

where $\alpha(s)$ and $\beta(s)$ are speeds along tangential and normal directions respectively.

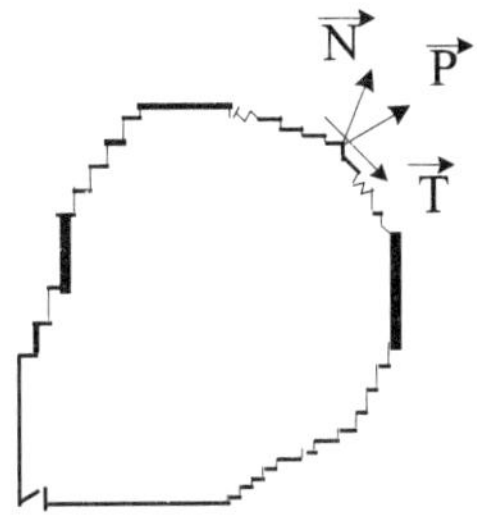

Fig. 26.3 Curve evolution along a specific direction is decomposed into normal and tangential components.

However, geometric curve evolution following (3) is really independent of the movement in the tangent direction. The deformation towards tangent direction is essentially reparameterization of the curve contour. Therefore, tangential deformation with time does not contribute *significantly* in the deformation of the curve. Hence, equation (3) can be restated as

$$\frac{\partial \vec{c}(s)}{\partial t} \cong \beta(s)\vec{N}(t). \tag{4}$$

This curve evolution can be explained through level set function. Let us recall the equation (2): $\varphi\ (x, y, t) = 0$. If we differentiate (2) with respect to time, it turns out to be

$$\frac{\partial \varphi}{\partial t} + \nabla\varphi \frac{\partial \vec{c}(s)}{\partial t} = 0, \tag{5}$$

and putting the curve evolution measure of (4) in (5), we get

$$\frac{\partial \varphi}{\partial t} = -\ \beta\|\nabla\varphi\|\,. \tag{6}$$

The equation (6) is the level set evolution equation where movement of the zero level set is defined. The speed term β is very important and throughout this deliberation we design this speed term that deforms the curve. Some curve points move fast while some move slowly depending on the speed so that, coming back to the problem with which we have started, we can deform an initial elliptic curve to fit to a circular object. The sign of β determines whether the curve embedded in zero level set expands or squeezes with respect to the initial position. The most important thing we note that this curve evolution deforms the entire contour together and the process does not do any individual pixel level processing to deform the curve. And we like that!

In most cases it is natural that a curve should deform as per its curvature. The curvature of a curve is a vector along the normal direction of the curve. Since, for curve evolution we have considered speed only along normal direction, the level set evolution speed can be taken as the curvature of the level set function. Therefore the equation (6) can be written as:

$$\frac{\partial \varphi}{\partial t} = -\kappa \|\nabla \varphi\|. \tag{7}$$

The parameter κ is the curvature of the level set function given by $\mathrm{div}\left(\nabla\varphi / \|\nabla\varphi\|\right)$ where div stands for *divergence* of the normal vector field. Detail numerical implementation of (7) is available in [7,8]. The update of level set function is implemented as follows:

$$\varphi_{n+1} = \varphi_n - \Delta t\left[\mathrm{div}\left(\frac{\nabla\varphi}{\|\nabla\varphi\|}\right)\right]\|\nabla\varphi\|. \tag{8}$$

The level set function at iteration n is given by φ_n and Δt is the time step. After few iterations the function φ seizes to be a signed distance function because of numerical inaccuracies. So, for accurate result, it may be necessary to impose the property of signed distance function on the level set function after every few iterations.

We can find numerous applications where curve evolution is important. In this paper we demonstrate the use of curve evolution in image segmentation. In the next section image segmentation using level set analysis is presented followed by results in Section 26.5.

26.4 IMAGE SEGMENTATION USING LEVEL SET

In the context of level set analysis the image segmentation problem is defined as the detection of object or region boundary. Given an initial curve it is evolved based on level set theory and the evolution slows, almost stops, as soon as the curve finds object or region boundaries. These boundaries are represented through higher edge gradient. Consider the Fig. 26.4(a) where there are four clusters of points representing, let us assume, four different objects. We would like to find the boundary of these point clusters using level set.

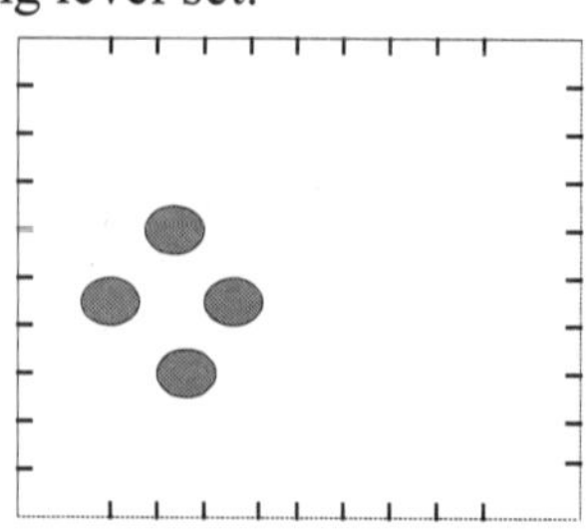

Fig. 26.4(a) Four point cloud clusters representing four different objects.

To start the curve evolution process we first draw a curve in and around these point clusters and then allow the curve to shrink. This initial curve encompassing the objects is shown in Fig. 26.4(b). Remember the curve deformation is effected within the level set function. For this example, the level set function is the signed distance function of the initial curve encompassing the point clusters.

Now while the curve is shrinking following (8) or in other words the zero level set is moving down along the level set surface, it is going to touch the boundaries of the objects. And once the curve touches the boundary we would like the curve to stick to it and at least that part of the curve should not deform further. Why? Because it found the object boundary! So, the speed with which the initial curve is evolving should slow down; in fact the speed should be almost zero when the curve is in contact with the object boundary. So, let us modify the speed function with a weighting function whose task is to reduce the speed where there is higher image gradient. Note that object boundary inside an image matrix means higher image gradient. The weighting function is expressed as:

$$g(I) = \frac{1}{1 + \|\nabla I\|^{p}}. \tag{9}$$

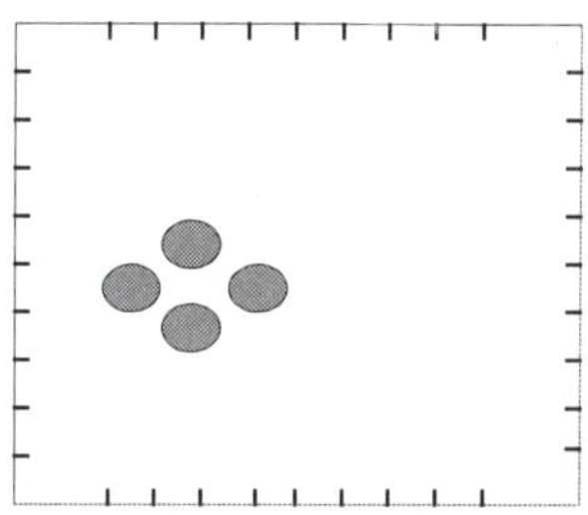

Fig. 26.4(b) The initial curve encompassing the point clusters is shown.

The gradient of image I is given by ∇I and p is a constant that controls the extent to which the level set speed is dampened. So the complete speed function turns out to be:

$$\frac{\partial \varphi}{\partial t} = -g(I)(c + \kappa)\|\nabla \varphi\|. \tag{10}$$

The speed function as specified in equation (7) is modified from κ to $(c + \kappa)$, c being an arbitrary constant. Putting the value of curvature the final curve evolution equation takes the following form.

$$\frac{\partial \varphi}{\partial t} = -cg(I)\|\nabla \varphi\| - g(I)\,\mathrm{div}\left(\frac{\nabla \varphi}{\|\nabla \varphi\|}\right)\|\nabla \varphi\|. \tag{11}$$

The results of curve evolution using equation (11) are shown in Figs. 26.4(*c*)-(*f*) after 100, 160, 215 and 270 iterations respectively with $c = 1$ and $p = 2$. Notice how the evolving contour after reaching the point cluster boundaries sticks to the object edge.

The synthetic image of Fig. 26.4 explains the level set theory elegantly. A very important point in the example of Fig. 26.4 is that one closed curve eventually separates out in four different closed curves. This shows that how zero level set curve can adapt the change in topology. Implementation of this type of change in topology is not possible in classical active contour model [4]. In the next section we present result of level set based image segmentation on real images.

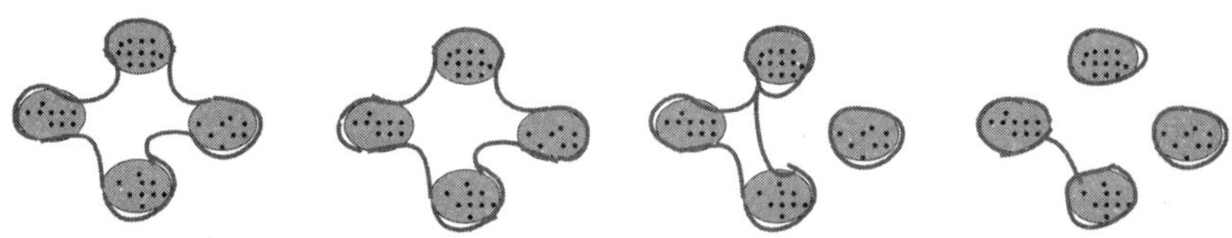

Fig. 26.4(c)-(f) Evolution of initial curve of Fig. 26.4**(b)** after 100, 160, 215 and 270 iterations.

26.5 RESULTS AND DISCUSSIONS

Let us examine the performance of evolution of zero level set on real images. Fig. 26.5(*a*) and (*b*) are images of tennis racket and tank with noisy background. The detected object boundaries using zero level set are shown with red dots.

Fig. 26.5(a) Boundary of tennis racket detected using level set. **(b)** Segmentation result of a tank image.

In both cases, the initialization starts from the boundary of the image and the zero level set is squeezed to take the object shape. Let us take another example of white blood cells shown in Fig. 26.6(*a*). This is part of a video sequence where movement of white blood cells within vein is photographed. The rectangular curve is the initialization for the first frame. The rectangular curve is deformed to capture the blood cell shape accurately. The cell shape detected in the first frame is now used to detect the same cell in subsequent frames of the video sequence. The result for the 5th and the 10th frames is shown in Figs. 26.6(*b*) and (*c*) respectively. In both cases the zero level set curve of 4th and 9th frames are used to detect the cell in 5th and 10th frames. The cell boundary detection in both cases is near perfect despite the inhomogeneous background of the picture containing image of vessel fluid including red blood cells. This shows the potential use of level set analysis for object tracking in a video sequence and may be extended for multiple object tracking [6].

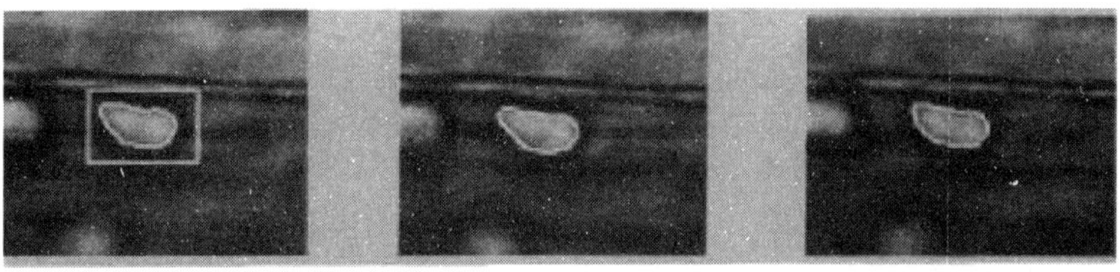

Fig. 26.6(a) White blood cell detected in the first frame with rectangular initial curve. **(b)-(c)** The same cell of Fig. 26.6**(a)** is detected in the 5th and 10th frames with initializations from 4th and 9th frames respectively.

This situation also points to a different scenario. So far we are considering situation where either the zero level set curve expands or squeezes. In order to capture the object boundary, especially for situations like tracking application, the zero level set curve may be expanded at some portion while it may be squeezed in some other portion. Let us explain this with a synthetic example in Fig. 26.7(*a*), where the initial curve representing the zero level set is drawn in red partly inside the white rectangle partly outside. The objective is to deform, both expand and squeeze the initial curve in order to capture the white rectangle. The result after 100, 150, 200 and 275 iterations are shown in Fig. 26.7(*b*)-(*e*) respectively. Note that ultimately in Fig. 26.7(*e*) the rectangular shape is detected accurately. Let us see what modifications are necessary in the level set evolution framework to incorporate both squeezing and expansion at different parts of the zero level set.

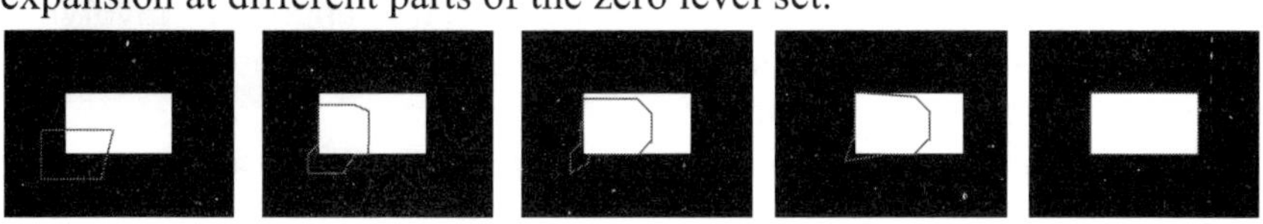

Fig. 26.7(a) Initial zero level set curve to detect the white rectangle. **(b)-(e):** Evolution of the zero level set after 100, 150, 200 and 275 iterations.

For the present implementation we have assumed that we have a priori knowledge of the intensity differential between the object and the background. This information is available from the histogram. Similar to analysis in [10], the mean image intensities for the segments inside and outside the zero level set are calculated. The difference between these mean intensities inside and outside the zero level set acts as a force to push the level set towards the object. The same idea can be extended for images with different intensity regions. The expansion, contraction mechanism can be visualized as evolution of independent zero level sets seeking separate intensity regions. An example on this concept with two different regions is shown in Fig. 26.8. The initializations are shown in Fig. 26.8(*a*). The segmented region is shown in Fig. 26.8(*d*) after 150 iterations. Fig. 26.8(*b*) and (*c*) are two intermediate states of evolved zero level sets.

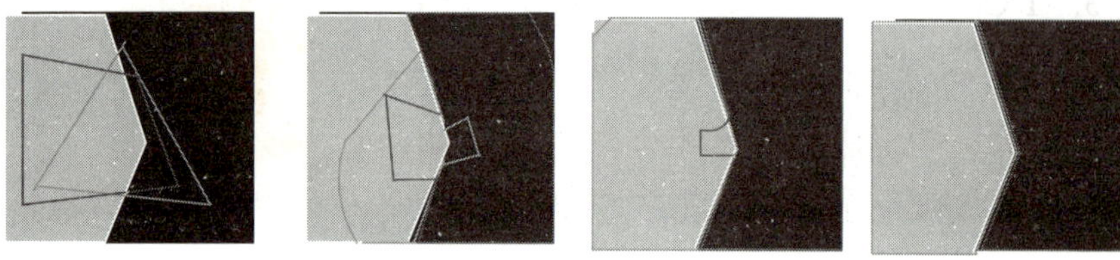

Fig. 26.8(a) Initial zero level sets. **(b)-(d):** Evolutions of two level sets at 50, 100 and 150 iterations.

This approach has several drawbacks and it is difficult to extend this concept for multiple regions without a priori knowledge of intensity difference. The region detection is also initialization dependent to some extent. The proof of convergence of this PDE based curve evolution is not explored in details. We are currently concentrating on improving these bottlenecks.

26.6 CONCLUSIONS

This paper presents a tutorial on level set analysis with specific application of image segmentation. Extension of curve evolution process for applications like tracking is also demonstrated. Unlike active contour [4] based pixel level manipulation technique, the level set approach evolves the curve in entirety. The performances of the algorithm on real images are demonstrated. Extension of the proposed approach for generalized image segmentation is indicated. However, the approach involving evolution of multiple zero level sets needs to be explored further to eliminate the dependence on a priori knowledge of image features. A suitable training scheme can generate necessary force for expansion contraction of zero level set as and when needed. An interesting extension would be in incorporating more image features in the evolution process especially variants of intensity and motion based features.

Acknowledgement

The author acknowledges the support of Virginia Image and Video

Analysis Lab, University of Virginia, USA especially for the use of white blood cell tracking data.

References

1. G Aubert and P Kornprobst, Mathematical Problems in Image Processing: PDE and the Calculus of Variations, Springer, Applied Mathematical Sciences, vol. 147, 2002.
2. D Breen and R Whitaker, "A level set approach for metamor-phosis of solid models," IEEE Transactions on Visualization and Computer Graphics, vol. 7, no. 2, pp. 173–192, April-June 2001.
3. I Cohen and I Herlin, "Tracking meteorological structures through curves matching using geodesic paths," ICCV98 Proceedings, pp. 396–401, Bombay, 1998.
4. M Kass, A Witkin, and D Terzopoulos, "Snakes: active contour models," International Journal of Computer Vision, 1(4):321–331, 1988.
5. A R Mansouri, D P Mukherjee and S T Acton, "Constraining active contour evolution via Lie groups of transformation," accepted for publication, IEEE Trans. on Image Processing, March 2003.
6. D P Mukherjee, N Ray, and S T Acton, "Level set analysis for cell detection and tracking," IEEE Trans. on Image Processing, to appear in January 2004.
7. Guillermo Sapiro, Geometric Partial Differential Equations and Image Analysis, Cambridge University Press, Cambridge, UK, 2001.
8. J A Sethian, Level set Methods and Fast Marching Methods, Cambridge University Press, UK, 1999.
9. M Y Wang, X Wang and D Guo, "A level set method for structural topology optimization," Computer Methods in Applied Mechanics and Engineering, 192 (2003), 227–246.
10. A Yezzi, S Kichenassamy, A Kumar, P Oliver and A Tannenbaum, "A Geometric Snake Model for Segmentation of Medical Imagery," IEEE Transactions on Medical Imaging, 16(2), 1997.
11. H Zhao, T Chan, B Merriman and S Osher, "A variational level set approach to multiphase motion," Journal of Computational Physics, 127, 179–195 (1996).

27

Remote Sensing Image Segmentation using M-band Wavelet Packet Frames and Neuro-Fuzzy Tools

Mausumi Acharyya[1,2] and Malay K. Kundu[3]
Machine Intelligence Unit
Indian Statistical Institute
203 B.T. Road, Kolkata - 700 108, India
email: mau_ach@yahoo.co.in, malay@isical.ac.in

ABSTRACT

The present article describes a feature extraction method based on *M*-band wavelet packet frames for segmenting remotely sensed images. Those wavelet features are first evaluated and then selected using an efficient neuro-fuzzy feature evaluation technique. Both the feature extraction and neuro-fuzzy feature evaluation processes are of unsupervised type. They do not require the knowledge of number and distribution of classes corresponding to various land-covers in remotely sensed images. The effectiveness of the methodology is demonstrated on two 4-band IRS-1A images containing 5-6 overlapping classes and a 3-band SPOT image containing 7 overlapping classes.

Keywords: *M*-band Wavelet Packet Frames, Adaptive Basis Selection, Fuzzy Feature Evaluation Index, Neural Networks, Remotely Sensed Image.

27.1 INTRODUCTION

A wavelet means small wave (oscillation), which has its energy concentrated in time (space). Wavelet transform is a tool for the analysis of transient, non-stationary, or time varying event. It is a two-dimensional expansion set for any one-dimensional signal. The wavelet expansion gives time-frequency localization, which means most of the energy of the signal is well represented by a few expansion coefficients. Wavelet system also satisfies the multiresolution conditions. This means that the lower resolution (coarser) representation of a signal can be calculated from its higher resolution information. Typically, the wavelet transform maps an image onto a low-resolution image and a series of detail images. The lower resolution image is obtained by iteratively blurring the original image; the detail images contain the information lost during this operation. The energy or mean deviation of the detail images are most commonly used features for texture based image analysis.

---

[1] Presently she is with the E-Radar Division, Electronics & Radar Development Establishment, Defence Research Development Organization, DRDO Complex, CV Raman Nagar, Bangalore 560 093, India.

[2,3] Machine Intelligence Unit, Indian Statistical Institute, Kolkata.

The major aim of the image processing /analysis research is to develop better tools, that may extract different perspectives on the same image, to understand not only its content, but also its meaning and significance. However, no image processing system can compete with the human visual system in terms of accuracy, but it can easily outperform the latter on the observational consistency, and ability to carry out detailed mathematical operations. With the passage of time, image processing research has broadened its approach from basic pixel based low-level operation to high-level analysis, to have a better semantic understanding of images. This is based on the relationship between image components and their context. What comprises an image, must be identified clearly before any further attempt is made for its detail analysis.

Segmentation is the technique for partitioning an image space into a finite number of non-overlapping and meaningful regions. The segmentation of different landcover regions precisely, in a remotely sensed image. This has been recognized as a complex problem for a long time. Remotely sensed images usually have inferior illumination quality and are mainly due to different type of environmental distributions. Spatial resolution of these images are also comparatively low. The natural scene mostly contains many objects (regions), *e.g.,* vegetation, water bodies, habitation, concrete structures, open spaces etc., but these regions are not very well separated because of low spatial resolution (spatial ambiguities). Moreover, generally the gray value assigned to a pixel is due to the average reflectance of different types of landcovers present in an area that corresponds to a pixel. Assigning unique class levels with certainty for all the pixel is thus a genuine problem of remotely sensed images. Fuzzy set theory provides a way of handling this uncertainties in a better way.

Texture is a concept used to indicate some spatial properties of image regions. Most naturally occurring patterns and natural surfaces exhibit texture. It is a fundamental characteristic of an image and plays an important role in the human visual system for recognition and interpretation of images. Despite of its pivotal role in the analysis of image data, there exist neither a formal /precise definition of texture nor an obvious quantitative measure to characterize it. Image texture can be qualitatively expressed in terms of coarseness, fineness, granularity, lineation, randomness and smoothness. The analysis of image texture content is extremely important in image analysis. It requires the understanding of how humans discriminate between different texture types and how to model algorithms to perform image analysis task in a best possible way. Another important aspect of texture is scale. The importance of scale in texture descriptions is clear from the fact there is a change in appearance of most textures when viewed at different resolutions, and also during the empirical division from macro to micro textures. Texture can also be defined as a local statistical distribution of pixel pattern (micro region) in observer's domain. Psychovisual studies reveal that the human visual system processes images in multiple scales. The visual cortex has separate cells that decomposes images into filtered images of various band of frequencies and orientation. Texture is especially suited for this type of multiresolution analysis, using both frequency and spatial information, because of its inherent characteristics. During the past two decades, wavelet analysis has become an important paradigm for multiresolution analysis, and have found important applications in various real life applications, ranging from seismology to image analysis and compression.

Remotely sensed images may contain information over a large range of scales and the spatial frequency structure also changes over different regions (*i.e.,* non-periodic signal). In remote sensing perspective, the resolution of the imagery may be different in many cases, and so it is important to understand how information changes over different scales of imagery. These reasons justify the use of multiresolution type analysis for this purpose and is most effective using wavelets. Moreover, wavelet theory is well suited in this area of study where signals are complex and non-periodic. Furthermore, wavelets are particularly good in describing a scene in terms of the scale of the textures in it.

Texture is an important property of all reflective natural surfaces which helps human visual perception system to segment and classify different objects in a digital image. In a remotely sensed image, texture is considered to be the visual impression of coarseness or smoothness caused by the variability or uniformity of image tone. These textural properties of a remotely sensed image are likely to provide valuable information for analysis (classification/segmentation), where different object regions are treated as different texture classes, *i.e.,* a multitexture segmentation problem. Note that segmentation of these images is necessary in order to identify regions of vegetation, habitation, water bodies, city area etc.

Effective classification and segmentation of images based on textural features is of key importance to many applications like image analysis, remote sensing, robot vision, query by content in large image data bases and many others. The wide variety of texture analysis methods that have been developed over the past two decades are reviewed in [1], [2]. Earlier approaches focused on first-order and second-order statistics of textures [3], [4], description using texture primitives and system rules [5]. There has been an extensive study on model based approaches like Markov random fields [6], [7], [8] and local linear transforms [9].

Haralick *et al.* [3] have used gray level co-occurrence features to analyze remotely sensed images. They have computed gray level co-occurrence matrices for a distance of one with four directions (0°, 45°, 90° and 135°). For a seven class problem they have achieved 80% classification accuracy. Rignot and Kwok [10] have analyzed SAR (Synthetic Aperture Radar) images using texture features computed from gray level co-occurrence matrices. However, they supplement these features with knowledge about the properties of SAR images. The use of various texture features have been studied for analyzing SAR images by Du [11]. He used the Gabor filters for extracting texture features and successfully segmented SAR images into categories of water, new forming ice, older ice, and multi-year ice.

All these approaches are restricted to the analysis of spatial interactions over relatively small neighborhoods, and are best suited for analysis of micro textures. In general, natural phenomena do not have a simple mathematical representation and do not even obey the restrictions imposed by several methods in order to use them suitably.

Psychovisual studies reveals that the human visual system processes images by decomposing them into filtered images of various frequencies and orientation at different scales that is capable of preserving both local and global information. This multiscale processing of the human visual system is the strong motivation for using methods based on these concepts for texture analysis [12], [13], [14], [15]. An extensive study has been made which certainly reveals the superiority of these multiscale processing over the more traditional ones.

Multiresolution techniques intend to transform images into representation in which both frequency and spatial information are present. Wavelet theory provides a more formal, precise and unified approach to multiresolution representations [16], [17]. The importance of scale in texture descriptions is clear from the change in appearance of most textures when viewed in different resolutions, and from the empirical division into micro and macro textures. These recent findings have motivated several important studies for texture analysis [18], [19], [20], [21], [22], [23].

The work of Mecocci *et al.* [24] have presented a wavelet-based algorithm combined with a *fuzzy c-means* classifier. Lindsay *et al.* [25] have used the 1D discrete wavelet transform (DWT) based on Daubechies wavelet filter. A wavelet-based texture feature set is derived in [26]. It consists of the energy of subimages obtained by the overcomplete wavelet decomposition of local areas in SAR images, where the downsampling between wavelet levels is omitted.

Simard *et al.* [27] studied the use of a decision tree classifier and multiscale texture measures to extract thematic information on the tropical vegetation cover from the Global Rain Forest Mapping (GRFM). The aim of the work by [28] is to show how coastline can be derived from SAR images by using wavelet and active contour methods. In a first step an edge detection method suggested by Mallat *et al.* [29] is applied to SAR images to detect all edges above a certain threshold. A block-tracing algorithm (BA) then determines the boundary area between land and water. Several other wavelet-based segmentation for geoscience and remote sensing applications have also been reported in the literature [30], [31].

Other approaches to segmentation of remotely sensed images include various fuzzy thresholding techniques reported in [32]. Genetic algorithm as a classifier has been investigated in the domain of satellite imagery for partitioning different land cover regions from satellite images, having complex/overlapping class boundaries in [33]. Muchoney and Williamson [34] have shown neural network classifiers to provide supervised classification results that significantly improve on traditional classification algorithms such as the Bayesian (maximum likelihood [ML])classifier.

All of these above methods use supervised classification where *a priori* knowledge about the images are essential. We apply a methodology to carry out this segmentation where no *a priori* knowledge about the image is available.

Applications of octave band wavelet decomposition scheme for texture segmentation to remotely sensed images have been studied in [24], [25], [26], [27], [28] as mentioned earlier. The octave band wavelet decomposition [17], [23] provides a logarithmic frequency resolution and are not suitable for the analysis of high frequency signals with relatively narrow bandwidth. Therefore, the main motivation of the present work is to utilize the decomposition scheme based on M-band ($M > 2$) wavelets, which, unlike the standard wavelet, provides a mixture of logarithmic and linear frequency resolution [35] [36] and hence can characterize a texture more efficiently. We conjecture that M-band wavelet decomposition would give improved segmentation results than the methods mentioned earlier. But the use of M-band wavelet decomposition gives rise to a large number of features, which incurs redundancy and confusion. Therefore, selection of the appropriate features using some feature selection algorithms is required.

The proposed methodology for segmenting a remotely sensed satellite image has two parts. The first part deals with extraction of texture features using M-band wavelet packet frame, followed by their neuro-fuzzy evaluation for selecting an optimal set of features. Note that the M-band ($M > 2$) wavelet transform is a tool for viewing signals at different scales and decomposes a signal by projecting it onto a family of functions generated from a single wavelet basis via its dilations and translations [35] [36]. Neuro-fuzzy computing [37] [38] which integrates the merits of fuzzy set theory and artificial neural networks (ANN's), enables the feature selection process artificially more intelligent. Incorporation of fuzzy set theory, as described above, helps one to deal with uncertainties in remotely sensed images in an efficient manner. ANN is used here for the task of optimization in an adaptive manner.

It may be noted that neuro-fuzzy hybridization is a widely used tool of soft computing paradigm. Soft computing is a consortium of methodologies which work synergistically and provides, in one form or another, flexible information processing capabilities for handling real life ambiguous situations. Its aim is to tolerate the imprecision, uncertainty, approximate reasoning and partial truth in order to achieve tractability, robustness, low solution cost and close resemblance with human like decision making. At this juncture, fuzzy logic (FL) and artificial neural networks (ANN's) and genetic algorithm (GA) are the three principal components where FL provides algorithms dealing with imprecision and uncertainty, ANN is used as the machinery for learning and adaptation, and GA is used for optimization and searching [39] [38].

The article is organized as follows. Section 27.2 presents the mathematical framework of *M*-band wavelets. Section 27.3 gives a brief overview of neuro-fuzzy hybridization. Section 27.4 discusses about filtering technique used in our investigation and the extraction of features. Section 27.5 provides the neuro-fuzzy feature selection algorithm. Segmentation and the quality measure is discussed in Section 27.6 while Section 27.7 analyzes experimental results and the article concludes with Section 27.8.

27.2 *M*-BAND WAVELET TRANSFORM

A. *M*-band wavelets

The standard dyadic (2-band) wavelets are not suitable for the analysis of high-frequency signals with relatively narrow bandwidth. To resolve this problem, *M*-band orthonormal wavelets [35] were developed as a direct generalization of the 2-band orthogonal wavelets of Daubechies [40]. These *M*-band wavelets are able to zoom in onto narrowband high frequency components of a signal and have been found to provide better energy compaction than 2-band wavelets [41].

The scaling function $\phi(x)$ is given by [35]

$$\phi(x) = \sum_k h(k)\sqrt{M}\phi(Mx - k). \quad (1)$$

Additionally there are $(M-1)$ wavelets which are given by [35]

$$\psi_l(x) = \sum_k g_l(k)\sqrt{M}\psi(Mx - k). \quad (2)$$

In discrete form, these functions can be indexed by scale parameter j and translation parameter k, and is written as [35]

$$\phi_{j,k}(x) = \sum_k M^{j/2}\,\phi(M^j x - k) \tag{3}$$

and
$$\psi_{j,k,l}(x) = \sum_k M^{j/2}\,\psi_l(M^j x - k),\ l = 1, \ldots, M-1. \tag{4}$$

The subspaces spanned by the functions $\phi_{j,k}(x)$ and $\psi_{j,k,l}(x)$ be respectively defined as, $V_j = \overline{span_k \phi_{j,k;}}\ \forall k \in Z$, and $W_{j,l} = \overline{span_k \psi_{j,k,l;}}\ \forall k \in Z$ [35]. It follows from equation (1) that the subspaces V_j have a nested property. If the scaling and the wavelet functions satisfy the orthonormality condition, the subspaces $\{W_{j,l}\}$ form an orthogonal decomposition of the l^2 function space and are related to the nested subspaces V_J by

$$V_j = V_{j+1} \oplus [\oplus_{l=1}^{M-1} W_{j+1,l}] \tag{5}$$

Thus a function $f(x) \in l^2$ can be expressed in terms of the sum of projections onto subspaces V_j and $W_{j,l}$ as

$$f(x) = \sum_k c(k)\,\phi_{j,k}(x) + \sum_{t=l}^{M-1} \sum_k d_l(k)\,\psi_{j,k,l}(x) \tag{6}$$

where $\oplus$ is the orthogonal plus. This is the discrete *M*-band wavelet transform (D*M*bWT). The expansion coefficients can be expressed as $c(k) = \langle f, \phi_{j,k} \rangle$ and $d_l(k) = \langle f, \psi_{j,k}^{(j)} \rangle$, $l = 1, \ldots, M-1$, where $\langle \alpha, \beta \rangle$ represents the inner product of α and β.

We can further extend our discussion in defining wavelet packets as a generalization of orthonormal and compactly supported wavelets [40]. From the subband filtering point of view, the difference between wavelet packet transform (DWPT) and standard wavelet transform (DWT) is that the former recursively decomposes the high frequency components as well, unlike the other, thus resulting in a tree structured multiband extension of the wavelet transform.

27.3 NEURO-FUZZY HYBRIDIZATION

The theory of fuzzy set has been introduced in 1965 by Zadeh [42] as a new way of representing uncertainties in everyday life. This theory provides an approximate and yet effective means for describing the characteristics of a system which is too complex or ill-defined to admit precise mathematical analysis. It is reputed to handle, to a reasonable extent, uncertainties (arising from deficiencies of information) in various applications particularly in decision making models under different kinds of risks, subjective judgment, uncertainties and ambiguity. The deficiencies may result from various reasons, *viz.,* incomplete, imprecise, not fully reliable, vague or contradictory information depending on the problem. Since this theory is a generalization of the classical set theory, it has greater flexibility to capture various aspects of incompleteness or imperfection in information about a situation.

Artificial neural networks (ANN) [43], [44] are signal processing systems that try to emulate the behavior of biological nervous systems, by providing a mathematical model of combination of numerous neurons connected in a network. These can be formally defined as *massively parallel interconnections of simple (usually adaptive) processing elements (called neurons) that interact with objects of the real world in a manner similar to biological systems.* The benefit of neural nets lies in the high computation rate provided by their inherent massive parallelism. This allows real-time processing of huge data sets with proper hardware backing. All information is stored distributed among the various connection weights. The redundancy of interconnections produces a high degree of robustness resulting in a *graceful degradation* of performance in case of noise or damage to a few nodes/links. Neural network models have been studied for many years particularly in the field of pattern recognition and image processing.

We see that fuzzy set theoretic models try to mimic human reasoning and the capability of handling uncertainty, whereas the neural network models attempt to emulate the architecture and information representation schemes of the human brain. Integration of the merits of fuzzy set theory and neural network theory therefore promises to provide, to a great extent, more intelligent systems (in terms of parallelism, fault tolerance, adaptivity and uncertainty management) to handle real life decision making problems. For the last ten years or so, there have been several attempts [37] [38] by researchers over the world in making a fusion of the merits of these theories under the heading *neuro-fuzzy computing* for improving the performance in decision making systems.

27.4 WAVELET FEATURE EXTRACTION

The notion of *M*-band wavelet, as described in Section 27.2-A, is used here to extract multiscale wavelet features of remotely sensed images. The methodology involves *M*-band wavelet packet filtering of an input image followed by adaptive basis selection. Subsequently, features are computed from this set of selected basis by using a nonlinear operator and smoothing filter. These features are then evaluated and selected using a neuro-fuzzy algorithm (described in Section 27.5).

A. *M*-band wavelet packet filters and adaptive basis selection

The objective of filtering is to transform the edges in a texture image into detectable discontinuities. The filter bank in essence is a set of bandpass filters which select frequency and orientation. In the filtering stage, we make use of orthogonal and linear phase M-band ($M = 4$) wavelet following [36].

The motivation for a larger $M(M > 2)$ comes from the desire to have a more flexible tiling of the time-frequency (scale-space) plane than that resulting form 2-band wavelet. It also enables to have some regions of uniform bandwidths rather than the logarithmic spacing of the frequency responses. Although the M-band wavelet decomposition results in a combination of linear and logarithmic frequency (scale) resolution, we conjecture that a further recursive decomposition of the high frequency regions would characterize textures better.

The M-band wavelet decomposition can be interpreted as signal decomposition in a set of independent, spatially oriented frequency channels. The discrete normalized scaling ($\phi_{j,k}$) and wavelet ($\psi_{j,k,l}$) basis functions are defined in terms of their filter responses as,

$$\phi_{j,k}(x) = M^{j/2} h_j(M^j x - k)$$

$$\text{and} \tag{7}$$

$$\psi_{j,k,l}(x) = M^{j/2} g_{j,l}(M^j x - k)$$

where j and k are the dilation and translation parameters and $l = 1, \ldots,$ $M-1$ is the number of wavelet functions. h_j and $g_{j,l}$ are respectively the sequence of lowpass and bandpass filters of increasing width indexed by j, which are expanded by inserting an appropriate number of zeros between taps and satisfy the quadrature mirror filter (QMF) condition and are called the analysis (synthesis filters).

The standard wavelet decomposition method require a down-sampling by a factor M at each scale. But this decomposition is not translation invariant which is desirable for image analysis tasks. A possible solution is achieved by using an overcomplete wavelet decomposition called a discrete wavelet frame (DWF). In the following we give a discrete M-band wavelet frame (DMbWF) decomposition, which is similar to discrete M-band wavelet transform (DMbWT), except that no downsampling is done between scales (levels of decomposition). It is mention worthy that there are other alternatives to alleviate this problem of shift (translation) variance by using complex wavelets [45].

Let $I(x, y) \in l^2(R)$ be an image in 2-D. Its DMbWF decomposition is given by,

$$
\begin{aligned}
c_j(x,y) &= [h_{j,x} * [h_{j,y} * c_{j-1}]](x,y) \\
d_{j,l}^{s_l^1}(x,y) &= [h_{j,x} * [g_{j,l,\,y} * c_{j-1}]](x,y) \\
d_{j,l}^{s_l^2}(x,y) &= [g_{j,l,x} * [h_{i,y} * c_{i-1}]](x,y) \\
d_{j,l}^{s_l^3}(x,y) &= [g_{j,l,x} * [g_{j,l,y} * c_{i-1}]](x,y) \quad \text{for } l=1,2,3
\end{aligned} \tag{8}
$$

where, $*$ denotes the convolution operator, and $c_0 = I(x, y)$ the original 2D signal. $h_{j,x}$ ($g_{j,\,l,\,x}$) and $h_{j,y}$ ($g_{j,l,y}$) are the lowpass (bandpass) filtering along x and y directions, respectively, corresponding to different scales. The number of subbands or frequency channels resulting from such decomposition (8) is found to be 16 (considering all possible combinations of l and the subband corresponding to c_j). $c_j(x, y)$ corresponds to the lower frequencies, the $d_{j,l}^{s_l^i}$ are obtained by bandpass filtering in a specific direction and thus contain the detail information at scale j.

We extend our discussion in defining discrete M-band wavelet packet transform (D*M*bWPT) as a generalization of D*M*bWT [40]. As mentioned earlier the difference between D*M*bWPT and D*M*bWT as described above, is that the former recursively decomposes the high frequency components as well, unlike the other, thus resulting in a tree structured multiband extension of the wavelet transform. At scale $j = J$, the image is first decomposed into $M \times M$ channels using all the filters h_j and $g_{j,l}$ with $l = 1, 2, 3$, and without downsampling. The process is repeated for each of the subbands for subsequent scales.

For extraction of textural features of a remotely sensed image, it is appropriate to detect the most significant frequency bands contained in the image. This leads naturally to a tree structured wavelet transform of the image. An M-band wavelet packet decomposition gives M^{2k} number of bases, for a decomposition depth of k. It is usually redundant to decompose all the subbands in each scale to achieve the full tree of decomposition. Also it is quite evident that an exhaustive search to determine the optimal basis from this large set is computationally expensive.

In order to find out a suitable basis without going for a full decomposition, we make use of an adaptive decomposition algorithm using a maximum criterion of textural measures extracted from each of the subbands [46] [49]. Then the most significant subbands are identified and it is decided whether further decomposition of the particular channel would generate more information or not. This search is computationally efficient and enables one to zoom into any desired frequency channel for further decomposition [47] [50] [48].

After decomposition of the image into $M \times M$ channels, as described above energy for each subband is evaluated. Among these subbands, those for which energy values exceed ε_1% of the energy of the parent band, are considered and decomposed further. We have further decomposed a subband if its energy value is more than some ε_2% of the total energy of all the subbands at the current scale. This step results in a set of 4-band wavelet packet bases. These bases corresponding to different resolutions are assumed to capture and characterize effectively different scales of texture of the input image. Empirically we have seen that a value of $\varepsilon_1 = 2\%$ and $\varepsilon_2 = 10\%$ are good choice for the images we have considered here.

B. Computation of features

After selection of the significant bases, a local estimator which constitutes a nonlinear operator followed by a smoothing filter, is applied to each subbands. This estimates a textural feature of a subband image in a local region around each pixel. A nonlinearity is needed in order to discriminate texture pairs with identical mean brightness and second-order statistics. There are a wide variety of textural measures. In this study we have used *energy* as the textural measures available. Since the magnitude of the correlation between the wavelet function and the image is all that is important, we have used *absolute values* of the wavelet coefficients as a generalized energy definition.

For a subband image $F_s(x, y)$ of subband number s, where $0 \le x \le M-1$, $0 \le y \le N-1$, the local energy $Eng_s(x, y)$ around the $(x, y)th$ pixel can be formally defined as

$$Eng_s(x,y) = |F_s(m,n)|, \tag{9}$$

This step is succeeded by a Gaussian low pass (smoothing) filter $h_G(x, y)$ to get a feature image. Formally, the feature image $Feat_s(x, y)$ corresponding to subband image $F_s(x, y)$ is given by

$$Feat_s(x,y) = \sum_{(a,b)\in G_{xy}} \Gamma(F_s(a,b)h_G(x-a, y-b)),$$

where $\Gamma(\cdot)$ gives the energy measure and G_{xy} is a $G \times G$ window centered at pixel with coordinates (x, y). This step results in a set of feature images $Feat_s(x, y)$, from which a set of feature vectors are derived. These feature vectors corresponding to the decomposed images at different resolutions are assumed to capture and characterize effectively different scales of texture of the remotely sensed image.

27.5 NEURO-FUZZY FEATURE EVALUATION

The wavelet features extracted in Section 27.4 are now evaluated in a neuro-fuzzy framework under unsupervised learning. The method is a modification of an earlier one [51]. This modification enables one to handle large data sets in an efficient manner. Note that for an image a large number of pattern vectors are generated as described in Section 27.4. These selected features are then used for the purpose of segmenting the different regions in remotely sensed images.

A. Fuzzy feature evaluation index and membership function

The feature evaluation index for a set of transformed features is defined as

$$E = \frac{2}{s(s-1)} \sum_{p} \sum_{q \neq p} \frac{1}{2} [\mu^{T}_{pq}(1-\mu^{O}_{pq}) + \mu^{O}_{pq}(1-\mu^{T}_{pq})]. \tag{10}$$

Here μ^{O}_{pq} and μ^{T}_{pq} are the degree that both the *p*th and *q*th patterns belong to the same cluster in the *n*-dimensional original feature space, and in the n′-dimensional ($n' \leq n$) transformed feature space respectively. μ values determine how similar a pair of patterns are in the respective features spaces. *s* is the number of samples on which the feature evaluation index is computed.

The feature evaluation index decreases as the membership value representing the degree of belonging of *p*th and *q*th patterns to the same cluster in the transformed feature space tends to either 0 (when $\mu^{O} < 0.5$) or 1 (when $\mu^{O} > 0.5$). In other words, the index decreases as the decision on the similarity between a pair of patterns (*i.e.,* whether they lie in the same cluster or not) becomes more and more crisp. This means, if the intercluster/intracluster distances in the transformed space increase/ decrease, the feature evaluation index of the corresponding set of features decreases. Therefore, our objective is to select those features for which the evaluation index becomes minimum; thereby optimizing the decision on the similarity of a pair of patterns with respect to their belonging to a cluster.

The membership function μ_{pq} in a feature space, satisfying the characteristics of *E* (10), may be defined as [51]

$$\mu_{pq} = 1 - \frac{d_{pq}}{D} \quad \text{if } d_{pq} \leq D,$$

$$= 0, \qquad \text{otherwise}, \tag{11}$$

where the distance d_{pq} between the *p*th and *q*th patterns can be written as

$$d_{pq} = \left[\sum_{i} w_i^2 (x_{pi} - x_{qi})^2 \right]^{1/2},$$

$$= \left[\sum_i w_i^2 \chi_i^2 \right]^{1/2}, \chi_i = (x_{pi} - x_{qi}), \tag{12}$$

The term $w_i \in [0, 1]$ represents weighting coefficient corresponding to ith feature, and x_{pi} and x_{qi} are values of ith feature (in the corresponding feature space) of pth and qth patterns, respectively. Note that, the higher the value of d_{pq}, the lower is the similarity between pth and qth patterns, and *vice versa*. D is a parameter which reflects the minimum separation between a pair of patterns belonging to two different clusters. When $d_{pq} = 0$ and $d_{pq} = D$, we have $\mu_{pq} = 1$ and 0, respectively. If $d_{pq} = \frac{D}{2}$, $\mu_{pq} = 0.5$. That is, when the distance between the patterns is just half the value of D, the difficulty in making a decision, whether both the patterns are in the same cluster or not, becomes maximum; thereby making the situation most ambiguous. Note that the computation of μ_{pq} in (11) does not require the information on class label of the patterns.

The term D in (11) may be expressed as $D = \alpha d_{\max}$, where $d_{\max}$ is the maximum separation between a pair of patterns in the entire feature space, and $0 < \alpha \leq 1$ is a user defined constant. α determines the degree of flattening of the membership function (11). The higher the value of α, more will be the degree, and *vice-versa*. $d_{\max}$ is defined as

$$d_{\max} = \left[\sum_i (x_{\max i} - x_{\min i})^2 \right]^{1/2}, \tag{13}$$

where $x_{\max i}$ and $x_{\min i}$ are the maximum and minimum values of the ith feature in the corresponding feature space.

The membership value μ_{pq} is dependent on w_i. The values of w_i (< 1) make the μ_{pq} function of (11) flattened along the axis of d_{pq}. The lower the value of w_i, the higher is extent of flattening. In the extreme case, when $w_i = 0$, $\forall i$, $d_{pq} = 0$ and $\mu_{pq} = 1$ for all pair of patterns, *i.e.*, all the patterns lie on the same point making them indiscriminable.

The weight w_i in (12) reflects the relative importance of the feature x_i in measuring the similarity of a pair of patterns. The higher the value of w_i, the more is the importance of x_i in characterizing a cluster or discriminating various clusters. $w_i = 1$ (0) indicates most (least) importance of x_i.

As mentioned earlier, our objective is to minimize the evaluation index E (10) which involves the terms μ^O and μ^T. The computation of μ^T requires (11)–(13), while μ^O needs these equations with $w_i = 1$, $\forall i$. Therefore, the evaluation index E (10) is a function of **w**, if we consider ranking of n features in a set. The problem of feature selection/ranking thus reduces to finding a set of w_is for which E becomes minimum; w_is indicating the relative importance of x_is. The task of minimization, as in [51], is performed using gradient-descent technique in a connectionist framework under unsupervised mode. This is described below.

B. Connectionist model

The network (Fig. 27.1) consists of an input, a hidden and an output layer [51]. The input layer consists of a pair of nodes corresponding to each feature, *i.e.,* the number of nodes in the input layer is $2n$, for n-dimensional (original) feature space. The hidden layer consists of n number of nodes which compute the part χ_i^2 of Eqn. (12) for each pair of patterns. The output layer consists of two nodes. One of them computes μ^O, and the other μ^T. The feature evaluation index E (10) is computed from these μ-values off the network.

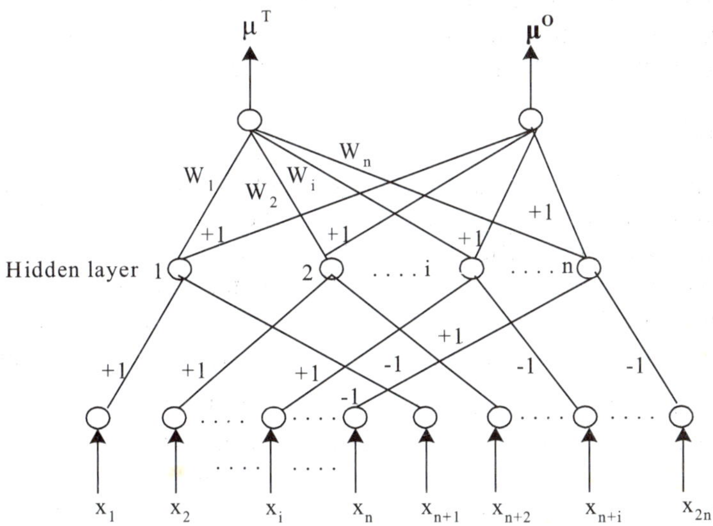

Fig. 27.1 A schematic diagram of the neural network model for feature selection.

Input nodes receive activations corresponding to feature values of each pair of patterns. A jth node in the hidden layer is connected only to an ith and $(i + n)$th input nodes via connection weights +1 and −1, respectively, where j, $i = 1, 2, ..., n$ and $j = i$. The output node computing μ^T-values is connected to a jth node in the hidden layer via connection weight $W_j(= w_j^2)$, whereas that computing μ^O-values is connected to all the nodes in the hidden layer via connection weights +1 each.

During learning, each pair of patterns are presented at the input layer and the evaluation index is computed. The weights W_js are updated in order to minimize the index E. The task of minimization of E (10)

with respect to **W** is performed using gradient-descent technique, where the change in W_j (ΔW_j) is computed as

$$\Delta W_j = -\eta \frac{\partial E}{\partial W_j}, \forall j, \tag{14}$$

η is the learning rate. Note that, $d_{\max}$ is directly computed from the unlabeled training set. The values of $d_{\max}$ and α are stored in both the output nodes for the computation of D. For details concerning the operation of the network, one may refer to [51].

C. Modified neuro-fuzzy algorithm for handling large data

As we have seen in Section 27.4, the number of patterns generated for an $N \times N$ image is N^2, *i.e.,* $s = N^2$. Each of these patterns corresponds to a pixel and has all the multiscale wavelet feature extracted in Section 27.4. Therefore, for selecting an optimal set of features out of them, the number of patterns to be presented to the connectionist system in one epoch, during its training, is $\frac{s(s-1)}{2} = \frac{N^2(N^2-1)}{2}$, which is a very large quantity. This incurs a very high computational time. In order to avoid this situation, *i.e.,* in order to make the neuro-fuzzy algorithm computationally more efficient, we, first of all, apply a clustering algorithm (e.g., *k*-means clustering algorithm) on the entire feature space, for grouping the data, and the cluster centers $\boldsymbol{cen_q}$'s are noted. Then two sets of samples, namely, $S = \{\boldsymbol{x}_1, \boldsymbol{x}_2, ..., \boldsymbol{x}_p, ..., \boldsymbol{x}_{N^2}\}$ and $S_c = \{\boldsymbol{cen}_1, \boldsymbol{cen}_2, ..., \boldsymbol{cen}_c\}$ are formed. That is, S is the entire training set, and S_c is the set of c cluster centers (for c clusters) obtained by the clustering algorithm. Now the similarity between the patterns and these cluster centers are computed, instead of computing it for every pair of patterns. These cluster centers are considered as representatives (prototypes) of all the points belonging to the respective clusters. Thus, the number of patterns to be presented to the network in one epoch becomes $\frac{s(s_c-1)}{2} = \frac{N^2(c-1)}{2}$, where $s = |S|$ and $s_c = |S_c| << s$.

Note that the clustering algorithm at this stage provides a first hand knowledge about the various landcovers in a remotely sensed image. Based on this knowledge, neuro-fuzzy feature selection algorithm is applied, for removing the redundant and confusing features, and thereby improving the segmentation result. Thus the algorithm for finding optimal $\boldsymbol{W}$ is as follows.

Algorithm for learning ***W***

- Cluster the patterns using an appropriate algorithm (*e.g. k-means* clustering algorithm) and the cluster centers $\boldsymbol{cen}_q$'s are noted.
- Calculate d_{max} from the unlabeled training set and store it in both the output nodes. Store β (user specified) in both the output nodes.
- Initialize W_j with small random values in [0, 1].
- Repeat until convergence, *i.e.,* until the value of E becomes less than or equal to certain predefined small quantity, or number of iterations attains, certain predefined number of iterations:
  - For each pair of pattern $\boldsymbol{x}_p$ and $\boldsymbol{cen}_q$, $\forall p, q$:
    * Present the pattern pair to the input layer.
    * Compute ΔW_j, for each j using the updating rule in (14).
  - Update W_j for each j with ΔW_j averaged over all the pattern pairs.

E (10), after convergence, attains a local minimum and then the weights ($W_j = w_j^2$) of the links connecting hidden nodes and the output node computing μ^T -values, indicate the order of importance of the features. Note that this unsupervised method performs the task of feature selection without clustering the feature space explicitly and does not need to know the number of clusters present in the feature space.

27.6 SEGMENTATION AND QUALITY MEASURE

Having selected the features, the main task is to integrate these features to produce a segmentation. We define a scale-space signature as the vector of features at different scales taken at a single pixel in an image,

$$\boldsymbol{Feat}(i,j)=[Feat_0(i,j), Feat_1(i,j), Feat_2(i,j), ..., Feat_k(i,j)]$$

These scale-space signatures are considered as feature vectors in a feature space.

Let us assume that there are M texture categories, C_1, ..., C_c, present in the image. If our texture features that have already been obtained are capable of discriminating these categories then the patterns belonging to each category will form a cluster in the feature space which is compact and isolated from clusters corresponding to other texture categories. Segmentation algorithm accept as input a set of features and put a class labeling for each pixel. Fundamentally this can be considered a multidimensional data clustering problem. We have used a traditional *k-means* clustering algorithm [52].

27.6.1 Quantitative Performance Measure

A quantitative index β [32] is used to evaluate the segmentation results. β is defined as the ratio of the total variation and within class variation. Let

n_i be the number of pixels in the *i*th ($i = 1, 2, ..., c$) region. X_{ij} is the gray value of the *j*th pixel ($j = 1, 2, ... n_i$) in the *i*th region, and $\overline{X_i}$ is the mean of n_i gray values in the *i*th region. Then β is defined as

$$\beta = \frac{\sum_{i=1}^{c}\sum_{j=1}^{n_i}(X_{ij} - \overline{X})^2}{\sum_{i=1}^{c}\sum_{j=1}^{n_i}(X_{ij} - \overline{X_i})^2} \tag{15}$$

where, n is the size of the image and $\overline{X}$ is the mean gray value of the image.

The numerator is constant for a given image and number of classes present in the image. Therefore, the value of β is dependent only on the denominator. The denominator, on the other hand, decreases with homogeneity of a region. So higher the value of β, better is the segmentation.

27.7 SEGMENTATION OF *IRS* AND *SPOT* IMAGES

In this section, the results on implementation of our algorithm on several remotely sensed images are provided. The images considered are two IRS-1A images and one SPOT image.

A: Data sets

IRS Images

The IRS-1A images (Fig. 27.2 and 27.6) were obtained from Indian Remote Sensing Satellite which is a circular sun-synchronous satellite, rotating around the earth at the rate of 14 orbits per day, at an altitude of 904 km and a repetition cycle of 22 days (NRSA 1986). This satellite is equipped with two different sensors LISS (Linear Imaging Self Scanner)-I and LISS-II. LISS-I has a spatial resolution of 72.5m × 72.5m while that for LISS-II is 36.25m × 36.25m. The IRS-1A images used for this work were taken using the scanner LISS-II in the wavelength range 0.45μm – 0.86μm. The whole spectrum range is decomposed into four spectral bands namely,

band 1 - blue band of wavelength 0.45μm – 0.52 μm,

band 2 - green band of wavelength 0.52μm – 0.59 μm,

band 3 - red band of wavelength 0.62μm – 0.68 μm and

band 4 - near infra red wavelength 0.77μm – 0.86 μm.

The images in Fig. 27.2(*a*)-27.2(*d*) cover an area around the city of Calcutta in these four bands. In all these figures the prominent black stretch across them is the river *Hoogly*. There is a prominent light patch on the bottom right corner, which is the *Salt Lake stadium* and the black patches nearby are the *fisheries*. In the upper right part of the images, there is a distinct line structure corresponding to the *airport runway*. In total there are five major classes in which the regions of Calcutta IRS images can be classified. These are *water bodies* (WB), *vegetation* (VEG), *habitation* (HAB), *city area* (CA) and *open spaces* (OS).

Figures 27.6(*a*)-6(*d*) show a part of the city of Bombay in the four aforesaid bands respectively. The elongated city area is surrounded by the Arabian sea. There is a *concrete structure* (on the right side top corner) connecting Bombay to New Bombay. On the southern part of the city, there are several islands including the famous *Elephanta islands*. The *dockyard is* situated on the south-eastern part of Bombay, which can be seen as a set of three finger like structure. On the upper part of the images, towards left, there is a distinct crisscrossed structure, which corresponds to the *Santa Cruz airport*. In total the regions of Bombay images can be classified into six major classes, *viz., turbid water 1* (TW1), *turbid water 2* (TW2), *concrete* (CONCR), *habitation* (HAB), *vegetation* (VEG) and *open spaces* (OS). The sea water is decomposed into two classes TW1 and TW2 for better classification since they have somewhat different reflectance properties due to variation in sea water density (as seen in Figure 27.6(d)).

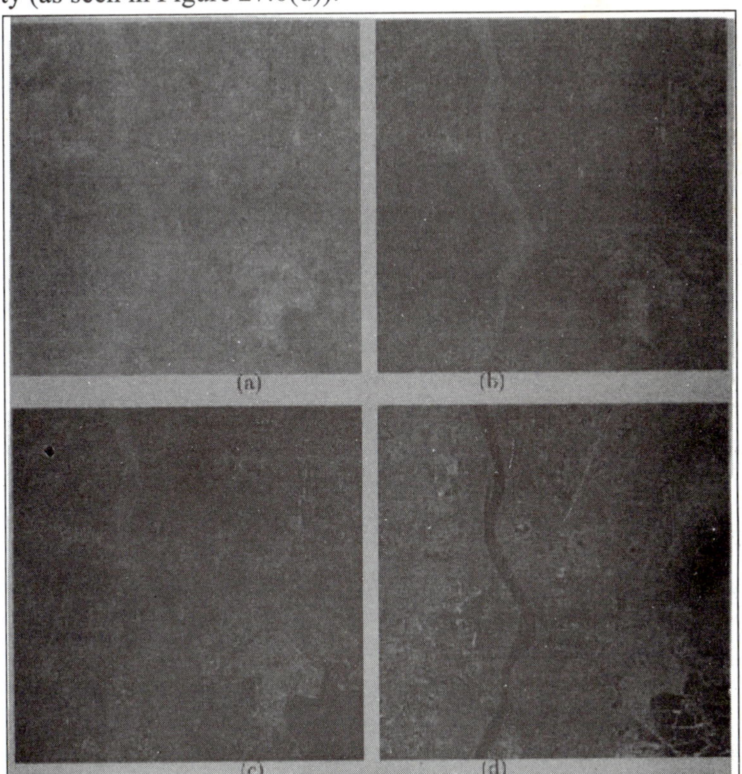

Fig. 27.2 IRS-1A image of Calcutta *a*) band-1 *b*) band-2 *c*) band-3 *d*) band-4

SPOT image

The SPOT image was taken by the French Satellites SPOT (Systems Probataire d' Observation de la Terre) [53], launched in 1986 and 1990. They carry two imaging devices that consist of a linear array of charge coupled device (CCD). Two imaging modes are possible, the multi-spectral and panchromatic modes. The image considered here has three bands in the multispectral mode. These are:

band 1 - green band of wavelength $0.50\mu m - 0.59\ \mu m$,

band 2 - red band of wavelength $0.61\mu m - 0.68\ \mu m$ and

band 3 - near infra red band of wavelength $0.79\mu m - 0.89\ \mu m$.

Figures 27.10(*a*)-27.10(*c*) are SPOT images of Calcutta and were taken in these three bands with a spatial resolution of $20.0\ m \times 20.0\ m$. In all these figures the prominent black stretch across them corresponds to the river *Hoogly*. There are two distinct black, elongated patches below the river, on the left side of the images. These are water bodies, the one to the left being *Garden Reach Lake* and the one to the right being the *Khiderpore dockyard.* Just to the right of these water bodies, there is a thin line starting from the right bank of the river and going to the bottom edge of the images, which corresponds to *Talis nala.* On the right side of the images, there is a triangular patch which is the *race course.* On the top right hand side of the images, there is a thin line, stretching from the top edge and ending in the middle of the image, which corresponds to the *Beleghata canal.* A bridge called the *Rabindra setu,* cuts the river near the top of the images. This image has seven major classes, which are *turbid water* (TW), *pond water* (PW), *concrete* (CONCR), *vegetation* (VEG), *habitation* (HAB), *open space* (OS) and *roads/bridges* (B/R).

All the images considered in this investigation are of size 512×512. Due to poor illumination, the actual object classes present in the input images are not visible clearly. So we have presented the histogram equalized images in Fig. 27.2(*a*)-27.2(*d*), 27.6(*a*)-27.6(*d*) and 27.10(*a*)-27.10(*c*), which highlight the different landcover regions. But the algorithms were implemented on the actual inputs.

B. Results

Here we demonstrate the effectiveness of our methodology over several remotely sensed images as described in Section 27.7-A. In order to validate the importance of neuro-fuzzy feature evaluation, we show how the feature dimensionality can be greatly reduced after feature evaluation. The test images have several fine (line) structures (roads and bridges). In order to detect these structures the window size has been kept small (3×3).

The total number of features considering all the bands are found to be 10 using the proposed feature extraction methodology described in Section 27.4. Figure 27.3 shows the segmented output of the IRS-1A image using all these 10 features considering the number of classes to be $c = 5$. The β index is found to be 3.65887. The neuro-fuzzy feature evaluation algorithm reduces the number of features to only one for which the segmentation result is given in Fig. 27.4. The value of β index is found to be 3.83431 signifying an improvement in segmentation quality. The *stadium* and *fisheries* as well as the *airport runway* are quite distinctly discernible in the segmented output (Fig. 27.4) as compared to Figure 27.3. We can comment on this finding that since we have considered all the 4 bands for feature extraction, most of the features so extracted contain very less information and hence can be discarded. It can also be inferred that out of these 4 bands only one band is significant and contains most of the image information. It is also evident from the Fig. 27.2(*a*)-27.2(*d*) that the image corresponding to the near infra red band (Fig. 27.2(*d*)) is the most significant band. The feature with which we have obtained the above segmentation result after neuro-fuzzy evaluation corresponds to band-4 and validates our comment. So we can easily disregard all the other bands and keep only the band-4 image for feature extraction. Comparing Figs. 27.3 and 27.4 we find that we get better segmentation output in the *saltlake stadium* area, also the compactness of the various classes present in the IRS-1A Calcutta image

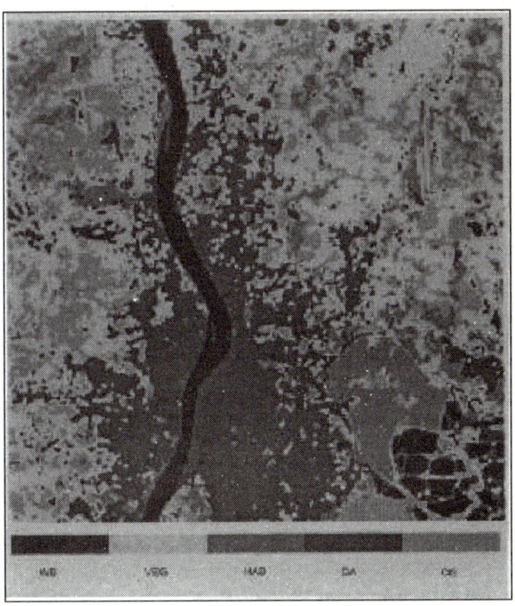

Fig. 27.3 Segmented output of Calcutta IRS-1A image with $c = 5$ and $\beta = 3.65887$

Fig. 27.4 Segmented output of Calcutta IRS-1A image with $c = 5$ and $\beta = 3.84578$

Fig. 27.5 Segmented output of Calcutta IRS-1A image using average and busyness as features with $c = 5$ ($\beta = 2.84578$)

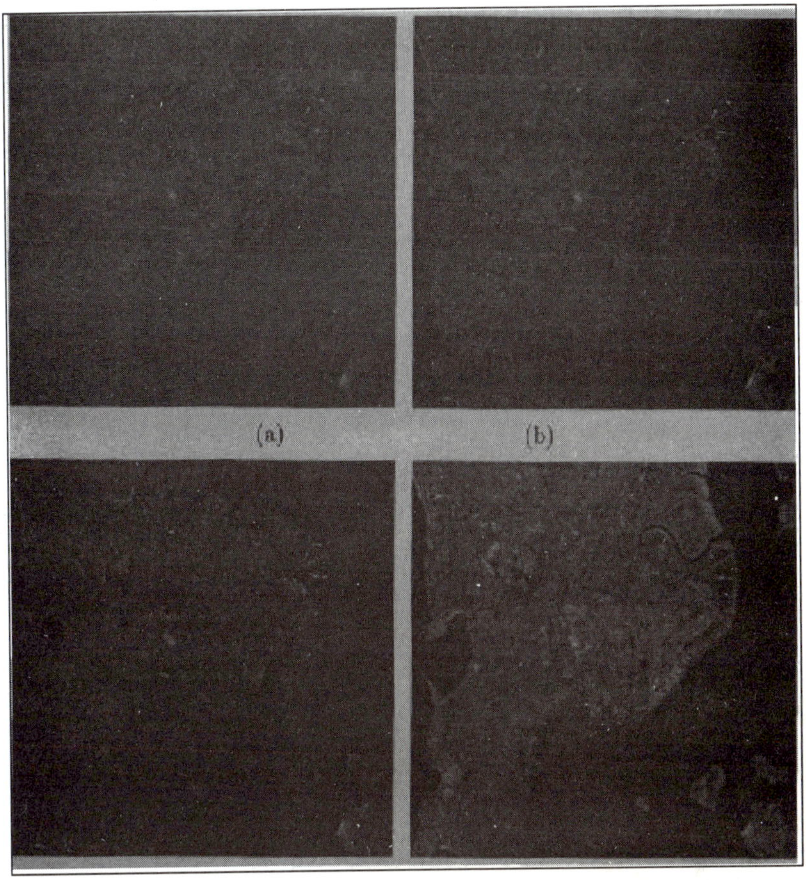

Fig. 27.6 IRS-1A image of Bombay *a*) band-1 *b*) band-2 *c*) band-3 *d*) band-4

increases after the feature evaluation step. For a comparative study we present the segmentation result (Fig. 27.5) obtained by using *k-means* clustering algorithm with average and busyness computed over 3 × 3 neighborhood [54] incorporating local information, as features. The figure shows clear improvement in segmentation output using our methodology both quantitatively (β value) and qualitatively (structural details).

The segmentation result of the IRS-1A image of Bombay is shown in Fig. 27.7 considering number of classes to be $c = 6$, and the β value is found to be 8.01462. The number of extracted features from all the 4 bands is found to be 12 as obtained by Section 27.4. The feature dimensionality is reduced to one after neuro-fuzzy feature evaluation. As in the previous case, β index (8.21309) shows better segmentation quality. In the segmented output after the feature evaluation step

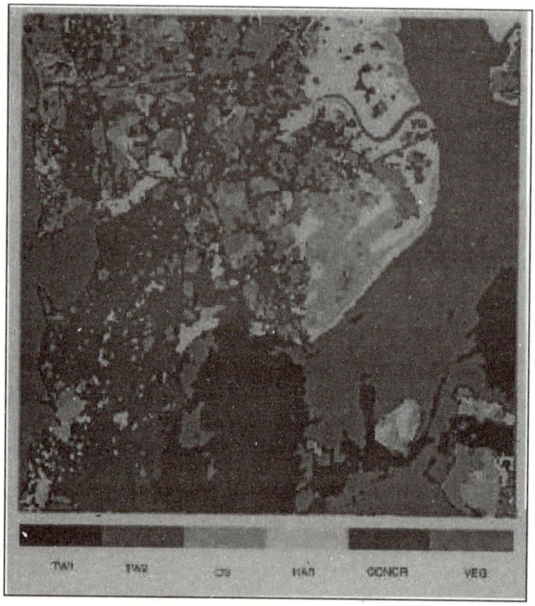

Fig. 27.7 Segmented output with $c = 6$ and $\beta = 8.01462$

(Fig. 27.8), it can be seen that the *dockyard,* the *concrete structure* connecting Bombay and New Bombay and *Santa Cruz airport* are very well detected. Even for this image of Bombay we can reiterate the above comments. Here also the feature obtained after the feature evaluation step corresponds to band-4 image and contains most of the image information. Comparing Figs. 27.7 and 27.8 we find that various objects and regions *(santa cruz airport, dockyard, roads and bridges* etc.) are identified more prominently. Moreover, the feature evaluation step increases the compactness of the various classes similar to the case of IRS-lA Calcutta image. In this case also a comparative study is presented. The segmentation result in Fig. 27.9 as mentioned above obtained by using *k-means* clustering algorithm with average and busyness as features. Here also we can find an improvement in segmentation.

In the case of SPOT image of Calcutta (Fig. 27.10(*a*)-27.10(*c*)), we have initially considered all the 10 features extracted by the wavelet based method. The segmentation result is given in Fig. 27.11 with $c = 7$ and a β value of 3.27832. After the neuro-fuzzy feature evaluation the number of features reduces to three. The segmentation result is given in Figure 27.12, and β value (3.45361) indicates better segmentation quality. It is to be noted that not only the *race course* but also a triangular outline (which is an open space) corresponding to the *track* of the *race course* are also detected. Here the *Rabindra Setu* has also been detected along

Fig. 27.8 Segmented output with $c = 6$ and $\beta = 8.21309$

Fig. 27.9 Segmented output with $c = 6$ with average and busyness as features ($\beta = 7.21309$)

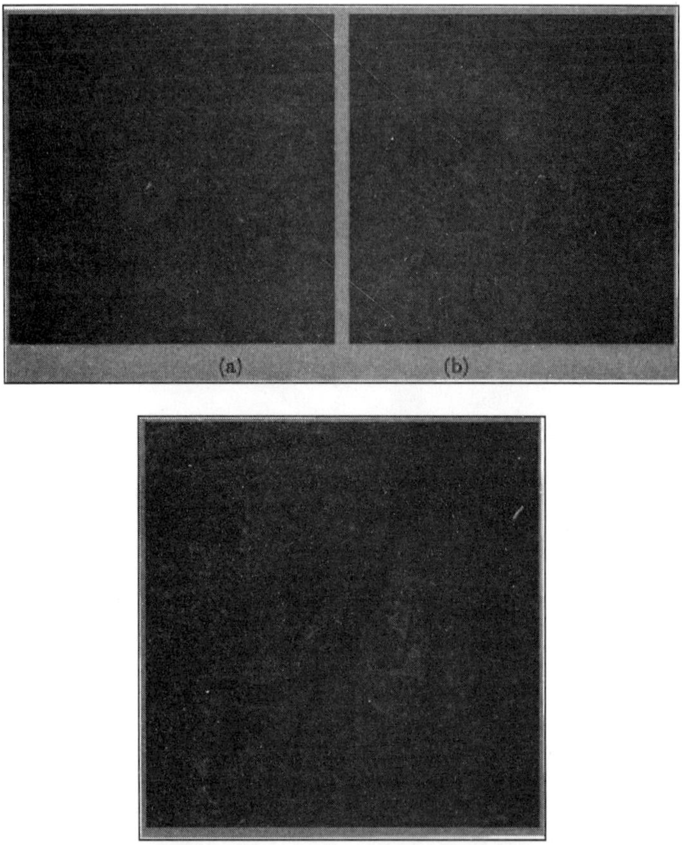

Fig. 27.10 SPOT image of Calcutta *a*) band-1 *b*) band-2 *c*) band-3

Fig. 27.11 Segmented output with $c = 7$ and $\beta = 3.27832$

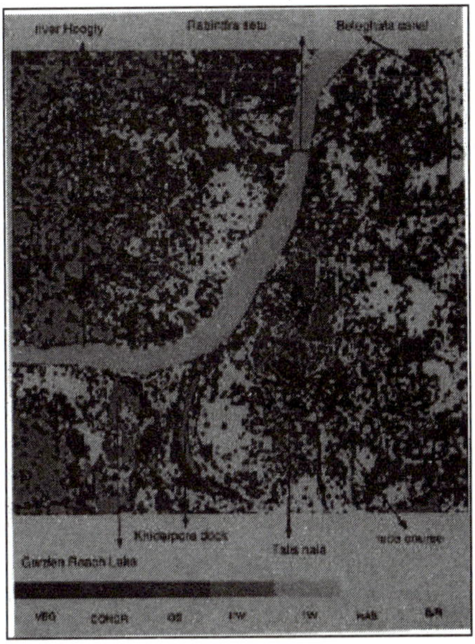

Fig. 27.12 Segmented output with $c = 7$ and $\beta = 3.45631$

with the *Talis nala* and *Beleghata canal.* Moreover, the *Khiderpore dock* and *Garden Reach Lake* are quite discernible. In this case all the three bands are important and furnish some information. The features obtained after the feature evaluation step correspond to each of the three bands. Comparing Figs. 27.11 and 27.12, it can be seen that the *race course* can be identified quite vividly (Fig. 27.12). In this case also the compactness of the various classes increases after the feature evaluation step. The segmentation result along with the β value obtained by using *k-means* clustering algorithm with average and busyness as features (as mentioned above) is given in Fig. 27.13 for a comparative study validating that the features extracted are characterize the remotely sensed images in a better way.

Table 27.1 *Performance evaluation of Nat l0a*

Methods/filters		Classification	Number of features
Proposed method *M*-band wavelet	without feature evaluation	71.7%	19
	with feature evaluation	79.5%	7
Heuristic Gabor filter bank (d) [56]		67.7%	20
Optimized Optimized representation Gabor filter [14] [57]		64.1%	15
Full rate QMF FIR filter f8a (d) [56]		60.3%	40
Critically sampled QMF FIR. f8a (d) [56]		57.7%	13

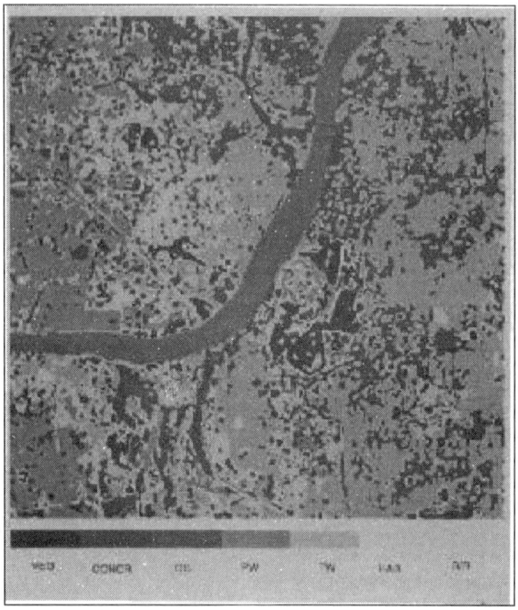

Fig. 27.13 Segmented output with $c = 7$ using average and busyness as features ($\beta = 2.45631$)

In order to prove the efficacy of our algorithm we have tested it on a synthetic 10-texture mosaic of size 256 × 512 comprising of ten different Brodazt textures (Fig. 27.14(*a*). The segmented output is presented in Fig. 27.14(*b*). Note that although the image contains 10 different Brodazt textures, some of them are not distinctly identifiable visually as depicted in Fig. 27.14(*a*). Interestingly, the proposed methodology has been able to identify more or less all the classes. Here the percentage of correctly classified pixels has been found to be 79.55%.

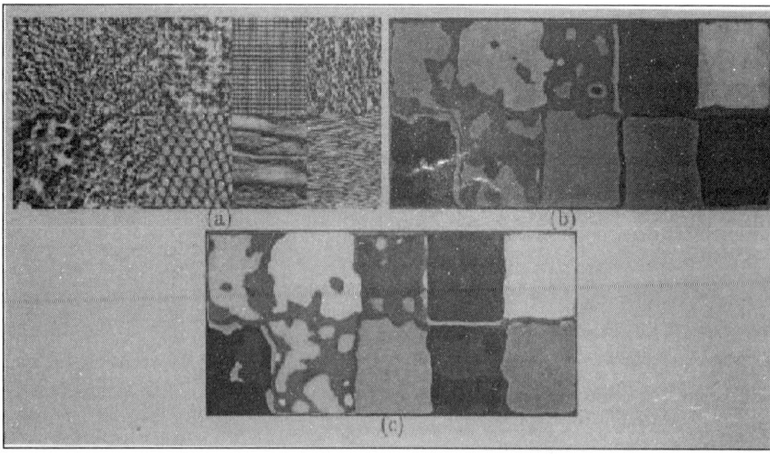

Fig. 27.14 (*a*) *Nat* 10*a*, segmented output (*b*) after and (*c*) before neuro-fuzzy feature evaluation

As part of the investigation, an extensive comparison has been made to show the superiority of the proposed methodology over various existing related algorithms. Note that several approaches to multichannel filtering for texture segmentation have been studied and a comparative performance evaluation is presented by Randen and Husϕy in [55].

27.8 CONCLUSION

In this article, we have presented a scheme to show how wavelet theory and neuro-fuzzy hybridization together can be applied in the domain of remotely sensed imagery for segmentation purpose. The use of wavelet theory via *M*-band wavelet decomposition of remotely sensed images provides an efficient representation of these images in terms of frequencies in different directions and orientations at different resolutions. This representation is obtained by segmenting some wavelet features from multispectral remotely sensed images. This facilitates an improved segmentation of the different class regions. The feature extraction method splits the lower as well as the higher frequency bands, and results in a tree structure. This enables the system to extract their characteristic features in the lower as well as the higher frequency bands of remotely sensed images. The neuro-fuzzy feature evaluation method helps in searching for important features efficiently from a remotely sensed image where the various classes are overlapping in nature. Both the feature extraction and neuro-fuzzy feature evaluation schemes are unsupervised and do not require any *a priori* knowledge about the number of classes, and spatial relationship of different regions in these images. Note that the neuro-fuzzy feature evaluation method presented here is a modified version of an existing one described in [51]. This modification helps in dealing with large data set efficiently. We have tested our algorithm on synthetic data comprising of natural textures. The results validates that our methodology is indeed superior to some of the related ones existing in the literature. Also the results presented using average and busyness as features and using *k-means* clustering algorithm for a comparative study show that our methodology is indeed effective in characterizing remotely sensed images in a better way.

The features obtained by the feature extraction method have been able to segment the remotely sensed images satisfactorily. It is been found that for the IRS-1A images that ultimately one feature is selected which corresponds to the band 4 of these images. However, for the SPOT image three features are selected. Almost all the desired classes are obtained in the segmented output satisfactorily. Moreover, the compactness of the various classes increases after the neuro-fuzzy feature evaluation step.

References

1. T R Reed and J M H du Buf, "A review of recent texture segmentation and feature extraction techniques," *CVGIP: Image Understanding*, Vol. 57, no. 3, pp. 359–372, 1993.
2. M Tuceryan and A K Jain, "Texture analysis," In *Handbook of Pattern Recognition and Computer Vision*, C H Chen, L F Pau, and P S P Wang, Eds., chapter 2, pp. 235–276. World Scientific, Singapore, 1993.
3. R M Haralick, K Shanmugam, and I Dinstein, "Texture feature for image classification," *IEEE Trans. on Systems, Man and Cybernetics*, Vol. 8, no. 6, pp. 610–621, 1973.
4. P C Chen and T Pavlidis, "Segmentation by texture using correlation," *IEEE Trans. on Pattern Analysis and Machine Intelligence*, Vol. 5, pp. 64–69, Jan 1983.
5. R M Haralick, "Statistical and structural approaches to texture," *Proc. IEEE,* Vol. 67, pp. 768–804, 1979.
6. G C Cross and A K Jain, "Markov random field texture models," *IEEE Trans. on Pattern Analysis and Machine Intelligence*, Vol. 5, pp. 25–39, 1983.
7. S Geman and D Geman, "Stochastic relaxation, gibbs distri-butions, and the bayesian restoration of images," *IEEE Trans. Pattern Anal. and Machine Intell.*, Vol. 6, pp. 721–741, 1984.
8. R L Kashyap and A Khotanzad, "A model-based method for rotation invariant texture classification," *IEEE Trans. on Pattern Analysis and Machine Intelligence*, Vol. 8, no. 4, pp. 472–481, 1986.
9. K L Laws, "Rapid texture identification," in *Proc. SPIE*, 1980, Vol. 238, pp. 376–380.
10. E Rignot and R Kowk, "Extraction of textural features in sar images: Statistical model and sensitivity," in *Proc. of IEEE Geoscience and Remote Sensing Symposium,* May 1990.
11. L J Du, "Texture segmentation of sar images using localized spatial filtering," in *Proc. of Intl. Geoscience and Remote Sensing Symposium*, 1990, pp. 1983–1986.
12. A K Jain and F Farrokhnia, "Unsupervised texture segmentation using gabor filters," *Pattern Recognition*, Vol. 24, no. 12, pp. 1167–1186, 1991.
13. C C Chen and D C Chen, "Multiresolution gabor filters in texture analysis," *Pattern Recognition Letters*, Vol. 17, no. 10, pp. 1069–1076, 1996.

14. A C Bovik, M Clark, and W S Geisler, "Multichannel texture analysis using localized spatial filters," *IEEE Trans. on Pattern Analysis and Machine Intelligence*, Vol. 12, pp. 55–73, 1990.
15. M R Turner, "Texture discrimination by gabor function," *Biological Cybernetics*, Vol. 55, pp. 71–82, 1986.
16. I Daubechies, *Ten Lectures on Wavelets,* Soc. Ind. Applied Math, Philadelphia, 1992.
17. S Mallat, "A theory for multiresolution signal decomposition: The wavelet representation," *IEEE Trans. on Pattern Analysis and Machine Intelligence*, Vol. 11, no. 7, pp. 674–693, 1989.
18. B S Manjunath and R Chellappa, "A computational approach to boundary detection," *Proc. CVPR*, pp. 358–363, 1991.
19. T R Reed and H Wechsler, "Segmentation of textured images and gestalt organization using spatial/ spatial frequency repre-sentation," *IEEE Trans. on Pattern Analysis and Machine Intelligence*, Vol. 12, pp. 1–12, Jan 1990.
20. J R Bergen and M S Landy, "Computational modeling of visual texture segregation," in *Computational Models of Visual Processing,* M. S. Landy and J. A. Movshan, Eds., pp. 472–481. The MIT Press, Cambridge, MA, 1991.
21. P H Carter, "Texture discrimination using wavelets," in *SPIE Applications of Digital Image Processing XIV*, 1991, Vol. 1567, pp. 432–438.
22. M Unser and M Eden, "Multiresolution feature extraction and selection for texture segmentation," *IEEE Trans. on Pattern Analysis and Machine Intelligence*, Vol. 11, pp. 717–728, 1989.
23. M Unser, "Texture classification and segmentation using wavelet frames," *IEEE Trans. on Image Processing*, Vol. 4, no. 11, pp. 1549–1560, 1995.
24. A Mecocci, P Gamba, A Marazzi, and M Barni, "Texture segmentation in remote sensing images by means of packet wavelets and fuzzy clustering," in *Proc. of the European Symposium on Satellite and Remote Sensing II,* Sept. 1995, Vol. SPIE 2584, pp. 142–157.
25. R W Lindsay, D B Percival, and D A Rothrock, "The discrete wavelet transform and the scale analysis of the surface properties of sea ice," *IEEE Trans. on Geoscience and Remote Sensing*, Vol. 34, no. 3, pp. 771–787, 1996.
26. S Fukuda and H Hirosawa, "A wavelet-based texture feature set applied to classification of multifrequency polarimetric sar images," *IEEE Trans. on Geoscience and Remote Sensing,* Vol. 37, no. 5, pp. 2282–2286, 1999.

27. M Simard, S S Saatchi, and G De Grandi, "The use of decision tree and multiscale texture for classification of jers-1 sar data over tropical forest," *IEEE Trans. on Geoscience and Remote Sensing,* Vol. 38, no. 5, pp. 2310–2321, 2000.
28. A Niedermeier, E Romaneesen, and S Lehner, "Detection of coastline sar images using wavelet methods," *IEEE Trans. on Geoscience and Remote Sensing*, Vol. 38, no. 5, pp. 2270–2281, 2000.
29. S Mallat and Sifen Zhong, "Characterization of signals from multiscale edges," *IEEE Trans. on Pattern Analysis and Machine Intelligence*, Vol. 14, no. 7, pp. 710–732, 1992.
30. D C Tseng, H M Tsai, and C C Lai, "Unsupervised texture segmentation for multispectral remote-sensing images," in *Proc. of the Intl. Conf. on Pattern Recognition, ICPR'98,* 1998, pp. 1630–1632.
31. P Thitimajshima, "Multiresolution fuzzy clustering for sar image segmentation," in *Proc. of the Intl. Geoscience and Remote Sensing Symposium, IGARSS'99*, 1999, Vol. 5, pp. 2507–2509.
32. S K Pal, A Ghosh, and B Uma Shankar, "Segmentation with remotely sensed images with fuzzy thresholding, and quantitative evaluation," *Int. Journal of Remote Sensing*, Vol. 21, no. 11, pp. 2269–2300, 2000.
33. S Bandyopadhyay and S K Pal, "Pixel classification using variable string genetic algorithms with chromosome differentia-tion," *IEEE Trans. on Geoscience and Remote Sensing*, Vol. 39, no. 2, pp. 303–308, 2001.
34. D Muchoney and J Williamson, "A gaussian adaptive resonance theory neural network classification algorithm applied to super-vised land cover mapping using multitemporal vegetation index data," *IEEE Trans. on Geoscience and Remote Sensing*, Vol. 39, pp. 1969–1977, 2001.
35. P Steffen, P N Heller, R A Gopinath, and C S Burrus, "Theory of regular *m*-band wavelet bases," *IEEE Trans. on Signal Processing,* Vol. 41, no. 12, pp. 3497–3510, 1993.
36. O Alkin and H Caglar, "Design of efficient *m*-band coders with linear phase and perfect reconstruction properties," *IEEE Trans. on Signal Processing,* Vol. 43, no. 7, pp. 1579–1590, 1995.
37. S K Pal and S Mitra, *Neuro-fuzzy Pattern Recognition: Methods in Soft Computing,* John Wiley, New York, 1999.
38. S K Pal, A Ghosh, and M K Kundu, Eds., *Soft Computing for Image Processing,* Physica Verlag, Heidelberg, 2000.

39. L A Zadeh, "Fuzzy logic, neural networks, and soft computing," *Communications of the ACM*, Vol. 37, pp. 77–84, 1994.
40. I Daubechies, "Orthogonal bases for compactly supported wavelets," *Comm. Pure Appl. Math*, Vol. 41, pp. 909–996, 1988.
41. H Zou and A H Tewfik, "Discrete orthogonal, *m*-band wavelet decomposition," in *Proc. Intl. Conf. on Acoustics, Speech, and Signal Processing,* 1992, Vol. 4, pp. IV–605–IV–608.
42. L A Zadeh, "Fuzzy sets," *Information and Control*, Vol. 8, pp. 338–353, 1965.
43. Judith E. Dayhoff, *Neural Network Architectures An Introduction,* Van Nostrand Reinhold, New York, 1990.
44. Richard P Lippmann, "An introduction to computing with neural nets," *IEEE ASSP Magazine*, Vol. 4, no. 2, pp. 4–22, 1987.
45. N G Kingsbury, "Complex wavelets and shift invariance," in *Proc. IEE Colloquium on Time-Scale and Time-Frequency Analysis and Applications,* 2000.
46. M Acharyya and M K Kundu, "Adaptive basis selection for multitexture, segmentation by *m*-band wavelet packet frame," in *Proc. 2001 Int. Conf. Image Processing,* Sept. 2001, pp. 622–625.
47. M Acharyya and M K Kundu, "Wavelet-based texture segmentation of remotely sensed images," in *Proc. 2001 Int. Conf. Image Analysis and Processing,* Sept. 2001, pp. 69–74.
48. M K Kundu and M Acharyya, "*m*-band wavelets : Application to texture segmentation for real life image analysis," *International Journal of Wavelets, Multiresolution and Information Processing,* Vol. 1, no. 1, pp. 115–149, 2003.
49. M Acharyya, R K De, and M K Kundu, "Extraction of features using *m*-band wavelet packet frame and their neuro-fuzzy feature evaluation for multitexture segmentation," *IEEE Trans. on Pattern Analysis and Machine Intelligence*, Vol. 25, no. 12, PP 1639-1644 2003.
50. M Acharyya, R K De, and M K Kundu, "Segmentation of remotely sensed images using wavelet features and their evaluation in soft computing framework," *IEEE Trans. on Geoscience and Remote Sensing*, Vol. 41, no. 12, pp 2900-2905 2003.
51. S K Pal, R K De, and J Basak, "Unsupervised feature evaluation: A neuro-fuzzy approach," *IEEE Trans. on Neural Networks,* Vol. 11, pp. 366–376, 2000.
52. J T Tou and R C Gonzales, *Pattern Recognition Principles,* Adision-Wesley, Reading, 1974.
53. J A Richards, *Remote Sensing Digital Image Analysis: An Introduction.,* Springer-Verlag, New York, 1993.

54. A Rosenfeld and A C Kak, *Digital Image Processing,* Academic Press, New York, 2nd edition, 1982.
55. T Randen and J H Husøy, "Filtering for texture classification: a comparative study," *IEEE Trans. on Pattern Analysis and Machine Intelligence,* Vol. 21, pp. 291–310, April 1999.
56. T Randen, *Filter and Filter Bank Design for Image Texture Recognition,* Ph.D. thesis, Norwegian Univ. of Science and Technology, Trondheim, Norway, 1997.
57. A C Bovik, "Analysis of multichannel narrow-band filters for image texture segmentation," *IEEE Trans. Signal Processing,* Vol. 39, pp. 2025–2043, Sept. 1991.

28

Some Results on Shape and Digitization of Bi-level Pictures

S K Parui and D Dutta Majumder

ABSTRACT

This paper presents a set of results on how the shape of black/white or bilevel pictures is affected through digitization. Pavlidis [1,2] proposes a condition on digitization so that the shape is preserved. Here some results are proved on shape preservation under a similar condition. Topological properties (like connectedness, surroundedness) are a subset of shape properties of bilevel pictures and their preservation is discussed here. It can be seen that the shape properties that are preserved under the proposed condition are much more than just topological properties [3].

Keywords: Shape; Digitization; Topology; Bilevel Pictures; Pixel.

28.1 INTRODUCTION

In the discrete grid, Pavlidis makes a pixel a black pixel if its centre falls in the input analogue (bilevel) picture. But here a pixel is made black if at least half of the area of the pixel falls in the analogue picture. With this new digitization scheme, it is proved that the topological properties of bilevel pictures are preserved after digitization.

28.2 SOME DEFINITIONS IN ANALOGUE AND DIGITAL CASES

Suppose, A is a subset in the Euclidean plane and d is a positive real number. Let $F\ (d, A)$ be the class of all closed discs D of diameter d contained in A. Let $C\ (d, A)$ be the set of the centres of the discs belonging to $F(d, A)$. In this report, we will mainly deal with those subsets A in the plane such that there exists a positive real number d satisfying:

(a) $F(d, A)$ is non-empty;

(b) A is the union of all discs in $F(d, A)$;

(c) $C(d, A)$ is path-connected;

(d) A is compact; and

(e) A^c can be expressed as a finite union at non-empty open sets $\bigcup_{j=1}^{m} B_j$

such that B_j satisfies conditions (a), (b) and (c) above for all j and $B_j \cup B_k$ is disconnected for $j \neq k$.

From above it is clear that A is path-connected and m is the *order of connectivity of A*. Let $Z(A) = \{d$: d is a positive real number satisfying conditions (a), (b) and (c) above$\}$. So, for a subset A satisfying conditions (a), (b) and (c) above, $Z(A)$ is non-empty. In that case, we define the *width* of A as $w(A) = \sup d\ d \in Z(A)$, provided $Z(A)$ is bounded.

A subset A in the plane is said to be an *analogue bilevel picture* if A can be expressed as a finite union $\bigcup_{i=1}^{n} A_i$ such that $A_i \cup A_r$ is disconnected for $i \neq r$ and A_i satisfies the five conditions above for all i. Each A_i is called a *component* of the analogue bilevel picture A. Let m_i be the order of connectivity of A_i. From condition (e),

$$\boldsymbol{A_i^c} = \bigcup_{j=1}^{m_i} \boldsymbol{B}_{i1},$$

where B_{ij} is non-empty and satisfies conditions (a), (b) and (c) for all j and $B_{ij} \cup B_{ik}$ is disconnected for $j \neq k$.

Proposition 1

For each i, B_{ij} is unbounded for exactly one value of j. For all other values of j, if any, B_{ij} is bounded.

Without loss of generality, let B_{ij} be unbounded.

Proposition 2

If A_i and $A_r (i \neq r)$ are two components of an analogue bilevel picture A, then A_r is a subset of B_{il} for exactly one j ($m \geq j \geq 1$).

If a component A_r is a subset of B_{ij} for $j > 1$, then A_i is said to *surround* A_r.

Proposition 3

If $m_i > 1$, then $\bigcup_{j=2}^{m_i} B_{ij} - \bigcup_{i=1}^{n} A_i$ can be expressed as a finite union $\bigcup_{r=1}^{v_i} H_{ir}$, where H_{ir} satisfies conditions (a), (b) and (c) for all r and $H_{ir} \cup H_{is}$ is disconnected for $r \neq s$.

H_{ir} are the *holes* of the component A_i. Note that a hole may be common to two or more components. If A_i has no holes, it is a *simply connected component*. Let $\boldsymbol{B} = \bigcap_{i=1}^{n} \boldsymbol{B}_{il}$. It is easy to see that B is unbounded. B is the *background* of the analogue bilevel picture A. It can be seen that B satisfies conditions (a), (b) and (c). The widths of the components A_i

and the holes H_{ir} are well defined and positive for all i and r. The *width* of the analogue bilevel picture A is defined as

$$w(A) = \text{Min}\{\text{Min}_i\, w(A_i),\, \text{Min}_{i,r}\, w(H_{ir}),\, w(B)\}.$$

If $Z(B)$ is unbounded, $w(B)$ is ignored in the above definition. Clearly, $w(A)$ is finite and positive.

Now, we will describe how an analogue bilevel picture is digitized. The digital output is a binary matrix. Consider a square or pixel of the grid. If less than half of its area is covered by A, then the pixel is assigned the value 0. Otherwise, it is assigned 1. Let S be the set of all 1-pixels. S is the *digital version* of A. We consider 8-connectivity for S and 4-connectivity for its complement or the background.

Let S_i ($i = 1, 2, ..., n$) be the *components* (8-connected) of S. Let m_i be the order of connectivity of S_i and W_{ir} ($r = 1, 2, ..., v_i$) be the *holes* of S_i. Let T be the set of pixels of the binary matrix which do not belong to any S_i or W_{ir}. T is the *background* and is assumed to contain the first and the last rows and columns of the binary matrix.

28.3 SOME RESULTS ON PRESERVATION OF TOPOLOGICAL PROPERTIES

So far we have discussed some topological properties (like connectedness, surroundedness, number of holes, number of components) of 2-dimensional shapes in both analogue and digital cases. Now let us propose a condition on the side size h of pixels of the digitization grid so that the topological properties of an analogue picture are preserved after its digitization. The condition will be developed on the basis of the following results:

Proposition 1

Suppose A_i is a component of an analogue picture with width $w_i = w(A_i)$. Then the digital version of A_i is non-empty and 4-connected with arbitrary position and orientation of the grid, provided $w_i > 2\sqrt{2}\,h$.

Proposition 2

Suppose H_{ir} is a hole of an analog picture with width $w_{ir} = w(H_{ir})$. Then after digitization with arbitrary position and orientation of the grid, H_{ir} gives rise to at least one 0-pixel and the resulting 0-pixels, if more than one in number, are 4-connected, provided $w_{ir} > 2\sqrt{2}\,h$.

Proposition 3

Suppose A_i and $A_r (i \neq r)$ are two components of an analogue picture A with width $w = w(A)$. Suppose S_i and S_r are the digital versions of A_i and

A_r respectively after digitization with arbitrary position and orientation of the grid and $w > 2\sqrt{2}\,h$. Then S_i and S_r are disconnected, that is, $S_i \cup S_r$ is not 8-connected.

Proposition 4

Suppose E is a hole and F is either a hole or the background of an analogue picture A with width $w = w(A)$. Suppose T_1 and T_2 are the sets of 0-pixels given rise to by E and F respectively. Then T_1 and T_2 are disconnected, provided $w > 2\sqrt{2}\,h$.

From the above four propositions, we can state the following proposition:

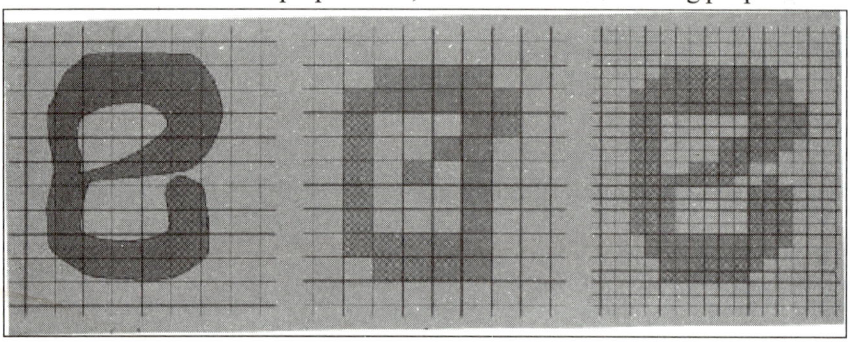

Fig. 28.1 (*a*) (*b*) (*c*)

Proposition 5

Suppose A_i is a component of an analogue picture A such that A_i has v_i holes $H_{i1}, \ldots, H_{iv_i}$ and A_i surrounds w_i components $A_{i1}, \ldots, A_{iw_i}$. Suppose the width of A is $w = w(A)$ and the digital version of A is S. Then after digitization with arbitrary position and orientation of the grid and $w > 2\sqrt{2}\,h$:

(*i*) each of $A_i, A_{i1}, \ldots, A_{iw_i}$ gives rise to one single component of S such that the digital version of A_i surrounds the digital versions of $A_{i1}, \ldots, A_{iw_i}$; and

(*ii*) each of $H_{i1}, \ldots, H_{iv_i}$ gives rise to one single hole of S which is a hole of the digital version of A_i.

From above, it is clear that the desired condition on digitization is $w > 2\sqrt{2}\,h$ under which not only the topological properties but all shape properties of the input analog picture are preserved. The only distortion after digitization in this case is lack of smoothness along the boundary. For example, under the condition $w > 2\sqrt{2}\,h$, the digitized version of Fig. 28.1(*a*) may be Fig. 28.1(*c*), but never Fig. 28.1(*b*).

Acknowledgement

Authors are grateful to Mr C A Murthy for the valuable discussions they had with him.

References

1. T Pavlidis (1980) Shape analysis and digitization In: Pattern Recognition in Practice (Ed. E S Gelsema and L N Kanal) North-Holland, Amsterdam, 123–129.
2. T Pavlidis (1982) Algorithms for Graphics and Image Processing, Springer-Verlag, New York.
3. S K Parui(1984) Some Studies in Analysis and Recognition of 2-Dimensional Shapes, Ph.D. Thesis, Indian Statistical Institute.

29

A Complete System for Document Image Segmentation

S. Mandal[1], S.P Chowdhury[2], A. K. Das[3] and Bhabatosh Chanda[4]

ABSTRACT

The objective of the document image analysis (DIA) is to provide a non-labour intensive, cheap and flexible way of storing, representing and managing the paper document in electronic form to facilitates indexing, viewing, printing and extracting the intended portions.

Segmentation of document image is the most important and crucial part of DIA. The success of DIA systems depends on the segmentation and classification. In this paper we present fully automatic segmentation and classification of documents using fast algorithms based on mathematical morphology.

29.1 INTRODUCTION

Document image segmentation is a part of Document Image Analysis (DIA) which is concerned with automatic interpretation of printed and handwritten documents, including, text, drawings, maps etc [1, 2]. Document analysis is used to extract geometric structures of a document. A document is broken down into several blocks which represents different constituent parts, such as text lines, headings, graphics and half-tones, with or without the knowledge regarding the specific format.

Although most of the documents are now created in electronic media rendering their storage, maintenance and distribution as flexible as possible the task of managing the available paper documents is daunting.

Due to its immense potential for commercial applications research in this field supports a rapidly growing industry including OCR and vision systems for DIA. Building a fully automatic DIA system remains a challenging problem for the researchers [3]. The sheer volume of data to be processed and complexity of the problem culminated in costly solutions. As most of the documents are produced using electronic media and more will be done in the same media in future - the present task of DIA is an ephemeral problem which demands a cheap and fast solution. Commercial document analysis systems are now available for storing business forms, performing OCR on typewritten text, and compressing

---

1 ,2,3 CST Department, Bengal. Engg. & Science University, Shibpur, Howrah

4 ECSU, Indian Statistical Institute, Kolkata

engineering drawings [1] but far behind the optimistic goal set in early 90's i.e., DIA systems should be fully automatic, cheap, and fast acting. It has been observed from the existing literatures, proposing similar objectives, that most of the segmentation tasks are so far done using computationally expensive algorithms which, we contend, is not suitable for real life adaptation.

This paper is organised as follows; Section 29.2 describes past work on segmentation. Section 29.3 deals with the proposed segmentation method while in section 29.4 the techniques are elaborated. Section 29.5 presents a document image model as well as experimental results and section 29.6 has concluding comments.

29.2 PAST WORK ON SEGMENTATION

There exits numerous techniques for extracting the geometric structure from the document image. Most methods may be categorized into (*i*) top down or module driven; (*ii*) bottom up or data driven and (*iii*) hybrid i.e., mixture of top-down and bottom-up approach.

Top down approach starts with an expectation of the type of the document (e.g., forms, letters or journal pages etc.) thereby it hypothesises a sequential interpretation at high level. It divides the document into major regions and divides them further into sub-regions. Top down is fast and effective for documents with specific formats. On the other hand the bottom up approach starts merging the evidence at the lowest level by layered grouping. It then progressively refines data and rise to upper levels until the entire image is completely assembled. This approach is slower but works without *a priori* knowledge of the format of the document. Hybrid methods are some combinations of top down and bottom up approaches at different levels and expected to work well as reported by Nagy [2].

The DIA starts with segmentation of the images into its constituent parts i.e., text, graphics and half-tones. In many works the document is divided into two segments: Text and non-text regions. Half-tone, in some work, is either treated as a part of the graphics or ignored totally [4]. In the first case, classifiers are subsequently employed to segregate half-tones from the graphics. From the text region, once again, paragraphs, lines and even words and characters are segmented. Each detected object is then assigned a label indicating the type of object. The spatial relationship is usually represented in hierarchical relations. Survey papers in this subject can be found in Nadler [5] and Kasturi et al. [6]. An early work on text/non-text block segmentation is done by Wahl et al. [7]. They used Run Length Smearing (RLS) and Constrained Run Length Smearing (CRL) to smear the text lines to black bands. The image is smeared in vertical and horizontal directions using predefined threshold values. Logical AND operation is done on smeared files and smeared again in horizontal direction with another threshold. This produces an image which, ideally, consists of blocks of connected components representing text, graphics and half-tones. A classifier is then used to identify the block into text, horizontal solid lines, vertical solid lines, graphics and half-tones. The major problem is that one has to specify three thresholds which are the functions of the text fonts, spacing between words, lines and characters etc. It also depends on the skew. No methodology is suggested for guiding the proper selection of these thresholds. Another drawback of the method is that the embedded text in half-tones and graphics are not detected.

Recursive projection profile cut (Nagy and Seth [8]) is another method to decompose a document image to a set of blocks. It employs an X–Y tree as the representation of a document layout structure. The X–Y tree is a nested decomposition of rectangular blocks to smaller blocks. So each node of the tree represents a block. For example the root node is the document image itself, i.e., largest rectangular block. At each level decomposition is induced by partitions into either horizontal or vertical directions; not both at the same time. A block is segmented into sub-blocks by making cuts in the projection profile corresponds to troughs of depth and width greater than a predefined threshold. This decomposition is recursive; at each step, the process must decide whether or not a cut needs to be made. The recursive subdivision of the document page is then converted to an X–Y tree. The segmentation process is recursive and may be carried out to any desired depth with the alternate horizontal and vertical segmentation. The macro divisions resulting out of the sub divided blocks are separated into six different classes by a classifier; these are small, medium and large characters, graphics and half-tones respectively. Drawbacks of this method are listed below.

- It works with the assumption that the document has a so called Manhattan layout and has a very low skew.
- Decomposition model for each class i.e., text, graphics etc., is different and at each step the system has to select the correct decomposition model; so mismatch may occur.

Algorithms based on connected component analysis are reported by Kasturi et al. [9], O'Gorman [10] and others. Kasturi et al. [9] describes an algorithm based on this approach to separate text from mixed text/graphics documents. The algorithm generates connected components and then Hough transform is used to group them together. The major steps are

1. *Connected component generation*: This is done by component labeling process which also computes the co-ordinates of the bounding rectangles.
2. *Filtering using area/ratio*: This is used to separate large graphical components. The filtering threshold is determined according to the most populated area and the average area of the connected components. The working set to be used by the next step is now reduced to text strings and small graphical components.
3. *Co-linear component grouping*: Hough transform is used on the centroids of the rectilinear bounding boxes of each component. This operation consolidates grouping of co-linear components.
4. *Logical-grouping*: Co-linear components are grouped to words by using information like position of each component, inter character and inter word gap thresholds.
5. *Text string separation*: The words along a text line is segmented from the rest of the image.

The algorithm is robust to changes in font size and style. It is by and large skew independent but sensitive to touching and fragmented characters. The inherent connectivity assumption weakens with images of degraded/worn out documents due to a large number of touching and fragmented characters. The algorithm is also computationally expensive like any other Hough transform based approach.

Connected component generation is also used by O'Gorman [11] to find out k nearest component of each connected object. The distance d and angle θ between centroids of each nearest neighbour pair is used to draw a histogram of the $d - \theta$ plot (known as docstrum). Several features like, skew, inter line gap and line heights are estimated from docstrum. Text lines are formed by transitive closure of nearest neighbour pairings along a line and text blocks are generated by merging text lines on the basis of their spatial proximity. The advantage of the method is skew independence and on the fly computation of some of the parameters used in the algorithm.

In contrast to the analysis of object properties algorithms have also been proposed in Baird et al. [12] and Pavlidis [13] that use the background white space for segmentation. Baird's method proceeds by finding out the maximal rectangles covering the background white space of a document page. The area outside the rectangular white background portion is then the subject for further classification. This approach also expects a low skew upright rectangular structure of the document. Zhou [14] extended this approach by removing constraints of right rectangle structure. The method works on the assumption that the input page can be divided into sub regions containing, ideally, unique types of data and separated by distinguishable white spaces. The steps of merging these white spaces to a set of blocks are

1. Identify the column gaps using vertical projection profile used locally to circumvent the problem of tilted text,
2. Grouping and merging of the set of white gaps over column intervals delimited by column gaps, and
3. Skew estimation which uses centers of column intervals.

The block classification is done based mostly on the behaviour of across scan-line correlations in text, graphics and half-tone regions. The major drawback of the algorithm is the assumption that local projection profile would be sufficient to find out the columns even in the presence of severe tilt.

Textural property of the document image is also used for segmentation as text and non-text regions presumably have clearly distinguishable textures. Jain et al. [15] exploits this property in his multichannel filtering approach for segmentation of documents using two dimensional Gabor filter. A set of Gabor filters is used to compute texture features in different regions. A clustering algorithm is then used to merge the pixels having similar texture features and followed by the placement of enclosing rectangles of those clustered pixels. The algorithm works directly on gray level image and it is skew insensitive. It can also segment text embedded in graphics or half-tones. However the problems are as follows:

(i) The process is computationally very expensive and

(ii) Choice of the filters and related parameters are difficult as Gabor filter does not relate to geometric shapes directly.

Most segmentation algorithm relies on the Manhattan structure, where blocks are all rectangular and are in the same orientation and the enclosing rectangles are either mutually exclusive or one completely contains the other. Propositions for treating blocks as polygons have come from Belaid [16] and Pavlidis [17]. Belaid detects the contour of the polygonal blocks by intersection of the elongated white spaces encircling each block. Pavlidis [17] modeled the blocks as set of gray islands inside the ocean of white space. A region growing technique is used to merge gray and white areas. The blocks are finally classified and grouped as text lines etc. Recursive morphological transforms are used by Haralick et al. [18] to isolate text and non text regions of a document. Morphological operators have special capabilities in dealing with shapes and suitable for segmentation algorithm relying on shape based information. Text is located and text band is formed by computing the frequency of zero to one transitions in [19]. Local thresholding is done on individual text bands fine tuning. Using some heuristics, text lines are then extracted. Rough logical structure of the document is found by analysing the typography which is used for an automatic document indexing system. Segmentation of text, graphics etc. is done using diagonal white run [20] and vertical edges. A diagonal white run (DRUN) is a set of adjacent white pixels that are diagonally connected and a vertical edge consists of the white area between the two consecutive DRUNs. The technique claimed to be layout independent. Sylwester et al. [21] did the segmentation using three basic tree operations; cut, glue and flip. An X-Y tree is constructed where the leaf nodes are individual characters. This X-Y tree is formed by successive horizontal and vertical cuts through white space in the page image. Consecutive characters are changed to word blocks by glue operation and text lines written horizontally are flipped to a vertical word block.

29.3 PROPOSED WORK

The work carried out for automatic segmentation of document page images provides a solution by developing morphology based fast algorithms to do, (i) skew correction and (ii) block level (text, graphics, tables, headings and half-tones) segmentation. The task, besides data acquisition, is carried out using fast algorithms of morphological operations [22]. The first step is skew detection and correction of the document (Binary version) by a new and extremely fast algorithm [23]. Half-tones are then extracted from the skew corrected image [24]. Instead of using the common approach of extracting half-tones from the binary image, we did it by processing the gray level image and the corresponding area in binary image is marked as half-tone. This prevents the problem of identifying bright half-tones as they appear as sparse

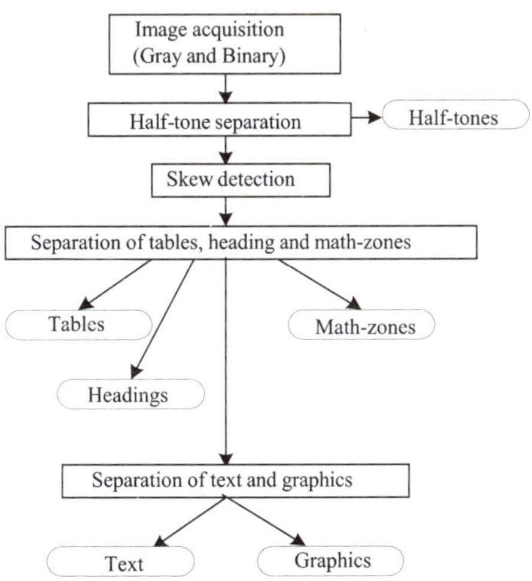

Fig. 29.1 Overview of the task carried out for segmentation.

foreground points in the binary image and loses the textural properties of half-tones.

Utilising the power of morphological operators to extract shape based features we extracted tables and headings from the document image [25]. This facilitates segmentation of regular text and graphics from residue image. Moreover, extraction of tables and headings from the text improves the possible OCR operation and interpretation of the segmented text.

Segmentation of displayed math-zone is done next. This is carried out by finding out three median lines; top, bottom and middle along the line (may be text) under test and checking the relative distribution of the components scattered along the medians as well as finding out very tall and short components.

The text and graphics separation [26] is done in a novel way exploiting the band structure of the smeared text lines and the respective inter-line gaps. This improves the performance of graphics segmentation where graphics, unlike many other works, is not assumed to be a collection of very big connected components made up only with lines and other graphics symbols.

For performance analysis of the proposed algorithms we define a document model in terms of its constituent parts and their inter-relationship. Finally, a quantitative measure of the segmentation error is proposed and implemented [27]. The major problem of validating the performance of the segmentation has been alleviated by using standard document image databases, UW-I and UW-II, from University of Washington as the experimental results are compared with the ground-truth information available in the said database.

29.4 SEGMENTATION STEPS

For fully automated segmentation besides the major steps, several small corrections have to be made on the fly depending on certain characteristics of the document to be segmented. We have deliberately avoided those details and present the basic approach.

Skew Correction: The image is closed with line structuring element to convert the texts to thick line elements. It is followed by open operation with small square shaped SE to remove undulations in the twice line elements. Then the bottom profile of each line is detected. This gives single pixels lines whose near extreme points (we pruned each line by 4/5 pixels to curb local variations expected in the beginning and end of lines due to the presence of characters with ascendants and descendants) are marked and the slope is calculated for each line. The average value of the slope is taken as the skew of the document. The process is shown in Fig. 29.2.

Half Tone Separation: Texture based half-tone segmentation technique is used in [15, 28] as it offers advantages like skew independence and no *a priori* knowledge of the format of the document. Our method is also texture based but extremely fast and exploits simple morphological open and close operations on the gray scale image. We define a new measure for Texture Based Identification. In the proposed method a square Structuring Element (SE) is used to open and close the image. The variation in gray values over the window is captured in a 2 dimensional accumulator array (a matrix) which is called Open-Close Function (OCF) matrix and defined as

$$MAT_{OCF}(i, j \mid k) = \Sigma_x \Sigma_y \#((f \circ k)(x, y) = i \wedge (f \bullet k)(x, y) = j)$$

where $f(x, y)$ is the original image matrix and $k(x, y)$ is the gray level SE. #{.} = 1 if argument is true and 0 otherwise. In our case $f(x, y)$ is the original gray scale image.

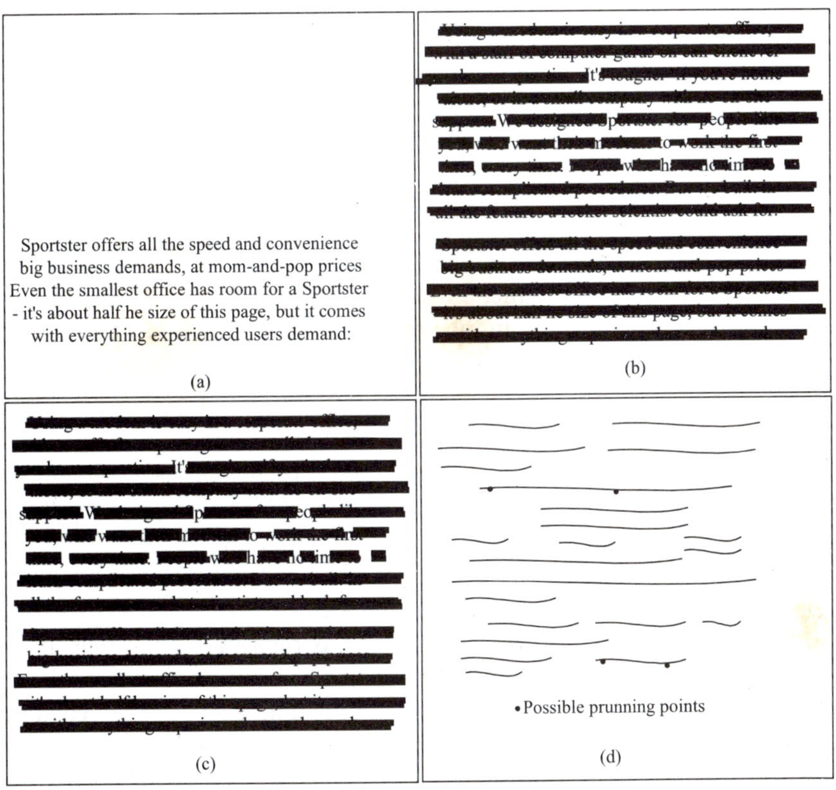

Fig. 29.2 Steps for skew detection a) Original image; b) Closed with line SE; c) Opened with small SE to remove undulating and d) bottom profile with pruning points.

To facilitate half-tone separation we would like to have minimum distortion in the half-tone portions and maximum in the text and graphics portions of the image for the gray level open and close operations. To ensure that the SE should be small but it should be reasonably large enough to hold a part of the text. Note that the gray values of pixels in the close version of the image is greater than or equal to its counterpart; i.e., the open version (so, $f \circ k \le f \bullet k$) thus for this reason the OCF becomes an upper triangular matrix. In OCF matrix the cells accumulate the number of pixels with specified variation in gray level. Its different regions reflect different sections of a document. An ideal OCF matrix is shown in Fig. 29.3 which exhibits that in ideal situation we will have 4 distinct regions in the OCF due to text (*T*), graphics (*G*), half-tone (*H*) and background (*B*).

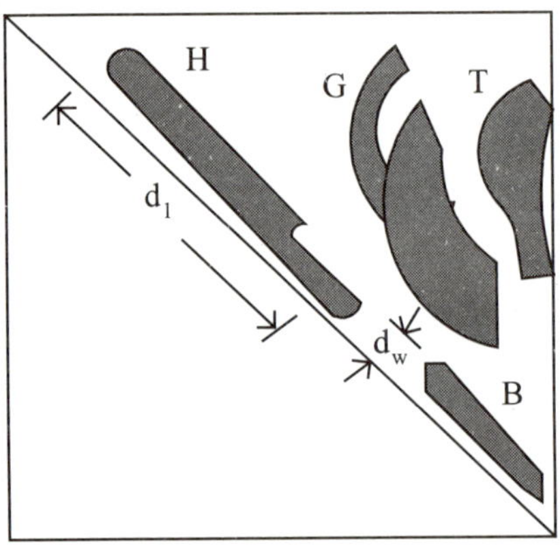

Fig. 29.3 Ideal OCF matrix shown as an image.

The OCF matrix is used to map different zones of the original document image as outlined below:

1. Blank out the irrelevant portions of the OCF keeping the required zone intact
2. Suppose $(f \bullet k)(x, y) = i$ and $(f \circ k)(x, y) = j$ then create a new image

$$g(x, y) = \begin{cases} 1 \text{ if } MAT_{OCF}(i, j \mid k) > T_h \\ 0 \text{ otherwise} \end{cases}$$

Note that T_h is a threshold count set to a suitable value to bypass low variation values.

The resultant binary image *g* (*x*, *y*) will outline the bounding rectangle of text, graphics or half-tone portion of the original image.

Text-graphics separation may not be very successful as there are lot of overlaps in these regions in the OCF for real images. However, half-tones can be extracted[5] out using the OCF as it is mapped (see Fig. 29.4) along the upper side of the diagonal forming a narrow but solid band structure.

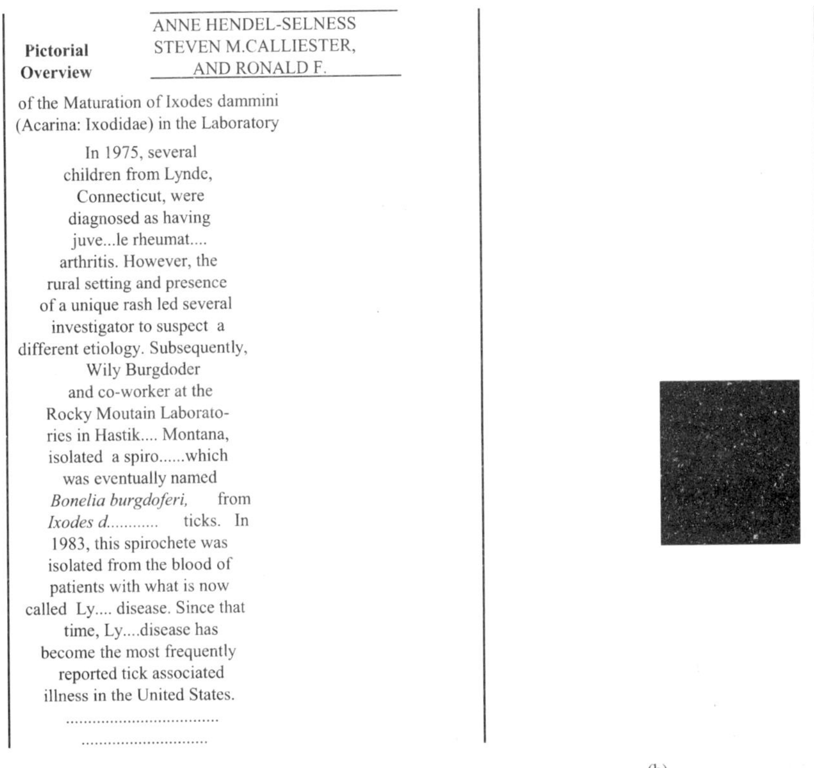

Fig. 29.4 Example of using OCF for isolating half-tone. (*a*) Original image in gray (*b*) Points mapped as half-tones using the relevant portion of the OCF matrix.

Table & Heading Separation: Once the half-tone is isolated from the image next we do the extraction of tables and headings. For table separation we have assumed that the contents of any table has a columnar structure and there is at least one horizontal header line present in the table. We have checked that almost all the tables conforms to this observation. Thus a table is identified by isolating horizontal lines and set up of a rectangular sliding window of certain height along those lines. The window is then moved back and forth in the vertical direction and projections are taken to check the presence of at least two or more columns. The idea is expressed Fig. 29.5.

---

5 by estimating d_l and d_w (see Fig. 29.3) using projections along the diagonal.

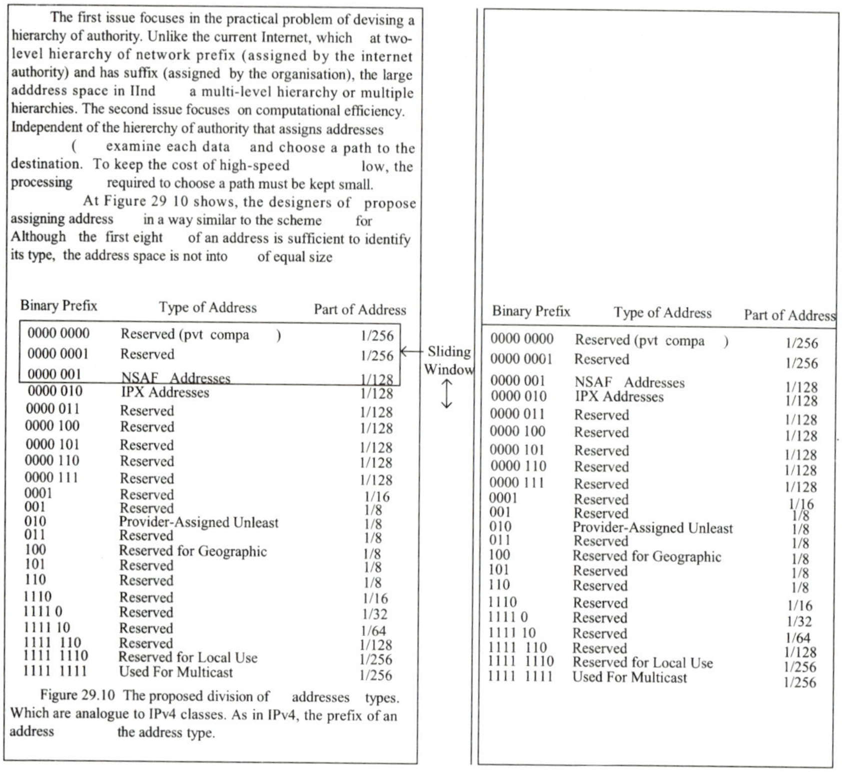

The first issue focuses in the practical problem of devising a hierarchy of authority. Unlike the current Internet, which at two-level hierarchy of network prefix (assigned by the internet authority) and has suffix (assigned by the organisation), the large adddress space in IInd a multi-level hierarchy or multiple hierarchies. The second issue focuses on computational efficiency. Independent of the hiererchy of authority that assigns addresses (examine each data and choose a path to the destination. To keep the cost of high-speed low, the processing required to choose a path must be kept small.

At Figure 29 10 shows, the designers of propose assigning address in a way similar to the scheme for Although the first eight of an address is sufficient to identify its type, the address space is not into of equal size

Binary Prefix	Type of Address	Part of Address
0000 0000	Reserved (pvt compa)	1/256
0000 0001	Reserved	1/256
0000 001	NSAF Addresses	1/128
0000 010	IPX Addresses	1/128
0000 011	Reserved	1/128
0000 100	Reserved	1/128
0000 101	Reserved	1/128
0000 110	Reserved	1/128
0000 111	Reserved	1/128
0001	Reserved	1/16
001	Reserved	1/8
010	Provider-Assigned Unleast	1/8
011	Reserved	1/8
100	Reserved for Geographic	1/8
101	Reserved	1/8
110	Reserved	1/8
1110	Reserved	1/16
1111 0	Reserved	1/32
1111 10	Reserved	1/64
1111 110	Reserved	1/128
1111 1110	Reserved for Local Use	1/256
1111 1111	Used For Multicast	1/256

Figure 29.10 The proposed division of addresses types. Which are analogue to IPv4 classes. As in IPv4, the prefix of an address the address type.

(a)

Binary Prefix	Type of Address	Part of Address
0000 0000	Reserved (pvt compa)	1/256
0000 0001	Reserved	1/256
0000 001	NSAF Addresses	1/128
0000 010	IPX Addresses	1/128
0000 011	Reserved	1/128
0000 100	Reserved	1/128
0000 101	Reserved	1/128
0000 110	Reserved	1/128
0000 111	Reserved	1/128
0001	Reserved	1/16
001	Reserved	1/8
010	Provider-Assigned Unleast	1/8
011	Reserved	1/8
100	Reserved for Geographic	1/8
101	Reserved	1/8
110	Reserved	1/8
1110	Reserved	1/16
1111 0	Reserved	1/32
1111 10	Reserved	1/64
1111 110	Reserved	1/128
1111 1110	Reserved for Local Use	1/256
1111 1111	Used For Multicast	1/256

(b)

Fig. 29.5 (*a*) Original image containing one table; (*b*) Detected Tabular portion.

Heading is considered as rectangular structure with height substantially greater than the nominal font height of the text portion. Using morphological operators heading detection is not a complex problem and detailed steps are not included.

Math-zone Detection: Many researchers in recent years have developed a number of approaches [29, 30, 31, 32, 33, 34, 35] for mathematical formula recognition and understanding. However, in almost all the cases it was assumed that the math-zones are already segmented from the document image using semi or fully automated segmentation logic. Chaudhuri and Garain [36] proposed a technique for detection of mathematical expression by detecting the presence of mathematical symbols in the text lines.

Kacem et al. [37] proposed a method for math-zone extraction using fuzzy logic without much emphasis on character recognition. It is based on finding the location of the most significant math-symbols and grouping of adjoining math symbols using contextual rules. Using fuzzy logic models created for math-symbols are identified in primary labelling and that is enhanced by a secondary labelling to locate subscripts and superscripts. The drawback of the approach is the overemphasis on the modelling of individual characters; overall spatial feature of the math-zone is somewhat neglected. This could lead to erroneous labelling in the presence of similar symbols in the math zone. Moreover the system is computationally expensive and needs re-training for modelling if there is a change in the document type.

Our method is unique in the context of segmentation of math-zones as no character recognition technique is used and the process is fully automated and exploits the usual spatial distributions of the black pixels in math-zones as they appear in a typical document.

Here we start with the segmented text and graphics which may have math-zones. Most of the elements in math-zone have little difference from normal text and some are pure text with no mathematical symbols. Naturally the segmentation depends on a couple of rules formed by observing general appearance of math-zones in common technical documents including journals. This is done by sampling 197 scanned pages containing mathematics in different possible forms. From the dataset we have identified that displayed-math (DM) zone may be classified into three primary types; namely, DM-I, DM-II and DM-III. We also have identified the following characteristics of the DM zones.

1. Subscripts and superscripts (S&S) are frequently present in math-expressions.
2. Tall symbols whose heights are significantly more than the median height of normal text characters may be present in math-expressions.
3. Math expressions are often written using 2-3 row height (virtual); this happens to accommodate S&S etc. and as a result vertical overlap of characters occurs. This is absent in a normal text line.
4. The math zones are generally aligned; central alignment is most frequent.
5. In math expressions the characters and symbols are less dense in comparison to normal text lines.
6. Presence of a horizontal line separating the numerator and denominator portions is common.
7. Multiple lines (with or without math-expressions) with nearby long vertical separator(s) may occur to represent matrices, determinants and conditional multiple assignments.

Characteristic 6 must be present in case of DM-II; whereas DM-III must have characteristic 7. Some or all other characteristics may be found in these two types of DM. Strong presence of characteristic 1 to 4 is an indication of DM-I.

The math-zone segmentation requires preprocessing like component labelling to remove very small components, like dots of *i*, *j* and small punctuations like comma, period etc. This is done to exclude them to be treated as S&S.

Next we do component labelling to find out the character level bounding box for each text line. It may be noted that we could draw three median lines by taking the median of the middle, top and bottom points of each character bounding box to represent middle median line (MML), top median line (TML) and bottom median line (BML) respectively as shown in Fig. 29.6. Characters appearing on the upper side of the MML without touching it are superscripts and those are on the lower are subscripts. Characters that crosses both the TML and BML are considered to be tall. The other features required to detect the type of display math may be computed easily; interested reader may see [38] for details.

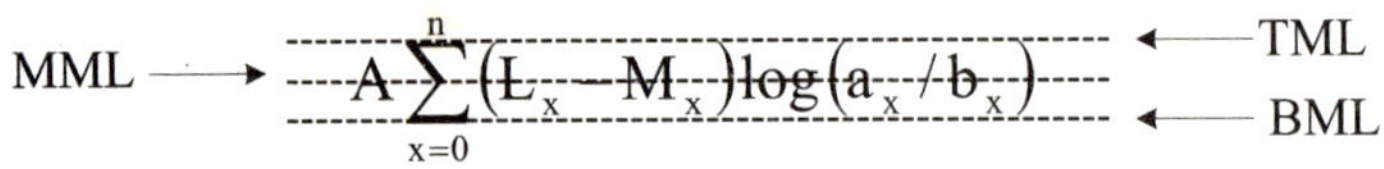

Fig. 29.6 Median lines.

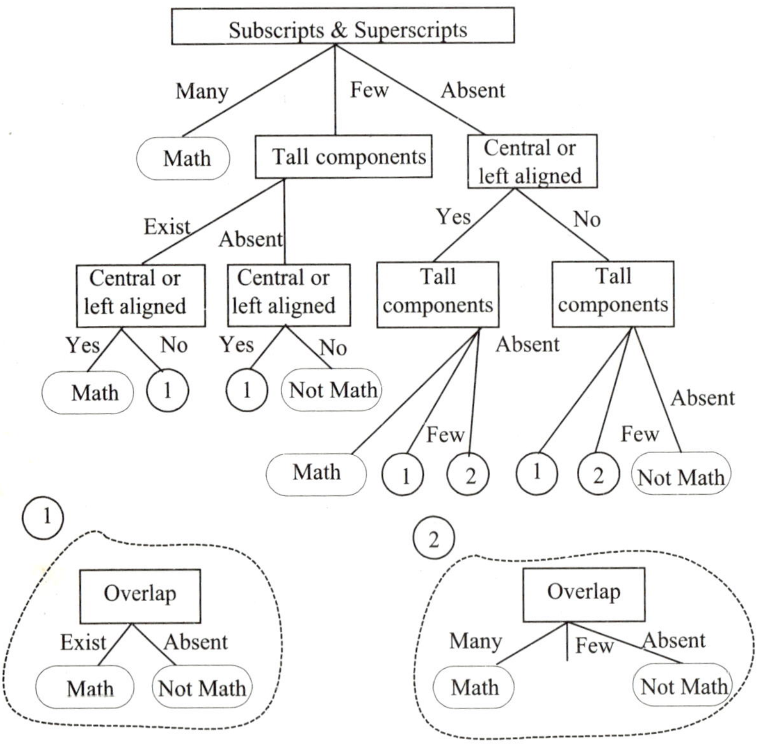

Fig. 29.7 Decision tree for DM-I.

Finally the decision trees used to find out three different types of displayed math are shown in Fig. 29.7, Fig. 29.8 and Fig. 29.9.

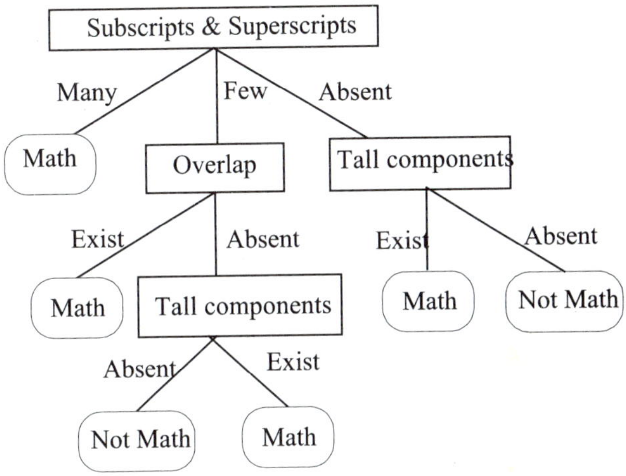

Fig. 29.8 Decision tree for DM-II.

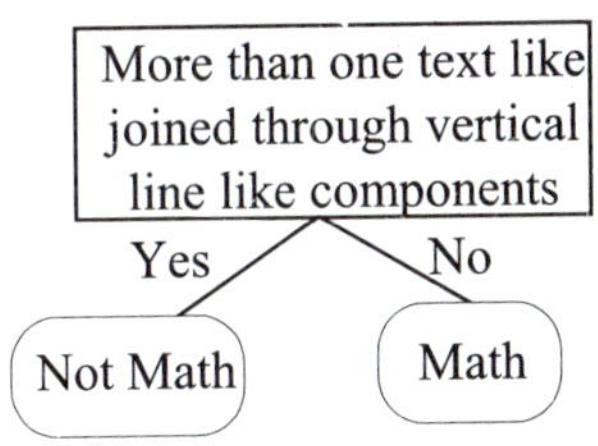

Fig. 29.9 Decision tree for DM-III.

Extraction three types of DM zones are shown in Fig. 29.10 and Fig. 29.11.

Text-Graphics Separation: Text separation is the next step where a novel method of detecting the text band structure is employed. Text/graphics separation algorithm have been suggested by many researchers and the algorithms are available in [9, 39, 40, 16]. In most cases computationally expensive algorithms have been used where in contrast we exploited the band structure of the alternate text lines using simple morphological operations.

It can be verified that the regular text portion of the document image exhibits a geometrical pattern that consists of horizontal bands of only white pixels (inter-line space) and that of black and white pixels (text lines) arranged alternately as shown in Fig. 29.12. Secondly, height of these bands are constants because text heights and inter-line gaps are kept constant during the generation of printed documents. Note that this

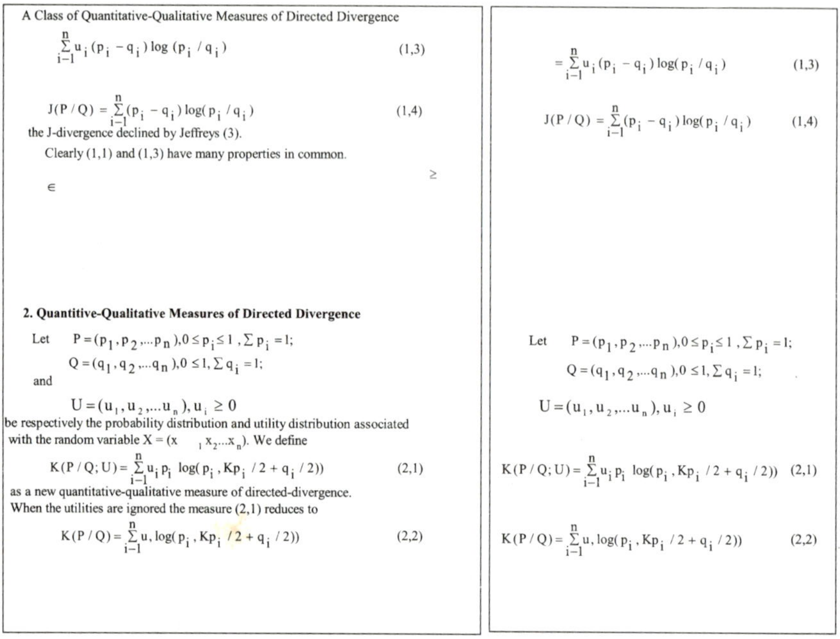

A Class of Quantitative-Qualitative Measures of Directed Divergence

$$\sum_{i-1}^{n} u_i (p_i - q_i) \log (p_i / q_i) \quad (1,3)$$

$$J(P/Q) = \sum_{i-1}^{n} (p_i - q_i) \log(p_i / q_i) \quad (1,4)$$

the J-divergence declined by Jeffreys (3).

Clearly (1,1) and (1,3) have many properties in common.

$\in$ $\geq$

2. Quantitive-Qualitative Measures of Directed Divergence

Let $P = (p_1, p_2, ... p_n), 0 \leq p_i \leq 1, \Sigma p_i = 1;$

$Q = (q_1, q_2, ... q_n), 0 \leq 1, \Sigma q_i = 1;$

and

$U = (u_1, u_2, ... u_n), u_i \geq 0$

be respectively the probability distribution and utility distribution associated with the random variable $X = (x \quad _1 x_2 ... x_n)$. We define

$$K(P/Q; U) = \sum_{i-1}^{n} u_i p_i \log(p_i, Kp_i / 2 + q_i / 2)) \quad (2,1)$$

as a new quantitative-qualitative measure of directed-divergence.

When the utilities are ignored the measure (2,1) reduces to

$$K(P/Q) = \sum_{i-1}^{n} u, \log(p_i, Kp_i / 2 + q_i / 2)) \quad (2,2)$$

(a)

$$= \sum_{i-1}^{n} u_i (p_i - q_i) \log(p_i / q_i) \quad (1,3)$$

$$J(P/Q) = \sum_{i-1}^{n} (p_i - q_i) \log(p_i / q_i) \quad (1,4)$$

Let $P = (p_1, p_2, ... p_n), 0 \leq p_i \leq 1, \Sigma p_i = 1;$

$Q = (q_1, q_2, ... q_n), 0 \leq 1, \Sigma q_i = 1;$

$U = (u_1, u_2, ... u_n), u_i \geq 0$

$$K(P/Q; U) = \sum_{i-1}^{n} u_i p_i \log(p_i, Kp_i / 2 + q_i / 2)) \quad (2,1)$$

$$K(P/Q) = \sum_{i-1}^{n} u, \log(p_i, Kp_i / 2 + q_i / 2)) \quad (2,2)$$

(b)

Fig. 29.10 (*a*) Input image with DM-I; (*b*) Result.

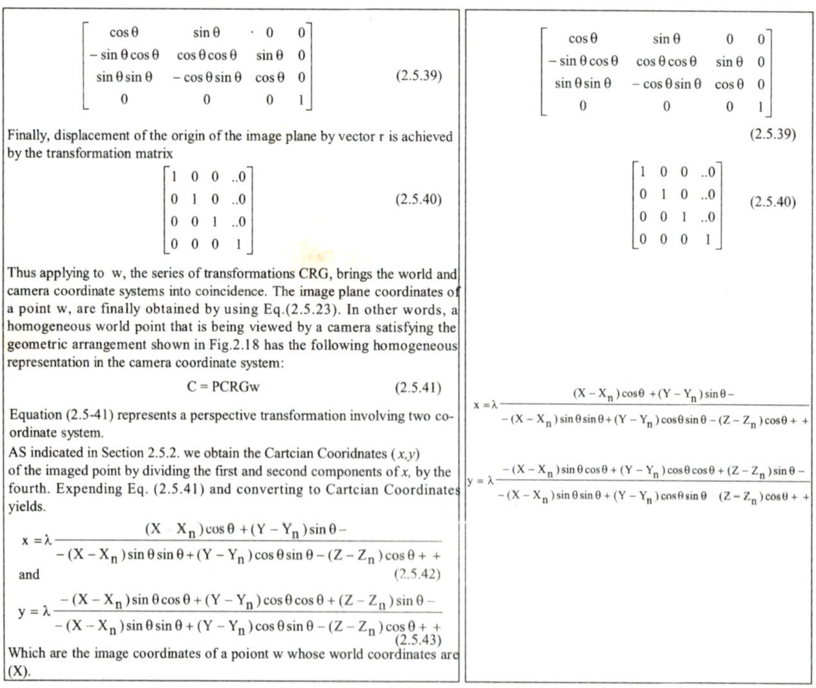

$$\begin{bmatrix} \cos\theta & \sin\theta & \cdot\ 0 & 0 \\ -\sin\theta\cos\theta & \cos\theta\cos\theta & \sin\theta & 0 \\ \sin\theta\sin\theta & -\cos\theta\sin\theta & \cos\theta & 0 \\ 0 & 0 & 0 & 1 \end{bmatrix} \quad (2.5.39)$$

Finally, displacement of the origin of the image plane by vector r is achieved by the transformation matrix

$$\begin{bmatrix} 1 & 0 & 0 & ..0 \\ 0 & 1 & 0 & ..0 \\ 0 & 0 & 1 & ..0 \\ 0 & 0 & 0 & 1 \end{bmatrix} \quad (2.5.40)$$

Thus applying to w, the series of transformations CRG, brings the world and camera coordinate systems into coincidence. The image plane coordinates of a point w, are finally obtained by using Eq.(2.5.23). In other words, a homogeneous world point that is being viewed by a camera satisfying the geometric arrangement shown in Fig.2.18 has the following homogeneous representation in the camera coordinate system:

$$C = PCRGw \quad (2.5.41)$$

Equation (2.5-41) represents a perspective transformation involving two co-ordinate system.

AS indicated in Section 2.5.2. we obtain the Cartcian Cooridnates (x,y) of the imaged point by dividing the first and second components of x, by the fourth. Expending Eq. (2.5.41) and converting to Cartcian Coordinates yields.

$$x = \lambda \frac{(X - X_n)\cos\theta + (Y - Y_n)\sin\theta -}{-(X - X_n)\sin\theta\sin\theta + (Y - Y_n)\cos\theta\sin\theta - (Z - Z_n)\cos\theta + +}$$

and (2.5.42)

$$y = \lambda \frac{-(X - X_n)\sin\theta\cos\theta + (Y - Y_n)\cos\theta\cos\theta + (Z - Z_n)\sin\theta -}{-(X - X_n)\sin\theta\sin\theta + (Y - Y_n)\cos\theta\sin\theta - (Z - Z_n)\cos\theta + +} \quad (2.5.43)$$

Which are the image coordinates of a poiont w whose world coordinates are (X).

(a)

$$\begin{bmatrix} \cos\theta & \sin\theta & 0 & 0 \\ -\sin\theta\cos\theta & \cos\theta\cos\theta & \sin\theta & 0 \\ \sin\theta\sin\theta & -\cos\theta\sin\theta & \cos\theta & 0 \\ 0 & 0 & 0 & 1 \end{bmatrix} \quad (2.5.39)$$

$$\begin{bmatrix} 1 & 0 & 0 & ..0 \\ 0 & 1 & 0 & ..0 \\ 0 & 0 & 1 & ..0 \\ 0 & 0 & 0 & 1 \end{bmatrix} \quad (2.5.40)$$

$$x = \lambda \frac{(X - X_n)\cos\theta + (Y - Y_n)\sin\theta -}{-(X - X_n)\sin\theta\sin\theta + (Y - Y_n)\cos\theta\sin\theta - (Z - Z_n)\cos\theta + +}$$

$$y = \lambda \frac{-(X - X_n)\sin\theta\cos\theta + (Y - Y_n)\cos\theta\cos\theta + (Z - Z_n)\sin\theta -}{-(X - X_n)\sin\theta\sin\theta + (Y - Y_n)\cos\theta\sin\theta \quad (Z - Z_n)\cos\theta + +}$$

(b)

Fig. 29.11 (*a*) Input image with DM-II and DM-III; (*b*) Result.

distinct shape characteristic is not present in other areas and exploited for extracting the text regions. This is done by an extension of the well known hit-and-miss approach.

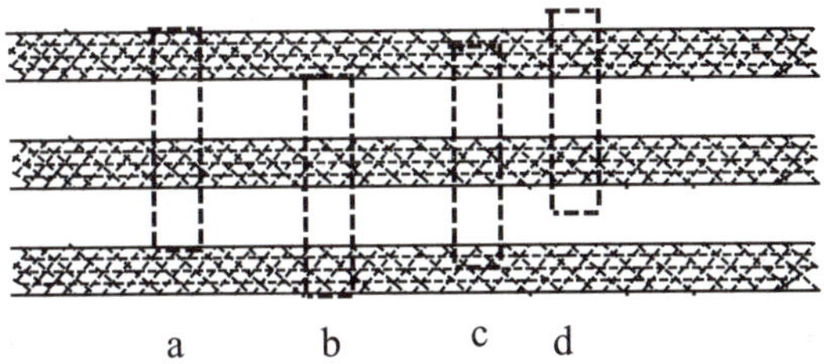

Fig. 29.12 Different positions of *W* with respect to band patterns in the text region of the document image; Situation (*i*) is shown in '*a*' and '*b*'; situation (*ii*) and (*iii*) are shown in '*c*' and '*d*' respectively. For description of the situations see text.

To get the text bands we do closing operation with horizontal structuring element (SE) to smear the text lines. We avoid merging of consecutive lines by keeping the height of SE as small as possible. This smearing of the text lines is followed by a smoothening step carried out by opening the image with a small square SE. Now we get a fairly regular horizontal band patterns representing text area. Now by scanning the image vertically the average value of the text height (h_t) and the gap height (h_g) is calculated. It may be noted that this preprocessing step is required for heading detection; so we start with the preprocessed image.

First we select a narrow vertical window which covers at least two consecutive text lines. A window of height $2(h_t + h_g)$ and of 1-pixel width is selected for this purpose where h_t and h_g *are* the average text height and inter-line gap height respectively. Ideally, this window can fit in the vertical profile of either (*i*) two black bands and two white bands, or (*ii*) two white bands, one black band and some portions of two other black bands, or (*iii*) two black bands, one white band and some portions of two other white bands. The situations are depicted in Fig. 29.12. In situation (*i*) (as shown in Fig. 29.12(*a*) and (*b*)) the number of transitions (from black to white and white to black) is 3; and it is 4 in the situations (*ii*) and (*iii*) (shown in Fig. 29.12(*c*) and (*d*)). Secondly, the ratio of number of black pixels to that of white pixels should be $\approx h_t / h_g$. Based on these observations we try to identify the band patterns (consequently text regions) within the closed document image using the following steps.

1. Place the window W over the closed image (aligning with the top left portion at start).
2. Compute the black to white as well as white to black transitions, and count the number nb of black pixels and number nw of white pixels within W.

3. If the number of transitions lies between 3 to 4 and the ratio nb /nw is close to ht /hg, then mark the origin 2(ht + hg) as text area.
4. Do (2) and (3) for all pixels by moving the window over the whole image.
5. Dilate with a narrow SE of height 2(ht + hg).
6. Use connected component analysis to find out and delete small components.

As a results of the operations mentioned above we get near rectangular text zones. This would roughly cover the whole text. But, some isolated text lines and short lines at the end of paragraphs may not be covered. The result of the text zone mapping using the proposed algorithm and its subsequent consolidation etc. is shown in Fig. 29.13.

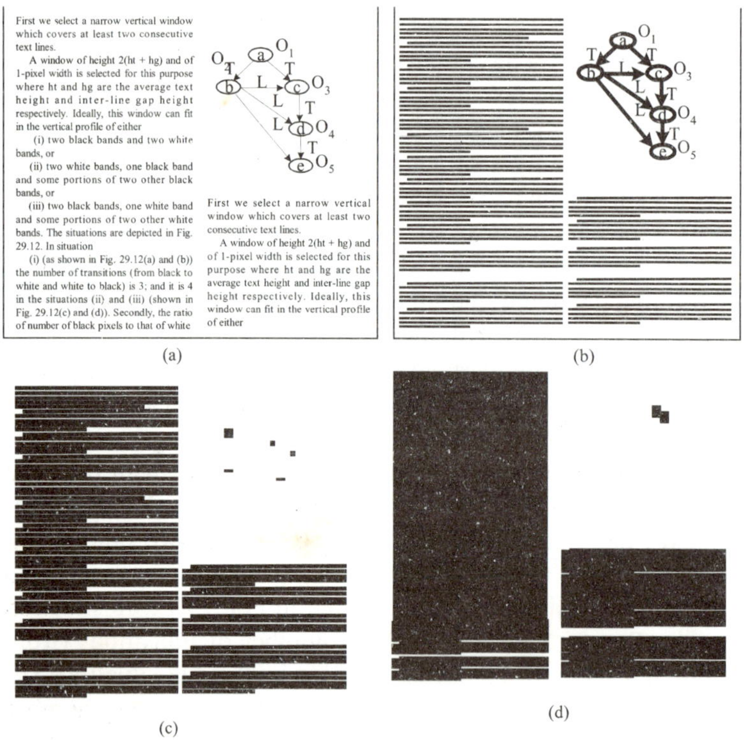

Fig. 29.13 Different phases of text extraction. (*a*) Original Image; (*b*) Consolidation through morphological operation; (*c*) Initial mapping of the text portion; (*d*) Final segmentation through morphological operations and connected component analysis.

29.5 DOCUMENT IMAGE MODEL AND EXPERIMENTAL RESULTS

In this section we specify a document image model based on the bounding boxes of its constituent parts for performance evaluation of segmentation algorithms.

Bounding boxes are usually represented by coordinates of diagonally opposite corner points (B_{i1} and B_{i2}). An example of such bounding boxes of five distinct zones is shown in Fig. 29.14a. First we derive two different bounding boxes bb_i and BB_i (as shown in Fig. 29.14b)[6]. bb_i is the smallest bounding box containing one of the components like texts, tables, graphics, headings, half-tones and BB_i is the largest bounding box containing bb_i and some part of the background (B) but not bb_j (where $i \neq j$). Thus BB_i has the following properties:

(i) $BB_i \supseteq bb_i$ and

(ii) $BB_i \cap bb_j = \phi$ for $i \neq j$

bb_{i1} and bb_{i2} represent top-left and bottom-right corners of bb_i. Similarly BB_{i1} and BB_{i2} represent top-left and bottom-right corners of BB_i.

We may construct a graph showing the relative location of a bounding box with respect to the others in a document page.

Layout features of document page image thus can be represented by a directed graph whose nodes represent various zones and edges represent their relative locations. Fig. 29.15a shows the graph

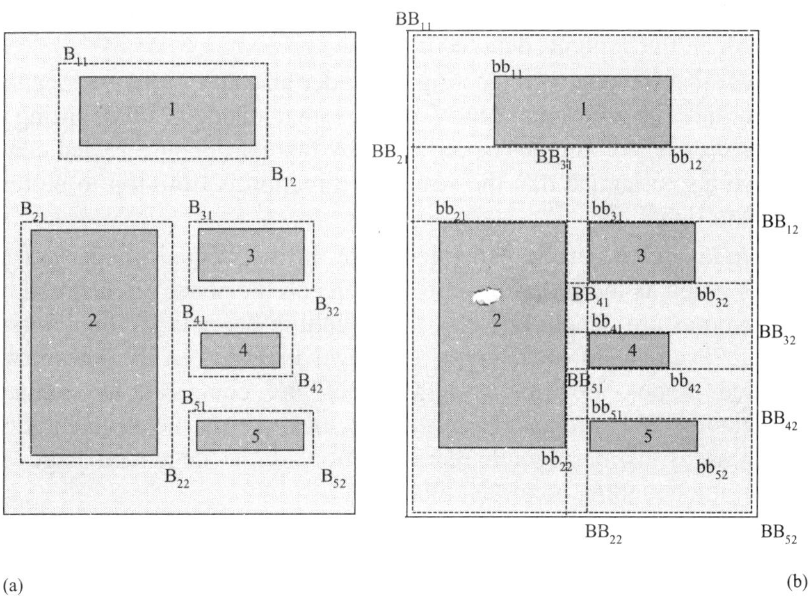

Fig. 29.14 Bounding box representation of constituent parts of a document page; (*a*) Bounding box information usually available in UW document image database; (*b*) Smallest and largest bounding boxes derived from B_{i1} and B_{i2}.

---

6 bounding box information is available from UW database.

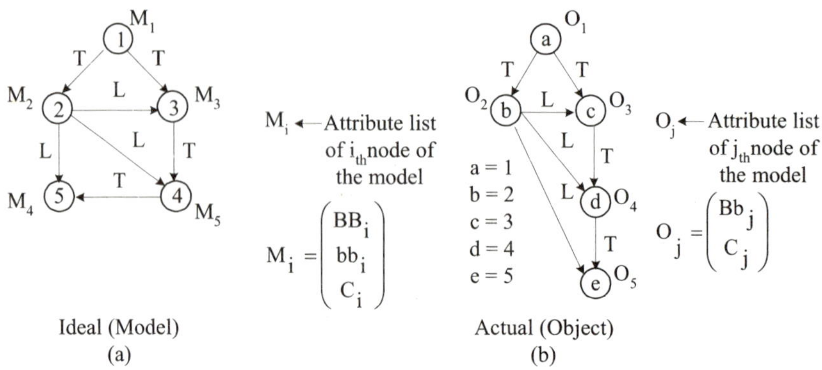

Fig. 29.15 Graphical representation of the page shown in Fig. 29.1 in the bounding box form. (*a*) Model graph of the page and (*b*) Actual (object) graph of the page obtained after segmentation.

representation of the example page shown in Fig. 29.14. Suppose we call it the model graph of the page. Each node M_i of the graph has the following attributes.

- Smallest bounding box (denoted by bb_i).
- Largest bounding box (denoted *by* BB_i).
- Type of the content (denoted by C_i).

Note that the edges connecting the nodes also carry relative location information. The notations T and L indicate that a node is either sitting at the top-of or left-of another node joined by that particular directed edge. We have also assumed that the scanning direction is from top to bottom and left to right.

Similar graph can be generated from the segmented image. Let us call this graph as the actual or object graph and the nodes are denoted by O_j. Attributes are denoted by Bb_j, the bounding box and C_j, the content type. An example of such graph is shown in Fig. 29.15b. These two attributed graphs, i.e., model and object, are compared to evaluate segmentation. We propose performance measure of the segmentation algorithms by using a graph representation of the document page, in terms of the bounding boxes as follows:

(i) Correct classification $cc_{ji} = \#(Bb_j \cap BB_i)$,

(ii) False alarm $ef_j = \#(Bb_j \setminus BB_i)$ and

(iii) Mis-classification $em_j = \#(bb_i \setminus Bb_j)$.

For performance analysis two graphs may be matched based on node types and relative locations associated with edges using graph isomorphism algorithms. As the number of nodes are very small (most of the cases the number is less than 10), we have implemented a simple algorithm to match the nodes explicitly.

We carried out the performance measure using around 200 samples taken from the UW-I, UW-II databases as well as our own collection of newly scanned images. The bounding box information is available from the zone and page bounding box information available for each image. The summary of the results is presented in Table 29.1 for 6 different zones. Note that the diagonal elements shows the correct classification rate for that zone. While column values other than the diagonal together give the mis-classification rate for that item. In a similar way false alarm is the row-wise summation of values excluding the diagonal element. Note that all experiments were carried out in a COMPAQ DS 20E high' end workstation and all the programs are written in C.

Table 29.1 *Performance of segmentation (in %) of different zones of the document*

		Actual					
		Text	**Graphics**	**Table**	**Heading**	**Displayed-math**	**Half-tone**
Classified	Text	91.30	1.16	4.26	1.42	1.63	
	Graphics	1.11	89.62	5.46	2.73		3.62
	Table	3.70	2.75	90.28	2.28		
	Heading	2.14			84.49	0.68	
	Display math	1.75			1.86	97.69	
	Half-tone		6.47		7.22		96.38

Note that the total segmentation time including skew detection and separation of text, tables, math-zones, half-tones and graphics is less than 25 seconds for a standard A-4 size document scanned at 300 dpi.

29.6 CONCLUSION

As concluding remarks we would like to point out the uniqueness of the work. Use of fast morphological algorithms for all stages of the proposed task is a specialty of this work. Time to detect skew in the proposed method is one of the fastest reported algorithms. This pushes us forward to our goal of low cost segmentation as de-skewing of the document takes less than 1 second irrespective of the complexity of the document.

The half-tone segmentation solution is also unique as we did it right from the gray image at a very low computational cost with a high percentage of success. Although working with tabular structure has been in the focus of many works for proper OCR operation most of the reported works are on processing the tables once they are detected manually. Idea of text graphics separation is totally new and can successfully work even in case of complex document.

Finally a scheme for performance analysis is proposed and tested with images from a standard database. We contend that our attempt in providing segmentation of document images using fast algorithm with morphological operations would lead to the improvement of timing performance of DIA systems without compromising the accuracy of segmentation.

References

7. L O'Gorman and R Kasturi, "Document image analysis systems," *Computer Mag, IEEE Computer Soc.* July, pp. 5–8, 1992.
8. G Nagy, "Document analysis and optical character recognition," in *Proc. 5th Int. Conf. on Image Ana. and Processing, Positano*, Italy, pp. 511–529, Sep. 20—22, 1989.
9. J Kanai and A Dengel, *Structured document image analysis: edited by H S Baird, H Bunke and K Yamamoto*, ch. IAPR 1990 workshop on SSPR, pp. 562–564. Berlin: Springer-Verlag, 1990.
10. S Chen, *Document Layout Analysis Using Recursive Morpho-logical Transforms*. Ph.D thesis, University of Washington, 1995.
11. M Nadler, "A survey of document segmentation and coding techniques," *Computer vision, graphics and image processing*, 28, pp. 240–262, 1984.
12. R Kasturi and L O'Gorman, "Document image analysis: a bibliography," *Machine vision and application*, Vol. 5, No. 3, pp. 231–243, 1992.
13. F M. Wahl, K Y Wong, and R G Casey, "Block segmentation and text extraction in mixed text/image documents," *CGIP* 20, pp. 375–390, 1982.
14. G Nagy and S Seth, "Hierarchical representation of optically scanned documents," in *Proc. 7th Int. Conf. on Pattern recognition*, pp. 347–349, 1984.
15. L Fletcher and R Kasturi, "A robust algorithm for text string separation from mixed text/graphics images," *IEEE Transaction on pattern analysis and machine intelligence.* 10 (6), pp. 910–918, 1988.
16. L O'Gorman, "The document spectrum for page layout analysis," *IEEE Trans. pattern anal. mach. intell.,* Vol. 15, No. 11, pp. 1162–1173, 1993.
17. L O'Gorman, "k × k thinning," *Computer vision, graphics and image processing*, Vol. 51, pp. 195–215, 1990.
18. H S Baird, S E Jones, and S J Fortune, "Image segmentation by shape directed covers," in *Proceedings 10th ICPR,* (Atlantic city, New Jersy, June), pp. 820–825, 1990.

19. T Pavlidis and J Zhou, "Page segmentation and classification," *Computer vision graphics and image processing*, Vol. 54, pp. 484–496, 1992.
20. J Zhou, A document analysis system. Ph.D thesis, State University of New York at Stony Brook, 1993.
21. A K Jain and S Bhattacharjee, "Texture segmentation using gabor filters for automatic document processing," *Machine vision and application*, 5, pp. 169–184, 1992.
22. O T Akindele and A Belaid, "Page segmentation by segment tracing," in *ICDAR'93*, (Tsukuba, Japan), pp. 341–344, 1993.
23. T Saitoh and T Pavlidis, "Page segmentation without rectangle assumption," in *Proc. of 11th IAPR Int'l Conf. on Pattern recognition,* Hague, Netherlands, Aug 30Sep 3, pp. 277–280, 1992.
24. S Chen, R M Haralick, and I Phillips, "Simultaneous word segmentation from document image using recursive morphological closing transform," in *ICDAR'95: Third International conference on document analysis and recognition,* Montreal, Canada, August 14—16, 1995.
25. F LeBourgeois and H Emptoz, "Document analysis in gray level and typography extraction using character pattern redundancies," in *Proc. of ICDAR'99*, (Ulm, Germany), 1999.
26. B Waked, C Y Suen, and S Bergler, "Segmenting document images using diagonal white runs' and vertical edges," in *Proc. of ICDAR* 2001, (Bangalore, India), pp. 194–199, 2001.
27. D Sylwester and S Seth, "Adaptive segmentation of document images," in *Proc. Of ICDAR* 2001, (Bangalore, India), pp. 827–831, 2001.
28. A K Das and B Chanda, "Fast binary morphological operations for sequential machines," *Image processing & communications*, Vol. 3, No. 1-2, pp. 49–62, 1997.
29. A K Das and B Chanda, "A fast algorithm for skew detection of document images using morphology," *Intl. J. of document analysis and recognition*, Vol. 4, pp. 109–114, 2001.
30. A K Das and B Chanda, "Text segmentation from document images: A morphological approach," *Journal of institute of engineers* (*I*)., Vol. 77, November, pp. 50–56, 1996.
31. A K Das and B Chanda, "Detection of tables and headings from document image: A morphological approach," in *International Conf. on Computational linguistics, Speech and Document Pro-cessing (ICCLSDP'98*); Feb. 18–20, Calcutta, India, pp. A57 – A64, 1998.
32. A K Das and B Chanda, "Segmentation of text and graphics from document image: A morphological approach," in *International Conf.*

on Computational linguistics, Speech and Document Processing (*ICCLSDP'*98); Feb. 18–20, Calcutta, India:, pp. A50–A56, 1998.

33. A K Das, S K Saha, and B Chanda, "An empirical measure of performance of document image segmentation algorithm," *Intl. J. of Document Analysis and Recognition*, Vol. 4(3), pp. 183–190, 2001.
34. K Yogesan, F Albregtsen, and H E Danielsen, "Gray level variance matrix: A new approach to higher order statistical texture analysis," in *The 3rd Int. Conf. on Automation, Robotics and Comp. Vis., ICARCV'*94, Singapore, Nov 9—11, pp. 658–663, 1994.
35. A Belaid and J P Haton, "A syntactic approach for handwritten mathematical formula recognition," *IEEE Trans. PAMI,* Vol 6., pp. 105–111, 1984.
36. A Grbavec and D Blostein, "Mathematical expression recognition using graph rewriting," in *Proc. of ICDAR*'93, (France), pp. 417–421, 1995.
37. J Ha, R M Haralick, and I T Philips, "Understanding mathe-matical expressions from document images," in *Proc. of ICDAR'*95, (Canada), pp. 956–959, 1995.
38. H J Lee and J S Wang, "Design of mathematical expression recognition system," in *Proc. of ICDAR'*95, (Canada), pp. 1084 – 1087, 1995.
39. J Y Toumit, S Garcia-Salicetti, and H Emptoz, "A hierarchical and recursive model of mathematical expressions for automatic reading of mathematical documents," in *Proc. of ICDAR'99,* (India), pp. 116–122, 1999.
40. M Okamoto and H Miyazawa, "An experimental implementation of a document recognition system for papers containing mathe-matical expression," in *Structured Document Image Analysis,* (Springer-Verlag), pp. 36–53, 1992.
41. R Fateman, T Tokuyasu, B Berman, and N Mitchell, "Optical character recognition and parsing of typeset mathematics," *Visual Commun. and Image Representation,* Vol. 7, no 1, pp. 2–15, March 1996.
42. B B Chaudhuri and U Garain, "An approach for recognition and interpretation of mathematical expressions in printed document," *Pattern Analysis and Applications,* Vol. 3(2), pp. 120–131, 2000.
43. A Kacem, A Belaid, and M B Ahmed, "Automatic extraction of printed mathematical formulas using fuzzy logic and propagation of context," *IJDAR,* Vol 4, no 2, pp. 97–108, 2001.
44. S P Chowdhury, S Mandal, A K Das, and B Chanda, "Automated segmentation of math-zones from document images," in *7th*

International Conference on Document Analysis and Recognition, Vol. II, (3-6 August'03, Edinburgh, U. K.), pp. 755 – 759, 2003.

45. K C Fan, C H Liu, and Y K Wang, "Segmentation and classi-fication of mixed text/graphics/image documents," *Pattern Recognition Letters*, Vol. 15, pp. 1201–1209, 1994.
46. A K Jain and B Yu, "Page segmentation using document model," in *Proc. ICDAR*'97, Ulm, Germany, pp. 34–38, August. 1997.

30

Knowledge Based Approach to Medical Image Processing: With Some Case Studies

Mahua Bhattacharya[1] & D Dutta Majumder[2,3]

ABSTRACT

In this paper in the first part we present a theoretical framework of the knowledge based approach to image processing and analysis systems, as a sub domain of pattern recognition, knowledge management and broadly artificial intelligence techniques and to indicate how this can be successfully implemented on different modality of medical images for diagnosis of diseases in order to assist the clinicians in their therapeutic planning. During last few decades pattern recognition and its sub areas such as speech / image processing, vision techniques have been developed for flexible interactive intelligent man–machine interfaces for several applications in science, society and industry. The operations on the image in the first level is carried out independent of the knowledge of the domain but specific to the structural and syntactic properties of the image. In the second level a semantic analysis of the image based on the results of the first level is performed. In the highest level the knowledge of the domain is injected where explicitly both the intrinsic anatomical properties of the organs and pathological structures with relational aspects are being represented. In second part we present some case studies of application of knowledge based methods using Dutta Majumder's mathematical theory of shape and shape metric and other approaches developed by the authors. These methods have been applied for decision making purposes using *CT*, *MR*, Mammographic and X-Ray images. The case studies presented in this paper are: (*i*) tumor gradation and cancer screening in *CNS* (*ii*) breast cancer gradation and screening using mammographic images (*iii*) quantitative measure of bone erosion process for osteoporosis and (*iv*) multimodal image registration and fusion of ventricular region for studying patient data for Alzheimer's diseases.

Keywords: Medical Image, Multimodality, Knowledge Based Approach, Segmentation, Benignancy, Shape Similarity Measure, Erosion Factor, Osteoporosis, Alzheimer's Disease.

30.1 INTRODUCTION & PERSPECTIVE

Physicians around the world are showing more and more interest in using computers, expert systems and knowledge based systems and other decision support systems in diverse clinical spheres. But Applications of AI and knowledge based approaches for medical image processing and therapeutic planning started only in the last decade or so. In present paper AI and knowledge based approaches to medical image processing

1 School of Information Technology, W.B. University of Technology

2 Indian Statistical Institute, Kolkata

3 Institute of Cybernetics Systems and Information Technology

with some case studies have been presented. For centuries mankind are interested to visualize human internal organ in their true form and shape. If the discovery of X-rays gave birth to radiology, the invention of Computerized Tomography (CT) and recently Magnetic Resonance Imaging (MR), Positron Emission Tomography (PET), Single Photon Emission Computed Tomography (SPECT) have revolutionized radiology. Three dimensional (3D) imaging is recent development that has brought us closer to fulfilling the noninvasive visualization. 3D imaging has evolved as a discipline of its own, dealing with the various forms of visualization, manipulation and analysis of multidimensional bio-medical structures. Since images in medicine are a very important information source in the process of diagnosis a knowledge based system for interpreting theses images is very much required that can fulfill the purpose of automatic symbolic description of them. The automatic interpretation of these images is particularly problematic due to the statistical and structural variations in the morphology and pathological and non pathological structures [1]. Conventional image processing techniques have certain limitations for its interpretation by the clinicians and the statistical techniques for pattern recognition have serious shortcomings as they do not consider structural information. But in interpretation of the whole image in order to identify both the normal and the pathological structures it is necessary to consider explicitly the knowledge that we have a priori about the properties of the organs and their anatomical relations as well as the shapes of the pathological structures. Due to these reasons the techniques developed in the field of artificial intelligence that lead us to develop the knowledge based systems that should be employed for understanding of clinically relevant properties of images. As an example one of the most important need for knowledge based image processing is indicated by efficacy of interpretation guided segmentation and vice versa particularly in medical image processing that lead to the development of cybernetic approach to the medical technology [4], [7]. Some algorithms that search for specific structures such as ribs [17] or nodules in chest X-ray images have been developed [15], [16].

The algorithmic way of processing and analyzing digital images has developed powerful means to interpret specified kinds of image but failed in providing general image understanding methods that work on all kinds of images [8]. This is mostly due to the fact that every picture can be interpreted in many ways so we need to build models in order to 'understand' the images. Another important goal of knowledge based image analysis is to make the knowledge of how to apply, compose and program image processing algorithms explicit and thereby help the non expert on the field of image analysis to do efficient image processing [5],

[6]. In knowledge based computation technique different levels of operations are performed on the image. The first level of operations on the image is independent of the knowledge domain and thus specific to the image on a syntactic level: like enhancement, extraction of boundaries, segmentation, obtaining of descriptors [33], [34], [35], [36]. In the second level a semantic analysis of the image based on the properties which are extracted in the low level process is done. In the high level process the knowledge which is possessed about the domain is injected by means of a model. The schemes for the representation of knowledge and the control strategies for obtaining the best correspondence between the model and the image must be considered. The literature [2] describes the low level processing which is executed by sequential modules and the high level part is a production system with a rule interpreter and a submodule for each object to be identified. Each submodule contains specific knowledge about the object and relational properties with respect to other objects; the submodules are executed independently and communicate through database. In knowledge based systems the organs and pathological structures are described by means of properties and relations relative to both to the intrinsic anatomical knowledge of the diverse organs and shapes of the lesions.

Advances in the frontiers of medical imaging, processing and application to diagnostics requires the incorporation of knowledge and the expertise of latest image manipulation method, that has taken place in the last thirty years. In mammography shape intensity and texture analysis techniques are used to facilitate the diagnosis of breast cancer. The use of multiple modality for the same patient whichever combinations are relevant in a particular case from CT, MR, PET, SPECT and USG requires sophisticated algorithms for image registration and fusion in which knowledge based approach is very useful [18], [31], [32].

In the last sections of the present paper we discuss four important case studies for diagnosis and therapy planning using knowledge based approach.

30.2. FUNDAMENTALS OF CYBERNETICS AND KNOWLEDGE BASED SYSTEMS: IMPACT ON MEDICAL IMAGES

The development of cybernetics as a modern discipline with a distinctive influence on almost all branches of science and technology follows from Norbert Wiener's (1948) publication. The subject of cybernetics emerged through the interaction of traditional sciences when the scientists and engineers faced a set of problems concerned with communication, control and computation in machines and living tissues. So one line leads to the study of automatic activity of living beings and the other line leads to that of machines including mechanization of thought process including mathematical logic, artificial intelligence and related subjects of computer science and information technology. *Dutta Majumder* [7], *Dutta Majumder & Bhattacharya* [4] combined the 'observer systems', 'observed systems' and the 'act of observing' in the environment into one unitary holistic discipline of a general dynamical system from the points of view of perspective, motivation, requirements, characteristics, attributes and behavior, formalizing a theoretical framework for cybernetic approach to medical technology [4], [7].

The cybernetic approach enables medical technology with artificial intelligence and expert system based computerized instrumentation for pathological study, diagnostics and therapeutic planning, a much better disease planning and patient management system at a much lower cost. This is realizable as the structural and functional information can have a reciprocal flow between the machines and living tissues.

The recent trend of research consists of combining more than one relevant modality of medical images (X-Ray, CT, MR, PET, SPECT, fMRI) for uncertainty management in diagnostics and therapeutic planning.

30.3 DESIGN OF KNOWLEDGE BASED SYSTEMS

Designing of a knowledge based system primarily consists of a relational database of object image and structural and functional information obtained by applying different techniques of image processing. To develop a framework for image understanding research from the point of view of knowledge level, information level and complexity level, knowledge organization and control structure in image understanding systems [IUS] are required. These systems may be defined using Low Level Vision [LLV], Intermediate Level of Vision [ILV] and High Level Vision [HLV] [3].

30.3.1 Low Level Vision

At the lowest level (LLV), pictures (sensor information–usually an intensity image) are segmented into regions of similar primary features to extract 'primitive information' from a scene. The process range from modeling the characteristics of incident and reflected light to detecting edges segments [3] and connecting them into lines or curves or regions with uniform properties [9]. Processing operation on image are performed for noise reduction, segmentation and other preprocessing tasks. The final objective of the process is to detect pathological structures, space occupying lesions, nodules and masses and these generally appear defined by region properties rather than contours. The segmentation process extracts structural information from the image by partitioning it onto coherent element regions. Before segmentation process an enhancement of the image by means of selecting masking techniques may be carried out. The segmentation process may be carried out based on thresholding of grey level histogram. Thus the original image is initially partitioned into a set of subregions, each of which is a connected region and is segmented in successive stages. The process ends when all the regions that have been generated is analyzed. The elemental regions that have been extracted constitute a first description of the image, into which by means of high level process we inject a clinical meaning. The elemental regions are described in terms of morphometric and relational properties like position, shape, orientation and relation to other region. The elemental regions with the values of their properties constitute the symbolic representation of the image on which the high level block is going to operate.

Image segmentation for extraction of the relevant image features like regions, edges, textures are considered by a data-driven, bottom-up analysis.[34].

Image interpretation: to find the scene elements, that is the invariants of a real, 3D world (shape from-X). This 3D-reconstruction from 2D-images is without prior knowledge is an ill-posed problem. Object recognition: to name the objects which are relevant in the specific domain using prior knowledge (models) about the expected objects.

30.3.2 Intermediate Level Vision

The next intermediate level of vision (ILV) consists of the procedures that use the results from LLV to produce structures in the picture or portions of the picture where complete knowledge regarding model features (topological structure) is available. The techniques are edge linking, segmenting, shape analysis and description and recognition. Techniques such as local graph search and global optimization using dynamic programming as developed in artificial intelligence can be employed to merge regions and to assign label sets to them .

30.3.3 High Level of Vision

The highest level (HLV) may be viewed as the process that attempts to emulate cognition, encompassing a boarder spectrum of processing functions. HLV may a relational database to store knowledge and vision strategy production systems which has to be on knowledge directed or

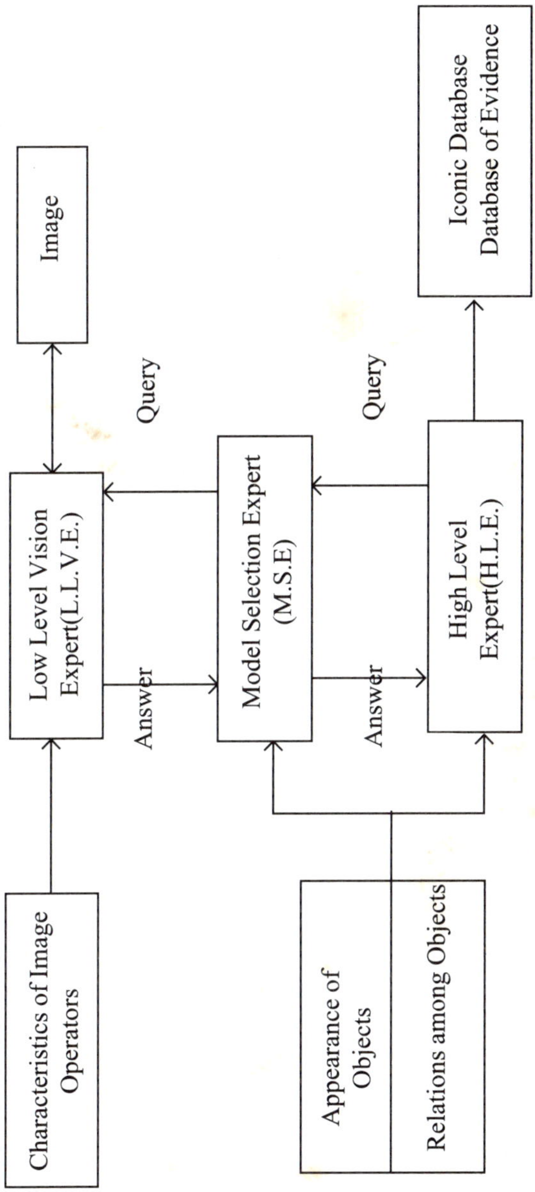

Fig. 30.1 A knowledge-based image understanding system with three levels of expertise for combining evidence.

goal oriented analysis. Though these three levels of processes applies to many vision systems, several systems omit or add one or more steps depending on the complexity of environments.

The processing is done on a semantic level, the knowledge about the domain and the region analyzer is distinguished. The descriptive anatomical knowledge about the domain both about characteristics of organs and pathological structures and the relations between them is represented by means of a semantic network in which the nodes constitutes the properties and the arcs represent relations and definitions of properties.

30.4 CHARACTERISTICS OF KNOWLEDGE BASED IMAGE UNDERSTANDING

The success of information and knowledge management depends on understanding and supporting the user's need to know. This requires understanding human's abilities, limitations and inclinations in seeking of information and knowledge. Since understanding is a knowledge based process for the several processing steps we need different kinds of knowledge [10], [13]. *Binford* [11] gave a good survey of the different IUS developed during the late seventies as feasibility studies. Some of them were proved to be good in some application areas as indicated in the earlier sections of this paper. *Michael Brady* [12], [14] described the extensive researches that have been conducted to extract a 3D features from 2D imageries.

30.4.1 Levels of Knowledge for IUS

Different levels of knowledge are required for image understanding systems:

Physical knowledge

The physical laws governing imaging processes in the multidimensional physical world along with the geometry of the camera, light source sensor and material of the object are important sources of knowledge. Information from shading, texture, motion, object contour and stereo vision can be combined with this knowledge to recover the 3D shape from the 2D object.

Visual perception knowledge

Proximity, similarity, continuity, smoothness, symmetry etc. are used for the grouping of primitive pictorial entities into more global ones. This knowledge plays an important role in segmentation and also in grouping primitive 3D features into global characteristics.

Semantic Knowledge

For recognition of objects, knowledge about properties and relations between them is essential. The above two types of knowledge are general and domain independent; semantic knowledge is domain specific.

Levels of Information

The Fig. 30.2 depicts information levels in an IUS and the processes developed so far to transform information across the levels. Here we also observe three levels of analytic processes. In the low level process (LLP) physical and neurophysiological knowledge is to be utilized to define extract and the most informative image features.

In the middle level process (MLP) the local features of the LLP are to be grouped into global image features using the perceptual knowledge, again the image features are to be transformed to scene features (2D features) using the physical knowledge, so that the matching can be performed with 3D object model. There are many possibilities for the grouping and for the 3D interpretations of a projected 2D image feature, so that AI techniques are needed.

The major task of high level process (HLP) is to find the object model which matches with the information extracted from the input image. The problems which may come into play are : (1) If the object is occluded by others, (2) 2D appearance may change due to moving objects so for image understanding sophisticated model representation and utilization of the semantic knowledge are required. It is easier to recognize man made artificial objects which have well defined open and closed curves such as line segments and disks. Different image processing techniques are employed to recognize the homogeneity of these objects. Texture analysis is useful to extract the well defined global image features. Even for recognition purposes the knowledge may be extracted from the other properties of objects like shape, texture and color.

But the limitations in knowledge extraction in the domain appears when information is approximate and for which knowledge may be imprecise. To handle the imprecision in the knowledge more powerful methods must be evolved which will be able to use approximate reasoning schemes. In case of medical image analysis using knowledge based approaches we have to handle the imprecision and uncertainties more carefully to design the automated expert system for diagnosis and therapy planning.

30.5 STRATEGIES FOR ANALYSIS OF MEDICAL IMAGES

Our objective is to offer the clinicians wider access to evolving medical image processing techniques for providing data for improved assessment and quantification of physiological processes. Our approaches are based on AI techniques knowledge based program where the scheme selects, organizes

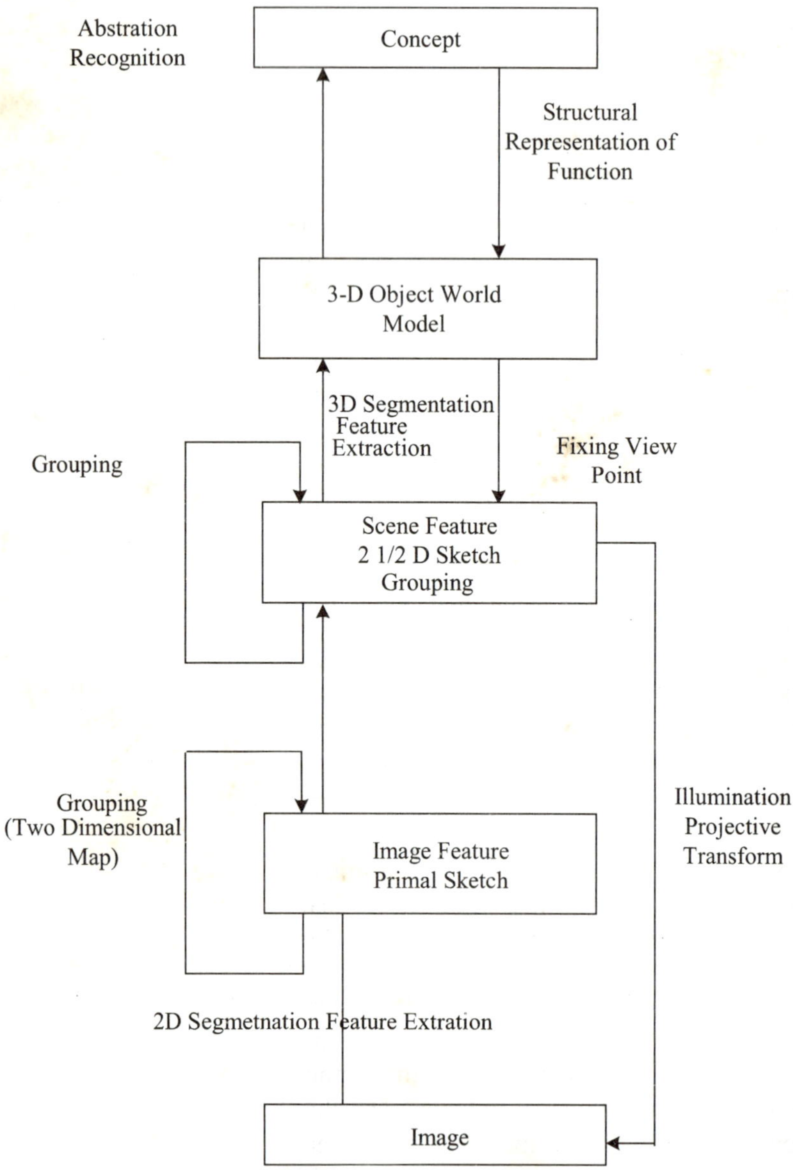

Fig. 30.2 Information levels in IUS. Facts about brightness values are explicit in the image; brightness changes, groups of similar changes, blobs, and texture are explicit in the primal sketch, surfaces are explicit in the $2\frac{1}{2}$-D sketch; volumes are explicit in the world model.

and executes the appropriate *medical image processing* algorithms. The methodologies suggested by us for the clinical end-users offer results, both in terms of robustness and reliability which we expect having of great use for improved therapeutic procedures to be determined by the physicians. The analysis and strategies proposed have been implemented by means of development of software which controls the recognition and classification processes stepwise.

30.5.1 Knowledge Based Approach to Segmentation of Medical Images

Accurately segmented and quantifying structures is a key issue in bio medical image analysis. The two conventional methods of image segmentation, region based and boundary based methods often suffer from a variety of limitations. One of the approach to minimize the limitation is to integrate the two methods so that knowledge of one can be used for others and vice versa. Knowledge can be intensity, texture and /or shape. Some of the earlier methods such as Sobel and Prewitt detectors [19], [20] used local gradient operators which only detected edges having certain orientation and performed poorly when the edges were blurred and noisy [22]. In the next course more sophisticated operators have been developed to provide some degree of immunity to noise and to detect more accurate location of the edges. In 1980 Marr and Hildreath [21] proposed the Gaussian filter which is the most commonly used smoothing filter in edge detection. Xiaolan Zeng, Lawrence H. Satib *et. al.* discussed knowledge based segmentation and measurement of the cortex from 3D MR images [26]. They have suggested a new approach of coupled surfaces propagation using level set methods for the segmentation and measurement of the cortex. The method has been described by evolving two embedded surfaces simultaneously each driven by its own image–derived information while maintaining the coupling, a final representation of the cortical bounding surfaces and an automatic segmentation of the cortex are achieved. Characteristics of the cortex such as cortical surface area, surface curvature and thickness are then evaluated. Theo *et al.* [25] used a system that exploited knowledge if cortical anatomy, in which white matter and CSF (cerebrospinal fluid) regions were first segmented, then the connectivity of the white matter was verified in regions of interest. Davatzikos *et al.* introduced the concept of a ribbon for modeling the outer cortex in cross–sectional brain images and then extended the model into 3D [23], [24]. A deformable surface algorithm was constructed to find the central layer of the cortex. Based on this parameterization, the cortical structure was characterized through its depth map and curvature map. This method explicitly used the structural information of the cortex. However close initialization and significant human interaction are needed to force the ribbon into sulcal folds.

30.5.2 Object and Shape Based Medical Image Analysis

Viewing of 3D objects allow one to focus on the object's decomposition into figures where both the global and the local shape information of objects are associated. In present and subsequent sections we shall discuss some application areas on medical image processing where we have executed several experiments on multimodal or unimodal medical imaging. We have developed methods related to the analysis of medical images in terms of the objects in them and their shape. The objective of the applications as described in the subsequent case studies include the extraction of objects, measurement of gradation of tumor/cancer growth in *central nervous system* (*CNS*) and to find the 'benignancy' index or 'malignancy index' detection of tumor lesion from mammographic images and to find the tendency of growth of the tumor lesion, quantitative measure of bone erosion process for osteoporosis, registration of different modalities medical images based on object matching, and diagnosis of Alzheimer's disease and other brain diseases via *shape change* of brain organs [18].

30.5.3 Mathematical Theory of Shape for Classification and the Concept of 'Shape Metric'

The features which are selected from shape analysis are associated with a boundary representation of the region of interest which is extracted as a digital contour from the image. The features associated with a boundary representation of an object are the length, the orientation of the straight line joining the extreme points on the contour, the area, and the number of concavities present on the contour. The features selected are invariant under any transformation of the shape. For a digital image the border is represented by a set of border pixel points where the boundary can be representation the boundary of the region of interest is ordered in a sequence of neighboring pixels and can be traversed in a vector scanning mode. As a pixel has eight neighboring pixels there are eight possible directions to move from one pixel position to its neighbor. Using Freeman chain coding representation the directional vectors between successive boundary pixels are encoded by numbers lying from 0 to...7 [39]. The sequence of a boundary can be represented by the chain of these numbers. The chain code representation of the border is utilized to find the distance function D between two contours and to measure the 'shape similarity' μ between the shape of two curves. The similarity measure is derived in terms of 'distance metric'. The regions having higher resemblance have higher degree of shape similarity. D. Dutta Majumder in his paper on mathematical theory of shapes [37] in relation to pattern recognition and computer vision enunciated a generalized formalism and concept of shape metric in the context of PR and CVS.

It is found that most of the approaches of analyzing shape particularly for practical applications in the areas of biology, cartography, engineering, geology, geophysics, each geometrical figure in R^K consists of N labelled points or landmarks and this is represented by an $N \times K$ matrix.

Two geometrical figures $X : N \times K$ and $X' = N' \times K'$ are said to be congruent if they differ by a rigid body transformation. We may use the words 'form' or 'shape –cum –size' as an equivalent class of congruent geometrical figures and can define them as the conceptual figures with location and orientations removed as developed in the following definitions [37]:

Definition 1

Two figures $X : N \times K$ and $X' = N' \times K$ have the same 'form' or 'shape' cum size if they are related by a rigid body transformation.

$$X' = X\Gamma + I_N\gamma^{\mathrm{T}}$$

Where $\Gamma = K \times K$ is a rotation. $|\Gamma| = 1$, I_N is the N vector of ones and $\gamma = K \times 1$ is a translation. The translation/rotation pair (γ, Γ) is a transformation from the special Euclidean group acting on R^K. In the absence of a common co-ordinate system we must compare the 'forms' of X and X' instead of the figures X and X'. Shape is the form with size removed. A shape is an equivalence class of geometrical figures modulo the special similarity transformation (no reflection) and we may write $[X]$ for the shape of X.

Definition 2

The two figures $X : N \times K$ and $X' = N' \times K'$ have the same shape $[X] = [X']$, if they are related by a special similarity transformation,

$$X' = \beta X\Gamma + I_N\gamma^T$$

$\beta > 0$ is a scalar. The triplet (γ, β, Γ) specifies the translation, scaling and rotation component of similarity transformations from X to X'.

Following the same logic the mathematical definition of shape for an open curve in 2D cases has been developed and then it is extended for a closed curve.

Definition 3

The object boundaries defined in digital region are assumed that they are closed and connected subset of Euclidean plane $\mathbf{R}^2$. No hole is permitted inside the region and the boundary of the region describes the region uniquely. Let R be the set of all regions. We can write a region A as (x_j, y_j) : for $j \in I$, where I is an index set.

Definition 4

R' is an equivalence relation of R for two regions A and B belonging to R and $(A, B) \varepsilon R'$ when any two regions A and B can be obtained by certain transformation of the other region.

Definition 5

A shape is an equivalence class generated by R' and in R. The two regions A and B have the same shape if $(A, B) \varepsilon R'$.'

Computational Methodology for Shape Analysis [38], [18]

Using the above formalisms Dutta Majumder and Bhattacharya developed the methodology and extensively applied them in different applications.

For a closed region it is necessary to have some reference points for chain generation of the border that does not depend on rotation of the pattern. The reference points are found from the intersection of boundary and major axis of the region as this is an invariant feature of a region. To extract the features from a region the classical least square method is used. Let x_j and y_j for $j = 1, 2, 3 \ldots\ldots. n$ be n points and the squared error of any straight line

$y = ax + b$ w.r.t. n points is given by

$$\sum_{j=1}^{n} (y_j - b - ax_j)^2$$

The Straight line with minimum squared error is

$y = a'x + b'$ where

$$a' = \frac{(1/n)\sum_{j=1}^{n} (x_j y_j - x_g y_g)}{(1/n)\sum_{j=1}^{n} (x_j^2 - x_g^2)}$$

and $b' = y_g - a'x$

where x_g & y_g are the centroid of the extracted contours of the region. The centroid x_g & y_g of the contour are given by n number of points on the contour as

Where

$$x_g = (1/n) \sum_{j=1}^{n} (x_j)$$

$$y_g = (1/n) \sum_{j=1}^{n} (y_j)$$

If this least square method is applied to the point (x_j and y_j) of a region it can be seen that the slope of the best linear fit $y = a'x + b'$ remains unchanged if the region is translated or dilated. But its relative slope may change if the region is rotated. This difficulty can be overcome by changing the definition of the mean squared error, that by taking the shortest distance between (x_j, y_j) and the line. We may consider the polar representation of the point (x_j, y_j) that,

$$x_j = r_j \cos\alpha$$

$$\text{and} \quad y_j = r_j \sin\alpha$$

r_j is a non-negative real number and α varies from 0 to 2Π. The shortest perpendicular distance from x_j and y_j to a straight line $y = x \tan\alpha + c$ is the absolute value of $c \cos\theta + r_j \sin(\theta - \theta_j)$. To find the axis of the region which makes an angle to the x-axis and passes through the centroid x_g, y_g the least square method is applied to the boundary points. In polar co-ordinate system the new squared error is $f(\alpha, c)$ should be minimum for required condition.

$$f(\alpha,c) = \sum_{j=1}^{n} (c\cos\alpha + r_j \sin(\alpha - \alpha_j))^2$$

The slope of the major axis (α^*) is obtained from the best linear fit solution by minimising $f(\alpha, c)$ passes through x_g, y_g and makes an angle (α^*) with x-axis and (α^*) satisfies the relation.

$$\tan 2\alpha^* = \frac{2\sum_{j=1}^{n}(x_j - x_g)(y_j - y_g)}{\sum_{j=1}^{n}(x_j - x_g)^2 - \sum_{j=1}^{n}(y_j - y_g)^2}$$

$$\cos 2\alpha^* \sum_{j=1}^{n}(x_j - x_g)^2 - \sum_{j=1}^{n}(y_j - y_g)^2 + 2\sin 2\alpha^* \sum_{j=1}^{n}(x_j - x_g)(y_j - y_g) \geq 0$$

Let us consider the best linear fit for the points belonging to a region. The two furthest points say *A* and *B* among the points of intersection of the major axis with the contour region are called the reference points and *AB* is the best line for the region. For a region belonging to an equivalence class the major axis and reference points are unique and invariant to position, size and orientation of the region. For a region belonging to an equivalence class the major axis is unique and invariant to rotation, translation and dilation of the region [37], [31].

Extraction of the Feature of the Boundary

To describe the extraction of features from a region we are considering n points on the contour such that the distance between any two consecutive points is the same. The direction code d_j denotes the direction. The string of direction code $d_1 = (d_{ij})^n{}_{j=1}$ is called an approximated border of the region l =1, 2 that depends on the starting point but not on the position and size of the region. The extracted border is represented by string number or directional code d defines a direction that makes an angle $(i - d)$ 45° with direction I where d is any real number lying between 1 to 8 and i = (1, 2 ...... 8). $d_1 = (d_{ij})^n{}_{j=1}$ be the contour representation starting from each reference point 1 and 2 and are denoted by d_1 and d_2 such that $d = (d_1, d_2)$ is the extracted feature from the region for two reference points described. The distance function **D** is derived on the basis of feature d.

Concept of Shape Metric and Computation of Shape Distance D* and Shape Similarity Measure μ

The possible directional codes are d_1 and d_2 for a length of a contour having n number of points. If d_2 is a rotation of d_1 then $d_2 = d_1 + \gamma$ for any real number γ when

$$d_{2j} = d_{1j} + \gamma \text{ for all } j.$$

From the direction code representation the distance function **D** is computed for each reference positions for l = 1, 2 between the contours to be matched one being the model contour and another one is the contour or region on interest in the image. Let d_1 and d_2 be the two elements of all the possible string sets.

Here $d_1 = (d_{1j})^n{}_{j=1}$ and $d_2 = (d_{2j})^n{}_{j=1}$ Now $d^1 = (d_1^{\,1}, d_2^{\,1})$ and $d^2 = (d_1^{\,2}, d_2^{\,2})$

For contour 1 the directional code representation are $d_1^{\,1}$ and $d_2^{\,1}$ for l = 1, 2 i.e. for two reference positions respectively, similarly for contour 2 the directional code representations are $d_1^{\,2}$ and $d_2^{\,2}$ for l = 1, 2 when the following conditions hold that $d_1^{\,2}$ is a rotation of $d_1^{\,1}$ and $d_2^{\,2}$ is a rotation of $d_2^{\,2}$. Similarly $d_1^{\,2}$ is a rotation of $d_2^{\,1}$ and $d_2^{\,2}$ is a rotation of $d_1^{\,1}$ then d^1 and d^2 belong to the same region. The distance function **D** is defined in terms of two string numbers d^1 and d^2 belong to a set as,

$$\mathbf{D}(d_1, d_2) = \sum_{j=1}^{n} \min((d_{1j} - d_{2j}), 8 - (d_{1j} - d_{2j}))$$

The distance function **D** is computed in terms of string number between the two contours. The directional code d gives the approximate description of the border and is independent of the size and position of the region d depends only on a starting point of the border. $d = (d_1, d_2)$, the set of two string numbers considering the two invariant reference points C and D on the contour, $d = (d_1, d_2)$, are information preserving and invariant under translation, dilation. The two contours C_1 and C_2 are considered having reference points (P_1, P_2) & (P_3, P_4) considering the distance function **D** with respect to the position of reference points (*a*) between (P_1 and P_3) : $\mathbf{D}\ (d_1^{\ 1}, d_1^{\ 2})$; (*b*) between ($P_1$ and P_4) : $\mathbf{D}\ (d_1^{\ 1}, d_2^{\ 2})$; (*c*) between ($P_2$ and P_4) : $\mathbf{D}\ (d_2^{\ 1}, d_2^{\ 2})$; (*d*) between ($P_2$ and P_3) : $\mathbf{D}\ (d_1^{\ 2}, d_2^{\ 1})$.

We define $\mathbf{D}' = (d_1, d_2) = \textit{infimum}\ \mathbf{D}\ (d_1, d_2 + \Upsilon)$ and $f(\Upsilon) = \mathbf{D}\ (d_1, d_2 + \Upsilon)$. But the computation on **D′** on the basis of the present definition of **D** is difficult since $\mathbf{D}\ (d_1, d_2 + \Upsilon)$ is not in general differentiable with respect to Υ so an alternative definition is proposed for **D** where all proposed desireable properties are retained and which is differentiable with respect to Υ so changing **D** we may write $\mathbf{D}\ (d_1, d_2 + \Upsilon)$ as

$$\mathbf{D}\ (d_1, d_2 + \Upsilon) = \sum_{j=1}^{n} \sin^2 (1/8)\Pi\ (d_{1j} - d_{2j} - \Upsilon)$$

and $f(\Upsilon)$

$$f(\Upsilon) = \sum_{j=1}^{n} \sin^2 (1/8)\Pi\ (d_{1j} - d_{2j} - \Upsilon)$$ all n points on the contour and

$f(\Upsilon)$ is optimum for $\Upsilon = \Upsilon_0$ when,

$$\Upsilon_0 = \frac{4}{\Pi}\left(\frac{\sum_{j=1}^{n} \sin(\theta_j)}{\sum_{j=1}^{n} \sin(\theta_j)}\right)$$

where $\theta_j = (1/4)\ \Pi\ (d_{1j} - d_{2j})$ let $\Upsilon_0 = \Upsilon_1, \Upsilon_2$, for Υ_1, belonging to $|0, 4|$ and $\Upsilon_2 = \Upsilon_1 + 4$. The value $\Upsilon = \Upsilon_0$ is obtained as $f(\Upsilon_0)$ and can be obtained from the infimum value of $\mathbf{D}\ (d_1, d_2 + \Upsilon)$. To compute $\mathbf{D}^*$ four values of **D′** namely $\mathbf{D}'(d_1^{\ 1}, d_1^{\ 2})$, $\mathbf{D}'(d_1^{\ 1}, d_2^{\ 2})$, $\mathbf{D}'(d_2^{\ 1}, d_2^{\ 2})$, $\mathbf{D}'(d_1^{\ 2}, d_2^{\ 1})$ are to be computed and $\mathbf{D}^* = \min\ (\mathbf{D}'(d_1^{\ 1}, d_1^{\ 2}) + \mathbf{D}'(d_2^{\ 1}, d_2^{\ 2}), \mathbf{D}'(d_1^{\ 1}, d_2^{\ 2}) + \mathbf{D}'(d_1^{\ 2}, d_2^{\ 1}))$

The normalised value of $\mathbf{D}^*$ is $\mathbf{D}^*/n$ and the shape similarity measure between the two shapes is given by,

$$\mu = 1 - \mathbf{D}^*/n$$

30.6 SOME CASE STUDIES OF APPLICATIONS OF KBCS APPROACH IN MEDICAL IMAGE PROCESSING FOR DIAGNOSTICS

In this section we present four important case studies of some real life applications.

30.6.1 Classification of Tumor Lesion of CNS (Central Nervous System) and Cancer Screening

The task of developing a knowledge based framework for screening test of detection and grading of malignancy and benignancy has been undertaken for decision making in oncology . The studies are mainly grouped into (*a*) Tumor/cancer detection in central nervous systems appearing in brain as space occupying lesion using CT and MR images (*b*) detection of tumor lesion growth in breast using mammographic images. In first part of the study we have concentrated on the problem to classify the different brain tumors obtained from CT and MR modality in two basic groups of tumors (*a*) the non-cancerous benign lesion and (*b*) the cancerous malignant lesion. The required knowledge base is modeled by correlating the medical image characteristics and tumor biology. The medical investigation predicts that benign lesions grow uniformly and nodule is approximately circular, contour is well defined whereas the malignant lesion grows fast, non-uniformly and the contour of the lesion is irregular in nature. If the growth of the tumor is assumed to be spherical in nature considering a known regular geometry a degree of mismatch between the contours of different tumor lesions and the 'spherical model' may be computed. A shape similarity/dissimilarity measure between the contours of the 'model' and the tumor lesions may indicate the low grade benignancy or high grade malignancy of tumors. The low grade homogeneous benign glioma are usually smooth masses with single radius where as malignant transformation have multiple protrusions. The concept of symmetry analysis of shape is utilized to classify the tumors mainly in two broad categories benign and malignant transformations. A shape of a contour is described on the basis of its structural features using chain code representation. The descriptors of the shape are information preserving. So that it is possible to reconstruct any reasonable information of the shape from the descriptors. In classification of tumors the idea of shape similarity measure is implemented by minimization of distance function D between the contours of tumor lesions and the model. These measurements give the indication of benignancy or malignancy of tumor lesions from a coarse to finer grading and will be helpful to the medical practitioners for preoperative diagnostic planning considering the condition of the patient.

Prior to the classification/recognition process the images were segmented and region of interest (space occupying lesions) have been extracted for analysis. A region can be represented by its boundary as external characteristics. The present approach of classification of tumor lesions is developed based on feature selections from shape of an object. In the segmentation algorithm the threshold is selected from the knowledge of sizes, their probability of occurrence and intensity distribution.

The knowledge based approach for the analysis and gradation of tumor regions using CT and MR modalities

From the tumor biology (*i*) benign lesion appears well defined, regular and circumscribed types, the feature concerning tumor contours is that benign transformations are usually smooth masses with single radius (*ii*) high grade malignant lesion are heterogeneous on gross pathology, irregularly shaped and diffused, tumor contour for malignant transformation have multiple protrusions (*iii*) Classification technique is based on boundary detection of lesion for 2D shape metric analysis (*iv*) The object boundary defined in digital region is assumed that they are closed and connected subset of Euclidean plane (*v*) The extracted boundary of tumor lesion is represented by direction code or chain codes (*vi*) 'Distance function D' and 'shape similarity measure μ' have been computed for each case from the knowledge of the contour of the lesion and the contour of the model (*vii*) A finer gradation technique for the tumor growth towards benignancy or malignancy has been evolved to assist clinicians which may replace the conventional grading system called 'Kernouhan grading' which is coarse (*viii*) Computer assisted screening procedure might be useful for improved therapeutic planning by determining the accurate preoperative stages for surgical cure.

Preliminary Results

The system is now of construction of the knowledge base for recognition/classification of tumor of human brain region using CT and MR images. A CT image is shown in Fig. 30.3 having benign cyst, an MR image is shown in Fig. 30.4 having tumor growth and in Fig. 30.5 shows a CT image having tumor lesion. For the shape similarity measure the model contour is considered to be circular in nature as contour of non cancerous benign lesion appears regular and spherical and its μ value is 1 assigning perfect noncancerous benign contour. For computer assisted screening procedure this is the priori knowledge to the computer. Computer can classify any contour of tumor lesion considering the degree of closeness or degree of similarity / dissimilarity of the region with the model contour. The low degree of similarity predicts the tendency of growth to be malignant and high degree of similarity predicts the tendency of growth to be benign in nature.

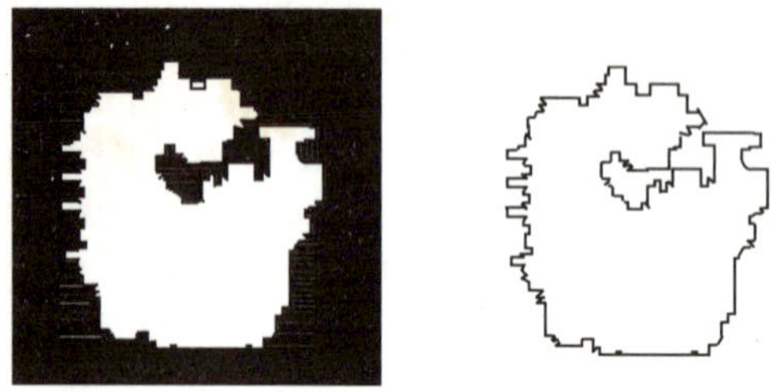

CT image of Brain Shows Benign Cyst — Segmented Cyst — Contour of Cyst

Fig. 30.3 Brain image having Cyst using CT image.

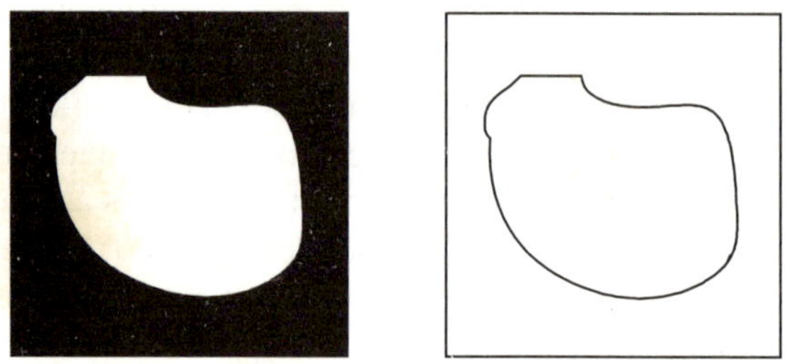

MR image shows Benign cyst — Segmented tumor — Contour

Fig. 30.4 MR image of section of human brain showing tumor growth.

Segmented tumor — Contour

CT image shows malignant lesion

Fig. 30.5 CT image of section of human brain showing tumor growth in human brain using CT and MR image.

Table 30.1 *Results: Study of benignancy / malignancy of the space occupying lesion appearing*

Case	Image dim.	Lesion dim.	Edge count	x_g	y_g
I	256 × 256	30 ×30	69	14.9	19.6
II	199 × 299	73 × 71	766	36.6	38.1
III	479 × 479	99 × 85	480	31.7	23.0
IV	479 × 479	179 × 140	905	58.3	8 .2
V	325 × 325	58 × 60	197	26.3	30.1

Table 30.2 *Measurement of Distance Function ($D = D_1, D_2,$) between the Contour of the model & the Tumor Lesion*

Case		D_1	D_2	Normalized D
I		8.1	10.6	0.27
II		34.5	285.2	0.41
III		66.2	141.3	0.44
IV		265.0	266.9	0.58
V		35.82	15.0	0.35

Table 30.3 *Gradation of Benignancy or malignancy of Tumor Lesion from shape Similarity Measure* (μ)

Case	measure of μ	Tendency of Tumor growth	Nature of tumor	Grade of Benignancy
I	0.72	Benign	Intracranial Cyst	Grade 3
II	0.59	Benign	Primary Neoplasm	Grade 5
III	0.56	Benign	Glioma	Grade 5
IV	0.41	Malignant	Primary Neoplasm	-
V	0.65	Benign	Lesion with edema effect	Grade 4

In the present study the tumor lesion having μ value less than 0.5 are detected to be malignant in nature. For all tumor lesions which having μ values greater than 0.5 are expected to be benign in nature. On that basis we have tried to find a new gradation technique of the benignancy of the lesion. Lesions having μ values lying from 1 to 0.9 are in grade 1, for μ values in between 0.9 to 0.8 lesions are in grade 2, for μ value in between 0.8 to 0.7 the lesions are in grade 3, for μ values in between 0.7 to 0.6 the lesions are in grade 4 and for μ values in between 0.6 to 0.5 are in grade 5. Higher grade of benignancy indicates the tendency of the transformation of lesion towards malignancy. This gradation is confirmed by the Medical Experts of related fields. The largest category of gliomas are usually found to be astrocytomas. A clinical grading is made according to the prognosis of the gliomas. This new gradation technique based on 'shape analysis' of the contour of the tumor lesion can be correlated with the tumor biology and the characteristics features of the medical images. The gradation of tumor lesions have certain impact in therapeutic planning which may be an indication to take preoperative steps by the clinicians. Different treatment planning are adopted depending on condition, such as degrees of cytoreduction surgery to reduce the volume of the tumor, radiation therapy and chemotherapy on which the mortality and the survival of the patient depends. According to the conventional clinical gradation of tumor growth the astrocytomas are generally graded in an ascending scale of malignancy and it has a range starting from grade 1 (low grade benign) to grade 4 (high grade malignant). The additional feature which is added to the histopathological gradation is the cell characteristics. In medical investigation of tumor lesion the chemical contrast are used to enhance the pathological part. The low grade astrocytomas have high absorption value of chemical and appear homogeneous, regular and circumscribed. High grade astrocytomas on both the CT and MR modalities have heterogeneous mixed densities. The neoplastic cysts (benign feature) and necrotic components (malignant or cancerous) show different enhancement criteria. Cysts have very smooth inner margin in both CT and MR images after using chemical contrasts. The gradation in medical treatment is modified according to the appearance of astrocytomas. These are summarized as : (1) an irregular, indistinct wall whose thickness varies when the malignant necrosis is at the central part of the lesion, (2) in benign case the lesion is nodular in nature and the enhanced image is homogeneous and (3) mixed type lesion having irregular outer edge and is distributed in a low density region. In diagnosis process of the tumor heterogeneous lesions grow rapidly and the edges of the boundary is irregular where as slowly growing tumors have homogeneous boundary. In classification of tumor lesions these distinctions add more important information in determination of the characteristic features for gradation. During growth of tumor lesion these features are in microscopic level. In 2-D shape metric analysis of the tumor boundary where the digital boundary is subdivided into very minute edge points, we get the measure of tumor growth in microscopic level. By employing this new shape based methodology the gradation technique gives more finer approach to classify the tumors by determining the degree of benignness. The shape similarity measure is based on the contour match between a 'model' contour and pathological tumor contour. Regular and spherical contour of non-cancerous benign appearance of tumor lesion which is assumed to be the 'model' of a perfectly benign lesion is the priori knowledge to the computer. On that basis computer can classify any contour of tumor lesions considering the degree of closeness of any shape of tumor lesion to the 'model' and can be able to find a finer gradation of tumor lesion detecting the degree of similarity / dissimilarity of the region with the 'model'. The low degree of similarity predicts the tendency of growth to be malignant and high degree of similarity predicts the benignancy of the tumor lesions. This automatic screening of tumor lesions using 'shape analysis' technique determine the practicality of the method which might be useful for improved diagnostics and therapeutic planning by determining the accurate preoperative stages of the patients for surgical cure.

30.6.2 Classification of Tumor Lesions Using Mammographic Images for Breast Cancer Screening

As explained in previous sections the present methodology is based on a concept of shape and its symmetry analysis to classify the breast tumors in cancerous and in non-cancerous transformations. To achieve the shape similarity measure the model contour is considered to have a tendency towards circularity in nature as the benignancy of the tumor lesion is approximated by the mathematical regularity of the region. The idea of shape similarity measure is implemented by minimizing the distance function between the contours of tumor lesions and the circular model considered. The distance function measure **D** and a a similarity measure μ between the shape of the tumor boundary and the boundary of the model are the determining factors to classify the tumor lesions in different grade of benignancy. Fifteen cases have been considered to implement the new shape based methodology for tumor classification. In experimental result five cases have been discussed. In Fig. 30.6, a digital mammogram has been shown having two space occupying lesion and the segmented lesion is shown in Fig. 30.7. Using Canny segmentation technique and by choosing the Gaussian smoothing factor and the upper threshold values t_2 and the lower threshold value t_1 the contours of the lesion have been extracted. Fig 30.8 and 30.9 show the approximated continuous contour of the tumor lesion.

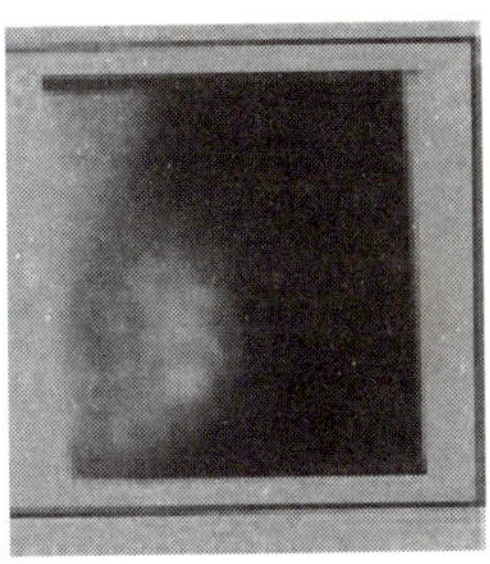

Fig 30.6 A digital mammogram showing two space occupying lesions.

Fig. 30.7 Segmented lesions.

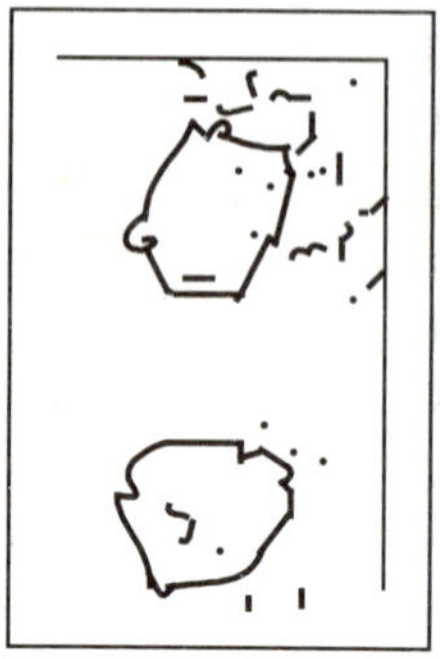

Fig. 30.8 Segmented lesions.

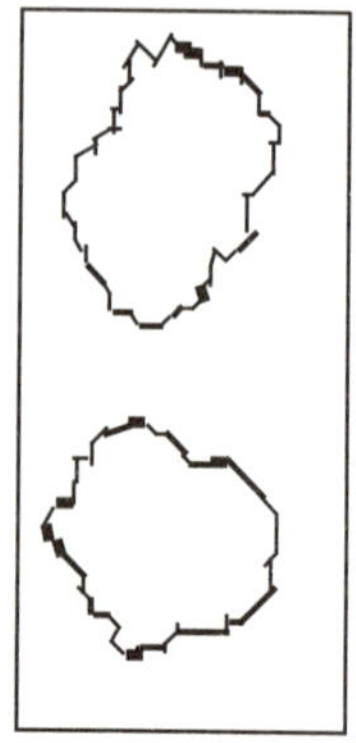

Fig. 30.9 Contours of the two lesions.

Table 30.4 *The Image Dimension, Edge Count and Centroid of the Contour*

Case	Image dim.	Lesion dim.	Edge count	x_g	y_g
I	216 × 255	43 × 45	191	21.5	21.4
II	216 × 255	55 × 45	247	19.3	22.3
III	480 × 480	73 × 95	341	36.4	35.9
IV	480 × 480	60 × 60	118	33.0	32.7
V	425 × 425	45 × 45	97	16.5	25.7

Table 30.5 *Computation of Shape Distance Function ($D = D_1, D_2$) between the Contour of the Model & the Tumor Lesion*

Case		D_1	D_2	Normalized
I		2.6	6.3	0.06
II		26.4	6.9	0.18
III		155.8	73.2	0.33
IV		4.8	30.1	0.68
V		25.8	12.3	0.3

Table 30.6 *Gradation of Benignness or Malignancy*

Case	Measure of μ	Grade	Tendency of growth
I	0.94	I	Benign
II	0.82	II	Benign
III	0.67	IV	Benign
IV	0.32	–	Malignant
V	0.7	III	Benign

In the present study lesion having μ value less than 0.5 are detected to be malignant and when μ value is more than 0.5 then we found that the lesion is benign in nature. For example in case I the degree of benignancy of tumor growth is the highest order compared to the other cases and the lesion is benign in nature and risk factor is lowest compare to the other cases. The of μ values for case II, case III and case V also indicate the benignancy of tumor growth but the tendency of growth for case III and case V towards malignancy is higher than the case I and case II as a result the risk factor for case III and Case V is higher than case I and case II. The μ value for case IV indicates the tumor lesion to be completely malignant in nature. A clinical grade is made according to the prognosis of the tumor growth in mammary gland. The attempt of this study is to find a new classification system for tumor growth enabling different levels of gradation from coarse to fine which may be practically and clinically useful to the medical practitioners to take preoperative decisions. 3D shape analysis of the tumor lesion may lead to a better evaluation for tumor classification.

30.6.3 Quantitative Measure of Bone Erosion Process (Osteoporosis) using X-ray Images at Different Sections of Spine

Osteoporosis is a common metabolic bone disease that manifests in loss of bone density. A major field of research in recent years is quantitative assessment of osteoporosis by radiographic photodensitometry and by other means [28]. Quantitative assessment of bone mineral density (BMD) loss using CT (quantitative CT or QCT) is performed by measuring the absorption co-efficient of bone in the spine where X or Gamma radiation are utilized [29], [30]. This measurement process is costly and its accuracy is dependent on repeated excessive radiations [27]. So a considerable effort is being made for the development of methods for quantitatively assessing the skeleton so that osteoporosis can be detected early, its progression and response to therapy monitored carefully, its risk effectively ascertained and treatment can be planned.

Attempt of estimation of percentage bone material loss due to osteoporotic erosion of spine from conventional radiographs is carried out using the mathematical theory of shape . Idea of using shape property in the study of bone erosion problem arises from the conviction that shape is a primal intrinsic property linked with the generative process. The outline of an eroded vertebra and a non-eroded (normal) vertebra have been considered for necessary shape analysis. In case of bone erosion the loss of bone contour occurs. Hence at micro level the bone erosion is estimated as a function of shape similarity/dissimilarity measure between the contour of an eroded vertebra and a normal one. Using this technique for quantitative analysis of bone erosion, the hazards and harmful effects of excessive radiation in human body can be avoided. This new approach is cost effective as the imaging modality is conventional radiographs, the most common and available imaging technique to investigate the bone diseases. To estimate the erosion process of spine at different anatomical level i.e. in the lumber, dorsal and in sacral region, a non-eroded sample of the respective region of vertebra is chosen as normal sample. In classifications of different significant regions the shape features selected are associated with a boundary representation of the ROI which is extracted as a digital contour from the digital image. The features associated with a boundary representation of an object are the length, the orientation of the line joining the extreme points on the contour, the area and the number of concavities of the contour. The patterns are invariant under certain transformations of shape. The chain code representation of the border is utilized to find a distance function {**D**} between two contours and to measure the shape similarity μ between the shape of two curves having any arbitrary shape. From the μ value the erosion factor ε is derived which gives an indication of the degree of bone erosion. A gradation of the degree of bone erosion is attempted to achieve from the measure of ε values.

$$\varepsilon = \frac{1-\mu}{1+\mu}$$

The erosion factor ε which gives an estimation of bone erosion can be derived from the expression of similarity measure μ. where the similarity measure is derived in terms of a 'distance metric'. The regions having higher resemblance have a higher degree of shape similarity.

Some Experiment with Osteoporosis in Human Vertebra

In the present investigation we have studied eleven cases of osteoporosis in human vertebrae of spine of four patients at different levels of lumber (L) and dorsal or thoracic (T) positions. We are presenting the bone erosion at spine for four patients. The case I, case II and case III depict the bone erosion at lumber section of spine of a female patient (patient 1). The case IV and case V describe bone erosion at lumber position of spine of a male patient (patient 2). Case VI, case VII, case VIII describe the erosion at dorsal positions of a male patient (patient 3) and case IX, case X and case XI depict the erosion both at dorsal and at lumber positions of spine of a male patient (patient 4). Human vertebrae vary in size and shape at different levels, they vary from person to person also. To avoid this complication for a particular patient an uneroded vertebrae at a particular position (say at lumber position) is chosen as standard and with respect to this normal uneroded vertebra the erosion factor of the other eroded vertebrae of same level is estimated.

To illustrate the bone erosion we have considered the different cases of osteoporosis at different levels of spine. Let us consider the radiological features of L_5 position which depicts the early stage of

Table 30.7 *Computation of Four Distance Functions between normal vertebra contours*

Case	γ_0	D'_1	γ_0	D'_2	γ_0	D'_3	γ_0	D'_4
I (L_4)	4.73	68.3	0.89	100.8	5.6	292.1	0.68	59.5
II (L_5)	5.75	178.5	0.29	7.2	5.57	178.5	5.9	285.8
III (L_5)	0.55	35.23	0.06	0.45	4.17	3.53	0.54	34.53
IV (L_4)	0.78	68.70	1.45	219.7	5.36	195.7	4.8	62.2
V (L_5)	5.9	267.81	6.9	112.5	5.18	123.3	1.94	249.1
VI (T_7)	1.71	116.82	0.64	18.9	7.45	12.3	1.82	128.7
VII (T_8)	1.98	147.90	6.2	135.10	.84	30.8	6.3	119.03
VIII (T_9)	1.32	62.32	1.68	95.6	1.72	100.1	0.2	1.54
IX (T_{10})	1.35	62.21	0.5	9.42	1.53	81.7	1.82	108.8
X (T_{12})	0.56	12.11	1.4	65.2	0.06	121.3	1.79	105.6
XI (L_1)	7.2	54.72	6.8	118.5	6.47	183.3	0.35	10.9

Table 30.8 *Estimation of Shape Similarity Measure μ, Erosion Factor ε and Grade of Erosion for different Osteoporotic Patients*

	I	II	III	IV	V	VI	VII	VIII	IX	X	XI
D^*		254.8	35.7	257.9	472.4	135.7	149.8	101.6	71.6	77.3	173.2
μ	0.8	0.52	0.95	0.66	0.4	0.55	0.51	0.61	0.72	0.6	0.7
ε	0.11	0.32	0.02	0.21	0.43	0.29	0.33	0.24	0.16	0.26	0.18

Table 30.9 *Range of ε values vs the grade of bone erosion*

Range of ε values	0.00-0.01	0.11-0.20	0.21-0.30	0.31-0.40	0.41-0.50	0.51-0.60	0.61-0.70	0.71-0.8
Grade of bone erosion	I	II	III	IV	V	VI	VII	VIII

Table 30.10 *Estimation of Grade of Bone Erosion for Different Osteoporotic Patients*

Case	I	II	III	IV	V	VI	VII	VIII	IX	X	XI
Grade	II	IV	I	III	V	III	IV	III	II	III	II

osteoporosis. This is case III. There exists opacity in the vertical bodyand no appreciable change in bone contour occurs. The value of ε is estimated for this vertebral L_5 region is 0.02 which is classified as the degree I of osteoporosis. Early changes appear in bone contour such as increased angulation of bones, the ε value is determined to be 0.11 and the degree of erosion is in grade II. In L_4 position and this is case I In L_5 position severe osteoporosis is detected where loss of bone density along with change in bone contour occurs. Highly increased angulation with crumbling of vertebra is noticed. According to proposed methodology the ε value is computed to be 0.43 and the erosion process is specified in grade V. This is case V. The grade of bone erosion at the T_7 and at the T_9

positions is determined III and the grade of bone erosion at the T_8 position is IV. The bone erosion at the T_7 and at the T_9 positions are mild than bone erosion at the T_8 position. All the results coincide with the view of medical / radiological experts. It is clear that the higher value of μ or the shape similarity measure indicate lower degree of erosion process. For μ equals to 1, ε is 0 i.e. no erosion occurs. μ equals to 0, ε is 1 which indicates the highest degree of erosion. The gradation of erosion process is classified as per ε value as indicated in Table 30.9. It may be mentioned, we have done this work in close collaboration with medical practitioners including orthopaedic/radio-logical experts. According to medical experts the internal contour of the vertebra does not depict any clear picture of severity of osteoporosis and has no particular role in diagnosis of the disease, rather the change in outer contour of an eroded vertebra with respect to an non eroded vertebra plays an important role. A clinical comment can only be made over the changes in respect of outer contour. From the conventional radiographs using our proposed method it is possible to assess the loss of bone density from the investigation of the radiological change, in respective region where the appearance of more dark region in the vertebra, indicates the less opacity and higher degree of erosion, with a meaningful (acceptable by clinicians) degree of accuracy. Clinicians in general make a guess of the bone density loss from the radiographic features. This new gradation technique proposed by us will assist the medical practitioners to take more accurate treatment planning by classifying the cases in clinically meaningful grades. Depending upon the degree of erosion clinicians treat the cases conservatively or surgically. But in most of the cases the therapeutic planning is done from the radiographic films only. This shape based approach for more finer gradation of bone erosion process will assist clinicians to make necessary treatment planning in a more accurate way.

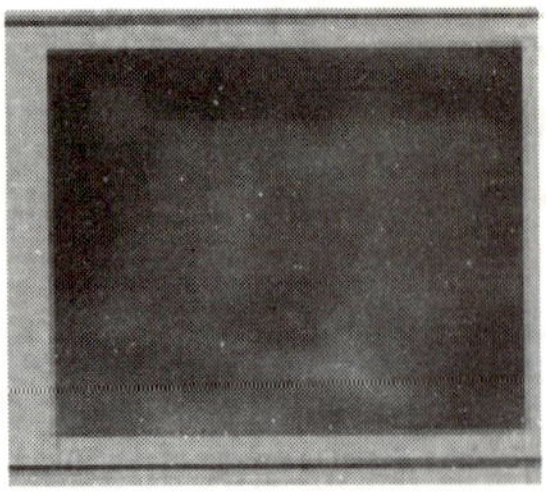

Fig 30.10 An eroded vertebra at L3 position

Fig. 30.11 T2 = 6, T1 = 3, s = 2

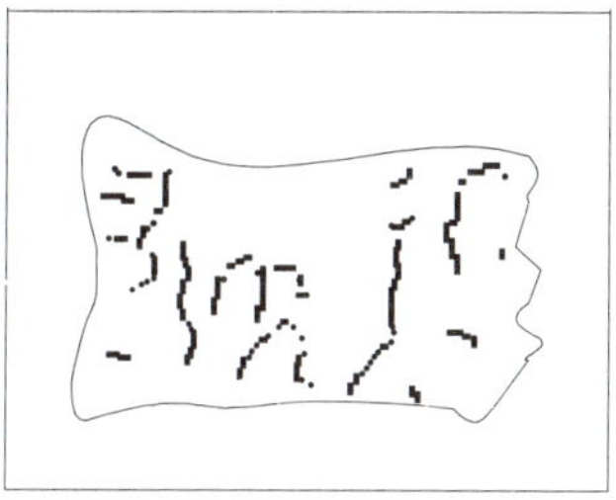

Fig. 30.12 T2 = 15, T1 = 5, s = 2

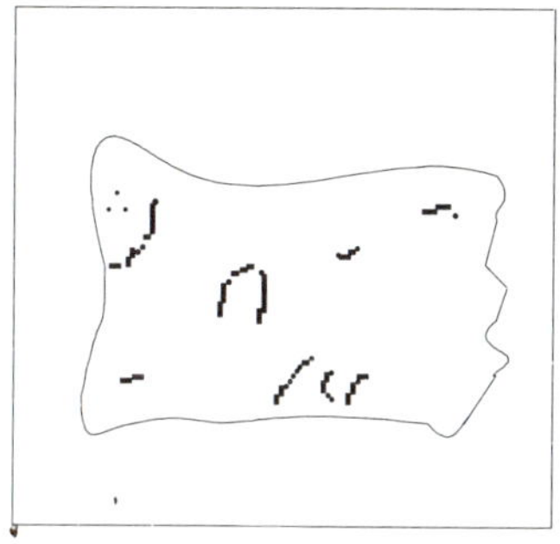

Fig. 30.13 T2 = 21, T1 = 7, s = 2

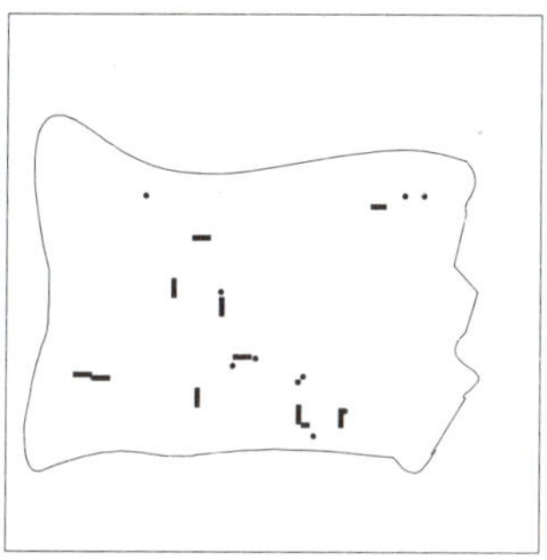

Fig. 30.14 T2 = 24, T1 = 8, s = 2

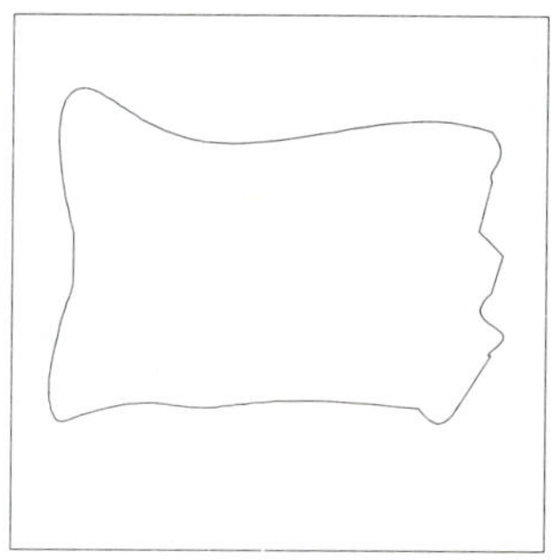

Fig. 30.15 T2 = 27, T1 = 9, s = 2

30.6.4 Multimodal Image Registration and Fusion Using Patient Data of Alzheimer's Disease

The present work concerns registration of CT, T_1 and/or T_2 weighted MR images of brain (axial section) of a patient suffering from Alzheimer's Diseases (AD) as part of an investigation carried out by the authors in a common reference frame and finally the 'best matching' was found using the generalized approach of shape. The goodness of matching was determined by selecting landmark points along the concavity of the contour of the ROI. Affine and projective invariance relations have been used to re-project the region of interest into another view. The visual recognition is achieved by alignment and the geometrical invariants extracted from the concavities present in the ROI. The concept of 'canonical frame' has been introduced in transformation of a set of co-ordinates and to match the segmented regions to be registered. In this model, affine and projective transformations are grouped on the basis of the degrees of freedom (DOF). As a result more features are associated to compute invariants for higher degree of freedom to improve the matching between the planar contour. The affine transformation needs at least three coplanar points and six DOF to construct invariants and for projective case at least four coplanar points are required whereas Euclidean group requires only two points to construct an invariant distance.

Results and Discussions

The digitized images of axial sections of the same region of brain of an Alzheimer's patient were obtained from T_1 weighted MR and T_2 weighted MR and CT modalities of pixel dimensions 173 × 230 as shown in figures. In both affine and projective planes the matching between the extracted contour of CT, T_1 and T_2 weighted MR images of Alzheimer's patient are estimated following 2D shape matching algorithms. The transformation has been done along the upper concavity of the ventricular region, the same transformation has been implemented considering the lower concavity. The projective transformation has been applied on the images. The dilation of the ventricular region is one of the determining clinical feature for Alzheimer's patient. In the present experiment the ventricular region of each image has been taken as the region of interest (ROI).

The registration process performs the integration of information from the multimodality medical imaging to a single reference frame and provides more accuracy in diagnostics procedures and improved therapeutic planning to the clinicians.

Finally the combination of information from the multimodal imageries as a fused image would provide the optimum information. The multimodal medical image fusion may provide integrated information to the medical practitioners for improved diagnostics and therapeutic planning.

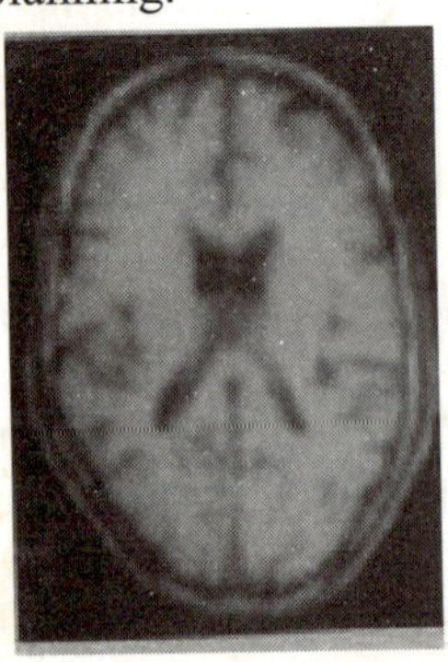

Fig. 30.16 T_1 weighted MR

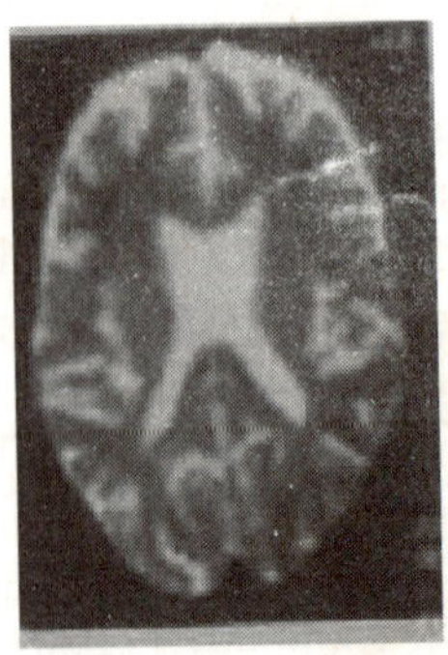

Fig. 30.17 T_2 weighted MR

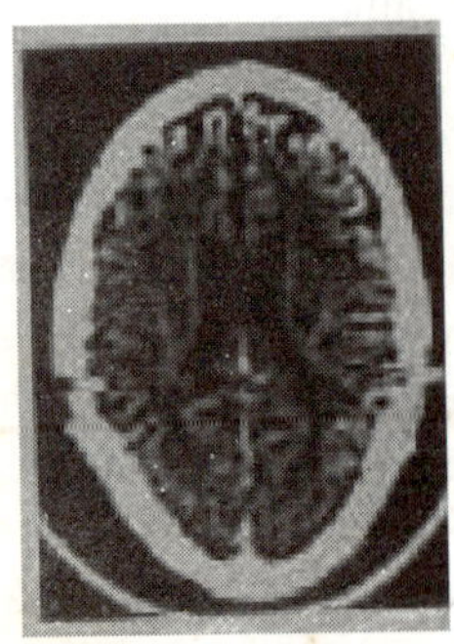

Fig. 30.18 CT image

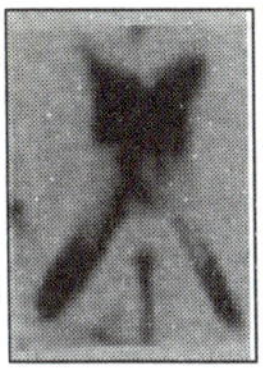

Fig. 30.19 Ventricular region of T_1 weighted MR image

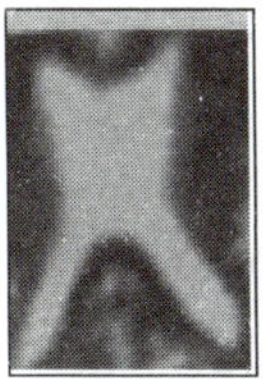

Fig. 30.20 Ventricular region of T_2 weighted MR image

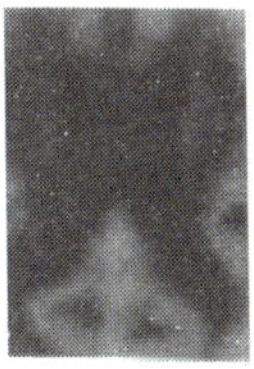

Fig. 30.21 Ventricular region of CT image

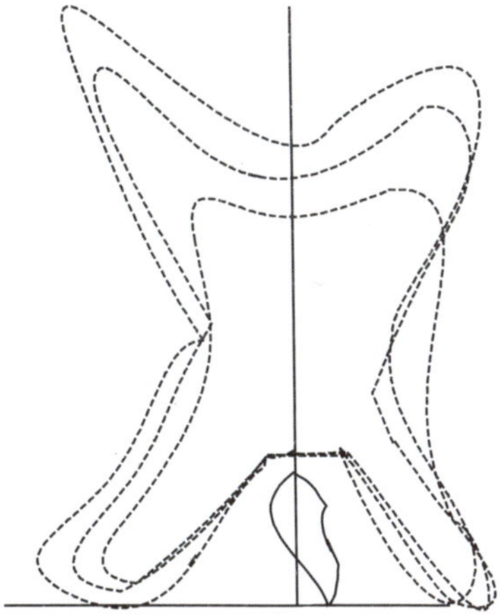

Fig. 30.22 Superposition of ROI of T_1, T_2 weighted MR and CT image in affine plane

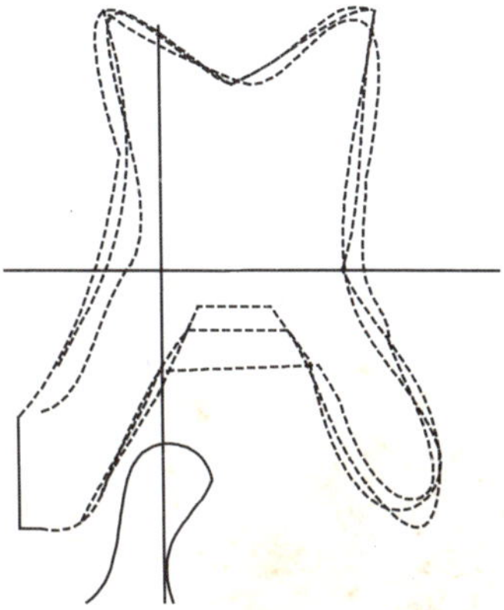

Fig. 30.23 Superposition of ROI of T_1, T_2 weighted MR and CT image in projective plane

30.7 CONCLUSIONS

In the first part of the paper we have developed a detailed theoretical framework for developing unimodal and multimodal knowledge based image processing and analysis including a cybernetic approach for human machine interfaces for medical systems for clinical applications. In the second part we have presented some case studies of real life application developed by us along with results. Better recognition will be resulted from the knowledge we possess about the domain to be more accurate, more precise. New system based on more powerful tools must be able to work with these levels of imprecision in the knowledge and will be able to use the approximate reasoning schemes.

The situations of conflict which may arise in the recognition process may be solved using relational knowledge. In designing of such systems if some regions are not recognized with a high value of certainty, the system must be able to perform a backword process, reconsidering decisions or retriggering a new segmentation process over certain areas of the image with another resolution level. The image may be considered as a multi resolution database that contains information in a wide range of resolutions or scales. Also the knowledge about the patient's history, other clinical descriptions may be injected into the system as this knowledge also can play a very important role in the decision making process for diagnostics and therapeutic planning along with future references.

Acknowledgement

Authors acknowledge with thanks DST, Govt. of India and All India Institute of Medical Sciences, New Delhi and Eko Imaging Institute, Calcutta and to West Bengal University of Calcutta Indian statistical Institute and Institute of Cybernetics Systems and Information Technology.

References

1. D Cabello, A Delgado, M J Carreira, J Mira, R Moreno-Diaz, J A Munoz and S Candela, 'On Knowledge Based Medical Image Understanding': *Cybernetics & Systems : An International Journal*, 21 : 227–289, 1990.
2. Nagao N & T Matsuyama, 'A Structural Analysis of Complex Ariel Photographs', Plenum, New York, 1980.
3. D Dutta Majumder, 'A Unified Approach to Artificial Intelligence Pattern Recognition, Image Processing & Computer Vision in Fifth Generation Computer Systems', *Information Sciences* 45 pp : 391–431, 1988.
4. D Dutta Majumder & Mahua Bhattacharya 'Cybernetic Approach To Medical Technology : Application to Cancer Screening and Other Diagnostics', *International Journal of Systems and Cybernetics, Kybernetes,* Vol 29, Number 7/8, pp: 871–895, 2000 *(Frank George Award Winning Paper).*
5. T Moto–Oka *et.al.*, 'Challenge for Knowledge Information Processing Systems (Preliminary Report on Fifth Generation Computer Systems)' in *Proceedings of the International Conference on Fifth Generation Computer Systems*, Oct. pp : 1–85, 1981.
6. J Allen, 'VLSI Overall System Design, FGCS State of the Art Report', *Pergemon Infotech Report*, pp: 33–39, 1983.
7. D Dutta Majumder, 'Cybernetics and General Systems Theory–A Unitary Science', *Kybernetes* 8 : 7–15, 1979.
8. D Marr, 'Analyzing Natural Images', *AI Memo* 334, *AI Lab, MIT* May 1976.

9. Takeo Kanade and Raj Reddy, 'Computer Vision : The Challenge of Imperfect Inputs', *IEEE Spectrum*, Nov. 1983
10. Martin D Levin, 'A Knowledge Based Computer Vision System, in Vision Systems' (A P Hauson and E M Riseman, Eds), Aa*cademic* 1978.
11. T O Binford, 'Survey of Model Based Image Analysis Systems', *International J Robotics* Res.l (1): pp: 18–64, 1978.
12. Michael Brady, 'Computational Approaches in Image Understanding', *ACM Computer Surveys* 14, No. 1, March 1982.
13. A Rosenfeld, 'Image Analysis : Problems, Progress and Prospects', *Pattern Recognition* 17, No. 1 Jan. 1984.
14. Michael Brady, 'Artificial Intelligence and Robotics' *Artificial Intelligence* 26, 1985.
15. M I Sezan, A M Tekalp, and R Schaetzing, 'Automatic Anatomically Selective Image Enhancement in Digital Chest Radiography', *IEEE Transaction Medical Image* MI–8, pp: 154–162, 1989.
16. N Walker and J Fox, 'Knowledge Based Interpretation of Images : A Biomedical Perspective', *Knowledge Eng. Rev.* 2(4), pp: 249 – 264, 1987.
17. H Wechsler and J Sklansky, 'Finding the Rib Cage in Chest Radiographs', *Pattern Recognition*, No. 9, pp: 21–30, 1977.
18. M Bhattacharya & D Dutta Majumder, 'Registration of Multi-modal Images of Alzheimer's Patient: A Shape Theoretic Approach' *Pattern Recognition Letter,* Vol-21, issue 6–7, pp: 531 – 548, 2000.
19. W K Pratt, *Digital Image Processing,* New York : Wiley – Interscience, 1978.
20. A Rosenfeld and A C Kak, *Digital Picture Processing* 2nd ed. New York Academic, 1982.
21. D Marr & E. Hildreth, 'Theory of Edge Detection' *Proc. of R. Soc. Lond. A Math. Phy. Sci., Bol B* 207, pp : 187–217, 1980.
22. Mitra Basu, 'Gaussian-Based Edge Detection Methods – A Survey', *IEEE Transactions on System Man and Cybernetics – Part C: Applications and Reviews*, Vol. 32, No. 3, August 2002.
23. C A Davatzikos and J Prince, 'An Active Contour Model for Mapping the Cortex', *IEEE Trans. on Med. Imaging*, 14 (1), pp: 65–80, March 1995.
24. C A Davatzikos and R N Bryan, 'Using a Deformable Surface Model to Obtain a Shape Representation of Cortex,' *IEEE Trans on Med Imaging* 15 (6), pp: 785–795, 1996.
25. P C Teo, G Shapiro and B A Wandell, 'Creating Connected Representation of Cortical Grey Matter for Functional MRI

Visualization', *IEEE transaction Med Imaging* 16(6), pp: 852–863, 1997.

26. Xiaolan Zeng, Lawrence H Satib, Robert T Schultz and James S. Duncan, 'Segmentation and Measurement of the Cortex from 3D MR Images' *Med Image Comp. And Comp. Asst Int. (MICCAI),* Oct, 1998.
27. Ronald O Murry, Harold G Jacobson, Dennis J Stoker, *The Radiology of Skeletal Disorders,* Churchill Livingstone.
28. M Lequesne *et.al. Partial Transient Osteoporosis,* Skeletal Radiology 2, 1977.
29. Ernst Klotz *et.al.* 'Automated Definition and Evaluation of Anatomical ROI's for Bone Mineral Determination by QCT', *IEEE Trans. on Medical Imaging,* Vol 8, no.4, December 1989.
30. H K Genant, *Osteoporosis Update* 1987, San Francisco, CA: Radiology Research and Education Fund, 1987.
31. Mahua Bhattacharya, 'Studies on Bio-Medical Image Processing of Different Modalities for Diagnostics and Therapeutic Planning' Ph.D. Thesis, 2000
32. D Dutta Majumder & Mahua Bhattacharya, 'Study on Mathematical Tools and Techniques for Medical Image analysis: A Bio Cybernetics Approach' : *Biomathematics–Modeling and Simulation*', Editor J C Misra, Narosa Publishing House, New Delhi, 2003.
33. Canny John, 'A Computational Approach To Edge Detection', *IEEE Trans. On Pattern Analysis and Machine Intelligence Unit.* Vol Pami-8, No-6, Nov 1986.
34. B Chanda & D Dutta Majumder, 'Digital Image Processing and Analysis' Prentice Hall of India, New Delhi, 2000.
35. J Basak, B Chanda and D Dutta Majumder, 'On Edge and Line Linking with Connectionist Models', *IEEE Transaction on Syst. Man and Cybernetics, SMC* 34, 1994, pp: 413–424.
36. B Chanda, B B Chowdhury and D Dutta Majumder, 'A Differentiation Enhancement Edge Detector and its Properties' *IEEE Transaction SMC,* SMC -15, pp: 162–186, 1985.
37. D Dutta Majumder, 'A Study on Mathematical Theory of Shapes in Relation to Pattern Recognition and Computer Vision' *Indian J of Theoretical Physics*, 43 (4), pp 19–30, 1995.
38. D Dutta Majumder and Mahua Bhattacharya, 'A New Shape Based Technique for Classification and Registration : Application to Multimodal Medical Images' *Intl. J. of Image Processing and Communication* 4, (3/4), pp 45–70, Warsaw Poland, 1998.
39. S K Parui and D Dutta Majumder, 'Shape Similarity for Open Curves', *Pattern Recognition Letters* 1, 1983.